DATE DUE

AG 1 00
NO 1 00

SAUDI ARABIA

Also by Geoff Simons

* *Also published by St. Martin's Press*

Saudi Arabia

The Shape of a Client Feudalism

Geoff Simons

St. Martin's Press
New York

SAUDI ARABIA

Copyright © 1998 by Geoff Simons

All rights reserved. No part of this book may be used or reproduced in any manner whatsoever without written permission except in the case of brief quotations embodied in critical articles or reviews. For information, address:

St. Martin's Press, Scholarly and Reference Division,
175 Fifth Avenue, New York, N.Y. 10010

First published in the United States of America in 1998

This book is printed on paper suitable for recycling and made from fully managed and sustained forest sources.

Printed in Great Britain

ISBN 0–312–21550–9

Library of Congress Cataloging-in-Publication Data
Simons, G. L. (Geoffrey Leslie), 1939–
Saudi Arabia : the shape of a client feudalism / Geoff Simons.
p.   cm.
Includes bibliographical references (p.   ) and index.
ISBN 0–312–21550–9 (cloth)
1. Human rights—Saudi Arabia.   2. Human rights—Religious
aspects—Islam.   I. Title.
JC599.S33S58   1998
323.4'9'09538—dc21   98–15228
                                                                              CIP

Contents

v

Contents

List of Figures

List of Tables

Preface

The West is indulgent towards Saudi Arabia ...

Few Western politicians are troubled to find that the Kingdom does not allow free speech, free association, trade unions or political parties. Washington does not group Saudi Arabia among terrorist states, even though the Kingdom has long supported Arab terrorists and US-approved terrorists (somehow the terrorist United States is also excluded).

It has not bothered successive American presidents, themselves keen to enlist God, that packs of religious bigots roam Saudi streets to terrorise ordinary men and women. And no Western leader is obviously concerned that Saudi Arabia tortures its dissidents, conducts secret trials, and drags weeping women to be lashed and beheaded in front of baying crowds of excited men.

The West is indulgent towards Saudi Arabia ... for one simple reason. The Kingdom has what the West wants (and while the oil is purchased the petrocash can be cycled back to fund arms manufacture and export). And so any cruelty, any repression, any gross violation of human rights can be smiled upon, ignored or aided – providing the oil keeps flowing. So Western indulgence rests on a plain and well-tried principle – that so long as we are granted secure access to a vital resource, anything and everything is permissible – the guiding light of every mercenary and pimp over the ages.

Then there is the matter of Islam, not to be criticised – say priest, prince and pundit – since we must at all costs allow cultural variation, tolerate religion and avoid 'Islamophobia'. After all, Islam, Judaism and Christianity have much in common. Indeed they do. All of these sky-god religions

- parade fairy tales and superstitious absurdities as eternal verities;
- celebrate the alleged Oneness of God by centuries-long schism;
- exhibit male-spawned themes of gross anti-sexuality in which women fare badly;
- rejoice in the everlasting torture of anyone who disagrees.

I suggest that cultural relativism is never sufficient to justify cruel and bigoted practices; and that modern political leaders, Saudi and Western, should never rate human rights below the price of a barrel of oil.

GEOFF SIMONS

Acknowledgements

Many people provided information for this book and I am grateful to them all. Some, for very proper reasons, preferred not to be mentioned here and I respect their wishes. I am able to express particular thanks to:

Mohammed H. Siddiq, for sending a copious supply of booklets, articles and letters;

IMMEL Publishing (London), for making available William Facey's *Riyadh: the Old City* (published in 1992), an impressive and invaluable research text;

Amnesty International, for supplying many Saudi-linked reports (on the treatment of minorities, the practice of torture, the incidence of executions, the abuse of Iraqi refugees, etc.); see, for example, *Saudi Arabia – Behind Closed Doors: Unfair Trials in Saudi Arabia*, November 1997;

The Minnesota Lawyers International Human Rights Committee (Minneapolis, USA), for sending their excellent report *Shame in the House of Saud: Contempt for Human Rights in the Kingdom of Saudi Arabia* (published in 1992);

The many journalists who, over many years and sometimes in conditions of danger, have worked to inform people about the nature of Saudi Arabia, a closed and repressive state. These journalists are cited in the 'Notes'.

I am grateful also to other people who supplied books, reports and articles: Mohammed al-Masari (for sending material from the Committee for the Defence of Legitimate Rights, CDLR), Hugh Stephens, Felicity Arbuthnot, Karen Dabrowska, Linda Melvern, Jonathan Hooper, Deborah Lamberti and Margaret Leddy.

None of the people who supplied information have any responsibility for the opinions expressed in this book; they are mine and mine alone.

I am particularly grateful to Christine Simons, who helped in many ways.

GEOFF SIMONS

Introduction

'... crazed with the spell of Arabia'
  Walter de la Mare

'... glorious Araby'
  George Darley

'... all the perfumes of Arabia ...'
  William Shakespeare

'Heart-beguiling Araby'
  Kathryn Tidrick

Arabia has long fascinated the Western mind. The stark environment, the fierce culture, the alternative ethic and religion, the mysterious Other – all have fed imagination and prejudice, at once fuelling romantic fancy and racial stereotype. Today, with modern technology conjuring a smaller world, it is harder to remain beguiled by dreams of distant lands. We can travel there in hours, if we wish, or otherwise need only seconds and minutes to communicate.

Today even the term *Arabia* is less prevalent than in the days of Doughty or Burton, since individual Arab states are separately named and the 'Arabia' that survives in language is more likely to be recognised as *Saudi*. Many forces – Western imperialism, Arab ambition, the House of Saud – have conspired to produce this narrower focus and to disguise the vision of an earlier age. A main consequence has been to obscure the integrity of the Arab Nation, a resonant ambition when the Ottomans finally collapsed at the end of the Great War. The present rulers of the Kingdom of Saudi Arabia have no interest in *an Arabia of all the Arabs ...*

Saudi Arabia, through its oil resource, is an important player on the world stage. It dominates the Organisation of Petroleum Exporting Countries (OPEC) and the Gulf Co-operation Council (GCC), and is a powerful force in the Middle East. At the same time, with its relatively small population, the Kingdom relies heavily on foreign labour and American protection. Moreover, the sociopolitical character of Saudi Arabia suggests important areas of instability that are given no publicity in the Kingdom and only minimal exposure by Saudi Arabia's Western sponsors. There are now problems with economic management, political evolution, and the Kingdom's self-appointed role as the focus of Muslim devotion.

Underlying most of these problems is the ubiquitous and pressing question of human rights. Despite all the efforts of the Saudi authorities to crush any sign of free expression, the constant abuse of human rights is frequently advertised by events in the Kingdom. For example, through 1997 the Western media reported

xiii

the case of the two British nurses, Lucille McLauchlan and Deborah Parry, accused of murdering the Australian nurse Yvonne Gilford. It is worth recording details of this case since what it reveals of the Saudi approach to ethics, politics and penal justice has much relevance in many other fields. Thus:

- McLauchlan and Parry were tortured by the Saudi interrogators (sexually abused; deprived sleep, food and water; denied access to a toilet);
- They were falsely told that *sharia* law did not apply to Christians, and so if they 'confessed' they would be allowed to go home;
- In late 1997 they were facing their twelfth month in captivity, with no verdict and forced to endure filthy prison conditions, poor diet and lack of exercise;
- It was reported that McLauchlan's health was deteriorating: her muscles were wasting, her teeth and gums rotting, and her hair falling out.

Such details helped to indicate the nature of *sharia* justice, at least in its Saudi version, as it applies in the Kingdom to many thousands of nationals and foreigners every year.

The McLauchlan/Parry case was not the first of its kind. In 1986 Monica Hall, a 36-year-old nurse working in Saudi Arabia, was falsely accused of killing a fellow Irishwoman, Helen Feeney. After 56 hours of psychological torture, with 'psychological disintegration' (her words) having taken place, Hall was writing a coerced confession of guilt. Her husband, paraded before her in manacles, was subjected to the same treatment. Monica Hall spent 19 months in jail before her trial (February 1988), at which no defence was allowed. She was sentenced to eight years, her husband to 10. In May 1989 the couple were 'pardoned' by King Fahd. Monica Hall commented in September 1997: 'For me it was a psychological catastrophe, which took six years to overcome'.

Defence lawyers are usually banned from Saudi courtrooms, defendants may be denied access to a lawyer, and judges acting on whim can dismiss defence evidence. The police, under promise of bonuses and promotion, are committed to securing a confession – by torture, prolonged incarceration, whatever ('Have you confessed? No? Then go back to jail'). Defendants are given no prior knowledge of the charges against them; or of when, if convicted of a capital crime (murder, rape, drug trafficking, armed robbery, apostasy, treason, sabotage, etc.), they are to be taken to what the locals call Chop Square for beheading. Thieves typically have their right hand cut off, not always with an axe. The journalist Kathy Evans (*The Observer*, 14 September 1997) describes one case: '*Then they cut a large V-shaped sign on his wrist pointing to his fingers and then, with what looked like an ordinary kitchen knife, began cutting into the wrist. When they finally cut through and dismembered the hand from the arm, he was rushed to hospital ... When he got back to his cell three days later, he was still in enormous pain, but the guards did not allow him to take any painkillers.*' For a repeat offence the left foot is amputated, then the left hand, and finally the right foot – all well in accord with the Koran (Sura 5, Verse 37). Those found guilty of adultery are likely to be stoned to death, but only with medium-sized stones because large ones will kill too quickly. If a pregnant woman is to be executed she is allowed to give birth and to breastfeed her baby for a period specified by the male judge before she is stoned to death or beheaded.

One purpose of the present book is to highlight the human-rights situation in Saudi Arabia in the context of *sharia* law. Thus Chapter 1 indicates how the Saudi regime suppresses free speech, maintains gross corruption and inequality, tortures and otherwise abuses all types of dissidents, operates a brutal penal philosophy, suppresses and abuses women, and maintains slavery both in Saudi Arabia and abroad. Observing the obvious principle that modern regimes cannot be understood without some awareness of their historical background, Part II provides an outline of the history of the region from pre-Islamic times to the present day. Chapter 2 offers some details of pre-Muslim religion, before indicating some important aspects of Muhammed (the 'Prophet') and the religion which he founded. (I have relied on two translations of the Koran – Rodwell (1937) and Dawood (1988). In-text quotations are from Rodwell.)

Chapters 3 to 6 provide a chronological history for the Muslim era, necessarily only sketched since many events are covered: the great Arab expansion that flowed from the birth of Islam, the creation of the influential Umayyad and Abbasid dynasties, the Arab decline, the Ottoman conquest and subsequent decay, the emergence of Wahhabist philosophy, the tribal contention for dominance in the Arabian peninsula, the military successes of the House of Saud, the contribution of Ibn Saud who founded the modern state of Saudi Arabia, the post-Ibn Saud dynasty, the influence and dominance of the Western powers, the exploitation of oil, Saudi intervention in Yemeni affairs, the Arab–Israeli Wars, the arms trade, the Iran–Iraq War (1980–8), and the 1990/1 Gulf crisis. In all these events an indication is given of the Saudi involvement, whether active or passive.

Another principal purpose of the present book is to highlight the extent to which the modern Saudi regime is threatened by domestic and other instabilities. Chapter 7 focuses on the economic problems facing the Kingdom, the difficulties for the dynastic succession and what these imply, and the consequences for Saudi Arabia of its self-styled custodianship of the holy sites of Islam. Finally an indication is given of aspects – peaceful and violent – of the dissident revolt against the Saudi regime.

I make no assumption that the demonstrable tensions and instabilities will lead to early substantial change in the Saudi regime. Buttressed by oil wealth and American indulgence, the House of Saud has survived many crises and could well continue for years or even decades in the same vein. But a similar observation could easily have been made about the Shah's Iran in 1978 and the Soviet Union in 1990. There often comes a point when a minuscule social or political event can provoke an avalanche of change (the 'Butterfly Effect' of chaos theory), a dramatic transformation unheralded in all the computer models. So it is difficult to predict the course of even the most stable societies; where the tensions are many and deep any attempt at confident forecasting is a hazardous enterprise.

It is easier by far to make sweeping value judgements, to note with disdain and horror the inhuman consequences of the prevailing Saudi social ethic. We may say that *a society that institutionalises the grossest religious bigotry, financial corruption, a profligate élite, torture and sadism, terror, slavery and the abuse of women is not worthy of respect, tolerance or support*; and then we may wonder why – despite all this – the feudal regime of the Kingdom of Saudi Arabia is courted, fawned upon and celebrated by Western pundits, priests and politicians.

Of course the answer is plain enough, though today rarely advertised. It is clear that sociopolitical élites, with power over human and other natural resources, have no interest in challenging the economic arrangements that keep their egos and their personal finances in such a healthy state. The present book is intended in part to applaud and support those many campaigners who assume without question the sacred truth of that most revolutionary of all principles – that an *ethical* approach to human problems in society is vastly more important than the cynical protection of social, political and financial privilege.

Part I
The Feudal Frame

1 Islam, Law and Human Rights

... the recompense of those who war against God and his Apostle ... shall be that they shall be slain or crucified, or have their alternate hands and feet cut off ... As to the thief, whether man or woman, cut ye off their hands in recompense for their doings ...

Koran, Sura 5, Verses 37, 42

Men are superior to women on account of the qualities with which God hath gifted the one above the other ...

Koran, Sura 4, Verse 38

Verily, in your wives and your children ye have an enemy: wherefore beware of them ...

Koran, Sura 64, Verse 14

PREAMBLE

In the worlds of commerce and official relations Saudi Arabia is typically portrayed as responsible, virtuous and stable. Thus the former British prime minister John Major could depict the Kingdom as 'a vital force for stability'; Sir Patrick Cormack, Conservative Member of Parliament and President, International Affairs, of *First Magazine*, can applaud Saudi Arabia's 'enlightened leadership';[1] Sir Alan Munro, former British ambassador to Saudi Arabia, can celebrate the 'warmth' of British-Saudi relations;[2] and Prince Charles can offer such blandishments to the House of Saud that a welcoming speech to the British feudalist can represent the United Kingdom as 'a brother country'.[3]

There is another Saudi Arabia, studiously ignored by comfortable pundits and politicians in Britain and elsewhere. This is the Saudi Arabia of the appalling human-rights record; where massive censorship cripples any attempt at free discussion; where trade unions and political parties are banned; where private and public corruption are endemic; where dissidents are dragged from their homes at night, imprisoned with no recourse to law, tortured and 'disappeared'; where, before baying mobs, people are whipped, mutilated and decapitated; where women are abused and repressed; where slavery, though nominally abolished, is

3

allowed a *de facto* and *de jure* existence; and where wealthy Saudis can arrange for children to be plucked off the streets in order to seal their bodily organs.[4] This is the Saudi Arabia, the dark world behind commercial calculation and official plaudit, that should be considered at the end of the twentieth century and beyond.

THE HUMAN RIGHTS FRAMEWORK

There is now ample evidence of the human-rights record of Saudi Arabia, with information and testimony drawn from many sources – academic study, legal commentary, statistical survey, journalistic account, political analysis, and testimony from Saudis themselves from both within the Kingdom and the exile community. For example, one human-rights body, the Minnesota Lawyers International Human Rights Committee, has referred to the 'deplorable human rights situation' that afflicts Saudi citizens and foreign residents in the Kingdom. Here attention is drawn to the character of an 'absolute monarchy with no penal code, no political parties, no freedom of religion, no trade unions, and no free press'; to the harsh repression of political and cultural dissent; and to the thousands of Iraqi refugees who, having fled to Saudi Arabia during the 1990/91 Gulf crisis, have been incarcerated in desert camps surrounded by barbed-wire.[5] There is reference also to the Saudi failure to adopt nearly all the significant international human-rights treaties and conventions (Appendix I); and to Saudi Arabia's 'frequent criticism of the human rights record of other nations' that belies 'its own reprehensible conduct at home – conduct which runs afoul not only of international standards, but also of Islamic law and its own domestic law'.[6]

In summary, and having completed a detailed investigation, the Committee urges the government of Saudi Arabia to take a number of specific steps:

- to comply with the mandates of the Universal Declaration of Human Rights;
- to publish and disseminate in Saudi Arabia Arabic-language versions of the Universal Declaration and of the Cairo Declaration on Human Rights in Islam (see Appendix II);[*]
- to take actions to prevent arbitrary arrest, imprisonment for nonviolent opposition to the government, and torture for any reason;
- to legislate to guarantee equal rights for women;
- to comply with international obligations for women's full participation in society and full control over their personal lives;

---

[*] The Cairo Declaration on Human Rights in Islam was agreed at the 19th Islamic Conference of Foreign Ministers (Cairo, 31 July to 5 August 1990). The Resolution (49/19-P) recognises 'the place of mankind in Islam as viceregent of Allah on Earth'; recognises the Declaration as a guide for all Member States; and agrees its purpose as providing general guidance in the field of human rights.

- to respect the cultural and religious rights of the Shi'a Muslim minority;
- to cease government discrimination against and persecution of the Shi'a minority;
- to protect the rights of foreign workers;
- to issue residency permits and exit visas directly to foreign workers, not to their employers; and to publicise how foreign workers may obtain redress for ill-treatment, fraud and other abuses;
- to guarantee freedom of movement in Saudi Arabia; to allow Saudi citizens freely to leave and enter the country; and to permit increased access to the country by foreign journalists and human-rights organisations;
- to promulgate a comprehensive penal code;
- to abolish the death penalty and other cruel and unusual punishments;
- to ratify the Covenants protecting civil, political, economic, social and cultural rights; protecting women and migrant workers; condemning torture and prostitution, etc.;
- to work with international organisations to settle the Iraqi refugees.

The character of absolute monarchy in Saudi Arabia has often been described. In this system there is no constraint on the power of the King: he appoints and dismisses all Cabinet ministers; all resolutions agreed by the Council of Ministers are ratified by royal decree; the fourteen provinces are governed by Saudi princes or other relatives of the House of Saud, all appointed by the King; and all other high public positions are occupied by relatives or associates of the royal family, again all appointed by the King. In this system ordinary Saudi citizens have no political or religious voice, while the King claims absolute power by virtue of descent and his selection by consensus among senior royals.

The justice system (see 'The *Sharia* Imperative', below) is administered by a system of religious courts, presided over by judges (*qadis*) appointed and dismissed by the King. Saudi Arabia has no bill of rights; trials are generally held in secret; and typically no legal counsel is permitted, the judge determining guilt or innocence and imposing the sentence. Confessions are typically obtained through torture, and political opponents are often arrested without warrants and held for long periods without trial. Members of the House of Saud and other powerful families are largely above the law, generally able to ignore legal constraints and sometimes to reverse unwelcome decisions made by the religious courts. In these circumstances there is no equality before the law: members of the House of Saud rate above other citizens, loyalists above critics of the regime, Muslims above non-Muslims, and men above women. Saudi Arabia has been represented by the International Committee for Human Rights in the Gulf and Arabian Peninsula (ICHR-GAP) as 'a country without human liberties and responsibilities'.

The United States, official hyperbole apart, is prepared to acknowledge the appalling human-rights record of Saudi Arabia. Thus a report issued by the US State Department in 1966 declared: '*The Government commits and tolerates serious human rights abuses ... Security forces continued to abuse detainees and to arbitrarily arrest and detain persons. Ministry of Interior officers abused prisoners and facilitated incommunicado detention in contradiction of the law, but with the acquiescence of the Government. Prolonged detention is a problem. The legal system is subject to executive and royal family influence. The Government prohibits or restricts freedom of speech, the press, assembly, association, and religion ... intimidation, abuse, and detention of citizens and foreigners of both sexes continued. Other problems include discrimination and violence against women, suppression of ethnic and religious minorities and strict limitations on the rights of workers'.*[7] The report notes that the Saudi government 'disagrees with internationally accepted definitions of human rights' and regards its interpretation of Islamic law as its sole guide in such matters. This candid depiction of human-rights derelictions is all the more remarkable in view of Washington's willingness to underwrite the Saudi tyranny in perpetuity.

One consequence of the 1990/91 Gulf crisis was to jolt Saudi Arabia into token improvements in human rights. There was talk of increased freedom of speech, a new consultative council (see Chapter 7), and a growing participation of ordinary citizens in political affairs. None of this came to anything. Aziz Abu-Hamad, Associate Director of Middle East Watch, indicated the importance that many observers attached to the long-promised constitutional reforms, in view of the absence of legal protection for Saudi citizens.[8] But the newly-announced Basic Law of Government, pledging in Article 26 that 'the state shall protect human rights according to *sharia*' was 'truly disappointing ... the Saudi government thus retains near complete discretion to define the content and scope of the rights it will respect'. The new laws clearly did no more than consolidate royal power, falling far short of internationally accepted human-rights provisions and even depriving Saudi citizens of the modest electoral rights they enjoyed sixty years ago: 'Their right to vote for national and provincial councils is eliminated; the Consultative Council is being stripped of the very little power it had left; rights of women and minorities are totally ignored; and existing severe restrictions on speech, assembly and association have been maintained. The new laws expand King Fahd's authority over both legislative and executive matters'.[9]

It was plain that no reforms would be allowed that in any way heralded a democratisation of the Saudi political process. King Fahd himself had been quick to denounce democracy and free elections as inappropriate to Saudi Arabia: 'Our people's makeup and unique qualities are different from those of the rest of the world'. The only purpose of constitutional change was to defuse domestic tensions by creating the impression that reform was possible; but now it was becoming increasingly clear that this ploy could not serve as a long-term strategy. The Nebraska-based Saudi dissident Mohammed H. Siddiq has emphasised that the nascent middle class will increasingly expect a degree of involvement in the political process ('the middle class immediately after the Gulf crisis became restive').[10] By contrast, Rashed Aba-Namay, of the Legal Department of the Ministry of Communications in Riyadh, suggests that the reforms introduced by Fahd will satisfy the Saudi people: '... rights and liberties need not necessarily have been enumerated in the constitution, because they are already implicitly protected by Islamic law. Human rights ... would be, therefore, identified, and protected by the *sharia* court'.[11] It all comes down to relying on the law of God, 'as provided by the Holy Book of God and the traditions of His Prophet'; moreover, declares Rashed, citing Article 26, the state 'protects human rights in accordance with the Islamic *sharia*'. He acknowledges the 'limited nature' of the reform:

> The right to be freely informed, free association and assembly are not mentioned ... which means that the right to form a political party or to contest government policy or to have free association in a public forum is still forbidden by the government. The prohibition of torture was not mentioned nor were other social issues dealt with such as the rights of women who are still banned from driving, must be veiled, restricted in the type of work they can do, and restricted from leaving the country without a husband or guardian.[12]

The deliberate omission of these and many other rights (some of which Rashed considers) means that the 'issues of human rights have never been dealt with forthrightly, and have been studiously avoided by the Saudi authority and its courts-based-Islamic *sharia* ... Easing the grip over the political life will best serve both the government's interests to govern peaceful and contented people as well as the interests of the people of Saudi Arabia'.[13] The problem is that no such easing of the grip over political life in the Kingdom is in prospect.

The only traditional access to political power, outside the House of Saud and its loyalists, has been via the mechanism of the feudal *majlis*, whereby kings or other royals hold open court to hear citizens' complaints. Hence the inflated propaganda surrounding the revised Consultative Council (*Majlis Al-Shura* – see Chapter 7), in essence an empty public-relations gambit designed to persuade domestic and foreign opinion that reform was in the air. In the event few were impressed by the tardy and inconsequential political changes introduced by an ailing Fahd. Nothing had been done to address the problems enumerated by the ICHR-GAP in 1991:

1 The Saudi government is not a signatory to either the Universal Declaration of Human Rights or the Universal Declarations of Civil and Political Rights, and of Economic and Social Rights.
2 Political parties are forbidden.
3 Freedom of the press is not a reality.
4 There are no labour unions to protect the rights of workers.
5 There is no written law governing criminal and political matters.
6 There is a state-established religion, Sunni Islam.

7   The right to freedom of movement and residence, both within and outside the country, is frequently restricted.

8   The government does not allow private educational institutions to exist. It controls all education and culture.

9   There is tight censorship of all foreign intellectual materials.

10 There is no bill of rights.

11 Prisoners are subject to torture and there is no oversight of the prison system to prevent that from occurring.

12 There is no access to participation in the government.

13 Individuals are subject to arbitrary arrest and imprisonment.

14 There is no right to peaceful assembly, association, and petition for grievances.

15 The government has institutionalised social and economic discrimination against ethnic and religious minorities.

16 The government enforces discriminatory treatment against women, even keeping silent about the rights that women do possess under the Koran.

All efforts to focus attention on such matters have been bitterly opposed by the Saudi government. For example, when on 3 May 1993 six legal, religious and academic scholars founded the Committee for the Defence of Legitimate Rights (CDLR), promulgating a declaration of Islam-based principles for reform, the Saudi authorities fired the men from their jobs, revoked their licences, denounced them in the press, imprisoned and tortured some, and forced others into exile. New laws have been introduced to attack the funds of reformers and to restrict their access to information. Suspects have frequently been intimidated, jailed and abused (see 'The Treatment of Dissidents', below).

The pattern has remained basically unchanged over the years. Whatever the hints or suggestions or shifts in rhetoric, the abuses of human rights have continued. Some years have seen intensified campaigns against dissidents, increased numbers of public mutilations, a more raucous vilification of women. The Saudi · state has often appeared trapped in the confines of a mediaeval absolutism, within the narrow dogma that seems unable to escape the compass of a Bedouin tent. In this context it is necessary to look at the various abuses in more detail; but, before that, it is now important to glance at the credal schemes – *Islam* in general and *sharia* in particular – used by the Kingdom of Saudi Arabia to give spurious justification to torture, intimidation and abuse.

THE ISLAMIC SOURCE

Islam – like most cults, mythologies and religions – is replete with superstition, fancy, hope and dread (see Chapter 2). It conditions believers to be receptive to supernatural explanations of mundane phenomena; it often magnifies human prejudice to absolute proportions; and it sanctions eternal torture (for example, the branding of men on their faces with red-hot metal – Koran, Sura 9, Verse 35) in the name of 'God, the Compassionate, the Merciful'. In August 1997 thousands of Muslims in the remote north-east of India flocked to see a sliced potato on which the words 'Allah' and 'Mohammed' were said to have magically appeared. One Momina Ahmed said that she was preparing lunch when the words, written in orange Arabic lettering, appeared on the newly cut surface. Something in excess of 10,000 pilgrims journeyed to her house in hope of seeing the potato.[14]* In June 1994 three Muslims killed an epileptic woman by forcing her to drink a gallon of salt water to rid her of 'evil spirits'.[15]

In Saudi Arabia the official version of Islam is not held to be inconsistent with reliance on soothsayers and wizards. Many of the princes employ resident soothsayers; and King Fahd himself, told by a fortune-teller that when the angel of death makes his appearance in his court the youngest of his children will not be at his side, has insisted that his son Abdul Aziz will never leave the court while Fahd is sitting on the throne. In January 1997 a theological debate required the adjudication of Saudi Arabia's highest religious authority, Sheikh Abdul Aziz ibn Baz. Were Muslims to be allowed to use ear drops and eye make-up without any infringement of the rules of fasting during the holy month of Ramadan? The worthy cleric deliberated: 'Some scholars believe it breaks the fast, but the eyes and ears are not orifices, so khol [make-up] and ear drops in no way amount to breaking the fast'. In June 1997 the company Nike Inc. was forced to apologise to Muslims, to donate $50,000 to a playground at a Muslim school, and to withdraw 40,000 pairs of sports shoes – because a logo on them resembled the word 'Allah' in the Arabic script.[16]

The resurgence of Muslim fundamentalism throughout the Arab world is today blocking the chances of significant reform in many moral and religious matters. The Saudi authorities, keen to pose as custodian of the faith for the entire Islamic world, are unlikely to moderate religious law in ways that would upset the *ulema*. In July 1993 the government, partly in response to fundamentalist pressure, created a new ministry of religious affairs, seen as a move to reinforce the country's official religious establishment at a time of growing challenge from a younger generation of radical preachers and Islamic scholars. The new ministry coordinates the funding and building of mosques, and pays the salaries of all the imams and others who work in a religious capacity. The religious police (the *Mutawa*, a highly repressive organ) arrest people on the streets, publicly chastise or whip them, and break into homes in pursuit of non-Islamic practices. The

---

* In August 1997 a Muslim family in Manchester (UK) was amazed – and delighted at their good fortune – when mother Hanifa Khan sliced into a tomato and found the Arabic word for Allah written inside. Said son Mubesher: 'It means that God can prove he is everywhere ... He's even in a vegetable ... a lot of people will probably want to come and see it'.

Mutawa are directly funded by the government, with the head of the organisation holding ministerial rank.

The Saudi government constantly celebrates the total lack of religious freedom in the Kingdom. With the Saudi version of Islam the official religion, all citizens are required to be Muslims and the practice of all other religions is prohibited. Foreign workers (for example, Jews and Christians) conducting clandestine religious services, particularly around non-Muslim religious holidays, have been harassed, arrested and detained. The report issued in 1996 by the US State Department cites the case of a Christian worship service broken up by police and *Mutawain*, with the man who hosted the service punished by lashing.[17] The strict Saudi interpretation of Islam (that is, the Wahhabist sect's interpretation of the Hanbali school of the Sunni branch of Islam) has consequences for Muslims who prefer other versions of the Prophet's creed. For example, believers are discouraged from visiting the graves of renowned Muslims. The Shi'a Muslim minority (about 500,000-strong) are subject to officially sanctioned social and economic discrimination, though marches on the Shi'a holiday of Ashura have recently been permitted (with some restrictions). Persons wearing religious symbols of any kind, including Muslim motifs, are likely to be confronted by the *Mutawain*, with non-Muslims who promote high-profile religious activity liable to public whippings followed by deportation.

The influence of the *ulema*, as the dominant Islamists in Saudi Arabia, has always derived from their close connection with the monarchy. This link has enabled the religious establishment to play a political as well as a religious role, helping to shape the course of state affairs that may have no obvious connection with religious authority. Thus the *ulema* have been consulted by the House of Saud in such non-religious matters as the royal succession (as, for example, when Saud was supplanted by Faisal) and over decisions with obvious religious ramifications (as when King Khaled and Crown Prince Fahd sought a *fatwa* in 1979 to legitimate the government response to the Great Mosque takeover). At the same time the official focus on one particular version of Islam has necessarily constrained the Saudi approach to *sharia* law (see 'The *Sharia* Imperative', below). There is debate about the degree of flexibility in the Hanbali school of law,[18] but little doubt among independent observers that a narrow Islamicism is poorly suited to the legal needs of a modern state wanting to play a role in the global culture.

The religious focus of the Saudi state is reflected in King Fahd's self-appointed title of Custodian of the Two Holy Mosques, an enhancement of the Saudi supervision of Mecca and Medina despite the more ancient Hashemite claims on such a role. This has meant that the House of Saud has rejoiced in its administration of the annual *hajj*, when as many as two million pilgrims can journey through Hejaz to worship at the holy shrines. In reality the *hajj* has been beset by political and religious problems: massacres, police brutality, banned minority groups, political protests, mass deaths through administrative incompetence, inadequate funding, and confusions over whether UN-sanctioned states (Iraq and Libya) should be allowed by the Saudi authorities to send pilgrims by air (see also Chapter 7). In June 1992 Iraq accused Saudi Arabia of starving to death ten pilgrims at a desert camp near Medina, and charged also that Saudi police had molested Iraqi women. Thus Abdullah Fadhel Abbas, the Iraqi religious affairs minister, declared that Iraq held King Fahd personally responsible for the 'killing of Iraqi pilgrims' and said: 'Their blood will not go in vain. We will demand compensation'. According to Fadhel, the pilgrims were denied food and water for five days: 'They were forbidden to leave the camp ... The condition of many of them is very serious ... more than ten of our pilgrims have died'.[19] In addition, he claimed, women were molested and pilgrims robbed.

In June 1994 the Saudi authorities banned the head of the Iranian pilgrims, Hojatoleslam Mohammad Reyshahri, from travelling to Medina – a serious prohibition for any Muslim in view of the sacred *hajj* duty acknowledged by all believers. Two years later, all Nigerians were banned from entering Saudi Arabia following a cholera outbreak in Nigeria. And those pilgrims encouraged to visit the holy shrines could not assume that their safety was guaranteed. There is already a grim catalogue of *hajj* disasters (Table 1.1).

Another problem that faced the Saudi authorities in 1997 was the Baghdad decision to ignore the seven-year-long UN air embargo and fly one hundred sick and elderly pilgrims to Saudi Arabia in observance of the *hajj* (the analogous

Table 1.1   Hajj-linked disasters (1980–97)

August 1980	Pakistani airliner flying out of Jeddah catches fire when a pilgrim on board lights a stove to brew tea; crash landing kills 301.
July 1987	Saudi security police suppress Iranian demonstration against the United States; about 400 people killed, with well over 600 wounded at Mecca.
July 1990	Stampede in tunnel leading to holy sites at Mecca causes deaths of 1426 pilgrims, mostly Malaysians, Indonesians and Pakistanis.
March 1991	Aircraft returning to Kuwait after off-season pilgrimage to Mecca crashes, killing 92 Senegalese soldiers and 6 Saudi airmen.
May 1994	Stampede in Mecca, during the ritual of 'stoning the devil', causes the deaths of 270 pilgrims, mainly Indonesians.
April 1997	Well over 200 pilgrims killed and 1300 injured in fire that surges through an encampment outside Mecca.

Source: Ed Vulliamy and Leslie Plommer, 'Hundreds of pilgrims die in inferno', *The Guardian*, London, 16 April 1997; Kathy Evans, 'Fear for Islam's holy pilgrims', *The Guardian*, London, 17 April 1997.

Libyan decision is profiled in Chapter 7). The United States UN envoy, Bill
Richardson, denounced the Iraqi decision and called for the Security Council to
condemn the violation. Saudi Arabia, notionally obliged to receive and protect
Muslim pilgrims, made no comment.

The Saudi decision to tolerate Libyan and Iraqi pilgrims, despite hesitating
over the risk to US–Saudi relations, has demonstrated the primacy of the clear
Islamic imperative in at least one area of official Saudi policy. This primacy is
shown also in many of the efforts to improve the human-rights record of the
Saudi regime in particular and of Muslim states in general. It seems unthinkable
for a state with a commitment to Islam to propose social and political reforms
outside a nominally Muslim context; and the same is true of individual Muslim
reformers. Change may be necessary but it has to be sanctified by an Islamic reference. Thus the petitions submitted to the Saudi regime urging reform characteristically invoke reverence for Islam as a justification for change. For example,
one 'Memorandum to the King' (November 1993) – signed by ex-ministers, journalists, merchants and government officials (*inter alia*) – includes in preamble a
brief commentary on the signatories: '*They address you out of their desire to
enhance its [Saudi Arabia's] safety and stability, progress and prosperity, out of
the obligation to the rulers, and out of obedience to Allah with regard to the religious duty of offering their advice to Allah, His Messenger, the leaders of the
Muslims and the common Muslims*''. This, typical of the genre, is no secular revolutionary tract, but a fervent appeal to piety and what is perceived as a purer
Islam. In this context three 'pillars' of the Ummah (Muslim community) are
identified: the *sharia*, the rulers, and the common people; with the summary of
the proposed plans recommending the creation of an organised framework for the
fatwa, 'taking into consideration the holy *sharia*, which is never erroneous or
immune from being changed, expressed in the texts from the Book [the Koran]
and the Sunnah ... the scholars unanimously agree that no-one, no matter how
high his status is, can monopolise the explanation of the true meaning of the
words of Allah and His Messenger, nor can he impose his religious views as
binding on the whole Ummah'. In short, it is possible within Islamic doctrine, to
justify reform; the King, whatever his status, has no legitimate power to block
such proper development of Islamic doctrine. The signatories, while seeking to
challenge the royal prerogative in religious affairs, are keen to preserve a clear
obsequious tone: '*We made a covenant with Allah that we only tell you the truth
and open our hearts to you as Allah has ordered us, and as a sign of our love and
loyalty to you*'.

In the same spirit the Cairo Declaration on Human Rights in Islam (see
Appendix II) stresses the religious roots of the document. The Islamic Ummah is
reaffirmed as 'the best nation' that God has made; human rights must be achieved
'in accordance with the Islamic *sharia*'; 'fundamental rights and universal freedoms' are 'an integral part of the Islamic religion ...'; all human beings are
descended from Adam and are God's subjects, and so on and so far. However

God does not love all people equally, but prefers those 'who are most useful to the rest of His subjects ...' (Article 1(b)); human life should be preserved 'throughout the term of time willed by God ...' (Article 2(c)) – does this permit capital punishment or not? And woman is equal to man (contradicting the Koran, Sura 4, Verse 38), though the husband is responsible for 'the support and welfare of the family' (Article 6(b)). Education should be framed to strengthen belief in God (Article 9(b)), and anti-Islamic propaganda is firmly prohibited as detracting from the 'unspoiled nature' of Islam (Article 10). Other items in the Declaration might be mentioned but Articles 24 and 25 characterise both the character of the document and its ultimate limitation: all the rights and freedoms stipulated in the Declaration are subject to the Islamic *sharia*, which is recognised as 'the only source of reference for the explanation or clarification of any of the articles' in the Declaration.

The central point is that it is not only Saudi Arabia and the other Muslim states that are trapped within the imaginative confines of a single text and the framework of law (see below) that supposedly flows from it and the surrounding commentary. The reformers are equally stultified *mutatis mutandis* by the same narrow vision. Islam has failed, as have all other pretentious and dogmatic creeds, to provide a consensual world view, even among acknowledged Muslims who notionally adhere to the same revealed doctrines. It is significant that Saudi Arabia is under philosophic threat primarily from other Muslims, rather than from secularists keen to expose the demonstrable absurdity of all state-imposed superstition. So, as befits all religious disputation, pious clerics cite a religious text to refute other pious clerics citing the same religious text. Neither side pauses to reflect on the source of the *critical principles*: since they cannot derive from the religious tradition itself –that would be transparently circular – they must derive from an extra-religious source (that is, from the independent human mind – so rendering the religious canon superfluous).

Riyadh has traditionally supported Muslim groups judged to be sympathetic to Saudi views; but politics and religion have often become entwined. Thus Shireen Hunter, deputy director of Middle East Studies at the Washington-based Center for Strategic and International Studies, has commented: 'It is an unbelievable irony that the West blames only Iran for the rise of fundamentalism. For years, the Saudis financed Islamic movements in Algeria, for instance, and the Muslim Brothers all over the place'.[20] Saudi money has been channelled to the Islamic Salvation Front (FIS) in Algeria, and to such groups as the outlawed al-Nahda movement in Tunisia and Hamas in the Israeli-occupied territories. Funds have been fed through the Mecca-based Muslim World League and its offshoot, the World Council of Mosques. Here and elsewhere Saudi Arabia has been happy to support disparate Muslim groups with independent Islamic views and radical political agendas.[21]

The complexities of Saudi policy in these areas, never publicised in the Kingdom, encourage debate about the character of Islam. It is obvious that the official Islam of Saudi Arabia has many extreme elements, and yet there is mounting fundamentalist pressure for a more robust interpretation of the Koran and the associated teaching. Thus Abdul Rahman Jibrin, a theological member of the CDLR, allegedly once declared that Shi'ites were apostates who merited death; while Mohammed al-Masari, the leader of the Committee, once described as 'prostitutes' those women who took to the wheels of cars in 1990 to protest against the ban on women drivers (the state-appointed Grand Mufti, Sheikh Abdul Aziz ibn Baz, pronounced them 'seditious'). In this context Muslim zealots are subjecting the House of Saud to unremitting pressure to adopt an even more extremist posture; and nor are Western *kafirs* (unbelievers) secure. In one instance, a Western journalist was berated by a Muslim devotee: 'You know some Arabic, the language God chose, and yet you are still a *kafir*. Convert before it is too late. Within 10 years, the *Ulema* will be in power everywhere [this announced in 1993]. Europe will collapse like the Soviet Union'.[22] The Saudi state has encouraged the spread of Islamic education – to the point that unemployable but zealous PhDs, highly knowledgeable in this or that item of useless doctrine – have been searching for a role. Hence a 1992 petition called for 're-inforcement of the rule of the *Ulema*, who are not sufficiently consulted by the government'; and demanded that every government department take on properly qualified Islamic scholars to perform a proper monitoring role for religious orthodoxy. At the same time the Saudi government still relies upon loyalist members of the clerical hierarchy to denounce the increasingly virulent critics of the House of Saud.

The efforts of the Saudi regime to profess Islamic virtue, while striving to fend off the appeals of the fundamentalists, have not been successful. A young Saudi woman returning after time in Europe commented: 'God help us ... Abroad I used to pray five times a day. Here, in this atmosphere of coercion, never! Here, Islam is not what it should be. It seems to be a crime just to be a woman, with those bearded policemen, so full of hate ... Now they even stop us from going into video stores, because we might tap our heels to the music. I would like to ask our political and religious leaders in what way they think they are different from the Iranian *mullahs* they so despise'.[23] Riyadh's appeasement of the fundamentalists continues to outrage liberal opinion; while the extremists, never satisfied, are encouraged to press for more concessions. Said one Saudi businessman: 'Islam, Islam, Islam! We are saturated with it. It was useful when we exploited it in the Arab cold war against the godless creeds of Nasserism, Ba'athism, communism. It did little harm during the boom days when we had full employment for everyone, including those who lengthened their beards, shortened their robes, and told us they were better Muslims than we are. Now it's different ... We must learn to think in non-traditional ways ...'[24]

To demonstrate its Muslim commitment the Saudi government has funded the building of more than 1500 mosques throughout the world, while some 210 Islamic centres have benefited from Saudi largesse. In addition, according to official figures, help has been given to 1079 Islamic schools, 200 institutes, 134 universities, 48 dispensaries, 76 hospitals and 87 Muslim associations.[25] The Holy Mosques at Mecca and Medina have been enlarged as a duty to the *hajj* pilgrims, a task which has involved the expropriation and development of the adjacent areas. In this the House of Saud has attracted further Muslim criticism. Thus the Medina-born, Nebraska-based Saudi dissident Mohammed Siddiq has protested at the 'major face-disfigurements' perpetrated by the Saudi authorities. Of the 'fraudulent treatments' of Medina and the Holy Masjid [Mosque] he declared:

1   The old city of Al-Medina, as they knew it historically, has been demolished and all, yes all, the historical and sacred sanctuaries that were around the masjid have been destroyed.
2   A large portion of the Holy Masjid was torn down and has been converted into a colossal structure that looks more like one of King Fahd's palaces rather than a masjid.
3   Last, but not least, these face-disfigurement operations have cost the *Ummah* of Islam more than US$25 billion.[26]

To such commentary are added the frequent criticisms of the House of Saud for its manifest profligacy and corruption (see 'The Corrupt Culture', below). Even in the immediate aftermath to the Iraqi invasion of Kuwait the wealthy Saudi Sheikh Eynani, an advisor to the Saudi royal family, was preoccupied losing more than $10 million at the roulette tables of a French Riviera casino, the Carlton Club at Cannes. In response to such a performance it is an easy matter for pious Muslims to quote the Koran (Sura 5, Verse 92): 'O believers! surely … games of chance … are an abomination of Satan's work!' King Fahd himself has reportedly lost more than $1 million in a single night of gambling at Monte Carlo. Siddiq has cited a poll conducted by a Saudi scholar indicating that 80 per cent of Saudis believe that Fahd has broken many Islamic laws, that he has been guilty of nepotism, and that his reign is the most corrupt of any in the history of Arabia.[27]

The Saudi regime, like Islamic authorities everywhere, claims that the Koran and the associated clerical commentaries are equipped to provide exhaustive guidance for every aspect of human life on earth. Thus there is an Islamic ethics, an Islamic politics, an Islamic economics,[28] etc. The central problem, common to all ideologies erected on a single text, is that the one sacred work is necessarily rooted in a particular historical context, with all the contingent circumstances of race, social status and general culture that this implies. The Koran itself (assuming that the various English translations convey a substantial part of the intended meaning), while exhibiting many interesting features, must be judged as derivative, narrow, repetitive and (to unbelievers and apostates) harsh in the extreme. Much has been made of the ethical improvements what Muhammed brought to

Meccan paganism; and, in various particulars, the point is well made. But the Koran, like all ethico-religious tracts, cannot represent the sum-total of humankind's ethical capacity. When a Muslim writer[29] or a Christian bishop[30] chooses to applaud the Koran, highlighting respectively the unique truth of Islamic teaching and the 'holiness and commitment' of the Muslim religion, there is much in text and tradition that is conveniently ignored. The culture-linked Koran – like the culture-linked Torah, Zend-Avesta and New Testament – is too limited by far to provide an adequate foundation for human rights in the modern world. We can applaud Muhammed for denouncing the pagan habit of burying female babies alive and for urging that the poor be helped; but who, outside the confines of a cruel bigotry, would applaud Muhammed's enthusiasm for hand-chopping and crucifixion in this life and torture with red-hot metals and fire in the next? It is easy to see how the limitations and harshness of Muhammed's Koranic teachings are embodied in the practical manifestations of *sharia* law.

THE *SHARIA* IMPERATIVE

The pre-Islamic period, known by Muslims as *Jahiliyah* (the time of ignorance), was characterised by unwritten tribal laws that were binding over the chiefs and their peoples. With the development of a primitive legal framework, custom and tradition were relied upon to shape barter conditions and other agreements among the tribal members. In Mecca, the principal city of Hejaz in the Arabian penin-sula, a public assembly evolved to stipulate and enforce the rules of conduct; a system of legal administration was established and the public offices were divided among twelve principal tribes. The office of *Hakam* governed the city and adjudicated on disputes, often with the assistance of volunteers (*Hilf-ul-Fudul*) who helped victims to seek redress. Even before Muhammed there were provisions for the payment of blood-money, cutting off the hands of thieves, and blackening the faces of adulterers. Women were regarded as inferior, as they would remain – a few heretical opinions apart – through the entire history of Islam. In one delineation the history of Islamic law has been divided into seven distinct periods (Table 1.2).

The main source of law in Saudi Arabia derives from the school founded by the Imam Ahmad Ibn Hanbal (780–855), as recognised in Article 6 of the 1926 Saudi Arabian constitutional instrument. Here 'reasoning' (*ijtihad*) is repudiated, analogy is rejected as a source of law, and particular prominence is given to the Koran and the Sunnah. This particular school was unpopular with the majority of Muslims, but was revived in the eighteenth century by the Wahhabists in the Arabian peninsula. Ibn Saud, the founder of modern Saudi Arabia, issued a royal decree to establish the authority of a number of Hanbali texts; and in 1928 the Supreme Judicial Council of Saudi Arabia passed a resolution to ensure that

Table 1.2   Seven periods in the history of Islamic law

The Meccan Period (610–622): Opposition to the rise of Islam gave Muhammed little opportunity to develop a framework of Islamic law.

The Medinan Period (622–632): A range of laws was promulgated with reference to the Koran and the other precepts of Muhammed.

The Republican Period (632–662): Laws based on the Koran and the Sunnah were supplemented by laws based on the consensus of the Muslim community.

The Umayyad Period (622–722): Muslim scholars struggled to develop a corpus of genuine Traditions while discarding the false ones.

The Formative Period (722–970): Various competing and conflicting schools of Islamic law were established – the Hanafi, Maliki, Shafi'i and Hanbali schools of Sunni Islam on the one hand; and the Shi'ite school on the other.

The Period of Research Fixation (970–1258): This period was marked by the 'closing of the door of reasoning (*ijtihad*)', whereby the jurists simply imitated the rulings of the old scholars.

The Ottoman Period (1288–1914): Islamic legal scholars produced commentaries, glossaries and compendiums with few additional contributions. After the Gulhane Charter (1839) a move was made to reform the existing legal system by adopting European codes.

Source: Sayed Hassan Amin, 1985.

courts in civil transactions relied upon Hanbali sources.[31] The principle of *ijtihad*, formerly repudiated, was reintroduced to allow an element of independent judgement.[32] At the same time the focus on the Koran as the ultimate source of *sharia* (Holy) law has remained deeply stultifying. Fewer than 200 of the Koran's 6000 verses – and these heavily culture-linked – focus on legal matters, far too narrow a base for a comprehensive and modern legal system.

The Saudi focus on the Koran as a source of law necessarily affords the *ulema* a central role in the government of the state. They are influential in:

- The judicial system;
- The implementation of the *sharia*;
- The nationally-distributed Religious Guidance Group;
- Religious education (law and theology) at all levels;
- Religious jurisprudence;
- Preaching and propaganda throughout the nation;
- Supervision of girls' education;
- Supervision of all mosques;
- Preaching of Islam abroad;
- Scientific and Islamic research;

- Administration of notaries public;
- The handling of court cases according to *sharia* law.[33]

The *ulema*-mediated system of Koranic (that is, *sharia*) law has deep implications for human rights in Saudi Arabia. In addition to the Koran and the Sunnah, account is taken of *Ijma* (the consensus of Muslim scholars on issues not addressed in the Koran or Sunnah, but where it is assumed that the consensus is consistent with them) and the *Qiyas* (rules derived by juridical analogy, as with *ijtihad* formerly rejected by the Hanbali scholars). In addition there is a growing body of Saudi law – defined by royal decrees, legislation promulgated by the Council of Ministers and approved by the King, and other approved rules and regulations issuing from government – that is assumed to follow *sharia* principles but which may enshrine nothing other than royal whim.

The 1975 Judicial Law, enacted under King Khaled's royal decree, nominally guaranteed the independence of the judiciary, established a hierarchy of courts, and made provision for public trials. The Supreme Judicial Council has administrative and supervisory jurisdiction over the four levels of *sharia* courts (Limited Courts, General Courts, Court of Appeals, and the Council itself). In addition a number of administrative and quasi-judicial tribunals, with powers conferred by royal decree, operate with nominal independence from the Ministry of Justice. Such tribunals include the Commission for the Settlement of Commercial Disputes, the Committee for the Settlement of Labour Disputes, and the Board of Grievances.

The principal of *legality* is taken as central to Saudi criminal law: 'The fundamental principle is that everything is permissible (*halal*) unless it is specifically prohibited, condemned, disapproved, or frowned upon'.[34] However, the absence of a well-defined penal code is seen as seriously undermining this principle of legality. Specific categories of crimes are recognised: boundary (*hudud*) crimes, such as the consumption of alcohol, theft, armed robbery, adultery and apostasy (fixed punishments specified in Koranic and other sources); equality (*qisas*) crimes, such as murder, involuntary killing, unintentional physical injury and maiming; and reform (*ta'azir*) crimes, such as usury, corruption and false testimony. *Hudud* crimes, generally carrying corporal or capital punishments, may require the testimony of four witnesses before a guilty verdict can be given; *qisas* crimes, implying equivalence, suggest that the guilty person may be punished 'in the same way and by the same means that he used in harming another person'; *ta'azir* crimes, signalling reform or chastisement, are punished with discretion.[35] Punishments are often severe (see 'The Practical Penology', below).

There are many perceived structural failures and abuses in the Saudi legal system. In reality, despite the 1975 Judicial Law, the independence of the judiciary is a fiction while the King retains ultimate authority: he appoints and dismisses every important figure in the judicial system – the Minister of Justice, all the Members of the Supreme Judicial Council, all the Judges of the Court of

Appeals, and every other judge in Saudi Arabia. Any individual who returns verdicts or takes decisions that are in any way uncongenial to the King can be instantly dismissed by royal decree. Experts in Saudi law, Saudi nationals and foreign workers have all provided testimony confirming doubts that the Saudi judicial system can deliver 'fair and unbiased decisions' in cases where the royal family has an interest.[36] Moreover, the court system is closely connected to the police functions of the Interior Ministry, rendering the courts directly amenable to police and security pressures.

The King – able to 'suspend, modify, ignore, or repeal any law or regulation'[37] – is largely outside the law, as are a host of favoured Saudi princes and their families. Since the King has unlimited power over the legislature, the executive and the judiciary the law can be constantly manipulated to the advantage of the House of Saud – so helping to define the *ultimately corrupt system*, in which the birth status of particular individuals is rated more highly than judicial institutions or ethical principles. In addition, just as members of the royal family are outside the law, so foreigners are treated differently from Saudis, non-Muslims are treated differently from Muslims, and women are treated differently from men. The cardinal principle of equality before the law, enshrined equally in the Universal Declaration of Human Rights and the Cairo Declaration on Human Rights in Islam (see Appendix II, Article 19(a)), is totally absent in Saudi Arabia. Moreover, the absence of an explicit penal code inevitably means that much penal action in the Kingdom is the result of arbitrary government initiative, royal whim and the corrupt use of police powers rather than due observance of clear judicial principle and established law. In this context there are no adequate provisions for the protection of human rights in the Kingdom.

Apologists for the Saudi legal system may claim that *sharia* law, based primarily on the Koran and Sunnah, offers a consistent and comprehensive judicial framework for modern society. Any such claim is patently absurd. Even within Sunni Islam, one of the two principal schismatic factions, there are several schools of Islamic law; and even within any one of the schools there is continuous debate about how certain teachings and doctrines should be applied. It is one of the enduring paradoxes of religion, risible to robust unbelievers, that the *One* God, the *One* Word, the *One* True Prophet (Saviour, Mahdi, Redeemer, Messiah, etc.) always generate dispute, contention, disagreement, war even, amongst the multifarious believers.

It is significant that various Saudi kings over the last few decades, while ever keen to declare the immutability of Koran and *sharia* law, have been compelled to attempt legal reforms, however desultory and unconvincing. It is significant also that Muslim scholars have been ready to contemplate the progressive evolution of Islamic law. Thus Muhammad Yusuf Guraya, a scholar working for the Government of the Punjab, has asked (of 'commandments in the sacred text'): 'Are they matters of conscience which will be tried in heaven, or are they subject to the action of a worldly court? How far is a Divine ordinance binding when the conditions under which it was promulgated have passed away?' And he notes that 'Under the impact of the West and under the influence of the predecessors, the modern [Muslim] scholars are forced to believe in the theory of the evolution of [*sharia*] laws'.[38]

Hence it is possible to imagine Saudi Arabia and other Muslim states evolving a system of law that is more appropriate for the emerging world culture. Any such change, necessarily radical, would have important consequences for the observance of human rights. To see just how far Saudi Arabia would have to progress in this area we need only glance at some human-rights issues in more detail ...

THE CLOSED SOCIETY

The Saudi regime responds to the possibility of criticism by banning free speech, by massive censorship, and by maintaining the tightest possible control over the expression of opinion – not only within the Kingdom but also beyond. This gross abuse of human rights is defended in official Saudi publications and in documents that seek to propagate an Islamic view of human society. Thus a leaflet issued by the Birmingham (UK)-based Islamic Propagation Centre International (IPCI) declares: *'Islam gives the right of freedom of thought and expression to all citizens of the Islamic state on the condition that it should be used for the propagation of virtue and truth and not for spreading evil and wickedness.'* This is the slogan of every repressive state – 'You are free to express those opinions that are congenial to the regime.'

The Saudi authorities are not prepared to tolerate criticism of Islam, the House of Saud or the government. People voicing such criticisms are liable to arrest and indefinite detention until they confess their crime or sign a statement promising that no further criticisms will be made. This restrictive situation has been specifically defined by government pronouncements. Thus a 1965 national security law and a 1982 media policy statement prohibit any dissemination of views that are critical of the regime. The policy statement instructs journalists to uphold Islam, to oppose atheism, to promote Arab interests, and to preserve the cultural heritage of Saudi Arabia. The Ministry of Information tells newspapers how to report controversial issues; and also appoints the editors-in-chief. Editors who do not reflect the defined government line on any issue are dismissed from their posts.

Saudi newspapers are allowed to publish news in sensitive areas, but only when the presentation of such items has been approved by the government-owned Saudi Press Agency (SPA) or by a senior government official. Every effort is made to censor any stories about Saudi Arabia in the foreign press that might be read in the Kingdom. Thus full-time censors are employed removing or blacking-out offending reports, glueing pages together, and banning certain issues of foreign publications or the publication in its entirety.

In addition to providing controlling finance for the print media the government also owns and operates the radio and television companies. Here the censors work hard to remove any unwelcome references to politics, criticisms of Islam, references to religions other than Islam, mention of pork or pigs, references to any alcoholic beverages, and all sexual material in songs and other foreign broadcasts. The legal status of satellite receiving dishes remains ambiguous: their import was prohibited in 1992, under pressure from the *ulema*, and in March 1994 the government banned the sale and installation of such equipment – but the dishes are still used and people are allowed to subscribe to satellite decoding services. All forms of public artistic expression are heavily censored. Cinemas are prohibited, as are all musical and theatrical performances unless specifically authorised. Academic freedom is non-existent, with permanent blanket-bans imposed on such topics as biological evolution, Freudian psychology, Marxist economics, Western music and Western philosophy. Some professors have testified that government and religious informers monitor their performance in the classroom.[39]

The denial of the right to free expression helps to abrogate most other rights, which in any case are either heavily restricted or totally prohibited. If people are not informed freely, and if they cannot discuss the government without fear of persecution, then they are in no position to demand even those rights included in the *sharia* or the supplementary texts. The Articles of Government (see Appendix III) make no guarantee of freedom of information, a deliberate omission designed to keep the media under government control. Thus Article 39 states: 'The information and publication media should express themselves in a courteous manner and abide by the regulations of the state and contribute to the education of the nation and support its unity. All acts that lead to sedition and disunity or undermine the state's security and public relations or insult the dignity and rights of the people will be prohibited'. For King Fahd himself *there is nothing in freedom of expression beyond the ability to contact an official*: 'The freedom of the individual in this country is secured by the Islamic faith in practice. Expression, rights and duties, as long as it is not harming others, and not violating Islamic teachings or existing rules, are permitted. The citizen is free to contact any official, and there is no door that would be closed to them by any official.'[40]

In this atmosphere of cultural repression the primary interest of the Saudi regime is in blocking any groundswell of critical opinion that might destabilise the House of Saud. Here the regime can rely upon the support of the conservative religious establishment: Muslim fanatics have been known to shoot at satellite dishes with .22 rifles.[41] And the support of the media can be largely guaranteed by appointing – and, where necessary, dismissing – the people who run newspapers, magazines and broadcasting stations. At the end of the 1980s King Fahd encouraged the establishment of a London-based satellite station, the Kingdom's own Middle East Broadcasting Centre, to transmit approved programmes to the whole of the Arab world. Royal staff directly run two newspapers, *Al-Sharq al-Awsat (The Middle East)* and the *Arab News*; with the Kingdom estimated to dominate as much as 95 per cent of the Arabic-language newspapers, magazines and radio and television stations throughout the Arab countries and beyond.[42] Here it is emphasised that the domination can be direct, when the royal family maintains total ownership, or indirect, when Saudi money or intimidation guarantees support for the Saudi regime.

The Saudi government has signed a range of 'media protocols' with the governments of several Arab states, including Egypt, to ensure favourable publicity for Saudi Arabia. This means an effective prohibition on articles that criticise Saudi domestic or foreign policy, the state of Saudi finances, and the behaviour of any members of the royal family. One Egyptian editor-in-chief has testified that he received instructions from Egypt's Ministry of Information not to criticise King Fahd, his family, or any policies of the Saudi government.[43] In the same way the Saudi regime has imposed its media policies on the smaller members of the Gulf Co-operation Council. The need of foreign advertisers to focus on the lucrative Saudi market further strengthens Saudi control over the media. Thus in 1994, following the declaration of a *ulema*-inspired ban on all women's magazines formerly available in the Kingdom, 19 out of 24 publications immediately collapsed since they were dependent on the Saudi market for their advertising revenues.[44] This means that by direct control (see Table 1.3) or by indirect means that are equally effective the Saudi regime is able to exert massive control over a broad media culture.

Table 1.3   Some Saudi royal-family media interests

Saudi Research and Marketing Company (SRMC) – publishes more than 15 daily, weekly and monthly publications; organisation owned by Prince Salman bin Abdul Aziz; the chairman of the board of directors is his son, Prince Ahmad.

Al-Hayat Press Corporation – branches in London, Riyadh, New York, Paris and Jeddah; owned by Prince Khaled bin Sultan bin Abdul Aziz, commander-in-chief of Arab forces in Gulf War.

Middle East Broadcasting Centre – created in 1991 by Saudi billionaire Salih Kamil to operate as London-based satellite TV station, the first for the Arab world; bought in 1993 by Walid and Abdul Aziz Barahim, brothers-in-law of King Fahd.

Arab Media Corporation – owns Rome-based Arab Radio and TV (ART) network, currently expanding from four satellite TV channels; 90 per cent owned by Salih Kamil; Prince Walid, a nephew of King Fahd, owns 30 per cent of ART and holds shares in Mediaset, with links to Silvio Berlusconi's Fininvest Group.

Orbit Television – Rome-based network broadcasting to some 23 countries; owned by Prince Fahd, a nephew of King Fahd; in June 1994 agreed to transmit BBC Arabic Service – controversy when network censored coverage of Masari case (see text).

The all-pervasive censorship of Saudi-linked media (eight Arabic- and two English-language dailies in the Kingdom; dozens of weeklies, monthlies and quarterlies) has discouraged investment from Saudi businessmen and financiers – making it even easier for the House of Saud to maintain its censorship grip. The whole spectrum of the Saudi élite – including 20,000 princes and princesses – remains immune from any hint of criticism. The scale of corruption (see below), the endemic bribes, the shady arms deals – all encouraging corruption in countries that deal with the Kingdom – cannot be questioned in the media; the profligacy of the princes, problems with the state's finances, the street protests of liberals and other dissidents, the presence of US forces and bases on Saudi soil – none of this can be reported or questioned; and particular cultural features of other states – for example, the GCC royals – are equally taboo.

In 1990 a Saudi citizen was sentenced to nearly a year in prison and more than 150 lashes for bringing books contrary to Islam into the Kingdom. The man was said to have breached internal security and to have disobeyed the will of King Fahd. Once the books had been seized, they were promptly destroyed by customs officials, so giving the prosecutor no opportunity to inspect them. None the less he condemned them as unlawful, whereupon the government-appointed judge rubber-stamped his version of events and found the man guilty. No corroborating evidence was given to support the prosecution.[45] The scheme was now well entrenched. Judgements in court would be made on arbitrary grounds, often in the absence of relevant testimony or decisive evidence. This situation continued to bear heavily on any attempt to obtain, express or disseminate information. A report, *Silent Kingdom* (from the London-based International Centre Against Censorship), noted in late 1991 that the ill-treatment and torture of people detained for 'crimes of opinion' remained 'routine'. Laws were being used to harass, dismiss and jail journalists and outside the Kingdom the Saudi regime was exerting pressure wherever possible to ban books and films, and to close down newspapers and magazines.[46]

The report, produced by Article 19 (after Article 19 of the Universal Declaration of Human Rights: 'Everyone has the right to freedom of expression ...'), notes that in Saudi Arabia 'anything contradicting the origins or the jurisdiction of Islam, undermining the sanctity of Islam ... or harming public morality' is subject to censorship. Artists and poets have been arrested, and books and films are routinely confiscated. In one case study considered by Article 19, a 40-year-old housewife, Zahra Al-Nasser, was detained in July 1989 for possessing a Shi'a prayerbook and a photograph of the late Ayatollah Khomeini. She died 'after three days of brutal torture'. In another case a certain Ghassan Mohammed Hussein Saleh was detained and abused 'for possessing a number of old books about genies, ghosts and magic'. The Article 19 group concluded that 'academic freedom' is unknown in Saudi Arabia.

The Saudi regime, highly nervous at any suggestion of free discussion, has even been driven to banning the quoting by press, radio or television of a particular Koranic verse. The royal family remains particularly embarrassed by the manifestly anti-monarchical statement recorded by the Prophet in Sura 27, Verse 34: 'Kings when they enter a city spoil it, and abase the mightiest of its people ...' Many Muslim fundamentalists, committed to their egalitarian version of Islam, are keen to cite 27/34 as a means of undermining the House of Saud. Hence the ban on this and any similar declaration, whatever its seeming authority. Sometimes Saudi agents even go so far as to track down dissident writers abroad and convey them back for a lengthy incarceration in the Kingdom. Thus when the Beirut-based dissident Nasser al-Said published *The History of al-Saud* in 1979 he was, according to his lawyers, kidnapped, flown back to Saudi Arabia in a private plane, and then jailed. In the same spirit, in the immediate aftermath of the 1991 Gulf War, some forty religious leaders were banned from speaking in the mosques.

In early 1992 the Saudi authorities offered a reward of 2m riyals (£310,000) to anyone who could supply information leading to the arrest of the authors of an illegal but best-selling cassette tape that was critical of the royal family and the Saudi regime. One source noted that 'scores of people, both civilians and clerics, have been detained, with many of them released after questioning'. One of the tapes, highly critical of Riyadh's principal foreign ally, suggests that the United States is a country where men marry men and where joggers can be seen 'running in the streets naked, like wild animals'; and it adds: 'God must destroy America the same way it did with Russia, for America is an arrogant nation where people do nothing but fornicate, men go with men and women ...' One of the main features of the subversive tapes is the blame heaped on Arab leaders for the supposed New World Order imposed by President Bush on the Middle East. Here the Arab kings and generals who aided the 1991 onslaught on Iraq are perceived as helping to crush a renascent Islam. In response to the tapes and other signs of dissident criticism, Sheikh Baz informed the newspaper *Al-Sharq al-Awsat* that Muslims only had the right to gently 'advise' their king. Obedience to the sovereign and the *ulema* was absolutely essential; anything less represented 'revolt' and was unacceptable to Islam. Even if the monarch took a decision that was evil in the eyes of God, nothing more than gentle advice and prayer was allowed.[47]

In October 1993 the Saudi government managed to secure agreement with Shi'ite opponents whereby the Shi'ites would stop publishing material abroad that was critical of Saudi Arabia's policies and human-rights abuses. It was reported that the London-based monthly *Arabian Peninsula* would cease publication and that the Shi'ites would refrain from further criticism. In return the Shi'ites would be allowed to return home, some prisoners would be released, and passports would be issued to members of the Shi'ite minority in the Kingdom. Commented a Saudi royal: 'You have always got to leave the door open that says you can still become a member of the mainstream, which is what we have done'; while officials noted that the move would be useful in neutralising the efforts of radical Sunnis trying to move up through the ranks of the clergy. In addition, Saudi Arabia was negotiating to take control of at least three Europe-based Arabic-language publications: *Al-Arab* (based in London), *Sourakia* (London) and *Muharar* (Paris).[48]

Sometimes the Saudi regime faces unwelcome criticism that is hard to stifle; as, for example, when the Saudi ambassador to London, Ghazi Algosaibi, publishes a 700-page novel that many have interpreted as a coded attack on the House of Saud;[49] When the erstwhile Saudi oil minister, Sheikh Yamani, attracts a high-level dissident group around him; and when Yamani's son, Hani Ahmed Zaki Yamani, publishes an intensively 'loyal' book that at the same time criticises Saudi corruption and urges fundamental reform.[50] Where the Saudis *are* able to act against independent voices, they do not hesitate – as when the Mufti of Lebanon, under Saudi pressure, forced police action against the distinguished publisher Riad al-Rayyes in order to ban unacceptable texts. Commented al-Rayyes: 'The "inquisition" of fundamentalist extremism has come to Lebanon to practise repression of a new kind ... as if Lebanon were Algeria with its fundamentalist movements, or Egypt with its al-Gama'a al-Islamiya, or Saudi Arabia with its Wahhabi fatwas'.[51] In December 1995 the Saudi ambassador in London, despite his own independent forays, appealed to Riyadh to cut off funds to Yusuf Islam (formerly the popular singer Cat Stevens) on account of his 'insulting' remarks about the Saudi regime: he had called for the release of Saudi dissidents, had opposed the 1991 Gulf War, and had declined to appear at the Saudi national day (23 September) celebrations. In April 1996 the Saudi authorities decided to cut BBC Arabic Service transmissions to the Middle East, following Saudi censorship of the reporting of the Masari case (see also Chapter 7). Masari himself was quick to applaud the divorce: 'It is the best thing. The BBC should not submit to Saudi censorship. There is no way you can get into the same bed with someone who has AIDS and get away safely. I believe the BBC filed a strong complaint against the censorship of services from Rome and the Saudis couldn't take it. The BBC World Service would do better to find a free channel not owned by the Saudis'.[52]

In April 1997 the leading American publishing house Simon and Schuster was forced by pressure from the Council on American-Islamic Relations (CAIR) to destroy thousands of copies of a children's book after complaints that Muhammed had been depicted unfairly – as a lover of beautiful women, a *bon vivant* and a fearsome warrior. The book, written by a notable historian, also offended the Muslims because it carried a drawing of Muhammed, forbidden in Islamic law. The publishers pledged to consult Muslim scholars about a revised version. (Saudi royals surprisingly agreed to sit for the court painter Andrew Vicari to produce portraits commemorating the Saudi contribution to the 1991 Gulf War – any depictions of the human form are supposed to violate Koranic law.) The Islamic attitude in general and the Saudi posture in particular are broadly consistent: censorship, artistic prohibition, the banning of free expression

– all this must be maintained in support of a narrow obscurantism, the obsession with a particular Koranic interpretation. In September 1996 the Saudi Ministry of Information was again warning commercial establishments (hotels, housing compounds, furnished apartments) against showing uncensored films; efforts were now intensifying to satisfy the fundamentalists that Muslim virtue could be safely protected in the Kingdom. Newspapers, magazines, books, radio and television broadcasts, films, education lectures – all would continue to be scrutinised, mutilated, stifled. The abuse of a central human right would continue.

THE CORRUPT CULTURE

Corruption in Saudi Arabia – involving such phenomena as business 'commissions', bribery, secret accounting systems, nepotism, croneyism, royal profligacy, etc. – is multifaceted and endemic. It is so much part of Saudi culture that those people with position or status who *fail* to enrich themselves at public expense are widely seen as unimaginative or incompetent; and foreign traders, acquainted with what is expected, find themselves making questionable accommodations in order to secure business – to the point that they themselves may be branded as corrupt in more fastidious states. There have been few attempts to rein back the massive scale of corruption in the Kingdom, with most of the financial and other abuses constantly reinforced by self-serving behaviour sanctified by traditional royal prerogative. Foreign commentators routinely acknowledge the scale of Saudi corruption but rarely propose ameliorative policies for commercial companies or national governments keen to preserve the Saudi connection. One American group urging radical reform is the Committee Against Corruption in Saudi Arabia (CACSA), a group based in McClean, Virginia, that has strong links with the business communities of Saudi Arabia and the United States: *'The group intends to drastically change the way Saudi Arabia's government and businesses are run and to change the way US corporations, policy makers, and strategic planners relate to the Saudi government and its business ...''.* A 6-Article CACSA Mission Statement, available primarily via the Internet, urges a peaceful and moderate approach committed to parliamentary democracy, legislative reform (including laws to protect human rights in general and women's rights in particular), and measures to correct 'the problems created by King Fahd's rule ...'.

A principal problem facing Saudi Arabia has been the traditional assumption that the national income of the Kingdom can be viewed as royal revenue: the national Treasury is the bank account of the House of Saud. This has meant that subjects of the King have enjoyed no rights beyond those agreed at royal whim – so successive monarchs have been able to disburse cash, land and oil to relatives and croneys with no thoughts other than enrichment of themselves and their class, and the security of their tyrannical regime. Thus the national revenue of

$234.8 million in 1954 was regarded as the King's income, with no independent control over the finances involved. It was inevitable in these circumstances that the system of royal prerogative established by Ibn Saud would lead to a magnified scale of corruption among his successors in the years that followed. Thus under King Saud, erstwhile Crown Prince under Ibn Saud, the royal court *'became a forcing house of waste, decadence, corruption and intrigue as a growing throng of princes and self-serving advisors plunged their hands into the bulging coffers'.*[53]

Throughout all the layers of royal officialdom, bribery and graft were the norm. Those in a position to pay royal employees withheld wages and pocketed the due earnings; wages and bills were delayed for months.[54] Expensive fittings for the royal palaces disappeared and were sold back 'to the royal commissariat from shops ... owned by the King's "advisors"'.[55] A royal deal with Aristotle Onassis, the Greek shipping magnate, was lubricated by vast commissions and by Onassis signing a contract with a special ink designed to evaporate.[56] King Faisal, Saud's successor, was well aware of the scale of corruption in the Kingdom but knew that any attempt at serious reform would damage the unity of the House of Saud. The corrupt culture installed by Ibn Saud continued as a defining element of the Saudi state under Saud, Faisal and the later kings; under Fahd, first as Crown Prince and then as King, the scale of financial corruption was further magnified. Thus in 1977 the Saudi government opted for nationwide switch-gear to be installed by Philips of the Netherlands, which by chance was represented by the Al Bilad company owned by Muhammed bin Fahd, the sixth son of the Crown Prince. It was revealed that the price agreed with Philips was about $6700 million, five times the consultants' estimates, a massively inflated figure in part because Muhammed was taking substantial 'commissions' from both Philips and its sub-contractors. One estimate suggests that Muhammed's slice of the deal would have amounted to $1300 million.[57] It was similarly revealed in 1979 that 'disguised commissions' of up to $5 a barrel were being paid on some contracted oil sales; in one investigated case, providing a Saudi prince with a $2.4 a barrel commission for 100,000 barrels a day for a year (amounting to around $100 million).[58] One prince has been known to demand 17 per cent commissions on multi-billion dollar engineering contracts.[59]

The corrupt acquisition of wealth by the Saudi royals has long been reflected in their profligate life-styles. Thus in 1988 King Fahd ordered a luxury 482-feet-long luxury yacht, the *Abdul Aziz*, which he hoped would meet his needs. Built in Denmark, the vessel cost around $100 million and came equipped with marble bathroom and gold-plated fixtures, two swimming pools, a ballroom, a gym, a sauna, a theatre, a fully-equipped hospital (two operating rooms and intensive-care unit), and four US-supplied Stinger missiles capable of shooting down air-craft. In early 1990 Fahd, accompanied by a 150-strong entourage, visited the French Riviera where he spent £1 million over two weeks of shopping, drinking, entertaining and gambling (in violation of Koranic teaching).[60] The party arrived in five private planes, Fahd in his own private Boeing 747 that cost £78 million with £60 million worth of extras, his wife in a similar plane, and the entourage in three smaller planes. He stayed at his palace seven miles from Nice, described by a journalist: 'Its walls are decorated with pure gold leaf. A pure silk Bedouin tent fills one enormous room. A computer centre is linked to the world's business centres and there are aircraft and missile radar systems too. Everywhere you look there are carved ivory pillars, marble floors and mountains of antique furniture. The gardens are half a mile long, stocked with trees and flowers from all over the world.[61]

It is reported that Fahd headed his fleet of 40 limousines on a spending spree. The purchases included: a truckload of Louis XIV furnishings (£750,000) chocolates (£20,000), clothes (£80,000) and a leaving tip to the people of Nice (£100,000). In 1990 Fahd's wealth was estimated at something in excess of $18 billion; he was known to possess at least twelve royal palaces, several yachts and jet aircraft, and fleets of Cadillacs and Rolls-Royce.[62] Fahd's fortune is only part of the royal wealth in Saudi Arabia. Innumerable princes are millionaires and some are billionaires, most having accomplished nothing except birth into the House of Saud. Thus Prince Turki is a billionaire, with a lifestyle so profligate that two of his aides were reported to have quit in disgust.[63] When Turki was visiting Harvard he booked 40 hotel rooms on two floors, and brought sand and trees into the hotel to create an oasis; his fleet of limousines caused traffic jams and he demanded that a local park be cleared of people so that he could hold a royal picnic. (All this happened at a time when the Saudi government was facing the 1990 Gulf crisis and urging the Saudi people to make sacrifices). In 1994 Prince Bandar, Saudi ambassador to the United States, bought the house in front of his own in suburban McLean, Virginia, in order to demolish it so as to provide a larger entranceway to his $8.6 million property. Then he purchased a neighbour's house for $4.7 million to serve while his own was being remodelled. Some observers thought he might have managed in the interval with his other 26-bathroom holiday house in Aspen, Colorado.[64] (And all this was taking place during the new 'austerity' measures introduced by the Saudi government in response to the financial crisis – see Chapter 7.)

In October 1994 King Fahd's wife, Al-Anud Bint Musaid Bin Jiluwi, arrived in Phoenix, Arizona, for a spine operation – and, having intended to stay there for three weeks, remained for two years. The Barrow Neurological Institute was adapted to meet her needs: the seventh floor was refitted and redecorated, the other patients were moved out, and the floors were fitted with priceless Persian carpets. A top-class chef was brought into the hospital, and the medical staff were taught the finer points of Saudi etiquette. A satellite dish was installed to keep the Saudi 'queen' in touch with events back home.[65] The proffered tips were so large (typically $100) that managers ruled they had to be returned. The 300-strong Saudi entourage astounded local traders, as royal Saudi women often spent as much as $30,000 on impulse buys of jewelry and other luxuries, while the local limousine company had 58 of its vehicles on permanent stand-by. The royal party then moved on to Los Angeles where a similar level of expenditure was anticipated.

In October 1997 it was deemed necessary for Saudi ministers and officials to visit the Saudi Defence Minister, Prince Sultan, recuperating from a knee operation in a Swiss clinic. For this purpose 100 Mercedes cars for the 300 Saudi personnel were conveyed on lorries from Germany, a scale of profligacy that reportedly angered the local Swiss car rental companies.

The royal wealth is widely spread. Seven of Fahd's palaces (worth around $11 billion) are in Saudi Arabia; with another half dozen or so in other countries. The dissident Mohammed Siddiq draws attention to Fahd's $2.5 billion Al-Yamamah Palace near Riyadh and to a Fahd 'cottage', four times the size of the American White House, in Marbella, Spain: '... what of the people? Are they not able to share in the wealth that is pumped from the ground of their nation? Do not worry. King Fahd has made it possible for the people to share in his wealth. He has built for himself twelve palaces which the people can admire from afar.'[66] As with the earlier Saudi monarchs, Fahd maintains his grip on national revenues by ownership of, or involvement in, the leading companies in the Kingdom. It was estimated in 1994 that members of the House of Saud and their relatives and in-laws were chairmen of 520 Saudi corporations, often doing no more than lending their names to organisations financed and run by the government or by loyalists happy to exploit the royal connections. Many Saudi princes are 'silent partners', promoting particular business interests and receiving huge sums in return. It is rare to conduct serious business in Saudi Arabia without significant royal involvement at some level and at some stage.

In addition to the royal business connections, where vast returns are given for minimal effort, the princes are granted salaries simply because of their links to the House of Saud. By 1984 each prince received a monthly salary of $20,000; and, if he held a job, he could be receiving a royal salary, an official salary and a princely salary. Senior princes expected to receive much more than the lowly sum of $20,000 awarded to the vast bulk of the 6000 or so standard princes. Moreover, it was traditional to regard every princess or royal child as a 'prince' for salary purposes – so an ordinary prince with ten children and two wives could be receiving around $260,000 a month, in addition to any official or commercial salaries he might pick up on the way. A top prince in the public eye might receive a grant of around $100 million a year.[67] Observed one economist in 1996: 'With "ordinary" princes on a monthly stipend of nearly $30,000 they cost us at least $4 billion a year'.[68] In general, the royal family decides what its needs are, and government ministers are obliged to behave accordingly. The bulk of the national revenue is paid to King Fahd before it is registered as state income. He then allocates money to the many members of the royal family in an improvised manner, ensuring that his own funds are maintained in a healthy state. He informs the Oil Minister how much he intends to maintain in his own accounts, and the minister is bound to agree his wishes.[69]*

The endemic Saudi corruption has inevitably spilled over into high-profile cases with international significance. Thus the Lockheed scandal, when vast payments were made to Fahd's friend Adnan Khashoggi, who had become 'the world's richest man' by serving as an agent for the US aerospace giants Lockheed and Northrop in the 1960s and 1970s, exposed the possibility of a royal Saudi involvement in financial corruption on a huge scale. Saudi Arabia was also deeply involved in the Iran–Contra scandal that rocked the American government. Similarly the 1991 scandal involving the Bank of Credit and Commerce International (BCCI) revealed a substantial Saudi involvement in the persons of Kamal Adham, Ghaith Pharoan and Hamad bin Mahfouz, all accused of gaining hundreds of millions of dollars from illegal transactions (Mahfouz settled out of court after denying all charges, Adham has paid back $115 million, and Ghaith Pharoan was given Saudi protection – and all friends of King Fahd.[70] The dissident Saudi Arabian diplomat Mohammed al-Khilewi resigned in June 1994 as first secretary in the Saudi mission to the United Nations, claiming to have documents revealing a catalogue of Saudi corruption: *'I am against the king himself and the corruption of his rule. He is a dictator who has stolen our rights and our money and is not doing any of the correct things for our people. There are no human rights in my country. There are no political rights. Even a political demonstration is illegal.'*[71]

In October 1994 British ministers in the House of Lords came under pressure to investigate allegations that Mark Thatcher, son of the former prime minister, was paid £12 million commission in the 1985 Al-Yamamah Saudi Arabian arms deal – a 'sorry mess', according to Lord Richard, the Labour leader in the Lords. It was known that huge commission fees were paid out to many brokers, middlemen, politicians and diplomats; and that details were contained in British Aerospace documents held in a Swiss bank. Intermediaries commonly played key roles in major arms deals: 'The difference with Al Yamamah is that the son of the British prime minister who negotiated the multibillion contract was one of those middlemen who benefited financially.'[72] To the Saudis, with their culture of deal-making through nepotism and connections, the involvement of the prime

---

* Individual Saudi royals are free to dispense funds on whim, according to their political and other sympathies. Thus Vanessa Redgrave relates how she needed money to continue a theatrical court case that grew out of her pro-Palestinian sympathies: 'I needed $150,000 to carry on ... I telephoned the Washington embassy of the Royal Kingdom of Saudi Arabia and asked for Prince Bandar Bin Sultan's secretary. The ambassador ... invited me to see him and his family in Virginia. I flew up from Boston ... I flew back ... with a cheque for $150,000 ...' (Vanessa Redgrave, *An Autobiography* (London: Random Century, 1991)).

minister's son was unremarkable; and it seemed clear to some observers that Mark Thatcher was onto a good thing. Said Steve Tipping, a former associate: '... I was never involved in Saudi Arabia. That was Mark's business. In the world of defence, Saudi Arabia is an essential market because you can make the silly rag-headed buggers buy anything.'[73]

In 1984 the Saudi intelligence agency Istakbarat secretly recorded telephone conversations between some of the leading participants in the Al-Yamamah negotiations. Mark Thatcher's possible use to the Saudis was discussed, and his bid set against a cheaper one from a certain 'John'. An Arab arms broker commented that 'Mark is more in power and he has influence with the military group and with the government'; and he added: 'These people will sell their families for money'.[74] In the event the Saudis opted for Mark Thatcher as their middleman. Sources indicated that he was paid 'a minimum of £12 million, but probably closer to £20 million'.[75]

The Thatcher issue was never resolved in the way that some politicians and others had demanded. There was evidence in the public domain about the nature of his commercial involvement, but no official enquiry and exposure. After the unresolved Thatcher episode, it was Jonathan Aitken, former Conservative minister with links to the highest echelons of the Saudi regime, that was most obviously involved in scandal associated with Saudi Arabia. Aitken, at one time part of the British government, had also acquired influential Arab friends. The Saudi Prince Muhammed had provided £2 million to enable the Aitken cousins to buy Hume Corporation from the Rothschild Investment Trust and launch Aitken Hume International, with Jonathan employed as the £40,000-a-year chairman of the new company. Adnan Khashoggi, the Saudi tycoon, with whose wife Soraya he allegedly had an affair, was another of Aitken's close associates; as was Wafic Said, the Syrian-born business 'fixer' and close friend of Mark Thatcher; and Said Ayas, the godfather to Aitken's daughter Victoria, and a man accustomed to handling worldwide investments for the Saudi royals.

The subsequent scandal involving Jonathan Aitken – with fresh evidence of corrupt Saudi largesse, an abandoned libel suit, a mystery over missing funds, and the final exposure of lies under oath – revealed yet again how vast Saudi funds had tempted ambitious individuals into perjury and corruption.[76] In March 1997 Thailand issued an arrest warrant for Adnan Khashoggi on charges of conspiracy to defraud the Bangkok Bank of Commerce (BBC); and three months later, Said Ayas, a victim of the fallout from Aitken's public humiliation, was under arrest in Saudi Arabia over the reported disappearance of £25 million from the accounts of Prince Muhammed. In October 1997 Said Ayas, aided by the 'Saudi underground', escaped house arrest and fled Saudi Arabia. Prince Muhammed was said to be furious.

The culture of corruption, endemic in Saudi Arabia through the entire history of the modern Kingdom, has always been able to infect the various strata of the Saudi regime and also the many susceptible opportunists abroad.

THE TREATMENT OF DISSIDENTS

The Saudi regime, preoccupied with the need for survival, has been forced to contend with many disparate groups – the Shi'a minority, Sunni fundamentalists, liberal reformers, Iraqi refugees, foreign agitators, women. All have been classed as *de facto* and *de jure* dissidents, destabilising factions within the narrow confines of an intolerant and feudal estate. And so all have been repressed: *'This regime so essential to the US was marked by a policy of internal repression which combined the most virulent tribal tyranny with the most advanced repressive techniques imported from abroad'.*[77] The oil interests and the associated Western governments were keen to support the Saudi regime in its resolve to crush any pressures for reform. As an official US government publication declared, the oil consortium (ARAMCO) believed that 'a strong, stable government' was essential to its long-term interests.[78]

In October 1953 some 13,000 workers went on strike in the oil-fields around Dammam; troops were used to crush the revolt, though minor concessions were made. In June 1956, when workers demonstrated against King Saud during a visit to Dhahran, many strikers were arrested and foreign workers were deported; a royal decree, banning work stoppages and strikes, was issued. In such disputes the American employees of ARAMCO could be relied upon to help the Saudi troops to identify the workers' leaders. In September 1962, at a time of a pro-Nasser revolt in the Saudi armed forces, US aircraft were called in; and in 1966 the Arabian Peninsula People's Union (APPU) claimed it was launching a struggle against the Saudi regime: 'we, who include soldiers, officers, doctors, engineers, writers, civil servants, merchants and workers are everywhere. We are the people'.[79] Over a period of a few months, from November 1966 to February 1967, the Union claimed to have blown up a key pipeline, a US military headquarters in Riyadh, a public security building in Dammam, parts of two royal palaces, and part of the massive Saudi airbase at Khamis Mushayat, near the Yemeni border. Saudi and US forces counter-attacked; and in March 1967 some seventeen people were publicly executed in Riyadh; hundreds of Yemenis were deported. The power of the APPU had largely been broken, but the Saudi regime judged it necessary to continue widespread repression in the years that followed. The British politician Reginald Maudling, one of several with business interests in the country, applauded the Saudi government for its 'clear ideas' on how to handle the matter of internal security. In 1973 there were around 2000 political prisoners in Saudi jails.

The British and American governments worked to aid the Saudi repression of any challenge to the regime. Western security forces were on permanent duty in the Kingdom, while Western technology was made available to support the activities of the Saudi secret police. In 1975 the General Intelligence Department (GID) of the Saudi government signed a contract with Scientific Control Systems (Scicon), a computing subsidiary of British Petroleum, for the installation of a comprehensive computerised intelligence system. In 1980 two linked computer centres in Riyadh and Jeddah were scheduled to begin operations. When the Saudi operators switched on their video screens they were greeted with the message: 'In the name of Allah the Merciful, the Beneficent – Welcome!', after which they could gain access to details of the political and business activities of (potentially) a million people in Saudi Arabia and abroad. Via some 27 computer-linked GID offices – at airports, frontier posts, industrial centres and major towns – data could be fed to the computer centres to facilitate the compilation of 'Surveillance Lists' and 'Black Lists' of foreign and Saudi citizens, and to enable appropriate 'executive' action (including surveillance, harassment, arrest and interrogation) to be taken.[80]

Such practical technological assistance, supplemented by continuous advice from the American Central Intelligence Agency (CIA) and the British intelligence community, encouraged the intensification of Saudi political repression through the 1980s and beyond. In January 1990 Amnesty International published a detailed 27-page report noting the scale of 'detention without trial of suspected political opponents'.[81] Here a 'clear pattern' was identified: arrests without warrant, long periods of imprisonment without trial, denial of access to family or legal counsel, weeks of solitary confinement, routine ill-treatment and torture. In 1982 Amnesty learned about the cases of more than 120 untried political detainees; during 1983 it held the names of more than 170 untried political prisoners; in 1984 some 62 people were imprisoned without trial for attempting to organise a political party; in 1985 another 100 were held in untried detention; in 1986 140 more were imprisoned (among them Makkiyya Abdullah Hamdan arrested after midnight for trying to discover the whereabouts of her husband detained three months earlier); in 1987 dozens of Shi'a Muslims were arrested and imprisoned without trial; in 1988 many alleged opponents of the regime were arrested and held in untried detention. Over this period Amnesty International frequently raised the issue of untried imprisonment with the Saudi authorities, stating that the practice was a violation of the Universal Declaration of Human Rights; no response was received. In November 1991 Sheikh Mohammed al-Fassi, extradited from Amman, was imprisoned without trial by the Saudi authorities for opposing the Gulf War and campaigning for democracy in Saudi Arabia. His arrest was reportedly ordered by the Saudi interior minister, Prince Naif, a younger brother of King Fahd. At the same time more than 54,000 Iraqi refugees – including many women and children, and the old and the sick – were being held in isolated camps in the Saudi desert, surrounded by barbed wire and cut off from the outside world. Commented American human-rights lawyers in a detailed report (May 1992): 'The Saudi government has never explained the basis for its arrest and continued detention of these Iraqis.[82]

The report also noted abuses in the Saudi legal system, the widespread use of arbitrary arrest and untried detention, the abuse of foreign workers, the treatment of women, and the persecution of the Shi'a minority. In connection with this last issue the Koran has been quoted (Sura 2, Verse 256): 'Let there be no compulsion in Religion' (though perhaps it should be set against Sura 3, Verse 79). In fact the Saudi regime has no tolerance for religious minorities and their rights to freedom of worship. The Shi'a are not allowed to build new mosques or to expand or remodel existing ones; in 1986 a makeshift Shi'a mosque in Dammam outraged the *Mutawa* who immediately ordered it destroyed. The Committee for the Propagation of Virtue and Discouragement of Vice has warned the Shi'a of severe punishment if they recited their call to prayer in its entirety (the *Mutawa* insist that the words 'I testify that Ali is one of God's believers' be omitted). The Saudi authorities have shot and killed people celebrating Shi'a religious holidays;[83] have closed Shi'a schools and arrested teachers; have arrested and beaten worshippers; have tortured Shi'a students; and have imprisoned many Shi'a Muslims without trial, adding to the complement of political prisoners held in Saudi jails without trial.

In all the cases of untried incarceration (some political prisoners are listed in Table 1.4), the prisoners are allowed no access to a lawyer or legal advice. Trials are typically held in private and the defendants are usually unable to challenge before a higher tribunal the lawfulness of their arrests, imprisonment or convictions. It is common for the prisoners not to be informed of the charges against them or allowed family visits. It is entirely up to the discretion of the unaccountable Saudi authorities how long the detainees will be held in prison, and how they are treated while there.

In May 1993 the Saudi authorities arrested about 400 of the supporters of the newly-formed Saudi Arabian human-rights group, the Committee for the Defence of Legitimate Rights (CDLR). According to the Arab Organisation of Human Rights (AOHR), more than 10,000 people had signed a petition supporting the Committee, a detail that failed to impress the House of Saud. Prince Salman ibn Abdul Aziz, governor of Riyadh and a brother of King Fahd, summoned six *ulema*, founding members of the Committee, to explain their behaviour. Said one CDLR spokesman: 'All he [Prince Salman] gave us was empty talk. He kept straying from point to point, going back and forth, it was useless. His reaction was as we expected. We hope that one day the Sauds will depart from this path, but at the moment they want to maintain a tribal state. We are in the last 10 years of the 20th century and yet they are trying to rule as in the first days of Islam.' The Saudi authorities did not stop at dialogue. A few days after the summoning of the *ulema*, scores of armed Saudi police raided a Riyadh university campus and arrested Professor Mohammed al-Masari, a leader of the banned CDLR, while other human-rights activists were also being arrested and interrogated by the police. Said the interior minister, Prince Naif: 'We rule by virtue of our Islamic principles. We have a higher respect for human rights than any other country in the world.'

In September 1993 Amnesty International published a 28-page report detailing the scale of Saudi intolerance (extending to 'arrest, detention and torture') of religious minorities (Christian worshippers and Shi'a Muslims) in the Kingdom.[84]

Table 1.4   Some political prisoners in Saudi Arabia (October 1992)

Name	Age/ Status	City	Job	Arrest Date	Prison
Mohammed Hilal al-Saued	33/Mar.	Saihat	Engineer	04/20/88	Dammam
Fouzy Abdulla al-Yousif	32/Mar.	Saihat	Engineer	04/20/88	Dammam
Fathi Hasan al-Habeeb	29/Mar.	Safwa	Engineer	04/22/88	Dammam
Ali Saeed Darwish	35/Mar.	Tarout	Engineer	04/21/88	Dammam
Abdullah al-Nemer	32/Mar.	Dammam	Clergyman	08/17/88	Riyadh
Jafar Ali al-Mobarak	37/Mar.	Safwa	Clergyman	04/22/88	Dammam
Abdullatif al-Nasir	29/Mar.	al Ahsaa	Clergyman	08/01/88	Dammam
Ahmed Abdulla al Saif	29/Mar.	Safwa	Engineer	04/22/88	Dammam
Zubair al-Safwani	26/Sin.	Safwa	Student	08/01/91	Riyadh
Zakaria al-Qatefi	25/Mar.	Almobaraz	Clergyman	N/A	Riyadh
Ali bu Auais	25/Mar.	Almobaraz	Clergyman	11/90	Riyadh
Abdulaziz al-Faris	24/Sin.	Tarout	Student	06/17/89	Riyadh
Ali Mohammed bin-Lail	25/Sin.	Safwa	Student	06/17/89	Riyadh
Salah Nasfan	23/Sin.	Safwa	Student	06/19/89	Riyadh
Husain Ali Sbait	25/Sin.	Safwa	Student	06/19/89	Riyadh
Hatem Jafar al-Sadiq	25/Sin.	Safwa	Student	06/19/89	Riyadh
Jafar al-Safwani	26/Sin.	Safwa	Worker	1991	Dammam
Mahdi al Qassab	28/NA	Qateef	N/A	1983	N/A
Ali Khalil al-Saigh	29/Mar.	Sanabis	N/A	04/21/88	Dammam
Abdulkareem Hmood	31/Mar.	Saihat	Employee	04/20/88	Dammam
Jafar Jasem al Hamad	26/NA	Saihat	N/A	04/20/88	Dammam
Adel Ali al-Khawajah	26/NA	Dammam	N/A	1988	Riyadh
Abdulghafoor Habib al-Dibasi	30/Mar.	Rabeiyah	Engineer	04/13/88	Dammam
Husain Abdulla al-Haiy	35/Mar.	Safwa	Employee	04/21/88	Dammam
Jafar al-Khabbaz	27/NA	Qateef	N/A	08/19/88	Dammam
Ali Saeed al-Jeshi	28/NA	Qateef	N/A	04/26/88	Dammam
Naji Jasim Tehaifa	28/NA	Awamiyah	N/A	N/A	Dammam
Saiyed Najeeb al-Hashim	21/NA	Rabeiyah	Student	04/22/88	Dammam
Mohammed al-Jerani	23/NA	Rabeiyah	Student	04/18/88	Dammam
Mostafa Ali al-Khatim	27/NA	Saihat	Worker	04/20/88	Dammam
Abdulkareem al-Hubail	34/Mar.	Rabeiyah	Clergyman	04/21/88	Dammam
Hani Abbas	25/NA	Rabeiyah	Student	08/02/88	Dammam
Hassan Ali al-Darura	31/Mar.	Sanabis	Salesman	1989	Dammam
Sayid Adnan al-Yousif	N/A	Safwa	N/A	N/A	Dammam
Husain Mansour al-Abbas	31/Mar.	Saihat	N/A	10/05/89	Dammam
Sayid Yaseen al-Sayigh	32/Mar.	Qateef	Clergyman	10/89	Dammam
Husain Nooh al-Mashami	37/Mar.	Saibat	Employee	1989	Dammam
Tuki Mohammed al Turki	33/Mar.	Sanabis	Employee	01/92	Dammam
AbdulKhaliq al Janabi	32/NA	al-Qudaih	N/A	01/92	Dammam
Naser Abdulla al-Yousef	30/NA	Saihat	N/A	04/20/88	Dammam

Source: Arabia Monitor, October 1992.

Here it is noted: '*Hundreds of men, women and children have been arrested and detained in Saudi Arabia since the Gulf crisis in August 1990, most without charge or trial, solely for the peaceful expression of their religious beliefs. Scores have been subject to torture, flogging or other cruel, inhuman or degrading treatment while in detention.*' The expression of religious belief by the Shi'a Muslims was being regarded as an act of political dissent: 'Consequently, they have been arrested, detained and tortured for advocating freedom of religion and thought and equal rights for members of their community'. In addition, there was 'a marked increase in the number of Christian worshippers being arrested and ill-treated solely for the peaceful expression of their religious beliefs'.[85]

The following year, Amnesty turned its attention to the enduring plight of the Iraqi refugees in Saudi Arabia. Now there were grounds for deep concern about the treatment of the Iraqi civilians (mostly women, children, the sick, the old) at the hands of the camp authorities in the isolated desert enclosures: 'Over the past three years, the organisation [Amnesty International] has received numerous reports of widespread human rights violations perpetrated with total impunity by the camp authorities. These include the arbitrary detention of refugees, their torture and ill-treatment (in some cases resulting in death in custody), possible extrajudicial executions and forcible return to Iraq. Various forms of collective punishment have also been systematically used against the refugees, particularly in response to protests about living conditions and treatment by the camp authorities.'[86] At the same time the arrests and untried detentions were continuing within Saudi Arabia, accompanied by the usual ill-treatment and torture of suspects. In April 1994 Anmar Mohammed al-Masari, the son of the CDLR spokesman, was arrested; in May university students, professors and other college employees were arrested; and in the same month about twenty Westerners at a party were arrested, and some beaten, by the *Mutawa*. In September the Saudi authorities acknowledged that 110 people had been arrested in connection with attempts 'to sow dissension and chaos', while the CDLR was claiming that more than 1000 political activists had been arrested by Saudi Arabian troops.[87] The Committee, now in enforced exile in London, was issuing frequent communiqués, press releases and monitors to publicise the scale of human-rights abuses in the Kingdom (see extracts in Table 1.5).

In 1996 the monitoring organisation Human Rights Watch, conducting systematic investigations of human-rights abuses in some seventy countries, noted that over the previous year Saudi Arabia had 'experienced further deterioration in human rights observance'.[88] Again particular attention was given to the treatment of dissidents by the Saudi authorities:

There was a four-fold increase in the number of executions, mostly of foreign suspected drug traffickers. One Islamic opposition activist was also beheaded … Arbitrary arrest, detention without trial and ill-treatment of prisoners remained the norm during the year, especially for those accused of political offences. Several hundred Islamist opponents were arbitrarily detained without

Table 1.5 Saudi arrests/raids/torture (1994/95)

Communiqué/Monitor	Case
23 April 1994	Abdul Rahman Al-Ashamwi, well-known poet and writer, arrested early hours of 13 April 1994; food slid under prison door to maintain total solitary confinement; has published 12 volumes of poems.
1 May 1994	Nasir Abdul-Karim, businessman and writer, arrested on 27 April 1994; Nabil Muhammed Kamaal, Mohammed al-Masari's brother-in-law, arrested on 28 April; Fouad Dahlawi, associate professor of electronic engineering, arrested and taken to undisclosed location.
13 August 1994	Sulayman Bin Ahmad Daweesh and Abdur-Rahman Bin Abdul Aziz Al-Daweesh arrested; cars searched and houses ransacked; no official explanation given; other detainees noted – Anmar al-Masari (111 days), Fouad Dahlawi (106 days), Rashaad Al-Mudarris (110 days), Nabil Al-Mudarris (106 days), Lu'ay al-Masari (103 days) and Muhammed Ben Fahd Al-Marshud (28 days)
9 September 1994	Abdullah Al-Hamid, formerly professor of Arabic literature, detained for more than two months without charge or trial; wrote *Al-Islah* (the reform), an epic poem about his detention; on the same day, 8 September 1994, Muhsin Al-Awaji, assistant professor of agriculture, arrested after the storming of his house.
18 September 1994	Thousands of arrests; armoured vehicles patrolling Buraida 'to terrorise and cow the population'; troops with tear gas and machine guns raid many homes; raids on mosques, one during speech by the Imam (Khutba).
28 October 1994	Abdul Aziz Ibn Al-Qasim, renowned judge, arrested and taken to unknown destination; his books and research documents confiscated; a dozen other detainees listed (one aged 74, another chained in front of his children; raids on houses and mosques.
6 March 1995	Muhammed Al-Qahtani, lecturer in Islamic Beliefs and Doctrines, arrested; Sa'eed bin Zueir, lecturer in Islamic Media Studies, arrested; Nassir Al-Umar, a prominent scholar, in hiding – the Riyadh houses of his parents and relations under siege.
4 June 1995	Humud bin Abdullah Al-Uqla Aash-Shuaibi, blind 75-year-old scholar and jurist, arrested by seventy men and taken to an unknown destination.
17 August 1995	Abdullah Al-Hudhaif, severely tortured until paralysed; after two weeks, prolonged beating caused a fatal haemorrhage.

Source: *CDLR Year Book* '94–'95, The Committee for the Defence of Legitimate Rights, London, November 1995.

trial. The ban on free speech, assembly and association were strictly enforced; violators were jailed, deported, banned from travel or dismissed from their government positions.[89]

On 11 August 1995 the Saudi authorities beheaded the CDLR human-rights activist Abdalla al-Hudhaif, convicted in a secret trial in which nine other Islamists were given lengthy prison sentences. The Saudi government, in announcing the verdicts, denounced its opponents for rebellion and heresy, both capital offences. Human Rights Watch noted that the trial had been marred by 'the use of coerced confessions, denial of legal counsel, and blatant interference by government officials': Hudhaif had at first been sentenced to twenty years in jail, whereupon the Ministry of the Interior protested the lightness of the sentence, secured a retrial, and insisted that Hudhaif be sentenced to death.

In this case the defendant was informed of the first court decision in May 1995, but the decision to execute him – reportedly made in early July and ratified by King Fahd on 10 July – was kept secret until 12 August, a day after the execution. The beheading was performed in secret, an exception to normal practice; and his family was denied access to the body to conduct the usual burial services, thus fuelling speculation that Hudhaif had been tortured before execution. The victim's primary offence, repeatedly cited in the court judgement, was that he had distributed CDLR publications; with reference made also to his 'disrespect and disobedience to the ruler of the community and to the nation's religious scholars, who have condemned this group [the CDLR] as an illegitimate entity, warned of its dangers and called for fighting it'.[90]

A 1996 Amnesty report, covering the period January to December 1995, confirmed the arrests of scores of political suspects: 'They included Shi'a Muslims and suspected Sunni Islamist critics of the government. Many were denied visits by relatives for weeks or months after arrest and had no access to lawyers. Others were released after interrogation about their political activities'.[91] Among those detained were six Shi'a worshippers, arrested for commemorating the death of the son of the late Ayatollah Khomeini of Iran. In April the Saudi authorities arrested Sheikh Jafar Ali al-Mubarak, a religious scholar, for refusing to sign an undertaking not to preach. Most of the detainees arrested during the year were suspected Sunni Islamist opponents of the government, adding to the more than 200 other political detainees arrested in earlier years and still being held without trial or access to legal counsel. One political activist, Ibrahim al-Rahman, was given 300 lashes as well as 18 years in jail: 'All appeared to have been punished for their political dissent rather than the criminal charges brought against them'. An Indonesian national was beaten to death in Mecca for overstaying his visa to Saudi Arabia.[92]

The Human Rights Watch report covering the events of 1996 confirmed that Saudi Arabia had 'continued to violate a broad array of internationally recognised civil and political rights'.[93] Again it was acknowledged that the Saudi authorities were using arbitrary arrest, incommunicado detention, torture, whipping and beheading 'to suppress and intimidate opposition'.[94] In March 1996 the authorities had carried out more arrests and detentions in the Shi'a community; and an American engineer was arrested and detained in three different Saudi cities for a total of thirty-eight days – his interrogators said they had no charges against him but simply wanted information about Saudi opposition groups. This man was kept in solitary confinement and denied adequate food and medication; for thirty days he was refused any contact with his family, a lawyer, or the US embassy. In March 1997 Nigel Rodley, the UN special investigator on torture, included Saudi Arabia in his annual report as one of the countries that regularly use torture. He commented that his mandate from the United Nations including investigating the use of corporal punishment – whipping, amputation and stoning – in Muslim countries which observe *sharia* law.[95] It is important to note the character of official punishment in Saudi Arabia.

THE PRACTICAL PENOLOGY

The Saudi approach to the punishment of crime and dissidence is marked by, at best, its extreme harshness and by, at worst, its sadistic cruelty. Thus a 32-page Amnesty International report (*Saudi Arabia – Behind Closed Doors: Unfair Trials in Saudi Arabia*, November 1997) notes that the Saudi criminal justice system 'is designed to cater primarily for the might of the state with total disregard for the individuals' right to fair trial'. As a summary prelude to copious examples of arrest and detention abuses, secret trials, torture, flogging and amputation, execution, and the abuse of women and other groups, Amnesty comments:

> Suspects are invariably arrested without a judicial warrant, held incommunicado beyond any judicial supervision, and detained for lengthy periods without trial ... Those charged are tried behind closed doors ... Disregard for the right to fair trial has been a key factor in Saudi Arabia's catalogue of gross human rights violations over the years. Thousands of political and religious activists, including prisoners of conscience, have been arbitrarily deprived of their liberty because of the lack of independent and impartial judicial supervision over the arresting and interrogating authorities. The lack of such supervision has also allowed security forces to make torture an institutionalised practice with full impunity.

In these circumstances of torture, secrecy and inadequate (or no) legal protection, conviction and sentencing is 'a simple exercise even when the penalty is of a grave nature such as flogging, limb amputation and death ...'.

Lashings, the cutting-off of hands, beheadings – all are frequently carried out by the Saudi authorities, usually for the entertainment of a baying crowd; and of course all the whippings and hand choppings are sanctified by holy writ. The Koran demands the lashing of adulterers, the killing (for example, by crucifixion) of those who act against God and his Apostle, and the severing of the hands and feet of criminals. Thieves, men or women, are to have their hands cut off 'in recompense for their doing' (Sura 5, Verse 43): Muhammed himself is said by the early traditionalists to have punished a woman guilty of theft in this way while on route to Mecca previous to its capture.[96*] And if such practices are not judged sufficiently robust the Saudi authorities practise torture on a massive scale against untried men and women.

The journalist Robert Fisk has described the lashing of women in Saudi Arabia. Girls are typically held down by a policewoman 'while they are whipped by a man'. According to two Asian embassies that have vainly tried to protect their nationals, more than 2000 women were flogged in the Gulf over a three-year period.[97] One Western medical worker, herself imprisoned on fraudulent charges of 'attempted seduction', testified that women in Saudi prisons are sexually molested on being arrested by the *Mutawa*. A Canadian nurse who worked in the largest hospital in Riyadh commented on the punishment meted out to women: 'The lashings are brutal and excruciatingly painful; they will bear the scars physically and psychologically for a long time'.[98] In the Saudi prison of Malaz an Indonesian maid being lashed in 1993, according to a fellow prisoner, 'had been starved and tortured for two years'; her mistress 'had placed hot irons on her arms and had beaten her on the head with high-heeled shoes, penetrating her scalp'. The same witness testified that domestic helpers, raped and abused by their Saudi employers, were being jailed and lashed when they attempted to escape. An Asian diplomat commented: 'The Saudis don't want us to talk about this. But I must tell you there is blood and there are scars. The way these girls are treated is simply cruelty; you could perhaps call it sadism.'[99]

The jailing of such women frequently follows perfunctory trials held in secret where the accused have no access to legal counsel. Confessions are often 'coerced' (that is, obtained through hours, days or weeks of torture) as a means of 'proving' guilt. In these circumstances there are no legal safeguards against the possibility of a miscarriage of justice. The judges, Saudi apologists declare, are bound to behave fairly since they would otherwise face divine retribution – so we can trust in the piety of the *sharia* court administrators. Said the Saudi interior minister Prince Naif, the Saudi version of *sharia* law – and there are *many* disputed versions in the Islamic world – is 'stern but just'.

---

* The then British minister Tony Benn relates a conversation in 1965 with the Saudi deputy minister of communications, Sheikh Ahmad Zardan: 'The only time he warmed up was when we told him about the great mail robbery and he said that in Saudi Arabia they cut off the hands of robbers and this was a very good idea that we ought to consider' (Tony Benn, *Out of the Wilderness: Diaries 1963–67* (London: Hutchinson, 1987), p. 225).

Sharia justice was well demonstrated in the case of Neil Tubo, a gay man beheaded for allegedly raping two Filipino seamstresses nearly twice his age. He claimed that the confession, that led to his conviction and execution, was beaten out of him by prison guards using sticks. On 4 December 1992 he was dragged out of bed, told he had two hours to finalise his affairs before being beheaded, and then driven to a square in front of a mosque in Jeddah where a huge crowd baying for blood had just finished its midday prayers. Of the hundreds of men and women beheaded in Saudi Arabia in the 1990s, few knew in advance the prosecution's case against them since there is typically no pre-trial disclosure; lawyers are not permitted in the secret courts; and foreigners often do not understand the proceedings because interpreters are either incompetent or are not provided at all.

In this context justice is perfunctory and arbitrary, administered at the whim of judge or *Mutawa*, often with no semblance of due legal process. Thus Fred Mallo, an accountant from the Philippines, was charged with a criminal offence after organising private Christian worship in a villa in Riyadh. He and his co-workers were jailed for a year and sentenced to 150 lashes each; while the *Mutawa* destroyed his piano, prayer books and all his religious literature. In jail, Fred Mallo and his colleagues were flogged, causing them swellings and prolonged discomfort on their backs, buttocks and rear limbs; after a year of this ill-treatment they were taken to the airport, with their heads shaved and their legs shackled, and bundled onto an airplane. The Saudi ambassador to Britain, Ghazi Algosaibi, explained: 'The people of Saudi Arabia are offended if somebody publicly practises something that tarnishes this image of ... the purity of the oneness of God'.[100] Another case was that of Arlene Herno and her husband, who went out for a pizza to celebrate her birthday with two women friends; at the restaurant they encountered a male Egyptian friend. Since men and women who are not close relatives are not allowed to have social contact, the *Mutawa* pounced. The result? The man was given 45 days in jail and 60 strokes; Arlene Herno was given 75 lashes.[101]

The cases are too numerous to describe exhaustively, but it is useful to remember the human details behind some of the bald statistics. James Rebenito, a 35-year-old migrant worker from the Philippines, took his first overseas job as a carpenter for the Saudi Ministry of Defence and Aviation at Al Uyainah in Riyadh. His employment began in 1991, but on 24 September 1994 he was arrested on a charge of murder, after which his wife struggled to follow up his case. One confidential report said that he was now (September 1995) blinded in one eye and his nails pulled out; another reported suggested that Rebenito had already been beheaded. Then Wilhelm Soriano, the Filipino administrator of the Overseas Workers Welfare Administration (OWWA), wrote that he was in good condition, but that under Saudi rules of court the trial could not progress until he confessed his guilt.[102] In early 1996 an Egyptian, one Mohamed Ali al-Sayyid, was led, heavily shackled, into a Saudi marketplace to be lashed for the 3800th time in three years. In 1991 he had been convicted in secret trial of theft and had been sentenced to 4000 lashes, to be administered in public at the rate of 50 every two weeks.[103] In 1995 some 192 prisoners, 11 of them women, were beheaded with swords; witnesses 'have recorded seeing many of the women dragged weeping to their deaths in front of baying crowds of men'.[104]

Torture in Saudi Arabia is routine. Amnesty International and other human-rights bodies have accumulated first-hand accounts and other evidence of the gross abuse and ill-treatment of untried prisoners. Thus two Thai carpenters, Pilarn Pucharoen and Boonsri Prakarnnung, were arrested in April 1980 and held in solitary confinement for more than two years. Prakarnnung testified that for more than two years he was not allowed to see sunlight; both testified that they had been tortured by whippings and electric shocks to force them to confess to complicity in murder. Keith Carmichael, a British subject, was arrested on 2 November 1981, held incommunicado, threatened with sexual assault by a prison guard, padlocked to the back of a chair, and beaten on the soles of his feet with a cane (forcing him to be hospitalised). The subsequent findings of an enquiry were not made public. Amnesty also notes the case of the Yemeni Salah Fariah Shukair, one of many whose right hand was severed by knife in a public square, and who after the punishment on 7 August 1982 was immediately hospitalised. Other cases relate to sentences of up to 300 lashes being carried out over days or months.[105] The officials wielding the cane are expected to hold a copy of the Koran under their cane arm, both for reason of piety and allegedly to moderate the severity of the inflicted wounds. Amnesty has also recorded the names of particular individuals who had their right hands judicially severed in public: Ali Hamud Muhammad (25 June 1982), Roland Debtin (12 July 1982), Hamdi bin Zuwai'al (31 December 1982), etc.[*] The penal philosophy established by Ibn Saud has been consolidated over the subsequent decades.[106]

A subsequent Amnesty report (November 1990) notes, of Yemenis returning from Saudi Arabia:

> At the time of arrest, many say they were kicked and beaten. The kinds of ill-treatment and torture alleged in detention centres are electric shock treatment, beatings on the head or all over the body, enforced standing, sleep deprivation, total submersion in water and *falaqa* (beatings on the soles of the feet) – all of

---

[*] In September 1997 the Rev. Robert McConachie (Kent, UK) recommended cutting the hands off thieves, citing St Mark (9:43): '*And if thy hand offend thee, cut it off. It is better for thee to enter into life maimed, than having two hands to go into Hell, into the fire that never shall be quenched.*' Did he favour chopping off one hand or both? 'Well, I would start with one and see if that had the desired result' (*The Daily Telegraph*, London, 10 September 1997, p. 5). In the same Christian spirit the Rev. Frank Collins, former SAS soldier and author of *Baptism of Fire* (Transworld, 1997) has opined: 'Yes, you can be a Christian and blow someone's head off.'

which fit the pattern of human rights violations in Saudi Arabia in recent years.[107]

In one case, a 28-year-old mechanic, Amin Ahmad Al-Shawafi, who had worked in the Kingdom for four years, was arrested outside Mecca, questioned about his political views and continuously beaten over his head and body. A doctor testified that he had been assaulted with a 'sharp instrument' and was now suffering from extreme paranoia. In another case, a 25-year-old skilled worker, Said Abdo Ibrahim al-Shami, who had worked in Saudi Arabia for 13 years, was arrested after his taxi driver told police that he had criticised the Saudi regime. He subsequently testified to Amnesty investigators that he was taken to the General Intelligence Centre in Abu Arish, submerged in water almost to the point of suffocation, beaten all over his body, and forced to stand on one foot for four hours. Amnesty has cited many cases where political prisoners were tortured to extract confessions or for punishment: 'Prisoners who later said their confession had been extracted under torture were often tortured again until they had 'changed their minds'. Among the methods reportedly used were *falaqa*, sleep deprivation and suspension by the wrists from the ceiling or a high window'.[108] Said the Saudi government: Islamic *sharia* in Saudi Arabia did not 'allow the extraction of confessions under duress, pressure, torture or in any manner contrary to human dignity ...'[109]

Independent legal observers have noted the direct encouragement that the Saudi penal system gives to the coercion of confessions through torture. Thus: *'The strict evidentiary demands of Islamic penal law require either the testimony of witnesses or a confession for conviction of certain offences. Consequently, Saudi police and prosecutors routinely demand that suspects confess to their alleged crimes. When suspects refuse, they are intimidated, harassed, repeatedly tortured, and may be held without trial indefinitely until they confess. It seems to matter little that Islamic procedure does not recognise coerced confessions as valid'*.[110] The neglect of the requirements for a valid confession is one of the most serious flaws in the day-to-day operation of the Saudi penal system. In September 1985 the Saudi police searched the house of a Filipino national, Benito Bernardino, and found marijuana in a roommate's briefcase. Bernardino did not know the whereabouts of his roommate, whereupon the police hit him in the face and kneed him on the chest. After an hour they took him to the Dammam Drug Detention Centre, where he was tortured for 12 days. After prolonged *falaqa*, sleep deprivation, forced standing and submersion, Bernardino involuntarily confessed to selling drugs.[111] Such methods are routinely used as punishment, to extract confessions, and to obtain information about other suspects. In one documented case a prisoner denied knowledge of his relatives' political activities, whereupon he was prevented from sleeping for five consecutive days and nights, suffered boiling tea poured in his face, was given *falaqa* beatings, and was suspended off the floor for six to eight hours. He was struck whenever he gave negative answers. In another case a man was held in a two-by-two-foot room containing a toilet with overflowing sewage. He was starved for three days, beaten, stripped, suffered icy water thrown at him, was given electric shocks, was whipped, and was subjected to *falaqa* beatings. He then signed the necessary confession papers.[112]

Many other cases could be cited. In one case a woman was forced to stand for long periods on a broken leg, while being beaten and having unknown substances injected into her with a syringe; in another a one-year-old baby suffered an injury, in front of its mother, which left it with a permanent mental disability; in yet another case a pregnant woman was tortured until she miscarried.[113] Cases of torture at the hands of the Saudi authorities are documented in many sources.[114] New reports of torture and ill-treatment of detainees have been received by Amnesty International through the 1990s. Deaths as a result of torture are equally well documented; as, for example, in the case of Muhammad bin Fahd al-Mutayr, a bank employee, who died as a result of severe beatings; and the 18-year-old Zuhair Ibrahim al-Awami and Abdullah Abbas (blood-stained urine) who died following heavy beatings. Amnesty continued to record judicial amputations and beheadings: for example, 66 men publicly beheaded in 1993 for allegedly committing murder, drug-trafficking, apostasy, kidnapping and sexual offences (homosexual behaviour, adultery, etc. viewed as capital offences). A compilation of essays from the London-based *Muslim Chronicle* includes gruesome pictures of Saudi torture victims.[115]

In March 1992 a Jordanian woman, referred to in reports as Safia, discovered in Saudi Arabia that she had lost her return airline ticket. While waiting for a replacement to arrive from Amman, she went shopping in Jeddah, properly veiled and accompanied by a male member of her host family as required by law. As she entered a boutique the *Mutawa* pounced, demanding to know her relationship with her male companion. Then she was first whisked to the *Mutawa* precinct station, where she was interrogated for four hours, before being taken to Breman Prison to be systematically tortured. There she encountered another hundred female inmates from various Arab countries, including Yemen, Morocco and Sudan. A 50-year-old Yemeni woman, able to produce a Yemeni-issued marriage licence but not a Saudi licence, was tortured over days for having sex with her husband to whom she had been legally married for 33 years. In the same prison a Moroccan nurse who had asked her bus driver to turn the lights on in her apartment as a security precaution had been arrested for alleged illicit sex and was being whipped by male guards at the rate of one hundred lashes a week. A Sudanese girl, sentenced to three months in jail, was still incarcerated after three years; her health deteriorated and she suffered a severe stroke. Safia, wrongly convicted of being intimate with an unrelated man and of being unveiled, was sentenced to thirty-nine lashes while thinly attired to sharpen the severity of the punishment.[116]

In summary, the most common methods of Saudi torture are *falaqa*, beating on the head and body, suspension by the wrists, electric shocks, enforced sleep deprivation, pouring caustic substances onto the skin, withdrawal of food and water, solitary confinement, sexual abuse, threats of further torture, threats against relatives, pumping of fluids into rectum, submersion almost to suffocation, etc. To such practices must be added the ever-present possibility of hand-severing and beheading in public. In 1996 an Egyptian worker in Saudi Arabia was sentenced to 4000 lashes, in addition to seven years' imprisonment, for burglary.[117] Human Rights Watch noted 'a marked increase during 1995 of reports of torture and ill-treatment of detainees during interrogation by the secret police and religious police'. Thus: 'To compel prisoners to provide information they were frequently beaten with bamboo sticks and plastic-covered truncheons. Ill-treatment included prolonged incommunicado detention, sleep deprivation for long periods, threats of violence and execution, and insults'.[118] Now it was known that Britain and the United States were providing some of the equipment used by the Saudis to torture prisoners.[119] In secretly taped interviews exposed in the UK Channel 4 *Dispatches* television programme 'The Torture Trail', Philip Morris of Royal Ordnance boasted he had supplied 5000 electric-shock batons to Saudi Arabia. At the same time the Federation of American Scientists, using the American Freedom of Information Act, revealed that between 1991 and 1993 some fourteen licences valued at $5 million were issued for exports to Saudi Arabia under the Department of Commerce category OA84C, covering 'saps, thumbcuffs, thumbscrews, leg irons, shackles and handcuffs; specially designed implements of torture; strait-jackets, plastic handcuffs'; a further fourteen licences valued at $5.4 million were allowed for 'stun guns, shock batons, electric cattle prods'.[120] An Iraqi victim of Saudi torture, interviewed for 'The Torture Trail' (11 January 1995), described how electric batons were used on him:

> The secret police handcuffed me and put legcuffs around my ankles. A bar was put between my legs. Then they started beating me up with the electronic sticks. For many hours they tortured me on the soles of my feet. Being hit with an electric baton not only made me vomit, but I lost control of everything. I lost control of my bowels, my water. I just could not control anything in my body. I was left in my own vomit and urine all night. That is how they want you to be during a torture.[121]

On 23 May 1994 a Pakistani national, Gulum Mustafa, was severely tortured by Saudi officials in Jeddah before he was transferred to Priman Prison. This man was given electric shocks when a metal baton was inserted into his rectum, leaving him bleeding, unable to walk, and denied medical attention. He has now been released and deported.

The Saudi treatment of foreign nationals, already cited, includes many cases of torture and abuse, as with the refugee Iraqis incarcerated in the desert camps of Saudi Arabia. (The populations of these refugees have been reduced but many thousands continue to suffer a years-long imprisonment. Amnesty International, relying on testimonies from former inmates of the Artawiyya and Rafha camps, has indicated the various forms of torture and ill-treatment: 'The victims have described systematic beatings all over the body, being forced to stand for prolonged periods of time, the administration of electric shocks and being dowsed with cold water while naked. In addition some have also endured *ta'liq* (hanging by the wrists from the ceiling or a high window), *falaqa* and deprivation of sleep for long periods'.[122] It is noted that the accounts are consistent with information gathered from independent sources including such non-governmental organisations as the Lawyers Committee for Human Rights (LCHR).

The detailed testimonies indicate what a largely hidden prison population was made to endure:

- Yarub Hassan Suri al-Khaffaji, stripped and made to lie on the hot bonnet of a car: 'I felt that my skin was being stripped off my body ... they began to beat me with their clubs and they lashed me. Lieutenant ... asked his soldiers to bring some sand which he put in my mouth by force. Then he forced me to drink urine'.

- Asad Ali Hussein, beaten on his hands with cables until the skin began peeling off: 'I was then hit on the back with an iron bar, and fell to the ground ... kicked me on the nose with his boots while four others kicked other parts of my body ...'. He was then dragged naked behind a truck until his left arm was dislocated.

- Zahir Rizqi Saber, stripped, tied to a wire fence and then beaten: 'The soldiers then cut my hair, mixed it with sand and water and forced me to eat it'.

- Ali Muhsin Abu-Zahra, stripped and threatened with rape: 'They also used other forms of ill-treatment and torture, including *falaqa*, beatings all over the body, and being jolted by an electric rod. They would do things to us ... including kissing the officers' boots and being urinated upon. I eventually signed a statement "confessing" that I had been a trouble-maker ...'.

We need hardly be surprised that such treatment resulted in 'numerous cases' of deaths. The interrogators of Muhammad Khudhayr Mubarak Tuma stripped him, beat him and, when he protested, sewed his lips together. Then he was made to crawl on his stomach with his hands tied behind him, and was beaten until he died. Hussein al-Jizani, seeking medical help for illness, was found in breach of the camp curfew and was then beaten through the night until he died. Eye-witnesses were arrested and forced to sign a statement saying that he had died of a heart attack. When some refugees chanted protests at camp conditions, 'Saudi Arabian soldiers ... indiscriminately opened fire at the crowd killing at least six people ... Further killings took place at Rafha camp ...' At the same time Amnesty International was recording many other examples of torture and ill-treatment of criminal and political prisoners in Saudi Arabia.

A 1996 Amnesty report (covering the period January to December 1995) again notes the well-documented methods of torture, the extensive use of amputation and flogging (for such crimes as theft, consumption of alcohol, and sexual offences), and 'a sharp increase in the number of executions, the vast majority carried out by public beheading'.[123] It is recorded that 192 prisoners, including seven women, were executed, mostly for alleged drug crimes or alleged murder. In such cases the defendants had no right to legal representation, and confessions extracted under torture were accepted by the courts. Scores of prisoners were being held on death row, including a Somali national, Abd al-Aziz Muhammed Isse, whose clear evidence that he was not in the country at the time of the crime was ignored by the court. The Saudi authorities bitterly resented any domestic or foreign publicity given to such cases – as with the broadcast film *Death of a Princess* in 1980, dealing with the public beheading of the Saudi Princess Misha'al and her lover in 1977 for adultery.[124] Here the indignant Saudi objections to the televised screenings resulted in some US broadcasts being blocked, a loss of some commercial contracts with Britain, and abject and disreputable apologies from some British politicians.

The scale of beheadings in the Kingdom is often reported in the Western media, but in general inobtrusively and with little or no comment. Thus the journalist Caroline Moorehead noted the soaring execution rate in the run-up to the 1991 Gulf War (*The Guardian*, 29 October 1990); and Amnesty International continued to record the annual execution tally. Typically, the beheading of a Pakistani woman, Rani bint Khamisallah Bishk, for alleged murder is given one column-inch (*The Independent*, 16 January 1993); as is the beheading of the Filipino maid Leonarda Akula for alleged murder (*The Independent*, 8 May 1993). In such cases it is useful to note that the executions usually take place outside mosques following the Muslim sabbath congregational prayers. In May 1993 Amnesty International reported 'an upsurge' in the number of Saudi executions, highlighting this contravention of UN General Assembly Resolution 32/61 (8 December 1977) calling upon member states to work for an abolition of the death penalty. Amnesty also stressed the character of the Saudi method of execution: the use of swords, firing squad and stoning: 'The method of execution by beheading is particularly violent for all those involved: the victims, their families and on-lookers. Although death by beheading is claimed to be swift and "merciful", in some cases several blows had to be administered before the victims were pronounced dead, thus causing untold suffering.'[125*]

---

* It should not be thought that Saudi Arabia is the only state in violation of GA Resolution 32/61, or the only state that employs brutal execution methods. The United States has increased its execution rate in recent years, and frequently kills people in an unconscionably cruel way. Thus the execution of Cuban immigrant Pedro Medina on 25 March 1997 caused a foot-long flame to burst from the side of his head. Said witness Michael Minerva: 'It was brutal, terrible. It was a burning alive, literally' (*The Guardian*, London, 26 March 1997).

On 18 February 1987 the Saudi government widened the scope of the death penalty via the mechanism of *ulema fatwa* (religious edict) Number 138, which extended the option of execution for people convicted of drug smuggling or of receiving and distributing drugs from abroad; King Fahd approved the ruling in March 1987. On 24 August 1988 the scope of the death penalty was again widened by *fatwa* Number 148, authorising the execution of people for acts of sabotage or 'corruption on earth' that 'undermine security and endanger lives and public or private property'. Such acts were deemed to include 'destruction of homes, mosques, schools, hospitals, factories, bridges, ammunition dumps and water storage tanks, resources of the Treasury such as oil pipelines, and the hijacking and blowing up of aircraft'. In September 1988 four Saudi citizens were executed in a retroactive implementation of *fatwa* 148. A year later, sixteen Kuwaiti nationals were executed under the terms of 148 for allegedly planting bombs in Mecca; the men were allowed no legal representation and their 'confessions' were extracted under torture.

On 13 December 1996 Abd al-Karim Maral al-Naqshabandi was beheaded in public for allegedly practising witchcraft against his employer, Prince Salman, a nephew of King Fahd. Having criticised the prince and so fearing for his life, al-Naqshabandi acquired a protective amulet to ward off evil, a common practice in the Middle East (allowed by the 14th-century Saudi jurist Ibn Taymiya). Later, when al-Naqshabandi refused Salman's demand that he give false evidence against an employee, he was thrown into solitary confinement and charged with using witchcraft to harm the prince 'in his religion, soul, money and rationality' (part of the 'evidence' was the amulet found in a desk drawer). After torture used to extract a false confession, al-Naqshabandi was decapitated in Chop Square in Riyadh.

In response to the Amnesty allegations and its recommendations for reform, the Saudi ambassador to Britain, Ghazi Algosaibi, commented:

> One billion Muslims believe that the Koran is the sacred word of God – and that punishments specified in the Koran are binding for all time. It is amazing that Amnesty International continues to show such obvious contempt for the beliefs of all Muslims by insisting that capital punishment as specified by the Holy Koran 'is the ultimate form of cruel, inhuman and degrading treatment'. One wishes and prays that those in charge of this organisation will spare some time and effort defending the victims and not the murderers ... one wishes that Amnesty International, which purports to believe in freedom, will allow other people the freedom of adopting the legal system of their choice.[126]

It was inevitable in these circumstances, with the Koranic punishments 'binding for all time', that the beheadings would continue. The Amnesty publication *AIBS Journal* (September/October 1993) pointed out that death by beheading was now being bestowed – following the ruling of *fatwa* 148 – on vandals as well as on many other categories of criminals. One man was executed in 1993 for brewing alcohol. And the rate of beheadings continued to increase. Thus by May 1995 about one hundred people had been executed in the year, exceeding the full annual totals for recent years. In April the journalist James McCredie witnessed one of the executions – *The huge black executioner arrives. The sharia judge is reading from his copy of the Koran. The crowd is growing restless and the children are fretting. Then a man wearing a stethoscope arrives and lays out the instruments to be used for amputations. The crowd is expectant but first there must be prayers. A veiled woman is sobbing. Then the executioner produces his curved sword, soon to whirl 'in a glittering arc': 'The head falls with a thud ... Bright arterial blood jets into the tray. The headless body topples over ... The legs and arms, still manacled behind the back, twitch vigorously ... A great "Aaah" goes up from the crowd ... The second man is being helped out of the van ...* '[127] Said the Saudi interior minister, Prince Naif, in response to Amnesty International: 'We apply the laws of God and don't pay attention to whoever says anything about that'.[128]

The reports, harrowing and impotent, continued to accumulate. Turks executed for smuggling the sex-stimulant drug Captagon into the Kingdom; a Saudi beheaded for allegedly trying to kill a policeman; a Saudi woman and her daughter beheaded one after the other in Dhahran; a 40-year-old Shi'a Muslim housewife, Zahra Habib Mansur, tortured to death by Saudi security men; a Pakistani girl, Del Ferouza Delaur, beheaded after allegedly carrying heroin of which she denied all knowledge; Fatimah bint Abdullah, beheaded for allegedly running a brothel and chewing the mild drug 'qat'; a man who stabbed another in a fight was beheaded in early January 1997 – the first execution of the year; and the two English nurses Lucille McLauchlan and Debbie Parry, sexually abused and intimidated into 'confessing' to the murder of the Australian nurse Yvonne Gilford in December 1996.[129]

In late 1997 it was reported (*The Sunday Times*, 19 October 1997) that two Pakistani girls, Mushrefah (aged 8) and Nargis (13), faced beheading for acting as 'drug mules' for their family. When Saudi officials detected that the girls had swallowed packets of heroin they and the rest of their family were formally charged with drug running, an offence which carries a mandatory death sentence. Held in appalling prison conditions the fate of the girls remains uncertain (as I write). Some commentators thought that Mushrefah might escape decapitation, because of her age, but that Nargis could well be executed. In 1992 the Saudis hanged a 15-year-old boy for abandoning his religious faith.

By mid-September 1997 some 101 people had been executed in Saudi Arabia in the year. Said the Saudi deputy interior minister, Prince Ahmed bin Aziz: 'Our experience in dealing with culprits has proved to be highly successful'. There would be no reforms, no acknowledgement that defendants should have access to legal representation or to legal advice, no acknowledgement that criminal trials should be held in public and independently reported, and no acknowledgement – despite provision in authoritative Islamic legal texts – that 'confessions' coerced through torture should be denounced and disregarded. The Holy Koran, 'binding for all time', would suffice.

THE SEXUAL SUPPRESSION

The Prophet was in no doubt about how women should be regarded: *'Men are superior to women on account of the qualities with which God hath gifted the one above the other'* (Koran, Sura 4, Verse 38). In another translation (Dawood, 1956) of the same Koranic text the declaration is equally unambiguous: *'Men have authority over women because Allah has made the one superior to the other'*. And the same verse urges men to hit their wives when they misbehave: '... chide those for whose refractoriness ye have cause to fear; remove them into beds apart, and scourge them' (Dawood: 'As for those from whom you fear disobedience, admonish them and send them to their beds apart and beat them'). If the women are then obedient, 'seek not occasion against them' ('... if they obey you, take no further action against them').

This then is the underlying attitude – sanctified by God – that informs the Islamic attitude to women. Women are inferior to men, should do as they are told, and can expect to be properly beaten if they do not. This is not to say that women are not assigned important rights (see below) or that they do not have a place in heaven (see Sura 9, Verse 73); but it does entail that it is always *men* who will decide the rights of women. It is this grossly sexist posture that afflicts the sociopolitical status of women throughout the Islamic world.

One issue that graphically illustrates male abuse of women in many Muslim communities is the practice of female circumcision, a cruel mutilation designed in part to expunge sexual feeling and to thereby protect female virtue. There is debate as to the extent to which ritual circumcision is an African, Arab or Muslim practice, but certain facts are plain. Strabo ('The Geographer', 63 BC to AD 19), of Amiseia in the Roman province of Pontos, mentions the excision of girls in Arabia centuries before the birth of Muhammed. But it is clear that, whatever the practice in many non-Muslim countries, Islam served to reinforce the custom of circumcision in Arab and non-Arab communities. Thus the researcher J. G. F. Riedel noted in the late nineteenth century the ritual of female circumcision on the Molucca Islands of Indonesia, *especially* by the Muslim population: 'The girls are bathed and placed across a stone and an old woman cuts away a portion of their *glans clitoridis*. It is said this is done to suppress and limit their desires before marriage. Burnt and pulverised sago leaves are applied as a styptic. Then the woman carries the girl in her arms into the hut which she must not leave till her wound is healed ... The custom is said to be Mohammedan in origin.'[130]

Professor and Mrs C. G. Seligman described nineteenth-century female circumcision among the Kababish, one of the most powerful of the Arab tribes (with strong Islamic influence) of the Anglo-Egyptian Sudan. Here it was the custom to cut off the entire clitoris and to carve away the whole of the vulva; the screams of the child (typically between the third and the sixth year) were drowned by the spectators, after which the girl's legs were tied together for two or three weeks. Another authority, F. J. Bieber, describes early twentieth-century practices among the Muslim Galla communities of Harai. Here girls of eight to ten years of age were infibulated in the 'stitching' (*mutscha durba*) process, where the inner labia were scraped until raw and bleeding, after which they were sewn together with horse-hair and the feet bound together for some days. A French physician, Dr Peney, describes elements of the ritual: 'the matron ... begins by slicing off the tip of the clitoris and the edges of the inner lips. Then the razor shears along the rims of the outer lips ... In order to drown the shrieks of the girl, the assembled guests and kin raise the loudest and shrillest din conceivable until the process is over ... when the flowing blood has been staunched, the girl is laid flat on her back, her legs extended and tied firmly together ...' Another researcher, Vita Hassan, recorded that female circumcision, practised as part of a religious ritual, was customary 'among all the Mohammedan tribes of the south from Berber to Sennaar, including Khartoum, Metemma, Shendi, Wad, Madani, Haraz, Sennaar and their environs'. One consequence of extensive circumcision was to impede the passage of the baby at birth: '... so the muscles from groin to reins are severed ... then this laceration is sewn together like the pre-marital wound, and the woman is once more impenetrable'.

The feminist writer Elizabeth Gould Davis has emphasised the Arab enthusiasm for female circumcision, where 'son of an uncircumcised mother!' is a particularly offensive epithet for one Arab to hurl at another.[131] One researcher has suggested that clitoral size, in addition to requirements of virtue, has encouraged excision: '... we have the proof on record of women with large clitorides who have seduced young girls ... It is to avoid such unnatural connections that the Asiatic nations, especially the Arabians, are in the habit of removing the clitoris.'[132] The explorer Sir Richard Burton describes the circumcision of Muslim women on the Arabian peninsula: 'The prostitutes of Aden all had the labia and clitoris completely excised and the skin showing scars and the traces of coarse sewing'.[133] It should not be thought that this nineteenth-century commentary has no relevance to the modern world.

In early 1994 Egyptian campaigners intensified their campaign for the eradication of female genital mutilation. Here the reformers were facing the entrenched belief among many Egyptians, both Christian and Muslim, that the excision of at least part of the clitoris and labia was necessary to preserve hygiene, femininity and sexual virtue.[134] The conservative Sheikh Youssef Al-Badri has claimed that medical evidence supports the theory that female circumcision improves the complexion and prevents 'sexual upheaval'; when provoked by a female reporter, he commented: 'Women who have had the necessary part removed have red complexions ... with cheeks as red as apples. Not like your yellow ones' (while a Badri supporter shouted at the woman: 'You shut up! I'll cut your tongue out and the tongues of those who gave birth to you!').[135] In June 1997 an Egyptian court ruled that a government ban on female circumcision being performed in hospitals and clinics was contrary to Islam. Said Badri: *'It's our religion. We pray, we fast, we do circumcision. For 14 centuries of Islam, our mothers and grandmothers have performed this operation ... God be praised, we have won and can apply Islam'*.[136]

In Saudi Arabia female circumcision is given no publicity and is rarely mentioned in foreign campaigns. It remains prevalent: a Saudi princess has recorded that her sister was circumcised when about 12 years old, and that the ritual had been carried out on the three sisters that followed her in age. A Western physician had protested to the father, so saving the youngest six daughters from the barbaric custom: 'Nura [the first sister] added that I was blessed not to have endured such a trauma'.[137] Nura had been circumcised according to long-standing custom: 'The oldest women gathered round the frightened child. Nura, nude from the waist down, was held by four women on a bedsheet that had been spread on the ground. The oldest of the women raised her hand in the air; with horror Nura saw that she had a razor-like instrument in her hand. Nura screamed. She felt a sharp pain in her genital region. Dizzy with shock ... she saw blood pouring from her wounds ...'[138] Nura's mother, as a pious and caring Muslim, had no doubt that the rite was the will of Allah.

With ritual circumcision still practised as a means of male dominance over women (though usually performed by older females in the group), women continue to be exploited in Saudi Arabia through prostitution and slavery (see 'The Survival of Slavery', below). It is interesting that education for girls has been prohibited in Mecca, but that prostitution has long been tolerated in the Holy City. Religious prostitution has survived in Arabia and elsewhere in the region over many centuries – to the extent that individual prostitutes would focus on the tomb or shrine of a Muslim saint, offering their services to pilgrims.[139] Even the most sacred rites of Mecca were not immune from such attentions: 'Some of the Banu Amir women used to perform the *tawaf*, the circumambulation of the Ka'ba, the sacred Black Stone, in Mecca, in a naked state, reciting in the meantime obscene verses'.[140] As late as the nineteenth century women in Mecca were still offering themselves as prostitutes for the Muslim pilgrims.[141] Moreover, one Muslim sect, the Ali-Ullaheeahs of Kerun, was known to indulge in an unusual form of Islamic celebration – ritual nakedness and sexual promiscuity at annual feasts.[142] And Islamic festivities were supported also by the Egyptian Ghawazee, entertainers and prostitutes, who often accompanied the Egyptian caravans of pilgrims to Mecca: 'They attend the camps, and all the great religious and other festivals; of which they are, to many persons, the chief attractions. Numerous tents of Ghazeeyehs are seen on these occasions'.[143] The prostitutes, having completed the pilgrimage to Mecca, were allowed to assume the title of Hadji.

The exploitation of women as prostitutes has mirrored the Muslim exploitation of women as wives, concubines and slaves. The Koranic verses address men, indicating how they shall deal with women. For example, a man may take four wives, providing he treats them equitably (Koran, Sura 4, Verse 3); and he is entitled to pick and choose who he sleeps with, among his wives and slaves, whatever their feelings on the matter: 'Thou mayst decline for the present whom thou wilt of them, and thou mayst take to thy bed her whom thou wilt ...' (Sura 33, Verse 51). Young daughters given in marriage cannot object when they reach puberty, however distasteful the marriage; men are instructed on how they may divorce their wives, but wives are given no equivalent entitlement; menstruation is 'a pollution' and women should not be approached until they are cleansed; if a woman is found guilty, by testimony of four witnesses, of 'whoredom' she shall be walled up in her house until merciful death releases her (Sura 4, Verse 19). These and other stipulations – for example, related to dowry provisions, property and inheritance entitlements, etc. – are well laid out in Koranic verses and the surrounding commentary; but often there is no more than a tenuous link between authoritative prescription in this or that text and what practices are actually observed in the world. In Saudi Arabia the harshest tenets of *sharia* law are duly observed but female Islamic rights are often ignored. Muslim states vary in their theoretical interpretation of holy writ; and equally in their day-to-day treatment of women.

Domestic violence against Saudi women is unsurprising, in view of the unambiguous Koranic advocation. The Saudi authorities deem it prudent not to maintain statistics on the extent of violence against women, but hospital workers report that many women are admitted for injuries caused by spousal violence; foreign women are often abused by their Saudi husbands, able to prevent their wives from obtaining exit visas.[144] Female domestic servants from abroad are frequently raped and otherwise abused by their Saudi employers (evidence has accumulated on forced confinement, withholding of food, beating, harassment, rape and other forms of abuse). Employers are largely immune from effective legal action in these cases, and complaining victims are likely to suffer further punishment and reprisal through the working of the penal system. There are no private support groups or religious organisations in Saudi Arabia to which abused women can turn for help. There are no active campaigning groups for women's rights.

Saudi women may own property and are entitled to support by their husbands or male relatives; but, in the absence of most social and political rights, women are seen in practice and in law as inferior subjects of the King. Women may not drive motor vehicles (see below) and are restricted in their use of public facilities. They may use city buses, providing they enter by separate rear entrances and sit in specially designated areas – clear examples of petty apartheid. Women are not allowed to travel in a car driven by a male who is neither an employee nor a close male relative; they are not allowed to undertake domestic or foreign travel alone; and are not allowed medical treatment in a hospital without the consent of a close male relative.[145]

Women appearing in public are expected to wear the *abaya*, a black garment that effectively shrouds the entire body (it is required that the head and face be covered). In recent years the *Mutawa* have instructed visiting Western women to wear the *abaya*. Some government officials and ministries still bar accredited female diplomats from abroad from appearing at official functions in Saudi Arabia, though Western governments maintain a diplomatic silence on such practices. The many discriminatory features of *sharia* law include:

- the stipulation that daughters shall only receive half the inheritance awarded to their brothers;
- the provision that a man's court testimony is equivalent to that of two women;
- the entitlement of a man to have up to four wives, with the Koranic equity demand left to the husband's discretion;
- the requirement that women seeking divorce must demonstrate legally specified grounds, where men may divorce without giving cause;
- the provision that children over a certain age are automatically awarded to a divorced husband or to the deceased husband's family;
- the exclusion of women from university courses in a number of subject areas (including engineering, journalism and architecture);
- the ban on women studying abroad unless accompanied by a spouse or a close male relative.

In addition to legal discrimination there are many *de facto* forms of discrimination that are equally oppressive. With women prevented from taking jobs in much of the public and private sectors, they make up only 5 per cent of the workforce. Women are most likely to be employed in education and health care, with minimal opportunities in business, banking, the media and retail sales; they are not allowed to accept jobs in rural areas if this entails living apart from their families. All workplaces are physically segregated by sex, though one concession has been made – female employees are permitted to communicate with clients or male supervisors by telephone or facsimile machine. In 1995 the Saudi government announced that women would no longer be issued business licenses for work in areas that might require them to supervise foreign workers, interact with male clients, or to deal on a regular basis with government officials.[146]

The entire social, political and employment structure of the Saudi state is seen to be hostile to women. Saudi women may only marry non-Saudi men with government permission, which is rarely given; female employees have been banned in many shops and offices; the *Mutawa* patrol the streets, looking for immodestly attired women, and have been known to hit women with sticks on their bodies and faces when the women are judged to be improperly dressed; fathers, husbands and brothers frequently chastise their women when they are thought to have behaved badly; a woman may be subjected to effective house arrest by her male relatives wanting to exact retribution; female prisoners are tortured in jail, as are men; when women protested against driving restrictions, King Fahd ordered all who taught at one university to be dismissed, some women were phys- ically attacked by male family members, and others were forbidden to leave Saudi Arabia (no local newspapers were allowed to cover these events); through- out education, employment and political opportunity there is massive and – in some particulars worsening – institutionalised discrimination against women. One detailed study concludes: '*Few countries in the world so severely restrict the lives of women, and all members of the United Nations are charged to promote and encourage respect for human rights and fundamental freedoms without dis- tinction as to sex. Saudi Arabia's notoriety in this regard sets it far apart from the majority of nations and creates an imperative for the Saudi Government to rectify the condition and standing of women in its society*'.[147] Another detailed study, by an academic who has worked with UN agencies on projects relating to women in the Arab world, concludes with the broad generalisation: 'What is needed, then, is a restructuring of thought and analysis that accepts the fact that women are equal to men and provides the vital element for the development of today's [Saudi] society'.[148] Then she adds sentiments that some observers might find con- tentious; suggesting that 'Islamic values are not an impediment to the participa- tion of women in the building of the country', and that intolerance 'is abhorred by the true spirit of Islam'.[149]

The studies are supplemented by personal accounts, written by Saudis born and bred in the oppressive system and by foreigners who witness the scale of abuse and discrimination. Thus a Saudi princess records that she is 'in chains', living a life reduced 'to a narrow segment of fear'.[150] She declares: 'The men feel they are what they have had to become. In Saudi Arabia, the pride of a man's honour evolves from his women, so he must enforce his authority and supervision over the sexuality of his women or face public disgrace ... The authority of a Saudi male is unlimited; his wife and children survive only if he desires. In our homes, he is the state ... women in my land are ignored by their fathers, scorned by their brothers and abused by their husbands'.[151] She describes also the stoning of a woman for adultery. The crowd was growing impatient, but then a 'very beautiful' young woman was dragged out of a police car, her hands bound, a dirty rag gagging her mouth, and a black hood at last drawn over her head. At first the woman was lashed on her back fifty times while rocks and stones of the approved size were being emptied from a truck. Then the enthusiastic men began to hurl rocks at the tormented woman, pausing at times to let the doctor check her pulse. It took two hours for her to die.[152]

The princess tells also of the child, already mentioned, who was kidnapped off the street to be used as an involuntary kidney donor. The father, at first relieved that his daughter had not suffered sexual assault, then learned that she had recently undergone major surgery: 'The child's scars were ragged, and infection had set in from filth ... the police ... suggested that the child had been taken to

India by a rich Saudi who had a child in need of a kidney transplant ... Widad [the Lebanese mother of the child] despised my land [Saudi Arabia] and the oil riches that had shaped a people who considered their wealth the conqueror of all life's obstacles. Sacred body parts were taken from innocent children and cash left to neutralise the anger of those injured!'[153]

The journalist Linda Blandford has also noted the Saudi attitude to women, here from the perspective of a foreign visitor: 'Saudis in Riyadh aren't used to having unescorted women flapping about'.[154] Here she learns about an arranged marriage, the characteristic infidelity of Saudi men, and the humiliation of the veil; and she records also the fate of Saudi princesses: 'Sad, pathetic beings for the most part. They're shut away in palaces, soaked in luxury and loneliness. Officially it's as if they don't exist ... Most princesses are doomed to a lifetime in parentheses ... slowly, very slowly, these sleeping beauties are stirring.'[155] Another sort of visitor to Saudi Arabia, Jehan Sadat, wife of Egypt's President Anwar Sadat, recorded similar impressions. Thus at the UN International Women's Year Conference in Mexico City in 1975, to which Jehan Sadat led the Egyptian delegation, the 'women's delegation' from Saudi Arabia was entirely composed of men; just as the Saudi delegation was that attended the similar conference in Nairobi in 1985. She remembers that when the wife of the Egyptian Vice-President, Magda al-Shafei, appeared in Mecca during the pilgrimage without a head covering the police hit her legs with sticks.[156]

Jehan Sadat notes also that only women professors, mostly from Egypt, were allowed to teach when the first Saudi university to admit women was opened in 1973; and that later the female students were not allowed to listen to male lecturers in the same room, but had to hear the lectures over closed-circuit television and ask any questions via a telephone link. Later, when Jehan Sadat appeared in public with her husband, confronting King Khaled and at least twenty Saudi princes waiting to greet them at the Jeddah airport, she realised it was an historic moment: '... it was well known that in such a conservative and deeply religious society as Saudi Arabia's, a Muslim woman did not appear in public in the company of men'. The Saudi embassy in Cairo had suggested that she wait on the plane until President Sadat, Khaled and the princes had together left the airport (this was the solution chosen by Mrs Tito, the wife of the President of Yugoslavia): 'But I had resisted ... "Anwar, on this trip I am deaf. I don't need anyone to tell me or to teach me what it means to be a good Muslim woman" ... the Saudi television cameras followed me as I left the airport reception with the Saudi princes ...'.[157] When Jehan Sadat flew on the royal plane from Jeddah to Mecca for the pilgrimage, she thought that at last Saudi women were being allowed to work as air hostesses, but then their accents revealed them as Lebanese. 'I hope soon they will be Saudis', she said; and a Saudi prince replied: 'Soon ... soon'.[158] The Saudi women are still waiting.

The repression of women in Islamic culture extends to every area of their personal lives; in no sphere are they allowed to act, think even, without reference to approved custom, *fatwa*, law. In some areas – such as dress, deportment, travel – the restrictions on women are well known; in other areas, only fully acknowledged within the confines of the orthodox Muslim family. Thus in one detailed text describing what is *halal* (permitted or lawful) and what is *haram* (prohibited or unlawful), the many constraints on female behaviour are indicated. Thus women are allowed to wear jewelry and ornaments but not to attract men or to arouse their sexual desires. An *hadith* declares: 'When a woman puts on perfume and goes among people so that its scent reaches them, she is an adulteress ...'; and women 'should not stamp their feet in order to make apparent what is hidden of their adornment'.[159] Women's garments must cover the entire body, and they must not be transparent or tightly fitting. Nor shall women pluck their eyebrows: 'The Prophet (peace be on him) cursed both the women who do the plucking and those who seek to have it done'; and the addition of any hair, real or artificial, to one's own hair (that is, the wearing of wigs and hairpieces) is also prohibited.[160]

A substantial compilation of *fatawa* on women, given by the Grand Mufti of Saudi Arabia, Sheikh Ibn Baz, and other scholars, deals in remarkable detail with every aspect of life. Abdul Malik Mujahid, contributing a Publisher's Note, observes that in addition to the common problems faced by men and women, women face 'a lot of special problems regarding their menses, post-partum bleeding, *istihada*, "a prolonged or continuous flow of blood from the vagina ... outside of the monthly menses", *hijab* [dress], mixing with men; rights and duties with respect to their husband, husband's household, children; inheritance, marriage, divorce and so forth'.[161] In this context women are told to observe what the male clerics tell them about their menstrual problems, how to behave if the doorbell rings during a prayer, and whether they should comb their hair before offering a sacrificial animal: 'It is only the scholars who can derive rulings from Shari'ah and give legal verdicts. Hence the people are commanded by Allah to have recourse to the pious scholars of religion ... In Saudi Arabia women have got the facility to put their questions regarding different kinds of problems faced by them in their day-to-day life, to the eminent scholars herein who are from amongst the best scholars of the world.'[162]

Any Saudi woman who is perplexed about how she should behave in particular aspects of her life is sure to gain much guidance from the *fatawa*. The following questions are just six of the 366 on which the learned male clerics (Sheikh ibn Baz, Sheikh ibn Uthaimin, Sheikh ibn Jibreen and others) provide authoritative answers:

Is there any difference in the manner that a man and a woman wash themselves after sexual defilement? Does a woman have to undo her braids or is it sufficient for her just to pour three handfuls of water over her hair?

What is the ruling concerning a woman dressing in a thin cloak that shows her clothing?

A woman had blood starting to flow while she was in the Mosque of the Prophet. She stayed in the mosque for a little while until her husband had finished the prayer and she could leave with him. Did she commit a sin?

While I was praying, my menses began. What should I do? Do I make up the prayers of the time of my menses?

If there is some sort of covering or wall between the men and the women in the mosque, does the Hadith of the Prophet still apply, 'The best rows for the men are the first rows and the worst rows are the last rows. And the best rows for the women are the last rows and the worst rows are the front rows'?

Is it allowed for a woman to wear a watch to know what time it is and not for the sake of beautification during her mourning period?

In such a fashion male clerics work to consolidate the rigid social framework in which women are expected to think and act. There is no suggestion in any of this that women should be allowed to develop as autonomous citizens, able to discuss and shape the copious rules that govern their lives. Here the closed society of Saudi Arabia, insulated from freedom of speech and easy access to foreign ideas, has so far managed to maintain the suppression of women; but some events in recent years have served to prise an opening in the hermetically-sealed walls of the Kingdom.

The 1990/91 Gulf crisis, whatever its other multifaceted consequences, had the effect of shaking the cultural obscurantism of the Saudi regime, not least where the status of women was concerned. More than half a million foreign troops had arrived in the Kingdom, nominally to protect the Kingdom from Iraqi aggression, but also to secure the House of Saud from the possibility of internal revolt. So it was that hundreds of thousands of Americans in uniform, many of them women, came to protect a culture in which the *Mutawa* and secret police would be enabled to break into houses to arrest and abuse women at parties talking to men who were not their fathers or husbands. The absurdity was obvious not only to many foreign journalists and soldiers but also to many Saudi women. In protest, thirty Western-educated women drove cars publicly through the streets of Riyadh, in direct challenge to the ban on women drivers.[163] The result was that the women were sacked from their jobs, a new *fatwa* was issued denouncing the women, and in some minds the women's cause had been set back many years.

The Saudi regime had faced a problem. The US forces flooding into Saudi Arabia in 1990 had included many women. Prince Khaled Bin Sultan, commander of the Arab forces through the period of the crisis, declared the problem: 'As the centre of the Muslim world, we could not afford to be as flexible as some other countries ... our tradition dictates that women wear long clothes and act demurely ... Saudi women are not much seen in the workplace, nor do they drive motor vehicles.' How, in such circumstances, could tens of thousands of young American women be accommodated in the feudal Kingdom? To prohibit the female influx would have been impossible not only from the diplomatic point-of-view but because the American war effort would have ground to a halt. Women were serving as drivers, mechanics, technicians, nurses, and even in combat; about a third of all US army vehicles were driven by women. Prince Khaled knew when he had to compromise: 'This was not an issue on which I could stick. Off-duty driving out of uniform was the real knotty point. So I hammered out a compromise with Schwarzkopf. I agreed to women driving in combat uniform on military missions, but I drew the line at their driving in civilian clothes for civilian purposes, such as shopping.'[164] And he notes also the requirement that the American women wear Saudi-supplied black robes over their uniforms during off-duty hours 'to make their presence more acceptable to our population'.[165]

The Riyadh demonstration, a brave protest at an absurd but symptomatic restriction, had achieved nothing. Passers-by were amazed to witness the women drivers; and for a while, according to Saudi ambassador Ghazi Algosaibi, the Saudi government 'was thrown into confusion'.[166] The traffic police and the *Mutawa* disputed who had jurisdiction in dealing with such an unprecedented matter, after which both factions escorted the women to a police station. They were later released after husbands or other male relatives had signed solemn pledges that no such violation of Muslim law would happen again. The Ministry of the Interior promised to observe the new formal legal opinion (Sheikh Baz's denunciatory *fatwa*), while Muslim preachers condemned the women's protest as a 'secularist conspiracy'. Soon Islamic cassette tapes were circulating denouncing the American female troops, the Saudi women drivers, and any person daring to sympathise with such blasphemers.[167] Another blow had been struck for religious propriety.

The women's protest was not the only cultural jolt to the Saudi regime through the period of the Gulf crisis. In early 1991 the Saudi authorities recruited two eminent Egyptian theologians to counter Iraqi claims that American women soldiers were guarding the Kaaba in Mecca. That female infidels should be allowed in contact with Islam's holiest shrine – a double desecration! In late January Iraqi radio began suggesting that the shrine had been occupied by US troops; and in January there were unconfirmed reports that the Iraqis had produced a photograph showing American women soldiers at the site. As a matter of urgency the two retired Egyptian clerics, Sheikh Mohamed Ghazaly and Sheikh Mohamed Mitwali Shaarawy, were flown to Mecca by private plane. It was hoped that televised prayers by the two old men would demonstrate to the Saudi people that the Kaaba was not polluted by any female infidel defilement.[168]

Apologists for Islam inevitably proclaim that there is nothing in Muslim teaching that is hostile to women. This strategy has three principal dimensions: quotations are used from the Koran and associated commentary to 'prove' that women's rights are protected (inconvenient texts – for example, Sura 4, Verse 38

– are ignored); texts are 'explained' in order to show that what *seems* to be hostile to women is in fact in their interest; and defects in other religions (especially Christianity) are cited to demonstrate that non-Muslim believers have no room to talk (as if to suggest that the gross sexism in St Paul cancels out the gross sexism in the Koran). Thus Ahmed Versi, editor of *The Muslim News*, can suggest that Islam 'is really a women-friendly religion' (the abuses of women under the Afghan Taliban and the Turkish regime, both self-avowedly Muslim, do not count since there are respectively Western-created and a pro-Western secular state).[169] Similarly Jamal A. Badawi, in an interesting booklet ('The Status of Women in Islam'), highlights the degrading treatment of women under Christianity; and then uses quotations from the Koran and elsewhere to 'prove' the superiority of Islam.[170] Even here the author is obliged to quote the Koran (Sura 2, Verse 228) to demonstrate the superiority of men over women ('men are a degree above them'). And the Muslim philosopher Mostafa Mahmoud, seeking to justify Islamic teaching on women, declares: '*We are simply dealing with facts: men have authority or transcendence over women by virtue of their natural attributes, fitness, and the controlling personality given to them by the Creator ... Islam, in fact, did no more than recognise this human rule ... Islam's position on women is justice itself.*'[171]

The anthropologist Mai Yamani, a former lecturer at King Abdul Aziz University in Saudi Arabia, has described the discernible stirrings of feminist consciousness in the Kingdom, albeit set against the constraints of social restriction, public segregation and family law.[172] Here she notes the growing number of women in business (with '2000 women on the Jeddah commercial register in January 1994'), but also the swelling ranks of female fundamentalists – a challenge to the male *Mutawa* – who, while not seeking the vote or the right to drive, are increasingly prepared to dispute male interpretations of Islam and *sharia*. The new 'feminism', a seeming betrayal of the liberal trends evident under King Faisal, appears to be deeply mired in Islamic constraint: 'Since the 1980s religion has become the platform on which the power game is played.'[173] In this there is no secure route to the social and political liberation of women in Saudi Arabia and elsewhere.

The constraints, abuse and discrimination continue. The authorities still maintain Saudi Government Railroad Organisation rule 1: 'It is absolutely unacceptable for women to travel by train without being accompanied ... by her father, brother, son or husband'. Women are obliged to board first and to sit with their minders in segregated compartments. In Riyadh a sign announces: 'Women are kindly requested to not enter or sit in the restaurant'; a side door is marked 'For Women Only'. Saudi women have been condemned for seeking to show how Koranic verses in fact support some of the rights for which they are struggling. Nor is it helpful for aspiring Saudi business-women to be banned from renting an office and to be prohibited from attending board meetings, even if they are major shareholders; a Saudi woman may finance a factory but may not visit it, since this would entail the mixing of the sexes. And in some areas the Saudi religious establishment is seeking to deny women some of their existing rights.

In August 1996 the Grand Mufti Sheikh Baz issued four *fatawa* reviving the old tradition of *sawaj al messiar* whereby men, already massively favoured in employment and inheritance law, are not legally obliged to support their wives financially. Since a man is legally entitled to have up to four wives the *messiar* arrangement allows him to enter into a relationship without the burdensome need to treat each of his spouses equitably. In short he is legally enabled to take a mistress without informing an existing wife (or wives). Saudi men have argued that the new law will help mop up the growing number of spinsters in the country. Said one middle-class Saudi man: 'It's a way of getting married to a lady without having the hassle of telling your existing wife ... polygamy without the obligations. It's only the first wives who are against it.'[174] At the same time women were still being denied any chance of employment in many industries, were being regularly abused on the streets by the *Mutawa*, and were being denied any opportunity to make a start in sport (for example, Saudi Arabia would not countenance sending a female team for any event in the Olympic games – should the International Olympic Committee ban male Saudi participation in these circumstances, or should it continue to underwrite sexual apartheid?).

The gross abuses continue, all within the shaping culture of this or that Muslim devotion. Consider the following (taken from a substantial file):

- In December 1996 nearly eighty children, many scarred and maimed, were abandoned or sold by their Muslim parents during the pilgrimage to Mecca; one 14-year-old girl, Hasina, told police that her hand had been cut off in Saudi Arabia.
- Some 400 former wives (married on a Thursday, bedded the next night, and discarded the next week) of the Kuwaiti ruler now live in neglect with no chance of remarriage.
- Iranian women with a lock of hair or a foot uncovered can be executed (84 lashes is the usual punishment).
- A Jordanian law stipulates that a convicted murderer's sentence will be reduced if his victim was an adulterous female relative.
- A Palestinian, Ali Musrati, killed his 16-year-old sister Amal by leaving her tied up in the road and running over her several times – in order to restore the family honour after she had run away several times.
- A Turkish mother and daughter were shot dead by male relatives for offending the Islamic code of dress.
- The Malaysian state of Kelantan, ruled by Muslim fundamentalists, has decreed that men and women must stand in separate queues at supermarkets.
- Mai Halima, who lived in a small village in Pakistan, was killed and dismembered by her husband after he saw her talking to a man.

- A young woman, Jamila, was stoned to death for adultery in Afghanistan under orders from the Taliban; in July 1997 women were told not to make noises on the pavements when they walked; thousands of young British Muslims were being taught the Taliban belief that women are the source of all evil.

Such events, all mediated directly or indirectly by various versions of religious commitment, show the fruits of the broad Islamic attitude to women. This remains a deep problem for Muslim reformers at a time of growing sensitivity to the rights of women throughout the world. Even the US State Department, under Secretary Madeleine Albright, has instructed American diplomats to consider the advancement of women's rights as a central priority of foreign policy. This did not mean that any pressure would be put on Saudi Arabia to improve its appalling record on the treatment of women. Said one US official: 'We're upping the profile on this issue, but it's not going to start trumping other considerations'; the United States was not 'going to be beating up on the Saudis' because of the status of women in that country.[175] Washington, as always, had much more important matters in mind than human rights.

THE SURVIVAL OF SLAVERY

If a state abrogates human rights to an extreme degree then it is likely that many of its citizens live in conditions approaching those of slavery; if people are abused and ill-treated, denied what is essential to their humanity, then they are at least *akin* to slaves. Thus the Saudi (Nebraska-based) dissident Mohammed Siddiq can declare: 'The Saudi ruler is truly unloving and unsympathetic towards his citizens ... He makes them feel embarrassed and the citizen is shunned, set aside as worthless and treated as though he/she is invisible. The House of Saud maintains that others are defective beings; therefore, they must defer to the dominance of the first-order son or grandson of Ibn Saud. In this scheme, others are servants/slaves who are only to be used.'[176]

It is unhelpful that the Koran (like the sacred texts of Judaism and Christianity) approves of slavery: 'O Prophet! We allow thee thy wives whom thou hast dowered, and the slaves whom thy right hand possesseth out of the booty which God hath granted thee ...' (Sura 33, Verse 49). Saudi rulers in the modern age were happy to take Muhammed at his word. In January 1957 the Mayor of New York, Robert F. Wagner, was robust enough to say that the Saudi King was 'not the kind of person we want to be recognised in New York City'; since Saud was 'a fellow that says slavery is legal, that in the Air Force you can't have any Jewish boys, and that a Catholic priest can't say mass'.[177] Slavery had long been a flourishing institution in Saudi Arabia, with the holy pilgrimage the main source of human merchandise. Nigerians, Sudanese and other nationalities would sell their children in Mecca, seemingly no affront to Muslim parenthood, in order to fund their journey home; and the slave trade helped to swell the sharif's wealth. Emirs and sheikhs maintained black slaves in their households, with slave children assigned to play with the youngsters of the Nejd. When Prince Faisal visited New York in 1944, his black slave Merzouk stayed with him at the Waldorf Astoria.[178]

In 1962 Faisal announced a ten-point programme for the new government that he was forming; and, under pressure from President John Kennedy and the United Nations, included the abolition of slavery: 'It is known that the Moslem *sharia* urges the manumission of slaves. It is also known that slavery in modern times lacks many of the stipulations imposed by Islam for the justification of slavery ... Now the government finds the time opportune for the total abolition of slavery'.[179] It is estimated that at the time there were around 30,000 slaves in the Kingdom, or one for every hundred of the indigenous population. The Saudi government had refused in 1956 to support the UN Supplementary Convention on slavery, and years later many of the traditionalists, including conservative *ulema*, insisted that the institution of Slavery be maintained: for did not the Koran indicate Muhammed's approval? But the royal princes would not give up their slaves without adequate compensation. Over the period of a year, according to Mecca Radio, the equivalent of more than $10 million compensation had been paid out to the wealthy royals and some 10,000 slaves freed.[180]

Saudi Arabia was the last country in the region to abolish the legal status of slavery. Moreover, because of the remoteness and cultural isolation of much of the country, some independent observers wondered whether slavery had in fact actually been eradicated. The Anti-Slavery Society, a non-governmental advisor to the UN Economic and Social Council, emphasised the difficulty of travelling within Saudi Arabia and pointed out that non-Muslims were not allowed residence in Mecca or Riyadh.[181] No government census had been published to indicate the scale of the slavery problem in the Kingdom, though Riyadh had claimed that an initial payment of £1,785,000 in compensation had resulted in the freeing of 1682 slaves. It was known that at the time of the 1962 decree King Saud had several hundred slaves and that many other exalted persons in the Kingdom were maintaining their own slave populations. One report suggested that the slaves in Saudi Arabia 'numbered many thousands',[182] with a semi-official estimate putting the figure at a quarter of a million, substantially more than the 30,000 already cited (Holden and Johns, 1981), of whom '60 per cent were foreigners who had been enslaved illegally'.[183]

A traveller in Arabia provided information to the Anti-Slavery Society on how the slave trade operated in the Kingdom. He commented on what was a well-known trade, 'with recognised centres for collection' and where the 'selling of slaves' was conducted openly: 'There is a recognised slave route from Dubai, Muscat, Buraimi, Al Hasa, Riyadh. Merchants make seasonal trips to Dubai and Muscat, returning with a group of 50 to 60 slaves at a time. They are put up for sale at Al Hasa and later, if unsold there, sold through brokers at Riyadh.' A trader described how slaves were kidnapped and a compensatory fee paid to the Sheikh of the tribe. The traders then handed over the slaves to the brokers for sale on the open markets: 'At Mecca there is a slave market called *Dakkat Al Abeed* (the slave platform) and at Riyadh the slaves are taken around following their dealer yoked like cattle, six or seven at a time.'[184]

A Saudi spokesman called the report 'tendentious' and 'fantastic ... based merely on hearsay and rumours derived from a "traveller" and sensational articles appearing in the Western Press'. Furthermore the Anti-Slavery Society was abusing its consultative status by submitting such an 'ill-founded and malicious' report to the Economic and Social Council. The Society responded by praising Faisal's 1962 decree, acknowledged that the transition from slavery to emancipation must be gradual, and commented: 'The Society understands that former slave-owners have been offered indemnification for the loss of property and that plans are being made for the resettlement of emancipated slaves. It would welcome an assurance that the envoys of slave-source countries are accorded facilities to enable them to find and to interview such of their nationals as may have entered Saudi harems in their childhood. It is at least possible that some of them may have found it impossible to adapt themselves to their new life and if given the chance might welcome repatriation.'[185]

The attitude of the Saudi government was soon apparent. It declined to respond to a questionnaire on slavery submitted by the Economic and Social Council, nor did it reply to the *note verbale* (11 March 1965) submitted to it by the non-governmental consultative organisation, Friends World Committee for Consultation. The Committee itself quoted an informant who, while acknowledging the freed slaves as 'the main problem' (so suggesting the government's 'considerable success in carrying out the reforms'), observed: '... a certain "black market" in slaves was still going on two years ago', after the 1962 decree. He was told in Taiz that it was still possible to buy both male and female slaves but that it was 'very much a hush-hush business'. He points out that in so large and loose-knit a country as Saudi Arabia, it is difficult to secure uniform application of the law.[186] We may consider the extent to which slavery persists under the auspices of a feudal Saudi Arabia, not only within the closed confines of the Kingdom but also at the hands of rich Saudis abroad.

The researcher Said Aburish declares of Saudi Arabia: 'The new slave state started in the late 1950s.'[187] Then it was that foreign workers, many of them impoverished and with no employment rights, began flooding into the Kingdom in search of a living. The Saudis responded to the foreign workers in the traditional way: 'To them they were real slaves ... It was not merely a case of abuse by individual Saudis which created the new slavery. The inherent unkindness of the Saudi *nouveaux riches* was compounded by the laws enacted to govern this situation and by the emergence of a new class of labour suppliers who traded mercilessly in human commodities.'[188] The determination to protect the rights of

Saudi employers created a new master-and-slave relationship that became enshrined in law. The Saudi employer has total discretion over how his imported labour is to be used; he is free to define the job (changing it on whim), the hours worked, and the scale and type of remuneration; he can 'discipline' a recalcitrant or incompetent worker, and 'retail' (sell) him to other employers. If wages are late or not paid at all, the worker has no recourse to law; whatever action he takes, he will be branded a trouble-maker and will find himself unemployable or in jail. Nor can a worker voluntarily seek employment with another businessman or organisation; he first needs to obtain an official 'release' from his current employer, after which he can be 'retailed' elsewhere, doubtless with communicated details of his shortcomings. The sourcing countries, often highly dependent upon Saudi largesse, are in no position to protect their exploited nationals in Saudi Arabia – which inevitably means the consolidation of 'officially sanctioned slavery'.[189]

The position of female workers, often beaten and sexually assaulted, is particularly dire. Typically they speak no Arabic and, as maids or nannies, they are confined in their employer's house; so, disciplined by food withdrawal and whipping, they may spend months without speaking to anyone. They have no recourse except for suicide (high among young Asian women in Saudi Arabia) or flight (when they are likely to end up in jail facing further torment).

The academic surveys and other studies confirm the picture painted by journalists, refugee employees and others. Thus the 1996 US State Department report confirms the helplessness of foreign workers at the hands of their Saudi employers: '... employers have significant control over the movements of foreign employees, giving rise to situations that might involve forced labour ...'. Sometimes workers are pressured to drop claims against their employers for unpaid wages; often a Saudi sponsor refuses to provide a worker with the necessary 'release' (a 'letter of no objection') to allow him to seek employment elsewhere; sponsors retain possession of the workers' passports, so they cannot travel abroad, even to return home, without permission from their Saudi employer. If abused workers abscond in desperation, like runaway maids fleeing sexual molestation, they are liable – if not jailed – to be returned to their employers against their wishes. The State Department study confirms the 'many reports' of Saudi employers who have refused to pay accumulated wages for months or even years. If workers protest they are liable to be deported or to be retained, with domestic and overseas travel prohibited, and further punished.

The study conducted by the Minnesota Lawyers Committee found that 'most foreign workers in Saudi Arabia' receive 'poor treatment'.[190] The situation is perceived as 'especially bad' for workers from developing countries 'and for female workers, in particular'. Workers may suffer from 'contract substitution' where new terms (for example, lower wages than those originally agreed) are unilaterally imposed by the Saudi employer; a worker demanding to return home may have no money for the return travel. Complaints about non-payment of wages are often considered to be 'violations', justifying cuts in wages and further delays. The Committee reports cases of partial payment (four-months' pay for seven-months' work) and complete non-payment. Filipino workers were being expected to work seven days per week, sometimes 12–18 hours per day.[191] Where Saudi employers have been demonstrably violating agreed contracts or the provisions of the Saudi Labour Code, the Saudi government usually has no interest in taking action. To divert worker criticisms, Saudi labour officials may present language problems (for example, refusing to provide a translator for a complaining foreign worker). When one female worker, to be employed as a seamstress, arrived at the house of her Saudi employer she found that her wage had been cut from $258 to $150 a month and that she was required to perform additional domestic duties; when she complained, she was beaten. A Saudi labour official cautioned the employer to pay the woman her agreed wages; the employer refused and no further action was taken. In addition, the woman was sexually harassed by staff in the Saudi Labour Office.[192]

The Committee's findings indicate the conditions of neo-slavery under which many foreign workers in Saudi Arabia are forced to live: enforced work for no wages; a man complaining to his employer about non-payment and then locked in a room for an entire month; four workers forced to live in a 12-metre-square concrete shelter; domestic servants locked inside their rooms at night, and inside the house when the family leaves; workers, sometimes employed for several years, forbidden from talking to members of the opposite sex for the entire duration; one man arrested by the police for making eye contact with a Saudi woman (the same man beaten by a *Mutawa* agent for speaking to a Filipino woman in a store); female servants not allowed to leave their employer's house during the entire period of their stay; workers denied permission by their employers to leave the country; wages withdrawn from an innocent man because of the working time he lost while being beaten by the police; a young woman forced to sleep on the floor, to work 18 hours a day, and to remain in the locked house when her employer was away; young women sexually abused, refused food and medical treatment, beaten, held for long periods in deportation cells ...[193]

A UK televised documentary, Channel 4's *Dispatches* (21 February 1996), focused attention on the abuse of domestic servants in Saudi Arabia. Furthermore, describing Saudi Arabia as one of the most repressive regimes in the world, it questioned whether important trade agreements make the British government deliberately uncritical of its human-rights record. In October 1995 the journalist Robert Fisk highlighted what Filipino and Sri Lankan maids were suffering at the hands of their Saudi employers: 'Beaten, burnt and sexually assaulted, they turn up in their dozens each year' at their embassies in Riyadh (and elsewhere in the Arab world). He notes the case of a Filipino nurse, arrested by the *Mutawa* and forced to sign a confession which she did not understand, who had committed the crime of talking to a male acquaintance in a Riyadh restaurant; she later discovered that she had 'confessed' to prostitution. Then she was taken to a Saudi prison and lashed 40 times by a male officer in the presence of laughing *Mutawa* officials.[194] In early 1997 the Philippines government, responding to dozens of tragic cases, warned young women going to work in Saudi Arabia that they could expect to be sexually harassed by Saudi men and slapped around by their Saudi mistresses: 'It has told its migrants that they could face a bleak, almost medieval, life of near-slavery.'[195] A booklet issued by the government declared: 'If you are a maid, you must cope further with being a woman. You have to ward off advances by your master, his brother, son and other male members of the household ... You may also have to bear pinching, slapping and scratching from your mistress. Mistresses get jealous of their maids for no reason at all and punish them for it'. It emphasises that there may be no rest days, that maids may not even be allowed to rest when they are sick, and that medical treatment may have to be paid for out of wages.

The slavery that wealthy Saudis find congenial at home is also often exported with them when they travel abroad.[196] The London-based *Kalayaan* ('Freedom') organisation has highlighted the plight of overseas domestic workers, many of them forced to accompany wealthy Saudis on visits to the United Kingdom. One Remy, hired in the Philippines, describes her time with a Saudi diplomat in London: 'My experiences of this were very horrific, and I could keep you here all morning telling you of daily threats and beatings. I became terrified of the husband and wife ...'.[197] Now it was obvious, to anyone who bothered to notice, that wealthy Saudis were exporting their home-grown slavery to the rest of the world. Thus an Egyptian maid, Shadia Eldeen, reported having been assaulted by a Saudi diplomat for whom she worked in London. At first she travelled with the family to Jordan, and then to Britain in the belief that she would be given her passport and allowed to return home: 'But when we came back, he said I would have to stay. He said that even if they cut me into pieces, no one would know about it for years. I told them I did not want to work for them any more. So he got a stick and they started hitting and beating me. Blood was running down my nose. They tried to stop me screaming but the neighbours came to the door. Then they left me alone.' No action was taken by the British authorities against the Saudi diplomat; just as no action was taken against two Saudi royals, Prince Saad and his wife Princess Nura, for the enforced confinement of two women, a Filipino and a Sri Lankan, in a Houston hotel (the judge declared that the Kingdom was protected by the Foreign Sovereign Immunities Act).

In early January 1997 two more Saudi royals, Prince Khaled al-Sudeiri and his wife Princess Latifa Aziz al-Saud, a sister of King Fahd, were being sued by three former Filipino women servants who claimed they had been beaten, starved and held against their will in Wimbledon, south-west London. One of the plaintiffs said that she was refused medical care when lack of food made her ill; another, trying to escape, was beaten in the street in front of other people. (This followed an earlier case where two German nurses, imprisoned by Saudis in a hotel in Park Lane, London, managed to produce a note, later found on the street: 'Help us, we are prisoners'.) In May 1997 the three Filipino maids were given leave to sue Princess Latifa in Britain, rather than being forced to take the case to the Saudi courts – where the result would have been predictable.[198]

The appalling human-rights record is the Saudi truth behind all the calculations of economists, oil prospectors, military planners and Western strategists. It is the reality also behind all the Saudi claims for Muslim virtue and leadership of the Islamic world: the Custodian of the Holy Mosques is the custodian also of profligacy, corruption and terror, the stalwart guardian of a feudal tyranny.

The situation is unstable, not least because an abundant world resource is not best managed via the narrow vision of a mediaeval obscurantism. And there are many other forces conspiring to weaken the feudal Saudi regime. Before considering these, it is useful to profile some relevant history.

Part II

Prehistory

2 Religious Roots

> ...*Whoso desireth any other religion than Islam, that religion shall never be accepted from him, and in the next world he shall be among the lost.*
>
> Koran, Sura 3, Verse 79

PREAMBLE

Several million years ago the Arabian peninsula was covered by a shallow sea that supported abundant lifeforms: molluscs, brachiopods and many others. As the creatures died in profusion over the centuries they sank to the bottom and became embedded in the seafloor. Eventually the water receded, the exposed terrain was compressed at high temperatures under layers of sedimentary rock, and vast reservoirs of oil and natural gas were formed over time. Eighteen thousand years ago the peninsula was a luxuriant grassland with an ample rainfall that sustained abundant vegetation and diverse wildlife. Then, with the end of the Ice Age and the retreat of the glaciers, the once fertile land was subjected to a prolonged drought: the rains rarely came, the rivers evaporated, and little survived of the rich flora and fauna. Now, with the fossils and dried-up riverbeds (*wadis*) telling of a different past, the land was little else than desert and desolation.

In one view the name *Arabia* derived from a Hebrew word, signifying a wilderness, a land of deserts and plains. The Arabs themselves have preferred to trace the name of one of their ancestors, Yarab, a son of Joktan, said to have been one of the earliest settlers in that region. But other observers have pointed out that Yarab is not included in the Old Testament listing of Joktan's sons (Genesis 10: 26–9), so perhaps the derivation should be sought elsewhere. Moses speaks of Arabah and identifies the region (Deuteronomy 1: 1), just as the Jewish historians and later prophets consider Arabah (Arabia), its traffic and its tribes. Thus Joshua includes *Arab* (15: 52) as part of 'the inheritance of the tribe of the children of Judah' (15: 20); Solomon is reported as receiving merchandise from all the kings of Arabia (1 Kings 10: 15); and Jeremiah (25: 17, 24), talking of the nations 'unto whom the Lord had sent me', includes 'all the kings of Arabia and all the kings of the mingled people that dwell in the desert'.

In the nineteenth century the Turks and the Persians called the Arabian peninsula *Arabistan*, with the natives themselves calling it *Jezirat el Arab* (the peninsula of the Arabs). One authority (writing 160 years ago) comments on the remarkable circumstance that Arabia, 'amid the changes and revolutions of 3000 years, still retains the precise appellation which it bore within a few centuries of the deluge'.[1] In fact Arabia, as a geographical entity, has been variously

71

defined in history; its boundaries have always been uncertain (even today's Saudi Arabia, like many other countries, remains in territorial dispute with several of its neighbours). Crichton, noting that the peninsula is surrounded on three sides by water, mentions the 'considerable variations' to which the northern frontier has been subject. Ancient geographers marked it by an imaginary line between the extreme points of the Arabian and Persian Gulfs, but many later adjustments were proposed for geographical and political reasons. Xenophon chose to extend the frontier northward to include much of Mesopotamia (Iraq); with Ptolemy, Diodorus and Strabo opting for boundaries defined by the Chaldean mountains in the east and the city of Thapsacus in the north. The Arabian geographer Abulfeda (writing in the fourteenth century) placed the northern boundary at Beles, almost at the latitude of Aleppo.

The Turkish geographers divided Arabia into a dozen provinces, while others proposed only two. Ptolemy (Claudius Ptolemaeus, 100–168) suggested a division that has remained familiar in modern times: *Arabia Felix* (the Happy Arabia), *Arabia Petrea* (Stony), and *Arabia Deserta* (Desert). Such demarcations, largely an arbitrary matter, were never recognised by the native inhabitants of Arabia. *Arabia Felix* was intended to embrace the celebrated Region of Incense on the coast of the Indian Ocean, a land of reported extravagance, costly artefacts and prodigious personal wealth (at least among the ruling élites). In the fifth century Marcian noted that the region contained four considerable rivers in those days, uncommon enough for the peninsula; and Strabo ('The Geographer', 63 BC–AD 19) remarked on the sumptuous temples and palaces. *Arabia Petrea*, the mountainous tract between Palestine and the Red Sea, was the site of many of the extraordinary events recorded in Jewish history: the allegedly divine issuing of laws to Moses on Sinai, the burning bush at Horeb, the caves that sheltered Elijah, the smitten rock that yielded water, the emotional turmoil of Job – such tales, and many more, granted Arabia an enduring religious significance long before the time of the Prophet. *Arabia Deserta*, separated from *Petrea* by the ridge of Mount Seir, extended north and east, and included the great central wilderness; by its nature, its emptiness and its desolation, *Deserta* made little imprint on the course of historical affairs.

Arabia Felix has been identified with the region of Yemen, *Petrea* with the modern Hejaz (dubbed the Muslims' *Holy Land*, by virtue of the holy cities of Mecca and Medina), and *Deserta* with the vast plains that extend through much of the peninsula and, in some demarcations, as far north as the Euphrates. For the most part the peninsula is a sterile table-land without a single navigable river; furrowed channels, dry in winter, become muddy streams in summer, suggesting the occasional lower stratum of water that can sometimes bring an oasis of relief in the empty waste.

Most of the interior of the peninsula is nothing more than a burning and totally inhospitable desert, merciless to plant and animal alike. The vast plains lie baked under an almost perpetually cloudless sky and stretch endlessly to a grim and uniform horizon. Sudden winds, dry and suffocating, whip the sand into columns and shape fresh hills, so perplexing the unwary traveller; while the quivering air can play tricks with the light, magnifying the appearance of distant objects in the undulating vapour, perhaps causing a meagre shrub to resemble a tree, a flock of birds a caravan of camels. Vegetation is today all but extinct in the vast reaches of the peninsula, though hardy brushwood, tamarisk and acacia survive sparsely, relying on the cold nightly dews. The prophet Jeremiah recorded (2: 6) the passage of the Israelites through Arabia, *'through the wilderness, through a land of deserts and of pits, through a land of drought, and of the shadow of death, through a land that no man passeth through, and where no man dwelt'*.

Modern Saudi Arabia constitutes about 70 per cent of the peninsula, so covering almost one million square miles (or somewhat more – the texts vary). The poorly defined borders conspire with a substantial nomad and immigrant population to make nonsense of dogmatic statistics. If traditional nomads regularly cross badly demarcated frontiers, of which state are they citizens? Today four distinct areas define the Saudi state: *Hejaz*, including the cities of Yanbu, Taif, Jeddah, and Mecca and Medina; *Nejd*, including the massive deserts – the southern Rhub al-Khali (the 'Empty Quarter'), the al-Nafud with its striking red and white sands, and the al-Dahna that links the other two deserts in a sweeping 1300-km arc of inhospitable sand; *al-Hasa* ('Sandy Ground with Water'), including the population centres of al-Khobar, Dammam, Dhahran and the massive al-Hofuf oasis; and *Asir* ('Difficult'), taken from Yemen in war (1934) and enjoying the most plentiful rainfall in the country.

The region has scarcely been blessed with abundant natural resources (oil and natural gas apart, discovered well into the twentieth century). Here are none of the fertile river valleys that favoured the development of civilisations elsewhere in the ancient world. It was not through prodigious capital wealth that Arabia came to influence the course of human history. Its ancient historical role was no more than to plant geographical markers in the development of Judaism, to which the Koran acknowledges its implicit but unambiguous debt. But in later times Arabia came to influence the world through two major forces: the impact of Muhammed, and the power of the vast energy sources laid down by the ancient sea. The oil and gas were waiting millennia before the birth of Muhammed, but his impact was felt first. It is useful to glance at the early Arabians, the precursors to the Prophet.

THE EARLY ARABIANS

Human settlements were established in the Middle East about 10,000 years ago, according to archaeological evidence found in the Fertile Crescent countries (Iraq, Syria, Palestine, Jordan and Egypt), Turkey and Iran. In these early societies the primitive hunters and gatherers eventually established permanent villages, began agriculture and animal husbandry as essential food sources, and so facilitated the progressive stratification of society. The nomads of the Arabian peninsula were influenced by such developments but, struggling for survival in a more hostile environment, were able to contribute little to the high civilisations emerging in Mesopotamia and elsewhere.

In much of Arabia, while settled communities were rapidly evolving in neighbouring countries, Neolithic hunter-gatherer groups survived as nomads or on a semi-settled basis. Arabian society south of the Nafud, unlike its northern counterparts, did not use pottery until around 2000 BC, a significant index of the level of development in contemporary society. Eventually an increased emphasis was given to the herding of goats, cattle, sheep and camels, but hunting remained important with agriculture given little thought in the difficult environment. The extant evidence for these early cultures includes arrowheads, stone blades and other artefacts, and the rock carvings at Jubbah (Nafud) and Hanakiyyah (western Nejd).[2] Stone circles and other stone structures have been found in northern Arabia and also, more sparsely, in various southern regions. To the north of Riyadh various stone tools (querns for grinding cereals, finely-flaked spear heads, and others) have been found in the environs of a village site of circular dry-stone walls. The site, dating to the 5th–4th millennia BC, has been judged typical of the settlements then developing in the better-watered parts of Nejd.[3] At the same time traders and agriculturalists were surviving in various parts of eastern Arabia.

The biblical evidence (already cited) for the existence of early Arab communities is complemented by Assyrian and Babylonian inscriptions of the ninth–sixth centuries BC. Here reference is made to the *Arubu*, tribal, camel-riding traders linked with oasis settlements in northern Arabia. Thus the Kurkh Stele, held in the British Museum, records the operations of the Assyrian Shalmaneser III against the Aramaeans (853–841 BC). In conflict with Argana, Shalmaneser was forced to confront many forces, including '1000 camels of Gindibu of Arabia'. Similarly the interventions of Tiglath-Pileser III in Syria and Palestine (743–732 BC), noted in a slab inscription from the South-east Palace of Nimrud, refers to Zabibe, the Queen of Arabia; just as a Nimrud prism, recounting Sargon's capture of Samaria (722 BC), makes reference to Samsi, the Queen of Arabia; and an inscribed tablet, recording Nebuchadnezzar's capture of Jerusalem (597 BC), complements the Old Testament account (Jeremiah 49: 28–33) of the Babylonian onslaught on the Arab tribes ('the men of the east. ... And their camels shall be a booty, and the multitude of their cattle a spoil ...'). In the fifth century BC Herodotus referred to the *Araboi*; Strabo and Pliny, in the first centuries BC and AD, wrote of the *Arabes*; and by the fourth century AD settlers in the Yemen used the term *Arab* to denote the pastoral nomads of central and western Arabia.[4] One authority (Crichton, 1838) suggests a distinction between the old extinct Arabs, the genuine or pure Arabs, and the mixed or naturalised Arabs.[5]

It is noted that the ancient Arabians, 'shut up for so many ages within their rocky peninsula ... appear to have occupied themselves entirely with their own feuds and factions'.[6] But, with an interest in their genealogies, some isolated facts were preserved – in songs and oral tales rather than in any substantial national literature. (Some have argued that zealous Muslims, in the manner of pious bigots in other religious cultures, might have been eager to destroy ancient literary works steeped in pagan idolatry. Crichton: 'This supposition ... is not supported by any fact that has yet come to light.') Arab tradition records that the most famous of the extinct tribes were those of Ad, Thamud, Jadis and Tasm, all descended from the biblical Shem. Many fabulous tales surround these early Arabs. Thus Sheddad, the son of Ad, completed the magnificent city begun by his father in the desert of Aden. A palace, built in supposed imitation of the celestial paradise, was constructed with alternate bricks of gold and silver, and protected by a roof of gold inlaid with precious stones and pearls. Trees and shrubs were built out of the same precious materials, with jewelled birds constructed with cavities to hold the richest perfumes, that wafted on the breeze. But a jealous god, enraged by a human creation that could rival paradise, issued a terrible noise from the sky to destroy the palace and its gardens. One legend continues to assert that the palace still stands in the desert, though invisible.

The tribe of Thamud was a race of giants, each so powerful that by stamping on the hardest ground he could plant himself knee-deep in the earth. It is of some interest that the sons of Anak destroyed by Joshua (11: 21) supposedly inhabited the same region, and that the Jewish rabbis made Japhet and his son of gigantic proportions. The tribes of Tasm and Jadis settled between Mecca and Medina, with little known of their culture or exploits; when the Arabs wish to signify that an account has dubious authority, they call it a 'fable of Tasm'. The extinction of the early tribes was necessarily attended by divine displeasure. Thus the posterity of Ad and Thamud had allegedly abandoned worship of the true God and lapsed into idolatry, stubbornly unwilling to heed the chastising drought or the words of the prophet Hud: 'O people! Understand and be converted, and suplicate remission for your sins! Then shall the heavens drop with rain, and your sustenance shall be renewed.' God then sent a hot and suffocating wind, accompanied by an earthquake, by which the pagan idols were shattered and all the houses of the tribe razed to the ground. There were some survivors, who came to form the tribe of the Latter Ad, but God remained angry enough to transform them into apes. In the same impious spirit the idolatrous tribe of Thamud refused to heed divine warnings. When the prophet Saleh demonstrated God's power by producing a camel and its offspring from a certain rock the tribesmen refused to acknowledge the miracle, deciding instead to hamstring the mother, to kill the offspring, and to divide the flesh among them. God sent a terrible noise from heaven to kill them all, the fitting response to stubborn idolatry. But not all the early Arab tribes were exterminated by God. The tribes of Jadis and Tasm became extinct when the Tasmite despot Abulfeda claimed priority over all the brides of the Jadisites. In the ensuing bloodbath there were few survivors. Other lost tribes (for example: Amalek, Abil, Waber, Jorham, Emim and Jasim) were similarly either obliterated in domestic feuds or extinguished under clouds of divine wrath.

In one historical view the 'pure Arabs' are those descended from a certain
Kahtan, regarded as a principal founder of the race: a member of such supposedly
genuine stock is styled *Al Arab al Araba* (an Arab of the Arabs). The genealogy
of the Kahtan patriarch recognises two distinct branches: Yarab, one of his sons,
founded the kingdom of Yemen; while Jorham, another son, established the
kingdom of Hejaz. Their names cannot be found in the Old Testament record; but
some observers have argued that the two sons were the Jerah and Hadoram mentioned by Moses as among the thirteen planters of Arabia. The posterity of Yarab
multiplied into many clans, with new accessions requiring fresh subdivisions. In
this context it is possible to identify nearly three score tribes of 'genuine Arabs',
many of whom were renowned long before the time of Muhammed. It is of interest that in dividing their nation into tribes the Arabs resemble the Jews, as they
did many other races in ancient times; and that, in this connection, perhaps *'the
Jews themselves were nothing more than a small Bedouin tribe, just like the rest,
which local conditions, agriculture, and so forth placed in opposition to the other
Bedouins'.*[7] It is known that many Jews settled in Arabia after the age of Joshua
and Moses, eventually forming powerful and independent tribes, until the sword
of the Prophet either extinguished their line or forced them into flight.

The 'mixed or naturalised' Arabs (the *Mostarabi*) were supposedly descended
from Ishmael and the daughter of Modab, the King of Hejaz and a descendant of
Jorham. Since Muhammed traced his descent to this source the Arabs have traditionally been keen to protect and adorn this genealogy. Here we learn that
Ishmael was the son of Abraham, by the Egyptian slave Hagar. When Ishmael
was fourteen years of age he was supplanted in the affections of his father by the
new-born Isaac, whereupon Ishmael and his mother were cast out to live elsewhere. Eventually, after great tribulation, Ishmael settled in Hejaz and founded a
nation; at Mecca his life had been providentially saved when an angel directed his
mother to water; and it was at Mecca that Hagar died and was buried. The legend
states also that God commanded Abraham to build a temple to commemorate the
miraculous intercession of the angel. Thus Abraham, aided by Ishmael, built the
Kaaba (or sacred house): the black stone set in the wall and still kissed by
Muslim pilgrims is supposed to be that on which Abraham stood. In this tale the
stone descended from heaven and, once positioned in its sacred site, rose and fell
of its own accord to meet Abraham's needs. Once allegedly white, the stone grew
black long ago through natural wear or, some said, to mourn the crimes of men.

Ishmael became the prince and first high-priest of Mecca, preaching for half a
century until his death when he was buried in the tomb of his mother Hagar; he
had lived for 137 years. Ishmael's eldest son Nebat then assumed the regal and
sacerdotal duties though Muhammed's lineage is traced to a younger brother,
Kedar. But Nebat was not destined to enjoy a peaceful reign. The Jorhamites
seized the secular power and the guardianship of the temple, which they maintained for about three centuries. Then they were attacked by other tribes and
driven from Mecca – not before committing every kind of sacrilege. Into the

Zemzem well were thrown all the treasures and sacred utensils of the temple, including the celebrated swords and cuirasses of Kolaah, golden gazelles presented by one of the kings of Arabia, a sacred image of the ram substituted for Isaac, and the heaven-sent black stone. For several centuries a separate line of Ishmaelite descent held sway at the sacred site. Table 2.1 lists the princes, the lineal ancestors of Muhammed, who held sacred and secular power in Hejaz for more than six centuries.

The early lineage, from Ishmael to Adnan, is highly uncertain – since the stated 40 generations are scarcely sufficient to extend over a period of 2500 years. But the line from Adnan to the Prophet, involving some 21 generations and nearly 160 different tribes, is viewed with more confidence. Those who regard Moses as a reliable authority will be happy to accept the national descent of the Arabs from Ishmael.

The recording of Muhammed's lineage is of natural interest to those keen to fill out a sacred tradition, but the history of the petty sovereigns is unremarkable. The tradition tells of bequests, sagacious judgements, acts of bravery and singular generosity (Hashim killed his own camels to feed the poor, Abdul Muttalib brought food-laden tables to mountain summits for the benefit of birds and wild beasts), the restoration of the holy artefacts (presumably retrieved from the Zemzem well), the fabrication of swords into an iron gate for the Kaaba, and so on. One particular feature is recorded in the tradition as marking out the lineal ancestors of the Prophet from all their collateral tribes – the extraordinary prophetic light said to illuminate their faces (a defining symbol 'inherited from father to son since the days of Adam'[8]). It is interesting to note that the intensity of the light varied according to the piety and virtue of the individual: in some dazzling to behold, in others a mere flicker.

The Arabs lived, as today, in both nomadic and settled communities. Where the conditions were favourable, as in parts of Hejaz and Nejd, villages and towns

Table 2.1   Lineal ancestors of Muhammed

BC	122	Adnan	AD	241	Galeb
	89	Maad		274	Lowa
	56	Nazar		307	Caab
	23	Madar		340	Mora
AD	10	Alyas		373	Kelab
	43	Modreca		406	Qusayy
	76	Khozaima		439	Abid Menaf
	109	Kenana		472	Hashim
	142	Nader		505	Abdul Muttalib
	175	Malec		538	Abdullah
	208	Fehr			

Source: Crichton, (1838) (some spellings adapted).

were able to develop, while the mobility conferred by camels gave the Arabs an increasingly significant trade and military role in the region. By the first millennium BC the agricultural settlements were emerging as important trading cities – in north-western Arabia, in eastern Arabia, in southern Nejd and elsewhere. Important cities, contemporaneous with the Mediterranean period, were established after 500 BC and derived benefits from the growing trade between the Indian Ocean and south-west Arabia on the one hand and the Fertile Crescent and the Mediterranean on the other. In this context it was inevitable that different Arab cultures would develop in the peninsula, according to the pressures of environment and tradition and to external pressures felt through trade and military adventure. Again it can be noted that specific well-defined groups inhabited the broad expanse of Arabia in ancient times.

One principal group survived in the rain-fed uplands of the south, in the region of what today is the Yemen.[9] The pastoral nomads have been depicted as the other main group, wandering with their livestock over the great deserts that stretch in largely unbroken desolation from the centre of the peninsula to the Euphrates in the north. These latter, often celebrated by those in search of the 'true Arabs',[10] were often subservient to transitory conquerors, forced to pay tribute in camels and in other ways. Thus the Old Testament notes (II Chronicles 17: 11): '... *some of the Philistines brought Jehoshaphet presents, and tribute silver; and the Arabians brought him flocks, seven thousand and seven hundred rams, and seven thousand and seven hundred he goats'*. The nomads (essentially Bedouins[11]) maintained their essential trading contacts with the settled communities, so encouraging cultural cross-fertilisation: both the settled and wandering Arabs became increasingly aware of Hellenic ideas, the complex fabric of Jewish belief, and the derivative claims of the early Christians. Again we encounter the suggestion that the ancient Hebrews were also Arabs, tribal dwellers in the Arabian peninsula.[12]

The trading interests of the early Arabians helped to define their access to foreign goods, the character of the developing population centres, and the influence of fresh cultural concepts. That the early Arabs were keen traders is well attested by the ancient caravan routes that crossed Arabia in all directions: commerce between the fierce nomads, who often pillaged for booty, and the more placid towns and villages was an influential feature of the Arab world. For example, the Old Testament (Genesis 37: 25) records how a travelling group of Ishmaelites participated in this trade, coming from Gilead 'with their camels bearing spicery and balm and myrrh, going to carry it down to Egypt'. It is likely that social disruption elsewhere helped the Arabs to take control of important trade routes. Thus the fall of the 'New Empire' in the Egypt of the eleventh century, which in turn led to the loss of overseas territories, enabled the southern Arabians to secure naval control of the Red Sea and thereby to dominate the incense traffic from the Hadramaut and the spice trade with India. The expanding trade led to contact with fresh ideas, some associated with monotheism: by the fourth century AD many of the Arab settlers had abandoned traditional animism and were turning to worship of a supreme deity dubbed *al-Rahman*, 'the Merciful'.[13] By now the ground was well prepared for the coming of Muhammed.

The character of early Arabian culture has been gradually revealed through archaeology,[14] linguistic studies,[15] and the discovery of extant texts in Arab and other cultures. Thus we know that by the end of the 2nd millennium BC a region of north-west Arabia was practising irrigation, the mining of copper, and sophisticated pottery manufacture; and that by 500 BC a southern group of Arabian languages, characterising the Sayhad cultures in the Yemen, had developed distinctive features. The pre-Islamic dialects of western and central Arabia are still being classified,[16] but already it is clear that Classical Arabic drew on many linguistic sources. The tribes developed their own dialects and variations, incorporating their own unique experiences and absorbing foreign influences. The various linguistic adaptations reflected many cultural interests: they celebrated the heroic histories – real or imagined – of the tribes; and reflected also on the human predicament in the face of an often hostile and unyielding environment. It was into this rich but often parochial culture – the fabric of a pagan diversity with an emerging proclivity to monotheism – that a new and challenging creed would explode upon the scene.

THE PAGAN CULTURE

The harsh Arabian environment encouraged an attitude that was practical rather than theoretical or metaphysical. For centuries the fierce Bedouin tribes of the Hijaz, Nejd and elsewhere contended in the desperate struggle for survival. Despite frequent contacts with Hellenic speculation and Judaeo-Christian eschatologies the Arab tribes preferred to focus on more immediate concerns: how were the basic necessities of life to be located, won and protected? The early Arab communities had favoured animism, perhaps an inevitable phase in human social evolution, and then evolved a pagan pantheon of deities, perhaps an advance, and the Arabs were prepared to worship at their shrines; but there was no complex mythological system setting such divinities and holy places in relation to immortal souls and an eternal afterlife. At most there was a belief in the ubiquitous *darh*, loosely meaning time or fate ('it is written'), an inevitable concept in human societies where all life was perennially insecure and brief. Instead of religious devotions and nicely fanciful speculations, much pursued by contemporary peoples with time on their hands, the Arabs preferred a stern social ethic that would aid survival.

To aid a practical communal spirit the Arabs developed the *muruwah* ideology, an attitude that to a large extent stood in the stead of contemporaneous religions and comprised a complex of elements: Westerners have translated *muruwah* as little more than 'manliness' but in reality the term has signified such things as courage in battle, patience and endurance in suffering, loyalty to one's fellows, and absolute dedication to the tribe. Under the demands of *muruwah* the Arab was required to obey his chief (*sayyid*) without question, with no thought of personal safety; to avenge any wrong committed against the tribe; and to spare no effort in protecting the vulnerable members of the group. One authority has described *muruwah* as 'bravery in battle, patience in misfortune, persistence in revenge, protection of the weak, defiance of the strong'[17] – the very qualities that were necessary for the survival of the desert tribe. And the doctrine imposed equivalent obligations on the *sayyid* of the tribe.

Chiefs were naturally assumed to show bravery in conflict and a remorseless will to destroy the enemies of the tribe. But in addition the *sayyid's* wealth and possessions were not to be hoarded to the detriment of the tribe: the central demand was the survival of the group – to which personal courage, the protection of women and children, the munificence of the *sayyid*, and the bitter prosecution of blood-feud or vendetta could all equally contribute. *Muruwah* encouraged egalitarianism, a pragmatic indifference to personal goods, largesse and generosity, and personal endurance in the face of adversity. Such qualities were set to continue under the scope of Islam, but supplemented by other obligations that more comprehensively addressed the needs of a changing society. By the end of the sixth century, during the last phase of the pre-Islamic *Jahiliyah* (the time of ignorance), *muruwah* was no longer adequate in isolation to answer the conditions of modernity.[18]

The pagan culture, its ethics and its primitive religion, was the result of a centuries-long evolution. First the animism: stones and trees were worshipped as either divinities in their own right or the abodes of spiritual forces; later such natural objects, revered in attitude and ceremony, were assigned imaginary links with celestial bodies – the first hesitant conjunction of the earthly and the heavenly. It has been suggested that the Bedouins had little serious interest in such divinities, perhaps because they were originally the gods of the agricultural tribes.[19] Still most Arabs believed that the universe was infested with benevolent and malevolent demons (*jinns*) and with formidable genii (*efrit*), who took a disturbing interest in human affairs. The worship of stones gave rise to idols that were no more than blocks of stone, such as those of the goddess Manat at Kodaid and the goddess El Lat (dubbed Alilat by Herodotus) at Taif. The gods and goddesses were numerous (Huart in his *History of the Arabs* lists fifty: including Atthar (the Sun), a female divinity; Sin (the moon-god filched from the Assyro-Babylonians); Ankarih; Haubas; El-Makun; and Khol – among the divinities of southern Arabia. For the north he includes Allat (the planet Venus); Ruda (the Evening Star); Itha; Raham; and Chai-al-Kaum (the good and rewarding god who condemns wine)). The Koran itself mentions a few pagan divinities; for example, the idols erected by the descendants of Cain (Wadd, Sowa, the lion-shaped Yaghut, Yauk, and the vulture-god Nasr). The Qurayshites esteemed the goddess el-Ozza – to the point that she was offered human sacrifices; and due obeisance was given to the storm-god Kozah, and to Isaf and Naila, still represented in

Mecca by standing stones. And it is useful to remember that the Kaaba at Mecca, the sacred house of Abraham, had developed as a focus of pagan devotion long before the birth of Muhammed: Islam, like Christianity, found it easier to absorb rather than to extirpate many existing pagan elements.

The sacredness of the Kaaba in pre-Islam Arabia is well conveyed in the story of the Abyssinian general Abraha who appeared before Mecca with the intention of destroying the venerated house of devotion. Suddenly he found himself unable to enter the city: the elephant on which he was riding knelt and refused to proceed further. Then Abraha's army was forced to retreat in panic, pursued by birds that released stones from their beaks to pierce the fleeing soldiers. The legend is recounted in the Koran (Sura 105): 'Hast thou not seen how the Lord dealt with the army of the elephant? / Did he not cause their stratagem to miscarry? / And he sent against them birds in flocks (ababils) / Claystones did he hurl down upon them / And he made them like stubble eaten down.' In such a fashion was the Christian King of Abyssinia and Arabia Felix repulsed from the site of the holy Kaaba. In fact we learn that the army was defeated by a smallpox epidemic (the Arabic word for smallpox also means 'small stones' on account of the gravelly feeling of the pustules); and that smallpox was unknown in Arabia before the time of Abraha's invasion.

We have learned about pagan religious practices from early Arab writers who themselves used written and oral sources for their work. Thus Hisham ibn Muhammad al-Kalbi (d. *c.* 817), in his *The Book of Idols*, considers various divinities; in particular, el-Ozza (or al-Uzza), a goddess mentioned in the Koran. He observed that el-Ozza was more recent than the goddesses Allat and Manah, since Arab children were named after the latter two before they were named after el-Ozza; but then the later goddess came to be particularly favoured among the Quraysh, who travelled to her sacred sites, offered gifts, and sought favours through sacrifice and other practices. As the Quraysh circumambulated the Kaaba, a long established ritual, they intoned the prayer: 'By Allat and el-Ozza / And Manah, the third idol besides / Verily they are the most exalted females / Whose intercession is to be sought.' Such goddesses were perceived as 'the Daughters of Allah', suggesting the emergence of monotheistic concepts in pre-Islam paganism. But the Koran (Sura 53, Verses 19–29) disparages these divinities, not least because they are female:

Do you see Al-Lat and Al-Ozza,
And Manat, the third idol besides?
What? shall ye have male progeny and God female?
This were indeed an unfair partition!
These are mere names: ye and your fathers named them thus:
God hath not sent down any warranty in their regard.
A mere conceit and their own impulses do they follow. Yet hath 'the
  guidance' from the Lord come to them.

Shall man have whatever he wisheth?
The future and the present are in the hands of God:
And many as are the Angels in the Heavens, their intercession shall be of no
avail.
Until God hath permitted it to whom he shall please and will accept.
Verily, it is they who believe not in the life to come, who name the angels with
names of females:
But herein they have no knowledge: they follow a mere conceit; and mere
conceit can never take the place of truth …'

Hisham al-Kalbi identifies also several idols in and around the Kaaba – of which
the greatest was Hubal: 'It was, as I was told, of red agate, in the form of a man
with the right hand broken off. It came into the possession of the Quraysh in this
condition, and they, therefore, made for it a hand of gold …'.[20] Seven divination
arrows, one carrying the word 'pure' and another 'consociated alien', were
shuffled before the idol whenever the lineage of a new-born child was doubted. If
the word 'pure' was shown, the child would be accepted; but appearance of the
words 'consociated alien' would cause the child to be rejected from the tribe. The
other divination arrows were variously concerned with the dead, marriage and
dilemmas over travel and other projects: 'Whatever result they obtained they
would follow and do accordingly.'[21] When Muhammed conquered Mecca (630,
see below) he encountered the idols arrayed around the Kaaba, whereupon he set
about piercing their eyes with his arrow, declaring at the same time (Koran, Sura
17, Verse 83): 'Truth is come and falsehood is vanished. Verily, falsehood is a
thing that vanisheth.'

The pagan Arabs, according to al-Kalbi, were fond of their idols. Worshippers
unable to build a temple or adopt an idol would erect a stone at a sacred site, and
then circumambulate it as they would the Kaaba. Such stones (*baetyls*) were
regarded as idols when they resembled a living form, and whenever a traveller
stopped at a place to spend the night he would select a fine stone 'and adopt it as
his god', using others to support his cooking-pot. Such improvised divinities were
symbolic of the holy Kaaba, which continued to invite pilgrimage and veneration.[22]

The Kaaba had significance also in ways that may be unsuspected and which
have been little advertised. In one view it was in the cloisters of the Kaaba 'that
Arab morals were developed and polished', not least because for centuries it was
here alone 'where men and women gathered together', mingling as they circumambulated and sang the holy songs. One authority offers a perhaps fanciful depiction: 'Each procession took three-quarters of an hour and was repeated several
times a day. Soon conflicts broke out between fathers and lovers; the would-be
suitors confessed their passion in amorous odes to the young girls who were
under the strict supervision of fathers and brothers. Many an intrigue was begun
there in the holy cloisters – and many a feud born.'[23] Moreover, there is further
scope in this traditional context for those observers intent on identifying and

interpreting sexual symbolism. Thus *el-Mehraub*, the arched niche in the wall of the mosque, a form that pre-dates Islam, and the Black Stone of the Kaaba have been regarded as symbols of the female genitalia (*kheshaushim*); just as the bulbous cupola, extensive in Eastern architecture, nicely symbolises testicle or mons veneris.[24]

There are also such vexed questions as clitoridectomy (suggested by some modern Muslims as an African rather than Arab custom, but for which there is substantial evidence from both African and Arab sources), religious prostitution, and the more general elements of sexual morality. It has been suggested that in ancient Arab tradition 'a woman was regarded impure unless declitorized; and no respectable man would accept her in marriage unless thus consecrated'. So *Ibn el-bezzreh* (son of an uncircumcised mother) emerged as a stock term of abuse, in concert with many other obscene expressions.[25] Prostitutes, the so-called temple harlots, were apt to frequent religious sites of pilgrimage, thereby intercepting substantial traffic. Mecca and Medina, popular in this regard in pagan times, continued to offer a wide variety of services during the Islamic era.

One authority, Muhammad Mazheruddin Siddiqi, suggests that the women in pagan Arabia enjoyed substantial licence in sexual affairs, commonly indulging in illicit unions and promiscuous indulgence. Marriage bonds were loose, family life had little stability, and women characteristically dressed in provocative style. Here there were few rules of propriety, the 'rude and barbarous Arabs ... freely entered each other's houses',[26] and paternity became a confused matter. Such a situation, against which the Prophet was to rail, was denounced also in Jewish texts. Thus the Babylonian Talmud declares (as, at least in part, self-serving propaganda) that 'there is no adultery as flagrant as the adultery of the Arabians':

Ten measures of immorality descended to the world; nine were taken by Arabia and one by the rest of the world.

By swearing and lying, and killing and stealing, and committing adultery, they spread forth and blood touches blood (Hos. 4: 2). As Rabbi Joseph translated: 'They beget children by their neighbour's wives, thus piling evil upon evil.'

That lie upon beds of ivory, and stretch themselves upon their couches (Amos 6: 4). Said Rabbi Abbahu: 'This refers to people who eat and drink together, join their couches, exchange their wives, and make their couches full of semen.'[27] (Italics in original.)

Thus, if such charges were even partly true, Muhammed was to confront a dissolute pagan ethic that needed drastic reform, in circumstances where the traditional *muruwah* ideology was no longer adequate in changing social environments, if family stability and communal cohesion were to be protected: it is not historically uncommon for sternly moral nomads to be horrified by the supposedly loose attitudes of more sophisticated urban dwellers.

The existing pagan communities also assumed matrilineal descent; that is, men and women were regarded as belonging to their mothers' groups, with tribes and individuals known as the sons of females.[28] Property was thus owned by the matrilineal group, with uxorilocal marriage the norm; that is, the women remained in the family house, while husbands visited them. Where such arrangements involved temporary unions, there was little distinction from prostitution, though a stable relationship could survive where a woman bore several children to the same man. At the same time there is evidence of patrilineal practices in pagan Mecca and other population centres. Here individuals were named after their fathers, with tribes depicted as the sons of males.

It is also significant that the unstable ethical situation and the diverse lineal conventions were accompanied by a notable development of religious attitudes, even before the time of Muhammed. Contact with Judaeo-Christian and other influences had increasingly exposed the shallowness of the pagan pantheon and the need for a more developed eschatology: there is debate about the precise impact of such key influences in pagan Arabia. *Allah* (God) is a contraction of *al-ilah*, which literally means 'the god' but which has been taken to signify 'the supreme god' or the 'God' denoted in monotheistic creeds. It is likely that the Meccan pagans used *Allah* to signify the main deity associated with the Kaaba, with the other gods and goddesses regarded as lesser spiritual beings. At one level this is not far removed from the central beliefs in Judaism, Christianity or Islam, where the assumption of a supreme godhead is not taken as incompatible with the existence of angels, demons, *jinns* or whatever.

In any event the social and religious ground was well prepared for the arrival of a new prophet: much of Arabia, as elsewhere, was in a state of mounting tension under the pressure of expanding trade, military ambition and fresh ideologies. It remained to be seen how a new creed could exploit the instabilities in a rapidly changing social environment. But one thing was clear: any new creed, even if offering a more adequate ethic and a fuller positioning of man in eternity, would not be able to extirpate all the old paganism. Many traditional elements might be set aside but it would still be necessary to strike deals with the important residue. Muhammed might be prepared to denounce the old female deities but he would learn to exploit the traditional power of the Kaaba with which they were indelibly associated; he might be prepared to remould rather than to abolish polygamy; to grow the old *muruwah* revenge ideal to cosmic proportions; and in the new Islamic order there might still be a place for *jinn* and angel, the ubiquitous spiritual creatures of the pagan world.

Islam, like Christianity, was set to develop as part old pagan and part social and religious innovation – with further meldings involving non-Arabian creeds (as when the Mazdaian demonology of Persia was reconciled with the Koranic genii). But innovation does not necessarily signal moral progress: the new is not always the better. Muhammed may have discouraged blood sacrifices on sacred stones. Some of us may think that to substitute for this the immolation of human sinners in a torture pit for all eternity is not much of an improvement.

MUHAMMED

The Context

For centuries before Muhammed, Mecca had been one of the most important population centres of Hejaz. It functioned as a religious sanctuary of extreme antiquity; and also as a staging post for trading caravans from the Yemen to Egypt and Syria. The tribe of Jurhum controlled Mecca for a lengthy period, after which the Khuzaah took power while allowing certain sacral privileges to remain with the traditional families. In due course the Khuzaah and their allies lost power to Qusayy, in firm alliance with the Kinanah, the Qudaah and the Quraysh, this latter the tribe of Muhammed (Figure 2.1). There were often tensions and conflicts within the Quraysh, leading to family divisions and subsequent pragmatic accommodations,[29] but the Quraysh came to enjoy primacy among the tribes. They came to be regarded as the first among all the Arabs, with the corollary that the subsequent caliphs had to be selected from their tribe.

The Quraysh included caravaners, camel drivers and men of business. They travelled to the harbours of south Arabia to meet the trading ships from India and Africa, transported the merchandise to Syria and elsewhere, and made large profits. Then they purchased the products of Syria and Egypt, and transported them into Arabia for sale in Mecca and in the other oases and population centres. It was found also that religious devotion could be commercially exploited: as the tribes of Arabia made their annual pilgrimage to Mecca to worship the pagan idols, the enterprising Quraysh organised a fair at which they could market the merchandise conveyed from Damascus and elsewhere. Thus the Quraysh were both experienced traders, wealthy men of the world, and guardians of the holy Meccan sites. Some members of the tribe had even visited the Byzantine court or paid their respects to the Great King in Persia. But the primacy of the Quraysh did not rest solely on commercial acumen and religious devotion: it was required also that they protect their tribe and their clients, and protect Quraysh primacy by avenging all insults, injuries and deaths, according to the strictures of the traditional *muruwah* ideology.

It has been suggested, and disputed, that the Quraysh maintained a mercenary army of black slaves, to supplement the fierce Arab warriors. The scale of such a military contingent can be debated but there is evidence that the Quraysh had numbers of black slaves who were expected to fight when required. Moreover, Arabs from other tribes were attracted to Mecca as confederates (*hulufa*) of the dominant Quraysh. We may assume that the wealthy merchants, accustomed to a comfortable life-style, would have encouraged others to carry out the necessary military tasks on their behalf. Thus it was through confederacy, involving both

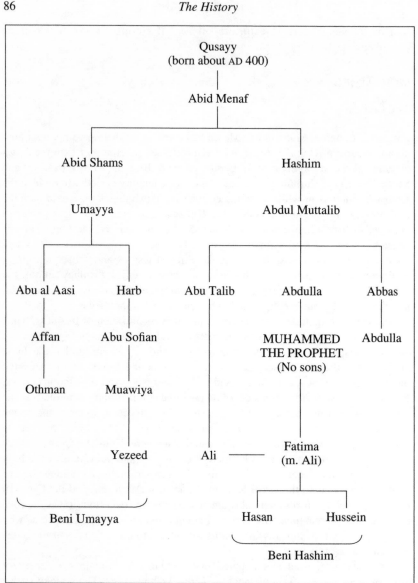

Figure 2.1   The genealogy of the Quraysh, the family of Muhammed
Source: Glubb (1978).

individual cavalier-brigands and tribes, that the primacy of the Quraysh was maintained. Money was required to sustain such an arrangement, but so also was the wise and patient statesmanship (the *hilm*) of the Quraysh.[30]

The senate (*mala*) was the principal organ of government in Mecca, an assembly of chiefs and notables of the various clans. This body had no coercive powers so, with any clan able to act independently, only the unanimous decisions were effective. At the same time, as with the boycott of the Hashim and al-Muttalib, it was possible to exert economic and other pressures on recalcitrant groups. For the most part the various clan leaders were prepared to overcome petty disputes in the interest of the greater good, aided as they were by a range of officials and functionaries: for example, the *nasi* (to administer the calendar), the *siqayah* (to supervise the water-supply, a primary concern), the *rifadah* (to supply the pilgrims), and the *liwa* (to safeguard standard-bearing in war). Taxes were levied on pilgrims and merchants, but the practicalities remain unclear.[31]

The great powers of Byzantium and Persia, and the smaller kingdom of Abyssinia (Ethiopia), regarded Mecca as within their sphere of interest. Trade was the main reason: the Byzantines wanted merchandise from the East, but the Persians controlled most of the trade routes, leading to permanent tensions and frequent military confrontations. The first Sassanid King of Persia, Ardashir, invaded eastern Arabia around AD 225, with a severe drought in the early fourth century said to have caused Arab raids across the Gulf into Persia. In AD 310 the Sassanid King Shapur II invaded eastern Arabia and marched across the peninsula to reach Medina. Thereafter the Persians relied on the compliant Arabs of Hirah, the Lakhmids, to protect their interests in the region. At the same time the continuing confrontation between the Sassanids and the Byzantines across the Syrian desert encouraged the emergence of Arab confederations to serve as buffers; for example, the Salih and the Ghassan in Syria and north-west Arabia, and the Lakhmids in north-east Arabia.

The Arabians were already accustomed to confrontation with foreign powers. In 30 BC, when Egypt became a Roman province, Augustus planned the extension of Roman power into Arabia and Abyssinia. Thus Gallus, a Roman of the famed Equestrian order, subsequently led 10,000 Romans, 15,000 mercenaries and more than 200 ships in the anticipated conquest of Arabia – only to retreat two years later with his army massively reduced by hunger and sickness, only seven men having died by the sword. Thereafter, according to custom and traditional practice, the Arab tribes continued to fight among themselves until an event occurred which was destined to generate a further foreign incursion into the peninsula: namely, the establishment of Christianity in Abyssinia around AD 300.

Two centuries later, in AD 525, the Abyssinians launched a successful invasion of southern Arabia. The Christian Elisbaas (according to Greek writers) or Caleb or Amda (according to the Abyssinians), having consolidated his power, made plans for the conquest of Yemen. He caused 700 small vessels to be built, and with these and larger ships provided by the Roman Emperor Justin, conveyed 60,000 men across the Arabian Gulf to the port of Ghalifica. A battle on the sea coast ended with the comprehensive rout of the Arab forces, with the Himyarite ruler, the Tobba, fighting on horseback in the sea, first hemmed in by his enemies and then drowning. The Abyssinian commander Aryat penetrated into Yemen with little opposition. Dthafar, unprepared for siege, immediately surrendered, and to secure his conquest Aryat razed many of the most important fortresses to the ground. After one battle the Himyarite Prince Dthoo Jadan, said to have been the first to cultivate the art of singing in Yemen, destroyed himself in defeat by plunging into the sea.

Aryat ruled Yemen as viceroy of the Negashi or King of Abyssinia from AD 525 to 537. Arabian historians claimed that the Abyssinian monarch ordered him to destroy a third of the land of the Himyarites, to massacre a third of all the males, and to send a third of all the females as slaves to Abyssinia; and it is asserted that he substantially fulfilled these instructions.[32] The chiefs of the victorious army were enriched with Yemeni spoils, but the soldiery were given the most arduous duties and scarcely the provision for subsistence. The resulting divisions among the occupying forces were terminated by single combat between Aryat and Abraha, who from the status of a Christian slave of a Roman merchant had risen to high rank in the Abyssinian army. After Aryat struck the first blow, he was treacherously slain by Abraha's attendant, Atwada, whereupon all the troops went over to Abraha. He ruled Yemen without opposition from AD 537 to 570.

The Yemeni ruler, a pious Christian, built an ornate church at Sanaa and tried to divert the Arab pilgrims from the Kaaba at Mecca, but the worshippers of the traditional paganism were unwilling to abandon their customs. Abraha then issued an order demanding that the Arabs perform the pilgrimage to Sanaa; despatched his missionaries to Hejaz and Nejd; and informed the King of Abyssinia that he intended to compel the Arabs to abandon the Kaaba in favour of the Sanaa church. The custodians of the Kaaba were outraged, fearing not only the collapse of traditional devotion but also the eroding of their own commercial advantage. Then, as a sign of the growing discontent, one of Abraha's envoys was murdered in Hejaz by a Kinana tribesman; and another man of the same tribe was bribed by the Kaaba guardians to desecrate the Sanaa church. Now an outraged Abraha, having resolved to destroy Mecca and the Kaaba, rode an enormous white elephant at the head of 40,000 men marching on Mecca. He routed the inhabitants of Tehama and seized all the cattle in the neighbourhood of Taif, including two hundred camels belonging to Abdul Muttalib, the grandfather of Muhammed. When Abraha appeared at the head of his vast army before Mecca, the Quraysh offered him money to abandon his plans, but to no avail. The Meccans fled to the mountains and nearby fortresses and importuned the gods, to good effect. The Lord, as we have seen (Sura 105), '*dealt with the army of the elephant*'. Abraha, with a small remnant of his army, returned to Sabaa where he died of a loathsome disease, probably smallpox.

Abraha was succeeded by his son Yascoom, offspring of Rihana whom Abraha had carried off from the Himyarites. His rule (AD 570 to 572) was marked by cruelty and tyrannic oppression: he raped the women, slaughtered the men, and made slaves of the children. This forced many of the Arab tribes to seek the protection of the Quraysh, whose apparent victory over Abraha had enhanced their reputation. (The Greek writers took a different view of Yascoom, dubbing him Serdius or Serdeed, and remarking on his justice and piety.) Yascoom was succeeded by his brother Masrook (reign: AD 572 to 575), a similar tyrant and the last of the Abyssinians to govern Yemen.[33]

Saif, the Himyarite husband of Rihana, had always retained the hope that the Abyssinians would be expelled from the peninsula. In AD 573 he journeyed north to the Byzantine court at Constantinople to plead the support of Emperor Justin II (Heraclius). But Justin, a Christian, was unwilling to aid the Jewish Saif: 'You profess the Jewish faith; the Abyssinians profess the Christian faith, as I do: consequently I cannot undertake anything to their injury to do you a service.' Saif then proceeded to Hirah, where in AD 574 he visited the court of the Persian monarch, Kesra Anowshirwan, to encourage a Persian invasion of Yemen to expel the Abyssinians. This initiative bore fruit, but Saif died before Kesra could fulfil his pledge to intervene, whereupon Saif's son, Maadi-Kareb, made a fresh appeal to the Persian monarch for action. The subsequent Persian invasion force, comprising mainly 3600 malefactors from the prisons, attracted the native Arabs who quickly rallied to the cause. Masrook died when an arrow pierced his skull between the eyes, and the demoralised Abyssinian army was crushed with immense casualties. Maadi-Kareb, the returned Himyarite, was installed as viceroy under obligation to pay tribute to the Persian monarch.

The news of the Persian/Arab victory over the Abyssinians in Yemen quickly spread throughout Arabia, whereupon princes and envoys rushed to offer their congratulations. Amongst the many envoys from Mecca was Abdul Muttalib, grandfather of Muhammed and a leading prince of the Quraysh, who supposedly expressed the greatest joy and addressed Maadi-Kareb as '*the head of all the Arabians; their spring-season, from which originated all their prosperity; their leader; the pillar on which they all depended; and the banner lifted aloft for the refuge of God's worshippers*'. A number of Abyssinians had survived the conflict. These Maadi-Kareb enslaved or massacred, until he fatefully changed his policy and unaccountably surrounded himself with Abyssinian guards armed with javelins. One day, while on a hunting expedition, they rounded on him, slew him, and then fled to the mountains. An Abyssinian faction gained power before being crushed by a fresh Persian invasion, again led by the Horzad ibn Narsee Wahraz who had defeated Masrook. It was now that the old Himyar dynasty became extinct; and Yemen, as well as its dependent lands, Hadramaut, Mahra and Oman, became absorbed by the Persian Empire.

It is recorded that the Persian rule was light, with local Arab rulers allowed substantial local autonomy. The external threat to Mecca and the Kaaba had been lifted; and the Quraysh, secure in their sacral and secular power, continued to prosper. Where the Persians held sway in Arabia the three principal religion-groups – Jewish, Christian and pagan – were equally tolerated, with few disturbances caused by the ambitions of the proselytisers. Christianity, despite the unpopularity of the Abyssinians, had established a secure presence, chiefly at Nejran with the Benool-Harith ibn Kaab. For a time a noble Christian family, named Oulad Abd-el-Madan ibn Deyyan, held power in Nejran and erected a church modelled on the Kaaba of Mecca. (Other writers depict the Nejran church as a vast tent, made out of three hundred hides, in which the poor and those in danger could find succour and refuge.)[34]

This then was the turbulent environment into which Muhammed was born: within a stratified social grouping where the Quraysh and its alliances, having struggled against many threats, remained the primary tribal force; where trade and foreign incursions had brought both wealth and cultural cross-fertilisation; where the numerous Bedouin tribes, in a state of almost constant warfare, were a law unto themselves; where the memory and prospect of foreign conquest continued to shape attitudes and expectations; where alien ideologies were increasingly exposing the limitations of the stern *muruwah* ethic; and where new religious ideas – primarily the Jewish, Christian and Arab monotheisms – were encouraging a radical reshaping of the old Arabian paganism. It remained to be seen how a new prophet, operating largely within the narrow confines of seventh-century Hejaz, would frame a new ethic and a new metaphysics for a new age.

The Life

Muhammed was born in or near the year AD 570, the year of Abraha's doomed confrontation with Mecca – so dubbed the Year of the Elephant. The early details of Muhammed's life are uncertain.[35] It seems likely that he was born either posthumously or to parents who did not long survive. The Koran (Sura 93, Verses 6–8) suggests the circumstances of his early life: 'Did he not find thee an orphan and gave thee a home? / And found thee erring and guided thee / and found thee needy and enriched thee.' The various historical accounts agree that Muhammed was put in the care of a tribal wet nurse, but this detail does not necessarily mean that his mother was dead at the time. It was the custom in Mecca for the upper classes, including the Quraysh, to give their children to the nomadic tribes with whom there were good relations, in order that the children would grow up in the healthy desert environment around Mecca, in Syria and south-western Arabia. Thus Muhammed was assigned to the wet nurse Halimah of the Hawazin tribe, and lived in a pastoral environment for two years or more.

It was inevitable that pious Arab chroniclers should embellish Muhammed's birth and early years, just as they did all the stages of his life. Thus Ibn Ishaq records the early signs that Muhammed was a special child:

> Jahm ... the client of al-Harith ... informed me that Halimah the apostle's foster-mother used to say that she went forth from her country with her husband and little son whom she was nursing ... in search of other babies to

nurse ... When we reached Mecca, we looked out for foster children, and the apostle of God was offered to everyone of us, and each woman refused him when she was told he was an orphan, because we hoped to get payment from the child's father ... Every woman who came with me got a suckling except me ... By God, I do not like the idea of returning with my friends without a suckling; I will go and take that orphan ... as soon as I put him to my bosom, my breast overflowed with milk ... my husband got up and went to the old she-camel and lo, her udders were full ... my husband said: 'Do you know, Halimah, you have taken a blessed creature?' I said, 'By God, I hope so'.[36]

It was recognised that such bounty, remarkable in a time of famine and destitution, came from God. Muhammed was growing up 'as none of the other children grew', and Halimah was reluctant to let him return to Mecca 'because of the blessings which he brought us'.

In one account, when Muhammed's mother died when he was six he came under the charge of his grandfather Abdul Muttalib, a Quraysh notable, who died two years later. Then Muhammed was cared for by his uncle Abu Talib, with whom on one occasion he journeyed to Syria and with whom, aged between fifteen and twenty, Muhammed fought in various tribal conflicts. It has been suggested that, despite the affluence of many of the Quraysh, Muhammed's family was impoverished. Thus the Koran (Sura 43, Verse 30) hints that Muhammed was not of great social standing at the time of the divine revelation: 'And they say, "Had but this Koran been sent down to some *great* one of the two cities ..."' (italics in translation). It remains that, whatever his position, Muhammed was born to one of the most celebrated tribes in Hejaz; and that he had significant blood ties to both Mecca and Medina. Abdul Muttalib's father, Hashim (bearing the name of the family that would come to serve as the guardians of the two holy cities, and in modern times provide monarchs for Iraq and Jordan), married a woman of Medina, a member of the clan of Adi ibn al-Najjar of the Khazraj tribe. It is of interest that Abdul Muttalib, seemingly unaware of his grandson's destiny, lived and died a pagan.

When he was about twenty-five Muhammed married Khadijah bint Khuwaylid ibn Asad, a Quraysh business woman fifteen years his senior. It is said that Khadijah, on hearing of Muhammed's honesty and high moral character, invited him to serve as her agent on caravan journeys; and that, impressed with his stewardship, she made an offer of marriage, which he accepted. They had seven children (al-Qasim, Ruqayyah, Zaynab, Umm Kulthum, Fatima, Abdullah and al-Tahir), but the boys all died young – a circumstance that was to complicate the Islamic succession. In one of the key authorities it is reckoned that the offspring arrived at regular yearly intervals, which would have made Khadijah forty-eight years old at the birth of the last, an unusual accomplishment which might have encouraged embellishment as a miracle but which attracted no comment in the various sources.

Muhammed had now established his own commercial reputation, albeit primarily via his marriage to a successful trader. At the same time he was already leading a mystical and solemn life, showing evidence of spiritual capacities that probably impressed Khadijah and others. Khadijah's cousin Waraqah, a pious man who became a Christian, may have influenced both her and Muhammed; and Muhammed himself was doubtless aware of the traditional sacral duties of the Quraysh as custodians of the Kaaba. Involved in the caravan business, Muhammed would also have heard the tales told by cosmopolitan travellers regarding the many competing religious ideas circulating in the Middle East; and it was likely that he had contact with the pious Hanifs, a tribal group in search of a religious alternative to Judaism, Christianity and traditional Arab paganism. Little is known about Muhammed's life at this time, though it is clear that he was developing both a commercial and a spiritual reputation. His marriage had already helped to determine the future of Islam, partly through its cosmopolitan influence on Muhammed's awareness and in part through the subsequent marriage of his daughter Fatima to Ali (Shi'a Muslims regard their descendants as the true heirs to the Caliphate). At the same time, in addition to contact with various religious groups, it is likely that Muhammed was acquainted with earlier religious writings (Koran, Sura 10, Verse 94: '... if thou art in doubt as to what we have sent down to thee, inquire at those who have read the Scriptures before thee' – unless this merely advises seeking guidance from those who have already read the Koran itself).

At the age of about forty, Muhammed – according to the traditional accounts – was called by God to be a prophet (*the* Prophet, according to Muslims). It was at this time that he experienced what believers are keen to interpret as contact with the supernatural, with the 'one true God'. In one version of this seminal event, Muhammed sees an angel (often reckoned to be Gabriel) who urges him to become the messenger of God. In another version the angel is heard telling him to recite certain verses; at first he resists, and then a physical presence compels him to utter sublime and ominous words that convey the anger of a passionate and omnipotent God resolved to punish mankind for the pagan idolatry of Arabia. Then Muhammed is supposed to have felt a great upsurge of emotion before falling into a deep trance, to awake as a transformed man convinced that he had been chosen as the Prophet of God.

Such events remain of the utmost importance to believers. This was the beginning of revelation 'for the Messenger of God', an instance of 'true vision' (*ar-ru'ya's-sadiqah*), coming 'like the breaking of dawn'.[37] When Muhammed returned home his wife was quick to believe everything he said: 'Rejoice, O son of my uncle, and be of good heart. By Him in whose hand is Khadijah's soul, I hope that thou wilt be the prophet of His people.' Thus Khadijah was an instant convert and quickly enlisted the surviving children. Muhammed, it is said, had been disturbed by his historic spiritual experience: 'I had been standing, but I fell to my knees; then I crept away, my shoulders quaking; then I entered Khadijah's chamber and said, Cover me (zammiluni), cover me, until the terror left me'. Gabriel, as noted, did not rely on verbal appeal but intervened also in a direct physical way ('Then he took me and squeezed me vehemently three times until exhaustion overcame me; then he said, Recite in the name of the Lord who created. And I recited'). Then, when Khadijah heard what had happened, she took Muhammed to Waraqah and he too believed what Muhammed recounted: 'This is the *namus* which was sent down (or "revealed") to Musa (Moses). Would that I were young here! Would that I might be alive when your tribe expel you! ... No man ever brought what you bring without being treated as an enemy; if your day had reached me, I should have helped you valiantly.'[38]

Muhammed's 'true vision' (to be distinguished, believers claim, from mere dreams) and early commitment (accompanied, as it was, by fear) were followed by what some mystics choose to call 'the dark night of the soul': he became exhausted by the trances and emotional turmoil, and doubts may have surfaced as a reaction to his experiences. During this time Muhammed was supported by his wife's undimmed faith and by Waraqah's belief (evidenced by his mention of *namus*, from the Greek *nomos*, signifying the law or revealed scriptures) that what had come down to Muhammed was to be classed with the revered Jewish and Christian scriptures. And he could also rely, at least for a time, on the tribal solidarity of the Quraysh, wont to support all members, however unusual or eccentric. Three years after the angelic vision, Muhammed supposedly received the divine order to preach, to proclaim in public – beyond his small domestic circle – what he had been newly taught by God (Allah). He then began teaching that God was One, that the ancient idols must be swept away, that the righteous dead would rise again to eternal happiness, and that the pagan idolators would be consigned to hell-fire. Muhammed claimed that the angel Gabriel sometimes spoke to him as one person to another, and that sometimes he heard an inner voice. With each fresh revelation Muhammed would recite a new verse, which his disciples would learn by heart and which would eventually come to form part of the Koran (see 'The Holy Koran', below). He further claimed that his faith was not new, but simply the correct religion of Abraham that had been distorted by the Israelites and the pagan idolators. And he made no claims to be anything more than a conduit for God's Word, to be reciting verbatim the words of a holy Koran laid up in paradise. He called the new creed *Islam*, surrender to God. Those who followed the true path would be known as *Muslims*, surrendered persons.

At first Muhammed met with little success: conversions were generally carried out in secret and there was growing opposition from traditional Meccans who still favoured the old paganism. They were proud of the Kaaba as an idol temple, believing that if Muhammed succeeded in destroying the prevailing beliefs the reputation of Mecca – and so its prized commerce – would suffer: there would be fewer pilgrims and so less trade. Moreover the upright Meccans did not enjoy being told by an upstart that their esteemed ancestors were now being punished in hell for their worship of false gods. After four years of ministry, Muhammed had only about seventy folowers and threats were being made on his life. He continued to enjoy a degree of tribal protection but some of his disciples were less fortunate. In 615, five years after the Gabriel vision, fifteen converts, no longer able to tolerate the frequent humiliations and threats of violence, embarked for the Christian enclave of Abyssinia. But this early *hijra*, seemingly undertaken for simple reason of prudence, has invited much discussion. Perhaps, it has been said, Muhammed removed some of his early followers to reduce the chances of apostasy: in Mecca there was always the chance that the disciples, succumbing to family and other pressures, might be tempted to deny their new faith. Perhaps the *hijra* to Abyssinia signalled no more than a trading enterprise; or perhaps Muhammed was seeking to win political support in Abyssinia, just as Abdul Muttalib might have tried to win the support of the invader Abraha. And perhaps the *hijra* indicated little else than an early Muslim schism, a sharp division of opinion within the embryonic Islamic community.

In any event it remains the case that the elders of Mecca had a strong vested interest in maintaining the prevailing pagan beliefs: as traditional custodians of the idols and other religious paraphernalia they attracted gifts, encouraged trade, and enjoyed many other considerations. The growing opposition to Muhammed transformed him from a simple preacher into a vigorous proselytiser, then 'into a religiopolitical warrior who found the old tribal custom of the *jihad* the best means of overthrowing resistance to his vision'.[39] The respectable Meccans probably argued (see Koran, Sura 43, Verse 30, quoted) that if Allah had wanted to convey an important message to mankind then he would have selected one of them as prophet. It followed clearly enough that Muhammed must be an imposter, a disruptive influence to be opposed by every possible means.

In 619 Khadijah died, and also Abu Talib, the uncle who had helped raise Muhammed. Beset by such losses, he wondered whether to seek converts farther afield, away from the growing persecution encouraged by the Meccan elders. In 620 seven men from Medina (then Yathrib), who had visited Mecca on pilgrimage, met the Prophet and were converted; the next year the men returned bringing more converts with them, and now Muhammed's attention was focused on Medina, 250 miles to the north. The Meccan elders, detecting these movements, decided that Muhammed should be killed, but he slipped out of his house and sought refuge with Abu Bakr, noting that 'God has given me permission to emigrate'. Then the two men fled the house and, seeking a secure place in the surrounding mountains, stayed in a cave until Abdullah, Abu Bakr's son, brought riding camels and told the fugitives that the way was clear. It is recorded that on 28 June 622 they reached the green fields and date palms of the oasis of Yathrib, subsequently named Medinat al Nebi, the Prophet's city. The journey from Mecca to Medina became known as the *Hijra* (Hejira), the 'flight' or 'escape', and it provided the first firm date in Muslim history, the start of the Muslim calendar. (The word *hijra* also took on a wider meaning, denoting the escape from any wicked community for one living in accordance with the Word of Allah – as with the earlier flight to Abyssinia.)

Soon after his successful flight to Medina, Muhammed married Ayisha, the daughter of Abu Bakr. She is said to have been about nine years old, while at that time the Prophet was fifty-three. Moreover Muhammed subsequently accumulated eleven wives, claiming that a divine revelation had permitted him to exceed the statutory four wives permitted to Muslims[40] (Koran, Sura 4, Verse 3: '*And if ye are apprehensive that ye shall not deal fairly with orphans, then, of other women who seem good in your eyes, marry but two, or three, or four; and if ye still fear that ye shall not act equitably, then only one*'). Perhaps Muhammed, in taking so many wives in his late fifties, hoped – albeit in vain – for a son.

Now, despite his ancestry, Muhammed was being drawn into armed conflict with the Meccan Quraysh, perhaps for control of the caravan routes. In 625 the Quraysh, fearing the growing threat that Muhammed and his followers represented to the established order, marched on Medina to extirpate the heretic once and for all. Muhammed himself was in no doubt that he had to fight to protect his sect and his beliefs: '... when Quraysh became insolent towards God and rejected His gracious purpose ... He gave permission to His apostle to fight and protect himself.'[41] The Muslims had no doubt that God was fighting on their side and that the conflict would represent a great test for believers. The archangel Gabriel, Muhammed declared, had instructed the Muslims to fight the idolators of Mecca, saying that all Muslims who died in battle would be admitted to paradise. Poor Bedouins, accustomed to little bounty in this life, were no doubt greatly attracted by the prospect of much in the next: by the promise of a future celestial realm blessed by flowing streams, fruit in abundance, and large-breasted maidens (Koran, Sura 78, Verses 31–4: '*But, for the God-fearing is a blissful abode / Enclosed gardens and vineyards / And damsels with swelling breasts, their peers in age / And a full cup*'). Muhammed now found that he had a growing number of devoted followers eager to die for the cause.

He began by launching raids on the caravan routes on which Mecca depended, a task for which Medina was strategically well placed. In 624 a vast caravan of about one thousand camels, journeying from Damascus to Mecca, was due to pass Medina. Once the intentions of the Muslims had become plain the caravan leader, Abu Sofian, sent a swift rider to Mecca to demand reinforcements. Muhammed, with more than three hundred men, set out to intercept the caravan at the wells of Bedr, but Abu Sofian changed his route to elude the Muslim force. Soon after the caravan had passed in safety the Meccan Quraysh confronted the Muslims in battle: the Prophet, it is recorded, called loudly on God for victory and so the outcome was assured. Some forty-nine Quraysh were killed and a similar number taken prisoner, with the forces of the Prophet rejoicing in their victory over the larger Meccan contingent. Soon afterwards, no doubt still flushed with their success, the Muslims decided to evict the Beni Qainuqa Jewish tribe from Medina (the Jews, already well equipped with committed belief, were firmly resistant to the insistent word of the new prophet). The tribe was surrounded and then forced to migrate to Syria, whereupon their property was confiscated for use by poor Muslims. Further conflicts broke out when it became clear that, despite Muhammed's growing influence, some of the local tribes were determined to maintain their allegiance to the Quraysh elders of Mecca.

In 625 the Quraysh organised to mount a massive onslaught on Medina. Abu Sofian's three thousand men, including two hundred cavalry, confronted Muhammed's seven hundred unmounted men who sallied forth with fanatical resolve to fight a battle at the foot of Mount Uhud, two miles north of Medina. On this occasion the mighty Allah of the Prophet did not prevail: the Muslims were routed, Muhammed himself was wounded, and his uncle Hamza killed. The surviving Muslims fled up Mount Uhud but Abu Sofian did not attempt to pursue them or to occupy Medina. Instead he shouted to the routed fugitives: 'Today is in exchange for Bedr. We will meet again next year.'[42] Then, two years later, 10,000 Meccans marched on Medina and laid siege to the desperate Muslim population, but here traditional Bedouin practice came to the aid of the Prophet and his followers: the Quraysh and their allied tribes, accustomed to fast moving desert battles, had no commitment to a prolonged siege. After three weeks the Mecca force withdrew and the Muslims were saved.

In 628, during a period of the year that the pagan Meccans regarded as sacred (and during which no fighting was allowed), Muhammed announced his intention of making a pilgrimage to Mecca. The Meccans, despite the traditional religious code, mobilised their forces to resist a possible Muslim attack. At Hudeibiya, not far from Mecca, Muhammed urged his followers to take an oath to fight to the death, should it become necessary (the Hudeibiya oath came to be revered in later Muslim lore). Emissaries were exchanged and a truce negotiated, with agreement that the Muslims should be allowed to make a pilgrimage the following year. When in 629 Muhammed entered Mecca he went straight to the Kaaba to touch the sacred Black Stone, an act that had immense political and religious significance. Muhammed had demonstrated his reverence for the symbol that lay at the heart of Meccan piety: at a stroke his reputation among the Meccans was massively enhanced, though doubtless some perceived that the Prophet was seeking also to appropriate for Islam the core of traditional devotion.

The following year, in January 630, a force of 10,000 Muslims again set out for Mecca. Abu Sofian, perceiving that resistance would be futile, journeyed to Muhammed's camp to offer surrender and then returned to Mecca to report the general amnesty. Of the four Muslim columns, only the one commanded by Khaled encountered resistance that violated the truce, and that token military confrontation was soon overcome: twenty-four Quraysh and four Hudhayl were killed, whereupon the survivors fled. With such small enemy casualties, and only two Muslim dead, Muhammed had achieved a great triumph – which came to be known as the *fat'h* (conquest *par excellence*, literally 'opening', meaning also God's bestowing of gifts). Such a *fat'h* had been long expected, though already optimistically recognised in earlier Muslim victories, but the final and absolute decision between the traditional Meccans and the followers of the Prophet came to be perceived as the supreme *fat'h*. The next generation of Muslims also used the word to denote their conquest of the Persian and Byzantine empires.[43]

Muhammed, now in full command of Mecca, remained in the city for fifteen to twenty days. The idols were cast out, not only from the Kaaba, now the focus of Islam, but from private houses and distant shrines (parties were sent out to destroy Manat at Mushallal, the long-revered el-Ozza at Nakhlah, and many others): it soon became plain that there would be no religious tolerance under the new Muslim order (Koran, Sura 3, Verse 79: '*Whoso desireth any other religion than Islam, that religion shall never be accepted from him, and in the next world he shall be among the lost*'). It was necessary also to deal with administrative matters. Priority was given to defining the sacred territory of Mecca, while most of the traditional Quraysh offices and privileges were abolished. Uthman ibn Talhah was permitted to retain the custody of the Kaaba, though under new instructions, and al-Abbas retained the right to supply water to pilgrims, now expected to show due devotion to Islam. During his brief spell in Mecca, Muhammed was compelled also to despatch military missions to quell recalcitrant tribes in the surrounding area. He preserved Medina as his capital but now held sway over the two great Arab cities and increasingly over the surrounding lands. The Prophet was now functioning as a supreme arbiter, aided by selected deputies and funded by both voluntary gifts (doubtless often donated through common prudence) and a levy on believers and tribes that yielded to his military power. Over a relatively short period Muhammed had secured control of the oases, caravan routes and markets over a vast expanse: the fierce and feuding tribal leaders over a wide area were forced to come to terms with the Prophet.

Muhammed made his last visit to Mecca in 632, when he gave a speech recorded as the final statement of his message: 'Know that every Muslim is a Muslim's brother, and that the Muslims are brethren'.[44] It followed that Muslims should not fight among themselves; and that in addition no efforts should be made to avenge the blood shed in pagan times. Muslims should however be prepared to fight all unbelievers until they are willing to declare: 'There is no god but God, and Muhammed is his Prophet.' At the end of his final sermon Muhammed is said to have looked up to heaven and cried out: 'O Lord, I have delivered my message and fulfilled my mission'. Three months later he grew ill, at times racked by pain and often delirious. On one occasion his wife Ayisha complained of a headache, whereupon Muhammed said, 'Nay, Ayisha, it is Oh *my* head'. He suffered also from fainting fits at this time, and sometimes wrapped a cloth round his head before leading prayers or addressing the people. When eventually he collapsed it was said that his wives hung lovingly over him, perhaps assuming that he would soon recover. When he died in Ayisha's arms some of his followers would not accept the death, believing that his soul had left his body temporarily and would soon return. Abu Bakr then reminded those present that Muhammed had always taught that he was a mere mortal like themselves; and he quoted the verse (Koran, Sura 3, Verse 138): '*Muhammad is no more than an apostle; other apostles have already passed away before him; if he die, therefore, or be slain, will ye turn upon your heels? But he who turneth on his heels shall not injure God at all: And God will certainly reward the thankful.*' (Some commentators have suggested that Abu Bakr invented these lines and inserted them in the Koran.)

When Muhammed died in 632 he had left no established Muslim code of laws (though many administrative provisions for Mecca and Medina[45]), and there was no obvious provision for the succession. Muhammed had left no sons, despite his many wives;[46] and no protocols had been established for the selection of the next leader of Islam and the growing Muslim movement. The authorities in Mecca and Medina quickly conferred, whereupon Muhammed's father-in-law, Abu Bakr, was appointed – or appointed himself – *Caliph* (meaning successor). It proved a temporary solution only: Islam – like Christianity – would come to be racked by schism for most of its later history.

A Prophet?

That Muhammed had a profound influence on the course of history in Hejaz, the wider region and indeed the world is beyond dispute. But this simple truism – that he was *deeply influential* in human affairs – says nothing more about the man, though it implies that he had exceptional qualities. It says nothing about his morality or his intellect; and it says nothing about whether his influence was wholesome or otherwise. Nor does it say anything about the veracity of his 'true vision', about the truth of the central Islamic tenets, or even about the existence of a supreme deity that – for mysterious reasons best known to itself – is reckoned by believers to take a surprising interest in the antics of one biological species among thousands living on a small planet in one galaxy among millions. In these circumstances more needs to be said, not least because of Muhammed's enduring influence in the modern world in general and on Saudi Arabia in particular. It is inevitable that any commentary derives from a particular perspective – ranging in one dimension from the piously hagiographical to the resolutely sceptical.

It is difficult enough even to establish the existence of a deity, before one begins to consider Muhammed's relationship with such an entity: and the proposition that we have no good reason to believe in God must be judged unhelpful to the broad Islamic agenda. For the typical Muslim believer there is no philosophical dilemma. The 'one true God' exists and that is an end of it: not for the committed follower of the Prophet the diffident anxieties of a Dr David Jenkins, the one-time Bishop of Durham in England, who can define Christian faith as 'risky commitment to a glimpsed possibility in the face of reasonable human hesitation about whether it is really possible' (in *God, Miracle and the Church of England,*

SCM, 1987). But Muslim assurance – like firm belief of any sort – cannot be reckoned *per se* an adequate signpost to truth: it is quite possible for one to have all the dogmatic conviction in the world, and still be wrong. In fact since religious devotees around the world (even within the same broad religious traditions) routinely contradict each other, some at least – possibly all – are in error.*

If (as I would argue) the term *'God'* cannot be adequately defined in a way that properly serves religious needs, much less shown to denote an existing entity in the universe, then the problem at the heart of Islam – at the heart of all theistic creeds – is obvious. If *'God'* emerges as no more than a largely meaningless symbol, having evolved into nothingness from the concrete symbols (rocks, trees, special 'people') of pagan times, then Muhammed cannot be rationally viewed as 'the Prophet of God', since the very term is incoherent. Hence any consideration of the significance of Muhammed must begin with an investigation of theism. Belief in God existed before Muhammed; if it is shown to be unsustainable then the Islamic edifice is built on sand.

It is possible to provide a philosophical criticism of theism in general and Islam in particular without resorting to the dogmatic abuse that has featured in much Western commentary over the centuries. What the Syrian writer Rana Kabbani has called 'the legacy of slander', 'the legacy of prejudice and ignorance', has deep roots in Christian apologetics.[47] Says Kabbani, of Western attitudes to Islam: 'There seems little doubt that the long history of denigration and ridicule, fed by Church Fathers, crusading knight, theologians, travellers, oriental scholars and contemporary novelists, is in itself a formidable obstacle to tolerant understanding.'[48] In the same vein Karen Armstrong, for seven years a Roman Catholic nun, charts the history of Christian abuse of Muhammed and Islam.[49] Here we are told, with good cause, that 'much of the old prejudice [about Islam] remains'; that the West has an 'inaccurate image of Islam', maintains a 'stereotypical view'; and that 'sometimes there seems to be a definite desire to blame the faith itself [Islam] for every disorder in the Muslim world'.[50] But the alternative approach, represented by Armstrong as 'more objective', necessarily involves much special pleading. If the acknowledged defects of Muslim societies are not to be attributed to the all-pervasive influence of Islam, then why should we give credit to Islam for the evident social advances in such societies? And by what token are some manifestations of Islam – evidently not the Wahhabism of Saudi Arabia – to be regarded as the 'most authentic' forms of the faith? Who is to decide? And on what authority?

If (as I would argue) it is implausible to declare that Muhammed was communing with supernatural creatures – Gabriel, God or whatever – then what are we to make of his 'true vision' and the words that he recited? It is easy to propose that Muhammed's experiences were a matter of psychiatry rather than

---

* I cannot here digress into philosophy. I consider, for example, the Teleological (Design) Argument for God's existence in *Is God a Programmer?* (London, 1988).

metaphysics. Today, in times that are in many ways more rational than was seventh-century Hejaz, medical science is well acquainted with a wide variety of visual and aural hallucination: people claiming to see and hear demons, angels, *jinns* or divinities are rarely assumed to be in direct communication with supernatural creatures. It has to be said that there is evidence that Muhammed suffered from a seriously disturbed psychology. One observer notes that he was 'a poor lad subject to a nervous disease which made him at first unfit for anything except the despised occupation of the shepherd'; and that the 'disease of his childhood returned upon him in his middle age; it affected his mind in a strange manner, and produced illusions on his senses'.[51] At times he thought himself possessed by evil forces:

> He thought that he was haunted, that his body was the house of an evil spirit. 'I see a light,' he said to his wife, 'and I hear a sound. I fear that I am one of the possessed.' This idea was most distressing to a pious man. He became pale and haggard, he wandered about on a hill near Mecca, crying out to God for help. More than once he drew near to the edge of a cliff, and was tempted to hurl himself down, and so put an end to his misery at once.[52]

Sometimes Muhammed would collapse on the ground, as if intoxicated, with the ensuing fit ending with profuse perspiration. His friends were often alarmed by his psychological state: 'Some ascribed it to the eccentricities of poetical genius; others declared he was possessed of an evil spirit; others said he was insane.'[53] Karen Armstrong notes Muhammed's 'terror and revulsion' when he was forced by the angel to recite the first words of the Koran. Thinking himself *jinn*-possessed, he wanted to end his life: 'Rushing from the cave, he began to climb to the summit of the mountain to fling himself to his death'.[54] For Armstrong, sensitive to what she claims is 'the deep unity of mankind's religious experience', Muhammed is behaving in such a fashion because he has experienced 'transcendence, a reality that lay beyond concepts and which the monotheistic faiths call "God"'.[55] There is no need for such a fanciful explanation.

The impulse to interpret certain extreme manifestations of human behaviour in supernatural terms is age-old: demons were to be expelled from the insane; epilepsy and plague signified divine intervention in human affairs; twins, the albino child and the blind 'seer' might be protected as sacred creatures, or cast from the rocks as children of demons. Muslims and other sympathetic commentators claim to know that God communicated with Muhammed through some angelic agent, and so conveyed the words of the divine Koran laid up in heaven. And the embellishments of the life of the Prophet did not stop there. His birth, like that of other great men, 'was rich in prodigies'.[56] A prophetic illumination surrounded him wherever he moved, bright enough not merely to serve his mother as a lamp but to illuminate the country as far as Syria. And no other divine light could be allowed: 'the sacred fire of the Persians, which had burned without interruption for a thousand years, was forever extinguished; the palace of Khoosroo was rent by an earthquake, and fourteen of its towers levelled with the ground; events that prefigured the failure of the royal line of Persia, and the subjugation of that country by the Arabs, after the reign of fourteen kings'.[57]

Muhammed was alleged to have spoken from the cradle while still a young baby; while he enjoyed an early visit from an angel to purify him from original sin. When he married Khadijah, legend has it, angels rejoiced in heaven, a celestial voice was heard proclaiming a benediction on their union, and the boys and girls of paradise were led out in their bridal garments. Later, to confound the sceptical Quraysh, Muhammed performed occasional miracles. One of these singular events has been referred to as 'the Splitting' – when he cleaved the moon into two parts. The Quraysh, wanting to discredit Muhammed, challenged him to shift the moon out of the sky in the presence of a large assembly. Muhammed accepted the challenge:

At this command the sky was darkened at noon; when the obedient planet, though but five days old, appeared fully-orbed, leaped from the firmament, and, bounding through the air, alighted on the summit of the Kaaba, which it encircled by seven distinct revolutions. Turning to the Prophet, it did him reverence, addressed him in very elegant Arabic, and pronounced a discourse in his praise, concluding with the formula of the Moslem creed. These salutations finished, it entered the right sleeve of his mantle, and made its exit by the left. Then descending from the collar of his robe to the fringe, it mounted into the air, separating into two halves. In this manner it resumed its station in the sky, the parts gradually uniting in one round and luminous orb, as before.[58]

Are we expected to believe that the moon behaved in such a fashion? The details are well rehearsed by the Muslim biographers of Muhammed. This of course is the perennial problem when human discrimination meets alleged authority. As soon as some textual items are embraced and others discarded, reason rather than blind obeisance is emerging as the proper arbiter.

On another occasion Muhammed made a nocturnal journey to heaven, an adventure later dubbed the *Mesra* and recorded in the Koran (Sura 17, Verse 1). The angel Gabriel awoke Muhammed, told him of the planned journey, and presented him with the means of transport – Borak, a milk-white creature with a human face, the body of a horse, hair of fine pearls, emerald ears, and two sparkling hyacinths to serve as eyes. The jewelled wings of the beast enabled Muhammed to soar over the hills of Mecca and then to pray on the top of Sinai where hoof-prints can still be discerned. Jerusalem ('the temple that is more remote') was visited next: after receiving the salutations of the ancient prophets, Muhammed tethered Borak at the gate of the temple and then ascended to heaven via a ladder of light. Here, in the seven layers of heaven (or the seven heavens), Muhammed encountered Adam in the form of a decrepit old man, angels in the form of men and beasts, and other wonders. Many of the angelic toilers – some watering the clouds, some chanting hymns – were enormous: for example, Azrael, the angel of death, had two eyes separated by a distance 'equal to 70,000 days' journey according to the rate of Arabian travelling ... he could have swallowed the seven heavens ... as easily as a pea'.[59] After such marvellous encounters Muhammed rejoined Gabriel, found Borak where he had left him, and returned to Mecca whose slumbering inhabitants were unaware that Muhammed had performed 'the labour of so many thousand years ... in the tenth part of a night'.

The subsequent recounting of the miraculous journey invited dispute, with many pious devotees believing every detail in the most literal fashion. The most pious Muslims thereafter maintained that to deny the physical reality of Muhammed's visit to paradise was as gross a sin as to reject the Koran. Armstrong, as befits modern circumspection, begins her brief account of the alleged journey with the words: 'Then it *seemed* to him that he was woken by Gabriel ...'[60] (my italics).

The devoted biographers claimed also that Muhammed was miraculous *in his very nature*. His every word and every act was scrutinised with the utmost reverence. Every hair dropping from his head to the ground was gathered with superstitious care; his saliva, when available, was collected and preserved; the water in which he washed was rendered magical by his touch; his bodily exudations were nutritious; he could see behind him without turning his head; his arm-pits gave off a delicate fragrance, as did his sweat from any part of his body; and he was miraculously exempt from vermin, that would neither touch his garments nor taste his blood. It seems obvious (at least to the present writer) that such miraculous qualities are nothing more than fanciful concoctions, created in pious awe by devoted believers to whom nothing marvellous about the Prophet was inconceivable. But the miracles and the magic were part of a broader fabrication – the notion that Muhammed was in communication with supernatural creatures of various sorts, the very essence of the Prophet's purpose. If (as here) such claims are discounted, it none the less remains true – as it is true of many other great historical figures – that Muhammed was a remarkable leader, shaping a generation, their descendants, and the wider world through the centuries that followed.

Muhammed, whatever his status as a 'spiritual' force, was manifestly a significant moral teacher, statesman, administrator and military commander. He consolidated much of the Hejaz and the wider Arab community in the peninsula, preparing the way for an explosive imperial expansion. There can be no doubt that Muhammed's fervent belief in God – however rooted in myth and gullibility – gave him immense confidence, after the early terrors and doubts, and invested him with all necessary charisma among a credulous and superstitious people. Hostile critics have impugned Muhammed's sincerity, suggesting that he simulated piety to win maximum support in ignorant communities. It is one hypothesis but unnecessary to explain Muhammed's great influence. The question of

Muhammed's sincerity is quite irrelevant to the veracity of Islamic opinion or the worth of the Prophet's moral pronouncements: *ad hominem* enquiry is of interest but secondary to any assessment of the broad Islamic contribution to human society. Central to any such assessment must be a measured awareness of the Koran – not the mythical 'archetypal Book' (Sura 43, Verse 3) laid up in heaven but the actual Koran, Muhammed's most significant legacy to the world.

THE HOLY KORAN

The Koran (derived from *Karaa*, to read; thus, the book to be read) made its first appearance scrawled on anything to hand – as Muhammed recited, dictated to secretaries or wrote (there is debate about his alleged illiteracy). So the holy verses were initially recorded on any item that could carry an impression or an indelible sign: date leaves, the bones of sheep and camels, scraps of parchment, and tablets of smooth white stone. It was Abu Bakr, Muhammed's successor, who first arranged for the scattered fragments of the Koran to be collected together. Zaid Ibn Thabit, a native of Medina and reputedly Muhammed's amanuensis, charged with the practical task, gathered together the holy fragments of God's Word 'from date leaves and tablets of white stone, and from the breasts of men'.[61] The copy thus compiled by Zaid remained with Abu Bakr during his brief caliphate; was later entrusted to the custody of Hafsah bint Umar, one of Muhammed's widows; and was regarded during the ten years of Omar's caliphate as the standard Koranic text.

In the circumstances of its creation who can know what fragments were lost or what items were added beyond Muhammed's contribution. Copies were made of the standard text, with 'various readings naturally and necessarily' springing up.[62] Disputes grew among the faithful as to which were the authentic verses, as to which were blessed with the authority of God. Thus the caliph Othman, sensing a growing threat to the unity of Islam, entrusted Zaid with the task of establishing a standard text, in which vital duty he was aided by three (others say twelve) Quraysh notables. Copies of the final text were then despatched to military stations throughout the empire, with all other versions of the Koran committed to the flames.[63] Subsequent translators, Muslim and non-Muslim alike, have arranged the suras (chapters) as they see fit. Thus, for the non-Arabic reader, there is some variation in both the meaning of the individual verses and the overall shape of the text from one translation to another. That any particular text is allegedly the Word of God has never protected it from ambiguity, uncertainty and pious disputation.[64]

The Koran has always been regarded by most pious Muslims as the one universal book, the complete guide for every aspect of moral and spiritual life on earth. Its sublime words allegedly demonstrate its divine origin – since no human being could compose anything so marvellous. Moreover, tradition claims, the celestial Koran – from which the Arabic version is copied – was inscribed with a pen of light on the Preserved Table in the seventh heaven. And even the earthly copies of the Koran, like Muhammed himself, have often being assigned a magical potency indelibly permeating the wonderful words. The most pious Muslims would not permit anyone of a different faith or of no faith to handle the sacred text, a crime that piety judged a capital offence. Appropriate words from the Koran have been inscribed on every-day garments and martial banners, in order to confer the proper magical protection; and on the walls of houses and mosques, to signal moral and spiritual duties. Thus Crichton notes, of pious Muslims: 'They bestow upon it [the Koran] the exalted epithets of the True Book, the Word of God, the Director of Men and Demons, the Quintessence of all Sacred Compositions, and not only the greatest miracle, but the spiritual treasury of 60,000 miracles.'[65] And there have even been attempts to discern divine significance in the number of verses, words and letters in the Koran (even in the number of times that a particular letter occurs) – a remarkably ambitious enterprise in view of the untidy origins of the text (we are told by Crichton that the first transcript 'was thrown in promiscuous detachments into a chest' entrusted to Hafsah). So: 'Of the seven ancient copies, the first reckoned 6000 verses, the second and fifth 6214, the third 6219, the fourth 6236, the sixth 6226, and the seventh 6225; but they agree in the common amount of 77,639 words and 323,015 letters.'[66]

The literary merits of the Koran cannot be praised too highly by pious Arabs, as they venture far beyond the accolade offered by N. J. Dawood, an Iraq State Scholar at London University in 1945 and one of many translators of the sacred text: 'The Koran is the earliest and by far the finest work of Classical Arabic prose.'[67] Thus Mostafa Mahmoud, a leading Arabic writer on science and religion, arguing that the Koran cannot have been composed by Muhammed, declares: 'With its form, phrases, and even letters, and with the knowledge, science, mysteries, stylistic beauty, and linguistic precision it contains, it is impossible to conceive that any man is capable of composing it.'[68] Then he draws attention to Sura 10, in which we are told (Verses 38–9) that the Koran 'could not have been devised by any but God'; and challenged, if we doubt this, to 'bring a Sura like it'. Thus Mahmoud: 'God is daring them to enlist the help of the jinn, the angels, and the geniuses among men to compose even one verse similar to those of the Quran.'[69] It is difficult for a non-Arabic-speaker (such as the present author) to rise to such a challenge – it is theoretically possible that something divine has been lost in translation – but since many of the Koranic verses are one line only, and since many appear banal or distasteful (*viz*: 'Praise the name of thy Lord, the Most High', '... the courses of women. They are a pollution', 'As to the thief, whether man or woman, cut ye off their hands ...'), the task of producing Koranic-style lines may not be unduly onerous.

There has been much debate – outside the narrow obeisance of Muslim orthodoxy – as to the originality of the Koran. In fact it is easy to argue that it derives substantially from Jewish and Christian sources, from various Apocryphal texts circulating at the time, and from various traditions and tales of Arabian and Persian mythology. Few who have read the Koran, even in translation, would deny that it exhibits not only keen moral sensitivity but also tiresome repetition and, in many particulars, a cruel intolerance.[70] This last, too rarely considered in sympathetic Western commentary (for example, Armstrong, Watt, *inter alia*), is exemplified in the frequent Koranic statements about the fate that sinners can expect in the next world. The corollary, that the virtuous believer (necessarily male) can happily contemplate the unrestricted indulgence of his bodily appetites in paradise, does nothing to mitigate a range of judgements that are at best harshly unforgiving (despite the slogan at the start of every Koranic sura: '*In the Name of God the Compassionate, the Merciful*') and at worst pathological. Some indication is given below (see 'The Islamic Frame') of the ethical content of the Koran. It is useful also to draw attention to Muhammed's condemnation of sinners (Table 2.2) and to the rewards that virtuous men might expect (Table 2.3) – the lists are not exhaustive.

The Koran is at least in part an unwholesome celebration of everlasting torment. The Day of Judgement, differently estimated in different texts, may last 1000 or 50,000 years, during which all human beings will be assigned to torture or to bliss. The tradition suggests that every soul will be forced to pass over the dread bridge, Al Sirat (the strait), which spans the terrible pit of hell and which is represented as finer than a hair and sharper than a sword. The virtuous, despite briars and thorns, will cross with ease; the wicked, already beset by pain and darkness, will plunge into the horrible abyss, where reside the everlasting torments of hell. Here it is that the damned are tortured by reptiles and other loathsome creatures, by sadistic demons, by hunger and thirst, by boiling water and the dreadful fire. Christians, Jews, idolators and others may expect an eternity of unremitting misery; whereas sinful Muslims may expect to fall only to the upper and milder levels of the seven hells. Here their sins may be expiated in as little as 900 years and perhaps in no more than 7000 – after which, 'when "the crimes done in their days of nature are purged away", and their skin burnt black, they will be released; the infernal soot and filth being washed off in the river of life till their bodies become whiter than pearls'.[71] While such matters are proceeding, we are told, the blessed are reclining in luscious gardens, enjoying a surfeit of fruit, wine, milk, honey and sex.

The intolerance of the sinner in the next life nicely reflects the intolerance of the infidel in this. Thus God urged his followers to be merciless with the infidels: 'Strike off their heads then, and strike off from them every finger-tip' (Sura 8, Verse 12); and 'When ye encounter the infidels, strike off their heads till ye have made a great slaughter among them, and of the rest make fast the fetters' (Sura 47, Verse 4). The Arabs of the desert would profess Islam or they would be slain (Sura 48, Verse 16). There is nothing in this of tolerance or forgiveness – except for those helpless peoples, often of different cultures and with different beliefs, who have been terrorised into submission: '... kill those who join other gods ...

Table 2.2   Muhammed's judgement on sinners

Statement	Source (Sura/Verse)
We will surely cast him into Hell-fire. And who shall teach thee what Hell-fire is? It leaveth nought, it spareth nought, Blackening the skin.	74/26–9
Nay, for verily he shall be flung into the Crushing Fire; And who shall teach thee what the crushing fire is? It is God's kindled fire, Which shall mount above the hearts of the damned.	104/4–7
Verily, those who vexed the believers, men and women, and repenteth not, doth the torment of Hell, and the torment of the burning, await.	85/10
Hell truly shall be a place of snares, The home of transgressors, To abide therein ages, No coolness shall they taste therein nor any drink, Save boiling water and running sores.	78/21–5
Downcast on that day shall be the countenances of some, Travailing and worn, Burnt at the scorching fire, Made to drink at a fountain fiercely boiling, No food shall they have...	87/2–6
Lay ye hold on him and chain him, Then at the Hell-fire burn him, Then into a chain whose length is seventy cubits thrust him; for he believed not in God, the Great.	42/30–3
Amid pestilential winds and in scalding water, And in the shadow of a black smoke, Not cool, and horrid to behold. For they truly, ere this, were blessed with worldly goods, But persisted in heinous sin.	56/41–5
For the Infidels we have got ready chains and collars and flaming fire.	76/4
Seize ye him, and drag him into the mid-fire; Then pour on his head the tormenting boiling water.	53/47–8
Hell – wherein they shall be burned: how wretched a bed! Even so. Let them then taste it – boiling water and gore, And other things of kindred sort.	38/55–8
But in the torment of Hell shall the wicked remain for ever: It shall not be mitigated to them, and they shall be mute for despair therein.	61/74–5
The fire shall scorch their faces, and their lips shall quiver therein.	23/106
Did the infidels but know the time when they shall not be able to keep the fire of hell from their faces or from their backs, neither shall they be helped! But it shall come upon them suddenly and shall confound them; and they shall not be able to put it back, neither shall they be respited.	65/40–41
...for those who have disbelieved garments of fire shall be cut out; the boiling water shall be poured down upon their heads: All that is in their bowels, and their skins shall be dissolved: and there are maces of iron for them ... 'Taste ye the torment of the burning.'	107/20–22

Table 2.3 Muhammed's judgement on the righteous

Statement	Source (Sura/Verse)
But for those who shall have believed and done the things that be right, are the Gardens beneath whose shades the rivers flow. This the immense bliss.	85/11
But, for the God-fearing is a blissful abode, Enclosed gardens and vineyards; And damsels with swelling breasts ... and a full cup.	78/31–4
Therein shall be a gushing fountain, Therein shall be raised couches, And goblets ready placed, And cushions laid in order, And carpet spread forth.	88/12–16
Surely, among delights shall the righteous dwell! Seated on bridal couches they will gaze around; Thou shall mark in their faces the brightness of delight; Choice sealed wine shall be given them to quaff, The seal of musk. For this let those pant who pant for bliss.	83/22–6
But mid gardens and delights shall they dwell who have feared God, Rejoicing in what their Lord hath given them. 'Eat and drink with healthy enjoyment, in recompense for your deeds.' On couches ranged in rows shall they recline; and to the damsels with large dark eyes shall we wed them.	52/17–20
And theirs shall be the Houris, with large dark eyes, like pearls hidden in their shells ... In recompense ... Amid thornless sidrahs, And tall trees clad with fruit, And in extended shade, And by flowing waters, And with abundant fruits ... And of lofty couches. Of a rare creation have we created the Houris...	56/22–34
But for those who dread the majesty of the Lord shall be two gardens ... With o'erbranching trees in each ... In each two fountains flowing ... In each two kinds of every fruit ... On couches with linings of brocade shall they recline, and the fruit of the two gardens shall be within easy reach ... Therein shall be the damsels with retiring glances, whom nor man nor djinn hath touches before them ... In each, the fair, the beauteous ones ... With large dark eyeballs, kept close in their pavilions ... Their spouses on soft green cushions and on beautiful carpets shall recline.	55/46–76
And ye shall not be rewarded but as ye have wrought, Save the sincere servants of God! A stated banquet shall they have of fruits; and honoured shall they be in the gardens of delight ... A cup shall be borne around then from a fountain ... And with them are the large-eyed ones, with modest refraining glances...	37/38–47
But a wine cup tempered at the camphor fountain the just shall quaff.	76/5
But the pious shall be in a secure place, Amid gardens and fountains, Clothed in silk and richest robes ... and we will wed them to the virgins with large dark eyes.	44/51–4
A picture of the Paradise promised to the God-fearing ... rivers of water ... rivers of milk ... rivers of wine ... rivers of honey...	47/16–17

wherever ye shall find them; and seize them, besiege them, and lay wait for them with every kind of ambush: but if they shall convert, and observe prayer, and pay the obligatory alms, then let them go their way, for God is Gracious, Merciful' (Sura 9, Verse 5). And to the charges that the Koran – the manifest word, not of God but of Muhammed, his scribes, earlier apostles, later editors *inter alia* – is derivative, intolerant and repetitious (see Tables 2.2 and 2.3) must be added the comment that it is self-contradictory. Compare, for example,

> *For truly to thee and to thy people it is an admonition; and ye shall have an* *account to render for it at last* (Sura 43, Verse 44)

and

> *The wicked shall not be asked of their crimes* (Sura 28, Verse 78).[72]

Such matters are important only because pious Muslims claim perfection for the Koranic text as an alleged verbatim duplicate of the ideal book protected in paradise. In fact the Koran – like any human creation – is partial, flawed and culturally limited (how odd that the celestial Koran, supposedly embracing all humankind, should focus so resolutely on human males and the camel!). The Koran is manifestly a derivative text, one in a series of apostolic works and plainly shaped by regional knowledge of the tales surrounding Arab paganism, Abraham, Noah, Moses, Jesus and others. Its harsh temper and much of its dogmatic reforming zeal were well suited to developing societies in the region. Today the Koran – for historical, political and psychological reasons (that can all be explored without any reference to metaphysics as a plausible credal system) – remains deeply influential throughout the world. Its shortcomings in terms of originality, form, rational insight, ethical sensitivity and cultural breadth may in fact help to protect the Koran's enduring power at the heart of Islam.

THE ISLAMIC FRAME

As soon as the death of Muhammed became generally known among the tribes of the Arabian peninsula the rudimentary Muslim alliance began to fall apart: many of the tribes renounced the Islam that sat uneasily with their residual pagan beliefs, and they refused to pay the tax; this development is known in Arab history as the Apostasy (*Riddah*). Muhammed had left no sons, despite his best efforts, and no body of rules to define the polity of the Islamic state. In these circumstances Abu Bakr, the aging caliph, had no option but to use force to subdue the dissident tribes, an arduous task in some regions: by the summer of 633 the Apostasy against Islam had been suppressed and much of Arabia was at peace. It was this unprecedented concord in the peninsula that was to serve as the secure springboard for the explosion of Arab imperialism into the lands beyond.

Muhammed had left a multifaceted legacy: the surviving impact of his own personality and authority; a reformed social ethic; a castigation of the ancient paganism (while retaining many of its features); and an uncompromising monotheism headed by a One True God that was simultaneously merciful/compassionate, duly sensitive to the bodily appetites of men, and brutally judgemental – all enshrined in the Koran, to believers the sacred word of God. The testimony of Muhammed, protected by the early Muslims as at least in part an oral tradition, was not consolidated until much later. It was inevitable that the tales would vary in the telling, as variations were added and accretions supplied that would have been quite new to the Prophet. The early Muslims, rejoicing in the poetic richness of the Arabic language, would have enjoyed the tellings and the retellings, perhaps discounting particular details but adding embellishments according to whim and fancy. It was inevitable also that the reputation of the Prophet would have grown over time, an expanding symbol of virtue and spiritual insight for all men.

To Muhammed's legacy of judgement, moral pronouncement and tales in the Koran, Muslim scholars began to compile the great corpus of Muhammed's alleged sayings (*hadith*: traditions) and customary practice (*sunna*). It is largely through the *sunna* – particularly revered by today's Sunni Muslims, 90 per cent of Muslims in the world – that devotees are enjoined to imitate the way that Muhammed is supposed to have behaved in every aspect of his life (speaking, loving, washing, worshipping, etc.). And it is on these three pillars (Koran, *hadith* and *sunna*) that Islamic Holy Law (*sharia*) has been developed over the centuries (see Chapter 1). But from the beginning there have been disputes within Islam on questions of textual accuracy and authority. Othman was not successful in securing a standard version of the Koran: various communities, not least the people of Kufa, rejected the 'finalised' edition and protected an alternative version that was still in use as late as AD 1000. Today various interpretations of the 'agreed' texts are disputed among Muslim scholars, even to the point that they argue about individual vowels and consonants.

There is dispute also about how to balance the respective contributions of Koran, *hadith* and *sunna*: for example, some devout Muslims have suggested that the *hadith*, possibly competing with the Koran for attention, might detract from the spiritual weight of the Holy Book. And there is the perennial problem that individual *hadiths* might have been invented or distorted in recollection. This in turn meant that a complex discipline of *hadith*-criticism developed – entailing the inevitable absurdity common to all religious exegesis: that pious *human beings* are driven to deciding exactly what constitutes *divine* truth. In such circumstances, with sinful and intellectually limited men struggling to resolve questions of absolute virtue and eternal truth, there have always been immense etymological and philosophical difficulties in deciding what message an alleged deity had conveyed to mankind.[73]

The Islamic Frame is a highly complex phenomenon: at once rich in residual superstition, detailed moral prescription, scholarly evaluation of text and tradition, political pluralism, legal discourse and poetic evocation. Muhammed himself set much of this in train: reforming marriage law (while consolidating the imagined inferiority of women – Sura 4, Verse 38), reforming inheritance law (while favouring men over women), protecting new-born girls from infanticide, condemning idolatry, reforming urban administration, generating lyrical verse to captivate his followers, etc.; while at the same time he encouraged acceptance of supernatural entities, encouraging belief in angels, demons, *jinns, inter alia*, as well as humble obeisance before the One True God.

The desert Bedouin, proud to be Muslim, might fear the threat of the bestial *ghuls* ('ghouls'), apt to live in caverns; despise the *jinn*-possessed *majnun*; and zealously seek the intercession of *awliya*, the ghosts of long-dead saints.[74] At the same time, smiling at such pastoral innocence, the educated urban Muslim – in Baghdad or Damascus, Cairo or Tripoli, Tehran or Jakarta – may contemplate the Islamic history of jurisprudence or philosophy. But a common part of the Muslim devotion, of whatever sophistication, is the persistent urge to judge, to proscribe this or that detail of behaviour, to applaud this or that piety – not just in terms of the simple *halal* (lawful) and *haram* (prohibited) at the most mundane domestic level,[75] but in terms also of male-only rewards and sadistic torments that run on through eternity. The Muslim commitment, at its best, is humane, scholarly and largely free of superstition; at its indelible worst it enshrines a deeply anti-human agenda.

3 Conquest and Decline

*Those who disbelieve our signs we will in the end cast into the fire: so oft
as their skins shall be well burnt, we will change them for fresh skins, that
they may taste the torment.*

Koran, Sura 4, Verse 59

*Take there none of them [infidels] for friends, till they have fled their
homes for the cause of God. If they turn back, then seize them, and slay
them wherever ye find them.*

Koran, Sura 4, Verse 91

*Believers! Wage war against such of the infidels as are your neighbours,
and let them find you rigorous.*

Koran, Sura 9, Verse 124

PREAMBLE

Muhammed had invested the Arabs with a new creed, albeit derivative, a new
solidarity, albeit temporary, and new confidence. Upon the 'five pillars'* of Islam
an ideology had been erected for the common man. There were no sacraments or
priests; no redeemer or saviour was interposed between devotee and godhead;
ordinary men (and, with less emphasis, women) were supposedly brought into
direct contact with the supernatural Absolute.

Now, under the bracing universalism of the new doctrine, the warring groups –
the pastoralists, the Bedouin nomads, the settled communities, the urban tribes –
were beginning to sense their nationhood. For the first time the Arabs of Hejaz
and beyond were able to contemplate a collective imperial ambition. There is
nothing like metaphysical absolutism to sanctify the slaughter of the infidel on a
prodigious scale. (Those who deny that force was a useful element in spreading
the Islamic Word of God should reread (or read) the Koran and note the early
Arab explosion into neighbouring lands. They might also remark the symbolic

---

* The five pillars: the profession of the faith (*shahada*) that 'There is no god but God and
Muhammed is his Apostle'; the daily worship (*salat*), later fixed at five prayers; the feast
of Ramadan (*sawn*); the giving of alms (*zakat*), one-tenth of the believer's income being
given to charity; and the pilgrimage to Mecca (*hajj*), to be undertaken at least once in a
lifetime.

sword on the national flag of Saudi Arabia, that country's Wahhabism as legitimate an Islam as the rest.)

THE ARAB EXPANSION

Explosion, eruption, tidal wave – the metaphors running through the literature
convey the scale and speed of the Arab imperial expansion in the decades following the death of Muhammed. The Prophet had elevated the Arabic language to the
status of the God-chosen vehicle for divine revelation, and it triumphed over all
other languages in the lands conquered by the Arabs. Arabic was soon spreading
far beyond the Arabian peninsula and a distinctive Muslim culture was effectively challenging other religions and philosophies over a wide region. In such
circumstances it was inevitable that the Muslims should see the hand of God in
their military triumphs (just as Christian conquistadors would later claim the
presence on the battlefield of long-dead saints in the genocidal wars in the
Americas).

The death of Muhammed brought the first great threat to the survival of Islam.
For a time it seemed that the fragile unity that the Prophet had imposed on the
fierce tribes of the peninsula would descend into a new turmoil. The acquiescence
of the Bedouin had been accomplished only through force and superstition, both
sustained largely through the sacral and secular power of Muhammed. Among the
tribes there remained widespread resentment of the exaction of tribute under the
terms of the *zakat* (alms) obligation, of the *salat* pressure for frequent prayer, and
of the Bedouin subordination imposed by the urban dwellers in Medina. Now the
disaffected tribes saw their chance. In a widespread repudiation that came to be
known as the *Riddah* (Secession, Apostasy), many of the tribes struggled to break
free from the Muslim hold. Thus the short caliphate of Abu Bakr (632–4) was
mainly concerned with the suppression of the tribal threat to the degree of Arab
unity that had been accomplished by Muhammed.

Many of the tribes were listening to what the Muslims regarded as false
prophets, men who had remained active during the time of Muhammed and who
now perceived a fresh opportunity. In fact, because of the great distances
involved and the limited missionary activity over a very brief period, perhaps
only a third of the peninsula would have been Islamised during the time of the
Prophet. Even Hejaz, the focus of Muhammed's activities, became Muslim only a
year or two before his death; so the delegates (*wufud*) who journeyed to pay him
homage may in fact have represented only a minority of the tribes. Some – such
as the Yaman, Yamamah and Uman – were jealous of the rising hegemony of
Medina and were eager to return to a time when its authority could be effectively
disputed. One of the 'false prophets', the Yemeni Mosailma (dubbed a 'liar' in
Muslim orthodoxy), had won a substantial following among the powerful Hanifa
tribe in central Arabia. In the ninth year of the Hejira he had headed a deputation

to Muhammed and become a Muslim, but on returning to his own region he had resolved to establish himself as an independent prophet. Another pretender to the role of God's Apostle was al-Aswad ibn Kaab – like Mosailma, first pagan, then Muslim and finally a religious preacher with independent ambitions. Aswad claimed to receive his inspiration from the angels Sohaik and Shorhaik, and to witness phantoms that materialised in his presence. In one judgement, Aswad 'was well versed in juggling tricks and natural magic, and astonished the multitude by spectral illusions ... for a time his schemes were successful'.[1] Aswad slew Shehr, to whom Muhammed had assigned one of the provinces of Yemen, whereupon the people of Nejran accepted Aswad's authority, the gates of Sanaa were thrown open to him, and most of Yemen came under his control. A group of Muhammed's supporters, conspiring with one Kaes ibn Abd-el-Yaghooth, terminated the usurpation of the Prophet's authority by breaking into Aswad's house one night and decapitating him; his wife, hearing his piercing shrieks in his death agonies, reportedly judged that he was merely under the influence of prophetic inspiration. The murder of Aswad was an effective solution to the problem: the next day the standard of Muhammed was again raised over Sanaa and Aswad was consigned to history as a liar and an imposter. But it was plain, even before Muhammed's death a few days later, that the *Riddah* repudiation was already gathering pace.

Mosailma, who was to pose a serious threat to Islam, had calculated that a pragmatic alliance with Muhammed might be the best course. In 632 he despatched a letter to Muhammed suggesting that they should divide the world between them: 'From Mosailma, the Prophet of God, to Muhammed, the Prophet of God! Now let the earth be half mine, and half thine!' – to which Muhammed, not prepared to share his spoils with any pretender, replied: 'From Muhammed, the Prophet of God, to Mosailma, the Liar! The earth is God's; he giveth the same for inheritance to such of his servants as pleaseth him, and the happy issue shall attend such as fear him!'[2] Muhammed lived only a few months more, during which time Mosailma built up his military power and, with the other recalcitrant tribes, posed a growing threat to the Muslim alliance. Abu Bakr, the new caliph, resolved that all 'seceders' from Islam, including Mosailma, offer an unconditional surrender or face a war unto destruction.[3]

The military commander Khalid ibn-al-Walid was assigned the task of suppressing the *Riddah* revolt. First he overcame the Tayyi, the Asad and the Ghatafan; and then he prepared to confront the Hanifa forces headed by Mosailma. The forces of Khalid, combined with those of the commanders Ikrama and Serjabeel, numbered about 40,000 men, against a somewhat larger Mosailma army. The subsequent battle fought at Akreba, near the capital of Yamamah, was decisive: after an initial reverse to Khalid's troops, with the loss of 1200 men, his forces rallied and counter-attacked, leaving 12,000 enemy dead upon the field. Mosailma was slain by a negro slave named Wahsha, allegedly with the same weapon that had killed Hamza, an uncle of Muhammed. The issue had been resolved. It seemed that there was only one 'Prophet of God' and it was not Mosailma; and that the Hanifa survivors of the battle suddenly found themselves eager to embrace Islam.

It had again been demonstrated that God and the angels had fought on the side of the Muslims; a propitious alliance that was again effective when Ikrama ibn Abu Sahil, one of Khalid's commanders at Akreba, was despatched to quell a rebellion in Oman and Mahara. It is said that, on his return and visiting Aden, a strongly secured door was revealed in the ground after a heavy fall of rain. In the cavity beneath was found a richly apparelled body decorated with jewels; in each hand was a tablet and at the head a sword carrying the inscription: 'This is the sword of Hood ibn Hood'. On the tablets were engraved the following words: 'If governors and judges oppress the earth! / The Great Judge who is in heaven will punish them / Ye should act according to the law of Muhammed.' It seems that the Prophet could rely even on underground messages proclaiming the wisdom of his rule.

Abu Bakr, the first of the four *rashidun* (orthodox) caliphs (Abu Bakr, Omar, Othman and Ali), had succeeded – via the efforts of Khalid and the other Muslim commanders – in unifying most of the Arabian peninsula. The so-called 'secessionists' had been brought back into the fold and many other tribes, recalcitrant in the age of Muhammed, had been converted to Islam. Now the ground had been prepared for wider conquest: the need to suppress the *Riddah*, and to block the possibility of further disaffection, had yielded an effective fighting machine that could now be launched against the neighbouring regions. It was the Arabian challenge to the authority of Muhammed's successors that made possible the military expansion far beyond the peninsula. When the last of the insurgents had capitulated, Arabia was nothing less than a militarised nation; the wild Bedouin tribes had been subdued but remained resentful, a persistent threat to Muslim unity. In 633 the decision was taken to enlist the tribes in wars of conquest against the civilisations bordering on the peninsula: in such a fashion it was hoped that the restlessness of the Arabians could be usefully channelled, removing the threat to Islam and possibly bringing wider benefits. The success of this policy would astonish the world.

The empires of Byzantium and Sassanid Persia then came under direct pressure from the new Arab ambition. In its long war with Rome (603–28), Persia had become exhausted before succumbing to Heraclius. The Zoroastrian State Church, soon to be challenged by Islam, was detested by the non-Persian minorities; and oppression of the peasants suffering under heavy taxation had generated widespread discontent. A 'religious communist'[4] – known to history as Mazdak – had urged the poor to plunder the rich, and his suppressed underground faction still had influence on public opinion. Here was a nation that was ill-equipped to withstand a violent onslaught from the Arabian deserts. The Byzantine or East Roman Empire had itself been weakened by its conflict with the Sassanids, which again paved the way for the success of the Arab forces.

In 633 Abu Bakr, having won volunteers for a Syrian expedition, despatched troop contingents to both Syria and Palestine. A small Byzantine force was defeated the following year but after a number of minor raids into southern Palestine the Arabs withdrew to the desert to await reinforcements from Medina. Heraclius, smarting under the victory of Yezzid ibn-abu-Sofian over Sergius, the patrician of Palestine, was now preparing to repel the Arab forces. Yezzid, whose brother Muawiya was destined to found the Umayyad Dynasty (see below), had launched operations in southern Syria in concert with such Arab commanders as Amr ibn-al-As and Shurahbil ibn-Hasanah. Khalid, who had already led success-ful incursions into Iraq, had been ordered by Abu Bakr to move his troops into Syria in support of the Muslim contingents. The Arab forces under Khalid then began a punishing march across the desolate terrain, eventually reaching the vale of Damascus to reinforce the Arab armies. One Rafi ibn-Umayr of the Tayyi tribe had acted as guide. The historical accounts give details of the desert journey headed by Khalid, dubbed the 'Sword of Allah'. The troops carried bags of water, five to eight hundred men riding camels that were later slaughtered to provide food for the troops and water for the horses. At one time Rafi, almost blinded by the sun, could not discern the signs of water and so instructed the men to hunt for box-thorn. Here it was, to the relief of the men, that fresh supplies of water were found.[5]

After almost three weeks' travel across the empty wilderness Khalid and his men reached the vale of Damascus to reinforce the Arab armies and to begin the successive routs of the enemy forces. Thus at Marj Rahit, some 15 miles from Damascus, he crushed the Christian soldiers of the Ghassanids on their Easter Sunday; then he conquered Busra (Old Damascus) before joining other Arab con-tingents for the decisive battle at Ajnadain. Here it was, on 30 July 634, that the Arabs crushed the forces of Theodore, brother of Heraclius, 20 miles to the west of Jerusalem. The Byzantine survivors fled in disarray from this humiliating encounter, some seeking refuge in Jerusalem and others in the stronghold of Gaza, but a brief siege forced surrender, whereupon the victorious Arabs ranged freely over Palestine and the surrounding area.

The Byzantine garrison abandoned Damascus after a siege of six months, forcing the civilian population to capitulate. Khalid laid down the terms that would apply to Damascus and the other Syro-Palestinian cities falling under Arab sway:

> In the name of Allah, the compassionate, the merciful. This is what Khalid ibn-al-Walid would grant to the inhabitants of Damascus if he enters therein; he promises to give them security for their lives, property and churches. Their city wall shall not be demolished, neither shall any Muslim be quartered in their houses. Thereunto we give unto them the pact of Allah and the protection of His Prophet, the caliphs and the believers. So long as they pay the poll tax, nothing but good shall befall them.[6]

Nothing could now stand in the way of the Arab conquest (see Figure 3.1). Any resistance was quickly overcome, with some towns capitulating even before Khalid's arrival: 'The people of Shayzar went out to meet him accompanied by players on the tambourines and singers, and bowed down before him.'[7] It was prudent to acknowledge that a new power, both sacral and secular, had exploded into history.

Now Heraclius was raising another army, 50,000-strong and again headed by his brother Theodore, in a bid to block the Arab expansion. In a careful strategic move Khalid abandoned Hims, Damascus and other important towns to concentrate 25,000 troops at the valley of Yarmuk, the eastern tributory of the Jordan. The final confrontation between Theodore's Byzantine forces and the Arab warriors occurred on 20 August 636, when the Muslim soldiers carrying Koranic words and symbols on their standards confronted Christian troops carrying crosses and with the chants and prayers of their priests sounding in their ears. The Cross did not prevail over the power of the Prophet. The Byzantine forces, supported by Armenian allies and Arab mercenaries, were comprehensively defeated, slaughtered where they stood or driven into humiliating flight. Theodore himself fell in the battle, and on hearing the dreadful outcome Heraclius reportedly commented: 'Farewell, O Syria, and what an excellent country this is for the enemy!'[8] The Arabs quickly occupied most of the Syrian towns, though Caesarea, receiving military supplies by sea, managed to resist the Arab onslaught for a few years. By 640 the whole of Syria had been brought under Muslim sway.

The 'easy conquest' of Syria was followed by the administrative absorption of the new territory under the banner of the Prophet. The Arab military commander abu-Ubaydah, Khalid's successor, specified the regulations for the control of the new lands; and was then carried off by a disease epidemic that killed 20,000 of his troops. When his successor, Yezzid ibn-abu-Sofian, died, Muawiya took power and tightened the Muslim grip on the region. It was found convenient to retain the division of Syria into the four military districts existing at the time of the Arab conquest: Dimashq, Hims, al-Urdunn (Jordan) and Filastin (Palestine); a fifth, Qinnasrin, was added by one of the Umayyad caliphs. The acquisition of Syria, significant in itself as an important territorial gain, served also as a springboard for further Arab imperial ambition: from Syria the Muslim forces swept across northern Africa, towards Armenia and northern Mesopotamia, and into Georgia, Azerbaijan and Asia Minor. Even Spain, in distant Europe, was soon to feel the impact of the Prophet.

Khalid had left his Iraqi forces under the control of the Bedouin al-Muthanna ibn-Harithah of the banu-Shayban. In 634 the Arabs in the region still remained vulnerable to Persian counter-attack: on 26 November the Muslims suffered substantial losses at the Battle of the Bridge (across the Euphrates) near al-Hirah, but al-Muthanna soon rallied the Arab forces to defeat the Persian commander Mihran at al-Buwayb on the Euphrates. The caliph Omar (Abu Bakr's successor, 634–44) then sent Sa'd ibn-abi-Waqqas, one of the Prophet's Companions, to

117

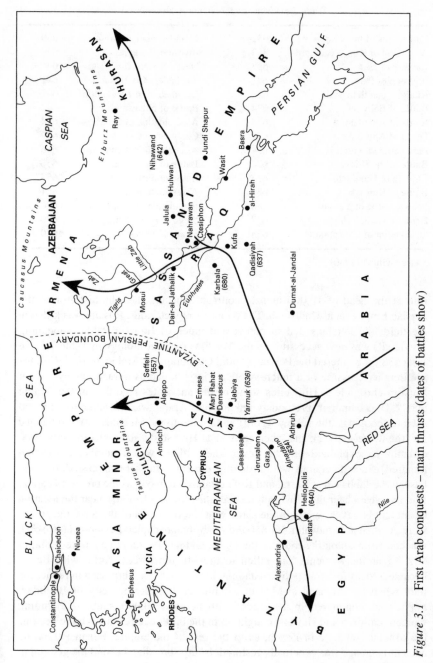

Figure 3.1 First Arab conquests – main thrusts (dates of battles show)

Source: Saunders (1965).

Table 3.1   Main events in the Arab conquest

Campaigns of the *Riddah*	632–3	Foundation of Kufa	639
Accession of King Yezdegird	632	Invasion of Egypt	640
Capture of Hira	633	Death of Heraclius	641
Invasion of Palestine	633–4	Surrender of Babylon	641
Khalid's march to Syria	634	Occupation of Alexandria	642
Battle of Babylon	634	Battle of Nihawand	642
Battle of Ajnadain	634	Assassination of Omar	644
Death of Abu Bakr	634	Conquest of Cyprus	649
First battle of Yarmuk	634	Assassination of Othman	656
Battle of the Bridge	634	Battle of the Camel	656
Capture of Damascus	635	Battle of Seffein	657
Battle of Buwayb	635	Assassination of Ali	661
Second battle of Yarmuk	636	Foundation of Qairawan	670
Battle of Qadisiyah	637	Siege of Byzantium	670–77
Occupation of Ctesiphon	638	Death of Muawiya	680

Source: Glubb (1980)

Iraq at the head of 10,000 men to confront Rustam, the administrator of the Persian Empire, at al-Qadisiyah. The Arabs were victorious: Rustam was killed in the field; the Persians fled in panic; and much of Iraq (in Pahlawi meaning 'lowland') was now accessible to the Muslims (see chronology in Table 3.1). In June 638 Sa'd entered the Persian capital Ctesiphon (in Arabic *al-Mada'in*), his preliminary crossing of a much-swollen Tigris hailed as miraculous by devout Muslim chroniclers. Hitti cites some of the anecdotes recorded in the Arabic texts.[9] Thus camphor, previously unknown to Arabs, was mistaken for salt and used for cooking; 'the yellow' (gold), unfamiliar to the Muslims, was exchanged for 'the white' (silver); and when an Arab at Hira sold a slave-girl for only 1000 dirhams he explained that he never knew 'there was a number above ten hundred'. Such diversions were little impediment to further conquest. A fortified base was established at Basra, and Kufa established in 639 as the preferred capital site; two years later the Muslim forces reached Mosul (*Mawsil*), near the location of ancient Nineveh; while in the same year the remnants of the Sassanid forces were crushed at Nihawand. By 650 the Arabs had occupied Persepolis (*Istakhr*), reached Kurasan on the route to the Oxus, and had begun to penetrate India; in 652 Byzantine Armenia had fallen to the Muslim forces. Kufa, with Basra, became a focus for Arab political and intellectual activity, surpassed in reputation only when the Abbasid al-Mansur established the glorious city of Baghdad. Persia was conquered in a decade, with perhaps 40,000 Arabs – including women, children and slaves – caught up in the bitter campaigns. Arabic became the official language in Persia, as in the rest of the empire, but in Persia the ancient language was eventually restored. Islam, spreading beyond the geographical limits of Arab power, was destined to remain a world force long after the decline of Muslim imperial ambition.

The Arabs had established an effective dominion over Syria, Iraq, Palestine, Jordan and other regions, but their rule was not uniformly secure throughout the empire. The Persians and some others had always presented stubborn resistance, though all their counter-attacks in Mesopotamia had been repulsed. Yezdegird, the last of the Sassanid emperors, was obliged at the age of twelve to confront the Arab invasion: he was forced to flee to the Zagros mountains before being overtaken by the pursuing Muslims and quickly slain, whereupon the Arabs poured eastward from the Euphrates. But Persia itself, though suffering military defeat, was never assimilated in the manner of Syria and Mesopotamia, fused together under Arab administration. The Persian forces had been crushed but Caliph Omar wisely ruled out any Muslim incursions into the heart of Persia. It was one thing to subdue Iraq, a region that had always resented the Sassanid presence, quite another for the desert Bedouin to battle through mountainous terrain to conquer a large population that would have little enthusiasm for imperial subjugation. The Persian people, well aware of their rich cultural heritage and their own imperial traditions, resented the barbarous race of 'lizard-eating Bedouins'.[10] But Islam had its own dynamic, able to penetrate regions that were closed to Muslim warriors. At first the Persians adopted Islam reluctantly (as *mawali*, inferior clients of the Arabs), but later with a growing cultural autonomy. Then came a moment of supreme Persian reprisal: one Abu Lu'lu'a, a Persian Christian slave taken to Medina, in 644 stabbed Caliph Omar six times in the back. The 52-year-old Omar, taking some hours to die, had time to rejoice that his assassin was not a Muslim and to set up an electoral college (including Ali, Othman, Zubair ibn al Awwam, Abdul Rahman ibn Auf and Sa'd ibn-abi-Waqqas, the conqueror of Iraq) to select the next caliph. It was decided that Othman would rule: he too was assassinated (in 656), as was his successor, Ali (in 661).

FROM UMAYYAD TO ABBASID

The death of Omar quickly exposed the growing political divisions at the heart of Islam. Now a new situation was developing in the young Arab empire, not merely because of the seismic shock of assassination but because the pace of Muslim advance had inevitably slowed. The scale and pace of the early conquests could not be indefinitely maintained: the enemies of the Arabs were beginning to recover from the initial cataclysm; and the Muslims themselves, prone to factional dispute and contention, were well prepared to challenge their fragile unity. The young Arab empire was on the brink of a crisis over the leadership succession that was set to create permanent divisions in Islam and whose effects would reverberate into modern times.

It was soon clear to the electoral college (*shura*) set up by the moribund Omar that there were only two serious candidates for Omar: Ali (ibn abi Talib) and Othman (ibn Affan), both of them members of the Quraysh and neither prepared to forgo his own ambitions in favour of the other. Ali came from the Beni Hashim clan and Othman from the Beni Umayya, the two principal Quraysh groups that had competed for power before Islam and during the lifetime of Muhammed (the Prophet himself had belonged to the Beni Hashim (see Figure 2.1) and his main rival, Abu Sofian, to the Beni Umayya). Hence a mere twelve years after the death of Muhammed the traditional family rivalries were again coming to the fore – with all the potential for confrontation and schism that this implied. With the very unity of Islam and the security of the Arab empire under threat it was easy to note the mounting instabilities: 'Quraysh had built it [the new state] and Quraysh were to destroy it.'[11] In the event such a calamity was avoided, but only at the cost of permanent schism.

The electoral college was torn: Abdul Rahman, without personal ambition, proposed that Othman be selected as the new caliph, perhaps in order to propitiate the rich and powerful Umayyads; but the supporters of Ali were angry that their man had been set aside in favour of the progeny of Abu Sofian, long associated with Arab paganism. Othman, duly elected, was handsome and wealthy but ineffectual: the new caliph, nearly seventy years of age, was soon showing the weakness that would help to end his rule (644–56). The military conquests continued but at an ever rising cost: Omar had dissipated much of the treasure from the conquered domains on the ground that, even with depleted reserves, God would continue to provide. The Arab armies were now receiving diminishing revenues; prices were rising; the Medinese denounced the alleged greed of the Meccans; and the Bedouins increasingly resented the centralised control exercised by the comfortable urban dwellers. At the same time pious Muslims were outraged by the banishment of the ascetic Abu Darr, and by Othman's supposed interference with the Koran in his efforts to provide a standard version.

With the general growth of popular discontent, there were popular rebellions in Persia (644–9) and elsewhere. Othman, responding with nepotism and indecision, continued to advance the ambitions of clan members, however incompetent and unsuitable. He had appointed his own half-brother, Waleed ibn Uqba, governor of Kufa and the military commander in northern Persia (when Waleed's father, Uqba, had been taken prisoner at Bedr and cried out, 'Who will take care of my little children?', Muhammed had replied, 'Hell-fire!'). Waleed, a drunkard, was soon removed from his post and replaced by Saad ibn al-Aasi, another Umayyad, as was the newly-appointed governor of Basra, Abdullah ibn Aamir. The revolts in Persia were crushed after a years-long struggle, but such distant victories did little to quell the growing disaffection among the Arab tribes. Othman continued to exclude members of other clans from high office, despite the Beni Umayya history of opposition to Muhammed and the establishment of Islam; and Othman himself accepted presents (bribes) from the appointed governors, including on one occasion the gift of a beautiful slave-girl offered by the governor of Basra. Othman, despite his clear failures, had succeeded in establishing a standard version of the Koran, had crushed the Persian rebellions, and had added parts of Armenia and other regions to the empire; but the discontent – fanned by such ambitious Qurayshites as Ali, Talhah and Zubair – continued to mount.

In 655 armed insurgents in Kufa signalled rebellion by shutting its gate against its Umayya governor, Saad ibn al-Assi, after which the sedition spread to Egypt. In Medina itself the Companions Talhah and Zubair, backed by Muhammed's widow Ayisha, worked to undermine the authority of Othman. His cousin Muawiya, seeing Othman's growing isolation, urged him to seek sanctuary in Damascus under the protection of the loyal Syrian army; but Othman replied that as caliph he would never leave the land where the body of the Prophet was buried. In 656 a contingent of insurgents from Egypt reached Medina, urged reform of the government, and demanded an audience with Othman. Then a letter, possibly a forgery, suggesting that Othman was planning the execution of the rebel leaders, was allegedly intercepted by the insurgents, which served further to undermine Othman's position. To demands for his abdication he declared: 'I will not put off the robe with which I have been invested by God:'

Othman, now an octogenarian, was trapped in his house, far removed from the help that would have been offered by Muawiya and his other supporters. On 17 June 656, while the caliph was reading the Koran, Muhammed, the son of Abu Bakr, broke into the residence and laid the first violent hand on Othman. His wife Nailah, trying to shield him from assassination, had several of her fingers hacked off before a number of the insurgents plunged their swords into the body of the caliph. One chronicler, Ibn-Battutah, claimed that when he visited Basra in 1377 the mosque still retained Othman's Koran, blood-stained at Sura 2, Verse 131 (which begins with the words: *'If therefore they believe even as ye believe, then have they true guidance; but if they turn back, then do they cut themselves off from you'*). This was a fateful time, when a Muslim caliph was slain by a fellow Muslim in Arabia's second holiest city. Now it was plain that the Caliphate, at the very heart of Islam, could be seized by the sword. There need be nothing in this of divine intercession; nothing of hereditary entitlement or political process. The assassinations of the first four caliphs, taken with the *Riddah* wars and the Arab conquest, show how indelibly bloody violence had stained Islam in its early years.

The scene was now set for further political struggle. Ali, the first cousin of Muhammed and husband of his daughter Fatima, seemed to be Othman's natural successor; but first he had to defeat his close rivals Talhah and Zubair, supported by Ayisha. In December 656, in the 'Battle of the Camel', Talhah and Zubair were killed, along with 10,000 Muslim soldiers, and Ayisha, who had fought on camel-back throughout, was captured and taken back to Mecca. But Ali's bloody victory had done little to enhance his reputation. It was remembered that he had opposed Othman's election and was in Medina at the time of the assassination. Had he tried to prevent the catastrophe? Did he intend to punish the assassins? Did he secretly welcome the death of the caliph? Now Muawiya was accusing Ali of complicity in the murder; already about sixty years old, Ali found himself increasingly beset by enemies. The victory over Talhah, Zubair and Ayisha had not secured the throne. Othman's bloodstained shirt (perhaps also the blood-stained Koran) and Nailah's severed fingers were smuggled out of Medina and conveyed to Damascus, there to be exposed in the mosque to stimulate public outrage. Now Ali would be forced to confront Muawiya ibn-abu-Sofian.

Ali was quick to receive the submission of Egypt, Iraq, Persia, Khurasan and much of Arabia; but Muawiya's Syrian army refused to support Ali's ambitions. A central question, with emphasis shifting away from Medina, was whether Kufa in Iraq or Damascus in Syria was to be the focus of Islamic affairs. Ali attempted peaceful overtures but these were rejected. Again it was obvious that the future of the caliphate would be settled by the sword.

The two armies, Ali and his Iraqis set against Muawiya and his Syrians, pitched their camps on the plain of Seffein on the west bank of the Euphrates near Raqqah. For 102 days some 150,000 Muslims waged a desultory war, with neither side eager to reach a general decision. About ninety actions or skirmishes are said to have taken place, with the humanity of Ali as evident as his valour: his troops were enjoined to spare the fugitives and to respect the virtue of the female captives.[12] Eventually the sporadic confrontation drew to a conclusion. On 28 July 657 Ali's forces were on the point of victory. The lines of the Syrians were broken; Ali fought on horseback with his ponderous sword and clad in the accoutrements of the Prophet; and the battle raged on through the night. Ali was said to have shouted *'Allah akbar'* (God is great!) every time he cut a man down, 523 times in all. Muawiya, sensing defeat, was said to be contemplating flight as he witnessed the loss of 7000 of his men. But then the shrewd Amr ibn-al-As, one of Muawiya's commanders, resorted to a ruse that snatched victory from the jaws of a bitter and humiliating defeat. He ordered the Syrian soldiers to fix 550 copies of the Koran to the points of their lances, and then to await the approach of the enemy. This signified that the contest should shift from the decision of arms to the decision of the Koran. The artifice was successful and hostilities ceased. Ali, having all but won the battle, agreed to let Muawiya arbitrate the case 'according to the Word of Allah' – which in reality could have meant anything at all.

Ali, now the effective caliph, appointed as his representative abu-Musa al-Ashari, a pious negotiator but with doubtful loyalty to Ali's cause. Muawiya appointed the wily Amr ibn-al-As, reckoned by later Arab chroniclers to have possessed rare political skills. The two arbiters, each equipped with a document of authorisation and four hundred witnesses, met in January 657 for their first public discussion at Adhrub on the main caravan route between Medina and Damascus. There is disagreement among historians about the details of the encounter, but the most favoured view is that the two representatives agreed to discount both Ali and Muawiya, to clear the way for a third party, but that then abu-Musa disloyally asserted that Ali's caliphate was invalid and that Muawiya should be seen as the legitimate contender. In such a fashion the authority of the *de facto* caliph was undermined and the pretender, merely the governor of Syria, was granted superior status. The view persisted that Ali had failed to act against the assassins of Othman, and abu-Musa's posture had discredited him further. Several thousand of his followers deserted him and became known as Kharijites ('outgoers' or 'secessionists'), now claiming connections with the original Kharijites and destined to have an influence through all the subsequent centuries of Islam.

Ali, though still determined to stand against Muawiya's claims, was now becoming increasingly insecure. Discontent was growing throughout the empire and he was no longer able to contain the local rebellions. He lost most of the Hejaz, the very heart of Islam, to a revolt; and was then forced to move against the Kharijites, who had adopted the slogan 'arbitration belongs to Allah alone' (*la hukma illa li-l-lah*) and launched a 4000-strong rebellion headed by Abdullah ibn-Wahb al-Rasibi. In July 658 he crushed the revolt but pockets of resistance remained. On 24 January 661, when Ali was entering the mosque at Kufa, he was attacked by a Kharijite, Abd-al-Rahman ibn-Muljam, wielding a poisoned sword. The blade, penetrating to Ali's brain, secured the third assassination of a caliph in seventeen years. The supporters of Ali, the *Shi'a* ('partisans of Ali'), made some efforts to continue the struggle against Muawiya, but to little avail. Soon the first dynasty in the long history of Islam would be established. The period of the four *rashidun* (orthodox) caliphs was at an end; the era of Muawiya, the first of the Umayyad caliphs, had begun.

Ali's son, Hasan, had been encouraged to make claims on the caliphate, but when Muawiya declared himself caliph in Jerusalem the young pretender agreed to renounce his claims in exchange for a substantial pension. The Shi'a then built the town of Najaf around Ali's supposed tomb: the Shi'a/Sunni divide had been consolidated and would remain a permanent schism in Islam up to modern times. The Arab state, weary of civil strife, was now prepared to accept the rule of the Umayyads, the establishment of a dynasty set to endure for eighty-nine years (see Table 3.2), a substantial period in the turbulent times of early Islam. The political confrontations had been temporarily abated in celebration of the *jama'a* (the return to harmony and agreement). The historical contribution of the *rashidun* caliphs was ambiguous: much was achieved (in particular, the consolidation of Islam over a wide area), but perhaps their historical appelation ('Rightly Guided Ones') seems generous in view of the violence and errors with which their names are indelibly associated.

Hasan had died at the age of forty-five (*c.* 669), possibly poisoned in revenge through marital or harem intrigue: he is said to have married and then cast off a hundred wives, so earning him the title 'great divorcer' (*mitlaq*). The Shi'as inevitably blamed Muawiya for his death, and so transformed Hasan into the

Table 3.2 Caliphs of Umayyad dynasty*

Muawiya I	661	Omar	718
Yezzid I	678	Yezzid II	721
Muawiya II	683	Hescham	723
Abdullah	683	Walid II	742
Merwan I	683	Yezzid III	743
Abdul Malek	684	Ibrahim	744
Walid I	705	Merwan II	744
Suleiman	716		

Source: Crichton (1838), vol. 1, p. 376.

'lord [*sayyid*] of all martyrs'. Hussein, Hasan's younger brother, refused to acknowledge the claims of Yezzid and schemed for his downfall. In response, Omar, the son of the celebrated general Sa'd ibn-abi-Waqqas, led 4000 troops against Hussein's paltry force. The rebels were quickly defeated, Hussein's head was conveyed to Yezzid in Damascus (before being returned to his family), and the Shi'as had won a new martyr. (The Shi'as annually observe the first ten days of Muharram as a commemorative lamentation; and an annual passion play is performed in two parts: *Ashura* commemorates the battle, while the second part recalls 'the return of the Head'. The death of Hussein had consolidated the establishment of the Shi'ite 'church'.)

With the success of Muawiya and the onset of the Umayyad dynasty, Arabia had lost its political primacy for the Arab nation, though Mecca and Medina, the holy cities of Hejaz, would retain their unique spiritual significance for Islam. Now the focus of political power had shifted from Medina to Damascus, where Muawiya was set to rule as caliph for almost two decades (until the accession of Yezzid I in 678). Muawiya is said to have circulated freely in the streets of Damascus without an escort, successfully defusing enemy plots and consolidating the loyalty of his allies; that there was no rebellion against him throughout the relatively long period of his rule was a remarkable accomplishment in the turbulent circumstances of the caliphate. Muawiya was not averse to bribery, in addition to calm conciliation, in order to gain allies. When his opponents rebuked him for his lavish use of bribes he replied: 'War costs more!' With Syria as a secure political base the young Umayyad dynasty seemed secure; but Iraq, characteristically restless, could only be kept in check by a series of ruthless governors; and some individuals, in Medina and elsewhere, continued to plot against Muawiya and the Umayyads. Ayisha, for example, continued her recalcitrant refusal to pay

---

* Merwan I broke the hereditary Umayyad line by transferring the caliphate to his son instead of to the younger brother of Muawiya II. None the less the Umayyad clan retained *de facto* political power at the heart of the caliphate.

due allegiance to the caliph – a stubbornness that ultimately spelt her doom. According to some historians, the illustrious widow of the Prophet was invited to an entertainment staged under the auspices of Muawiya. Her chair, it is said, was set over a deep well or pit carefully covered with leaves; when Ayisha sat down she 'sank to everlasting night' – so at least one thorn in the body politic was effectively removed. But this was of little help to Muawiya: soon afterwards the caliph 'quitted this abode of clay for the mansions of eternal retribution'. He had at last organised the succession, after almost two decades of more or less peaceful rule.

Muawiya had resolved, without dispute from the *shura*, that his son Yezzid would inherit the throne; but leading Muslims, recalling the rampant nepotism through all the early years of the caliphate and no doubt also noting Yezzid's feeble and dissolute character, were not eager to uphold the hereditary entitlement to the caliphate. At least Yezzid had the wit to retain his father's advisors, a detail that presumably enabled him to despatch the threat from Hussein. Not only Hussein's head but perhaps seventy more were struck off in the suppression of the rebellion; while the female captives, stripped naked and thrown on the backs of camels, were conveyed in chains to Damascus and then to Medina. The final action of Yezzid, the climax to an undistinguished reign, was to quell further insurrections which had broken out in Mecca and Medina, partly as a result of Hussein's death and the slaughter and humiliation of his followers.

Some of the rebels, pursued by Syrian troops, took refuge behind the walls of Medina and for three days in the year 682 the city suffered massive pillage and slaughter, during which it is estimated that some 6000 inhabitants perished. In Mecca the supporters of Hussein proclaimed Abdullah, the son of Zubair, the next caliph; and for forty days the rebels defied all the efforts of the besiegers. The walls were severely battered; great stones thrown from the catapults demolished several pillars of the temple; and even the linen veil covering the Kaaba was set on fire and reduced to ashes by flaming naphtha launched from one of the siege engines. Some 10,000 men, seeing the futility of further resistance, deserted the cause of Abdullah, whereupon he allegedly rushed into the thickest of the enemy and died an honourable death. Yezzid, before these events, had been 'enrolled among the dignitaries of the infernal regions' (according to a Persian text); but now the recovery of Mecca and Medina, in time-honoured fashion, had reasserted the legitimacy of the Umayyad dynasty. But it was still judged necessary to suppress any revolts with the utmost harshness. For example, Hejaje, governor of Iraq, was said to have butchered 120,000 people of rank over a period of twenty years; and at his death the various prisons under his jurisdiction were found to contain no less than 30,000 men and 20,000 women.

In November 683 Yezzid died and again turmoil broke out over the political succession. The sickly child Muawiya II, son of Yezzid, was proclaimed caliph but died a few months later, soon after Abdullah ibn Zubair, son of the Zubair who had opposed Ali, had registered his claim to the throne. The new Zubair was set aside and the defence of the Umayyad dynasty now depended upon Merwan al-Hakam, a cousin of Yezzid. In 684 Merwan was proclaimed caliph in Damascus, only to die a year later, when his son Abdul Malek ibn Marwen took the throne. Such contention had further weakened the Umayyad dynasty, and it seemed increasingly unlikely that the untried Abdul Malek would be able to bring stability. Now Abdullah was making fresh claims, and in Mecca he chose to proclaim himself a rival caliph. The Persian provinces were in revolt; and in turbulent Iraq the Shi'as and the Kharijites were again challenging the hegemony of the caliphate.

Abdul Malek, now emerging as a shrewd and competent politician, worked to consolidate what forces remained loyal to him, and then launched an invasion of Iraq – which was by now showing increasing allegiance to the anti-caliph Abdullah. In December 691 Abdul Malek took Kufa, killing Abdullah's brother in the process. The loss of Iraq seriously weakened the position of Abdullah in Mecca, and in 692 Abdul Malek felt strong enough to despatch an army to recapture the Holy City and so reassert his authority over the heartland of Islam. Already Kufa – lost to the rebel Mukhtar who had promised his followers the coming of the *Mahdi* (the redeemer) – had been retaken, with Mukhtar and his principal lieutenants slaughtered. Now it was time to tackle Mecca. The army encamped round the city prepared for a siege that was destined to last for eight months. The Umayyad commander, Hajjaj ibn Yusuf, had placed wooden rock launchers, the dreaded mangonels, on the surrounding hills and Mecca was forced to endure a constant bombardment. Abdullah, faced with a seemingly impossible situation, consulted his mother, whereupon this bold daughter of Abu Bakr declared: 'If you are conscious of your right, you will die like a hero!' Perhaps the disconsolate Abdullah found this judgement some consolation. On 3 October 692 he donned his armour and rushed out of the battered Meccan stronghold to confront Abdul Malek's Syrian army. History records that he was first hit by a missile in the face, and then fell, sword in hand, riddled by arrows. So perished yet one more contender for the caliphate. Mecca again changed hands and, as was seemly for the times, Abdul Malek was happy to receive Abdullah's head in Damascus. It was time to signal a second *jama'a* of peace and reconciliation.

Walid ruled uneventfully as caliph until succeeded by his brother Suleiman ibn Abdul Malek in 716. It was under Suleiman that the second great siege of Constantinople was launched, though this two-year-long effort was no more successful than the first Arab attempt to take the city. Again flaming naphtha ('Greek fire') was ejected from nozzles and poured from the battlements onto unfortunate soldiers struggling to mount the walls. A harsh winter (716–17) further impeded the Arab efforts, their lines covered by thick snow for three months; and their forces suffered an attack in the rear when the Bulgars were persuaded to enter the war by the Isaurian Emperor Leo. In 717 Suleiman died in Damascus while fighting continued to rage outside Constantinople, whereupon the new caliph, Omar ibn Abdul Azeez, ordered the Arab armies to return to Syria. Omar took steps also to end the historic feud between the Beni Hashim and the Beni Umayya, and quickly established a reputation as a conciliator (for example, when Iraq again suffered a Kharijite rebellion he invited the insurgents to send delegates to Damascus to explain their grievances). But his failure to resolve differences through peaceful negotiation was set to contribute to the eclipse of the Umayyad dynasty.

There was now a growing discontent with the Omar caliphate: revolts were crushed, only to flare up again; and the perennial claimants to the throne exploited every opportunity to encourage disaffection with the regime. Now another branch of the family of Muhammed was coming to the fore: the descendants of the Prophet's uncle Abbas, seeing their opportunity, created a political organisation with its centre at Kufa. Omar had died after a brief reign, and his successors (Yezzid II and Heschan, another son of Abdul Malek) were merely marking time before the creation of a new dynasty. In 743 the caliph Hescham died, and the Umayyads began their irreversible decline. Walid II, the next caliph, was reputedly a drunkard and a blasphemer; unable to survive the turbulence of caliphate politics he succumbed after fifteen months, and on 17 April 744 his head was paraded through Damascus on the point of a lance. His successor, Yezzid III, who had organised the revolt, died in October of the same year after a mere six months in power. Now the Abbas emissary Abu Muslim, sent to Khurasan to raise an army, marched to the west to engage the Umayyad forces in a number of battles. In a series of confrontations (749–50) the demoralised Umayyad armies were defeated; the last Umayyad caliph, Merwan II, was chased into Egypt and there killed. In Kufa the new leader of the Arab nation was proclaimed: Abdul Abbas, the founder of a new dynastic line (see Table 3.3).

The new dynasty was quick to move its capital from Syria to Iraq, a decision that was to involve the creation of Baghdad in 762. This meant that Muslim power was now focused on the former Sassanid territories (southern Iraq, Persia, Khurasan and the land that stretched into central Asia), rather than on the Mediterranean countries or the Hejaz. The Umayyads had moved political power away from Mecca and Medina; now the Abbasids had consolidated the shift of power away from Hejaz and the Holy Cities. And with the new territorial focus there was increased Persian influence – to the point that some early observers saw the cultural transformation in Islam as a victory for Persian Aryans over Arab Semites. The Arab presence in the movement was still substantial but now Islam was increasingly cosmopolitan, a development regretted by the Arab purists but one that made Islam more credible as a creed for all mankind.

The Arab tribes had been at the heart of the early imperial expansion, but now Persians were streaming into the public service: a new class of officials, merchants and landowners was evolving, with the *ulema* corresponding 'socially, though not religiously, to the priesthood of Christendom'.[13] A new office (Wazir or Vizier), with the authority of a vice-caliph, was created and the caliph himself was encouraged to retreat, in the manner of the old Sassanid shahs, into the heart

Table 3.3   Caliphs of Abbasid dynasty

Abdul Abbas	749	Rhadi	934
al-Mansur	754	Mottaki	941
Mahadi	775	Mostakfi	944
al-Hadi	785	al-Moti	946
Haroun al-Raschid	786	al-Tai	974
al-Amin	809	al-Kadir	991
al-Mamum	813	al-Kayem	1031
Motassem	833	Moktadi	1075
Vathek	842	Mostader	1094
Motawakkel	847	Mostarshed	1118
Montasser	861	al-Rashed	1135
Mostain	862	Moktafi II	1136
Motazz	866	Mostanjed	1160
Mohtadi	867	Mostadi	1170
Motamed	870	al-Maser	1180
Motaded	892	Daher	1225
Moktafi I	902	Mostanser	1226
Moktader	908	Mostasem	1242
Kaher	932		

Source: Crichton (1838), vol. 2, p. 11.

of his palace, secure from the common eye. Now much of the traditional Arab egalitarianism of the caliphate, celebrated in the Koran, was being distorted by a fresh cultural authoritarianism. The shift towards oriental despotism, already evident under the Umayyads, was accelerated under the Abbasids; now the new caliphs 'seemed to have inherited the sacred absolutism of the kings of Nineveh, Babylon and Persia'.[14] The official executioner stood by the throne and symbolised the caliph's total power over his subjects, unprotected as they were by any law or constitution. One of the first decisions of Abdul Abbas ('*Saffah*', shedder of blood) was to order the murder of Abu Muslim and all those who had helped the Abbasids to power: there must be no residual threat to the crown. Thus the accession of the house of Abbas to the caliphate was attended with circumstances of 'unparalleled cruelty'[15] – the scene was set for a dynasty line that would survive for five centuries.

On 9 June 754 Abdul Abbas died of smallpox, and was succeeded by his brother Abu Jafar who was proclaimed caliph in Kufa with the title of al-Mansur (the Victorious). The most celebrated act of Abu Jafar was the creation of Baghdad. According to legend he had spent 'the sweetest and gentlest night on earth' at the site of a priest's church. He was pleased by everything he saw, whereupon he declared: 'This is the site on which I will build. Things can arrive here by way of the Euphrates, Tigris and a network of canals. Only a place like this will support the army and the general populace.' He allocated funds for the building of Baghdad, even laying the first brick with his own hand: 'In the name of God and praise to Him. The earth is God's; He causes to inherit of it whom He wills among His servants, and the result thereof is to them that fear Him ... Build, and God bless you.'[16] The new city was set near an old Persian village near the old Persian capital of Ctesiphon. Baghdad (later dubbed the 'Round City' or the 'City of Peace'), soon to emerge as the greatest metropolis of the time, had a diameter of two miles, three concentric walls, and great highways that radiated from the caliph's palace at the centre of the city to the four corners of the Muslim empire. The Tigris and Euphrates fed the irrigation canals, enabling the surrounding countryside to support the large city. Grain was brought from Jazira in northern Iraq, camels plied overland from Persia, and ships could sail down the Tigris to Arabia and other lands. Tribute and taxation accumulated in the vast treasure-houses of Baghdad, while the great city of the caliph developed as the heart of an immense trading network.

Astrologers had been consulted to determine the most propitious season to begin the building of Baghdad, though the suitability of the site needed little comment. The Tigris itself was a great waterway, in parts 250 yards wide and often as much as 46 feet deep. The environs were rich in gardens and villages, and the region could support a large population: some 800,000 men and 60,000 women attended the funeral of Hanbal, a popular saint. Baghdad was to reach the peak of its glory under the caliphs Haroun al-Raschid (786–809) and his son al-Mamum (813–33), though even under these monarchs there were already signs that the empire was beginning to decline (North Africa had become largely autonomous around 800). Baghdad for a time was the undisputed focus of Muslim power, wealth and religious devotion; often depicted by subsequent chroniclers as a city of pleasure (the nineteenth-century English explorer Sir Richard Burton dubbed Baghdad 'the Paris of the ninth century'). There were mosques and palaces, patios and pavilions, walkways and gardens; and philosophy, science and a literary revolution (the great Arab poet Abu Nuwas was a friend of Haroun al-Raschid). *The Thousand and One Nights* – the great compilation of tales immortalising the exploits of Aladdin, Ali Baba, Sinbad the Sailor and many others – dates to this period, many of the stories originating from far afield (Persia, India, Turkey, Greece). Haroun and his son appear in many of the tales, though some of the main protagonists – such as King Shahryar and the prime minister's daughter Shahrazad (Scheherazade) – carry Persian names, again signalling the Persian influence at the heart of the caliphate.

In 809 Haroun al-Raschid died, whereupon the power struggle between his sons Amin and Mamum threw the empire into confusion. Amin reigned for a time and fought to consolidate his power despite the depleted treasures of the capital: 'to supply the deficiency he was obliged to commit to the crucible his gold and silver plate'.[17] Thus he hoped to fund the soldiers in defence of Baghdad against Mamum, who had proclaimed himself caliph in Khurasan. Amin had managed to fund some 5000 mercenaries, but the number was insufficient to protect him: at the height of the turmoil, and under siege by Mamum, Amin was assassinated by a slave and the display of the monarch's head on the walls of Baghdad indicated to Mamum that one particular struggle was at an end.

The new caliph then began a glorious reign. At his marriage a thousand immense pearls were showered on the head of the bride; while gifts of lands and houses, settled by scattering lottery tickets among the populace, announced to the amazed witnesses the scale of the royal bounty. Mamum encouraged literature and the arts in general, inviting learned men from all parts of the world to the Baghdad court. At the same time some observers questioned his religious devotion. For did he not favour the heretical doctrine that denied to the Koran the authority of a divine revelation? And did he not spend the last years of his life demanding, sometimes through persecution, that the people accept the odious doctrine that the Koran was no more than a human creation? The errors of Mamum are remembered, as well as his boundless cultural enthusiasm.[18] But by the end of his reign the Muslim decline was evident. The period of the Abbasids had done nothing to heal the divisions at the heart of Islam; and even the world-shaking Arab conquests, though impacting dramatically on all later centuries, had only piled up the forces that would in due course rend apart the empire. The Arabs, fuelled by a potent fanaticism, had burst out of the desert peninsula to confront ancient empires and to sweep across many lands. The sudden ascent of the Arab nation had happened with startling speed; its decline, inevitable and irreversible, would take much longer. The Abbasid caliphs were witnesses to the accelerating pace of Arab decline. There was nothing they could do to prevent it.

THE ARAB DECLINE

The corrosive tensions within the caliphate were evident throughout its entire history. The violent deaths of the *rashidun* caliphs, the persistent revolts under the Umayyads, the mounting disruption under the Abbasids – all signalled the failure of the Islamic state to impose order on the empire. Religious turmoil continued under the nominal victories of the Muslim rulers. The teachers of Islam, in confrontation with Christian dogma and Jewish apologetics, were forced to deepen and refine their own philosophy; now the Muslim scholars were forced to grapple with such questions as the character of God, the scope of revelation, and the extent of human autonomy in the context of the divine plan. Such disputation did much to erode the simple Islam of the early empire: the Abbasids, from the outset, had to cope with mounting dissension at the heart of the faith and with mounting religious revolt throughout the empire. The dissent that was manifest under the Umayyads continued under the Abbasids; and, linked to political ambition, threatened to rend the Muslim state.

In 742, under Umayyad rule, a dissenting Manichaean preacher was executed; while, a generation later, the Caliph Mahadi (775–85), an Abbasid, established a pious inquisition designed to root out the *zindik* heretics, who were forced thereby to flee into the Turkish lands of Central Asia. Some sects anticipated the 'second coming' of the religious agitator Bin-Afaridh who, executed by Abu Muslim, had claimed divine revelation and urged his disciples to worship the sun. The 'Veiled Prophet' Mukanna, masked in green silk (to temper his divine glow, according to his supporters; to hide his deformities, according to his detractors), fought the caliph's armies until besieged in 780, when he cast himself into the flames rather than be taken captive. In 838 the prophet Babak (or Papak) was executed by Caliph Motassem, after a campaign of religious terror that had lasted twenty years. Such events were not designed to bring pious harmony to a Muslim empire supposedly resting on the divine revelation enshrined in a single text.

It has been argued that the remarkable cultural developments in Islam – as epitomised by the scientific and artistic progress under Raschid and Mamum – themselves contributed to the decline of the Islamic empire. Mamum established the so-called House of Wisdom, responsible for translating foreign works: Hunain ibn Ishaq was in charge of translating Greek works into Arabic (Aristotle and Plato among the philosophers, Galen and Hippocrates among the physicians); it was from Baghdad that Galen's seven-volume *Anatomy*, translated into Arabic, reached western Europe via Sicily and Spain (Hunain himself produced ten treatises on the eye, the earliest known text of ophthalmology). At the same time the Arabs were making prodigious strides in mathematics; introducing the zero concept, establishing the positional method of computation, inventing plane and spherical geometry, devising logarithms, and discovering the range of trigonometrical relations ('algebra' and 'algorithm' derive from Arabic roots, and the term 'algorithm' is a corruption of the inventor's name, al-Khawarizmi). Mamum witnessed the building of an astronomical observatory: Arabs accurately computed the circumference of the earth, six hundred years before the European Christians were prepared to admit that it was not flat; and the Arab *Compendium of Astronomy* was used as a standard text in Europe up to the sixteenth century. Raschid established a free public hospital – with doctors and chemists subject to government inspection; and Mamum opened medical schools in Baghdad at the very heart of the Islamic empire.[19] But, it is argued, such staggering cultural progress failed to consolidate the Muslim state: the world-shattering Arab conquest had succeeded because of the simple martial qualities of the desert Bedouin, not through the congenial pursuit of intellectual enquiry.

The Muslim regions of northern Africa had become largely autonomous around 800; and the caliphate lost Khurasan in 820. Now the Muslim rulers of the empire were forced to witness the progressive contraction of their domain. Even in Baghdad it was plain that the central authority of the Muslim state was being eroded. Thus Mamum's successor, Motassem (833–42), experienced such local hostility to the caliphate that at one stage he was forced to transfer the capital to the town of Samarra, lying further north on the Tigris. Now numbers of imported slave-boys from Turkestan had been built up to constitute the main strength of the local army: it was this alien bodyguard of 10,000 Turks, eager to repress the Baghdad population, that forced the half-century-long Samarra exile on the Abbasid caliphate. In 837 the Byzantine Emperor Theophilus crossed the Taurus and captured the Muslim town of Zebetra, whereupon the Byzantines mutilated many men, gouging out eyes and cutting off ears and noses, and carried off more than a thousand Muslim women as slaves. The following year Motassem, bent on revenge, led 200,000 troops against the Byzantine forces, slaughtered thousands, and carried off women and children as slaves. Four years later the caliph was dead, with the empire witnessing further rebellions and corrosive disaffection.

A sequence of weak caliphs progressively weakened the Muslim state: some were at first elevated and then deposed by the army; all seemed ineffectual as they witnessed the progressive decay of the empire. Most of Persia had been lost to rebellion; a Turkish soldier, Ahmad Tulun, proclaimed himself master of Egypt and Syria; and a terrible slave revolt – the Zanj (or Zindj) insurrection – began in Basra, advanced through lower Iraq, and shook the entire Muslim world. The black Zanj slaves, supported by dissident Muslim missionaries, were led by Ali Muhammed (an Iraqi Spartacus), who claimed to be a descendant of the caliph Ali. Here again was a self-appointed *mahdi* (redeemer); his followers called him Master of the Zanj (*Sahib az-Zanj*), while his enemies dubbed him the Rascal (*al-Khabith*). After pillaging the countryside for food and weapons the slaves captured Basra in 871 and took a number of other towns in southern Iraq; but in 883 the caliph's forces finally defeated the Zanj armies, killing Ali and his officers.[20]

The weaknesses in the Muslim empire were now plain. Independent states were being consolidated in Egypt, Persia and elsewhere; and other contemporary revolts, taking inspiration from the Zanj insurrection, had merged into a more general rebellion, the Qarmat movement, that contributed further to the destabilisation of the Muslim caliphate. The slave uprising had been crushed and other revolts suppressed, but with every success there were fresh reverses. A Fatimid anti-caliphate was established in Egypt in 909, challenging the religious primacy of the Abbasids; and in 945 the Buyid clan from north-west Persia seized power in Baghdad, so finally extinguishing the effective political power of the Abbasids. In the tenth century the Isma'ilians, revolutionary supporters of the Ali tradition, broke for ever the spiritual unity of the Muslim *umma*, and another layer of schism became enshrined at the heart of Islam.[21]

The perennial family jealousies, the endless tribal rivalries, the personal ambitions, the residual pressures of ancient empires, the competing ethnic claims in the massively expanded empire, the many incompatible ingredients poured into the cultural melting-pot – all contributed to the eventual emasculation and dissolution of the Arab empire. Separate dynasties gradually broke away from the authority of the caliphate – to yield autonomous regimes in territories that had all at one time been held in subordination to the central Muslim state: the Safavids in eastern Persia (867–1495), the Samanids of eastern Khurasan (819–1005), the Tulinids in Egypt (868–905), the Aghlabids of Tunisia (800–909) and others. The indelible influence of the Prophet continued to be felt in all the territories of the erstwhile empire: the people and their rulers in the once subject lands continued – for the most part – with their Muslim devotions, even during the decay and final overthrow of the caliphate. A few areas broke away from Muslim control or retained pockets of religious independence: notably Spain, subject to a Christian reconquest, and various self-sufficient enclaves of Judaism, Christianity and Zoroastrianism in other lands. The influence of the Prophet and the Koran, though benefiting greatly from the persuasive power of the Arab sword, had proved much more durable than the ambitions of security authority.

The Abbasid caliphs had degenerated into mere 'shadow-caliphs', pathetic imitations of the great Raschid and Mamum, still nominally in control of the Baghdad regime but no longer active players on the political scene. Turkish and Circassian slaves, the so-called Mamluks (*mamluk*, 'owned'), increasingly arrogant in their supposed defence of the state, had established a *de facto* Turkish control of the neighbouring lands in the name of the Abbasid dynasty. In 1094 the Byzantine Emperor Alexius I appealed to Pope Urban II to send urgent military aid to block the growing Turkish authority. It was the pope's response to this desperate appeal that precipitated the Crusades. In 945 the Abbasid caliph Mostakfi (944–6) had surrendered all power to Ahmad ibn Buwaih, a Persian tribal chief hostile to the dynasty, and was quickly proclaimed *Amir al-Umara* and *Muiz al-Dawla* ('one who cherished the state'). On 29 January 946, now at the end of his patience, Buwaih broke into the palace, dragged the caliph from his throne, and then drove him through the streets to the jeers of the soldiers. Then his eyes were put out with red-hot irons and he was thrown into jail where he died five years later. Buwaih subsequently installed Moti as a new puppet caliph. So ran the Buwaihid period of Iraqi history (945–1055), terminated when the Seljuk Tughril Beg entered Baghdad to impose yet another authoritarian regime.

The Seljuk leaders (primarily Tughril Beg, Alp Arslan, Malik Shah and Sancar, the last of the great Seljuks) had assumed most of the main powers of the Abbasid caliphs. Now it was the sultans, deriving from the Turkish Ghuzz (or Oguz) in the steppes north of the Aral Sea, who were taking the important decisions on matters of administration and military affairs at the heart of the disintegrating Islamic empire. The caliphs retained certain religious responsibilities, being allowed to comment on matters of Muslim observance, Koranic exegesis, and proper personal behaviour. But such entitlements, though of residual spiritual significance, were more or less irrelevant to the running of the state. The Seljuks soon set about revising the Perso-Islamic administrative framework, injecting Persian culture, and largely eliminating the Arabic language in most cultural and governmental activities. Even communities with a large Arab majority found themselves administered by officials who knew no word of Arabic. Moreover the

Seljuks were well prepared to limit the Abbasids' areas of nominal religious autonomy: it was a keen Seljuk aim to erase all Shi'ite influence in religion, politics and military affairs – which in turn led to the expulsion of Shi'as from their official posts and the reorganisation of Muslim schools to reflect the new orthodoxy.

The Seljuks, who had effectively brought to an end the great age of the Arab Nation, were no different from all the previous historical conquerors in having no permanent hold on power. The fractures in the empire, the competing family and ethnic factions, the civil wars, and unanticipated threats from across the frontiers – all conspired to undermine the Seljuk hegemony. The fabric of the Seljuk order was finally destroyed in 1194 when the caliph al-Nazir, of the Turkish dynasty of Khwarizm Shahs, defeated the ruling sultan in Baghdad. Already the Arabs had been challenged by the launching of the Christian Crusades: soon they would be forced to suffer the greatest calamity of all – the tidal wave of a fierce people from Mongolia destined to overwhelm Islam almost completely.

In 1095 Pope Urban II, keen to exploit the Byzantine call to block the Turkish advance through Asia Minor, demanded the launching of a military expedition – not so much to aid the Byzantines as to expel the Muslims from Palestine, the cradle of the Christian religion. The first response to his appeal was the People's Crusade, a vast rabble of men, women and children that fought and looted its way to Constantinople before some 20,000 of them were massacred on 21 October 1096 by the Turks near Nicomedia. It was hoped that the more professional Christian armies would fare better. In the event the Christian onslaught, despite many a pious proclamation, was nothing more than plunder, rape and massacre. Thus the Franj (to the Muslims all West Europeans were *Franj*, Franks) 'passed through several villages, all of them Christian, and commandeered the harvests, which had just been gathered, mercilessly massacring those peasants who tried to resist. Young children were even said to have been burned alive.'[22]

The Egyptian Fatimids and other Muslim dynasties were now taking steps to repel the mounting threat from the Western infidel. Following the request for military aid Nuraddin in Jerusalem despatched Shirkuh and his (Shirkuh's) nephew Salah el-Din (Saladin) to Egypt. When Shirkuh, appointed wazir, died suddenly in 1169 his place was taken by Saladin, who now began building up the necessary power to expel the Franks from Muslim lands. Soon, accepted by orthodox Muslims, he had gained control of the governments of Egypt, Syria and Iraq and was in a position to challenge the Christian power in Jerusalem. In 1187 Saladin overran Palestine, a decisive victory that horrified the European powers. The Franks were able to retrieve little from the ruins of their defeat, and the peace of Ramla in 1192 did nothing more than consolidate the Muslim victories. The virtuous Richard the Lionheart set about massacring 3000 Muslims when talks broke down, while his pious soldiers were busy examining the entrails of the corpses for swallowed gold.[23] Now Saladin's empire included substantial parts of North Africa, Syria, Kurdistan, Egypt and Iraq; and, according to the contemporary Arab historian Ibn al-Athir, with further conquests planned. A few months later, on 3 March 1193, Saladin, the mighty conqueror of the Christian Crusaders, died in Damascus.

The Crusades, though in large part unsuccessful, had further weakened the Muslim world; now the fragmented and weary followers of the Prophet would find it even harder to resist a fresh cataclysmic onslaught on Islam. It was the Mongol horde that was to represent the ultimate 'disaster', 'catastrophe' and 'scourge' for the Muslim world. Al-Athir writes that this episode was 'so horrible that I shrank from recording it ... To whom, indeed, can it be easy to write the death-blow of Islam and the Muslims ... this thing involves the description of the greatest calamity ... which befell all men generally, and the Muslims in particular ... since God Almighty created Adam.' Nebuchadnezzar had slaughtered the children of Israel, but 'what was Jerusalem in comparison to the countries which these accursed miscreants [the Mongols] destroyed, each city of which was double the size of Jerusalem? ... these whom they massacred in a single city exceeded all the children of Israel ... these spared none, slaying women and men and children, ripping open pregnant women and killing unborn babes ...'.[24] Thus Genghis Khan, leaving misery and desolation in his wake, sought to extend the Mongol Empire, rocking Islam to its foundations and succeeding in extinguishing the moribund caliphate once and for all. The perennial feuding at the heart of Islam, the corrosive effects of successive invasions, the inability of the 'shadow-caliphs' and their masters to impose order on the Muslim world – all prepared the way for the ultimate dissolution to be forced on Islam by Mongol power.

It is hard to exaggerate the scale of the devastation wrought by the Mongols (or *Tartars*: a European effort to link the Mongols, because of their hellish deeds and infernal cruelty, with Tartarus where sinners were tormented in the underworld of Greek mythology). Many of the Muslim cities were well fortified and it was thought that a series of lengthy sieges would weary the Mongol invaders. But the Mongol siege tactics, aided by skilled Chinese engineers, were highly effective. Mangonels were drawn up to bombard the walls, after which slaves were forced to lead assaults on the weakened defenders. Then all the inhabitants would be driven outside the city, the women to be raped and thereafter all the people – men, women and children – to be butchered. Finally the town would be comprehensively plundered, before being razed to the ground. Genghis Khan is said to have declared: 'All cities must be razed, so that the world may once again become a great steppe in which Mongol mothers will suckle free and happy children.'[25]

On 1 July 1251 Mangu, a grandson of Genghis Khan, was elected by the Mongol tribal council to serve as the supreme khan, a decision that led to some tribal dissent but not sufficient to weaken the Mongol onslaught on Iraq, Syria and Egypt. In March 1257 Hulagu, Mangu's brother, sent an ultimatum to the caliph Mostassem (1242–58), demanding that he surrender and come to pay homage; but Mostassem, as a Muslim ruler, found it impossible to acquiesce before the threats of an animist heathen, however formidable. In January 1258 the Mongol siege of Baghdad began. The pattern was familiar: in three days the mighty mangonels had reduced the walls of the city to ruins, while at the same time the Mongol engineers were breaking the irrigation dykes to flood the city. Mostassem was dragged to Hulagu's camp, while all the pathetic inhabitants of Baghdad who had not drowned in the rising floodwaters were ordered to assemble on the plain outside the city. All were massacred, shot with arrows or hacked to death, their corpses piled in heaps. Then the Mongol soldiers plundered the Baghdad mosques, palaces and colleges, slaughtering any Muslims still struggling to hide in the rubble of the city. It is estimated that some 800,000 civilians – men, women and children – were killed over a period of days in the streets and houses of Baghdad and on the plain outside the city. The subsequent murder of Mostassem and his sons required that they be rolled in blankets (or sewn up in sacks) before being trampled under the hoofs of Muslim horses – because of the Mongol dread of shedding the blood of sovereign princes. In such a miserable fashion the Abbasid caliphate was finally extinguished in 1258, and all the glories of mediaeval Baghdad were reduced to ruins.

The Mongols, well satisfied (as were many Christians) with the sacking of the great city at the heart of Islam, marched off carrying the Muslim treasures that had accumulated over five centuries. In January 1260 the Mongols took Aleppo in Syria, and that ancient city was forced to suffer all the massacres, plunder and devastation that had ravaged Baghdad and countless other Muslim towns. Damascus, one of the great surviving Muslim centres, surrendered in wise prudence without a fight; whereupon three Christian leaders – the Mongol commander Kitbuga, the King of Armenia and the Frankish Count Bohemund of Antioch – paraded in the streets of the ancient Muslim city, forcing the followers of the Prophet to bow to the cross. It was easy for the Christian devotees to represent the merciless Mongol campaign, with all its cruelty and destruction, as a fitting adjunct to the Frankish expeditions.

Then the fortunes of imperialism were yet again thrown into reverse: not even the Mongols could secure an empire. With the death of Mangu, reported to Hulagu in 1260, Mongol authority was plunged into disarray. At the same time the Mamluks, well aware that Mongol attention was diverted, raised a Muslim army and advanced under the Sultan Kutuz to confront Kitbuga. At the historic battle of Ain Jalut ('Goliath's Spring') near Nazareth, Kitbuga was killed and the terrible sway that the ancestors of Genghis Khan had held over the world was broken forever. The Mongols had destroyed a feeble caliphate that had still served as a focus for Islam and Muslim identity. Any residual semblance of a widespread Arab empire, rooted in the Word of the Prophet, had been finally dissolved; but the Hejaz, home of the Holy Cities, remained intact as the secure focus of comprehensive Muslim devotion. Mecca and Medina, though ineluctably associated with the life and work of Muhammed, had been consigned to the fringes of Umayyad and Abbasid culture. The political masters in the Hejaz had come and gone, but the spiritual guardianship of the holy places had been retained largely by the descendants of the Prophet. Again Islam, of whatever merit and in whatever shape, had proved to be a more durable focus than all the ambitions of secular rulers. Now Mecca and Medina, with the rest of the fragmented Muslim world, were about to experience yet another conquest from beyond the frontiers of the Arabian peninsula.

THE OTTOMAN ERA

The Turks were originally nomadic horsemen from the central and eastern Asian grasslands, the homelands also of the Scythians, Huns and Mongols. Like the Mongols the Turks were a fierce warrior race whose skill with the bow gave them considerable military prowess. Many of the tribes were a racial mixture, some resembling the Chinese in skin colour and facial features, others the Caucasians of the southern steppe. Under the Seljuk Tughril Beg the Turks captured Baghdad in 1055; and the first major Seljuk victory over Christian armies followed in 1071 with a shattering defeat of Byzantine forces. With the collapse of the Seljuk sultanate under the Mongol onslaught many of the local Turkish rulers carved out principalities for themselves. Among these was Osman of Sogut, a region near modern Eskisehir in western Anatolia, whose dynasty became known as the *Osmanli* in Turkish and *Othman* in Arabic; these terms were duly transmuted into 'Ottoman' in the languages of western Europe. In 1326 Osman died during the Turkish siege of the Byzantine city of Brusa, subsequently captured by his son Orhan. Thus Brusa became the first effective capital of an Ottoman sultanate that was set to survive until 1922; though the capital became Adrianople in 1364 and Istanbul (Constantinople) almost a century later.

In the seventh century the Ottoman Turks began a westward trek that was to bring them in contact with the borders of the Middle East, there to encounter Islam and the caliphate regimes. Gradually the Ottomans adopted the Prophet, and the groundwork for a vast new Muslim empire was established. In 1345 the Ottomans crossed the Dardanelles into Europe at the invitation of Emperor John V. Paleologus in his effort to suppress a usurper; but then Turkish imperial ambitions gained their own momentum. By 1366 the Ottomans had expelled the Byzantines from Anatolia and were mounting fresh expeditions against other Byzantine strongholds. Constantinople, the Byzantine capital, finally fell to the Ottoman forces on 29 May 1453 and Sultan Fatih ('Conqueror') Mehmet II occupied what was now the new capital of the Muslim empire of the Ottomans. The scene was set for further Turkish conquests.

The Turkish expansion led to the first Ottoman–Mamluk war (1485–91), a series of skirmishes in which neither side used its main forces. The Mamluks managed to retain their Cicilian towns, while the Ottomans secured many of the mountain passes. The resulting peace (1491–1516) ended with the eventual

Ottoman conquest of the Mamluk empire. From its secure Anatolian heartland the Ottoman state was now spreading over three continents: Asia, Europe and Africa. Sultan Selim I, in a highly successful campaign (1516–17), had captured Syria, Palestine and Egypt; and soon his great successor, Suleiman the Magnificent (1520–66), was to invade Iraq as far as the borders of Persia and to penetrate also into central Europe, adding Hungary and other regions to the empire (Figure 3.2).

This turbulent period had also witnessed a Persian national revival under the Safavids, a dynasty (1501–1736) founded by Ismail I who conquered most of Persia and added much of Iraq to his empire; in 1508 Baghdad and Mosul were taken, with the bulk of Iraq added to the Persian conquests. Soon, however, the Safavids were forced to confront the expanding Ottoman empire. The Turkish Selim I (1512–20) was the first Ottoman ruler to launch a comprehensive onslaught on the Mamluk and Safavid territories. The Mamluks were under pressure from Portuguese imperial expansion: the capture of Socotra in the Gulf of Aden (1507) and of Hormuz on the Persian Gulf (1508) had strengthened Portugal's strategic position. Ismail, though reluctant to encourage any European advance, agreed to help the Portuguese in return for their support against the Ottomans, whereupon Selim responded by supplying the Mamluks with guns, gunpowder, naval supplies and shipwrights. The Mamluks, despite this aid, suspected that Selim would eventually move against their empire and so they struggled to remain aloof from the Ottoman–Safavid conflict.

In 1516 the Ottoman armies began to move through Anatolia, inducing the Mamluks to transport their main forces across the Euphrates to avoid a conflict with Selim for which they were ill prepared. At the same time various leading Mamluk officials, sensing the drift of events, sent secret messages to Selim offering support in the likelihood of an invasion and asking for financial consideration in return. When Selim received news that the Mamluk sultan al-Gawri was leading a force into Anatolia, the scene was set for an Ottoman response and a corresponding expansion of Turkish power. In the event the Ottomans conquered the Mamluk empire with amazing rapidity: leading Mamluk officials deserted; the local peoples had no interest in supporting the losing side; and Ottoman weapons and tactics proved highly effective.[26] The only major battle took place on 24 August 1516 when Mamluk forces were comprehensively defeated at Marc Dabik, near Aleppo. Then Selim quickly swept through the rest of Syria, occupying Aleppo (28 August), Hama (19 September) and Damascus (27 September). The local populations, including the former governors of the provinces, were quick to welcome the conquerors; local desultory efforts to mount resistance were unsuccessful; and Selim, conciliating the main towns and provinces, was able also to win the support of the Bedouin tribal leaders and the heads of the various Muslim and non-Muslim religious factions.

The Ottoman armies then crossed the Sinai peninsula in five days (11–16 January 1517); and overwhelmed Tuman Bay's Mamluk forces on 22 January, killing 25,000 men. Tuman Bay survived and, organising guerrilla

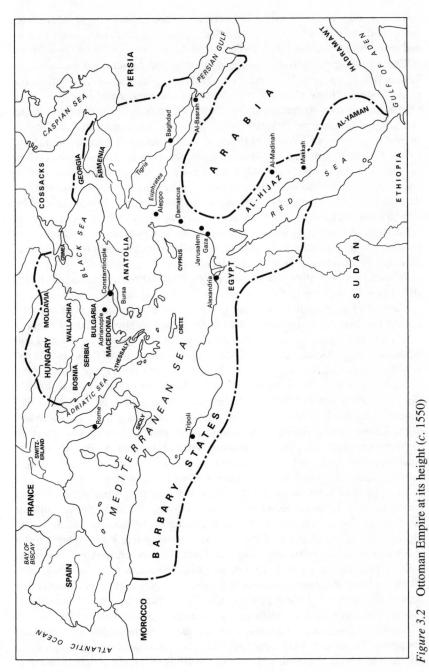

Figure 3.2 Ottoman Empire at its height (c. 1550)

resistance, managed to delay the fall of Cairo by a mere three days: the city was devastated and thousands more were killed. Sporadic guerrilla resistance continued in the Nile Delta and Upper Egypt, but in due course most of northern Africa fell under Ottoman control.[27] It was now, after the capture and execution of Tuman Bay on 13 April 1517, that Selim received testaments of loyalty from the major Bedouin chiefs. On 3 July the shareef of Mecca offered his loyalty to the Ottoman conqueror, so sanctioning his control of the Holy Cities of Islam without the need for a further military expedition. In return, Selim appointed the Muslim shareef as governor of Jeddah and Hejaz, as well as acknowledging his traditional role in Mecca and Medina, so establishing a precedent for his successors. Then the Ottoman fleet conveyed to Alexandria the provisions that Selim needed to march his army back to Anatolia; after which the caliph al-Motawakkel and two thousand Egyptian merchants, artisans and religious leaders were transported by ship to Istanbul, so beginning the process whereby many of the principal figures at the heart of Islam were absorbed into the Ottoman system: the religion of the Prophet was infused with a new vigour, while Persian and Arab officials came to influence the developing Turkish administration.

It is said that after the Ottoman fleet returned to Istanbul the caliph transferred all his powers to Selim and his successors (in contemporary chronicles there is reference to Istanbul being the 'seat of the caliphate'); but other evidence tells against the idea, not least because the Ottomans had no obvious family connection with the Prophet and because al-Motawakkel later journeyed to Cairo and there continued caliphal duties until 1543. The Ottoman use of the term 'caliph' may have signified no more than a claim to secular power, the mark of the acknowledged ruler. More significant, with respect to Islam, was that the title 'Servant and Protector of the Holy Places' came to be used by Selim and his successors. Thus the Turkish sultans emphasised their role as leaders and defenders of the Islamic world, signifying their undisputed authority over all Muslims. In the eighteenth century, after the Treaty of Kucuk Kaynarca, Russia allowed the weakened Ottomans to retain certain religious rights over the Crimean Muslims, a caliphal claim recognised by the Russians but not by many Islamic scholars.

In April 1534 Suleiman despatched Ibrahim Pasha, the Grand Wazir, to begin the conquest of Iraq; and soon Ibrahim was marching out of Aleppo to confront the Safavids. While a second army was marching to support Ibrahim, Suleiman himself was taking charge of Ottoman forces moving into Persia – however, a harsh winter causing substantial human and material losses forced him to concentrate on Iraq with its more favourable weather. The weary Ottoman army, after journeying over the Zagros mountains and the Mesopotamian plains, managed to occupy Baghdad with little opposition; already the Sunni leaders, encouraged by Suleiman's approach, had organised a local revolt against the oppressive Shi'as. Now most of Iraq was in Suleiman's hands, though some Bedouin groups held out around Basra until 1538. Any possibility of a Safavid advance through Syria into Iraq had been removed, and most of the lands of the old caliphate had now been brought under the control of the Turkish sultan. The orthodox Islam of the Sunnis had been rescued from Shi'a oppression, while Suleiman's supremacy in the Muslim world had been confirmed.[28]

Suleiman, the tenth Ottoman sultan (1520–66), is recognised as signalling the apogee of the Ottoman Empire.[29] He has been represented as a great *ghazi* warrior, lawgiver, scholar, poet and patron of the arts. Suleiman ruled over a vast territory, serving (in particular, for this book) as the protector of the Muslim holy places in Hejaz. He was in fact much more than a secular potentate: his assumption of caliphal powers, indicating more than the authority of a normal monarch, gave Suleiman a spiritual primacy among Muslim princes. None the less it was still possible for pious disciples of the Prophet to question Suleiman's lineage: the Shi'as continued in their zealous conviction that only the legitimate descendants of Ali, Muhammed's cousin and son-in-law, could properly assume the mantle of caliph.

Such considerations did nothing to diminish Suleiman's state authority. To bolster his vast secular power he was able to invoke the aura of Koranic authority over the business of government: few were prepared to question his claim to be a *de facto* caliph. He made plain his reverence for Islamic holy law (*seriat*) and his willingness to seek advice from the religious establishment of religious divines (*ulema*). The *ulema*, led by the Chief Mufti (*seyhulislam*) and exempt from taxation and other impositions, were generally well disposed to underwrite the sultan's secular authority. At the same time the *ulema*, with its powerful inner circle (the *ilmiye*), developed as a constitutional check on Ottoman autocracy, even in due course evolving the capacity to make or break sultans: of twenty-one sultans whose reigns ended between 1612 and 1922, some thirteen were deposed by the proclamation of an opinion (*fatwa*) by the Chief Mufti on a matter of Holy Law.[30]

When Suleiman died in 1566 the Ottoman Empire began its long decline, beset by a chronology of vicious and incompetent sultans and by the growing challenge of imperial ambitions elsewhere. In 1619 Bakr (the Su Bashi), a captain of Janissaries in Baghdad, staged a revolt and took over the city. An Ottoman army was soon despatched to restore order, whereupon Bakr invited Shah Abbas I of Persia to take over Baghdad. The sultan, prepared to conciliate, offered Bakr the governorship of the city if he remained loyal; but Abbas, his ambition stirred, took Baghdad on 12 January 1624, slaughtered all the Sunni inhabitants of the city, tortured Bakr to death, and boiled in oil all the Janissaries who had supported Bakr.[31] The Turks attempted to retake Baghdad, failing in 1625 but succeeding in 1638 when the sultan Murat IV occupied the city and then sent troops over much of Mesopotamia to slaughter what Sunni Muslims could be found. On 17 May 1639 a peace was at last negotiated between the Ottomans and the Safavids, defining the borders between Iraq and Persia, and securing the Ottoman trade routes to the Persian Gulf. Such developments did little to delay the centuries-long decline of Ottoman power.

Many factors contributed to the decline of the Ottoman state: the inevitable encroachments of other powers, the usual problems of dynastic succession, and the characteristic problems of administering a vast empire. The harem system, guaranteeing sufficient contenders for the throne, also encouraged a disruptive competition for power that weakened the internal unity of the state. Sons competed for the throne and sometimes did not wait for the death of the monarch: by the fifteenth century, fratricide among the putative rulers of the Ottoman state had become an acknowledged part of the political process (a *kanun* issued by Fatih Mehment not only allowed such action but approved it as a means of avoiding civil strife). But the habitual contact with harem women did little to prepare future sultans for affairs of state; while endemic corruption, fostered by court intrigue, was now affecting both government and the management of the military establishment. From the seventeenth century onwards the sultans found themselves in charge of vast anarchic forces, far removed from the great disciplined state that had originally extended the frontiers of the empire. At the same time the European powers were growing in strength and influence, by the end of the seventeenth century presenting a multifaceted challenge to Ottoman authority.

In 1694 the turbulent desert Arabs succeeded in capturing Basra, only restored to the sultan after a Persian onslaught on the region. Now the Bedouins and the semi-nomadic Kurds were also raiding the caravan routes between Aleppo and Baghdad, so further hampering Ottoman trade. In 1704 Hasan Pasha Mustafa, the son of the cavalry officer Mustafa Beg, was appointed governor of Baghdad; and for almost two decades he struggled to maintain the power of the Ottoman sultan over the restless desert tribes. Thirty years later, Nadir Quli Khah, the successor to the Afghan chief Mahmoud Khan Ghilzai, laid siege to Baghdad and reduced the city to starvation. When the Ottomans eventually retook the city they found 100,000 people dead in the streets. But again Turkish authority in the region was challenged. Persian horsemen attacked the Ottoman forces, leaving their commander Topal Othman Pasha ('Othman the Lame') dead in the field, with the bulk of the Turkish army exterminated. Repeated Ottoman attempts to impose Turkish authority on the region failed – until, in 1831, bubonic plague devastated the Baghdad population and reduced the city to impotence. Twelve pashas – Mamluks and Turks – had ruled Iraq during the period 1750–1831, during which the fortunes and power of the Ottoman state had continued to deteriorate.

After the early phase of the *rashidun* caliphs (Abu Bakr, Omar, Othman and Ali), lasting from 632 to 661, the political heart of Islam had shifted irretrievably to beyond the frontiers of the Arabian peninsula. The world-shattering Arab conquests, won essentially by the desert Bedouins, soon became fractured by internal dissent and the predations of competing imperial ambitions. Arab culture, though influenced by other traditions, continued to survive in Arabia and far beyond, but with Islam increasingly enjoying the protection of imperial states – mainly

Ottoman Turkey – that claimed no blood ties to the Prophet. It was the Ottomans that came to shape one of the most enduring Muslim states in the history of Islam: some thirty-six sultans – all in the direct male line of Osman of Sogut – reigned from 1300 to 1922. Frequent wars and endless civil conflicts, plus a range of civil structural faults, had progressively weakened the Ottoman state. The war with Venice (1645–64) had exposed and exacerbated serious weaknesses in the empire; and soon afterwards the Russo-Turkish war (1676–81) had resulted in most of the Turkish Ukraine being lost to Russia. The long slow decay had begun, but it would take the twentieth-century Great War to finally extinguish the Ottoman Empire.

With the decline of Ottoman power a Muslim reform movement, founded by Muhammed ibn Abdul Wahhab in the eighteenth century, gradually gained strength in Central Arabia – and was soon winning adherents among the most powerful tribes in the peninsula. At the beginning of the nineteenth century a fanatical Wahhabist tribal chief, Muhammed ibn Saud, swept northwards, plundering and killing throughout Syria and Iraq. As early as 1802 the Wahhabists had captured Mecca and Medina, and quickly laid claim to the powerful soul of Islam. The Ottomans responded by crushing this dramatic Arab attempt at a fresh autonomy: the Wahhabists were defeated after fighting that began in 1812 and lasted for six years. But this was the beginning, not the end, of the Saudi story. After centuries when the political heart of Islam had shifted around regions beyond the Arabian peninsula, but where a spiritual focus of the Muslim world had always survived in Hejaz, a new phase in the history of Islam was about to commence – a phase ineluctably associated, for good or ill, with a new brand of Muslim fundamentalism, with the House of Saud, and with the imperial ambitions of great powers.

4 Saudi Ascendancy

'Well,' I interrupted, 'what about the propagation of Islam by the sword? For you cannot deny that in many countries it was so propagated. What right had Muhammad – what right has any prophet – to slay where he cannot convince?'

'A prophet has the right to slay if he knows that it is necessary,' answered the young Sayyid, 'for he knows what is hidden from us; and if he sees that the slaughter of a few will prevent many from going astray, he is justified in commanding such slaughter.'[1]

PREAMBLE

The bulk of the Arabian peninsula (around 80 per cent of it) was transformed in the twentieth century into Saudi Arabia – in effect, the Arabia of the House of Saud. The state so constituted in the early 1930s is not the only one today that bears the name of one particular dynastic line. We also have The *Hashemite* Kingdom of Jordan, less frequently remarked, and among the 200-plus states of the world there may be others whose names derive from unique family ascendancy.

The process, wherever it occurs, is always the same: for years, perhaps decades or even centuries, there is violent struggle among ambitious tribal factions. Allies are cultivated, territory is secured, and as many of the enemy as possible are put to the sword or in some other fashion despatched to paradise or the infernal regions. Such events are invariably accompanied by loud moral proclamation and devout invocation to this or that brutal deity. God, as is well known, is happy to underwrite copious blood-letting and always prefers to be on the winning side. To this general principle the origins of Saudi Arabia are no exception.

It is helpful also, in the case of Islam, if territorial and other ambitions can be underwritten by demonstrable blood links to the Prophet. Here the Hashemites, a principal rival faction to the House of Saud in the twentieth century and before, have been well favoured by historical circumstance (we need only indicate the Prophet's full name: Muhammed ibn Abdullah ibn Abdul Muttalib ibn Hashim – see Figure 2.1), a detail that had to be accommodated in Western imperial ambitions. One of the consequential perquisitions of the House of Hashim was that one Hashemite or another, by virtue of being a shareef (*serif*) or descendant of Muhammed, ruled as Emir of Mecca from 1073 to the twentieth century, controlling Mecca, Medina and much of the rest of Hejaz, and occupying various regional West-friendly thrones in modern times. It was Shareef Hussain ibn Ali, a

Hashemite, who was destined to become the main adversary of the House of Saud in the struggle to control twentieth-century Arabia.

In one depiction the history of the House of Saud is divided into three main phases. The first begins around 1744 when Muhammed ibn Saud, the petty ruler of Diriyah in Nejd, formed a political alliance with the religious revivalist Muhammed ibn abd al-Wahhab (see below). The movement spread rapidly, coming to the notice of the wider world at the beginning of the nineteenth century. In 1801 the Wahhabis sacked the Shi'ite holy city of Karbala in lower Iraq; and, to demonstrate their unique brand of piety, overthrew the domes of various tombs, including that of the Prophet's grandson, al-Hussein. Five years later they succeeded in expelling the Turks from Mecca and Medina, a temporary reprieve. The second principal phase of Saudi history can be regarded as starting in 1818 and extending throughout the rest of the century. Here again the Saudi faction, still wedded to the Wahhabist version of Islam, continued to struggle for power – this time mainly against the rival House of Rashid in Hail. In 1902, with the beginning of the third phase of Saudi history, Abdul Aziz ibn Muhammed ibn Saud (later to be known to the world as Ibn Saud), captured Riyadh and laid the basis for the struggle destined to establish the Saudi state through the bulk of the Arabian peninsula three decades later.[2]

THE WAHHABIST SOUL

Muhammed ibn Abdul Wahhab was born in 1703 (or, in other accounts, in 1691) to the Beni Tameem tribe in Nejd. His father – a man of learning, 'at any rate by Central Arabian standards'[3] – instructed him in the principles of Islam, to the point that the young Muhammed resolved to devote himself to a life of piety. He studied devoutly in Medina, Basra and Damascus; and gradually became convinced that the Turks and the Persians had allowed many abuses to creep into their practice of Islam. In 1742 he returned to Nejd and began to preach a religious revivalism based upon a fundamentalist return to the Koran, rejecting all the subsequent accretions that could not be justified by the clear authority of the holy text. It was plain that Abdul Wahhab was a true zealot, 'a John Calvin, so to speak, of Arabia come ... to re-create and re-purify the God-fearing, military – religious state of the Prophet'.[4] Finding little encouragement in his native village, he moved to Diriyah, there to encounter Muhammed ibn Saud, the first truly significant historical figure of the House of Saud (see Figure 4.1) and the man with whom Abdul Wahhab was set to forge such potent political links.

The historical Wahhabis have been adherents to the legal school of Ahmad ibn Hanbal (d. 855), the founder of the most conservative of the four orthodox schools of Islamic law. Here the doctrine urges an uncompromising acceptance of the letter of the *hadith*; with, following the teaching of the Syrian Taqi al-Din Ahmad ibn Taimiyah (1262–1328), no higher authority than the Koran and the

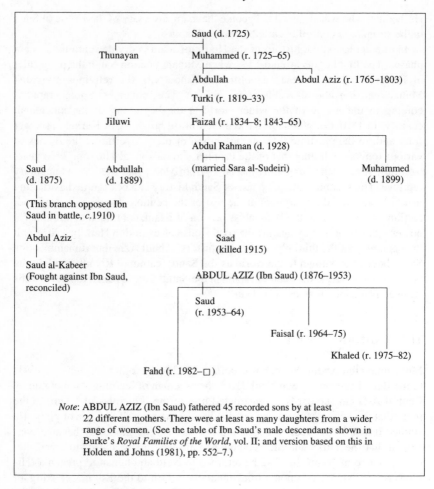

Saud (d. 1725)

Thunayan   Muhammed (r. 1725–65)

                            Abdullah   Abdul Aziz (r. 1765–1803)

                            Turki (r. 1819–33)

            Jiluwi   Faizal (r. 1834–8; 1843–65)

                            Abdul Rahman (d. 1928)

Saud   Abdullah   (married Sara al-Sudeiri)   Muhammed
(d. 1875)   (d. 1889)   (d. 1899)

(This branch opposed Ibn
Saud in battle, *c.*1910)

Abdul Aziz   Saad
                                            (killed 1915)
Saud al-Kabeer
(Fought against Ibn Saud,   ABDUL AZIZ (Ibn Saud) (1876–1953)
reconciled)
                                 Saud
                                 (r. 1953–64)

                                            Faisal (r. 1964–75)

                                                        Khaled (r. 1975–82)

                 Fahd (r. 1982–☐)

Note: ABDUL AZIZ (Ibn Saud) fathered 45 recorded sons by at least
22 different mothers. There were at least as many daughters from a wider
range of women. (See the table of Ibn Saud's male descendants shown in
Burke's *Royal Families of the World*, vol. II; and version based on this in
Holden and Johns (1981), pp. 552–7.)

Figure 4.1 Simplified family tree of House of Saud
Source: McLoughlin (1993), p. 206

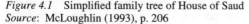

tradition of the community and no tolerance for such innovations as saint-
worship and pilgrimages to shrines. In this context Wahhabism – one of many
arbitrary versions of Islam – was seen as conveying a puritanical and simple
message, a vigorous and uncompromising return to the essence of early Islam.
Here we learn that God is absolute, characterised by an incomparable unity
revealed in the Koran (supposedly God's Word) and in no theological text deriving from human beings. In such a view any person who did not accept the unity
or oneness of God was necessarily a non-Muslim and a polytheist – an infidel
who ought to be 'mercilessly killed as enjoined by the Koran'.[5] Here the

Prophet, while an acknowledged non-divine human, was seen as infallible, able to intercede with God on behalf of true Muslims and in ways approved by God: this was contrasted with *tawassul*, the abominable attempt of false Muslims to derive power from God, often in the name of the so-called saints. A Canadian Islamist, Wilfred Cantwell Smith, has summarised the Wahhabist focus on the community as properly concerned with the law of God: 'The classical Law ... is the sum and substance of the faith ... Obey the pristine law, fully strictly, singly; and establish a society where that law obtains. This ... is Islam; all else is superfluous and wrong.'[6]

The doctrine is essentially egalitarian, theoretically denouncing all discriminations based on race, colour or social standing. Group chanting associated with religious observance is condemned, as are – predictably in this context – dancing, music, erotic literature and similar debauched indulgences. The traditional domes and other ornaments associated with Muslim graves are to be condemned; though it is permitted to visit graves as a sign of respect for the dead or as a reminder of the fragility of human life. Prayers are permitted, provided there is no appeal to the dead for intercession with God on behalf of the living. No person, with the possible exception of the Prophet, has a special relationship with God: so all the false mystics, sheikhs of religious orders, so-called saints and Shi'ite imams stand condemned. Even Muhammed, held in unique regard, is constrained by the harsh puritanism of the Wahhabist doctrine. Thus innovation (*bid'ah*) that has led to excessive honouring of the Prophet – for example, overt reverence for Muhammed's birthday – is denounced. It follows that only strict condemnation is merited by such phenomena as the rosary, ornate minarets and decorated graves; and the harsh puritanism necessarily prohibits tobacco, jewels, silk and precious metals used for personal adornment.[7] (We may reflect on the relevance of such Wahhabist puritanism to the conduct and deportment of today's Saudi royals.)

The Wahhabist is expected to obey the ruler or imam, providing the ruler himself follows God's holy law; while the imam is expected to propagate the doctrine in such a fashion that in due course it will embrace all mankind – an agenda that clearly mirrors the imperialism of the Koran. The Wahhabist *mutawi* ('obedience causer'), a recognised official, is entitled to force people to pray, to pay alms (*zakat*), and to fast at the prescribed times; while *jihad*, going far beyond the familiar notion of 'holy war', is expected to signify the continuous crusade deemed necessary for the extension of the faith. This comprehensive interpretation of *jihad*, justifying periodic wars against polytheists, has been taken as explaining the modern Saudi Arabian government's department of 'ordering good and forbidding evil' (*al-amr bi-al-ma'ruf wa-al-nahy 'an al-munkar*).[8] (There are clues here to the puritanical intolerance of Saudi Arabia, albeit underwritten by shameless hypocrisy – see Chapter 1.)

The Wahhabists perceived that many Muslims had fallen away from the strict ethical and spiritual rigour stipulated by the Prophet. Polytheism, a throw-back to pagan times, had become widespread; and, as in pre-Islamic times, the people were again worshipping trees, stones, tombs and the associated buildings. Sacrifices were being made to the *jinn* – food placed before them and in the four corners of the house – in the hope of good fortune; and superstitious oaths, to forces other than God, were commonplace. Men and women claiming the ability to treat the sick would urge animal sacrifices: for example, completely black lambs or the small-eared goats that had been popular as sacrificial items since Semitic antiquity. In this connection Winder (1965) quotes the nineteenth-century Wahhabist chronicler Uthman ibn Abd Allah Ibn Bishr (d. 1873): 'Then the practitioners would say to them, "Do not mention God's name when you sacrifice it; and give the sick person this part of it, and eat from it such and such, and leave that part." And perhaps God would cure the sick person in order to lead them on and to deceive them; or perhaps the time had come for him to be cured. Anyway those practices increased among the people, and much time passed. For this reason they fell into serious things; nor was there among them anyone to forbid those practices or to proclaim to them the approved and the disapproved things.'[9] It was into this lapsed atmosphere that Sheikh Abdul Wahhab came to proclaim what he perceived as the original pure message of Islam. His words pleased the people, 'but they did not forbid what the ignorant did or do away with what the innovators had introduced'.[10]

The new doctrine none the less quickly gained a following; accessible as it was, like any simple fundamentalist appeal. The Wahhabists were the first Arabic-speakers to challenge the Ottoman hegemony; and the new creed soon spread beyond the frontiers of the Arabian peninsula (the Ikhwan al-Muslimun movements in Egypt and elsewhere were inspired by Wahhabist ideals), so helping to inspire various brands of Arab nationalism. It is easy to see why Wahhabism has been depicted as a type of 'second coming' of Islam, a rebirth of the divine creed conveyed by the Prophet: just as Muslims have designated the pre-Islamic period the *Jahiliyah* ('period of ignorance'), so the Wahhabists used the same term to denote the period before their arrival.

It is significant also that the Wahhabist creed was insufficient in isolation to gain a wide following: as with the Prophet, Abdul Wahhab was happy to welcome the persuasive power of the Muslim sword, as wielded by Muhammed ibn Saud. This proved to be a highly effective union. The Wahhabists well knew that recalcitrant tribes were more likely to accept a new Muslim doctrine if they were first reduced to the status of conquered peoples; and Ibn Saud, forever locked in military confrontation with other tribes, was quick to recognise that a merciless and harsh deity would prove a useful ally. It was the union of Wahhab and Saud more than two and a half centuries ago that came to define modern Saudi Arabia in terms of a harsh intolerance managed by a feudal dynasty. Without the House of Saud the Wahhabists might have been no more than a simple Muslim sect; without the Wahhabists there might have been no Saudi ascendancy.

THE SAUDI ASCENDANCY

The 1744 pact between Abdul Wahhab and the House of Saud, an arrangement secured by the marriage of Saud's son Abdul Aziz to a daughter of Wahhab, was destined to shape the course of Arabian history. Diriyah, later to be sacked, became the centre of the new movement, the effective capital of what came to be acknowledged as the First Saudi State. At first the future of the new religio-political pact was uncertain. The Wahhabists (*muwahhidun*, 'Unitarians') quickly won many followers in the towns of Lower Nejd but also stimulated resistance from many of the petty dynasts who saw their own status threatened by the ambitious rulers of an expanding Diriyah. Moreover, the threat was now something more than the familiar rivalry of ancient tribes: the Wahhabist dogma had contributed a potent new element, one that combined a fervent spirituality with fierce military ambition.

Much of the early opposition to Diriyah expansion came from Riyadh (so named since 1726). After typical tribal rivalries, one Diham ibn Dawwas and his brothers were forced to flee Manfuhah and to seek refuge in Riyadh, then ruled by Zayd ibn Musa. When Zayd was killed in 1733 he left as heir a child whose mother was a sister of Diham. Four years later, following the flight of the slave Khumayyis who had seized power, Diham ibn Dawwas declared himself guardian to his sister's child and assumed the reins of power. Under Diham, Riyadh staunchly resisted the encroachments of Diriyah expansion and began its development as an important trading and political centre. Some of the surrounding settlements became enclosed by the fortified city, which contained also the central palace (*qasr*) as the seat of government. When Diham died in 1773 Riyadh was forced to submit to Diriyah hegemony, whereupon the once thriving city lapsed into obscurity until converted into a garrison town in 1820 by the Egyptian occupiers; and, four years later, into the new Saudi capital.

The resistance of Diham to Diriyah expansion was at times ambiguous: it is noted that at first he considered the appeals of Wahhabism and the pressures exerted by Ibn Saud (in 1753 and 1762/63 he called truces, only to break them). Facey (1992) cites the chroniclers who recorded the three dozen clashes between the Diriyah and Riyadh forces between 1746 and 1773, encounters that involved substantial loss of life: through this period there were around 1700 Diriyah and 2300 Riyadh fatalities.[11] As the alliances in the region shifted from year to year, the battle lines were not always clearly drawn: at one time Ibn Saud formed an agreement with Manfahah, one of Riyadh's main rivals, though Diriyah itself sometimes had difficulty in maintaining its alliances as town loyalties shifted through internal factional dispute.

A number of the Nejd towns, fearing Diriyah hegemony, were now moving against the Wahhabist ('Reform') movement. In 1754, when Diham ended the year-long truce, he was enjoying the support of Manfuhah, Tharmida, groups in Thadiq and Huraymila, and sympathetic factions in al-Washm and Sudair.

Significant battles took place near Huraymila (1755), Manfuhah (1756/57) and elsewhere; and in 1758 Diriyah forces staged a successful ambush outside Riyadh, destroying plantations and hastily building a fortified base from which to launch further military operations.[12] It was now clear that the House of Saud, sustained by the pious commitment of the new Islam, was gaining ground. Abdul Aziz repeatedly defeated Riyadh forces in 1762/63 and successfully raided a large caravan, so expropriating wealthy Riyadh merchants. Diham, in the face of these reverses, again agreed a truce, pledged support for Wahhabist teachings, and swore allegiance to the House of Saud. It was not the most propitious time for such concessions: Diriyah itself was now under threat from other groups, notably Hasan ibn Hibatullah of Najran, though after losing several hundred men and suffering a cannon bombardment the town survived.

In 1765 Muhammed ibn Saud died and was succeeded by Abdul Aziz, a desta-bilising circumstance that invited further attacks from Diham (in 1771/72 two of his sons were killed in battle). Now a demoralised Diham resolved to abandon the Riyadh that for so long he had struggled to protect. Abdul Aziz again attacked Riyadh (1773), at a time when morale was so low that concerted resistance was impossible. Ibn Ghannam, quoted by Facey, describes the events of the moment:

> ... panic fell upon Diham ibn Dawwas and terror filled his heart and he lost hope. He intended to evacuate Riyadh ... He gathered together the leading personalities and told them of his plan. They tried to dissuade him but they did not succeed, so they left him and dispersed, and the terror and panic grew ... Abd al-Aziz and the Muslims advanced on Riyadh wanting to destroy it ... their minds made up to besiege the town for days and nights until God should grant them the fulfilment of their hopes ... Diham ibn Dawwas left, fleeing from the town with his sons and bodyguard and most of the people ... about 400 of them perished on the road from exhaustion in the intense heat. The Muslims hastened after them and saved all the weak and the poor with water. But they killed all the strong among the people of error ... Everything in the town ... was plunder from God.[13]

Riyadh had now lost its independence: the bulk of its property had been con-signed to the public treasury of Diriyah; it is likely that its defensive walls were at least partially razed; and the growing prominence of the city had been abolished, albeit temporarily. People still inhabited the site but the political and commercial significance had given way to mundane agricultural activity. The supplanting of Riyadh by Diriyah as an important regional power was one phase in the gradual ascendancy of the House of Saud. Now the authority of the Saudi dynasty could be restored, where it had lapsed, in the towns of Sudair, al-Qasim and elsewhere.

It was inevitable in these circumstances that the burgeoning Saudi ambitions would generate reactions among tribes involved in their own disputes over land and other concerns. For example, the Beni Khaled of al-Hasa, who had invaded

Qasim in 1774, struggled to contain the expansion of the House of Saud. The following year a coalition of tribes (the people of Kharj and Wadi al-Dawasir in alliance with the Najran tribes) tried to resist the advance of Reformist factions, but within a decade most of the recalcitrant groups in the region had submitted their rights to Saudi hegemony. By 1780 Saud, the son of Abdul Aziz and a future ruler of Diriyah, had vanquished the Beni Khaled and the Muntafiq of the Iraq marshes. A few years later al-Hasa had capitulated and military initiatives had been launched against Qatar and Kuwait. In 1793 the Factory of the British East India Company had moved to Kuwait to escape the unsettled conditions around Basra. Between then and 1795 the British helped Kuwait to repel Saudi assaults on the town, a policy that provoked the Saudis into disrupting the East India Company's desert mail. But the British quickly realised the prudence of maintaining good relations with an important rising power in Arabia: Samuel Manesty, the head of the British Factory, despatched John Lewis Reinaud to Diriyah in an effort to improve relations with Abdul Aziz. The policy of Western propitiation of the House of Saud that would last into modern times had begun.[14]

The Sublime Porte in Turkey, increasingly alarmed by the advance of the Reform Movement in various parts of its Arabian territories, sent a military expedition in 1796 under Thuwayni, the Muntafiq chief. The Saudis captured the entire enemy camp, carried off the weapons, and put the soldiers to flight. A second military initiative fared no better: a force directed against Diriyah failed to reach the town and was forced to return to its Iraq base after agreeing a humiliating truce. It was now clear that the waning power of the Ottomans, with the empire still set to run for a further ignominious century, provided the Saudis with fresh opportunities in the Arabian peninsula. Now, after strengthening their position in eastern Arabia, they penetrated Qatar, Oman and the southern Gulf coast. With Hasa, Buraymi and other towns as secure bases the Saudis formed alliances with the seafaring Qawasim and began predations on shipping that provoked British reprisals.

In 1795 a Saudi expedition to Turbah in south-western Nejd added to the concern of the Ottomans, whereupon the Porte urged Ghalib ibn Musaid, the Shareef of Mecca, to discourage Saudi ambitions. Ghalib was ambivalent: while recognising his role in the Ottoman scheme he was forced to acknowledge also the Islamic purity of the Wahhabist movement and the martial valour of the pious Saudis. In 1796, doubtless with many a reservation, he led a military expedition into Nejd, there to be comprehensively defeated with great loss of weapons and equipment. By now the increasingly confident Saudi forces were approaching Najran and the borders of Yemen. In 1798 the Shareef Ghalib suffered a further humiliating rout, when both weapons and large sums of money fell into Saudi hands, whereupon Ghalib appealed to Abdul Aziz for peace. By 1800 Saudi forces were fighting on the Syrian borders and penetrating the Iraqi marshes. Now, under the invitation of a pliant Ghalib, the Wahhabists were making pilgrimages to Mecca with the aim in part of putting the spiritual centre under

Reformist pressure. In March 1802, following further skirmishing inside Iraq, the Saudis laid siege to Kerbala, sacred to the Shi'ites, eventually occupying the city and destroying its traditional shrines. A year later the 82-year-old Abdul Aziz was assassinated in the mosque at Diriyah, probably by a victim of the sack of Kerbala. The successor to Aziz was his son Saud ('the Great'), who came to be known for his simple life-style, his accessibility to the people, and the justice of his government.

In 1803 the Wahhabists conquered Mecca, taking Medina the following year: the treasuries of the two holy cities were plundered, and all the sacred tombs, seen as heretical to the reformers, were destroyed. Now much of the Hejaz had fallen under the sway of the Wahhabist conquerors. In the south of the Arabian peninsula the Yemeni Hamoud, chief of the Abu Areesh, continued to resist the pressures of the new faith; but when Abd al-Hakal of the Beni Aseer, the one-eyed Abu Nookta, launched a massive Wahhabist attack Hamoud sought refuge in flight. Again the pious devotees of the new faith had won a comprehensive victory but were prevented from gaining absolute dominion over Yemen by the stout walls of Mokha. Abu Nookta continued to harass Yemen but failed to gain control over the commerce of the country. In 1809 Hamoud and forty horsemen, dressed as Wahhabist Bedouins, managed to enter Abu Nookta's camp at dawn; there Hamoud slew Abu Nookta and many of his men. Yemen had now been rendered safe from attack.

Saud ruled until his death in 1814, by which time the Arabian empire of Diriyah reached its zenith. But the Saudi victories had not been consolidated: the Shareef Ghalib, with nice political acumen, had managed to steer a course between the demands of his nominal Ottoman overlords and the pressures of the Arab Wahhabists; and with the loss of Mecca and Medina, symbolically and commercially important, the Sublime Porte was resolved to suppress the Reformists once and for all. In 1813, as a final reverse to Saud before his death, Muhammed Ali Pasha restored Mecca and Medina to Ottoman control and made himself master of Hejaz. On 23 October Muhammed Ali was received in Jeddah by his son Tusoon Pasha and Shareef Ghalib, now again well prepared to recognise Ottoman hegemony in the region. But Ghalib's political contortions were at an end: on 12 November he was seized with three of his sons and sent to Constantinople where his copious frauds and extortions were exposed. Ghalib, perhaps fortunate to escape with his life, was sent into exile. Saud was soon to die and Ottoman power was again becoming dominant in the peninsula.

In 1814, with the accession of Abdullah, the son of Saud the Great, the tide of war began to turn in favour of Muhammed Ali, the ruthless governor of Ottoman Egypt. The following year the Saudis were defeated in southern Hejaz, where-upon Muhammed Ali contemplated launching a fresh attack on Yemen. Hamoud was still in control of the sea-coast but on learning that the Ottomans were advancing in the Hejaz he despatched an envoy bearing presents for the Pasha, ensuring him of his readiness to support the Turkish interests. But the Wahhabists were still able to inflict defeats on the Ottoman forces; and there is little doubt that Hamoud, like all the other opportunists in the protracted conflict, was well prepared to support the winning side.

At this time (1814) Sheikh Tami, chief of the Beni Aseer and the successor to Abu Nookta, was one of many local commanders fighting against the Ottoman contingents. In May the Turkish forces were attacked at Konfoda by around 10,000 Arabs led by Tami himself. The Turkish commander fled to the harbour, closely followed by many of his soldiers: the Arabs then pursued many of the refugees into the sea, putting them to the sword close to the guns of their vessels. The Wahhabists were happy to find a rich booty in the Konfoda garrison: Turkish baggage, munitions, guns, many camels and four hundred horses.[15] Tami was later defeated by Muhammed Ali at Tor Castle, a massive fortress built by Abu Nookta: in chains, Tami was delivered to Constantinople, where he was promptly beheaded. Now Ibrahim Pasha was appointed by the Ottomans to extend Turkish power in Arabia, a project that was largely successful. The power of the Wahhabists was broken, Diriyah was conquered, and the Saudi Abdullah was captured. The campaign was marked by 'the most barbarous cruelties, committed in violation ... of the most solemn promises, on some occasions with the object of enriching the leader by the plunder of the very tribes which had contributed to his successes ... to obtain possession of the wealth of his vanquished enemies, or to gratify the insatiable desire to shed human blood...'.[16]

Abdullah, faced with the advance of Ibrahim Pasha and his Egyptian Ottomans, decided to retreat to Diriyah in anticipation of the likely siege. In Durma, en route to Diriyah, the Egyptians had slaughtered everyone over ten years old: the pious defenders of Diriyah knew what to expect if the city were to fall. The anticipated siege lasted from March to September 1818, when, with the fall of Diriyah, the First Saudi State collapsed in ruins. Abdullah was conveyed in humiliation, first to Egypt and then to Istanbul, where he was publicly beheaded; at the same time, many prominent Saudis were exiled, mutilated and executed. The Ottomans had resolved that there would be no further insurrections by the upstart Arab dynasty. Some of the Saudi towns (for example, Hariq and Hilwah, south of Diriyah) struggled to hold out, but their resistance was quickly crushed. In some distant provinces groups of Wahhabists managed to survive unmolested, but for the time being there was no real prospect of an organised national resistance to Ottoman control.

The British in India had welcomed Ibrahim Pasha's siege of Diriyah: if the 'predatory habits' of the Wahhabists could be extirpated from the Arabian peninsula, so much the better for British trade in the region. It was for this reason that Captain George Forster Sadleir, an officer of the British Army in India (HM 47th regiment), was sent from Bombay to consult Ibrahim Pasha in Diriyah. The mission was unsuccessful, though Sadleir gained fame for being the first European to have crossed the Arabian peninsula. Moreover, he left a record of what he found in the erstwhile capital of the First Saudi State: 'The site of Deriah is in a deep ravine north-west of Munfooah, about ten miles distant. It is now in ruins, and the inhabitants who were spared, or escaped from the slaughter, have principally sought shelter here ... Munfooah ... was surrounded with a wall and ditch which the Pacha ordered to be razed. ... Riad is not so well peopled. ... The inhabitants were at that time in a more wretched state than at any prior period since the establishment of the power of the Wahabees. Their walls, the chief security for their property, had been razed ... The year's crop had been consumed by the Turkish force...'.[17]

The failed mission to strike an agreement between the British and Ibrahim Pasha in Arabia ended on a sour note – for seemingly trivial reasons. An elegant sword and a letter of congratulation had been conveyed to Ibrahim Pasha, but there was uncertainty about how he should address the British governor-general of India in the return communication. Ibrahim objected to the normal usage, 'noblest of the noble' (*ashraf al-ashraf*), as having an unwelcome religious connotation; and 'most glorious of the glorious' (*amjad al-amjad*), Sadleir's proposed alternative, was perceived as no improvement. Since no British officer could tolerate anything but the most exalted language in any address to the governor-general, an impasse was reached. Then Ibrahim proposed to offer Sadleir three Arabian horses in return for the gift of the sword (two for governor-general Lord Hastings and one for Sadleir). Alas, the first items that arrived at Sadleir's quarters were three sets of used and shabby 'saddle furniture' – an obvious affront to British dignity. Around such petty details do the plans of great nations founder. Sadleir's mission had taken more than a year, and had accomplished nothing.

The British still had an interest in crushing piratical assaults on their commerce in the region. Thus a large expedition headed by Sir William Grant Keir was launched against the pirate centre of Ras al-Khaimah: a force of nine warships and eighteen transports, with land forces of 1645 Europeans with artillery and 1424 sepoys and 600 Masqati troops, began a siege of the pirate base in preparation for an early assault. On 9 December 1819 the town was stormed, the defenders suffering perhaps a thousand casualties against five British fatalities and fifty-two wounded. Security (*aman*) was granted to the enemy commander, Hasan ibn Rahman, prior to his 'confinement' and subsequent release.

Other 'Pirate Coast' towns were similarly attacked; until, on 8 January 1820, the British drew up a 'General Treaty of Peace' to discourage plunder and piracy on the seas. Local chiefs were encouraged to sign; by this device, policed by a substantial British naval force off the coasts of Arabia, the incidence of 'piracies' quickly diminished. The British had begun their calculated process of treaty-making to achieve a dominant position in the Persian Gulf. Wahhabist efforts to exploit the possibilities offered by British trade had been much reduced; but this alone did little to impede the robust Saudi pursuit of commercial and strategic advantage.

In 1819 Ibrahim Pasha had left Nejd in a state of ruin: many towns were razed and agriculture had been devastated. Prominent Saudis had been exiled or executed, with only a severely depleted House of Saud left to pick up the pieces. The First Saudi State, based on Diriyah, had come to an end, but this was far from the end of Saudi ambitions. In the autumn of 1819 Muhammed ibn Mushari ibn Muammar, a scion of the family that had ruled the Nejd town of Uyainah in pre-Wahhabist days, made efforts to revive Diriyah and to gain control of the whole of Nejd. His role was ambiguous and short-lived. Related to the House of Saud by marriage, he was able to attract local support, but there were suspicions that he also enjoyed the approval of the Egyptians and had been nominated by Ibrahim Pasha to rule Nejd as a puppet governor. Ibn Muammar's early efforts to rebuild Diriyah, a residual symbol of Saudi ambition, increased his popularity, particularly among the refugees and the Saudis who had escaped the Egyptian onslaught.

There were other contenders for power. Thus Majid ibn Urair of the Benu Khaled, who had established a local power base, was encouraged by groups opposed to ibn Muammar's expansion in Nejd to invade the interior. Skirmishing around Riyadh was inconclusive, a peace was arranged, and when some of Majid's troops mutinied he was forced to return to Hasa where his family continued to reign until 1830. The threat to ibn Muammar had been removed, and he continued to gain support – not least from Turki ibn Abdullah ibn Muhammed ibn Saud, a cousin of Saud the Grèat and a man destined to lay the basis of the Second Saudi State at Riyadh. In 1820 Turki's brother Zaid and ibn Muammar's son Mushari fought on the same side in Huraymila to suppress a revolt against Muammar's burgeoning regime. Then another contender for power, Mushari ibn Saud ibn Abd al-Aziz, marched on Diriyah bearing the important asset of substantial foodstuffs. Ibn Muammar, reluctant to fight a member of the House of Saud, recognised him as imam and relinquished many of his own powers. Now, with a Saudi in control of Diriyah, many refugees returned home to what had been the capital of the First Saudi State. Then it emerged that Muammar's seeming compliance had been no more than a ruse. After soliciting the support of local groups (the Hamad family in Huraymila, Faisal al-Dawish and others), he launched a sudden attack on Diriyah, capturing Mushari, and then marched to Riyadh, putting Turki and other members of the Saudi family to flight. Then yet again the pendulum swung.

The Egyptians had watched the unfolding events with mounting alarm. Muhammed Ali's plan of indirect rule had failed, and now there was the renewed prospect of a Saudi resurgence. A renewed occupation of Nejd was ordered, which began with the arrival in Unaizah of a force led by Abush Agha who quickly subjugated the entire district of al-Qasim. Muammar promptly assured the Egyptians of his support, whereupon they confirmed him as the local ruler and encouraged Turki to lead a force against Diriyah where he managed to take Muammar prisoner. Turki, enjoying growing local support, then marched on Riyadh to demand Mushari's freedom. When this was denied him Turki ordered the execution of Muammar and his son, and then began preparations for the inevitable siege by the Egyptians. After three or four days the besieged forces, facing overwhelming odds, requested *aman*, a guarantee of safety in exchange for surrender. Abush agreed but failed to stop Turki making good his escape. The new commander of the Egyptians, Hussain Bey, despite the *aman*, ordered the killing of many of the defenders; and then began the systematic destruction of the Nejd commercial, political and intellectual life. Again a comprehensive attempt would be made to prevent a national resurgence against Ottoman control. Thus in 1821 Diriyah, now partly rebuilt, was razed again, while a reign of terror spread throughout the region: plunder and killings were encouraged, palms were destroyed, and two more garrisons were established (at Unaizah and Riyadh). Mushari and Omar ibn Abd al-Aziz, two who might have led a Saudi revival, were dead; Turki ibn Abd Allah was now the only surviving member of the House of Saud with a chance of renewing the fortunes of the royal family.

The oppression of Nejd continued under Hussain Bey. On one occasion he instructed those inhabitants of Diriyah who wanted land to assemble near his quarters, where some 230 of the applicants were slaughtered by waiting troops; all the property of these civilians, including that of the women and children, was confiscated by the troops. At the same time military contingents sent out to the main population centres imposed heavy taxes, demanded the sacrifice of women's jewelry, imposed arbitrary arrests and imprisonments, carried out torture and mutilation, and ordered widespread killings. When villagers fled to the desert the soldiers plundered their homes before destroying them. A nephew of Abdul Wahhab was jailed in Huraymila, while Hussain Bey's judge (*qadi*) plundered his library, burning those books that he could not carry away. When Hussain Bey was ordered back to Egypt he first collected hostages from all the main towns and imprisoned them in a Tharmida fortress as a calculated insurance for his successor. At the same time (1821) the scourge of cholera – doubtless conveyed by invading troops – reached Nejd for the first time.[18]

The loosening of Egyptian control led to some relief, and to widespread anarchy. The chronicler ibn Bishr records that the devil was in control and ordered 'cursing, revelling, whoring, darkness, murder and all sins and enmities'. Conflicts, perhaps long suppressed, broke out in the towns; feuds began again; and the Bedouins resumed their tribal skirmishes and their raids on the urban settlers. Again many of the prominent men of the region were killed.

In 1822 Hasan Bey abu Zahir, Hussain Bey's successor, arrived in Nejd and soon began to establish a semblance of order – without resort to cruelty. In a letter to the Tharmida garrison he ordered the release of the hostages imprisoned by Hussain, and declared in a public proclamation: 'I have come to fight the Bedouins so that they will pay their taxes, and I will return to the settled people what the Bedouins have wrongfully taken. I want nothing except the taxes.'[19] But the business of tax gathering remained problematic. Military units sent to collect the specified revenues were frequently attacked; for example, a detachment led by Ibrahim Kashif was intercepted by Subai tribesmen and suffered 300 fatalities, with Kashif himself killed in the encounter. Hasan Bey attempted to impose harsher tactics, demanding back taxes and punishing some recalcitrant Bedouins; but resistance was mounting and in one pitched battle some sixty Arabs were killed. Now the degree of order established by Hasan was beginning to melt away. The Ottomans remained relatively secure behind their fortress walls – in such principal towns as Buraidah, Rass, Shaqra, Unaizah, Tharmida and Riyadh – but as soon as they ventured beyond the fortifications into unfamiliar territory the occupying forces suffered heavy losses. The scene was set for a further Saudi revival: Wahhabism remained deeply entrenched among the people of Nejd, and the House of Saud was widely acknowledged as the royal family destined to bring the true Word of God to Arabia.

Now Turki ibn Abd Allah ibn Muhammed ibn Saud was able to gather growing support from many of the groups that had resolutely resisted the Turkish occupation. In 1823 he laid siege to Riyadh, but to no avail, while an Egyptian counter-siege of Arqah was equally unsuccessful. The temporary impasse was brought to a conclusion when the Egyptians found themselves forced to evacuate much of northern Nejd, thus increasing the isolation of the Riyadh garrison. Turki quickly gained the allegiance of such towns as Sudair, Washm, Huraymila and Manfuhah, where 600 Egyptian troops had been stationed under Abu Ali al-Bahluli al-Maghribi; and by August 1824 the Saudi forces were again in a position to besiege Riyadh. This time Turki was successful: he took command of Riyadh under the terms of an agreement that all the Egyptian troops would be granted safe conduct out of Nejd. Turki now resolved to establish Riyadh as the capital of the new Saudi state, rather than to rebuild the ruined Diriyah. From 1824 to the present day, Riyadh has remained the capital of the Saudi nation.

Riyadh, despite siege and other conflict, had escaped the comprehensive ruin that had afflicted many of the other Arabian towns. Turki was able to take over the defensive walls and *qasr*, much in the state they had been in the time of Diham ibn Dawwas; it is likely that renovation, rather than comprehensive rebuilding, was required. At the same time Turki resolved on the construction of a new Great Mosque, an essential requirement if Riyadh were to be properly viewed as the capital of the Second Saudi State. Another phase had begun in the long course of the Saudi ascendancy (see Table 4.1).

In 1825 Turki organised his forces for an attack on the recalcitrant region of Kharj, south of Riyadh. The small town of Najan was quickly overcome but the more substantial Dilam centre proved to be a greater obstacle. Dilam's defenders, led by Zuqm ibn Zamil, marched north to confront Turki but were powerless against the superior Saudi forces. After several encounters, Zuqm was forced to flee back to Dilam, soon to be besieged by Turki until peace terms were agreed. Zuqm's supporters were granted their lives and their property, while Zuqm himself was made captive and taken to Riyadh. Other towns in Kharj quickly fell under Turki's control, so facilitating his expansion of Saudi power. Salamiyah and Yamamah, having offered little or no resistance to the Saudi advance, were

Table 4.1   Some main events in the Saudi ascendancy

1745	Pact between Abdul Wahhab and the House of Saud.
1745–1818	First Saudi State.
1746–73	Thirty-five recorded military clashes between Riyadh and Diriyah.
1753	Truce between Riyadh and Diriyah.
1762–3	Truce between Riyadh and Diriyah.
1773	Death of Diham ibn Dawwas, opponent of Saudi expansion.
1803	Abdul Aziz ibn Muhammed ibn Saud assassinated.
1811	Muhammed Ali, Ottoman governor of Egypt, prepares reconquest of Hejaz.
1814	Death of Saud the Great, leading to accession of Abdullah ibn Saud.
1815	Defeat of Saudis in southern Hejaz.
1816	Ibrahim Pasha arrives in Hejaz.
1818	Destruction of Diriyah, Saudi capital, leading to end of the First Saudi State.
1820	Turki ibn Abd Allah ibn Muhammed ibn Saud appointed as governor of Diriyah.
1821	Hussain Bey, Ottoman commander, destroys partially rebuilt Diriyah.
1822	Hasan Bey abu Zahir, Hussain's successor, arrives in Nejd.
1824	Victorious Turki, after regrouping Saudi forces, establishes Riyadh as Saudi capital, and so starts the Second Saudi State.
1834	Turki assassinated, leading to accession of his son Faisal. Rashid rewarded by Faisal for alliance against dissident Saudis.
1836	Muhammed Ali launches fresh invasion of Hejaz.
1837	Egyptians retake Riyadh; in July Faisal begins siege.
1838–42	Khaled ibn Saud rules Riyadh as quisling of Egypt.
1841	Abdullah ibn Thunayyan, great-great-grandson of founder of House of Saud, organises revolt.
1843	Faisal regains control of Riyadh: ibn Thunayyan dies in prison.
1843–65	Faisal reigns in Riyadh: 'golden age' of the Second Saudi State; rivalry between sons Abdullah and Saud erupts into open; Abdullah becomes Imam.
1871	Saud takes power in Riyadh.
1874	Abdullah seizes power from Saud.
1874–84	Abdullah rules in Riyadh.
1876	Birth of Ibn Saud (Abdul Aziz ibn Abdul Rahman).

Table 4.1   (continued)

1887	Saudis forced to accept Rashidi governor of Riyadh.
1889	Saudis and Rashidis meet to discuss peace agreement.
1891	The child Ibn Saud, allegedly travelling in a saddlebag, leaves Riyadh for exile.
1899	Sheikh Mubarak of Kuwait concludes secret deals with Britain.
1901	Mubarak, in alliance with Saudis, launches attacks on Rashidi territory.
1902	Ibn Saud launches successful attack on Riyadh.
1903–4	Ibn Saud extends military and political power.
1904	Ibn Saud forces clash with combined Turkish–Rashidi contingents.
1913	Saudi forces march on Hofuf and disarm Turkish garrison, leading to expansion of Saudi State to the Gulf.
1916	Ibn Saud defeats the Ajman tribesmen with British support; the Hashemite Hussain ibn Ali proclaims the Arab Revolt against the Turks and in support of the British.
1922	Britain welcomes prospect of Saudi victory in contest with the Hashemites for control of Hejaz.
1924	Ibn Saud enters Mecca and assumes custodianship of the Holy Mosques; the long Hashemite custodianship is at an end.
1925	British, regarding Ali as finished in Hejaz, negotiate with Saudis; on Christmas Day the Nejd–Hejaz conflict is declared over, and Ibn Saud is proclaimed King of Hejaz and Sultan of Nejd; quickly receives international recognition.
1928	Ibn Saud given pledge of support by Ikhwan leaders against Faisal ibn Duwish; House of Saud continues to consolidate power.
1932	Ibn Saud suppresses revolt in Hejaz; on 23 September he proclaims the Kingdom of Saudi Arabia.

soon paying homage to the fresh authority in the region; and now Turki was able to organise under his control the central districts of Nejd (that is, Arid, Kharj, Hautah, Mahmal, Sudair, Aflaj and Washm). Some districts (for example, Qasim, Jabal Shammar and other provinces) had still not been brought entirely within the Saudi fold, and it is likely that Turki still paid a prudent tribute to the Ottoman authorities; but now the Wahhabists of Nejd were once more under the control of a worthy Saudi imam.

The earlier refugees, now heartened by the turn of events, were encouraged to return home. Among them was Mushari ibn Abd al-Rahman ibn Mushari ibn Saud, later to plan the assassination of Imam Turki. Another was the theologian Sheikh Abd al-Rahman ibn Hasan ibn Muhammed ibn Abdul al-Wahhab, described by the authority W.G. Palgrave, who visited Riyadh in 1862, as the 'court chaplain'.[20] With Abdul Rahman promptly made *qadi* of Riyadh, other appointments served to strengthen the Saudi grip on power. Thus Omar ibn Muhammed ibn Ufaisan was made emir of Kharj; Ahmad ibn Nasir ibn Sani treasurer of Sudair; and Yahya ibn Sari emir of Mahmal.

Turki, having secured the bulk of Nejd, turned next to al-Hasa. In 1830 a heavy defeat of a Beni Khaled coalition crushed the Beni Khaled rule in Hasa; while the Riyadh authorities under Turki now felt equipped to confront Bahrain, Oman and the Trucial Coast. Three years later the Sultan of Oman was again paying tribute to Riyadh, as were many other freshly conquered tribes. Thus the Dawasir tribesmen at Qarain, close to Shaqra, offered to pay two years' back taxes; and Turki's assigned representatives had little problem collecting taxes from the tribes of Subai, Suhul, Ujman, Qahtan and Mutair. Turki was now swelling the Riyadh treasury, consolidating his own political position, and building a reputation as a great Saudi ruler. He appointed judges, theologians and other officials; was much concerned with the support of widows and orphans; and duly attended the Koran study sessions, supervised outside the *qasr* by the *qadi* Sheikh Abdul Rahman. Turki was regarded as conciliatory in victory, though demanding the highest standards of equity, fair-dealing and commitment to agreements. He interpreted his devotion to Islam as a pious commitment to the good of the people. Thus in a famous address he emphasised man's dependence on God to highlight the sin of oppressing the citizens. Turki's rule was reportedly just but stern: the people could appeal directly to him but wrong-doers were promptly sent into exile. He espoused the doctrine – somewhat eccentric in view of the history of Al-Saud – that the imam held power by virtue of Islam and not by the power of the sword. Soon Turki was to learn that naked force could bring to an end the most pious of regimes.

Already Turki had been forced to confront a range of problems. In the early 1820s the destruction of agriculture had caused serious food shortages with the corresponding escalation of prices; in 1826/27 a drought added to the regime's difficulties. In 1828 there was a further outbreak of cholera, first recorded in Nejd in 1821; now a local eruption of the disease in Washm grew into a major epidemic that reached its peak in 1832. The much-quoted chronicler ibn Bishr recorded the gravity of the new affliction:

In this year [1832] there occurred the great plague which spread all over Iraq ... and Basra and Zubair and Kuwait and the surrounding areas. This was not like the previous plague ... instead this was a very infectious illness which we pray to God to deliver us from. Many died as a result and whole tribes and families died out. Houses were emptied of their inhabitants. If the disease entered a house, it would not leave while an eye remained moving. The corpses of the people remained in the houses with no-one to bury them ... Towns stank from the decaying bodies. Animals wandered around the towns with no-one to feed them or water them, until most of them died. Some of the children died from thirst or hunger. Many of them threw themselves into the mosques because their families, if they felt the pain, drove them into the mosques hoping that someone would come to save them.

Thus the towns were left empty and desolate. But then the epidemic died out and the survivors moved back into the towns to defend them against the looters from such low-caste tribes as the Sulabah and the Hutaim who, unlike most of the other nomadic Arabian groups, did not graze but functioned as the tinkers, carpenters, trackers and scavengers of the desert.[21]

Turki was facing also the characteristic difficulties of imperial ambition: many internal groups continued to resent Saudi hegemony, and formerly secure alliances were coming under stress. In 1833 Abd Allah ibn Ahmad of Bahrain had abandoned his allegiance with Riyadh and began to make hostile moves against the Saudis. With the ending of a great Bedouin war around Murabba, in which Turki did not intervene, he addressed the Bahrain question by deploying a Wahhabist force led by his son Faisal. The Amair, stimulated to revolt by Bahrain, were quickly routed, though fighting elsewhere continued for some time. In 1834, while Faisal was still engaged in military operations in the eastern regions of the peninsula, the Imam Turki was assassinated by followers of Mushari ibn Abdul al-Rahman, who now ruled in his place. Turki had been killed as he left the Great Mosque after prayer, exiting via a special door that he used unseen by his people. He had been deep in thought as he read a letter, not noticing a man who pulled out a pistol and shot him. An earlier revolt by Mushari (1830/31) had come to nothing: Turki had forgiven him and even provided the would-be usurper with a new dwelling in Riyadh. Now, his uncle assassinated, Mushari appeared in public, threatened the population with reprisals, took command of the *qasr* and the treasury, distributed gifts to win support, and demanded that the people swear allegiance to their new imam.

Faisal ibn Turki was now determined to avenge his father's death and to claim his rightful position at the head of the Saudi state. In Hufuf he laid his plans and demanded support, whereupon he was promptly proclaimed the legitimate imam by many notables, including Abd Allah ibn Ali ibn Rashid of Jabal Shammar; Abd al-Aziz ibn Muhammed ibn Abd Allah ibn Hasan, governor of Buraidah; Turki al-Hazzani, emir of Hariq; Hamad ibn Yahya ibn Ghaihab; and Omar ibn Muhammed ibn Ufaisan, emir of Hasa. On 28 May 1834 Faisal's forces moved stealthily from Hasa and infiltrated Riyadh, with the help of the people, to occupy various buildings opposite the *qasr*. The usurper Mushari, taken by surprise, ensconced himself in the citadel with about 140 men and plenty of supplies; but not all the defenders were loyal. Some let down ropes to assist the entry of Faisal's men into the *qasr*, so ensuring the success of the siege. Mushari's forces were soon overwhelmed, with the chroniclers recording the valiant efforts of a slave of immense strength and great courage who fought long to protect his master. The unnamed slave was eventually killed by the sword; and Mushari himself, now severely wounded and unable to fight, was found lying in a dark room. Faisal entered the citadel and was told that Mushari was now seeking refuge in the mosque. There Faisal declared to him: 'You betrayed and murdered a patriarch and imam of the Muslims without any right. Now the law requires your death.' Mushari was taken from the mosque and killed. His reign, fragile from the start, had lasted a mere forty days.

Faisal moved swiftly to consolidate Saudi rule over the districts, inviting first the *qadis* to Riyadh and then the emirs, governors and Bedouin chiefs. And again the tax gatherers were sent out into the desert. Now the new Saudi regime was being forced to confront not only the destabilising effects of the assassination but also a resurgence of Ottoman ambitions. Muhammed Ali was planning to include Nejd in an Egyptian empire embracing Hejaz, Syria, Iraq and the rest of the Arabian lands. Thus in 1836 an Egyptian demand for taxes and allegiance arrived in Riyadh; when Faisal, reluctant to risk yet another Egyptian intervention, equivocated, Muhammed Ali set about organising a new invasion. Now he could rely upon Khaled ibn Saud, a son of Saud the Great, who was well prepared to rule as an Egyptian puppet. The Egyptian strategy worked. Faisal's mobilisation against the new threat was unconvincing; in Riyadh the supporters of Khaled managed to occupy the *qasr*; and Faisal was driven to desperate measures of bribery to maintain support. Faisal regained the *qasr*, only to abandon it yet again and flee to Hufuf as the Egyptians approached the Saudi capital. Again Riyadh was relinquished to foreign control, with the puppet Khaled set to rule for four years (1838–42). And yet again the pendulum swung. Khaled and his successor Abdullah ibn Thunayyan proved increasingly unpopular, paving the way for Faisal's return to power in 1843.

In 1838 Faisal had been captured by Khurshid Pasha and imprisoned in Egypt, where he was forced to languish until escape could be accomplished. It has been suggested that Muhammed Ali's grandson, Abbas Pasha, helped to arrange the escape because he himself had dreams of empire and believed that the Arabians would make worthy partners in such an enterprise. In the event Faisal, his brother Jalwi, his son Abd Allah and a cousin Abd Allah ibn Ibrahim lowered themselves some seventy cubits from their prison to the ground, where mounts were waiting. The daring escape was seemingly disguised from Ibrahim Pasha for two days and the search party, with Abbas a member, accomplished nothing. Faisal then journeyed from Cairo to Arabia, and had little difficulty winning support away from Ibn Thunayyan, then nominally in control of the Saudi state. Manfuhah welcomed Faisal and he then began negotiations with his surviving supporters in Riyadh, where Ibn Thunayyan was soon forced to endure a 20-day siege. Then he struggled to escape but was intercepted, to die in a Riyadh prison. Faisal, after a six-year absence, was acknowledged as the legitimate imam.

Faisal now began his second reign (1843–65), widely regarded as the golden age of the Second Saudi State. His rival, Ibn Thunayyan, had been killed by his jailors seeking vengeance for the deaths of relatives; and Faisal was free to consolidate his power and to introduce social reform on a scale not seen since the time of Saud the Great. Torrential rain was now ending the long drought, and so seemingly signalling divine approval of the new regime. Ibn Bishr records that the rains also brought devastation: 'God ordered the sky to open ... there was a flood which filled the wadis, and the towns were destroyed ... The water came into the middle of the houses and even flowed into the Friday Mosque, and more than a third of it collapsed.' But such catastrophic events did nothing to impede the substantial social advance that characterised Faisal's second period of rule. Harry St John Bridger Philby (1885–1960), chief of the British political mission to central Arabia (1917/18), commented that it was in Faisal's reign that 'must be sought the real beginnings of the modern Wahhabi state'. Faisal was now ruling a territory 'considerably smaller in extent than that of his great ancestors, but perhaps more compact and better woven together on the loom of Wahhabism ... The Arabia of Faisal was Wahhabi, in a sense unknown to the heyday of the Wahhabi empire; and Faisal's reign was one of consolidation and progress in education and other acts of peace ...'. It was an 'irony of fate', noted by Philby, that this significant reign should lead up to 'a final tragedy of dynastic dissension'.[22]

The growing stability under Faisal did not prevent sectional ambition. Many of the tribes were still restless under Saudi rule; there were foreign pressures from the Egyptians, the Turks (and their surrogate Shareef of Mecca), the British and others; and it was during Faisal's reign that the Rashid dynasty of Hail achieved a degree of independence that increasingly threatened Saudi hegemony in the region. The shareefs of Mecca, resenting Saudi power, constantly encouraged the Rashids to cultivate their independence at the expense of Riyadh; and soon after the deaths of Faisal and Talal, Ibn Rashid's son and successor, the tribal hostilities grew as Hail began to eclipse Riyadh in political importance and reputation. Twenty-five years after the death of Faisal, the Second Saudi State ceased to exist.

Colonel Louis Pelly, Britain's envoy to Faisal in 1865, describes his impressions of the increasingly infirm imam. All the parties, he noted, admitted that the Emir Faisal ibn Saud was 'a just and stern ruler who had been unprecedentedly successful in curbing the predatory habits of his tribes; and who was desirous of inculcating among them more settled habits, and of turning their minds toward agriculture and trade'. No-one, Pelly observed, seemed to like Faisal, 'but all seemed to admire him, and he was spoken of with a sort of dread in which respect and hatred were curiously mixed'.[23] At his first meeting Pelly found the imam seated on a small carpet, his back supported by a cushion. Faisal, quite blind, rose with difficulty and requested Pelly to sit by him on the carpet: '... his face was remarkable, with regular features, placid, stern, self-possessed, resigned ... He was dignified, almost gentle; yet you felt that he could be remorselessly cruel.' Pelly arrived for a second audience before Faisal was

ready, and when he appeared he was supported by two female slaves: 'On crossing the threshold two male slaves received him from the females, keeping one on
either side and so guiding him to his seat. His welcome today was extremely
cordial.'[24] In early 1865 Faisal became paralysed, in addition to his blindness
and general infirmity; in June the eldest son, Abdul Allah, became the *de facto*
Saudi ruler; and in December Faisal ibn Saud, after clinging tenaciously to life
over many months, finally died. His two reigns have been judged as giving
'form and coherence to the [Saudi] dynasty from the time of Muhammed Ali's
invasion of Arabia until the present [20th] century when Faisal's grandson
Abdul al-Aziz, King Ibn Saud, regained what Faisal's sons were destined to lose
– and much more'.[25] Faisal had judged the limits of his power, and so worked to
consolidate a more compact Saudi state. It is arguable that, though the fortunes
of Al-Saud would again ebb in the decades that followed, Faisal had laid some
of the foundation stones for the Saudi Arabia that would emerge as a coherent
state in the twentieth century.

The death of Faisal generated a further period of turmoil and disorder.
Tensions between Faisal's two eldest sons, Abdullah and Saud, created an atmosphere of instability and uncertainty. Little attention was now being paid to the
supra-tribal ideals that had characterised the earlier Saudi states at their heights;
and the resulting factional disputes impinged heavily on the lives of the people.
Abdullah, the rightful heir, became imam and to mark his accession began to
build a new palace fortress, known as the Masmak, in Riyadh. The Masmak,
restored in modern times under the direction of the Department of Antiquities and
Museums, has survived as the only major building of the old city. But the building of a new fortress did little to enable Abdullah to resist court intrigues. In
1867/68 Abdullah took action to contain the Ulman faction and the Wadi al-
Dawasir settlements; he supported Qatar against pressure from Bahrain and Abu
Dhabi; and in 1868 struggled to enforce Oman's tributary relationship with
Riyadh. At the same time Saud contrived to enlist these and other potential
enemies of the Saudi state in alliance against his brother. In 1871 Abdullah was
ejected from Riyadh and Saud took power. The deteriorating state of affairs is
summarised by the historian Ibn Isa: 'The bond of authority was loosened; dis-
orders increased; famine and high costs grew worse; people ate the putrid bodies
of donkeys; many died of hunger, and the people were largely given over to
famine, hunger, trials, plunder, killing, dissension, and rapidly stalking death.'[26]

Saud entered Riyadh with Bedouin troops, Ujman tribesmen, who began an
orgy of looting and plundering. The town of Jubaylah was destroyed, its palm
trees cut down and many of its people killed. Ibn Isa notes that Saud scattered the
'people among the towns of al-Arid, so that no inhabitant was left in Jubaylah';
while another authority, Hamad al-Jasir, confirms Saud's plunder of the town,
including the destruction of palm trees and houses. Saud, not content with the
capture of Riyadh, pursued Abdullah until, towards the end of July 1871, he
defeated him with a Bedouin force at Barrah, 50 miles north-west of Riyadh.

to shape – for good or ill – the later history of the Arabian peninsula: a baby, Abdul Aziz, soon to be known to the world as Ibn Saud, was born to Abdul al-Rahman ibn Faisal.

The death of Imam Saud in 1875 led to another period of family feud. Abdul Rahman, Faisal's fourth son, immediately declared his accession against the interests of his brothers Abdullah and Muhammed. However, when Saud's sons combined in stalwart opposition and murdered one of his principal supporters, Fahd ibn Sunaytan, in the mosque at Riyadh, Abdul Rahman decided that there were larger goals than personal ambition. He joined his brothers Abdullah and Muhammed; it was agreed that Abdullah should again take power; and Saud's sons were forced to seek refuge in their family stronghold in Kharj. There they lived more or less securely, feeling strong enough in 1878 to instigate a revolt against the Turks in the Eastern Provinces, occupying Dammam and laying siege to the Turkish garrison at Qatif (the siege 'owed its relief, primarily to the appearance of Her Majesty's ship *Vulture* cruising against pirates'[27]). Now Abdullah had been recognised as imam for the third time; 'it was', noted Philby, 'the eighth change in the supreme authority that Riyadh had witnessed since the death of Faisal only eleven years before'. And this was not an end to the question of the succession. In 1887 the sons of Saud travelled from Kharj to lay siege to Riyadh, whereupon Abdullah, taken prisoner, appealed to Ibn Rashid for help. This was the development that brought an end to the Second Saudi State: Ibn Rashid had amassed a large army to besiege Riyadh; the sons of Saud were compelled to return to Kharj; Abdullah was taken to Hail; and the Rashidi governor Salim ibn Subhan was installed in Riyadh.

The sons of Saud, nominally confined to Kharj, then began plotting against Salim, who thereby resolved to end this threat once and for all. In August 1888 he and 35 men descended on Kharj: Abdul Allah was killed in the open, Muhammed was caught after a robust defence, Said was caught trying to escape to a near-by Bedouin camp, and only Abdul Aziz – on a mission to the Ujman – managed to escape. Muhammed ibn Rashid, shocked by this turn of events, swore that he had not ordered it. Even though the action had strengthened Rashid's hold on Nejd, Salim was dismissed from the governorship of Riyadh and replaced with Fahhad ibn Uwaid ibn Rukhaiyis. Now there was no significant threat to Rashid's control of Riyadh, and in consequence he could afford to be magnanimous. Early in 1889, after Abdul Rahman had visited his ailing brother Abdullah, the 'imam' requested that he be allowed to return to Riyadh. Ibn Rashid granted permission, even referring to Abdullah as the 'governor of Riyadh', and supplied him with horsemen and a suitable entourage. Ibn Rashid was risking little. Abdullah, increasingly ill from dropsy, finally reached his former capital; three days later, on 27 November 1889, he died. Abdul Rahman, the youngest of Faisal's sons, acceded to the headship of the family and was confirmed as governor by Ibn Rashid. At the same time Salim ibn Subhan had been allowed back to the capital as the Rashidi garrison commander.

Abdullah managed to escape, taking refuge in Ruwaidah, and then gained suppo
from fresh Ottoman efforts to increase Turkish influence in the region.

The Ottomans invaded the Eastern Region, occupying Qatif and Hufuf, on the
pretext of helping Abdullah against Saud, whereupon Abdullah formed a pragmatic alliance with Ottoman supporters in Hasa. He also took comfort from the
plight of Saud, now being ejected from Riyadh under pressure from Abdullah ibn
Turki, brother of the late Faisal. Saud then sought refuge in Dilam in the Kharj
district, and made a desperate attempt to regain his position in Hasa despite the
Turkish presence. At the same time Abdullah was growing suspicious of Ottoman
intentions, sensing that he was being restrained in Hufuf. In a bid to escape the
stifling Ottoman constraints, he managed to flee Hufuf and reach Riyadh where
he was welcomed by a city now racked by famine. Abdullah struggled against his
brother for two years but accomplished nothing: after reverses at Dilum and then
at Durma and Huraymila in 1872/73 he faced a further disastrous confrontation
with Saud at Jizah, whereupon Saud entered Riyadh for the second time and
declared himself imam. But Saud's troubles were far from over. In 1873 he suffered a serious defeat in confrontation with the Utaybah tribesmen, perhaps in
agreement with Abdullah, who abandoned him in the midst of a battle.

These events served to undermine Saud's will to continue the struggle. He had
emphasised the importance of tribal loyalties, against the wider perspective of the
Unitarian philosophy urging a religio-political ideal that transcended traditional
tribal loyalties; and had then fallen victim to inter-tribal tensions. Saud then
retired to the Riyadh citadel where, seriously wounded, he spent most of the rest
of his life. In January 1875 he died of smallpox.

Saud had reduced Nejd to instability and retrogression. Unable to rely on the
loyalty of local leaders he had increasingly resorted to nepotism as a means of
retaining power. Under the weakened central control the various districts developed their own autonomy; for example, Qasim and Jabal Shammar were no
longer effective parts of the Saudi state; in the early days of Saud's rule Bandar
ibn Rashid of Hail had sent twenty mares to Riyadh to signal his loyalty, but no
gesture of significance had followed that early gift. And other events were conspiring to weaken further the ebbing power of the Saudi state. The opening of the
Suez Canal in 1869 had made it easier for the Ottomans to extend their power,
and soon the Wahhabist strongholds in the west were again lost to Ottoman pressure. Under Saud the Saudi state had become weak and fragmented, no longer
sustained by the national ideal and with no obvious strategy to achieve and consolidate a supra-tribal polity. The residual Saudi state now encompassed little
more than the main Nejd districts; and even here there were constant tensions and
divisions. The death of Saud, after a further futile attempt to reassert Saudi
authority, left much of Nejd in chaos and dissolution. The Ottomans were making
further encroachments and were destined to remain in the Eastern Region unti
1913, and then it would be political forces far broader than mere Arab ambitic
that would end Ottoman power for ever. But in 1876 there occurred an event

In July 1890 Abdul Rahman, after a period of seeming acquiescence under Rashidi rule, staged an abortive revolt in Riyadh. Salim and the rest of the garrison were attacked and overwhelmed, though Abdul Rahman spared Salim's life in consideration for members of the Saudi family ensconced in Hail. Ibn Rashid responded promptly, mobilising a force to confront Abdul Rahman, now isolated by the defection of some factions already resentful of the growing Rashidi hegemony in the region. The siege of Riyadh lasted a month, after which Ibn Rashid called for negotiations. Muhammed ibn Faisal went out from Riyadh to begin talks with the Rashidis; he was accompanied by Abdul Rahman's ten-year-old son, Abdul Aziz, appearing for the first time in the affairs of the House of Saud. The negotiations yielded substantial agreement: Abdul Rahman was allowed to continue his governorship over Riyadh (and over Kharj, Aflaj and Mahmal), Salim and the other captured Rashidis were released, and Ibn Rashid released the imprisoned members of the Saudi family. Muhammed ibn Rashid himself then returned to Hail, after which it was possible to represent the outcome as a victory for Abdul Rahman. Ibn Rashid's power had not been compromised, but he was soon to face another serious threat to his authority.

There were still simmering resentments at the prospect of an expanding Rashidi hegemony. In December 1890 the Qasimi tribes, who had considered supporting Abdul Rahman against Ibn Rashid, began to mobilise. It was not long before opposing Arab armies were massed on the plain of Mulaidah, a twelve-mile strip of land west of Buraidah. At the beginning of the battle, which lasted a month or more, it seemed that the Qasimi alliance would triumph; at one stage Ibn Rashid was forced to retreat to his base camp, but then resolved on a classic military tactic. In January 1891 he feigned retreat while organising for a surprise offensive. As part of the plan Ibn Rashid set fire to bundles of brush tied to camels, thereby stampeding several thousand of the animals towards the enemy lines: the Qasimi army lost many men, thousands of casualties including perhaps 1200 killed, among them many leading figures. Some of the survivors fled as far as Kuwait, Iraq and Syria. Abdul Rahman, preparing to support his Qasimi allies, was devastated by the news from Mulaidah; now at a loss he and several members of his family headed back into the desert. The battle of Mulaidah was, as Philby noted, 'the last twitch of the dying Wahhabi state'. Again, however, this was far from the end of Saudi and Wahhabist ambitions.

After Mulaidah, Abdul Rahman managed to rally his forces, albeit briefly, and to retake Kharj and Riyadh; but Ibn Rashid promptly sent forces to defeat the Saudis at Huraymila and to recapture Riyadh. In 1891, according to Ibn Isa, Muhammed ibn Rashid 'went on to Riyadh and ordered the destruction of its walls, and the destruction of the new palace and the old palace'. The inhabitants of Riyadh were forced to raze the fortifications of the city; half the date plantations were destroyed; and the buildings associated with the rule of the Wahhabist emirs were left in ruins. Abdul Rahman's final defeat forced him, with the surviving Saudis, into a bitter exile, abjectly fleeing with his young son Abdul Aziz and his daughter Nura conveyed in camelbags. First the Saudis sought refuge with the al-Murra tribe, desert Bedouins, in the east of the peninsula; while Abdul Rahman sought permission to live in Bahrain, far beyond the reach of the Rashidis. It is of interest that during the period with the Bedouin, Abdul Aziz (Ibn Saud) was treated for rheumatism in Bahrain: the sickly teenager was to grow into a powerful man with great energy and endurance (see Table 4.2).

The Saudis then moved to Qatar, but only on a temporary basis and under pressure from the Turks, who were reluctant to countenance any Saudi resurgence. In 1893 the women and children were given permission to settle in Kuwait, under the protection of the ambitious Sheikh Mubarak, while the men were to remain with the al-Murra in the region between Jabrin and Hasa. After some delay, caused by Mubarak's reluctance to anger the Rashidis, the Saudi men were allowed to rejoin their families in Kuwait. The situation was again volatile. In 1897 Muhammed ibn Rashid, the master of Riyadh and the lord of Central Arabia, died – to be succeeded by a Rashidi with designs on Kuwait. Now Sheikh Mubarak and Abdul Rahman had a common interest in campaigning against the Rashidis, now facing turmoil over the succession in their Hail stronghold (in the final quarter-century of the House of Rashid most of the seven rulers of Hail were destined for violent deaths). Mubarak was soon conducting secret negotiations with Britain as a way of exploiting great-power ambitions in the region: in 1899 he achieved a treaty of protection against the Turks and others, in return for a pledge to cede no territory, or to otherwise deal with any foreign powers, without first obtaining the permission of Britain.[*]

By the end of 1900 the Kuwaiti/Saudi alliance felt strong enough to confront the Rashidis. A large force was sent into al-Qasim, winning support from towns and tribes in the region and in southern Nejd; the young Ibn Saud, the eldest surviving son of Abdul Rahman, was selected as the future governor of Riyadh. Ibn Saud, now in his mid-twenties (and having married his second wife, Wadhba, of the Beni Khaled, the previous year), was sent south to create a diversion by attacking Riyadh. Here Ibn Saud was initially successful: after some fighting he managed to occupy the town and to lay siege to the fortress where the governor and his men had taken refuge. But the Kuwaiti/Saudi forces elsewhere were suffering severe reverses. In March 1901 the Rashidis were victorious at the bloody Battle of Sarif, near Tarfiyyah, forcing Ibn Saud to withdraw from Riyadh and to rejoin his father in the retreat to Kuwait. The Sarif rout, suffered in a broad

---

[*] This was a cynical British move. Mubarak's earlier requests had been refused since Kuwait was under the nominal sovereignty of the Turkish sultan. Since Lord Curzon had recognised in 1892 that Kuwait owed allegiance to Turkey, Mubarak was 'strictly speaking, a usurper' (Ireland, 1937, p. 40). However, on 23 January 1899, the small region of Kuwait was brought into treaty relations at the direction of Curzon, reluctant to see Kuwait become a Russian port or a German terminus of the Baghdad railway (see also p. 178).

Table 4.2   Some main events in the life of Ibn Saud

1876	Birth of Ibn Saud (Abdul Aziz ibn Abdul Rahman).
1887	End of Saudi rule in Riyadh.
1888	Salim ibn Subham, Rashidi governor of Riyadh, attacks sons of Imam Saud in Kharj.
1889	Abdullah, now seriously ill, allowed by Ibn Rashid to return as 'imam' to Riyadh; he dies three days later (27 November).
1890/91	Qasimi alliance defeated by Ibn Rashid; Saudis take refuge with al-Murra tribe in east of peninsula.
1894	Ibn Saud takes first wife; she dies within six months.
1899	Ibn Saud remarries; many other wives, dozens of children, to follow.
1901	Sheikh Mubarak of Kuwait, in alliance with Ibn Saud, launches strike against Rashidi territory.
1902	Saudi forces raid Nejd; Ibn Saud recaptures Riyadh, then returns to Nejd.
1904	Ibn Saud defeats Turks and Rashidis at Bukairiya.
1905	Ibn Saud visits Trucial Coast.
1906	Abdul Aziz Ibn Rashid killed in battle with forces led by Ibn Saud at Rawdat al-Muhanna; leads to chaos in Rashidi stronghold in Hail.
1910	Captain William Henry Shakespear meets Ibn Saud; Sara Sudeiri, the mother of Ibn Saud, dies.
1912	First major Ikhwan settlement.
1913	Ibn Saud expels Turks from Hasa; enters Hufuf as a conqueror.
1914	Secret Saudi/Turkish treaty; denied by Saudis.
1915	Ibn Saud and British agree treaty.
1916	Start of Arab Revolt against Turks; Hussain ibn Ali declares himself 'King of the Arabs'.
1920	Saudi forces attack Kuwait.
1921	Final defeat of Rashidis by Ibn Saud.
1922	Ibn Saud, British and others at the Conference of Ujair.
1924	Ibn Saud, invades Hejaz; enters Mecca.
1925	British continue negotiations with Saudis; Medina and Jedda fall to Ibn Saud; Ibn Saud proclaimed Kind of Hejaz and Sultan of Nejd.
1927	Ibn Saud convenes conference of Ikhwan leaders and *ulema*; Britain recognises Ibn Saud as King of Hejaz and Nejd.
1928	Death of Ibn Saud's father, Abdul Rahman.
1929	Revolt flares up in Hasa, but is quickly crushed.
1932	Ibn Saud proclaims the Kingdom of Saudi Arabia (23 September).

Table 4.2   (continued)

1933	Saudis sign oil concession with the United States.
1934	Saudi Arabia fights brief war with Yemen.
1935	An assassination attempt is made against Ibn Saud.
1936	Saudi/Egyptian relations are restored; Saudis sign treaty with Iraq.
1938	Oil begins flowing in commercial quantities at Dhahran.
1939	First shipment of oil from Ras Tannura.
1942	Winston Churchill declares Ibn Saud to be 'boss of bosses' in the Middle East.
1943	US Lend-Lease aid is delivered to Saudi Arabia; British aid to Saudi Arabia reaches more than £8 million (complaints are voiced that it is being spent on princely cars and palaces).
1945	Ibn Saud meets Churchill and Roosevelt; Saudi Arabia declares war on Germany.
1946	Ibn Saud visits Egypt.
1947	ARAMCO is founded; one of Ibn Saud's last sons is born (see also 1952).
1951	Saudi/US agreement achieved on Dhahran base; Ibn Saud performs his last *hajj*; a favourite son, Mansour, dies in May after an operation in Paris; another son, drunk at the time, shoots dead a British engineer.
1952	Egypt convulsed by Nasser revolution; Saudis send forces to Buraimi in dispute with British; Ibn Saud's last son reportedly born in June, but dies in infancy.
1953	Council of ministers formed in Saudi Arabia with a view to managing the succession; Ibn Saud dies and is buried at Riyadh in an unmarked grave, his clothes sold in the market-place.

Source: McLoughlin (1993).

salt-pan area, had been a diasaster for Saudi ambitions: here it was that 'the rain mingling with the blood of the fallen flowed in a broad red stream into the snow-white basin of salt'.[28] The Kuwaiti/Saudi forces struggled to regroup in Kuwait in anticipation of the certain Rashidi counter-attack.

In September 1901 Rashidi forces approached Kuwait, to be confronted by soldiers bearing green banners adorned with the unsurprising slogan 'There is no God but God and Muhammed is His Prophet'. In the event it may not have been considerations of piety but British military power that finally deterred the Rashidis from making an attack on Kuwait. A British naval force was positioned off the coast, while the British at the same time were landing guns and ammunition in substantial amounts. In these circumstances the Rashidis appeared content to withdraw with only moderate booty of livestock in compensation. Ibn Saud, probably heartened by this evident Rashidi reticence, was now resolved on offensive action: the time had come for the Saudis to take and hold Riyadh once and for all.[29]

He proposed to his father and Sheikh Mubarak that he be allowed to take a force to confront the small garrison at Riyadh, at a time when the bulk of the Rashidi force was preoccupied far away. In October 1901 Ibn Saud, with about sixty relatives and followers, left Kuwait for Riyadh, at first hiding out for a month or more on the edge of the Empty Quarter. In early January 1902, towards the end of Ramadan, the Saudis celebrated the Id al-Fitr at Abu Jifan, then reached the Jubayl plateau within fifteen miles of Riyadh. During the night of 15–16 January Ibn Saud moved through the palm groves and gardens until within striking distance of the Qasr al-Masmak fortress. He then selected Abdullah ibn Jiluwi and a few others, instructing the remainder to await word of victory within 24 hours or then to return to Kuwait to announce the deaths of Ibn Saud and the rest of his advance party.

They then commandeered houses overlooking the great gate of the Masmak, and waited for dawn. It is recorded that the men slept a little, having locked up the women of the houses, and otherwise passed the time by eating dates, drinking coffee and reciting verses from the Koran. Shortly after sunrise the Masmak gate opened and the Rashidi governor Ajlan emerged to inspect the horses, whereupon Ibn Saud and his men rushed out to confront him. After a fight in which Ajlan was wounded by gunfire, Ibn Jiluwi hurled himself forward to reach the postern in the great gate before the aperture could be closed after the retreating Ajlan. In such a fashion Ibn Jiluwi and others gained access to the fortress. Ajlan and several of the defenders were promptly killed; the garrison was made secure; and the Riyadh populace awoke to a proclamation ringing out from one of the Masmak towers: 'To God the sovereignty, to Abdul Aziz ibn Abdul Rahman al-Faisal al-Saud the rule!'[30]

The population of Riyadh quickly swore their allegiance, perhaps unaware that a great new era in the turbulent history of Arabia had begun. The British Political Agency in Bahrain received the earliest known report (July 1902) of these significant events. It notes that Ibn Saud had reconquered his country and that all those who professed to be pacific should give up their arms. In the light of the victory Abdul Rahman returned from exile to Riyadh. At a public meeting at the Great Mosque, attended by the *ulema* and Riyadh notables, he renounced his rule in favour of his son, Ibn Saud, and presented him with the revered sword of Saud the Great, the symbol of Saudi leadership.

Riyadh had yet again been occupied by the Saudis, but a new Rashidi assault was inevitable. In the event Abdul Aziz ibn Rashid, the ruler of Hail, seemed reluctant to confront the Saudi capital directly. After bypassing the Riyadh area, an important battle took place in November 1902 in the area of Dilam. In this encounter the Rashidis were taken by surprise, first decimated by concentrated rifle-fire and then forced to confront the massed Saudi cavalry. By the end of the day Ibn Saud had achieved his first victory over the Rashidis in open conflict. Skirmishing continued over several months, with Ibn Rashid again briefly besieging Riyadh in April 1903; but the Rashidis were operating far from their Hail stronghold, and gradually Ibn Saud was extending his authority to the major settlements north and south of Riyadh. In late 1903 Zifli was occupied and Sudeir joined the Saudi camp; in 1904 Washm was taken, with Anaiza and other regions also succumbing to Saudi pressure. Of the Anaiza success Ibn Saud himself commented: 'After we had said the morning prayer we sent against them Abdullah bin Jiluwi, with him 100 men of the people of Riyadh to assist ... We broke them and slaughtered of them 370 men ... And by Almighty God, but two bedouin on our side were slain.'[31] Ubaid ibn Rashid, a cousin of the Rashidi ruler of Hail, found himself facing the sword of Ibn Saud. The ruler of the House of Saud later described the event: 'I struck him first on the leg and disabled him; quickly after that I struck at the neck; the head fell to one side, the blood spurted up like a fountain; the third blow at the heart, I saw the heart, which was cut in two, palpitate like that ... It was a joyous moment. I kissed the sword.'[32]

Ibn Saud continued to extend his power and influence. Through much of 1905 he worked to enlist the support of tribes in the Eastern Region, still occupied by the Ottomans. In el-Qasim there were further confrontations between the Rashidis and the Saudis, both now finding that Turkish control in the region was quickly evaporating. The following year Ibn Rashid was killed in a clash with the Saudis, so temporarily ending the threat from Hail. As the Ottoman garrisons, decimated by disease and desertion, pulled out of Qasim the influence of the Saudis grew. Ibn Saud continued to consolidate his power over the tribes, overcoming their traditional resistance to paying taxes, receiving emissaries, and accepting governors appointed by Riyadh. And Ibn Saud also embarked on a policy of forming alliances through marriage (see also 'Towards Saudi Arabia', below), an effective strategy that eventually led to a staggering expansion of the House of Saud.

Over a period of four years, from the time of the occupation of Riyadh (1902), Ibn Saud had established himself as a major candidate in the struggle for national supremacy. The Rashidi threat and other problems had been largely overcome; the tribes had been either enlisted to the Saudi cause or suitably constrained within particular regions; and Ibn Saud had established his control over the Ikhwan (or Brothers), the zealous tribesmen ever committed to *jihad* (holy war) and keen to emulate the supposed practices of the Prophet. For a time Ibn Saud had problems with vacillating leaders, apt to change sides as Saudi fortunes ebbed and flowed. Thus Faisal ibn Dawish changed his allegiances several times in the period 1907/8, encouraging Ibn Saud to reflect on how such instabilities could be avoided in the future. Perhaps one answer was the establishment of the Bedouin *hijar* (agricultural/military/religious settlements), encouraging the limitation of traditional nomadic patterns. Other problems derived from the persistence of recalcitrant tribes, eager to maintain their independence and to flout distant authority; and from the growing ambition of Hussain ibn Ali, appointed by the Turks as the Grand Shareef of Mecca in 1908. It seemed clear that Hussain, having suppressed the Idrisi chief Muhammed who had occupied Abha and Asir, was well prepared to act as puppet for his Turkish masters.

In 1910 the forces of Hussain encountered a small Saudi deployment led by Ibn Saud's brother Saad, busy recruiting allies among the Utaiba. Saad was captured and a prompt ransom demand was sent to Ibn Saud. When an attempt at negotiation failed, Ibn Saud paid the ransom and agreed to recognise Turkish sovereignty, only to repudiate the agreement, once Saad was free, on the ground that it had been made under duress. With Ibn Saud and his brother now reunited, various other problems were addressed. Pressure was maintained against dissident groups; for example, the town of Laila was besieged before the Hazzani rebels were overwhelmed and their chiefs promptly executed. In May 1913 Ibn Saud led about 300 men against the Turkish garrison of Hufuf, where he exploited the element of surprise to overwhelm 1200 defenders. On the morning of 9 May the garrison was disarmed and the Saudi state had reached the Gulf. Ibn Saud had by now extended his power and influence over much of the Arabian peninsula. On the brink of the Great War, and a decade after Lord Lansdowne had declared British supremacy in the Gulf, Britain had a growing interest in the development of useful relations with the House of Saud.

BRITAIN AND THE ARAB REVOLT

The possibility of British protection for Ibn Saud had long been considered. Over a century before, with the Arabian peninsula perceived as little more than a barren and uninviting territory, the East India Company had shown no enthusiasm for protection of its residual interests in the region. The file dockets of the British Foreign Office still made reference to 'Turkish Arabia' – an area assumed to be the 'sacrosanct preserve of the Ottoman'.[33] But with the prospect of a European war now looming large, the British Empire could not tolerate the possibility of Turkish Arabia falling into the German camp. The man chosen to explore the idea of improved relations with Ibn Saud was Captain William Henry Irvine Shakespear – in 1904, aged twenty-four, the youngest consul in the Indian administration; in 1909 Britain's Political Agent in Kuwait; in 1910 involved with his first talks with Ibn Saud; and in 1915 killed with the Saudi forces at the battle of Jarrab.

Ibn Saud had already requested British protection from Turkish encroachments, a written appeal that London thought it wisest to ignore. But with the expansion and consolidation of Saudi power in the peninsula it seemed that aid to Ibn Saud would at least give Britain the chance of controlling his ambitions. In 1911 Captain Shakespear reported to Sir Percy Zacharia Cox, the Gulf Political Resident, his impressions of Ibn Saud. He 'gave the impression of being endowed with a particularly straightforward, frank and generous nature. He treated me most hospitably and in the most genuinely friendly manner. He and his brothers did not show a trace of the fanatical spirit which might have been expected from the ruling Wahhabi family ... I frequently discussed matters of doctrine, custom and religion which are held to be anathema by the Wahhabi sect and I was always answered with calm and intelligent reasoning.'[34] In 1914 Shakespear observed that the Arabs had found a leader 'who stands head and shoulders above any other chief and in whose star all have implicit faith'.[35]

It is clear that Ibn Saud, for his part, was happy to exploit the growing British recognition of his political importance in the peninsula. He frequently urged the establishment of formal relations between the British and himself, and was evidently prepared to consider arrangements varying from simple financial subsidy to formal protectorate status; but Britain moved cautiously, reluctant even at this late stage to antagonise the Turks. London, while negotiating with the Ottomans in the attempt to prevent Turkey being drawn into an alliance with Germany and Austria–Hungary, was still wedded to a policy of (in the words of a senior official in the India Office) 'pretending that Saud does not exist'.[36] As late as 18 May 1914 Sir Edward Grey, Foreign Secretary, was insisting that Ibn Saud 'must be dealt with as a Turkish official or not at all'.[37] In such circumstances it is hardly surprising that Ibn Saud, while keen to exploit British attention, was equally happy to make deals with the Turks.

An Ibn Saud–Turkish agreement, a copy found in Basra by the British, stipulated that Ibn Saud was to be acknowledged as the 'Wali and Commandant of Nejd'; that he should allow Turkish troops to be stationed at specified locations; that he should allow the flying of the Turkish flag on public buildings and allow the use of the Turkish postal system; and that he should have no dealings with any other foreign powers, joining with Turkish forces to resist aggression. At the same time Ibn Saud continued to negotiate with the British; and on 26 December 1915 he and Sir Percy Cox signed an Anglo-Saudi treaty, whereby the British recognised Nejd and Hasa as 'the countries of Bin Saud and his fathers before him' and of his descendants, with the qualification that any such heirs should not be antagonistic to Britain. Here, as with the Saudi–Turkey deal, Ibn Saud agreed to have no relations with foreign powers, not to cede or lease any territories without British permission, and not to make aggression against any of the Gulf powers with which Britain had treaties (a matter of concern to Abu Dhabi, Qatar, Muscat, Dubai and Kuwait).[38] If Ibn Saud needed any inducement to come to an agreement his signature on the treaty brought him an immediate loan of £20,000, 1000 weapons and 200,000 rounds of ammunition, and a later subsidy of £5000 a month. Such pragmatic British largesse was useful to Ibn Saud in confrontation with his domestic opponents. By 1917 the British were actively supporting the planned Saudi campaign against Hail, while efforts were made to reconcile Ibn Saud's dispute with Shareef Hussain ibn Ali of Hejaz, also a nominal ally of the British.

The British government had appreciated the possible advantages in encouraging Hussain's anti-Turkish sentiments, just as it chose to offer inducements to Ibn Saud. Even before the outbreak of the European war Lord Kitchener, then High Commissioner in Egypt, had considered requests for a British accommodation with the Shareef of Holy Mecca. Hussain himself worked hard through 1915 to secure the assurances he needed from the British government, though it seemed clear that at that time London 'had no clear policy towards the Arabs or for the future of the Ottoman provinces in Asia after Turkey's defeat'.[39] Hussain, with others, had an obvious interest in the matter of independence; but with hindsight it seems clear that the British were motivated by nothing more than a cynical pragmatism, and that their indifference to any claims for Arab liberation would inevitably come to be seen as unprincipled. Sir Percy Cox had been keen to enlist Ibn Saud against the Ottomans, but with the death in January 1915 of Captain Shakespear, the British representative at the Saudi court, the emphasis shifted to the Hejaz Hashemites under Shareef Hussain. Since the Ottoman sultan had already called for a *jihad* against the Allies, London well saw the advantage of being able to parade its own pious Muslim leader, none less than the Shareef of Holy Mecca.

In October 1915 Sir Henry Macmahon, Cairo's envoy, made a vague reference to an independent Arabia, to include parts of Syria, Muslim control of Mecca and Medina, and other territories – in return for a successful insurrection against the Turks. Sir Mark Sykes (later to betray Arab dreams of independence via the notorious Sykes–Picot Agreement) was already urging the importance of the Arabs to the Allied war effort; with Lord Curzon counselling at the same time that no promises should be made because the Arabs were 'a people who are at this moment fighting against us as hard as they can'.[40] None the less, Macmahon seemed to pledge (letter to Hussain, 24 October 1915) an element of Arab independence, subject to various qualifications; for example, it had to be recognised, in connection with the Vilayets of Baghdad and Basra, that Britain's interests would require 'special administrative arrangements to protect those regions from foreign aggression, to promote the welfare of their inhabitants and to safeguard our mutual interest'. Already the ground was being laid for a post-war British colonialism.

In May 1916 Shareef Hussain, heartened at the prospect of British financial and political support, launched the Arab Revolt; on 16 June he overcame the small Turkish garrison at Mecca, and looked to the possibility of a wider Arab involvement. Hussain's irregulars, led by his sons Abdullah and Faisal, and under the guidance of the British army officer T. E. Lawrence, were now staging a rebellion that many nationalists hoped would win support throughout the Arab and Muslim worlds. Hussain and Faisal had reported that they would be joined by an uprising of 100,000 Arab troops (Hussain himself had claimed that 250,000 troops, almost all the combat troops in the Turkish army, would join the Arab Revolt). None of this materialised. No Arab units of the Ottoman forces, and no political or military leaders, defected to the Allies. Outside Hejaz 'there was no visible support for the revolt in any part of the Arabic-speaking world'.[41] Hussain had been forced to rely on a few thousand tribesmen, massively supported by British funds.[42] Half a century later, when a Bedouin sheikh was asked if he remembered Lawrence, he replied: 'He was the man with the gold.'[43] The Bedouin tribesmen, the core of Hussain's military contingent, were ill-equipped to cope with the modern tactics of the Ottoman forces; though skilful and courageous guerrillas they were often demoralised and near to collapse as a fighting force. Moreover, the problems of the Arab Revolt, despite its clear but minor contribution to the Allied victory, helped also to weaken Hussain's political position.

It is arguable also that the Shareef of Mecca did little to secure his own position. In October 1916 he arranged for the notables in Mecca to proclaim him 'King of the Arabs', a move that alarmed not only Britain but also the Saudis. London was unable to accept such pretensions since it had already made pledges to other Arab protégés; to Hussain's European allies he could only be styled 'King of Hejaz'. To Ibn Saud, with his own substantial ambitions, any suggestion of subservience to Hussain was anathema, not least because by now both of them were in the pay of the same European power. Hussain's move also made it easier for Ibn Saud to attract some of the tribal leaders away from their allegiance to Hejaz. In 1917 he gained the support of the chief of Khurmah, which encouraged Hussain to attempt an occupation of the oasis the following year. In May 1919 the resulting battle of Turubah gave Ibn Saud a victory over the the forces of the King of Hejaz. (There is some irony in the fact that each of the belligerents was in the pay of a different British department: thus the Foreign Office and the India Office were at war.) Ibn Saud hesitated to pursue his advantage since he feared losing his British subsidy and still had to settle accounts with Ibn Rashid. In November 1921 he decisively defeated the Rashidis and annexed their territory; when, in March 1924, the subsidy was finally ended there were no further constraints on Saudi ambition.

Hussain, anguished at European betrayal of Arab independence, refused to ratify the Treaty of Versailles or to enter into a treaty relationship with Great Britain. At the same time he was drawn into dispute with Egypt over questions about the Mecca pilgrimage. And in March 1924, just when Ibn Saud was feeling free to pursue his own interests, Hussain declared himself Caliph, the Ottoman caliphate having been abolished with the collapse of the Turkish military effort. This fresh move of Hussain, seemingly taken with reluctance, gained for Ibn Saud the manifest support of the Indian Muslims of the Caliphate Committee and thereby strengthened the Wahhabist claims on the leadership of the Islamic world. In October 1924, after vainly appealing for British support, Hussain recklessly abdicated as a device for bringing matters to a head; but all he accomplished was to create a vacancy.

On 13 October 1924 the Saudi forces occupied Mecca; and then laid siege to Hussain's successor, his son Ali, at the port of Jeddah. On 22 December 1925

Ali abandoned hope of any accession to the kingship of Hejaz; on Christmas Day the confrontation between the Saudis and the Hashemites was declared at an end; and in January 1926 the Mecca notables conferred the kingship of Hejaz on Ibn Saud. His political problems were far from over; but soon the way would be clear for the creation of a modern Saudi state occupying most of the Arabian peninsula.

TOWARDS SAUDI ARABIA

Much of the Muslim world was at least ambivalent about Saudi successes. The Wahhabists, despite their pretensions to a pure form of Islam, attracted only minority support among believers. Moreover, Ibn Saud's military campaign in Hejaz had placed various obstacles in the way of the annual pilgrimage to Mecca; while one report, perhaps exaggerated, declared that the Saudi bombardment of Medina had damaged the tomb of the Prophet. When, in June 1926, Ibn Saud convened an Islamic Congress in Mecca it was poorly attended by official delegates, and some of the questions raised proved to be extremely contentious. The *hajj* of that year also produced unfortunate confrontations between Wahhabists and Egyptian Muslims, seriously embarrassing those Muslims working for Islamic solidarity.

At the same time the expansion of Saudi power (in particular, the final conquest of Hejaz and Jebel Shammar) had brought Wahhabist forces into contact with Iraq and Transjordan, both now ruled under British auspices by the sons of Hussain. Now the geographical situation was often indeterminate. The subdivision of the old Ottoman territories had yielded international frontiers that largely ignored the detailed circumstances of economic geography, while the traditional nomadic groups could easily evade control by traversing the borders between different jurisdictions. Raids on adjoining territories continued to occur, sometimes provoking British intervention by armoured vehicles and the Royal Air Force. In the mid-1920s, despite earlier agreements, the full scope of Ibn Saud's territorial ambitions still seemed unclear.

In the post-war years the British government worked to manipulate various crucial jurisdictions in the Middle East, partly as a consequence of the mandates issued by the League of Nations and partly as a response to the traditional pressures of colonial instinct. Now Faisal ibn Hussain, having lost the throne of Syria after defeat by the French in 1920, was made monarch of Iraq; while Abdullah ibn Hussain was made emir of Transjordan – causing Ibn Saud to declare that he was now surrounded by his enemies. Efforts to define the limits on regional ambitions had done very little to settle the competing claims. Some tensions had been defused but at the cost of storing up massive problems for the future (see also Chapter 6). In this context the 1922 Conference of Ujair (or Uqair) was of particular significance.

During the final stages of the Great War the British had imposed a naval blockade on Kuwait to block supplies reaching the Turks via the desert route. At the same time Sheikh Salim, successor to his brother Jabir (Mubarak's first son), was told that Kuwait should refrain from any action prejudicial to British interests. Salim then proposed the building of a fort near Jabal Manifah to indicate the southern limits of his territory, whereupon Ibn Saud laid claim to the area and ordered a settlement to be built on land claimed by Salim. A British statement upholding the 1913 Anglo-Turkish agreement, a treaty favouring the territorial position of Kuwait against Ibn Saud, did nothing but exacerbate the problem. In October the Ikhwan responded by attacking Jahra, which Salim was forced to protect. In the ensuing battle the Saudi forces were decimated: at a cost of two hundred Kuwaiti fatalities there were eight hundred enemy dead on the field, with another five hundred Ikhwan to die later from their wounds. The Saudis withdrew, burying men as they died on the long journey home.

The British had not intervened in the battle, though they had watched developments with some alarm. Now they perceived that a new initiative was necessary to define the geographical frontiers in the region. Sir Percy Cox proposed that the Subaihiyah wells, now the site of an Ikhwan camp, should become an effective 'no man's land' between the two sides, and an uneasy truce ensued. On 27 February 1921 Salim died, to be succeeded by Sheikh Ahmad al Jabir (Mubarak's grandson), whereupon Ibn Saud immediately suggested that there was no need for a formal boundary between the two states. This declaration did not satisfy the British and at the 1922 Ujair conference Sir Percy Cox made efforts to resolve the frontier problem. The Kuwaitis, the Saudis and Faisal in Iraq had an obvious interest in the outcome.

The Iraqi delegate Sabih Beg proposed a boundary that ran close to Riyadh, thus taking in the northern half of Arabia ('As God is my witness, this and only this is the true boundary and cannot be disputed'). Ibn Saud, keen to exploit the situation, countered with a grandiose claim that took in much of Syria, a substantial part of Iraq and the whole of Kuwait. Sir Percy Cox soon lost patience with such extravagant demands and declared to Ibn Saud that he would not tolerate 'these impossible arguments and ridiculous claims'. He, Sir Percy Cox, would determine the frontiers.[44] He then proceeded to draw a line on the map, denying most of Ibn Saud's claim and giving Sabih Beg three hundred miles less than he had demanded. Cox had reprimanded Ibn Saud, the Sultan of Nejd and the future King of Saudi Arabia, as though he were a naughty child. A witness to these events, the military attaché Colonel Harold Dickson, later remarked: 'I was astonished to see him [Ibn Saud] reprimanded like a naughty schoolboy. ... Ibn Saud almost broke down and pathetically remarked that Sir Percy was his father and mother who made him and raised him from nothing to the position he held, and that he would surrender half his kingdom, nay the whole, if Sir Percy ordered.' Cox then responded by depriving Kuwait of nearly two-thirds of her territory and donating it to Nejd. Years later, Sheikh Ahmad commented to Dickson on how this action had shaken his faith in Britain; and Philby later commented in a letter to the Dicksons on how the British 'in their folly' prefer to maintain an artificial political barrier between Kuwait and Arabia.[45]

The Ujair conference succeeded in establishing frontiers that have survived to the present day, though not without problems: many of the tribes resisted the new constraint on their traditional movements; and the Cox initiative – perhaps not quite 'a true judgement of Solomon'[46] – was arguably one of the contributing causes of the 1991 Gulf War. Ujair was significant also because it put the question of oil on the agenda. Thus one of the advisors to Ibn Saud urged Cox to allocate more grazing room for the Saudi tribes, 'because we think that oil exists there', whereupon Cox replied: 'That is exactly why I have made it a Neutral Zone. Each side shall have a half share.'[47] Moreover, one of the men who attended the conference was a certain Major Frank Holmes, a New Zealand mining engineer and businessman, anxious to exploit the possibility of oil in Arabia. A few months later Ibn Saud signed his first oil concession agreement: for the right to prospect in the eastern provinces of Arabia, from the Kuwait frontier to the boundaries with Qatar, Major Holmes and the London-based Eastern General Syndicate company agreed to pay Ibn Saud the sum of £2000 a year.

In 1924, with the republican government in Turkey announcing the end of the Ottoman caliphate, King Hussain of the Hejaz declared that he was now the new Caliph of the entire Muslim world. He was not the only contender. Sultan Muhammed VI Vahideddin, recently exiled by the Turks, was still regarded in some quarters as caliph; and claims were also being made by King Fuad of Egypt, the Sultan of Morocco and various Malayan princes. But Hussain, as Custodian of the Holy Cities, reckoned that he had a uniquely powerful case; he was, moreover, an acknowledged descendant of the Prophet. At the same time Hussain banned the Ikhwan from making the *hajj*, on the ground that they would be a risk to other pilgrims, a decision that provoked a great council in Riyadh to address the issue. Speakers declared that Hussain's act was grounds for war; and that the *hajj* would be made by force if necessary. Now it emerged that in India the Caliphate Committee, representing 70 million Muslims, was bitterly opposed to Hussain's posture.

In September 1924 some 3000 Ikhwan, led by Sultan ibn Bijad and Khaled ibn Luwai, attacked Taif, the summer capital of Hejaz, overlooking the route to Mecca and the Red Sea Coast. Prince Ali, Hussain's youngest son, fled the fortress with many of the defenders, only to be pursued by the Ikhwan tribesmen. Around 300 of Hussain's supporters were slaughtered on the road to Mecca; Taif was plundered; and then most of its buildings were razed to the ground. It is said that the Ikhwan smashed all the mirrors in the houses, simply because they had never encountered such things before. The results were various: '... perhaps a fragment of mirror on a wall, somebody's share of the loot – or a window acting as a door because Bedouin do not see the point of windows – or half a door instead of a whole one … a quarter or a third of a carpet on a floor, because one big one has been cut up into fair shares.'[48]

The demoralised Hussain, having abdicated in favour of Ali, sailed to Aqaba, later to live his final years in Cyprus and Amman; he died, forgotten and isolated, in 1931. Ibn Saud instructed the Ikhwan, on pain of execution, not to loot and destroy, as they had done in Taif; but this did not prevent the destruction of the idolatrous graves of false saints and the confiscation of all musical instruments and human portraits (forbidden in Wahhabist doctrine).[49] Ibn Saud entered Mecca as a pious pilgrim, intent on demonstrating to the Muslim world that he was a fit custodian of the holy places. In December 1925 Ali joined his father in exile and Ibn Saud's victory was complete. On 8 January 1926, in the Grand Mosque of Mecca, he was proclaimed the new King of the Hejaz. One of his first acts was to promulgate by decree a Consultative Council (*Majlis al Shura*) 'of the *ulema*, the dignitaries and the merchants' to serve as an intermediary between Ibn Saud and the people.

It was not long before the Ikhwan were restive. Ibn Saud was now making it clear that the rewards to the tribesmen for their war effort would be limited. No Ikhwan chief was to be made a governor in Hejaz, so infuriating such leaders as Ibn Bijad of the Utaiba who had set his eye on the governorship of Mecca, and Ibn Dawish who had imagined a similar role in Medina. So incensed, the Ikhwan made their way back to Nejd, raiding across the borders whenever they had the opportunity, and as a result inviting bombing raids and hot pursuit by the Royal Air Force. In June 1926 the Ikhwan picked a quarrel with Egyptian pilgrims at the *hajj* over the issue of an ornate camel-borne litter (*mahmal*) sent from Cairo to Mecca. In the ensuing confrontation a number of men were killed or injured, with many other pilgrims insulted and abused. The resulting diplomatic breach with Egypt lasted for a decade until the death of King Fuad. Now it seemed that the Ikhwan were increasingly a force unto themselves, with Ibn Saud dependent upon their military power but seemingly unable to impose discipline.

In January 1927 Ibn Saud convened a conference of some 3000 Ikhwan at which the *ulema* were invited to rule on the mounting Ikhwan grievances. At this time the pious tribesmen had many problems: not least a planned telegraph network, obviously a work of the devil; Faisal's intended visit to godless England; the unwelcome persistence of the Shi'a; and the need to prevent foreign tribes ('infidel' Muslims) using Saudi land for grazing and transit. The *ulema* supported the Ikhwan in many particulars but still acknowledged the scope of Ibn Saud's discretion as imam. In September the Ikhwan complained that a British police post, well inside Iraqi territory, was a base for an attack on the Saudis. Ibn Saud duly protested but Mutair tribesmen took matters into their own hands, attacking the Busaiyah workmen (only one survived) and then launching raids into Iraq. Now the British were concerned that the Turkish Petroleum Company might be unwilling to build a planned pipeline and railway.

In 1928 the Saudis negotiated with Sir Gilbert Clayton, the British representative, in Jeddah when Ibn Saud appealed for an end to the RAF attacks on his people. Here it was that Lieutenant John Bagot Glubb, later to command Jordan's famous Arab Legion, first met Ibn Saud: 'Yesterday we again met Ibn Saud. his manner was much changed since our first meetings and he seemed depressed and bitter. To Clayton he said, 'When the English first came to Iraq I congratulated my people. They were surprised and asked me why. I had always abused the Turks as unbelievers, they said, yet here were people who were even worse because they were not Muslims at all. I told them the English were honest and my friends. Now I must admit that we have despaired of the English and their hair-splitting.'[50] None the less the Treaty of Jeddah was negotiated in May, providing recognition of Ibn Saud's frontiers and independence. The following year he insisted that the British dismantle the police posts in Iraq, possibly to pacify the Ikhwan. The tribesmen continued to mount raids across the frontiers, until intimidated in early 1929 by a strong British military force (troops, armoured cars and aircraft) blocking the northward march. On this occasion the frustrated Ikhwan committed the blunder of turning south to plunder other Nejdi tribes, so compromising Ikhwan claims of fundamentalist virtue and alienating their fellow Wahhabists. Now it was time for Ibn Saud to confront the recalcitrant Ikhwan factions.

At first he hoped to avoid open conflict and tried to coax the rebel tribes, the Mutair and the Utaiba, into accepting a judgement of the *sharia* court with regard to various Ikhwan outrages committed against the camel-traders and others. To this end he persuaded Faisal ibn Dawish to come unarmed to negotiate a solution. This achieved nothing. Ibn Dawish, accompanied by a bodyguard of eight men, visited Ibn Saud in his camp, spent a night in the King's tent, and then returned to his own side to report what had transpired. In one account Ibn Dawish commented that Ibn Saud's army was full of fat townsmen ill-suited to battle: 'They are about as much use as camel bags without handles.'[51] None the less the King was now preparing for battle. Fresh supplies of water were collected, and he made the appropriate payments to the tribal chiefs and their warriors: six gold pounds to each chief and three pounds for each of their men. After dressing for combat and mounting his war horse Ibn Saud exhorted his followers: 'Trust in God and prepare to fight!' Soon would begin the last major battle in Arabia between contending Bedouin forces.

On 30 March 1929 Ibn Saud launched his men against the Ikhwan forces at Sibilla, not far from Jarrab where Captain Shakespear had died fighting the Rashidis. Ibn Saud's brothers, Abdullah and Muhammed, and two of his eldest sons, Saud and Faisal, served as commanders; and they were happy to rejoice in a glorious victory. Ibn Saud threw symbolic handfuls of sand in the direction of the Ikhwan lines, the war banners streamed out, and at the King's command the horses and camels charged towards the enemy positions. In less than half an hour the battle was over, finally settled by machine-gun fire when the Ikhwan forces were caught in a vulnerable deployment. Faisal ibn Dawish was seriously wounded and Ibn Bijad in retreat. The battle was decisive but Ikhwan survivors still struggled to organise rebellion against the expanding power of the Saudi state.

At the same time some tribes saw the wisdom of making peace with Ibn Saud. Thus the Ajman, forced to acknowledge the Saudi victory at Sibilla, agreed to negotiate the terms of a new relationship. But when the Ajman chief, Dhaidan ibn Hithlain, met Fahd, the son of Abdullah ibn Jiluwi, Ibn Saud's cousin, the encounter led to disaster. After some argument between the parties Ibn Hithlain was first put in chains and then murdered – at a time when he was carrying safe-conduct papers signed by both Ibn Saud and Jiluwi. Faisal ibn Dawish, having recovered from his wounds, was once again leading the Mutair against the Saudis; with the Utaiba having taken control of the territory between Hejaz and Nejd. Now Ibn Saud was forced to confront recalcitrant factions in various regions.

The Ikhwan, though constantly harried by Saudi forces, continued their raids – even into Kuwait. Here it was that Faisal ibn Dawish encountered the British, well equipped as they were with aircraft and armoured vehicles. On 10 January 1930, in the car of Colonel Harold Dickson, the British Political Agent, he rode from his camp to surrender his sword to Air Vice Marshal Sir Charles Burnett at the local RAF headquarters. Finally the Ikhwan, variously a mainstay and an embarrassment to Ibn Saud, had no option but to end their predatory habits. In February Ibn Saud met with Iraq's King Faisal aboard the sloop *Lupin* in the Gulf, the remnants of the Ikhwan armies were disbanded, and various imprisoned rebel leaders, including Ibn Bijad, were consigned to obscurity. Ibn Saud was now growing increasingly unassailable, though conscious that his position depended to a large extent on British good will. Said Sir Andrew Ryan, the first British Minister to Jeddah: 'I believe that he was in his heart hostile to all Western influences including that of Great Britain but he knew that British friend-ship was a condition of his survival.'[52]

The internal opposition to Saudi rule in Arabia continued up to the time of the proclamation of the Kingdom of Saudi Arabia (23 September 1932) and beyond. Even in 1932, when Ibn Saud was undeniably supreme, he was forced to deal with the Ibn Rifada rebellion in Hejaz. Saudi cavalry and armoured cars inter-vened decisively: some 350 rebels, including Rifada and his two sons, were killed, after which the head of Rifada was first given to children to play with and then displayed in the bazaar. Yet again it was well demonstrated that no effective challenge could be mounted to the tightening Saudi grip on power in the penin-sula. Ibn Saud had waged a series of wars, often with foreign assistance, in which he had defeated powerful tribes and notable families. When victorious he ruled in part through terror, often spiking the heads of his enemies and displaying them in public. Between 1916 and 1928 there were some two dozen Bedouin revolts against Saudi power in general and against the mounting ambitions of Ibn Saud in particular. These rebellions were invariably suppressed by the Ikhwan, often in circumstances of mass slaughter involving women and children; Ibn Saud's cousin, Ibn Jiluwi, personally beheaded 250 Mutair tribesmen. One authority, Said Aburish, notes the scale of the slaughter:

> The tribes of Ajman and Najran show the after-effects of these massacres to this day, for there is a gap of a whole generation. The Shammar tribe suffered 410 deaths, the Beni Khalid 640 and the Najran a staggering 7000. And the cities were not far behind ... It was an atmosphere where the sword of the executioner had a recognizable name, the *rakban*, or 'necker', and it was as well known and feared as the guillotine during the French Revolution.[53]

It is noted, by General John Bagot Glubb, that Ibn Saud used 'massacre to subdue his enemies'; and that in this fashion more than 400,000 people were killed and wounded.[54] More than a million inhabitants of the peninsula were forced to flee to other Arab countries: Iraq, Syria, Egypt, Jordan and Kuwait – with political parties crushed, educated Arabs persecuted, and the entire Shammar tribe exiled to Iraq. Provincial governors, generally lacking education, were encouraged to rely on terror: '*By the time they had subdued the country, they had carried out 40,000 public executions and 350,000 amputations, respectively 1 and 7 per cent of the estimated population of four million.*'[55]

It is important also to note the role of sex in the life of Ibn Saud: partly as a matter of personal indulgence and partly as a matter of political policy. Ibn Saud's attitude to women ('I've never had a meal with a woman,' 'Learning does not become women') was unambiguous: they were for pleasure and breeding, nothing more. As one example, he married Hassa al Sudeiri, divorced her (after which she married his brother), wanted her back, forced his brother to divorce her, and then remarried her. He also had the maximum four wives allowed by the Koran, but also maintained four concubines and four slaves to feed his appetites; and the various groups were frequently replaced by others as he grew tired of them. It was the habit of Ibn Saud to execute the chiefs of vanquished tribes and then to force the widows into marriage with him. In such a way he married into more than thirty tribes – and so cemented their loyalty in part through terror and in part through the enforced blood ties. Ibn Saud also boasted that he had deflowered several hundred virgins, before giving them away as presents;[56] and during a visit to Egypt he is said to have declared: 'The country is full of pretty women and I would like to buy some of them ... How about £100,000 worth ...?'[57] This was the man – lecher, warrior and mass murderer – who on 23 September 1932 proclaimed the Kingdom of Saudi Arabia.

It was of course an act of supreme arrogance: to assume that an entire nation with an ancient history should be defined in perpetuity by the name of one family. And it also signified the contemporary reality: that the bulk of the Arabian peninsula had been converted into a Saudi family fiefdom. All political parties were banned; minority groups were terrorised and tortured; the *rakban* ('necker') was in constant use; and women, trapped in a mediaeval bigotry, were endlessly abused. This was the newly formed state in 1932 around which the Great Powers manoeuvred. And it is easy to see the principal reason why the Kingdom of Saudi Arabia was now uniquely equipped to concentrate foreign minds. Apart from the strategic geography of the peninsula, a matter that had been of importance for centuries, there were now hints of a new energy resource. Soon it would be known that Saudi Arabia was lying above the biggest oil reserves in the world. So it was that the United States, after so effectively supplanting British imperialism in the Gulf as elsewhere, came to serve as the main protector of a brutal feudalism. So it was that the abundance of Saudi oil helped to enrich the principal Western plutocratic elite and to fuel another expanding imperial ambition.

5 The Oil State

*I have conquered my Kingdom with my own sword and by my own efforts;
let my sons exert their own efforts after me.*[1]

Go into battle sure of victory from God.[2]

*...those who treasure up gold and silver and expend it not in the Way of
God ... their treasures shall be heated in hell fire, and their foreheads and
their sides, and their backs, shall be branded with them ... taste therefore
your treasures!*

Koran, Sura 9, Verses 34–5

PREAMBLE

The foundation of Saudi Arabia, not the first Saudi state but the largest, was destined to mark the beginning of a new and important phase in the Middle East. The
tumultuous births of nations that endure over time – in the twentieth century,
Israel, India, Pakistan, People's China and others – are always significant, for
good or ill, in the regions concerned and for the wider world, but the emergence
of a unified state over 80 per cent of the Arabian peninsula was set to have an
immense local and global impact. This was not primarily because of the singular
qualities of Ibn Saud, a formidable leader (but also, in world terms, an ignorant
man), but because of oil.

It is interesting to note that but for the sword of Ibn Saud, that copiously
bloodied tool that he was wont to kiss with relish, there might have been a
Rashidi Arabia or a Hashemite Arabia (to our conditioned ears such historical
options do not sound well). The Saudi Arabia that emerged in 1932 was set to
loom large in political affairs that far transcended the parochial matters of a
single nation state.

Oil was what it was all about. This is what gave the Saudis plutocratic privilege and political pull. This was what allowed the Saudis an influence far
beyond the natural wisdom of any one Arab dynasty. This was what induced
the Great Powers to circle in predatory calculation. This was the context in
which the House of Saud continued to sustain a brutal Islam, one idiosyncratic
version among many, to repress dissent with the instruments of sword and
torture chamber, to bicker with neighbours over frontiers, to participate in a
procession of wars, and to serve an ambitious superpower in the role of client
feudalism.

IBN SAUD – THE FINAL YEARS

In 1932 the kingdoms of Hejaz and Nejd (and its dependencies), over both of which Ibn Saud held sway, were abolished to constitute the Kingdom of Saudi Arabia; but this was far from an end to territorial adjustment. There would be wars with Yemen over disputed territory; and endless disputes with other neighbours over shifting demarcations in Arabian sand. Riyadh, formerly capital of the dual monarchy, was now capital of the Saudi state; its suburbs and its royal palaces multiplied while the expanding city struggled to adapt to the administrative requirements of the modern world. Traditional practice had sanctified the central judicial and political role of the monarch, prepared to meet his subjects for adjudication and other matters at his daily *majlis*; but now an element of delegation was inevitable. A Ministry of Finance, the first domestic ministry, was created as a focus for economic management. This, with other developments, encouraged ambitious and talented men to gravitate to the capital. This in turn encouraged further expansion and the disproportionate focus of services and enterprise that is typical of capitals throughout the world.

There now also began the more systematic exploration of the Arabian peninsula in search of oil, water and other resources. Harold Philby explored the Rhub al-Khali (the Empty Quarter) in 1932 and published an account the following year.[3] Ibn Saud had been reluctant to grant permission for such an expedition (at one time telling Philby to 'shut up!' as he pressed his case), but he came to see the advantage of having basic facts about his kingdom.[4] Abdullah ibn Jiluwi was instructed to assist Philby in preparing for the hazardous journey; and in due course the party set out with masses of equipment (not forgetting copies of the London *Times* so that Philby would not be deprived of the crossword).

Philby's efforts were soon overtaken by more substantial investments in the exploration of the peninsula. In 1933 a new oil concession was signed with the American company Socal (Standard Oil of California), following negotiations in Jeddah. Major Frank Holmes had allowed his own concession (made a decade earlier) to lapse by not paying the annual rent of £2000 after the first two years. Socal took over his interests and after discovering oil in commercial quantities in Bahrain began comprehensive prospecting elsewhere in Arabia. One consequence of these developments was American pressure for scrapping of the Red Line Agreement (Figure 5.1), framed in 1928 to define the region within which the Anglo and American oil majors would have control over all oil reserves and production.[5] The scene was set for American domination of the Saudi oil industry. Socal was already employing Philby as a consultant and managed also to secure the services of the American engineer Karl S. Twitchell who had begun surveying Hejaz in April 1931. Financial pressures were now encouraging Ibn Saud to sign a deal with Socal. Revenues from the *hajj* were massively reduced and there were mounting costs connected with Saudi administration, the Rifada rebellion and the uprising in the Asir region, which in 1934 led to open war with the Yemen (see below).

Figure 5.1   Red Line Agreement

The American contractors won the concession against desultory British competition (British doubts are encapsulated in the tale told of the oil company director who said he was prepared to drink all oil found in Saudi Arabia). Ibn Saud himself was said to be highly sceptical that oil would be found in his domain; and perhaps he harboured hopes that the real prize – an abundant supply of water – might be located. At the same time he reportedly tried to interest the British in taking up the concession, only abandoning the effort when the British minister Andrew Ryan encouraged Ibn Saud to accept the American offer. The British-controlled Iraq Petroleum Company could only offer £10,000 whereas the Americans were proposing £50,000 in gold.[6] The final Socal/Saudi deal was concluded in May 1933: £35,000 down, £20,000 after eighteen months, £5000 rental per year, £50,000 more if oil were discovered and a further £50,000 a year later, all the advance payments to be set against royalties.[7] Socal now had the exclusive right to explore a vast area of Saudi Arabia (the 'eastern part' of the Kingdom). The main agreement made no provision for prospecting in the Kuwait Neutral Zone but a secret annexe stipulated the payment of extra revenues if oil in commercial quantities were discovered in that area.

Ibn Saud's need for revenue at this time can be set in the context of a wide range of problems facing the new Saudi state. Thus Harold Dickson's dispatches frequently drew attention to the apparent instability of the regime: Ikhwan chiefs were being conveyed out of Riyadh by night for murder elsewhere; syphillis was spreading among the tribesmen; one of Ibn Saud's wives was caught *in flagrante delicto* with one of his sons; Ibn Saud was demanding protection money to safeguard Kuwaiti pilgrims; his brother Muhammed and Saud al-Kabir were expelled from Riyadh to prevent court intrigue; and so on.[8] Though one may look in vain 'for confirmation of most of this',[9] the economic problems were not difficult to fathom. With inadequate revenues, despite Socal, to meet the escalating national costs, Ibn Saud and his Finance Minister announced a moratorium on debts, confiscated various goods, prohibited the outflow of gold, maximised customs receipts, and took a variety of other measures to cope with the worsening financial situation. By 1933 the Asir rebellion in particular represented a severe drain on treasury resources; and at the same time there was an increasing likelihood of war with Yemen (see below).

In February 1934 the anticipated conflict broke out, whereupon Ibn Saud offered commands to his sons Faisal and Saud. After minor early reverses the Saudis were victorious, though Philby despaired at the resulting peace terms, seemingly far too generous to the defeated Yemenis (retorted Ibn Saud: 'You fool! Where will I get the manpower to govern Yemen? Yemen can only be ruled by its own ruler'[10]). At the resulting Treaty of Taif (21 May 1934) the Imam Yahya retrieved lost coastal areas while the Saudis secured Najran, the port of Jizan, and the uplands of Asir. Whatever Philby's doubts (and tears), the agreement endured for a substantial period. It is of interest that the conflict stimulated European interest. When Faisal, with his troop contingents, reached the Yemeni port of Hodeida, he became aware of war-ships sent by the colonial powers of Britain, France and Italy. Soon it would be plain that the European powers and the United States would have reason to attend closely to Saudi fortunes.

Now there were further mounting tensions on the eastern frontiers of the kingdom, in areas that impinged directly on states that had signed treaties with

Britain. In April 1935 the Saudis formally presented their claims to the British, proposing that the kingdom should have jurisdiction over crucial regions in the Qatar peninsula while also defining its border with Abu Dhabi. The protracted negotiations, in London and elsewhere, induced one British official to complain in March 1937 of Ibn Saud's creeping ambitions. Moreover, British resentments were mirrored elsewhere. In May 1935 three Yemenis had attacked Ibn Saud at the Kaaba; though the assassination attempt failed, prevented by the prompt intervention of Ibn Saud's guards, it highlighted the persistent insecurity of power and the need for constant vigilance.

The kingdom continued to experience financial problems, mitigated to some extent by the ending of the world recession. Government expenditure remained uncertain: the police could not rely on continuous pay, and many government officials remained dependent on the vagaries of pilgrim revenues. At the same time Ibn Saud, conscious of broader world issues, was frequently discouraged by the course of political events through the 1930s. He was alarmed that Britain was prepared to tolerate the Italian aggression in Abyssinia; and had little confidence that Britain – granted the League Palestine mandate but capable of favouring the Jews via the seemingly partisan Balfour Declaration – would have any interest in safeguarding Arab rights in the region. Even so, with the rulers of Yemen, Iraq and Transjordan, he urged the Palestinians to moderate their rebellion in the mandated territory, while his opposition to the establishment of a Jewish state remained plain: 'If I said to you that there was one atom in my body which did not call upon me to fight against the Jews I would be telling an untruth ... I would prefer that my possessions and my offspring should cease to exist rather than that the Jews should establish a foot-hold in Palestine.'[11] The Palestine question would continue to occupy Ibn Saud for the rest of his life.

In March 1938, following the Coronation visit of Ibn Saud's sons to London, Princess Alice and her husband the Earl of Athlone paid a return visit to Saudi Arabia. This occasion, the first on which Ibn Saud had ever deigned to receive a woman in public, was significant also in that American oilmen were just bringing oil on-stream at the Dhahran Well, Dammam No. 7. The British royal visit was ill-equipped to take such a momentous event on board. It was judged prudent to cultivate good relations between London and Riyadh, not least because of the Italian naval presence in the Red Sea and contacts that were developing between Saudi Arabia and Nazi Germany; but the significance of the Saudi oil resource was not yet weighing heavily in Whitehall deliberations. The British minister Reader Bullard had several meetings with Ibn Saud, well aware that London's Palestine policy would contribute little to good relations between Britain and Saudi Arabia.[12] Such contacts at least maintained pragmatic contact between the two kingdoms and succeeded in maintaining Riyadh's distance from the Axis camp.

The prospectors of what was now the California Arabian Standard Oil Company (Casoc) had spent nearly five years on a largely fruitless search, but with seven wells drilled into the Dammam Dome the decision was taken to deepen Well No. 7. The oil flowed and went on flowing: 16 March, 2130 barrels; 17 March, 2209; 18 March, 2128; 19 March, 2117; 20 March, 2149; 21 March, 3372.[13] It was not difficult now to envisage the prodigious wealth of Saudi Arabia. In May 1939 Ibn Saud was happy to inspect his first drilling rig, his first oil pipeline, and his 8000-ton tanker, the *D. G. Schofield*. Already Casoc had paid him £200,000 and all the signs were that this was only a beginning. But then another ambitious man embarked upon a grandiose scheme of conquest that – at least in the short term – dashed all Ibn Saud's hopes: on 1 September 1939 Adolf Hitler invaded Poland and what would rapidly escalate into the Second World War had begun. The international oil markets were in turmoil; expensive tankers could not be risked plying round to the Persian Gulf; Dammam No. 7 and its erstwhile prolific companions were all but closed down; and Ibn Saud was forced to wait for better times.

In the event the King of Saudi Arabia proved to be far from hostile to Nazi Germany. Diplomatic relations were opened with Berlin and in February 1939 Ibn Saud assured Hitler by personally-delivered letter 'that it is our foremost aim to see the friendly and intimate relations with the German Reich developed to the utmost limits'.[14] At the same time Ibn Saud was informing Fritz Grobba, head of German operations in the Middle East, that at heart he 'hated the English'. Some of Ibn Saud's advisors (for example, private secretary Yussuf Yassin and royal doctor Midhat Sheikh al Ardh) were markedly pro-German, cheering broadcast news of German victories; but, in one judgement, Ibn Saud never allowed his pro-Axis advisors to deflect him from the judgement 'he had always held that Britain was the power best fitted to help him; and even in the darkest moments of British retreat, he forced his courtiers to listen to the radio news bulletins from London and to applaud whenever they gave news of a British victory'.[15] Winston Churchill was later to praise Ibn Saud for 'his steadfast, unswerving and unflinching loyalty' to Great Britain and her allies throughout the course of the war. But this was either ill-informed rhetoric or pragmatic accommodation in desperate circumstances. Ibn Saud was well prepared to maintain cordial relations with both sides, uncertain as to the outcome and unwilling to be trapped on the losing side.

A Saudi arms agreement with Mussolini had already been concluded; and in July 1939 Ibn Saud negotiated with Hitler for 4000 rifles, ammunition and the building of an arms factory near Riyadh. Japan, sensitive to the abundance of Saudi oil, had also concluded a treaty of friendship and trade and was bidding for its own oil concession. But friendship with fascist Italy, Nazi Germany and imperial Japan did nothing to erode Ibn Saud's enthusiasm for good relations with Great Britain. The British representatives in Jeddah were constantly treated to Ibn Saud's affirmations of his undying loyalty to the British Crown. Ibn Saud, in the words of one historian, was 'clearly adept at being all things to all men'.[16] And when he judged the likely outcome of the war he carefully eased his politics onto the winning side. The German arms deal came to nothing; and the Japanese quest for an oil concession was gently declined. The British, tipped off by Ibn Saud that Philby planned an anti-war tour in the United States, detained him in Bombay in August 1940; though later (April 1941) Ibn Saud was happy to give refuge to the pro-Nazi Rashid Ali al Kilani who had planned rebellion in Iraq.

It is easy with hindsight to see how Ibn Saud worked to cultivate good relations with both sides during the Second World War; but it is equally plain to understand how his anti-Jewish posture made him particularly sympathetic to many of the Nazi aims. Perhaps Hitler's 'final solution' to the Jewish Question was excessive, as Ibn Saud suggested to Lord Belhaven in Bahrain in 1939, for it was necessary only 'to have shorn them of their possessions' since the Jews were 'a race accursed by God, according to His Holy Book, and destined to final destruction and eternal damnation'.[17] Such an attitude necessarily informed Ibn Saud's view of Palestine, where it seemed obvious that Jews were using terrorism and other methods to steal Arab land. At the beginning of the war Philby proposed an ambitious scheme whereby, for a sum of £20 million, Jewish immigration to western Palestine would be allowed, with the Arab inhabitants shipped out to Saudi Arabia and other sympathetic countries. It is hard to imagine how Ibn Saud could have countenanced such a scheme but, according to Philby (January 1940), the King said he would give 'a definite answer at the appropriate time'; Philby later told his wife that the scheme had been agreed.[18] Again it appears that Ibn Saud's pragmatism and perhaps his mercenary instinct were more persuasive influences than what the Koran might or might not say about the Jewish race. The whole affair is clouded in mystery. Ibn Saud later expressed much indignation at the idea of such a bribe, and how could he ever negotiate on such a basis ('we cannot be protected from the treachery of the Jews')? It is of some interest that Washington was well acquainted with the scheme, considered as it was during a time when the United States was becoming increasing involved in the affairs of Saudi Arabia (see below).

In 1941 President Roosevelt was invited by the State Department to extend the Lend-Lease provisions to Saudi Arabia, not least as a device for protecting American oil interests through the period of the war. On 18 July he responded in a brief note to Jesse Jones, the Federal Loan Administrator: 'Will you tell the British they can take care of the King of Saudi Arabia. This is a little far afield for us.'[19] But the US administration was becoming increasingly aware of the massive war drains on American energy resources; it was essential that Washington considered the availability of foreign oil supplies, not just for the duration of the war but in the post-war period when fresh war needs and escalating domestic demand would arise. On 18 February 1943 Roosevelt reversed his earlier peremptory decision and brought Saudi Arabia within the terms of the Lend-Lease framework. Ibn Saud was now learning that even though oil production might be restricted under the constraints of war elsewhere there were significant compensations to be won. During the first three years of the Second World War Britain had

donated an annual £3 million in goods and coin; and Casoc had made two payments of £750,000 in anticipation of future oil sales. In addition the Lend-Lease
provision made some $33 million (in cash, goods and bullion) available to Ibn
Saud, a useful boost to a state treasury hit by falling pilgrim revenues and tribal
demands in Nejd through drought and famine. Lend-Lease and other revenues
were also useful for specifically royal expenditure: work began on a new palace
in the gardens of al-Kharj near Riyadh and the growing number of profligate
Saudi princes required appropriate funds. The princes Faisal and Khaled, developing their taste for American automobiles, requested fourteen more for family
use and were upset when only two were made available.[20] The British complained
of such 'extravagance' and 'abuse of His Majesty's Government's generosity';
while an American report commented on the 'chaotic' state of Saudi financial
controls. None the less it remained essential for the United States and Britain to
maintain cordial relations with Ibn Saud, straddling as he did the largest oil
reserves in the world.

The United States, immeasurably strengthened by the military stimulation of
the American economy, then devised a $57 million post-war aid package for
Saudi Arabia, a scale of calculated largesse that an impoverished Britain could
not hope to match. At the Yalta Conference (February 1945) Roosevelt mentioned to Churchill that soon he would be meeting Ibn Saud: the British, despite
all Churchill's efforts, were gradually being eased out of their traditional relationship with Saudi Arabia. On 25 January 1945 Ibn Saud met King Farouq of Egypt
at Yenbo, an encounter that encouraged the birth of the League of Arab States
(the Arab League) in March of that year. Then, in early February, the King of
Saudi Arabia, accompanied by a party of 48 people, headed for the Jeddah pier to
board the USS *Murphy*, which would take them to the Great Bitter Lake in the
Gulf of Suez for a planned meeting with President Roosevelt aboard the USS
Quincy. It was natural in these circumstances that Ibn Saud, conscious of his duty
to feed his companions on the trip, should ensure that a flock of sheep was
brought along.

When Ibn Saud disembarked from the *Murphy* he presented each member of
the crew with $40, and offered gold daggers and swords to the senior officers;
whereupon the ship's captain presented the King of Saudi Arabia with binoculars
and machine guns. Then Ibn Saud, in poor physical shape, had to be hoisted
aboard the *Quincy*. Various topics were discussed, with Palestine given particular
attention. When Ibn Saud was reminded of the sufferings of the Jews during the
war he commented: 'Give the Jews and their descendants the choicest lands and
homes of the Germans who have oppressed them.' To this suggestion Roosevelt
had no obvious answer: in other respects he was meticulous in observing Ibn
Saud's Wahhabist sensitivities, refraining from alcohol and leaving the room
whenever he needed a cigarette.

Churchill's subsequent meeting with Ibn Saud, at a hotel in the Fayyum Oasis,
appeared to have been conducted with somewhat less aplomb. The British

premier began by declaring his awareness that Ibn Saud's religion required that he deprive himself of smoking and alcohol, and then he added: 'I must point out that my rule of life prescribes as an absolutely sacred rite smoking cigars and also the drinking of alcohol before, after and if need be during all meals and in the intervals between them.' Thereafter, for several hours of discussion, Churchill indulged in whisky and pungent cigars in the presence of the pious Custodian of the Muslim Holy Cities.[21] Churchill also presumed to suggest that now there should be some response to the years of British subsidy to Ibn Saud: if Britain had helped the Saudi King for so long then why should favours – in particular regarding a Palestine deal – not now be asked? Ibn Saud did not take well to Churchill wielding what the King chose to call the 'big stick'. Such pressure, exerted by the British premier over the Palestine Question and other issues, was poorly calculated to influence the proud Arab monarch.

On 5 April 1945 Roosevelt formally confirmed in writing his promises to Ibn Saud of protection for the Palestine Arabs, undertakings solemnly made 'in my capacity as Chief of the Executive Branch' of the US government. A week later Roosevelt was dead. His successor, Harry Truman, felt no obligation to promises that may or may not have been made ('I have to answer to hundreds of thousands who are anxious for the success of Zionism; I do not have hundreds of thousands of Arabs among my constituents'). But Saudi relations with Britain and the United States were set to survive both Churchill and Truman: oil would always retain its considerable political persuasive power.

At the end of the Second World War Ibn Saud was 70 years of age, there was unrest in many surrounding countries (Yemen, Palestine, Lebanon, Syria, Iraq and Jordan), Egypt was redoubling its efforts to expel the British, Iran was running into crisis over its confrontation with Western oil interests, and Saudi Arabia itself faced new tensions with Britain over border disputes in the eastern regions of the country. Oil revenues were flowing into Riyadh, but even these caused fresh problems. Saudi political administration drastically needed reform but the traditions of a feudal dynasty, burdened with a massive and growing nepotism, were ill-equipped to drag Saudi Arabia into the modern age.

On 14 May 1948 the State of Israel came into existence; and Ibn Saud, still sensitive to Roosevelt's earlier assurances of protection for the Palestinian Arabs, was outraged. Throughout the Arab world there was turmoil, with massive demonstrations, attacks on American legations, and angry talk of an economic war against the United States. Ibn Saud expressed his 'shock' at what he perceived as betrayal by Washington; and cancelled a portion of the $15 million loan agreed with the American Export–Import Bank. Such a mild response did little to trouble the Washington strategists, now intent on shaping a post-war strategy for US global hegemony. In such a scheme it would prove possible to cultivate both Israel and Saudi Arabia as crucial US allies.

The Arab attempts to reverse the UN-sanctioned creation of Israel were doomed from the start – not only because of the vigour with which the Jews

defended their newly-acquired Arab land but also because the Arabs themselves were often poorly organised and indifferently motivated. Egypt acquired
the Gaza Strip, just as the ruler of Transjordan, Abdullah, acquired parts of the
west bank of the Jordan River. In the event the Arabs, accustomed to mutual
distrust and individual politicking, were unable to act with the co-ordinated
response to the loss of Arab land that the situation required. Ibn Saud – while,
with Faisal and his other sons, bitterly resenting the Jewish occupation of
ancient Arab territory – had no wish to further the ambitions of the Hashemites
and other groups traditionally hostile to the Saudi state. In 1950 there was little
Saudi interest in Abdullah's campaign for international recognition of his
combined Palestinian and Transjordan territories; and when Abdullah was
assassinated the following year by an Arab nationalist the Saudis showed little
regret.

It is significant also that Ibn Saud, who had secured his kingdom by the sword,
was not averse to opportunistic land grabs of his own. On 14 October 1949 Saudi
Arabia notified the British government that it was laying claim to some 50,000
square miles of desert stretching eastwards from Hasa, a substantial extension of
Saudi territory. Ibn Saud was now attempting to acquire land extending along the
Trucial Coast towards the Strait of Hormuz, a move that would bring parts of
Qatar, Abu Dhabi and Muscat within the Saudi domain. The region, mostly
wasteland in the southern part of the peninsula but including a few gardens and
oases around Buraimi, quickly escalated as a minor conflict with Britain. Here
London was determined to act on behalf of the Trucial Sheikhdom of Abu Dhabi
and the Sultanate of Muscat and Oman, whose foreign policies it managed with
legal consent.

The area in dispute had long been a source of conflict, with the Saudis couch-
ing their claim in ancient and historic terms. Ibn Saud's ancestors had occupied
the region for many years: some Buraimi dwellers had periodically considered
themselves to be Saudi subjects, and old documents were available to demonstrate Buraimi links with the traditional rulers of Riyadh. In more recent history
the region had changed hands several times. In 1952, not long before the death of
Ibn Saud, the Saudis captured the Buraimi Oasis; and then in 1955 the Sheikh of
Abu Dhabi and the Sultan of Muscat and Oman expelled the Saudis from the
area, forcing large numbers of tribesmen to seek refuge in Saudi Arabia.[22] The
dispute was not about history or even land *per se*; again it concerned oil.
American prospectors now had thoughts that substantial energy reserves lay
under the neglected gardens, dilapidated huts and small oases of the region.
Suddenly the inhabitants of Buraimi were attracting the fresh attention of the
Saudis, the British and the ubiquitous Americans. It was a matter that would soon
attract the attention also of the United Nations and Secretary-General Dag
Hammarskjöld (see 'King Saud', below).

The Saudi claims on Buraimi, though suitably packaged in historical reference, were encouraged by the oilmen of the Arabian–American Oil Company

(ARAMCO).* They had an obvious interest in prospecting as widely as possible and it was plainly useful to underwrite their enterprise with the authority of Ibn Saud. It was soon clear that the Saudis themselves were not certain what land they actually possessed or had legitimate claim to, whereupon ARAMCO organised a group of Arabist scholars and researchers to explore the options. The result was what might have been predicted. The researchers compared poetic chronicles with tax records for the Buraimi area, and then generated a useful compilation indicating that Saudi Arabia could legitimately claim not only Buraimi but also some 200 miles of 'beaches, banks and islands' along the Trucial Coast.[23] For the enterprising American oilmen it was a happy conclusion.[24]

Ibn Saud's powers were now fading fast. While the ARAMCO entrepreneurs and oilmen manoeuvred for commercial advantage the once redoubtable King of Saudi Arabia anguished over his arthritic knees and diminished sexual prowess. Ibn Saud's forty-third and perhaps final son, Hamoud, had been born in 1947 – a solitary arrival after the eight additional sons born between 1940 and 1943, when Ibn Saud was approaching 70 years of age.[25] The commander of the USS *Murphy*, asked to return a medicine chest left behind by the King's doctors, first glanced inside and discovered a vast array of aphrodisiacs. It is recorded that Ibn Saud's concubines – at least in his last years – were young girls, on the ancient theory that contact with young flesh can infuse a fading libido with new vitality. The King of Saudi Arabia, the founder of a nation courted by presidents and monarchs, ended his days in a desperate paedophilia.

In 1947 a medical report on Ibn Saud, by E. A. White of the American Legation in Jeddah, noted exit and entry bullet wounds, a sabre scar, partial blindness, good teeth, a good heart and an obese abdomen. The hypertrophic arthritis was not expected to curtail another '10 to 15 years' of life. But three years later another US medical report noted that Ibn Saud was 'considerably aged and enfeebled' and 'increasingly senile', by then permanently confined to a wheelchair. The King's final years were lived through growing depression and demoralisation, as he was forced to acknowledge his almost total blindness, his physical immobility, his sexual impotence, the deaths of loved ones, delinquency in his own family, political confusion at the heart of the Kingdom, and intolerable international affairs over which he had no influence. He missed the 1950 *hajj*,

---

* Within a decade of the significant oil strike of March 1938 the American oilmen were helping to shape Ibn Saud's foreign policy. Standard Oil of California (Socal) had already sold a share in their Arabian concession to the Texas Oil Company in exchange for Texaco deals elsewhere. After the Second World War, Standard Oil of New Jersey (Esso, now Exxon) and Socony-Vacuum (Mobil) invested in the Arabian venture, with the entire enterprise then called the Arabian American Oil Company (ARAMCO), the largest US corporate group outside the United States. The ARAMCO share distribution was Socal, 30 per cent; Texaco, 30 per cent; Esso, 30 per cent; and Mobil, 10 per cent (Lacey, 1982, pp. 290–1).

allowing his son Saud to deputise for him; in 1951 Ibn Saud performed his last *hajj*, in great heat and in great personal discomfort. By 1953 any journey to Mecca in the summer heat was impossible for an obese monarch suffering constant pain. His last act was to sign a decree authorising the establishment of a Council of Ministers, which US embassy officials hoped would end the chaos in the Saudi administration.

Ibn Saud died in the small hours of 9 November 1953 in the arms of Faisal, his second son. Clad in a simple shroud the King's mortal remains were buried in an unmarked grave, his clothes sold in the market-place. The Saudi flag was lowered nowhere in the kingdom: since it bore the alleged word of God it could be lowered for no man.

THE DYNASTY CONTINUES

King Saud

Crown Prince Saud ibn Abdul Aziz, the eldest son of Ibn Saud, had already exploited his position as the likely successor to the King. In the desert outside Riyadh he had built for himself the Nasriyah Palace, within whose gates an avenue of tamarisk trees ran through a garden of flowers, lawns, caged birds and a blue-tiled pool fed from wells tens of thousands of feet below the ground. At dusk some 25,000 coloured light bulbs illuminated the main palace and mosque, the palace walls glowing a bright orange in the darkened desert. Saud, as predicted, succeeded his father as the King of Saudi Arabia, whereupon in November 1953 he ordered the Nasriyah Palace to be razed: the £4 million complex was now deemed too modest and only a £10 million replacement would suffice.

The new building was enclosed by a 7-mile pink wall with massive porticoed gates giving access to massive esplanades, swimming pools, boating pools, fountains and palm groves. The veritable township included a hospital, mosques, barracks and the inevitable multicoloured lights focusing around neon inscriptions from the Koran. The entire complex, designed by Lebanese architects, was said to consume more water and electricity than the whole of the rest of Riyadh.[26] At the same time King Saud was determined that the capital of the state should reflect its status as the heart of a modern nation. Traditional architectural modes gave way to modern imported ones, with cement and reinforced concrete structures appearing everywhere. At the end of 1953 the Riyadh Municipality (*Baladiyah*) was created to manage the development of the city, planning essential services, allocating land, and specifying the regulations for building and commerce. But town planning, where it existed at all, was haphazard, and private developers were allowed much discretion. One visitor remarked in 1956: 'Wherever one goes and in whatever direction one looks, new buildings of every sort and for every purpose are springing up. There is no attempt of any kind at town planning. Anyone who wants to build a house, large or small, does so, and apparently without the slightest regard to his neighbours ... the resulting confusion, general untidiness, bad roads and clouds of dust raised by the ubiquitous bulldozers produces an overall effect of complete chaos. No doubt, when it is all finished, it will look very different, but the old walled town that Philby knew and loved ... will have vanished.'[27] The eastern stretch of walls, including the celebrated Thumayri gate, were the last to disappear; old mud buildings quickly fell before the developers; and by March 1954 a new 'town palace' of masonry stood with the ruins of the old palace all around. King Saud had stipulated that the new buildings were to house the Governorate of Riyadh (*Qasr al-Hukm*), the Palace of Justice (*Qasr al-Adl*), and an auditorium where Saud could receive visitors. Even the Great Mosque was demolished, to be supplanted by a concrete structure with colonnades and two tall minarets in stark contrast to the earlier building.

In the event the efforts of King Saud were to become an embarrassment, a period of history best forgotten by friends of the House of Saud. It is true that in October 1979 the then King Khaled urged his Minister of Information to declare that 'the name of the late King Saud should not be omitted from stories of the Kingdom's history: some people skip King Saud when reciting the chronology of Saudi rulers, because they think to please His Majesty King Khaled. It is exactly the contrary.' In fact it was Saud who was largely responsible for the pre-stressed concrete work around the Prophet's tomb at Medina; and responsible also for the abolition of the taxes that pilgrims had traditionally paid in Mecca. In Jeddah the construction of modern *hajj* reception and medical facilities was ordered by Saud, just as he initiated the complex road systems that aided the growing numbers of pilgrims to the Holy Land.

It was the construction of a vast infrastructure that led to Saud's downfall. He wanted to be remembered for introducing comprehensive health, welfare and education provisions in a society still largely mired in feudal tradition; and it was this untramelled ambition that almost bankrupted Saudi Arabia in the process. Concrete megaliths to accommodate the swelling bureaucracy, several dozen hospitals, many schools, two new universities (Riyadh University founded in 1957 as a 'College of Arts'; Medina University established in 1961 as a theological seminary), several thousand miles of metalled highway[28] – it was all too much to afford, even for a state blessed with prodigious oil revenues.

Saud had been Crown Prince for twenty years, and though he was destined to rule for eleven he never rose to the challenge of being Ibn Saud's immediate successor (Table 5.1). He was profligate with the state revenues, recklessly dispensing hard cash from sacks when he journeyed by car into the desert. Like his father he sired more than a hundred offspring (fifty-three sons and fifty-four daughters), so massively complicating the entitlements of nepotism and succession. Moreover, in struggling to wrest some control over Saudi oil management away from ARAMCO Saud merely assigned powers to a fresh set of mercenary

Table 5.1   Modern Saudi dynasty

Ibn Saud	1932–1953
Saud	1953–1964
Faisal	1964–1975
Khaled	1975–1982
Fahd	1982–

foreigners. He began by drawing up plans for an independent Saudi tanker fleet: with Saudi oil transported in ships of the Saudi-Arabian Maritime Tanker Company it would be possible for the Saudis to control their own markets and prices. A Saudi Marine Training School was established to generate a class of Arabian tanker men, so that over a period more and more oil would be transferred from ARAMCO to Saudi vessels. But the visionary scheme foundered on the personal ambitions of powerful individuals. In reality a partnership emerged that served the private interests of Abdullah Suleiman, Ibn Saud's erstwhile Finance Minister, a group of Jeddah merchants, and the Greek shipping magnate Aristotle Onassis. The Arabian monarch had done little to establish Saudi control over its own massive energy resources.

The aim was to conduct negotiations in secret. In Jeddah Onassis was given two gold-sheathed swords and two horses, while Mrs Onassis was invited to the royal harem. The comprehensive rights of ARAMCO's 1933 concession were ignored, though it was inevitable that details of the new scheme would leak out. On 24 April 1954 the US ambassador George Wadsworth protested to King Saud that the planned use of the Onassis tanker fleet represented a direct threat to American interests. Now it seemed that Saud would continue with his plan to break the ARAMCO monopoly over the prospecting, extracting and transporting of Saudi Arabian oil. In response the ARAMCO partners resolved on a boycott of all Onassis tankers around the world, at the same time telling King Saud that when the first Saudi–Onassis vessel arrived at the Ras Tanura terminal it would not be admitted.

Such measures seemed insufficient to deter Saud. In mid-1954 a group of Riyadh functionaries celebrated the Hamburg launching of the 46,000-ton tanker *Al Malik Saud al Awal* (*King Saud the First*), the Onassis *Baunummer 883* now announced as the flagship of the new Saudi tanker fleet. One problem was an initial dispute about whether pious Wahhabists could allow a woman anywhere near the launching of the new ship; eventually Princess Anne-Marie von Bismarck was allowed to break a bottle over the bows. But alcohol was prohibited. The Saudis insisted that the bottled fluid should be nothing less than holy water from the sacred Zemzem spring in Mecca (since such fluid does not build up pressure when shaken it took three attempts to shatter the bottle). Such are the problems that sexism and piety present to the launching of oil tankers. Now the United States was planning to orchestrate problems of a more substantial kind.

In Iran premier Mossadeq had been ousted by a CIA-backed *coup d'état* in 1951 for daring to expropriate Iranian oil for the nation. Now the US Secretary of State John Foster Dulles thought it worthwhile to remind King Saud of this precedent. In an internal document Dulles commented: 'King and advisors should ask themselves where they would stand after three years or even one year without the oil revenues' ... the effects would be nothing less than 'disastrous'.[29] Now King Saud was having doubts, not only because of American pressure but also as a result of tensions between various parties to the new arrangements (for example, Onassis was objecting to claims by the middleman Spiros Catapodis for an initial payment of $2.8 million for setting up the tanker deal). Stavros Niarchos, Onassis's arch-rival, was helped by the US government to ensure that King Saud became well aware of the scandal that Catapodis was creating in Europe. The upshot was that Saud dropped the whole scheme, the dispute was taken to international arbitration, and all ARAMCO's rights and privileges were reinstated. Washington had demonstrated that it was the United States, not Saudi Arabia, that had ultimate rights over Saudi oil resources.

The Buraimi issue served as a further example where international pressure was the decisive factor in resolving a dispute within the Arabian peninsula. Here the Saudi claims, bolstered by ARAMCO-supplied documentation, were taken to international arbitration in the autumn of 1955. Soon it was clear that legal conventions were being flouted: one of the judges, a Saudi, had illicitly advised a witness, and an attempt was made within the courtroom to influence pro-Saudi testimony. The British representative, Sir Reader Bullard, resigned from the proceedings in protest; and in October 1955 Britain resorted to the time-honoured method of settling international disputes. A British military contingent from Oman occupied Buraimi without serious resistance, and then promptly expelled the Saudis. It was not the end of the matter.

In January 1959 the UN Secretary-General Dag Hammarskjöld visited Saudi Arabia at the invitation of King Saud, whereupon Saud and Faisal declared that they intended to take the Buraimi issue to the Security Council. Hammarskjöld commented that such a move would only freeze the positions of the contending parties; and that, with the approval of the British, he would attempt a solution of the problem. Meetings began in September 1959 between Abdur Rahman Azam, Saud's personal representative, and Harold Beeley, the deputy head of the British Mission to the United Nations.[30] In August 1960 it was agreed that Hammarskjöld should appoint a special representative to report and mediate; and that a resumption of diplomatic relations between Britain and Saudi Arabia should be discussed.[31] No early solution was achieved: it was not until the early 1970s, under the reign of King Fahd, that the Buraimi dispute was finally settled. Sheikh Zayid kept Buraimi but Saudi Arabia was content to acquire another compensatory slice of desert territory.

It had soon become apparent that Saud's administration was running into problems. He had created the Council of Ministers specified in Ibn Saud's last decree, but paid little attention to its advice. Saud preferred to discuss issues with his sons and court sycophants, sensitive to flattery and increasingly unable to deal with legitimate political criticisms. Disagreements in the House of Saud became public knowledge, and canny advisors despaired that essential government reforms were not being implemented (for example, the ageing Philby complained of the 'appalling corruption' at every level of the Saudi administration, and of the young princes learning their morals 'in the gutters of the west' – following Philby's strictures Saud publicly spat upon him³²).

Saud had disbursed oil revenues with profligate abandon, often with worthy but unrealistic intentions. At the same time, like many Saudi rulers, he had tolerated the worst excesses of nepotism, corruption and personal indulgence. Riyadh had now become 'a centre of ludicrously ostentatious personal wealth and a growing network of governmental graft and corruption'.³³ The *ulema* were alienated from the regime, as were many young Saudis attracted by Nasser's radical nationalism. In 1958 the royal princes, the sheikhs and the *ulema* combined to force Saud to relinquish power to his younger brother, the Crown Prince Faisal. Another phase of the modern Saudi dynasty had begun.

King Faisal

Saud had been forced to step down by a motley group, including 72 out of 1500 princes led by a character dubbed Muhammed 'Twin-Evil', an elder brother to Saud and an alcoholic Bedouin with an instinctive propensity to absolutism. Faisal was selected as Saud's successor as the candidate most likely to follow the path of Ibn Saud and to provide the family with a much-needed aura of respectability. The Saudi historian Abdallah Anwar commented: 'He [Faisal] eliminated obvious corruption and continued the subtle variety.' Faisal was, above all, committed to the sanctity of Islamic law: 'What does man aspire to? He wants good. It is there in the Islamic *sharia*. He wants justice. It is there, in the *sharia*. He wants security. It is also there. Man wants freedom. It is there. He wants propagation of science. It is there. Everything is there, inscribed in the Islamic *sharia*.'³⁴ The extent to which any such elements existed in the kingdom could be debated, but no-one doubted that Faisal was a very different man from the profligate brother that he had supplanted.

Faisal, living an austere and frugal life, refused to live in any of Saud's neon-lit palaces; his wife of thirty years' duration bore five of his eight children; and his governorship of Hejaz earned him wide respect. At the same time Faisal has been represented as a 'subtle manipulator ... extremely adept at concealing his misdeeds, regardless of their enormity and immorality, behind a veil of phoney correctness'.³⁵ He introduced a period of economic restraint in an effort to improve the nation's chaotic finances, but the measures were unpopular among the domestic constituency accustomed to Saud's profligate largesse. In consequence various factions combined to restore Saud to power on the understanding that some form of representative government would be introduced. In December 1960 Faisal resigned as prime minister and Saud enjoyed a brief new period of rule, but the Yemeni *coup* in September 1962 posed a direct threat to the Saudi monarchy and forced an ailing Saud to return power to Faisal. In November 1964 Saud was formally deposed and Faisal became King, now freshly empowered to emphasise the traditional and religious elements in Arab culture.

During the mid-1960s King Faisal, as a bitter opponent of communism and Zionism (which he tended to equate), struggled to form an Islamic Front as a rival to Egyptian socialism. It was Egypt, he declared, and to a lesser extent Syria, that were responsible for the growing communist influence in the Middle East. But what Faisal perceived as the mounting Zionist threat encouraged a Saudi accommodation with Egypt, particularly in the aftermath of the 1967 Arab–Israeli war; by the time of the next Arab conflict with Zionism (1973) the Saudi–Egyptian alliance, negotiated between Faisal and Egypt's Anwar Sadat, was sufficiently robust to provide a political foundation for Arab strategy.[36] But hostility to Israel inevitably created fresh tensions with the United States, a confusing posture for a Saudi King 'whose pathological anticommunism would make Ronald Reagan blush'.[37] One consequence was that Faisal always moderated his support for the cause of Arab liberation, as for example in the struggle of the Palestinians for a national homeland.

At the Arab summit in Rabat in December 1969 Faisal disappointed the other Arab leaders by refusing to increase the financial aid to Arab states confronting Israel. The Saudi government continued to help the Palestinian al-Fatah guerrilla organisation, in preference to the Marxist-oriented Popular Front for the Liberation of Palestine, but Faisal refused to countenance use of the 'oil weapon' to put added pressure on Western states supporting Israel. Washington suspected that the Saudis would be reluctant to antagonise the United States and that in any case it would be difficult to use the oil weapon to decisive effect. After the death of Nasser in 1970 Saudi relations with Egypt and the United States improved, ARAMCO announced vast expansion plans, and Washington moved inexorably towards greater dependence on oil from the Middle East. Faisal himself, despite mounting Arab pressures, tried to maintain a distance between politics and the oil trade; there was no need, he always believed, for political philosophy in a land blessed with the word of God revealed through the Prophet. When one historian interviewed King Faisal in 1966 on the question of socialism he commented: 'We have the Holy Koran and the *sharia* Law. Why do we need socialism, capitalism, communism or any other ideology.'[38]

Faisal might have mentioned oil. At the time of his accession to power in 1964 oil was earning Saudi Arabia about half a billion dollars a year; by 1970 the figure had risen to more than $1.1 billion; and by 1974 around $27.8 billion. Under the rule of King Faisal the oil revenues had increased by a factor of more than 50. In one context this meant that the Saudi population of not more than 6 million had three times the national income of the nearly 40 million Egyptians.

Thus at the beginning of the 1970s the Arab world turned increasingly to Saudi Arabia as a power that might realistically challenge the growing Israeli dominance in the region. Nasser, the strong arm of Arab nationalism, was no more; many of the oppressed, in their poverty and desperation, turned to Faisal as 'the new hero of the Arab world'.[39] He was poorly equipped for such a role.

The dissident Said Aburish considers the four acts during his lifetime, of which Faisal 'made much'.[40] Mention has already been made of his long marriage to Iffat, his fourth and last wife, an apparent exercise in fidelity uncommon among typical Saudi rulers. Aburish wonders why Faisal did little to discourage 'the overindulgence of his brothers and relatives, for which the state paid', as if Faisal could have controlled such matters. (One Saudi writer estimates that Ibn Saud's forty-odd sons married some 1400 women.) Then Faisal took pride in his abolition of Saudi slavery in 1962, late enough by all accounts. Little discussion is offered by most Saudi apologists of the fact that Faisal protected slavery for most of his life, to the point that in 1936 he renegotiated a Saudi–British treaty to prevent any need for Saudi Arabia to abolish institutionalised slavery. Faisal's record in this context is, at best, mixed: the thousands of nominally freed slaves remained where they were; and then, as now, foreign workers were forced to endure virtual enslavement in the homes of their employers.

Faisal's introduction of control on the royal purse was, according to Aburish, 'no more than a blatant propaganda lie'. Friends and family were compensated in 'more subtle ways', with the family continuing to exploit the treasury but in ways that were more difficult to trace. Public land was offered to family and friends, to the extent that 80 per cent of Saudi Arabia was rendered 'Aradi Emeria' (land of the emirs). The celebrated Saudi Oil Minister Sheikh Ahmed Zaki Yamani admitted to his biographer, Jeffrey Robinson, that he owned more than $300 million worth of Faisal-donated land.[41] One estimate suggests that land given away by Faisal amounts in value to between $35 billion and $50 billion.[42] Later kings followed this habit – to the invariable advantage of the House of Saud.

It has also been emphasised by supporters of Faisal that he ordered the opening of the first schools for girls in the country (see also Chapter 1). These were of limited scope, totally unconnected with any efforts to improve the lot of Saudi women. Asked when he would grant rights to women he replied: 'When we grant them to men.'[43] The Saudi opposition politician Abdel Ameer Mousa commented that Faisal should be remembered for the number of people he imprisoned and for torture – 'In this regard, he was the worst one of them all.'

Faisal supported the Yemeni monarchy with funds and arms against Nasser (see 'The Yemen Wars', below), and so weakened Egypt's efforts to unite the Arab world behind a radical agenda. In general Faisal continued the traditional Saudi policy of buying support, typically from reactionary regimes that were resistant to any modern or nationalist aspiration. He also subverted Arab opinion by bribing journalists and buying newspaper companies, a ploy that has continued up to modern times. It was characteristic of Faisal that he should support the

Pakistani army and its repressive Chief of Staff General Zia al Huq against the elected premier, Ali Bhutto – a policy that encouraged the overthrow and execution of the radical Pakistani leader. (As early as 1959, when Faisal was Prime Minister, the Egyptian magazine *Al Musawar* described how the CIA had worked with Saudi personnel to create Egyptian political groups opposed to Nasser.)

The 1973 oil embargo against the West, adopted when Egypt started the October War against Israel, was only undertaken by Faisal under massive Arab pressure throughout the Middle East. Though driven to such action, he was 'horrified';[44] and 'rescinded the action as soon as possible'.[45] Faisal had no wish to damage relations with Washington. To the *Time* correspondent Wilton Wynn he declared: 'US relations are a pillar of Saudi policy.' For its part the United States was happy to accept Saudi Arabia as its regional proxy. In the context of Arab–Israeli relations it was inevitable that the pragmatic accord between Washington and Riyadh would be frequently tested. Thus as events had drifted towards war in 1973, Faisal resolved to demonstrate at least token support for Palestinian rights. Yamani was despatched to Washington to declare that oil and politics could no longer be regarded as inseparable. Yamani indicated that the current limited production of 7.2 million barrels a day could be increased to 20 million provided that the United States was prepared to create 'the right political atmosphere'. Early in May, Faisal was commenting to Frank Jungers, the ARAMCO president, that he could 'not stand alone much longer' in the Middle East as a friend of the United States.[46]

The Arab (Egyptian–Syrian) attack on Israel on 6 October 1973 came as a shock to Faisal and his armed forces. Faisal had urged Sadat not to resort to the military option, and now he was worried about the possible consequences for the traditional feudal regimes of the Arabian peninsula. The Saudis, with little option under Arab pressure, deployed a contingent in support of the Arab Foreign Legion; and saw a single day's action on 19 October. Henry Kissinger despatched letters to the various parties, including one to Saudi Arabia, whereupon Faisal replied: 'The US should force Israel to withdraw from Arab territories and to grant the Palestinian people their rights in their territory and homeland.' There was of course no prospect of any such response from Washington. The UN Security Council passed Resolution 338, demanding an end to the fighting; and Israel tightened its grip on occupied Arab land. Faisal was content that he had supported the Arab cause with arms, however minimal; and that he could be proud of how the Saudis had exploited the oil weapon. The Israelis had not been ejected from Arab territory, and Washington had not welcomed Saudi support for the Palestinian cause. But little harm had been done to US–Saudi relations. It would soon be business as usual.

Now, however, Faisal's reign was running to its close. His rule would be ended not by ambitious relatives seizing power or by natural infirmity and death – but by assassination. It has been pointed out many times that the history of the House of Saud 'is riddled with feuds, conspiracies, betrayals, violent deaths and the exploits of pretenders, a fact largely obscured by the relative absence of dynastic troubles during Ibn Saud's long reign'.[47] Events that followed the death of Ibn Saud – such as the wresting of power from Saud in 1964, family ruptures, and the assassination of Faisal – were characteristic of Saudi dynastic history. On 25 March 1975 King Faisal was killed by one of his nephews, Faisal ibn Musaid – a particular embarrassment that a family member should have resorted to such a crime.

The assassin's father, Musaid ibn Abdul Aziz, was a relatively obscure son of Ibn Saud, a brother of Abdul Muhsin, the governor of Medina. Faisal ibn Musaid, having spent time as a student in the United States and as an over-indulged young man in Beirut's political *demi-monde*, was soon depicted as having shared the streak of insanity that ran through his family. His Wahhabist elder brother Khaled, whose mother was a Rashidi with ample reason to hate Ibn Saud, had led a violent demonstration against the opening of a television station in Riyadh in 1965. To the fanatical Wahhabist it was plain that television was a radical step too far, akin to heresy. When the police arrived to quell the demonstration Khaled and his followers refused to disperse. It was not enough that Faisal had decreed that all love scenes in films would be edited out, even to the point that any shows of physical affection in cartoons would be banned. Khaled had one aim: television, however censored, was a gross violation of the Koran.

When the police officer trying to restore order realised that the leader of the demonstration was a Saudi prince he sent word to Faisal and awaited orders. Faisal gave instructions that force must be resisted by force; Khaled, a scion of the House of Saud, was not above the law. In the event, in conditions of mounting chaos, he was shot dead by the Chief of the Security Forces. A few years later Khaled's brother Faisal went to the United States as a student, beginning at San Francisco State, then to the University of California at Berkeley and finally to the University of Colorado at Boulder – where in 1970 he was arrested for conspiring to sell LSD. In 1971 King Faisal, horrified at the youth's behaviour, prohibited him from leaving Saudi Arabia again.

On the morning of 25 March 1975 a television crew was assembling to tape a small gathering in a modest office of the King in Riyadh. Ahmed Zaki Yamani was there, as were the Chief of Royal Protocol and other officials. As various dignitaries began filing into the room a young man ran towards King Faisal. Then he pulled a .38 pistol from under his robes and fired three initial shots, the first tearing open the King's jugular vein. A short time later Riyadh Radio made an official announcement that King Faisal was dead, killed by a 'mentally deranged' assassin who had acted alone.

A medical panel subsequently ruled that Prince Faisal ibn Musaid was, 'although mentally deranged, sane at the time of the murder' – so opening the way for his public execution. On 18 June 1975 the Saudi prince was paraded in front of the Palace of Justice in the main square of Riyadh; and then, wearing white robes and a blindfold, made to crouch over the execution block. In a moment a man wielding a huge sword beheaded him, whereupon the prince's head was displayed on a stake for a time before being removed with the body.[48] King Faisal, via two dreams that he related to his aunt in January 1975, had judged that he would not live out the year.[49]

King Khaled

King Faisal's successor, Khaled, did not want the job but agreed to become King to avoid family rupture and the possibility of a reversion to the Saudi tradition of blood-feuds.[50] Khaled was reportedly more interested in falconry than in kingship; he represented the traditionalists in the family; and in 1938, dining with Adolf Hitler on the night that Czechoslovakia ceded his claim to the Sudetenland, Khaled was evidently impressed by his German host (later he commented that Hitler was a much maligned man).[51] Khaled, despite his traditionalist disposition, was not an unpopular man. His weekly *majlis* were well attended, and he often entertained as many as a thousand relatives and followers for dinner after sunset prayers. His pursuit of falconry in the desert brought him close to the bedouin tribes, in contrast to Faisal who had been more interested in central government and the problems of international affairs.

Perhaps the most important Saudi development during Khaled's rule was the emergence of the so-called 'Sudeiri Seven' (or Al Fahd, Figure 5.2), the seven sons of Hassa al Sudeiri whom Ibn Saud married, divorced, allowed to marry his brother, forced to divorce, and then remarried. Three of the sons (Fahd, Sultan and Naif) were ministers for some time, with the rest appointed governors and deputy ministers. What has been represented as the Sudeiri *coup d'état* within the House of Saud meant that one particular faction had managed, through careful calculation, to lay hands on all the principal levers of power within the state. Thus Fahd, later to become King, became Khaled's Crown Prince; Sultan was secure as Minister of Defence (his son would later become famous in the 1991 Gulf War – see Chapter 6); Naif was Minister of the Interior; and Salman was given the governorship of Riyadh. In such circumstances fresh tensions emerged in the House of Saud, as the traditional seniority system was disrupted. The sons of the late King Saud were denied jobs in the government, a gross affront to normal expectation; and the sons of King Faisal, while allowed nominal positions, were denied effective power. The Foreign Minister, Prince Saud ibn Faisal, reportedly complained to King Hussain of Jordan that he was no more than an office boy.[52] In one reckoning the Sudeiris and their sons, only one of the principal Saudi factions among several, occupied some 63 key government posts. None the less, agitations elsewhere in Al Saud continued to apply some constraint on the worst excesses of Sudeiri ambition.

Khaled's years were punctuated also by the Muslim fundamentalist revolution (1978) in Iran, a cataclysmic problem in view of Ayatollah Khomeini's

Fahd	Sultan	Abdul Rahman	Turki	Nalf	Salman	Ahmed
1920–	1927–	1931–	1933–	1934–	1936–	1940–
King	Minister	Vice Minister	Former Vice	Minister	Governor	Deputy Governor
1982–	of Defence	of Defence	Minister of	of Interior	of Riyadh	of Mecca
	1962–	1978–	Defence/ Now	1975–	1962–	1975–8
	Second Deputy		black sheep			Vice
	Prime Minister		awaiting			Minister of
	1982–		rehabilitation			Interior
						1978–

Bandar	Fahd	Turki	Khaled
Ambassador	Governor	Works in	Chief of
to USA	Tabouk	Ministry of	Saudi
	Province	Information	Arabian Air
			Force

Fahd	Sultan	Abdul Aziz
Deputy	First Arab	Works in
Governor	astronaut/	Ministry
Eastern Province	Works	of
	in Ministry	Petroleum
	of	
	Information	

Muhammad	Faisal	Saud	Abdul Aziz
Governor	President	Deputy	18 years old
Eastern	Youth	Chief	
Province	Welfare	Foreign	
	Organisations	Intelligence	

Figure 5.2   The 'Sudeiri Seven' (the Al Fahd)

fanatical espousal of a rival version of Islam. Now the Iranian revolution was impacting on the Shi'a Muslims in Saudi Arabia, who represented around 15 per cent of the population. In time-honoured fashion a desperate Khaled, backed by his family and the traditional Wahhabists at the heart of the regime, set about incarcerating hundreds of Saudi Shi'as and Muslim fundamentalists newly tainted by a fresh Islamic vision. *Now it was necessary for Saudi Arabia, Kuwait, the United States and others to bolster the worthy Saddam Hussein of Iraq as a virtuous opponent of Iranian ambition.* It was necessary also, in these alarming times, to allow Saudi Arabia to sink ever deeper into the protective maw of American strategic policy.

The Khaled reign lasted six years, during which period substantial social changes occurred in Saudi Arabia against the backdrop of a pious and traditional monarch. It is significant also that Khaled's pious limitations were compounded by poor health. When in 1978 aero-engineering companies were invited to tender for Khaled's personal 747 aircraft the specification required that the plane could fly non-stop from Riyadh to Cleveland, Ohio – in order that the King could receive emergency heart treatment in the Cleveland Clinic. He had already had major heart surgery, and in 1978 went to Cleveland for a bypass. When Khaled's private 747 Jumbo jet was eventually delivered it contained an operating theatre and other appropriate facilities for doctors, carrying plasma and emergency resuscitation equipment.[53] It seems that devotion to the Koran – Khaled kept a small green leather-bound copy in a pocket and often mouthed verses – was insufficient to ensure good health.

The regime also witnessed the building of new tower blocks in Riyadh, Jeddah, Dammam and elsewhere, replacing the low-cost housing programme that had displeased Khaled on inspection ('I am not happy to see my people living in matchboxes'). The new apartments properly observed the Koranic requirement that men and women should entertain in their own separate reception rooms, with extra bedrooms for children of different sexes. But some of the new schemes were beset by problems: how, the Ministry of Housing wondered, could bedouins and their goats be cajoled to the eighteenth floor of a tower block? Such difficulties, it is reported, have left many apartments unoccupied.

In many other areas Khaled played the traditional role of the omnipotent Saudi monarch, much of his activity focusing on the management of the family. Newborn offspring were brought to him for inspection, young men were directed to the armed forces or to government service, proposed marriages and divorces were submitted for his approval, and fund disbursement and land distribution were royally supervised. By the early 1980s ex-ministers and junior princes were being given some £1000 a month with the thirty-one surviving sons of Ibn Saud individually receiving around £10,000 a month. The land gifts made by Faisal continued under Khaled, with tribal chiefs traditionally bribed to offer tracts of territory to the House of Saud. In such a fashion Khaled expanded the vast system of patronage that benefited mainly his relatives and supporters, using traditional practices to enrich privileged men beyond their dreams.

Khaled represented conservative and religious values, keen to conduct Muslim leaders to Mecca in order to pray and perform their seven perambulations around the Holy Kaaba. He was largely a stable and unthreatening monarch, but could explode in fits of rage. When Gaddafi criticised Saudi supervision of the *hajj*, Khaled declared: 'Gaddafi is a criminal with no conscience ... a madman with a childish mind ... an atheist. ... He is facing his final days.' And when the film *Death of a Princess* was shown on British television (see Chapter 1), Fahd proclaimed that law-breaking foreigners should suffer the same penalties as criminal Saudis. Under Khaled foreigners caught brewing or selling alcohol were caned publicly in the streets; in earlier times they might have been quietly expelled from the country.

In November 1979 Khaled was deeply shaken by the heretical seizure of the Grand Mosque in Mecca, exposing to him in the most graphic terms the mounting instability at the heart of the kingdom. He wept when he visited the 461 young soldiers wounded in the siege. Much of this was deeply incomprehensible to a traditional monarch ill suited to the management of Saudi influence in the modern world, and even before a new ruler emerged to manage the kingdom effective power had already passed into other hands.

King Fahd

On 13 June 1982 King Khaled, aged 69, died of a heart attack at his home in Taif. Now Fahd was on the throne, though he had already exercised considerable power for many years. Within a few hours of Khaled's death Fahd had named himself the ruler of Saudi Arabia; Abdullah became Crown Prince and First Deputy Prime Minister; and Sultan was appointed Second Deputy Prime Minister. Many observers, in Saudi Arabia and elsewhere, were well aware of the problems that Fahd had inherited; few thought him well equipped to solve them. He has been depicted as 'neither a firm ruler nor a decisive man', though talkative and with an inherited taste for opulence and wealth.[54]

In 1985, during a visit to the United States, Fahd surprised Vice President Bush by arriving two hours late for a White House meeting; and then talked endlessly about a Saudi soccer team when it was hoped he would discuss Gulf politics. The same indifference to punctuality caused Prime Minister Fukuda of Japan to wait for two hours in a hotel lobby; and compelled King Hussain of Jordan to circle Riyadh airport for an hour because Fahd had failed to arrive on time. By the late 1980s, at more than 6 feet tall, he had reached 300 pounds in weight, was suffering severe respiratory and back problems, and could not be trusted in the coach of the Queen of England (1987) before it had been reinforced to prevent it turning over. At more than one meeting, unable to stand for any length of time, Fahd addressed crowds from a seated position.

As soon as Fahd acquired important elements of power from Khaled he resolved that the Sudeiri Seven would be installed as the rightful rulers of the kingdom; when he became King he emphasised that Ibn Saud's decree intended that only 'legitimate' sons would inherit the crown, so excluding a clutch of sons born to assorted slaves and concubines. It was inevitable that the competing claims of various sons outside the Sudeiri Seven would store up problems for the succession in later years.[55] Fahd, as the supposed champion of the Saudi technocrats, had inherited various problems apart from the question of the succession; but, in the words of one journalist, he had not 'inherited the talent' to deal with them. He could, however, be relied upon – like most Saudi rulers – to further the global ambitions of the United States.

In 1984 the CIA director William Casey met Fahd on the King's 495-foot yacht, the *Abdul Aziz*, off Marbella; Admiral John Poindexter was also involved, as was Lieutenant Colonel Oliver North representing the National Security Council. President Ronald Reagan was later (1985) to have secret talks with Fahd to discuss Saudi contributions to the Nicaraguan Contra terrorists to aid the overthrow of the legitimate government. The previous year, William Casey was already contriving a scheme whereby North could clandestinely sell arms to the Iranians and then launder the money to the Contras' benefit. The CIA plot needed a middleman and so Fahd was selected as the perfect go-between to enable Washington to deal illegally with the Iranians. Fahd, the pious Custodian of the

Holy Cities, had no objection to such clandestine and illegal action: *Irangate* was up and running.

Within months the Saudi ambassador to France, Jameel al-Hojailian, had arranged a secret meeting in Germany with members of the Iranian revolutionary government. Now the Saudi businessman and arms dealer – on occasions seen laughing and shaking hands with Fahd – was negotiating on behalf of the CIA with the Israelis and the Iranian arms dealer Albert Hakim. The appropriate lines of communication had been established and Washington had developed the mechanisms for introducing a lethal dose of terrorism to yet another part of the Third World. This was not the only way in which a Saudi monarch was prepared to aid the United States in using terror to further its global ambitions.

Prime Minister Margaret Thatcher had met Crown Prince Fahd ibn Abdul Aziz in 1981, shortly before his accession to the throne. Then, despite what many saw as his premature grip on the reins of power, the British premier felt constrained to make a subsequently much-quoted observation: 'You say that this man runs the country? He didn't have a word to say for himself.' But Fahd had done no more than show typical deference to Khaled in his presence; when no longer in the company of his elder brother he spoke volumes. Few doubted his real power, or the fact that he ate and drank too much. At the same time he acquired the reputation of a workaholic in his earlier years, despite his prodigious girth and worsening health. Like his many brothers he had a penchant for ostentation and extravagance, expecting to enjoy his quota of palatial dwellings, luxury and all the affluent privileges of a Saudi royal.

King Fahd has used oil money repeatedly to buy political support in the Arab and Muslim worlds; and he has remained conscious of the need for protection from the West (see Chapter 6). The Syrian journalist Nihad al-Ghadiri chose to embellish Thatcher's observation with a touch of Arab rhetoric: '*He's an empty hulk, a mountain of nothingness. Even his evil deeds don't reflect him; he's achieved the impossible, people don't take what he and his family do seriously. Nobody talks about corruption in Saudi Arabia any more; they take it for granted.*'[56] To critics such as Said Aburish, King Fahd is no workaholic, but a lazy parasite, a gambler and a womaniser (though not on the scale of Ibn Saud). In the casinos of Lebanon he often lost hundreds of thousands of dollars (despite the Koranic prohibition of 'games of chance' – Sura 5, Verse 92). Fahd maintains seven huge palaces worth a total of around $11 billion in Saudi Arabia, a 100-room palace in Marbella, one outside Paris, another in Geneva, and a mansion near London on which he spent $30 million. His Boeing 747 includes a sauna, chandeliers and gold bathroom fixtures, while at the same time he maintains a $50-million yacht and many cars, including a specially-converted Rolls Royce Camargue. In the mid-1990s King Fahd's personal wealth was estimated at something in excess of $28 billion.

The Kingdom of Saudi Arabia is today ruled in the manner of a mediaeval autocracy (see also Chapter 1). Ministers are dismissed on whim (sometimes only hearing about it first on television); in December 1992 Fahd dismissed seven members of the Council of Ulemas because they refused to issue a decree condemning critics of the government. As one example, the Minister of Health, Ghazi Algosaibi, was expelled from office after writing a poem complaining that Fahd would not see him. On another occasion Fahd telephoned the Minister of Information, Ali al Shaer, to instruct him to stop an Indian film being televised since the King was not enjoying it. When, at another time, Fahd announced he would be arriving in Jeddah a thousand sheep were slaughtered in anticipation; he then changed his mind, and on two further occasions repeated the promise and the cancellation – 3000 sheep were needlessly slaughtered, though dire consequences would have followed any official neglect of such important Islamic custom.[57]

Fahd, as already noted, helped various American factions to circumvent congressional constraints on the funding of terrorism in Nicaragua. There has also been demonstrable Saudi involvement in a host of business scandals, not least those involving the Bank of Credit and Commerce International (BCCI). Parties to the BCCI collapse included Kamal Adham, Ghaith Pharoan and Mamad ibn Mahfouz – all friends of Fahd. Under Fahd the commercial corruption endemic to Saudi business practice increased apace, with critics desperately demanding reform and an end to the blatant nepotism and the use of the Saudi Treasury as Fahd's personal bank account. Today the problems in Saudi society and political administration continue to mount, encouraging many observers to comment on the terminal decay of a feudal anachronism (Chapter 7).

THE BRITAIN FACTOR

The involvement of Britain in the affairs of the Arabian peninsula began long before the establishment of the Kingdom of Saudi Arabia. As always the strategists of London were interested in exploiting local commercial opportunities in particular areas; and, more broadly, in protecting extended trade routes from India and elsewhere. This imperial posture often involved military support and financial subsidy for specific groups in long-standing traditional contention with their neighbours; as, for example, when Saudi ambition came into collision with small domains in the eastern parts of the peninsula, or with other Arab pretenders to leadership of the Arab nation (we have already noted the absurdity that British funds were often simultaneously supporting the Saudis and the Hashemites in contention for possession of Hejaz and for leadership of the Islamic world. The funds, significant at the time, seem derisory by modern standards. Thus in the early 1920s Ibn Saud received an annual revenue from internal sources amounting to a total of £150,000, with a British subsidy of £60,000 (this may be compared with Saudi Arabian revenues of some £10 billion in 1974 and hundreds of billions of pounds in the 1990s). At the same time it is of interest that Ibn Saud resisted offers of British help in creating the nucleus of a modern army, as Britain had done for the Hashemites of Iraq and Transjordan, in part because Wahhabist puritanism remained highly suspicious of most twentieth-century technological innovation (the Saudi *ulema* discussed at length the contentious question of whether the bicycle could be permitted within the realm of a pious Muslim state).[58]

The imperial ambitions of Britain in the Arabian peninsula were set in a wide historical context. The Empire, via the motivation of commercial enterprise, had extended successfully around the globe; and when, as part of this grand scheme, Chinese peasants were successfully transformed into opium addicts, revenues were being amassed from the slave trade and Indian nationals were being tied on the end of canon, great fortunes were accumulated by pious English families who took pains every Sunday to proclaim the humanitarian vision of capitalism and the gentle virtues of the Christian religion. Britain had survived the First World War and the 1919 Versailles Conference as a superpower; but one alarmingly dependent on borrowed money organised by the Wall Street house of J. P. Morgan & Company: in 1919 the London politicians, custodians of a deeply racist and zenophobic tradition, found that they owed the United States some $4.7 billion in war debts (the total national debt had increased some 924 per cent to around £7.4 billion).[59] Such a circumstance was scarcely calculated to sustain British imperial ambition – in Arabia and elsewhere – in the decades that followed. The scene was set for the transfer of effective imperial arrogance from one great repository of Christian virtue to another.

Powerful American oil interests – in particular, the Rockefeller Standard Oil companies – were quick to note the newly-carved Middle East boundaries intended to give commercial advantage to the impoverished British Empire. Many of the oil-rich Arab states and Iran were now effectively controlled by British interests through covert government ownership of Royal Dutch Shell and Anglo-Persian Oil Company. It is significant that the mandates conferred by the Eurocentric League of Nations now offered a last gasp to ailing empires that desperately needed an economic boost. In April 1920, with no American presence, the British Prime Minister Lloyd George and the French Prime Minister Alexandre Millerand signed the San Remo Agreement, which gave France 25 per cent of oil exported by the British in Iraq (equivalent to the 25 per cent German Deutsche Bank share of the Old Turkish Petroleum Gesellschaft that was expropriated from the Germans as part of the war spoils). In return the French allowed the British oil companies to run an oil pipeline through French Syria to a Mediterranean oil port. In March 1921, to consolidate the newly-won British influence in the region, Winston Churchill – keen to express his enthusiasm for using poison gas against 'turbulent tribes',[60] Arabs and others – created the British Colonial Office Middle East Department as an effective replacement for the 1916 Arab Bureau; whereupon the US government protested on behalf of American Standard Oil companies keen to get their hands on Arab and Iranian oil. The British Foreign Secretary commented curtly to the British ambassador in

Washington (21 April 1921) that the American companies should be allowed no oil concessions in the British Middle East.[61] This was not a posture that could be long sustained, but in the short term Sir Henry Deterding's Royal Dutch Shell had tied up the oil concessions in the Dutch East Indies and in much of the post-war Middle East. In the longer term the Anglo-American struggle for primacy in the global oil industry was resolved by the creation of the immensely powerful Anglo-American oil cartel, later dubbed the 'Seven Sisters', in 1927. The British and American governments ratified the accord that became known as the 'Red Line Agreement' (see Figure 5.1).*

The Achnacarry Agreement preserved the illusion of parity between British and US oil interests in the Middle East, but only for a brief period. The Second World War further devastated British economic ambition and immeasurably strengthened American economic power around the world. Soon a range of other factors were conspiring also to further undermine British influence in the Middle East. At the end of the first Arab–Israeli war, following the UN-sanctioned creation of Israel, Britain's military power in Arabia proper was confined to the use of two airbases in Iraq and two in Jordan. On 1 May 1951 Mohammed Mossadeq in Iran managed to secure the passage of a bill through parliament (*Majlis*) nationalising the Anglo-Iranian Oil Company. When the popular Mossadeq was overthrown in a *coup d'état* organised by the CIA and MI6, Britain struggled without success to restore its former share of oil activity in the region. In fact the British capital investment dropped from 49 to 14 per cent, with the British share of oil production falling from 53 to 24 per cent. The US share moved from 44 to 58 per cent, with American companies now controlling 42 per cent of the capital. The socialist Mossadeq had provided an immense boost to US oil interests in the region. Dwight D. Eisenhower, US President at the time, later recorded that Mossadeq had secured a 99.4 per cent vote of support by the Iranian people, that a pro-Shah court subsequently (21 December 1953) sentenced him to a three-year term of solitary confinement, and that now Iranian oil was back where it belonged – within the grip of international corporations: '... the Iranian government [newly imposed by CIA/MI6 terrorism] reached an agreement with an international consortium to buy Iran's oil. Under a special ruling by the [US] Department of Justice, American oil companies participated in this consortium without fear of prosecution under antitrust laws. For the first time in three years Iran was quiet [well managed under the CIA-organised secret police, Savak] and still free.'[62]

---

* By 1932 the cartel formalised at Achnacarry, the Scottish castle of Sir Henry Deterding, in 1927 included all the seven major companies in the Anglo-American sphere: Esso (Standard of New Jersey), Mobil (Standard of New York), Gulf Oil, Texaco, Standard of California (Chevron), Royal Dutch Shell and the Anglo-Persian Oil Company (British Petroleum). The cartel, the most powerful in modern history, then devised a ruthless strategy to curtail the oil ambitions of 'outsiders'. In one depiction of this enormous commercial innovation the Anglo-American 'Special Relationship' was rooted in the agreement over oil (Engdahl, 1993, p. 88).

These events, coupled with the creation of Israel as an American beachhead in the Middle East, gave further impetus to the shift of power from British imperial involvement (in part through the disguise of the League mandate) to the emerging US hegemony. In another area of influence the British had been concerned with the security of the Suez Canal Zone, a consideration that had required a re-negotiation of the 1936 Anglo-Egyptian Treaty; but the 1946 talks foundered on Egyptian insistence that Sudan be included as a region under the jurisdiction of the Egyptian Crown. in 1947, at a time when the Israel Question was coming before the United Nations, the British–Egyptian talks were abandoned when Commonwealth countries were showing no interest in the possibility of providing forces for the defence of Egypt. On 16 October 1951 the Egyptian parliament unanimously abrogated the 1936 treaty, so escalating the Anglo-Egyptian tensions. The Nasser ascendancy, the 1956 Suez crisis and the associated US condemnation of the British posture served to further erode Britain's waning influence in the Middle East.

The collapse of the British imperial posture in the second half of the twentieth century, to an extent encouraged by American ambition, did not leave Britain totally without commercial and political influence in the Middle East in general and in Saudi Arabia in particular. Specific issues (such as the on-going Buraimi question and the 1980 televised film *Death of a Princess* – see Chapter 1) have produced temporary political dislocations that in the longer term have seemed rel-atively minor compared with the shared interests in politics and trade (in particu-lar, the sale of arms – Chapter 6). British relations with Saudi Arabia gradually deteriorated after the Second World War as the US oil corporations developed their activities in the region; and as border questions (in addition to Buraimi) con-tinued to disturb regions with residual British connections. The revolution in Yemen in 1962 (see below) underlined an identity of interest between London and Riyadh, though Saudi Arabia still encouraged the withdrawal of British forces from the south of the peninsula.[63] By the 1990s, even with Anglo-Saudi relations vaunted as 'excellent' and with massive trade in arms (frequently involving high levels of financial corruption), it was plain that the United States had emerged as the undisputed hegemonic power in the region.

THE US FACTOR

The United States had many reasons for wanting to supplant Britain as the main Western power in the Gulf. The British Empire was fast waning and in the alarm-ing context of the Cold War the vacuum had to be filled. The strategic geography of Saudi Arabia was important; and above everything the matter of oil loomed large. The United States – as by far the most energy-profligate nation on the planet – had a growing requirement for cheap energy. And this was not merely the demand of a domestic constituency accustomed to burning vast quantities of gasoline with high relish: all the lineaments of war, the enabling tools of US hegemonic ambition, depended on untrammelled access to fuel. There was never any doubt that as soon as the vast oil reserves of Saudi Arabia had been discovered that particular part of the world would always be viewed by Washington strategists with unusual affection.

In 1942, at a time when Ibn Saud was happy to contemplate suitable deals with the Axis powers (who, he doubtless surmised, might win the war), the King of Saudi Arabia entertained the first American government mission to Riyadh. Karl Twitchell, the geologist and oil company contact, led a group of Americans who had never visited the Kingdom before. The US Minister to Egypt, Alexander Kirk, was there; as were a small bunch of agricultural experts brought along to address Ibn Saud's interest in finding water in Nejd. The Americans found themselves squatting in desert robes, sampling Saudi culinary fare (including a whole roast sheep), and watching Crown Prince Saud's latest fad – a scratchy cinematic show featuring such stars as Roosevelt and Churchill signing the Atlantic Charter on the USS *Augusta* in August 1941.[64]

The purpose of the American expedition was plain. The United States had entered the war, and Saudi oil reserves were reckoned increasingly important for both the current military enterprise and the energy-hungry peace that would follow. It was time, judged Washington, for America to play an ever more influential role in the region: 'Its distrust of Britain was only marginally exceeded by its fear of the Soviet Union.'[65] And there was also the matter that Caltex (renamed the Arabian–American Oil Company, ARAMCO, in 1944) was paying increasing amounts to subsidise a Saudi treasury hit by war problems and diminishing pilgrim revenues; if Ibn Saud were denied further payments, difficult for Caltex to meet, he might turn again to the British, a possibility to be avoided at all costs. At the same time the Americans could view the situation with optimism. The war was already crippling Britain; and US companies were taking an ever greater share of oil-industry activities in Iraq, Bahrain, Kuwait and Saudi Arabia itself. The upshot, already noted, was that President Roosevelt, reversing earlier reluctance, agreed on 18 February 1943 to extend Lend-Lease funds to Saudi Arabia. In September, to consolidate the burgeoning relationship, Prince Faisal and his younger brother Khaled (now King) visited Washington, enjoyed full state honours as guests at Blair House, and were taken to Los Angeles and San Francisco in a private railway carriage. The British, suitably disconcerted, invited the Saudi royals to visit London on their way home; and then had the crass insensitivity to arrange for Mrs Churchill, instead of the British Prime Minister, to greet the desert princes reared in a culture of male supremacy.

The contest between Washington and London for influence in Saudi Arabia was unequal from the start. The war had impoverished Britain and enriched the United States (London had even been forced to concede gold reserves and imperial territories to Washington). Now the US oil companies were expanding their activities throughout the Middle East, with substantial US government encouragement: new areas were being prospected, new wells drilled, plans drawn up for a new refinery at Ras Tanura and for a pipeline from Dhahran across Arabia and Syria to the Mediterranean. Now it was plain that Saudi Arabia, by dint of US economic power, was rapidly being converted into a *de facto* American protectorate – a development that was set to have profound political consequences for the region over the decades ahead. Britain was powerless to prevent this inevitable drift. Churchill and Roosevelt cabled each other to express disquiet about the other's designs on Arab oil, while the Saudis were happy to exploit such differences.[66]

In January 1957 the US President, alarmed by increased Soviet penetration of the Middle East, announced the 'Eisenhower Doctrine' as a mechanism for branding the phenomenon of 'international communism' as the greatest threat to the region, and offering financial aid to any government prepared to resist it. The Hashemites in Iraq and President Chamoun in Lebanon readily accepted such aid; King Saud of Arabia expressed his willingness to support the so-called Eisenhower Doctrine, but with less enthusiasm than other Arab leaders. Saudi troops were despatched to Jordan as a sign of support for King Hussain after his dismissal of his national government; in Lebanon the US embassy and the CIA supported the pro-Chamoun forces in the parliamentary elections (while 14,000 US troops invaded Lebanon[67]); and, in an improbable attempt to represent the Saudi monarch as an effective rival to Nasser in the Arab world, King Saud was invited to Washington on a state visit.[68]

The Eisenhower Doctrine, despite Nasser's demonstrable hostility to communism, was manifestly an attempt to isolate Egypt and to counter the growing influence of Arab nationalism. There was no need to invoke the Doctrine for Iraq, Iran and Turkey, already linked to the West via the Baghdad Pact, US military agreements and various other mechanisms. But efforts to build up King Saud 'as a counter-weight to Nasser'[69] showed little understanding of the growing feelings in the Arab world. It is significant also that Saud himself assumed the role of US emissary only with reluctance. He appeared more sympathetic to the Russians than to the Israelis and the British, and commented to Eisenhower that reports of Egyptian and Syrian leanings towards the Soviet Union were exaggerated.[70] When Saud returned from Washington in February he attended a summit conference in Cairo with Nasser, President Kuwatly of Syria and King Hussain of Jordan; the resulting communiqué made no reference to the Eisenhower Doctrine but rejected any concept of a political 'vacuum' in the Middle East and applauded the idea of 'active neutrality'. Then (12 March 1957) the US envoy James P. Richards, a Democratic Congressman, was despatched on a tour of the Middle East to drum up support for the Doctrine: with only Lebanon's Chamoun giving unqualified support, in gratitude for CIA-inspired terrorism against his opponents, the journey was scarcely profitable.

The Eisenhower Doctrine, initially funded to the tune of $200 million, was mainly the creature of Secretary of State John Foster Dulles, not remembered best

for his political subtlety. The Doctrine was essentially a 'black-and-white' formulation, allowing no room for compromise or political neutrality. It was evident
that any Arab state that endorsed the Doctrine would have to make a public stand
not only against the Soviet Union but also against Egypt, an Arab neighbour; and
that, moreover, support for the Doctrine would imply absorption within the anti-
Soviet Dulles ideology. It was not a brand of US extremism well calculated to
win Arab friends. The Richards tour did no more than exacerbate Egyptian and
Syrian hostility to the United States; as did US help to King Hussain of Jordan in
suppressing his political opponents in April 1957. At the same time King Saud of
Saudi Arabia was prepared to support Hussain in ousting politicians sympathetic
to Egypt and Syria, so splitting the four-power alliance (Egypt, Syria, Saudi
Arabia and Jordan) symbolised by the Cairo conference in February. The
repression in Jordan, supported by King Saud and the United States, has been
represented as 'the first major set-back'[71] for Nasserism in the Arab world.

There remained unease in the Arab world among the supporters of the
Eisenhower Doctrine. The governments that had supported the Doctrine
(Lebanon, Jordan, Iraq and Saudi Arabia) were now increasingly unhappy, in the
light of Arab nationalist agitation, to be seen to be underwriting US policy in the
region. While various Arab leaders were growing increasingly sensitive to
American ambition, the US State Department continued to advertise its antago-
nism to Arab nationalist aspirations. Thus a spectacular US airlift to Amman did
little to help King Hussain's reputation in the Arab world, while US hostility to
Syria gave impetus to propaganda urging Arab independence. In this context
King Saud of Saudi Arabia, increasingly uneasy about the appearance of any
public difference with Nasser, began exerting diplomatic pressure to encourage
Arab governments hostile to Syria to moderate their views and to edge away from
US policy. In September Saud visited Beirut in an attempt to improve relations
between Syria and Lebanon; Jordan, responsive to Saud's efforts, was now
asserting that it would not interfere in Syrian affairs; and on 12 September Saud
reportedly urged Eisenhower to adopt a more moderate policy on Syria.[72]

Now King Saud, seemingly heartened by the broad Arab response to his new
initiatives, was developing what Washington must have regarded as an unhelpful
strategy. On 21 September a Saudi minister in Cairo commented that Syria represented no threat to its neighbours; two days later Crown Prince Faisal repeated
the point after meeting Eisenhower and Dulles in Washington. On 25 September
King Saud, now in Damascus, condemned any possibility of aggression against
Syria and reasserted the solidarity of the Arab nation; on the following days the
Iraqi Prime Minister, Ali Jawdat al-Ayubi announced that 'complete understanding' had been reached in talks between Syria and Iraq. On 27 September Saud
announced, at the conclusion of his visit to Damascus: 'I deplore every aggression on Syria and on any other Arab country from whatever source it comes ... I
will oppose with my Syrian brothers and with the other Arabs any aggression
against them and against their independence irrespective of its source.'[73] By now

even the Americans were being driven to acknowledge that earlier alarmist comment on Syria's pro-Soviet leanings had probably been exaggerated. On 3 October President Eisenhower admitted that the 'original alarm of countries like Lebanon, Jordan and Iraq and, to some extent, Saudi Arabia, seems to have been quietened by what they have learned'.[74]

Saud's success in restoring the image of Saudi identity with Arab nationalism was short-lived. Soon, in an effort to reclaim the leadership of the Arab cause, Nasser was deploying Egyptian troops in northern Syria alongside their Arab brothers – an initiative that the Saudis could never have matched. Now Syria and Egypt were discussing the possibility of political union, a 'desired national aim' applauded by Nasser in July and by Syria's President Kuwatly in August ('Syria's dearest wish was to achieve a union with Egypt which would serve as the nucleus for universal Arab unity'). King Saud's mediation efforts had served a purpose but were now outflanked by the improving relations between Egypt and Syria; and behind all the manoeuvring was the lingering suspicion that Saudi Arabia, still much courted by the United States, was continuing to operate as an American proxy.

There can be little doubt that Saud was deeply ambivalent in assuming the posture of Arab nationalist. As head of a traditional feudal society he had little interest in any Arab espousal of progress to socialist independence; and he remained highly dependent on US protection in the event of any republican or communist threat from outside or within the country. Moreover there was even evidence that agents for King Saud had paid £1.9 million for the assassination of Nasser,[75] a circumstance unlikely to endear the Saudis to nationalists throughout the Arab world. The Americans had praised Saud on his visit to Washington in early 1957 (said the US ambassador to Saudi Arabia: Saud 'is a good king ... who has the welfare of his people primarily in mind'); with such praise even extending to a partial defence by Ambassador Wadsworth of the Saudi slave trade.[76] Agreement had been reached on the US leasing of the Dhahran base for another five years; and in return a wide range of military aid was offered. The 15,000-strong Saudi army was to be doubled, and supplied with, US arms, artillery and jet fighter planes; US training and equipment would help to establish a Saudi air force and navy; and in 1958 Saudi Arabia was provided with a $25 million Foreign Assistance Act grant.

Under the terms of the 1957 agreement American forces remained at the Dhahran base until 1962 and then withdrew, only to return less than a year later, with a permanent military combat force alongside its military training mission, as a result of the North Yemen revolution (see 'The Yemen Wars – I' below). Now US policy required that Saudi Arabia be equipped not only to crush any internal revolt that might threaten American interests but to intervene in neighbouring states that might choose political systems unsympathetic to the regional needs of American capitalism. These US requirements were reflected in the scale of Saudi defence expenditure from the mid-1960s onward. It has often been pointed out

that these circumstances are a direct reflection of the needs of the West, in particular the needs of the United States: 'Without the West there would be no House
of Saud. The Saudi people or their neighbours or a combination of both would
bring about its end. But the West has always had reasons to support the Saudi
monarchy and to guarantee its existence and the West's, particularly America's,
continued need for oil will keep this support intact for the foreseeable future.'[77]
This situation has various consequences, not least the deterioration of the House
of Saud's relationship with its own people in the light of its failure to support
Arab and Muslim interests when these run into conflict with Western policies
(see Chapter 7).

The American involvement in Saudi Arabia grew with the increase in oil production, the expansion of the Dhahran airbase, and the building of the Trans-
Arabian Pipeline (TAPLINE) to the Lebanese port of Sidon. The increased
security requirements led to CIA assistance for Saudi secret police operations;
with, for example, expanded CIA activity in such organisations as the inter-Arab
TAPLINE Government Relations Department and the American Friends of the
Middle East (AFME). CIA staff (such as Kim Roosevelt and Harry Kern) were
seconded to Saudi Arabia, either to carry out their own independent operations or
to train their Saudi equivalents in such arts as interrogation, surveillance and
other counter-espionage activities. Saudis were sponsored for education in the
United States, as the usual mechanism for acquainting client states with the
boundless virtues of American culture (the perceived contrasts between
Wahhabist fundamentalism and free-market hedonism often led to disturbing
tensions, not least the attempts by Saudis in the 1960s and 1970s to overthrow
their government).[78]

The accession of Faisal in 1964 gave the Americans fresh opportunities to
develop the Saudi connection. Washington approved of his disciplined and
austere manner, advised him on national budgetary affairs, stimulated his hostility
to Arab nationalism, and encouraged his efforts to build an anti-communist
Islamic front. During the Kennedy administration various tensions had developed
between Washington and Faisal, already wielding significant power during
Saud's reign. In 1962 Kennedy had unexpectedly recognised the republican pro-
Nasser regime; though in 1963 he sent US fighter aircraft to Saudi Arabia to deter
further Egyptian expansion, and ignored flagrant Saudi abuses of human rights
when hundreds of pro-Nasser sympathisers were arrested and imprisoned in
Saudi Arabia. Between 1967 and 1973, with vastly increased Saudi repression
inside the country, there were many attempts to overthrow the government –
efforts defeated largely because of the help given by the Americans to strengthen
the Saudi internal security apparatus.

The US–Saudi relationship was further complicated by the Arab–Israeli wars
(see below). In 1967 the Israeli defeat of Nasser strengthened the position of
Faisal in Saudi Arabia (which left him free to intensify the internal repression);
but the 1973 war, leading to the oil embargo reluctantly imposed by Faisal and

other Arab leaders, served as a deep embarrassment to Saudi Arabia and other pro-West states in the region. American intransigence (for example, giving Israel $2.2 billion worth of arms) had left Faisal with little choice, though he worked to lift the embargo as soon as possible. In February 1974 Washington agreed to sell Saudi Arabia vast quantities of arms, while Faisal struggled to reach an accommodation in talks with Henry Kissinger. On 19 March, having been fêted in Pakistan and elsewhere as a heroic Muslim leader, Faisal felt able to lift the oil embargo. When Richard Nixon visited Saudi Arabia later in 1974 he was personally received as a friend by Faisal himself. Nixon later commented:

... thanks to his intelligence and the experience of many years in power, Faisal was one of the wisest leaders in the entire region ... Faisal's stature in the Arab world and the substantial financial support he provided to Syria and Egypt gave him a vital role in maintaining the momentum toward peace. I was also able to discuss with him the serious global impact of the high oil prices caused by the recent Arab oil embargo and to encourage his moves to moderate oil prices ... Faisal said at the departure ceremonies, 'Anybody who stands against you, Mr President, in the United States of America or outside the United States of America, or stands against us, your friends in this part of the world, obviously has one aim in mind, namely, that of causing the splintering of the world, the wrong polarization of the world, the bringing about of mischief ... Therefore, we beseech Almighty God to lend His help to us and to you so that we can both go hand in hand, shoulder to shoulder in pursuance of the noble aims that we both share, namely, those of peace, justice, and prosperity in the world.'[79]

If Washington strategists had doubts about Faisal's pro-West instincts then perhaps these remarks were helpful; what was less helpful to American strategy was that Faisal was assassinated the following year. And this was not the only trauma to assail the House of Saud. In January 1979 the Shah – nominally protected by the United States – was overthrown in Iran; in November there was a rebellion at the Grand Mosque in Mecca; and in December the Soviet Union invaded Afghanistan in support of the regime of Barbak Kemal. Now King Khaled had to acknowledge the limits to US power and also a range of problems that money could not solve.

The House of Saud was forced to recognise significant areas of opposition inside the country. The policies adopted by Faisal over Iran and Afghanistan had clearly failed, and within Saudi Arabia there were growing demands for political change: a group of Faisal's sons even went so far as to present King Khaled with a 33-page document calling for reform in both domestic and foreign policy (see Chapter 7). Now it seemed that Washington was under pressure to reassure the nervous Saudi rulers: in addition to private messages of support a US State Department spokesman announced on 13 September 1980 that the United States remained committed to the protection of Saudi Arabia against 'all internal and external attempts to destabilise it'. By now President Sadat was allowing an anti-Khaled group, the Islamic Revolution in Arabia, to beam radio broadcasts into Saudi Arabia; while Washington attempted to reassure the House of Saud by staging military displays at Dhahran and warning the new regime in Iran against any anti-Saudi actions. Soon Iran would be at war with Iraq (Chapter 6), dragging Saudi Arabia (and various other countries) into a military involvement that threatened further political destabilisation.

The United States remained committed to the defence of Saudi Arabia; and to the calculated application of political pressures that increasingly angered many Saudi dissidents struggling to achieve reform. America was now the biggest importer of Saudi oil, and reliant also on Saudi financial backing for clandestine operations that would not have received Congressional approval. Thus in the two years that followed the Congressional block on funds for the Contra terrorists in Nicaragua some $30 million was provided by Saudi Arabia in monthly instalments, most probably through the National Commercial Bank of Jeddah, independent of the monitoring brief of the Saudi Arabian Monetary Agency and often used by the Saudis for secret deals.[80] In these circumstance the illicit Contra funds – typically used to torture and kill school-teachers, nurses and factory workers – were fed to Miami via BAC International in the Cayman Islands.[81]

With the Saudis continuing to buy American arms the US–Saudi business connections continued to develop. American banks were now overflowing with Saudi money, a fact that contributed significantly to the Third World debt crisis; while American arms manufacturers were happy to make military hardware available to Saudi Arabia via sale or leasing arrangements. Thus substantial quantities of F-15 fighter aircraft, Stinger missiles, C-130 transport planes, M-60 tanks and much else was provided. It was now assumed that US corporations would derive much of their income from Saudi revenues derived from oil sales. Thus such firms as IBM, Proctor and Gamble, TWA, FMC Corporation and United Airlines were 'so dependent on Saudi business' that they enthusiastically lobbied Congress to approve arms sales to Saudi Arabia.[82] And it was inevitable in these circumstances that Saudi money would be used to buy political influence throughout the American Establishment. The Saudis funded senators and congressmen, and provided funds for Ronald Reagan's second presidential campaign. The former Secretary of Defense Clark Clifford, the former Vice President Spiro Agnew, the former CIA Chief Richard Helms, various former US ambassadors to Saudi Arabia and many other were involved with Saudi officials at the highest levels – in circumstances where King Fahd and President Reagan derived immense political advantage from the prevailing US–Saudi culture of corruption.[83] Some voices were raised in protest. Thus the former ambassador James Atkins continued to attack the scale of Saudi corruption, while the Israelis frequently expressed alarm at the volume of arms shipments to a potentially hostile Muslim state. US dissidents such as Atkins were routinely ignored; and the Reagan administration assured Israel that the most vital components of the AWAC systems then being made available to Saudi Arabia would remain under US control. A former US ambassador to Saudi Arabia was happy to note that the United States had achieved an AWAC 'flying base in the region and the Saudis would have the privilege of paying for it' (to the tune of $8.5 billion).[84]

The situation was plain. The United States had established Saudi Arabia as a client state, an effective protectorate, that was sufficiently alarmed by the surrounding political turbulence – much of it fostered by Washington – to require constant US reassurance. It was not unhelpful to this general scheme that Washington was happy to support Saddam Hussein through the 1980s and to continue arming Israel – so feeding Saudi anxieties, guaranteeing a copious flow of cheap energy to the United States, and ensuring prodigious arms sales. It remains to be seen whether this neat symbiotic connection – of benefit primarily to corporate America and a clutch of Saudi royals – can long continue in the years ahead. As Saudi Arabia languishes somewhere in the feudal dark ages, increasingly beset by corruption and disaffection, oil provides a temporary hedge against the accumulating realities of the modern age. We can debate just how long this unstable and ethically derelict situation will prevail (Chapter 7).

BLACK GOLD

In one imaginative view Saudi Arabia was the only country in the world whose development of oil 'resulted from purely philanthropic sentiment'.[85] It was Charles R. Crane, one-time Minister to China, who in the winter of 1926/27 offered the Imam Yahia of the Yemen a free prospecting survey of his land. This remarkable offer came to involve the engineer Karl Twitchell in various surveying expeditions from 1927 to 1932; and prompted King Ibn Saud to invite Crane to visit him in Jeddah.[86] On 30 March 1931 Twitchell was cabled by Crane to journey to Jeddah with a view to prospecting for water, since Ibn Saud's main interest was to find artesian wells in Hejaz and Nejd. In July 1932 Crane issued a letter allowing all the prospecting data obtained at his expense to be used but stating emphatically that he did not wish a statement ever to appear suggesting 'that there were ulterior commercial motives behind his philanthropic activities in Arabia'.[87] Twitchell was soon presenting the commercial potential of Saudi Arabia to possible American sponsors.

Various companies showed no interest in Twitchell's representations, arguing that little was known about Saudi Arabia and that British groups already operating in Africa, India and Asia might be interested. When US oil companies were approached Terry Duce of the Texas Company suggested that Twitchell should contact the Near East Development Company and the Standard Oil Company of California. It was significant that the Iraq Petroleum Company (the parent company of the former and the most powerful oil conglomerate in the world) had missed its chance to acquire important Bahrain oil concessions and did not want to be caught napping again. None the less it was the Standard Oil Company of California that first underook to negotiate an oil concession in Saudi Arabia. It was the farsightedness of Standard Oil's M. E. Lombardi that 'resulted in obtaining American control of what is probably the second greatest oil reserve in the world today' [1947].[88]

On 29 May 1933 the negotiations for the oil concessions were concluded at Kazam Palace in Nazla, a suburb of Jeddah. Najib Salha, a Saudi official, acted as the sole interpreter and secretary; he was presented with a briefcase as reward for his services, while the oil company donated fountain-pen sets to the other Saudi officials; and Twitchell was given his own 'reward' (he does not disclose details) by the Saudi Arabian government. Standard Oil then made an initial loan of £30,000 in gold sovereigns to the Saudi government, a substantial amount in the context of the prevailing American depression and the recently announced US 'bank holiday'. Standard Oil then formed the 'California Arabian Standard Oil Company', later changed to the 'Arabian–American Oil Company' (ARAMCO). On 25 August the loan was physically handed over, with every sovereign counted at the Netherlands Trading Society in Jeddah (the concession terms were printed in the *Umm al-Qura* newspaper of Mecca, a principal organ of the Saudi government). Within weeks a modern oil village had been established at Dhahran, providing schools and sanitation facilities, and paying for Saudi soldiers to police company property.

It was not long before the scale of the Saudi oil reserves was established. In 1943 the oil geologist E. I. De Golyer calculated the proven reserves at around two billion barrels, with possible reserves amounting to ten times this amount.[89] Standard Oil obtained a second oil concession in 1939, at a time when Germany was showing interest and Japanese offers were being made. By now Ibn Saud was well content to deal with his American friends: cash had been advanced far beyond the current production royalties, there was the seductive prospect of Lend-Lease donations, and in August 1946 the US Import–Export Bank offered a substantial loan. In addition the Americans were advising on the development of water resources, the layout of irrigation systems, and many other matters. The United States was gaining many benefits in return, not least the provision of a one-billion-barrel reserve, to be sold at 25 per cent under the market price, for the US Navy.

The establishment of American oil interests in Saudi Arabia was destined to shape the entire balance of power in the Middle East. At the time of the early granting of oil concessions there was no US diplomatic representation in the country, and only about fifty Westerners in Jeddah. Now the feudal desert kingdom was suddenly infested with oilmen, according to Philby, 'descending from the skies on their flying carpets with strange devices for probing the bowels of the earth in search of the liquid muck for which the world clamours to keep its insatiable machines alive'.[90] Standard Oil, keen to expand, soon formed a partnership with Texaco, being developed by Cap Rieber who in 1936 bought a half share in both the Bahrain and Saudi concessions. In May 1939, Ibn Saud and his party, having visited the new oil developments, were entertained on the tanker *D. G. Schofield*, named after the founder of Standard Oil of California. The King was sufficiently impressed with the unfolding of events that he soon expanded the concession to 444,000 square miles of Saudi territory – as big as the total area of Texas, Louisiana, Oklahoma and New Mexico.[91] Three months later, Bert Fisher, the US Minister in Egypt, was accredited as the American diplomatic representative in Saudi Arabia. It was a propitious time for such a political development. Four months later the Second World War began, to the mounting alarm of the Saudi royals, now highly aware that many nations were casting covetous eyes on the abundant energy supplies in the Middle East.

In February 1943 'Star' Rodgers, chairman of Texaco, and Harry Collier, president of Socal, visited the US Secretary of the Interior, Harold Ickes, with a view to bringing Saudi Arabia into the Lend-Lease framework. It was not long before Roosevelt abandoned his initial doubts. In June the Under-Secretary of the Navy, William Bullitt, explained in a memorandum that it had become a vital interest of the United States 'to acquire petroleum reserves outside our boundaries'; the British must not be allowed 'to diddle them out of the [Arabian] concession and the British into it'. Perhaps the United States were 'forty years late in starting – but we are not yet too late'.[92] Now it was suggested that the US government should establish a 'Petroleum Reserve Corporation' to acquire a controlling interest in ARAMCO, whereupon Roosevelt authorised the acquisition of the entire Arabian concessions. Socal and Texaco predictably rejected any such scheme and soon it was shown that no nationalisation deal between the Roosevelt administration and the oil companies would be possible. Texaco and Socal themselves built the government-envisaged Trans-Arabian Pipeline (TAPLINE) facility, though its operation would be fraught with difficulty: it was an easy target for terrorists, a Syrian bargaining counter against America, and a constant advertisement for US involvement in the region; in April 1975 the TAPLINE facility was closed down. The overall effect of Ickes's efforts to secure an enhanced government control over the Arabian concessions was to strengthen the hand of the companies.

It was now clear that Texaco and Socal had out-flanked the other 'five sisters', now worried that they would be undercut by cheap Arabian oil. At the same time the two holders of the Arabian concessions were not averse to strengthening their position by building links with other companies; by September 1946 there were discussions about how Exxon and Mobil could join ARAMCO. Efforts were made to break the 20-year-old Red Line Agreement with a so-called 'Open Door' policy, which led to immediate problems with the French company Compagnie Française de Pétrole (CFP) and Calouste Gulbenkian whose arrangements were earning him around $20 million a year. In due course the old Red Line Agreement was finally abandoned, the 'Open Door' approach triumphed, and Exxon and Mobil were given access to the Arabian concessions. The price of entry for the new companies proved to be trifling in view of the immense returns: 'The Saudi Arabian oil proved to be the biggest bargain in the history of the business.'[93]

It was not long before Ibn Saud decided he wanted a bigger share of the 'biggest bargain'. In 1945 the oil minister Perez Alfonso of the Acción Democrática in Venezuela was watching closely the development of US oil needs, the rapid depletion of reserves, and the introduction of rationing in Texas. Soon he was insisting that the Venezuelan government should have a *'fifty-fifty'* share in all oil profits. When Ibn Saud heard about this radical notion he began demanding a larger share of the vast revenues deriving from Arabian oil. ARAMCO and officials from the US State Department met to agree a revised deal, not least because of what they perceived as the mounting Communist threat in the Middle East. It was all a tax fix, a 'Golden gimmick' which in effect transferred an extra $50 million from the US Treasury to Ibn Saud.[94] It also meant that the oil-producing companies, now artificially insulated from the real market and disregarding the tax laws in what was a 'flagrantly improper' way,[95] were being allowed to pay lower US taxes than any other group of companies. In such a fashion the oil companies, now unambiguous paymasters to Saudi Arabia and other oil-producing Arab states, had emerged as an essential adjunct to American foreign policy. Hence an important part of the foreign policy of the West was delegated to the board rooms of corporate America. It was not a state of affairs that much surprised radical observers around the world.

The political significance of oil was now becoming increasingly obvious to the producing states, increasingly aware also of the advantages of some sort of collaboration. Thus after the revolution in 1958 the Iraqis began negotiations with the Iraq Petroleum Company (IPC) and encouraged support from other Arab countries. The following year the first Arab Petroleum Congress was convened in Cairo, with observers from Iran and Venezuela. On 9 September, following a further round of company-inspired price reductions, five countries (Saudi Arabia, Iran, Iraq, Kuwait and Venezuela), responsible for 80 per cent of the world oil exports, met in Baghdad to consider a joint strategy. The result was the foundation of the Organisation of Petroleum Exporting Countries (OPEC), conceived substantially as a mechanism for opposing the power of the oil companies, as shown in particular by unacceptable price fluctuations in the market. Thus the OPEC members could 'no longer remain indifferent to the attitude heretofore adopted by the oil companies in affecting price modifications'; the members would demand 'that oil companies maintain their prices steady and free from all unnecessary fluctuation', and would 'endeavour, by all means available to them, to restore present prices' to their previous higher levels.

The producer countries had learned the company philosophy of combining for added strength; and it was inevitable that the move would attract criticism from the West. But the companies quickly learned to cope with the new development. Tensions within OPEC itself, deriving in part from the disproportionate oil reserves from one country to another, made it possible for the companies to play the individual countries against each other. Now the situation was mixed. The creation of OPEC had an influence on the vexed question of oil price stability, but the companies retained immense power to control the flow of oil. In the late 1960s the producing countries were able to demonstrate their increased power in various ways. Closing the Suez Canal (from 1967 to 1975) and intermittently closing the Syrian pipeline caused a shortfall of some 25 million tonnes of oil for Europe.[96] Among the consequences were an increase in the price of oil supplied by Libya, able to deal with independent firms outside the magic circle of the major companies; and a 'leap-frog' effect as the three major producer countries (Saudi Arabia, Iraq and Iran) managed to negotiate price increases. Saudi Arabia was now spending substantially on defence, social infrastructure and aid (through the Saudi Development Fund and various international agencies). In less than a generation what had been a poor desert kingdom had emerged as a major financial power, a key member of the International Monetary Fund (IMF) and the World Bank, able to shape OPEC's market posture by varying the Saudi level of oil production.

ARAMCO continued to develop as the major oil-industry group operating in Saudi Arabia, but it could not ignore some constraints on its power. OPEC policies had to be considered, as did the activities of specific independent companies, other countries, and particular powerful individuals. In Saudi Arabia itself the geologist Abdullah Tariki, highly resentful of US hegemony, saw ways of chipping away at the effective ARAMCO monopoly. In 1957 he had become director-general of petroleum and mineral resources to the Saudi government, a sensitive position that failed to prevent him talking of 'American economic imperialism'. Talks with Taro Yamashita, chairman of the Japanese Petroleum Trading Company, suggested to Tariki how Saudi Arabia might be able to form a 'joint venture' for exploration of the continental shelf offshore from the Saudi–Kuwait Neutral Zone, well outside the ARAMCO-run concessions. Tariki's proposals were accepted by King Saud and Crown Prince Faisal, though Tariki was amazed to learn that an agreement had already been signed by the Saudi government and Yamashita, granting the Japan Petroleum Company 'the right to search and prospect oil in the Saudi Arabian territory'; Taro Yamashita had undertaken to pay His Excellency Kamal Adham, Faisal's brother-in-law, an annual 2 per cent of the share of the total net profit accruing from the new concession. An initial payment to Adham of $250,000 had also been agreed, with a further $750,000 to be paid when enough petroleum had been found 'to permit sound business enterprise'.[97] In May 1958 the Japanese company outbid the international competition for 50-per-cent rights for the Kuwait offshore Neutral Zone concession, guaranteeing exclusive drilling rights for the area.

The Japanese moved swiftly, and soon encountered problems. On 3 April 1958 natural gas erupted under a mobile platform, ignited, and fuelled an eleven-day fire that was finally extinguished by Texas engineers. But the Japanese persisted and by early 1960 were producing 6000 barrels a day from the first well. Two years later, some 34 wells were working; and by 1964 the Japanese were producing 240,000 barrels of Arabian oil a day. Yamashita was happy to report to shareholders that Japanese oil ventures in the region had 'a high future full of big dreams and hopes'.[98] And Tariki continued to wage his campaign against the US-dominated oil combines: it was an effort that did little to erode the ARAMCO position of virtual monopoly.

Much has been made of ARAMCO attitudes to Saudi nationals and its Saudi staff. In one account the US oilmen typically regarded Saudi natives as thieves and made fun of their religious beliefs, dress and love of dates; blood used for transfusions for ARAMCO Americans reportedly required more careful inspection than blood used for Saudi nationals; and an effective apartheid operated throughout ARAMCO-funded cafeterias, cinemas and athletic events.[99] Devout Muslims were discriminated against in job interviews, and every effort was made to 'Americanise' successful applicants; jeans were favoured over native dress, and chewing Wrigley's gum was welcomed as showing a willingness to emulate the American way of life.[100] The overweaning ARAMCO presence on Saudi soil raised (and continues to raise) a host of matters relating to corruption, profiteering, racism and abuse of human rights. At best ARAMCO officials have constantly demonstrated the petty and unthinking racism that has always characterised the colonial occupation of different ethnic groups. At worst ARAMCO has handed over 'trouble-makers' for torture and execution by the local emir:

> ... non-acceptance of ARAMCO's methods ... on occasion took the form of strikes ... ARAMCO worked with the local province emir to punish the strikers ... they provided him with a list of 600 workers who had petitioned them to improve living conditions. The workers were imprisoned; most were tortured and many of them were never seen again ... individual workers were known to disappear after they questioned their pay or their entitlement to promotion. There is no record of anyone in ARAMCO objecting to the surrender of workers to the merciless sword of Prince bin Jalawi.[101]

There is a human price paid for the acquisition of Saudi oil that is rarely reported in the trade journals or by comfortable Western politicians.

THE YEMEN WARS – I

Over the centuries the rulers of Nejd and Hejaz often came into conflict with the regimes in the southern parts of the Arabian peninsula (Chapter 1). In modern times political events in Yemen frequently impinged on the interests of the Saudi state, inviting a political response not only from Riyadh but also from other powers with their own strategic agendas. After the Second World War it was inevitable that Saudi Arabia would become involved in the years-long struggle for power in Yemen (Table 5.2) from 1962 to 1970 and which today (1998) is still not resolved (see Chapter 6).

The Free Yemeni movement was founded in 1943 in Aden, with the support of Yemeni businessmen demanding constitutional government and a limitation on the traditional powers of the royal family. Five years later Abdullah Ahmed, supported by the movement, managed to overthrow the existing regime and to take power. He in turn, after proclaiming himself Imam, was soon ousted by the Crown Prince Ahmed. The new Imam Ahmed quickly demonstrated his power by beheading Abdullah Ahmed al Wazir and some thirty-two members of his government, displaying their heads on the gates of Sanaa, and by consigning other politicians (including the future leaders Abdullah Sallal and Abdullah Nomaan) to the dungeons in chains (Sallal was incarcerated in this way for seven years).

In April 1956, after crushing an attempted *coup d'état* by one of his brothers, the Imam Ahmed went to Jeddah in Saudi Arabia to sign an agreement for mutual aid with King Saud and Nasser. Soon, sensitive to the growth of Arab nationalism and anti-imperialist feeling, the Yemeni leaders were supporting the newly-formed United Arab Republic and encouraging Egyptian support for opposition to the British plan for a South Arabian federation. Ahmed's support in 1958 for Nasser and the United Arab Republic had invited Saudi antagonism, since by then King Saud had emerged – with obvious American encouragement – as Nasser's principal Arab opponent. And at the same time Nasser was edging away from the conservative South Arabian League, which had strong links with the Protectorate sheikhdoms and with Saudi Arabia itself. It was not long before Ahmed, alarmed by Nasser's support for socialist revolution and his hostility to monarchy, was broadcasting his opposition to the Egyptian radicals. In December 1961 Ahmed broadcast a 64-line poem (his own), attacking Arab socialism as ungodly and – without mentioning Nasser by name – condemning his claim to speak for all Arabs. Nasser responded by urging revolution in Yemen.[102] These developments may be seen as complementing Nasser's campaign against Saudi Arabia and against what he regarded as the colonial British presence in Aden.

On 19 September 1962 the Imam Ahmed died and was succeeded by the Crown Prince Muhammed al Badr. Now the scene was set for a Yemeni civil war that would ineluctably drag in various interested foreign parties. On 26 September army officers tried unsuccessfully to assassinate the new Imam, Sallal agreed to join the revolutionaries as a future president, and army officers seized the radio station and the palace. In Sanaa Sallal's Revolutionary Council proclaimed the end of the Imamate and the creation of the Yemeni Arab Republic, at the same time well aware that previous *coups* had been crushed by surviving royalists and Saudi intervention. To forestall any such repetition the revolutionaries set about massacring supporters of the Imam and members of the royal family – by shooting, since beheading by sword was now deemed anachronistic. The new regime turned also to Nasser to enlist his support against any possible intervention from Saudi Arabia or the British in Aden. On 5 October the

Table 5.2　Struggle for power in Yemen (1948–74)

1948	
19 February	Imam Yahya, aged eighty, is assassinated and the Zeidi chief Abdullah Ahmed al Wazir, supported by the Free Yemeni movement, is proclaimed Imam.
1950	
17 June	Yemen joins Arab League Collective Security Pact.
1955	
2–5 April	Imam Seif el-Islam Ahmad and Crown Prince al Badr Muhammed defeat army revolt led by Emir Sair al-Islam Abdullah.
1956	
3 April	Yemeni regime makes claim on British Aden protectorate.
1957–1962	Soviet Union and China supply arms to Yemen. Soviets begin port construction at Hodeiya (Port Ahmed).
1962	
19 September	Crown Prince Saif al-Islam Muhammed al Badr assumes Crown after death of Imam Ahmed. Start of republican rebellion.
27 September	Proclamation of 'Free Yemen Republic' led by Abdullah al-Sallal.
29 September	Communist-bloc nations recognise new republic.
31 October	Abdullah al-Sallal proclaimed president.
1962–1965	Civil war: Egypt (60,000 troop strength by 1965) assist government; Saudi Arabia supports monarchists.
1965	
24 August	King Faisal of Saudi Arabia and President Nasser of Egypt agree ceasefire and to end their involvement in civil war.
1966	
22 February	Egyptian aircraft support republican attack on royalists; Nasser announces that Egyptian troops will stay in Yemen until agreed plebiscite on future government is held; Saudi Arabia accuses Egyptian planes of bombing Saudi settlements near the Saudi–Yemeni border.
1967	
5 November	Abdullah al-Sallal is overthrown by Rahman al-Iryani in *coup d'état* within the republican government; Egyptian troops have now been withdrawn following Egypt's serious defeat in Sinai.
1968	
February	Troops from Southern Yemen attack royalist forces.
28 February	Saudi Arabia renews support for royalists, claiming that this is necessary to counter support for republicans from Southern Yemen, Syria and Soviet Union.
1970	
14 April	King Faisal agrees to recognise the republican government of Yemen providing a number of royalists are included in the government.
1972–1973	Border clashes continue on the Saudi–Yemeni border.
1974	
13 June	Colonel Ibrahim al-Hamidi stages military *coup d'état*.

first Egyptian troops embarked on their journey to Yemen. Nasser was later to admit that his speedy response to Sallal's cry for help was a 'miscalculation', Nasser's 'Vietnam' – 'We never thought it would lead to what it did.'[103]

As soon as the Saudi intelligence service, doubtless aided by the United States, became aware that Egyptian forces were on their way to Yemen, Saudi Arabia began to pour in money, troops and armaments in support of the royalist forces. Sallal sent troops to intercept the Saudi forces and serious fighting began on the Saudi–Yemeni frontier; on 21 December 1962 King Hussain of Jordan pledged support for the royalists; and, as the republican regime proclaimed that government forces were preparing to invade Saudi Arabia, Nasser found himself dragged into a full defence agreement with the Yemeni republicans (Nasser's 'Vietnam' had begun). By 1964 some 40,000 Egyptian troops were fighting in Yemen; and before the final truce was agreed some six years later the Egyptian military presence had grown to more than 70,000 men, almost half the entire Egyptian army.[104]

The republican regime repeatedly claimed that the royalist resistance and the Saudi–Jordanian intervention had been crushed, but the fighting continued and the royalists appear to have retained the initiative from the outset.[105] The Saudis in particular, because of their proximity, were providing much more effective support than Nasser could bring to the Sallal regime; and in consequence he became increasingly committed to withdrawal, provided that the Saudis and Jordanians would do the same. Thus in December 1962 he proposed to withdraw his forces and that Riyadh and Amman should end their support for the royalists; but Faisal and Hussain, seriously alarmed at the paradoxical US recognition of the Sallal government, were now determined to shore up the monarchist effort in Yemen.[106] President Kennedy, surprisingly rebuffed, handed the problem to the United Nations, now forced to contemplate a general mobilisation of the Saudi forces. In March 1963 the UN Assistant Secretary-General, Ralph Bunche, visited Yemen; and four months later the first UN observer teams arrived in the area. By now there were reports that Egyptian aircraft were bombing the Imam's troops in Saudi territory. In September the UN Secretary-General, U Thant, commented that the UN peace-keeping efforts had come to nothing. This meant that Nasser, increasingly alarmed at the drain on his resources, could contemplate only one option: he would begin a unilateral withdrawal from Yemen.

Sallal, unsurprisingly, struggled to keep Nasser involved in the conflict; while Faisal rejected the efforts of yet another UN envoy sent by U Thant to Riyadh, Sanaa and Cairo. Now there were stories of poor republican morale, with government forces even prepared to sell arms surreptitiously to royalist supporters; it was intimated that Sallal's men were 'republicans by day and royalists by night'.[107] In these circumstances it was inevitable that the British would support the royalists and their Saudi backers, while even the United States, after its earlier unexpected support for Sallal, was slowly moving into the Riyadh camp. The Saudis remained committed to restoring the Imam to the Yemeni throne and Nasser seemed powerless to halt the drift of events.

On 13 January 1964 Nasser called the first of a series of Arab summit conferences: the heads of some thirteen Arab states assembled in Cairo, with focus on the main issue sure to unite them all – what was perceived as the growing threat from Israel. But where Nasser was successful in organising an Arab consensus over the question of Palestine he was still faced by recalcitrant Saudi opinion on the matter of the Yemeni conflict. To avoid the possibility of Yemen being 'controlled by a foreign state', the Saudis were still only willing to contemplate a settlement that excluded Sallal. None the less there was an improvement in relations between Egypt and Saudi Arabia. Already the Egyptian propaganda attacks against Riyadh had been halted; but Nasser, suffering 'my Vietnam', still had no option but to maintain the futile military effort in Yemen. Washington, after the assassination of Kennedy, was now particularly supportive of the Saudis, and highly suspicious of Sallal's frequent visits to China and the Soviet Union.

When, in July 1964, Britain announced that Aden and the other territories of the South Arabian Federation would be granted their independence not later than 1968, a delighted Nasser redoubled his efforts to improve relations with Saudi Arabia. There had been no option, he argued, but to answer the call of the legitimate Yemeni government; and possible attacks across the Saudi–Yemeni border, no more than an excess of local military zeal, were part of no Egyptian strategy to invade Saudi territory. By now it was plain that Sallal was making no headway against the Saudi-backed royalists; and Egyptian casualties alone were reckoned at around 10,000 dead, wounded and captured.[108] At last Faisal was prepared to agree a ceasefire and to secure the agreement of the Imam. King Saud, hinted Faisal, would soon be dethroned: days later it was announced that Faisal had become King of Saudi Arabia, that a ceasefire had been agreed, and that a conference for 'national reconciliation' would soon be convened. But the ceasefire was short lived. After barely a month the forces of the recalcitrant Imam again launched hostilities against the republican regime and its Egyptian supporters.

The Yemeni civil war, with all its implications for Saudi and Egyptian involvement, was destined to drag on intermittently until 1970. Then it was – following an Arab summit conference in Khartoum, sobering Arab defeats at the hands of the Israelis, and the pointless dissipation of yet more blood and treasure – that Nasser finally managed to extricate himself from his 'Vietnam'. By now Nasser was in no position to spurn the possibility of support from Arab regimes that he had so roundly castigated in earlier years. The Khartoum agreement, despite Sallal's objections, let him withdraw some 20,000 troops from Yemen. By 1968 Egypt had withdrawn the bulk of her troops, and the rest were to follow; a year later the Saudis finally ended the protracted support for the Imam; and in May 1970 the formation of a national coalition, to include royalist ministers, brought the civil war to an end.

Saudi Arabia had continued to support the Imam even after the withdrawal of the Egyptians in the last months of 1967; but once the Imam's supporters were no longer facing the Egyptian demon their power quickly declined. Now the moderate republicans were prepared to agree terms with the Saudis and the royalists.[109] By now the radical Southern Yemen seemed to be a greater threat to Arabian stability than the Yemen Republic (YAR). On 5 February 1970 Hohsin al-Aini formed a new republican government in Yemen, and on 21 March visited Jeddah for a Saudi-sponsored conference. On 23 May the royalist Ahmed al-Shami led a royalist delegation to Sanaa, and he was subsequently appointed a member of the three-man Republican Council. In July al-Aini visited Saudi Arabia; Riyadh – soon followed by Britain, France and Iran – recognised the Sanaa regime; and 'moderates' held the majority of posts in the new Yemeni government.

The Yemeni civil war had terrified the Saudis, dramatically reminding them of the fragility of their own royalist regime; Nasser had been bled dry, his substantial influence massively reduced; and the Great Powers had inevitably perceived the whole affair as yet another troublesome conflict of the Cold War (the CIA, active throughout the war, sometimes carried out operations in Saudi Arabia of which Faisal was totally unaware[110]). The outcome was a fragile peace destined to be shaken yet again by the 1990 Gulf crisis, by the character of the 1991 Gulf War, and by today's unresolved tensions. Saudi Arabia, by virtue of history, its shared border and its own inherent instabilities, was destined to maintain its involvement in Yemeni affairs throughout the 1990s.

THE ARAB–ISRAELI WARS

The enduring conflict between Israel and the Arab states, caused over the last half century by the progressive Israeli theft of Arab land, has always placed Saudi Arabia in deep quandary. The Prophet himself came into military and ideological confrontation with the Jews of Arabia,[111] and despite Islam's global impact the religion founded by Muhammed has remained in many particulars an Arab creation.[112] Saudi Arabia, as the site of the holy centres of Islam at Mecca and Medina, remains indelibly marked by the anti-Jewish Arabism that has both historical roots and substantial modern reinforcement. At the same time, despite the Islamic criticisms of the perfidies of the free market (for example, usury and the neglect of the poor), Saudi Arabia has remained an essentially pro-West protector of capitalist (mainly American) enterprise at the heart of the Arab world. With the United States the principal ally of Israel and the main benefactor of the immense Saudi oil resource, the quandary of Saudi Arabia has been manifest for half a century.

These circumstances have obliged the United States to walk a similar tightrope, though not always with skill or insight. Political contradictions have frequently emerged, almost invariably resolved in favour of Israel (for example, the US-dominated UN Security Council allows Israel to ignore SC resolutions, such as 242, 465, 476, 478, 672, 673, 681 and 799, where genocidal sanctions are imposed on an Arab state such as Iraq for minor infringements). The American attempt to back the two horses – Israel supported by the plutocratic US Jewish lobby, and the US oil interest sited in the deserts of Arabia – began before the founding of Israel. Thus the correspondence of President Roosevelt with King Ibn Saud, and their meeting after the Yalta conference in early 1945, showed that Roosevelt had made commitments to the Saudis that conflicted with his promises to the Jews.

Thus Bartley Crum, an American on the Anglo-American Committee of Inquiry on Palestine, commented that a secret State Department file showed that 'since September 15, 1938, each time a promise was made to American Jewry regarding Palestine, the State Department promptly sent messages to the Arab rulers discounting it'. A few months after Roosevelt's death the US Secretary of State James F. Byrnes released a letter from the President to Ibn Saud (5 April 1945) recalling Roosevelt's assurances that he 'would take no action, in my capacity as chief of the Executive branch of this government, which might prove hostile to the Arab people'.[113] The tensions that this dual policy represented for both Washington and important parts of the Arab world, particularly Saudi Arabia, were bound to produce conflicts in the year that followed. The Arab–Israeli confrontation – often encouraged by Washington as useful to American interests – had persisted throughout the entire history of modern Israel, frequently erupting into violence. Over a period of almost exactly half a century five wars have occurred, of varying intensity and with varying degrees of Saudi involvement:

- The First Arab–Israeli War, or Israel's War for Independence (14 May 1948 to 7 January 1949);
- The Suez–Sinai War (29 October to 6 November 1956);
- The Six-Day War (5–10 June 1967);
- The October War, Yom Kippur or Ramadan War (6–24 October 1973);
- The 'Peace for Galilee' War (1982).[114]

In all these cases Saudi Arabia offered support to the Arab cause, but reluctantly and to minimal effect. On 15 May 1948, while the Palestine Arab forces and elements of the regular armies of Transjordan, Iraq, Lebanon and Syria were struggling unsuccessfully to evict Israeli settlers from Arab land, Saudi Arabia offered no more than token support. Again, with Egyptian, Syrian and Jordanian troops integrated under Egyptian command during the Suez–Sinai War, there was no Saudi involvement. When the Israelis attacked Egypt in June 1967, with high-level clearance from the United States,[115] a substantial transformation of the shape of the Middle East had begun. Syria, Jordan and Egypt were attacked almost simultaneously; and by the end of the short war Israel had occupied Syria's Golan Heights, Jordan's West Bank and the rest of Jerusalem, and the entire Sinai peninsula. Israel, in less than one week, had doubled the extent of its territories – all of them land formerly occupied by Arabs. Again the Saudis had done little to resist the Israeli onslaught on Arab territory.

King Faisal was reportedly grieved at the loss of Jerusalem to Israel; and, as the Custodian of Islam's Holy Places, he felt obliged to retrieve the lost lands. But his sense of personal responsibility and his abiding hatred of the Jews (identifying Zionism with communism) were far removed from any practical political posture. In fact much of Faisal's hatred of Israeli adventurism derived from the resulting boost to Arab radicalism, a threat to all the feudal monarchies in Arabia. Israel was stimulating the growth of revolutionary Arab factions that were increasingly representing a hazard to Saudi Arabia and other God-fearing states. Faisal urged a *jihad* against the Zionist occupiers of the Muslim Holy Places; and, as a more practical gesture, convened a summit conference at Rabat, Morocco. Representatives from the entire Islamic world (with the exception of the Baathist states of Syria and Iraq) attended, unanimously agreed the appropriate measures, and applauded Faisal's efforts. Nothing, however, emerged from Rabat to restore the pre-war geography of the Middle East.

On 6 October 1973 the Egyptians launched a comprehensive attack on the Israeli positions facing them across the Suez Canal. This was the time of Yom Kippur, the Jewish feast of Atonement, and the Egyptian forces were seeking revenge for the reverses of the Six-Day War. President Sadat had confided to Faisal that no option remained to the Arabs but war, and the Saudi King had agreed. By early 1973 the Saudis had made preparations for the anticipated conflict: between $300 million and $500 million was now available to fund Egyptian arms purchases; up to $500 million was offered for balance-of-payment support; and the $250 million annual subsidy agreed at the 1967 Khartoum conference still stood. Now there were pledges also on the option of an oil embargo.[116] At the same time the cautious Faisal was desperately hoping for an American initiative to defuse the mounting tensions. In April 1973 the Saudi oil minister, Ahmed Yamani, visited Washington to discuss matters with Secretary of State William Rogers, Secretary of the Treasury George Schulz and National Security Advisor Henry Kissinger. Yamani emphasised that the Saudis were keen to prevent an oil embargo, but Washington had to adopt a more even-handed policy in the Middle East. Kissinger was dismissive: Arab oil embargoes had not worked in the past, and if the Egyptians resorted to war the Arabs would get thrashed.[117]

In the event the war took place, Faisal announced the oil embargo on 20 October, and two days later a ceasefire was imposed by a joint US/Soviet initiative. The war cost Egypt and Israel about $7 billion each, with negotiated disengagement agreements accepted by Egypt, Israel and Syria following 1974/5 talks; but it was not until 26 March 1979 that Israel returned the Sinai peninsula to Egypt. The social impact of the oil embargo was 'panic' in the United States: the public purchased whatever gasoline it could find, there were calls for rationing, and the economy plunged into recession.[118] In December 1974 nine of the world's most powerful bankers threatened the Mayor of New York, Abraham Beame, that unless he handed over the city's pension funds to the banks they would ensure the ruin of New York. He soon capitulated, public spending (including on schools and hospitals) was slashed to fund the bank debt, and thousands of workers were laid off: 'The nation's greatest city had begun its descent into a scrap heap.'[119]

The effectiveness of the oil weapon had been amply demonstrated. Saudi Arabia had shown that it was prepared to act decisively in the interest of the Arab cause; but with hindsight this dramatic episode seems little more than a historical aberration. Perhaps Faisal was the key element; under Khaled and Fahd there were no dramatic initiatives to reverse Israeli gains or to embarrass their American backers. Thus in 1982 Israel launched a massive invasion of the Lebanon, killing in some estimates around 20,000 civilians. This adventure, like earlier Israeli aggressions, had prior American approval.[120] The Saudis were horrified at this further desecration of Arab land and at yet more slaughter of Arab men, women and children; but they proposed no radical response. The desultory funding of Arab terrorist groups continued, but there was no suggestion of a multinational Arab response to this new Israeli aggression; and there was no suggestion of a fresh oil embargo against Israel and its backers. Saudi Arabia, from the Western perspective, was in safe hands, well prepared to consolidate its client status and to follow the American lead in the Middle East. Soon this policy of obeisance would involve Saudi Arabia – as an indirect or direct participant – in new wars; and would stimulate mounting disaffection with the kingdom. The wars of the 1980s and 1990s were destined to advertise, rather than disguise, the long-term instability of the client feudalism.

Part III
The Modern Client

6 Wars, Rumours of Wars

> *War is prescribed to you: but from this ye are averse. Yet haply ye are averse from a thing, though it be good for you ... God knoweth; but ye, ye know not.*
>
> Koran, Sura 2, Verses 12–13

PREAMBLE

In 1997, following President Clinton's description of the United States as the 'indispensable nation', US Secretary of State Madeleine Albright was happy to talk about 'the global system we are constructing'.[1] In this sublime scheme, underwritten by a Christian deity seemingly employed by the State Department, individual countries around the world are assigned their appropriate roles. They may not always like it but, where blandishment fails, Washington can always resort to force or the threat of force. In this context where once American arms were 'directed primarily against the Soviet Union', they may now be 'directed against everybody'.[2] In fact there are many ways in which the United States seeks to impose its will on weaker but necessary players in *the global system we are constructing*. These include propaganda, terrorism, force, threat of force, aid, withdrawal of aid, exclusion from global institutions, financial pressure, *inter alia*.[3] The rulers of Saudi Arabia are content – despite occasional political dislocations – to co-operate with the Washington strategists charged with the task of managing these global arrangements.

Saudi Arabia is essential to American strategy for the obvious reasons of oil and geography: Washington requires reliable access to cheap and abundant energy both to keep its automobile-fixated domestic population relatively docile and to project its military power around the world; and Saudi Arabia is usefully sited at the heart of the most oil-rich region of the planet. It is possible also for Saudi Arabia to be used in various other ways that are helpful to the Washington strategists. For example, Saudi oil money can be sent to US-backed terrorists in circumstances where a more direct and open American involvement might be politically embarrassing and financially costly. Thus Saudi Arabia has sent money to Washington-backed insurgencies in Nicaragua, Angola, Afghanistan and elsewhere in return for sophisticated US weapons and American military protection.[4] The arrangement has worked well, and continues to work well, for US strategic planners keen to extend American power around the globe and for a Saudi royal family equally enthusiastic about preserving its resolutely feudal and profligate life-style.

237

It is important to note that Saudi Arabia is not the only state required to function in such a role. Thus through the Reagan years the United States not only constructed 'a semi-private international terrorist network but also an array of client and mercenary *states* – Taiwan, South Korea, Israel, Saudi Arabia, and others – to finance and implement its terrorist operations' (italics in original).[5] And US government efforts were discernible also in the building and operation of various right-wing groups dedicated to a pro-America world agenda. For example, in 1966 the World Anti-Communist League (WACL) was formed by the merger of the Anti-Bolshevik Nations (ABN) organisation and the Asian People's Anti-Communist League (APACL).[6] The WACL developed to include a wide range of national groups, including fascist parties, groups sponsoring death squads and drugs-related activities, and groups associated with the US military/intelligence community. For the purposes of the present book it is significant that the League also included representatives from governments in power, including, those of Taiwan, South Korea, South Africa, Chile and Saudi Arabia.[7] Thus the Saudi royal family was prepared to support an international US-friendly organisation associated with terrorism, death squads and drug trafficking. Saudi Arabia has worked to protect American interests on a global basis in various ways that go far beyond the provision of cheap energy and a strategic geography at the heart of the Middle East.

The arrangements have long been in place. Thus the Saudis were providing support for the Afghan rebels against the pro-Soviet regime through the 1970s, even before the 1979 Soviet invasion.[8] In the same way Saudi funds were fed to the Angolan insurgents over many years, a US-approved initiative that helped to frustrate the peace-making efforts of the United Nations and indefinitely prolong the suffering of the Angolan people. For such services the Saudis were rewarded by massive US arms deals that often had no more than symbolic significance (since Saudi Arabia typically lacked the trained manpower to operate the military technology). Where US–Saudi arms deals were politically controversial – for example, possibly posing a threat to Israel – special efforts were made in Washington to negotiate a way through the problems. Thus Major-General Richard Secord, an experienced US organiser of clandestine arms deals, helped to steer the AWACS aircraft sale to the Saudis through Congress as a reward for the Saudi support given to the Contra terrorists in Nicaragua.[9]

It was also useful to the United States, in addition to selling arms to Saudi Arabia and so keeping US arms manufacturers well funded, to be able to consolidate an American military presence in the region. Between 1970 and 1979 Saudi Arabia purchased $3.2 billion worth of US weapons and military services; while by 1978 some 675 American military personnel and around 10,000 civilian defence personnel were constructing military facilities in Saudi Arabia.[10] The royal family had been very reluctant to demonstrate open collaboration with the chief Western ally of Israel, but events had allowed Washington to pressure the Saudis into a more active involvement in US military plans. Egypt, Oman and

Bahrain were already permitting American air and naval forces to use limited base facilities, with the Washington planners keen to expand such provisions. The Iran–Iraq War (see below), and the resulting Saudi anxieties, gave the United States a useful excuse for increased military penetration of the region. A key element in the scheme was the sale of five AWACS aircraft and the necessary support system of bases providing fuel, spare parts and munitions. The American military analyst Anthony Cordesman commented: 'No conceivable improvements in US airlift or USAF rapid deployment and "bare-basing" capability could come close to giving the US this rapid and effective reinforcement capability.'[11] The Washington military planners were happy to note that this enhanced US penetration of the region would be paid for by the Saudis themselves.*

Through the 1980s the Saudis spent around $50 billion on a regional air-defence system designed to meet NATO (that is, primarily US) requirements; it was part of the deal that American forces would have access to all system facilities in the event of a military crisis. By the end of the decade the US Army Corps of Engineers had built a $14 billion military network across Saudi Arabia, including military bases at Khamis Mushayat, Tabuk and King Khaled Military City; naval facilities at Ras al-Mishab, Jeddah and Jubayl; three military schools; a headquarters complex for the air force, the ministry of defence and aviation and the navy; support provisions for F-15 and F-16 fighter planes; and a headquarters/training complex for the Saudi National Guard. (We may speculate that the bulk of the new facilities were completed in good time for what some independent analysts judge was the planned US war against Iraq – see below.)[12]

The Saudis remained reluctant to advertise the increased US penetration of their country in particular and the region in general; and it suited Washington to note and accommodate such reticence. The Americans had no wish to further undermine the Saudi regime by fuelling Muslim complaints that Western infidels were gaining undue influence over the Custodian of the Holy Places. But US strategy was plain. The new military facilities, designed and constructed at Saudi expense, were now available and would be used by US forces when necessary. Said Secretary of Defence Casper Weinberger in a classified 1984–88 Defence Guidance report: 'Whatever the circumstances, we should be prepared to introduce American forces directly into the region should it appear that the security of access to Persian Gulf oil is threatened.'[13] In September 1985 *The New York Times* reported a classified State Department study prepared by Secretary of State Richard Murphy: the Saudis remained reluctant to agree formal arrangements for US military access to Saudi territory but had made it clear that 'access will be

---

* Just as the enlarged American military occupation of Europe, following the 1997 talks for the eastward expansion of the US-dominated North Atlantic Treaty Organisation (NATO), will be paid for in large part by the newly-occupied countries themselves.

forthcoming for United States forces as necessary to counter Soviet aggression or in regional crises they cannot manage on their own'.[14] Thus Washington had persuaded the Saudi government to allow '*the quiet construction of what amounts to an advanced, surrogate US military facility that is so tailored to meet US requirements that American aircraft staged from it with no trouble*' during the 1991 onslaught on Iraq.[15] Here the reference is to King Khaled Military City, 'built in secret in the desert ... a huge military oasis complete with missile silos and nuclear-bomb-proof underground command bunkers', with integrated air, missile, naval and command facilities that in some cases were superior to the analogous systems back in the United States.[16] The United States had succeeded in establishing a complex of bases in Saudi Arabia from which US power could be quickly projected to any part of the Gulf region.

It was possible also for Washington to exploit Saudi Arabia via its membership of such international organisations as the Arab League, founded in 1945, and the Gulf Co-operation Council (GCC), founded in 1980 as 'what amounted to a club for the rich'.[17] The GCC in particular (comprising Saudi Arabia, Kuwait, Qatar, Bahrain, Oman and the United Arab Emirates) was inevitably dominated by the Saudis, so providing a useful channel for American influence throughout the wealthy sheikhdoms of Kuwait and most of the Arabian peninsula.

There are thus many ways in which the United States is able to exploit the Saudi connection as part of the wider strategic framework being developed by the Washington planners. In this context the arms trade is pivotal: the US armaments trade to Saudi Arabia keeps the American arms factories humming, encourages regional instability as Israel struggles to maintain a military advantage, provides the revenues for further prodigious military research, and so guarantees the essential buttress for the American Establishment and its proxies around the world. In such circumstances the continued militarisation of the American economy is essential, so providing massive profits for arms-linked corporations and their comfortable placement in many government sectors.

These circumstances were well demonstrated through the period of the Iran–Iraq War (see below), where Saudi Arabia saw advantage in following the US policy of *supporting* Iraq; and the 1991 Gulf War (see below), where Saudi Arabia followed US policy in *opposing* Iraq. Here it is worth noting that the US–Saudi symbiosis is essentially a relationship between two national but disparate élites (respectively plutocratic capitalist and plutocratic feudalist). It should not be necessary to emphasise that such a narrow symbiosis is not necessarily of immediate or ultimate benefit to the national populations of either the United States or Saudi Arabia, or to the wider world community. In reality the opposite is the case: to the manifest horrors of the arms trade must be added the obvious injustices that help to define capitalist and feudal hierachies. The US–Saudi symbiosis is one of various shaping factors in a world where gross and well-protected affluence co-exists with massive segments of human deprivation.

THE ARMS PLOY

Arms sales to Saudi Arabia increased over a period of decades in line with the increased Saudi revenues from oil. For example, in the two decades from 1950 the United States sold Saudi Arabia around $176 million in military hardware and services; between 1971 and 1975 the figure was some $2.5 billion.[18] The equipment sold was not always ideally suited to Saudi needs. In May 1965 US Secretary of Defense Robert McNamara offered a $100 million package of armaments, including the F-5 aircraft, the *Hawk* missile, and radar and communications systems. Through the summer the British and French made competing offers, until in November King Faisal opted for a UK–US package comprising 36 English Electric *Lightning* interceptors and a number of Raytheon *Hawk* missiles supported by American radar and communications systems. It has since been suggested that the $300 million deal was ill-suited to Saudi needs. The *Lightnings* were short-range jets originally designed to protect the relatively small British airspace, with the Saudis needing air protection over an area nine times as large; and the Saudis lacked the maintenance crews and pilots for such sophisticated technology. Similarly the *Hawk* missiles were intended for close-in defence of static areas, not to be dragged long distances over difficult terrain. The Saudis would have been better served by US F-5 or F-104 jets and British or French air-to-air missiles.[19] The situation was to be repeated many times over subsequent years: the arms manufacturers have always been more interested in making sales than in assessing purchaser needs.

As the United States gradually supplanted Britain as the principal foreign influence in Saudi affairs, US corporations benefited enormously in obvious financial terms and the position of Saudi Arabia was strengthened in the Middle East. The so-called 'petrodollars' were effectively recycled into US corporate accounts while Riyadh became increasingly dependent upon military technology which, though little understood, could now be afforded on an increasing scale. To a large extent the Saudi government was encouraged to compensate for relatively low levels of military personnel by massive military expenditure on hardware and other spending per man in the armed forces. Thus by the early 1990s Saudi spending per soldier had reached an annual figure of $223,592, compared with $66,000 for the United States and $6,960 for Iraq.[20] By 1976 the US Army Corps of Engineers was involved in some $20 billion of military construction in Saudi Arabia, including the 'military cities' of al-Batin (near the Iraqi border), Tabuq in the north-west and Khamis Mushayat in the south-west. The foreign headquarters of the US Army Engineers were transferred from Germany to Saudi Arabia, providing further evidence that the Arabian peninsula was being militarised according to far-reaching US strategic planning.

By the late 1970s Saudi Arabia had become America's best arms customer, a seeming paradox in view of the US alliance with Israel. In early 1974 Washington revealed plans for a sale to the Saudis of $500 million worth of F-5s and naval equipment, with an offer of F-4s to replace the British *Lightnings*, but

the Saudis were said to be hesitant about the massive costs involved. In November the Assistant Defense Secretary Robert Ellsworth and George Vest, then director of the State Department's politico-military bureau, flew to Riyadh to press for Saudi purchases, over the next decade, of 440 helicopters, other aircraft, 26 new ships, tanks, other armoured vehicles, and additional equipment to create a paratroop brigade. Such weapons, declared a Pentagon report, would enable Saudi Arabia to 'deter aggression and defeat an enemy'. Saudi Arabia was soon agreeing to purchase, as a preliminary order, 300 *Hawk* missile batteries, for delivery before 1980, at a cost of $270 million. At the same time the Saudis were considering a French offer of 38 Mirage III/5 fighter-bombers and missiles, to cost $860 million; in 1976 an order was placed for 48 Dassault F-1s as part of an 'arms for oil' barter deal, while the Saudi Air Force agreed to buy both the French *Matra Magic* air-to-air missile and American *Sidewinder* missiles.[21] Some of the main events through this period and later are shown in Table 6.1.

At the same time the US arms manufacturers were forced to contend with the Jewish lobby in the United States (Morris Amitay, the lobby's main spokesman, had boasted: 'We've never lost on a major issue'). Under Jewish pressure on Congress the 1975 order for 2000 *Sidewinder* air-to-air and 1500 *Maverick* air-to-surface missiles (already reduced from totals of 5000 and 2880, respectively) was reduced by late 1976 to 1500 (then 1000, then 850) *Sidewinders*, and to 1000 (then 650) *Mavericks*.[22] An editorial in *Near East Report* (the newsletter of the American-Israel Public Affairs Committee, AIPAC), reporting that Saudi arms orders for 1976 amounted to more than $7.5 billion, commented that 'the Arabs' already had a three-to-one advantage over Israel in weapons and firepower.[23] Hubert Humphrey, well funded by the Jewish lobby and chairman of the Senate foreign assistance subcommittee, was holding public hearings on Saudi arms purchases; and other Senators were working to reduce or block particular US deals with Saudi Arabia. One House committee member, New York's Ben Rosenthal, suggested that anti-Israel Arab personnel were receiving military training on US hardware supplied to the Saudis, and that US equipment had been transferred to Egypt during the 1973 war: 'In fact, intelligence sources report Egyptian pilots already have been getting "orientation" or, if you will, "training" flights on Saudi F-5s. The Saudis transferred a squadron of Bell 205 Iroquois helicopters to Egypt during the [1973] war … That was in violation of the transfer clause in the purchase agreement with the United States, but this government did nothing about it.'[24*]

Some US Senators – for example, Democrats Joseph Biden of Delaware and Richard Clark of Iowa – proposed a total block on all arms sales to Saudi Arabia, Kuwait and Iran, as a way of *not* singling out the Saudis for special treatment. This proposal was defeated but anti-arms lobbying continued from AIPAC and other pro-Israel factions. Under this pressure President Carter agreed to review some of the agreed US–Saudi arms deals; in particular, the agreement to sell 580

---

* This compares with Saudi transfers to Iraq during the 1980s – see below.

Table 6.1 Sample Saudi arms deals (1974–97)

February 1974	Washington reveals plans for sale to Saudis of $500 million worth of F-5 aircraft and naval equipment.
November 1974	Ellsworth and Vest fly to Riyadh to promote massive US arms sales to Saudi Arabia over the next decade.
January 1977	Frost & Sullivan, New York market analyst firm, predict that Saudi Arabia will buy up to $3 billion more military equipment from United States over the next five years.
1978	Battle in US Congress over President Carter's decision to sell 60 F-15s to Saudi Arabia.
1982	Congress approves AWACS deal worth $8.5 billion, despite massive pressure from the American-Israel Public Affairs Committee.
1985	Saudi Arabia buys 480 Sea Eagle anti-ship missile-arming Tornado IDS fighters from Britain.
1986	Saudis buy 200 Alarm anti-radar missile-arming IDS fighters
17 February 1986	Massive Al-Yamamah agreement signed by Saudi Arabia and Britain – see main text below.
15 December 1986	British Aerospace hands over first PC-9/*Hawk* trainer, bought under Al-Yamamah agreement (deal total: 132 aircraft).
March 1987	Royal Saudi Naval Force expresses interest in buying up to 10 conventional submarines; Britain and France compete for contract.
June 1988	Saudi Defence minister visits UK to close Al-Yamamah deal: agreement includes 48 Tornado IDS fighters, 12 British Aerospace transport aircraft, 20 *Hawk*-100 trainer aircraft, 40 *Hawk*-200 fighters.
July 1988	Saudi Arabia buys 88 British Westland *Black Hawk* helicopters as part of Al-Yamamah deal; Britain sells 3 Sandown-class mine-countermeasure ships to Saudis, with option for 3 more.
1990	Saudi Arabia buys 461 Piranha armoured personnel carriers worth $400 million from Britain.
1991	Saudi Arabia buys from British Aerospace: 4 125–800 jets, 30 *Hawk* trainers, 36 Tornado ADV combat aircraft, 12 Tornado IDS combat aircraft, 88 Westland WS-70 helicopters; Penn Pharma supplies nerve gas antidotes; Shorts supply 40 Shortland S-55 armoured personnel carriers; Transac supplies 60 armoured personnel carriers; also supplied are 10,000 S10 unit respirators for NBC suits.
1992	British Aerospace supplies 12 125–800 utility aircraft, 480 ALARM anti-radar missiles, 480 Sea Eagle anti-ship missiles, 560 Sky Flash air-to-air missiles; Shanning Group supplies medical units worth $11 million; Vosper Thorneycroft deliver 6 Sandown-class minehunters.

Table 6.1 (continued)

11 September 1992	President Bush agrees sale of 72 McDonnell Douglas F-15 fighter aircraft to Saudi Arabia.
1993	By 1993 Saudi arms purchases from Britain (1988–92) total $3116 million.
28 January 1993	Saudi Arabia confirms agreement to buy 48 Tornado aircraft as part of £4 billion to £5 billion arms deal.
April 1993	Vosper Thornycroft and Fal Group of Companies (Riyadh) offer joint venture services for naval arrangements.
November 1993	Britain proposes to Saudi Arabia that she buy £2 billion package of armoured vehicles.
January 1994	Saudi budget cuts of 20 per cent seen as threat to UK jobs.
February 1994	Declining oil prices force US to restructure $9.2 billion repayment as part of $30 billion US–Saudi deal; Boeing and McDonnell win $6 billion airbus contract in Saudi Arabia.
July 1994	Fresh speculation about the possibility of Saudi financial support for development of Islamic atomic bomb; CIA begins investigation.
October 1994	Slump in oil prices threatens UK–Saudi deal worth £20 billion; 40,000 jobs said to be at stake.
February 1995	Saudi Arabia considers purchase of 385 Challenger 2 battle tanks from Britain.
October 1995	Saudi Arabia to buy 61 civil aircraft from Boeing and McDonnell.
January 1996	Reduced role for King Fahd seen as possible threat to UK arms sales in Saudi Arabia.
February 1997	Saudi Arabia cancels US deal for 102 F-16 fighter aircraft after leak of details.
July 1997	French and British compete to secure £1 billion Saudi order for battle tanks.

more *Hawk* missiles (worth $1.06 billion) that would have brought the Saudi *Hawk* arsenal to almost one thousand missiles of this type. Rosenthal reminded Carter of his campaign rhetoric intended to secure Jewish support: 'There is no reason to think these missiles will increase security and stability in the Middle East. There is no reason to think they can be used only for defence ... No administration which was sensitive to the climate in the Middle East would let the sale go forward.'[25] Carter later approved the sale of 45 F-15s and 15 F-15 trainers, worth $1.5 billion, to Saudi Arabia as replacement for the ageing British *Lightnings*, and he also subsequently approved the sale of further *Hawk* batteries, C-130s and various infrastructure contracts.

Saudi Arabia continued to acquire substantial quantities of US military hardware, though often in circumstances of political controversy. (Arms deals often had wide ramifications, as when in February 1966 the British government announced that it would buy fifty F-111s from General Dynamics, costing $725 million, with some of the cost offset by a deal with Saudi Arabia that Washington had agreed to forgo. In one account, here the Saudis 'had been persuaded to buy British planes they did not want, to allow Britain to pay for American planes that they could not afford'.[26] This was a classic case of where a seemingly straightforward arms agreement had much wider aspects.) Throughout the period the Jewish lobby, for obvious and understandable political reasons, persisted with its blocking tactics. Successive American presidents, inclined to deal with the Saudis, were forced to navigate the obstructions erected by the AIPAC and other pro-Israel groups. For example, President Carter offered the Saudis additional F-15s on certain conditions, none of which posed the Saudis problems and some of which were already enshrined in existing Offer of Sale requirements. One such condition was that military equipment was not to be transferred from the purchaser Saudi Arabia to other states, though if this were to happen it was not clear that Washington would block further lucrative arms deals.

The Jewish lobby lost on the 'major issue' of the F-15 agreement, but in any event the scale of US–Saudi arms deals was slightly on the decline towards the end of the 1970s. Where $2.5 billion worth of arms had been sold to the Saudis in 1976 the figure was $900 million in 1978, though this total did not include a Litton Industries deal worth $1.5 billion for the design and supply of a nationwide command, control and communications system. And *non-equipment* deals often added considerably to Saudi expenditure. In 1978, with US purchases of Saudi oil amounting to around $6.4 billion, Riyadh spent some $4.9 billion on all military-linked deals in the United States. Thus America was able to recoup much of its Saudi oil costs.[27]

At the same time the Saudis themselves were having to cope with a range of political problems linked to the acquisition of Western arms. Washington had often encouraged Saudi purchases as necessary defensive measures against such states as Iran and Iraq – at times when there were no obvious threats from those quarters. But Saudi Arabia remained sensitive to tensions within the Arab world; and in particular to the problems of a Middle East necessarily destabilised by the survival of Israel at the heart of the Islamic world. In such circumstances it was necessary for Riyadh – or at least for the Saudi royals – to pursue Saudi interests without alienating widespread Muslim opinion in the region by acquiescing in a *de facto* surrender of military sovereignty to the United States. It was a task only partly accomplished (see Chapter 7).

Thus Khaled Bin Sultan, a nephew of King Fahd and eldest son of Saudi defence minister Prince Sultan, has candidly described the extent of American control over Saudi defence interests.[28] Khaled, later to gain publicity as a commander in the 1991 Gulf War, admitted that 'Just as ARAMCO ran our oil industry, so Raytheon [the vast US arms corporation] ran our defense. ... These two important American companies controlled vital sectors of the Kingdom. Vast powerhouses of wealth and expertise, closely associated with the US government, they were directed by powerful boards back in the United States. In Saudi Arabia, few people were prepared to talk tough with them.'[29] In 1972, when Khaled was named project officer for the *Hawk* systems, the Americans who ran Raytheon from their Jeddah headquarters, had access to the highest ranks of Saudi royalty – a clear sign of US influence with the Saudi government. Khaled resolved to establish 'some control' over Raytheon: 'I believe it was to the benefit of both parties that I made Raytheon understand that it was not dealing with a banana republic ... we were now a self-respecting country well able to monitor the performance of the company which, more than any other over the years, had helped us build and equip our air defense forces.'[30*]

The extent to which the Saudis managed to establish real authority over the US on-site arms contractors (and other American firms deeply enmeshed in the Saudi economy) can be debated. It is still the case that the vast bulk of the military expertise is provided by American personnel; and that in fact individual arms deals are tailored primarily for US strategic and financial advantage with the Saudi interest a poor second. For example, it has been argued that US–Saudi arms agreements have been designed 'to provide Saudi Arabia with no advantages in any future military conflict with Israel' but instead to focus training and software support 'on potential conflict with Yemen, Iraq or Iran'[31] – an approach that is well suited to US strategic needs. Here it is proposed that the 1982 AWACS system, supplied only after much argument in the United States, included computer software and other features designed not to disadvantage Israel and to maintain US military control: 'The computer software was configured to reduce the effectiveness of the Saudi system against the type of US-manufactured jet fighters used by the Israeli Air Force. Secondly, the Saudi system was made heavily dependent upon the United States.'[32] The aircraft cannot fly for more than a month without US support, and some key systems require US support after operating for only a few days; some of the essential maintenance procedures can only be performed in the United States.

It is also of interest that the controversial AWACS systems were designed to carry a 'digital look down link' allowing the US military to collect the electronic intelligence data gathered by the Saudi AWACS and the wider air defence system. In addition, the AWACS design was configured to permit the controlled deployment of US aircraft in the region without the political embarrassment of

---

[*] Khaled visited the United States to begin the negotiations that led to the Saudi–Raytheon deal for the Improved Hawk systems; and three years later (1976) began negotiations with Litton Industries for the design and construction of the nationwide command, control and communications (C3) system (Khaled Bin Sultan, 1996, Chapters 7 and 8).

complex airbase facilities in Saudi Arabia itself. The air-strategy specialist Anthony Cordesman explains:

> In fact, each main Saudi air base had the basic support equipment for 70 US F-15 fighters in addition to supplies for its own F-15s. The package meant that Saudi Arabia would have all the necessary basing, service facilities, refueling capability, parts and key munitions in place to accept over-the-horizon reinforcement from USAF F-15 fighters. No conceivable improvement in US airlift or USAF rapid deployment and 'bare basing' capability could come close to giving the US this rapid and effective reinforcement capability ... The facilities that would become part of the Saudi system would also help to strengthen US ability to deploy forces from the eastern Mediterranean and project them as far east as Pakistan ... No conceivable build-up of US strategic mobility, or of US staging bases in Egypt, Turkey, Oman, Somalia or Kenya could act as a substitute for such facilities in Saudi Arabia.[33]

Again this serves to demonstrate the arrangement, already indicated, that the AWACS configuration was designed to enhance the US strategic posture on the basis of Saudi expenditure alone. The pro-Israel lobbyists had no cause to worry that the AWACS would adversely affect the strategic situation in the Middle East; the reverse was the case. President Reagan, keen to agree the deal, commented: 'I remain fully committed to protecting Israel's security and to preserving Israel's qualitative edge over any combination of potentially hostile forces in the region.' In reality the AWACS agreement, by further extending the US military reach, actively contributed to Israeli security. If the Saudis were aware of this central consequence of their vast AWACS investment they made no mention of it.[34]

The 1982 AWACS deal (worth $8.5 billion) was the largest single armaments deal in US history; but, despite the in-built protection for Israel, the AIPAC, in concert with various Christian fundamentalist and neoconservative ideologues, maintained vigorous opposition to further substantial US–Saudi arms agreements. The pro-Jewish lobbying was again having a decisive effect. In February 1985, during a visit of King Fahd to the United States, Washington announced that a vast new US–Saudi arms deal would be postponed pending further study. It was this procrastination that opened the door for the Al-Yamamah Offset agreement between Britain and Saudi Arabia, the largest British arms deal ever.[35]

In 1985 the British and Saudi governments negotiated the formal 'Al-Yamamah' agreement.[36] The following year a Memorandum of Understanding was signed to confirm a deal, worth around £5 billion, covering the sale of 72 Tornado aircraft, 30 *Hawk* aircraft and 30 PC-9 turboprop trainers. As part of the agreement the British government pledged to encourage UK companies to invest a total of £1 billion in Saudi Arabia over a 10-year period. A second formal understanding, known as Al-Yamamah II, was confirmed in July 1988 and soon depicted as the world's largest ever arms export deal. Technical payment difficulties prevented contracts being signed until January 1993. Then, after Prime Minister John Major visited Saudi Arabia, one contract worth £5 billion was signed for the sale of 48 Tornado aircraft: this deal reportedly saved 19,000 jobs at British Aerospace (Warton, Lancashire); was worth some £250 million to Rolls Royce (military engine division), securing 300 production jobs for two years; and provided subcontracting work for Lucas, Dowty, Smith Industries and others. It soon became apparent that Al-Yamamah was associated with a plethora of official statements, memoranda, intentions, contracts and formal understandings; with payment provisions linked closely to oil prices, so bringing problems when prices fall. In these circumstances, and considering the mounting financial pressures in Saudi Arabia, Britain has found itself competing for payment with the United States and France on signed contracts that are nominally unambiguous. (In 1989 the UK parliamentary House of Commons Public Accounts Committee was obliged to investigate claims that vast and unwarranted 'commissions' had been paid to middlemen in connection with Al-Yamamah. Robert Sheldon MP, chairman of the Committee, subsequently announced that no impropriety had been found – see also Chapter 1.)

The official UK presentation of Al-Yamamah indicates the strong defence component in the context of the wider commercial framework. Thus Charles Masefield, Head of Defence Export Services in the Ministry of Defence, comments: 'The Al Yamamah Offset is a pioneering programme which aims to promote profitable commercial ventures which contribute to the development of the Saudi Arabian economy through technology transfer. Typical projects promoted by the programme range from a Glaxo pharmaceutical factory, through participation by UK companies in the nascent Saudi defence industry, to a specialist commercial training venture. The programme ... is flexible enough to assist companies over a broad range of business opportunities, in all sectors of the Saudi economy. It is also a Government-to-Government programme ...'. In the same document, produced by the British Offset Office, it is stated that British Aerospace is the prime contractor for the Al Yamamah Project; and that there is an associated Economic Offset programme designed to encourage technology transfer to Saudi firms through joint ventures or licensing agreements ('All joint ventures in Saudi Arabia require Government approval').

The British Offset Committee, chaired by Sir Charles Masefield, comprises representatives from various government and commercial organisations (Figure 6.1). It meets with the counterpart Saudi Offset Committee, chaired by Prince Fahd ibn Abdullah, Assistant Minister of Defence and Aviation, every 6 to 9 months. Thus the Al-Yamamah Project involves close and multifaceted interaction between Britain and Saudi Arabia through both government involvement and corporate enterprise. Such a multilayered and intimate interaction necessarily implies substantial areas of shared interest with both commercial and military implications.

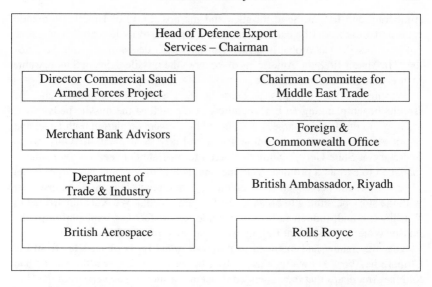

Figure 6.1 Members of British Offset Committee for Al-Yamamah Project

The restrictions imposed by Washington on arms sales to Saudi Arabia, the circumstances that had facilitated the complex UK–Saudi Al-Yamamah agreements, had resulted in a marked cooling of the relationship between Washington and Riyadh. General Norman Schwarzkopf subsequently described aspects of his 1988 visit to Riyadh after his appointment as Commander-in-Chief of the US Central Command: 'For my first trip I'd scheduled Saudi Arabia, Egypt, and Pakistan, the Saudis being the gulf region's most important stabilising force, and the Egyptians and Pakistanis the second- and third-largest recipients (after Israel) of US military aid. In Cairo and Islamabad, Pakistan's capital, the meetings were genial and direct ... In Riyadh my reception was cooler.'[37] He notes that for years the US Congress had limited the sale of arms to Saudi Arabia on the theory that even moderate Arabs would end up using armaments against Israel. Thus the Saudis had moved towards Britain (for fighter aircraft), to France (for air-defence radar), to Brazil (for artillery) and to China (for the CSS-2 missiles).[38]

It was in July 1985 when Prince Bandar ibn Sultan negotiated a $3 billion deal for Chinese CSS-2s, following a US refusal to supply short-range Lance missiles and F-15E Strike Eagle fighter bombers. When news of the Saudi–Chinese agreement broke in the news media in the spring of 1988 the Chinese foreign minister Wu Xueqian announced that Beijing had provided the missiles as 'conducive to stability' in the Middle East. The first CSS-2s were delivered in late 1987 and installed at Al Joffer (60 miles south of Riyadh) and Al Sulaiyil (400 miles farther south).[39] The missiles, housed on launch pads rather than in the more secure silos, were sited deep in the 'Empty Quarter', offering some protection from Iraqi and Iranian Scud missiles and the possibility of Israeli commando raids and air attacks (the earlier Israeli development of its Jericho-2 long-range ballistic missile was probably a factor in the Saudi decision to purchase CSS-2s).[40] In March 1988 the Americans discovered the missile fields in Saudi Arabia by means of satellite surveillance.

Washington was unhappy to learn of such Saudi developments, and the Israelis began planning an F-15 bombing strike against the missile pads. Now, unknown to the world at large, US-supplied F-15s were on alert in both Israel and Saudi Arabia, in full preparation for a military confrontation. Only when Secretary of State George Shultz – forced to mediate between the two sides – managed to extract a promise from the Saudis that they would not target Israel were the Israelis persuaded to abandon their bombing plans. Soon afterwards, with the story beginning to break in the US news media, Wu Xueqian arrived in Washington and, though failing to provide a 'satisfactory' explanation of the missile issue, promised that Beijing would act in a 'responsible' way.

That the Saudis had intended to purchase *some* types of missiles from the Chinese had been known to Washington. In fact in one account the Saudis had told the Americans that they intended to acquire a short-range version of the HY-2 Silkworm coastal-defence missile for supply to the Iraqis, an acceptable policy since the United States was supporting Saddam Hussein in his war against Iran (see below).[41] It is likely that the subsequent crisis was fuelled as much by American pique at learning that the Saudis were prepared to dissemble as by any possible intention of King Fahd to target Israel with long-range CSS-2s. Khaled Bin Sultan, a nephew of Fahd, later gave a Saudi version of the CSS-2 missile purchase (discussed in a chapter happily entitled 'Capturing the East Wind').[42] Here it is declared that Fahd himself, rather than his military commanders, hatched the idea, since 'we needed a weapon powerful enough to deter any potential enemy from attacking us'. Saudi Arabia, suggests Khaled, had acquired 'growing responsibilities' in the region, in the Muslim world, and in the wider global environment. It is acknowledged, contrary to the assurances given to Washington, that Israel was *not* ruled out as a possible target in certain circumstances: '*In brief, the aim was to give us the capability to counterattack in the event of an attack on us by either Israel or Iran, both in their different ways hostile neighbors at that time.*'[43] Khaled expands the point:

> Since the 1973 war – indeed since the 1967 war – Israel had attempted to impose its will on the region, brutally repressing the Palestinian population of the Occupied Territories and carrying out numerous acts of aggression against Arab states ... it is no secret that Israel has acquired nuclear weapons, together with long-range strike aircraft and ballistic missiles ... to deliver them, and is developing military satellites to improve its targeting and intelligence gathering in the Arab world ... our security and self-respect demand that we acquire some minimal deterrent capability.[44]

The comments regarding Iran are doubtless less contentious, at least to American ears, in view of Washington's posture in the Iran–Iraq War (below) and the on-going depiction of Iran as one of America's selected 'pariah states'.

The Saudis had turned to Britain (with Al-Yamamah the result) and to China (for the CSS-2s) because of the frequent American ambivalence about supplying armaments to a potentially anti-Israel state. Between February 1986 and April 1988, large volumes of arms were supplied to Saudi Arabia, but in the same period Congress imposed a block on five major deals – including the supply of F-15s, Maverick missiles, Stinger missiles, armour-piercing uranium ammunition, and AWACS ground-support equipment. At the time a Saudi official commented: 'We would prefer buying weapons from the USA. American technology is generally superior. But we are not going to pay billions of dollars to be insulted. We are not masochists.'[45] (Arms provision to Saudi Arabia sometimes featured surprising aspects. After much haggling over the supply of fuel tanks for Saudi F-15s Washington dropped its objections, whereupon McDonnell Douglas subcontracted Israel Aircraft Industries to produce them at the IAI factory outside Tel Aviv.[46])

A fresh Middle East arms race was being fuelled, with the United States willing to supply hardware and services (with fluctuating and inconsistent limitations) to various countries in the region, but with Saudi Arabia increasingly unwilling to accept any one state as its sole armaments supplier. At the beginning of 1988 it was reported that the Saudis were offering Pakistan $800 million to help develop 'an Islamic hydrogen bomb', on the condition that Iraq be denied access to the resulting technology. (Various countries were now supplying Pakistan with nuclear-research facilities. Washington, while claiming to deplore this trend, was prepared to negotiate a $3.2 billion deal with Pakistan that included forty F-16 aircraft.) It remained plain that, whatever the domestic influence of AIPAC and the rest of the Jewish lobby in the United States, Washington and Riyadh would continue to have a common strategic interest in the Middle East and the wider world community. The Saudis would continue to strive for a degree of independence from the United States but their 'bottom-line' reliance on American protection and military expertise necessarily confirms their continued client status.

The American strategic role in the Middle East and the nature of the US relationship with Saudi Arabia were both graphically illustrated during the Gulf wars of the 1980s/90s (see below). Such events demonstrated the extent to which Washington was prepared for active military involvement and the extent to which it would try to dominate the political postures of the regional powers. In more particular terms the wars, in large part shaped by US foreign policy, impacted on such matters as American access to Middle East oil, the enhancement of a permanent US military presence in the region, the extent to which a United States funded by foreign powers could adopt the role of mercenary, and the extent to which arms shipments to states in the region would be affected.

In June 1990, soon after the ending of the Iran–Iraq War and less than two months before the Iraqi invasion of Kuwait, Washington revealed plans to allow a $4 billion arms sale to Saudi Arabia – to include AWACS systems, armoured vehicles and anti-tank missiles. A US government official, anticipating Jewish-lobby objections, commented: 'The Saudis are our allies too. We've sold them similar stuff in the past and, anyway, Israel no longer has automatic most favoured nation [status] up here.' It was expected the Saudis would be spending more than $3 million on General Motors hardware, including 1117 light armoured vehicles; with 2000 TOW anti-tank missiles to be purchased from Hughes Aircraft; Boeing stood to gain a $600 million contract to modify five AWACS aircraft and eight KE-3 tanker aircraft for the Royal Saudi Air Force. Less than a year later the 1991 Gulf War was 'providing US defence contractors with the kind of advertising money can't buy'.[47] Export orders for the Raytheon Patriot missile systems were expected to double in 1992 to $2 billion, with the $1.6 million Tomahawk cruise missile, scheduled for cancellation in 1992, given a new lease of life. The war was particularly encouraging for various industry sectors: 'The good news from the Gulf has been particularly heartening for America's $55 billion a year defence electronics industry ...'.[48] There remained some strategic questions to be resolved in the post-war US–Saudi alliance.

The Saudis were now wanting to supplement their sophisticated air-defence system with an offensive army capability for mobile warfare, similar to that demonstrated against Iraq. The Bush administration, anticipating a bruising battle with Israel and the US Jewish lobby, was suggesting that it would be inappropriate to supply the Saudis with the training and weaponry that would be necessary. At the same time the Pentagon was pressing for Saudi-based facilities for the stockpiling of enough armour to equip a 150,000-strong corps with a logistical organisation similar to that of NATO in Europe. American officials acknowledged that the competing demands had put US–Saudi relations under strain: the Saudis were blocking Pentagon plans; the Saudi ambassador to Washington, Prince Bandar ibn Sultan, had refused to meet the State Department's chief negotiator, Richard Clarke; and the Saudis were refusing to sign new defence agreements with Washington.[49]

There were soon further signs of tension. In November 1991 McDonnell Douglas confirmed that Saudi Arabia was going ahead with a $5 billion deal to buy 72 F-15 fighter bombers – an announcement that brought a sceptical government response and the promise of Israeli protest. Moreover, the Pentagon was hostile to the deal: if McDonnell plant was kept active with F-15 production Congress would be less likely to fund the controversial new Advanced Tactical Fighter. A few months later it also emerged that the Saudis had improperly transferred US-supplied weapons to such states as Iraq and Syria in recent years (for example, passing on American bombs to Iraq in 1986, at a time when Washington also was supporting Saddam Hussein).[50] In July 1992 President Bush resolved to press ahead with the sale to Saudi Arabia of 72 advanced US fighters, F-15Es and F-15Hs, despite domestic opposition in Congress and elsewhere. It was not clear whether the Democratic presidential nominee, Bill Clinton, having pressed for 'strong international limits on the dangerous and wasteful flow of conventional arms to troubled regions', would cancel the Saudi deal. Now the Saudis, having negotiated Al-Yamamah with Britain, were threatening Washington with further deals with non-US companies in the event of American blocks on arms purchases. After the 1991 Gulf War the Secretary of State James Baker had announced a new policy 'to reduce arms flow into an area that is already over-militarised'; and then the United States sold a record $41 billion of arms, $16 billion worth of which were destined for the Middle East. It was not long before President. Bush was agreeing fresh arms deals with Saudi Arabia. On 11 September 1992 Bush announced that 72 F-15s would be sold to the Saudis in a deal worth $9 billion that was expected to save 20,000 jobs, mainly at the St Louis factories of McDonnell Douglas. This deal in turn put pressure on Al-Yamamah, with UK Ministry of Defence and British Aerospace executives being secretive about the future of the project. In October 'a source close to the Saudi royal family' suggested that Al Yamamah was unlikely to proceed: 'The Saudis will buy where the political strength is. Saudi interest in buying British died with Mrs Thatcher's resignation and, although it revived temporarily during the Gulf war, Britain could never hope to beat the American competition.'[51] In the event, perhaps as a result of Prime Minister John Major's visit to Riyadh in January 1993, the massive British Aerospace deal was salvaged 'in the nick of time'; it was hoped that the agreement, signed by Fahd and Major (and worth up to £5 billion) would save up to 19,000 jobs.[52]

In June 1993 it was reported that the Saudis had promised to keep oil prices low in return for continued American protection of the Kingdom – little more than a reaffirmation of the US–Saudi symbiosis. Later in the year the British government was urging Saudi Arabia to buy £2 billion worth of armoured vehicles, including Challenger 2 tanks, Warrior armoured vehicles and AS90 self-propelled howitzers (a projected deal dubbed by one source 'a mini-Al-Yamamah for the army'). Jonathan Aitken, the now-discredited defence-procurement minister, was said to be playing a large part in the British battle for Saudi orders. One problem was that Riyadh, faced with mounting economic difficulties, was ordering budgetary cuts – a further possible threat to the Al-Yamamah programme. Said one Saudi commentator: 'The British will have to face it just like any others, payments may be slowed and delayed, as with the American orders.' Some optimistic observers were suggesting that the complicated oil-barter system, negotiated for the Tornado deal, would protect payments to British Aerospace; but with oil prices falling the Saudis were unable to increase the amount of oil (500,000 barrels a day) allocated to the British deal without upsetting other OPEC producers. Some oil analysts argued that the Saudi budget cuts would now have to be larger than the planned 20 per cent: in early 1994 the Saudi economy was heading for a $9 billion deficit at a time when the Kingdom's liquid reserves were down to $7.5 billion. Now Washington was confirming that the Saudi debt of $9.2 billion owed to five leading US arms manufacturers was being restructured in acknowledgement of Saudi repayment difficulties.

The Saudi financial problems served only to intensify the foreign competition for arms deals with the Kingdom. In February 1994 the Saudis opted for a $6 billion offer from Boeing and McDonnell Douglas to supply up to 66 aircraft for the Saudi national airline, after President Clinton and top US officials had lobbied against a rival bid from Europe's Airbus consortium. (Said an Airbus spokesman: 'There's certainly been an extraordinary amount of pressure from the US government.') The general US–Saudi agreement – at that stage uncluttered with details of prices, delivery dates or even the airline's specific requirements – was announced by Bill Clinton, with Prince Bandar ibn Sultan at his side, in a White House ceremony: 'The purchase is a vote of confidence in American quality, in American workers and the competitiveness of our exports.' Airbus Industrie, the French Airbus component, then began an investigation into whether Washington had violated GATT regulations in its pursuit of the agreement ('We are studying closely Article 4* of the GATT code').

In July 1994 there was further media speculation about earlier Saudi support for an 'Islamic nuclear bomb'.[53] Here the Saudi diplomat and nuclear expert Mohammed Khilewi, having sought political asylum in the United States, stated that by the mid-1980s an Iraqi–Saudi pact had been agreed, whereby the Saudis would help to fund Iraqi nuclear developments and some of the weapons would be given to the Saudi armed forces. Khilewi suggests that at least $5 billion of the $25 billion given by Saudi Arabia to support the Iraqi war effort was intended for the nuclear programme. In this account the Saudis also attempted to buy experimental nuclear reactors from China, and by 1989 had opened their own research facilities. The American CIA was reportedly investigating the various assertions. Said a White House official ('off-the-record'): 'Can you imagine what would happen if we discovered Saudi had a bomb? We would have to do something about it and nobody wants that. Best not to ask tough questions in the first place.'[54]

By 1995 there were further signs that Saudi financial problems were threatening Al-Yamamah agreements and Saudi deals with other countries. The Saudi government – despite reassurances given by King Fahd to UK Foreign Secretary Douglas Hurd in October 1994 – was responding to slumping oil revenues and domestic unrest by imposing a severe cash squeeze on all government contracts. Now there was mounting evidence also that the Saudis were increasingly resent-

---

* Article 4 of the GATT code on civil aircraft sales prohibits inducements relating to 'defence and national security policies and programmes'. It was not known what inducements Clinton had offered when he telephoned King Fahd to clinch the deal. There was obvious political interference. What precisely had Clinton offered?

ing Western pressure for arms deals ('Weapon-toting West bleeds Saudis dry').[55] One Saudi establishment figure reportedly declared: 'Clinton, Major, tell them to stop coming here pushing arms down our throats. The United States is a dangerous lover. It will bleed you dry.'[56] At the same time the Saudis knew that they could not alienate Washington, 'their great protectors, even when the same protectors are seen as doing them harm'. It now seems increasingly obvious to Saudi observers that Saudi Arabia was being massively exploited as a means of financing the Western military establishments.

Still the Western governments, locked into militarised economies, continued to press the Saudis for yet more arms purchases. In early 1995 Saudi Arabia was said to be considering buying tanks from Britain or France after reports that the US-built Abrams was not performing well in desert conditions; and speculation continued about the possibility of more Al-Yamamah-linked deals. In November it emerged that strained UK–Saudi relations were threatening further British sales; and the semi-retirement of King Fahd after thirteen years was creating fresh uncertainties about prospects for future arms deals.[57] In early 1997 the Saudis cancelled a US deal for 102 F-16 fighters after details of the $15 billion deal were leaked in the United States and then criticised by Israel; and in Britain the limitations and uncertainties of Al-Yamamah were becoming increasingly obvious. In addition to Saudi repayment difficulties, projects in the Kingdom were required to be joint ventures involving technology transfer: which meant, for example, that British Aerospace was employing 1500 Saudis to assemble aircraft instead of carrying out such tasks in Warton, Lancashire; by mid-1997 it was obvious that Al-Yamamah earnings, even if paid on time, would steadily decline. In Britain and elsewhere questions had long been asked about the character of the arms trade in general and to Saudi Arabia in particular. For example, there was the question of disguised taxpayer support for weapons exports;[58] and the persistent matter of human rights, still largely unaddressed under the hypocrisy of New Labour's 'ethical' foreign policy.

The Western arms ploy is plain: to exploit Saudi Arabia as a milch-cow as a means of funding armaments development and so maintaining the West's global military hegemony. Touted by Western governments as a stable and reliable commercial partner, Saudi Arabia is in fact running into multifaceted crisis (Chapter 7). It remains to be seen how long the symbiosis of Western imperialism and feudal plutocracy can survive. Before considering the mounting problems facing the Saudi dynasty, it is useful to glance at Saudi Arabia's US-friendly involvement in three important wars of the last two decades.

THE IRAN–IRAQ WAR (1980–8)

For centuries there have been periods of conflict between Iran (Persia) and Iraq (Babylon, Mesopotamia): the 1980s war was far from the first Iran–Iraq confrontation. As in the wars of the past, various outside powers, not obvious parties to the conflict, had an interest in the outcome – and so became involved in many ways. The recent Iran–Iraq War was one in which Saudi Arabia, Kuwait and the United States, amongst others, were deeply involved – as committed allies of Saddam Hussein. It is useful to remember that when the Iraqi dictator is condemned by Western critics for his abuses of human rights and his aggressions against neighbouring countries, for most of his high-profile period in power he was financed, supplied and praised by Riyadh and Washington. It is even likely that Saddam Hussein was helped to power by American interference in Iraqi affairs.

In 1963, at a time when the ambitious Saddam Hussein was urging the need in Iraq for a special security body* modelled on the Nazi SS, the army staged a *coup d'état* and overthrew the first Iraqi Baathist government. General Abdul Karim Kassem, the country's populist leader for five years, was forced to surrender, whereupon he was summarily tried, tied to a chair, and then shot dead. These events – the planning and staging of the *coup* and its aftermath – were largely orchestrated by agents of the American CIA. Said Ali Saleh Saadi, Minister of the Interior in the new regime: 'We came to power on a CIA train.' These were the events that firmly set Saddam Hussein on the road to power.[59]

The CIA, according to its fashion, also prepared lists of people to be killed by death squads after the *coup*. The researcher Said Aburish claims that 5000 Iraqis were killed (including doctors, lawyers, teachers and professors), of whom he has collected the names of 600.[60] Saddam Hussein, then living in exile in Cairo, was encouraged by the CIA to supply some of the names of people to be executed. There then followed an orgy of torture and execution on a horrendous scale (Aburish: 'Saddam Hussein, who had rushed back to Iraq from exile in Cairo to join the victors, was personally involved in the torture of leftists in the separate detention centres for the *fellaheen* [peasants] and the *muthaqafeen*, or educated class'[61]). Kassem had angered Washington by withdrawing Iraq from the US-sponsored anti-Soviet Baghdad Pact, by nationalising part of the oil industry, and by resurrecting Iraq's claim to Kuwait. In such circumstances the anti-communist Saddam Hussein, eager to take power in his own right, was an obvious collaborator with the CIA in a *coup* against the regime and in the subsequent elimination of leftist politicians and academics.

The American enthusiasm for Saddam Hussein was set to persist through the 1970s and 1980s: where Saddam had already demonstrated his anti-communist credentials throughout most of his early career, he subsequently displayed a reliably anti-Iranian posture that was appreciated by the Washington strategists. On 4 November 1979 some 3000 Iranians stormed into the US embassy in Tehran to

---

* This body was the *Jihaz Haneen* (the 'instrument of learning') that would protect the Baathist Party, target 'enemies of the people', harassing and intimidating unfriendly factions, and so secure power by terror. This was the blueprint that Saddam would convert into a grim reality in the years that followed.

demonstrate the new regime's hostility to American imperialism. At the same time revolutionary Iran, espousing its own robust version of Islam, was posing a new threat to the feudal oil monarchies of the Gulf. Then, when the Soviet Union invaded Afghanistan on 25 December 1979, Saddam was one of the several Arab leaders who condemned this new communist aggression; and on 25 March 1980 he signed an anti-Soviet pact with Saudi Arabia in support of North Yemen's efforts to resist a Soviet-backed attack from South Yemen. The Iraqi leader was now pledging Iraqi military help 'to liberate South Yemen from communist agents and their masters'.[62] Clearly, reasoned the astute Washington planners, Saddam Hussein was a man to be trusted.

The Saudis too were happy to embrace Saddam as a staunch defender of Arab interests in the Gulf. According to Ghazi Algosaibi, the Saudi ambassador to Britain, King Fahd had developed a very close relationship with the Iraqi leader: 'The relationship between him and the Iraqi president went beyond friendship to real brotherly feeling.'[63] Fahd had first met Saddam in 1975 at the OPEC summit in Algeria: 'They immediately developed a friendship, as a result of which relations between the kingdom and Iraq became extremely warm following a long period of acute tension. Within a few months the two leaders were able to end the border dispute between the two countries, which had resisted all attempts to solve it over the years. Both leaders respected each other's ability to fulfill and honour their promises.'[64] It is now clear that Saddam and Fahd discussed Saddam's intention to invade Iran; and that despite the Saudi anxieties (Fahd: 'I hope that you will hesitate, because war is easy to begin but difficult to end'), Saudi Arabia 'threw all its weight behind Saddam Hussein' as soon as the war started.[65]

Saddam had judged that he would be able to rely on financial support from Saudi Arabia and Kuwait, and that Washington would not be hostile to a military campaign against a regime keen to depict America as 'the Great Satan'. He would, he judged, be able to wage a brief and highly successful war; whereupon he would be widely seen as the leader of the Arab world, the liberator of Arabs in Iranian territories and the friend also of the Iranian Kurds struggling for recognition. On 2 September 1980 Iraqi and Iranian troops clashed near Qasr-e Shirin and soon afterwards Iranian artillery began shelling the Iraqi towns of Khanaqin and Mandali. On 6 September Iraq threatened to seize vast swathes of Iranian land in the Zain al Qaws area, supposedly already granted to Iraq in a 1975 accord, if not ceded within a week. Iran responded with increased artillery fire, and Iraqi troops moved forward to capture a number of border posts. Then, in a televised speech to the National Assembly (17 September), Saddam claimed full control of the Shatt al-Arab, and heavy fighting broke out along the waterway. Three days later Tehran called up reserves and on 22 September the Iraqi armies mounted a general offensive. What observers, with little attention to history, were later to call the 'first' Gulf war had begun. It would last for nearly a decade.[66]

Saudi Arabia at once became Iraq's primary financier. By the end of 1981 Riyadh had already provided some $10 billion worth of financial support to

Saddam, with Kuwait contributing a further $5 billion. During the war years the Saudi and Kuwaiti support for the Iraqi war effort was to reach about $50 billion; and it seemed clear that where loans were involved at least part of them would not have to be repaid in the future.[67] Riyadh and Kuwait also worked to manage the sale of some oil on Iraq's behalf and allowed the use of their territory and ports for the shipment of goods to Iraq, now virtually land-locked following the outbreak of hostilities in the Gulf. An Iraqi oil pipeline was built across Saudi territory to allow oil to be pumped to the Red Sea, thus enabling Baghdad to continue substantial oil exports. Algosaibi records the various ways in which Saudi Arabia supported the Iraqi war effort:

> King Fahd ... urged that the other countries of the Gulf Co-operation Council provide every kind of aid to Iraq. The kingdom's assistance to Iraq included monetary gifts, oil loans, the transport of Iraqi oil to the Red Sea in a pipeline passing through Saudi territory, the financing of arms deals, intelligence co-operation, the provision of Iraq with information obtained by AWACS aircraft,* the placing of Saudi ports and roads at the disposal of the Iraqi army, and the provision of food.[68]

Fahd assumed that Saddam was duly grateful. When the Saudi monarch visited Baghdad, the Iraqi leader bestowed upon him much public praise and the highest Iraqi decoration.

The Saudi involvement in the war was essential to Iraq; without such support it would have been impossible for Saddam to weather the mounting pressures on his military logistics and on an Iraqi economy that would otherwise have been starved of oil revenues. Riyadh allocated 200,000–400,000 barrels of oil a day from the Neutral Zone to support the Iraqi war effort, encouraged other Arab states to back Saddam, and even urged the Western powers to provide military support to Iraq and to waive its imposed limitations on the use of arms sold to Saudi Arabia – so that military equipment could be transferred directly to Iraq.[69] Britain and America were happy to oblige. Britain provided Iraq with a wide range of equipment, much of it embargoed, as direct military support for Saddam Hussein, as revealed in the later Scott Report.[70] Here the equipment supplied included a Plessey-made electronic command centre, NBC (nuclear, biological and chemical warfare) suits, radar guidance systems and much else. The United States offered interest-free credits for wheat purchases, parts for chemical weapons plants and sophisticated electronics systems. John Cooley, the veteran ABC correspondent, has claimed that US ships in the Gulf jammed Iranian radar to assist Iraqi bombing raids on Iranian oil terminals.[71] Washington now believed that Saddam Hussein should be fully supported in his efforts to tame the

---

* This necessarily implied American support for Iraq.

ayatollahs – to the point that the Americans became actively involved in military operations.

Richard Murphy, the US Assistant Secretary of State for Near Eastern and South Asian Affairs, was one of a number of State Department personnel who worked out a complex scheme to aid Saddam: 'Our primary goal was to end the war because it was generating instability. No matter what anybody says now, with perfect hindsight, this is what it was all about. We wanted to see an end to this unpredictable war, before it got out of hand. We wanted to contain Iran.'[72] To this end, according to Murphy, Washington organised 'an interagency effort, with the participation of Defense, CIA, and State' to support Iraq. As one contribution, CIA Director William Casey devised an intelligence-sharing arrangement whereby the Iraqis could be supplied with sensitive intelligence data gathered by US AWACS aircraft based in Saudi Arabia. The CIA also established a top secret Washington–Baghdad link to supply the Iraqis with data from US satellites (Casey himself met with a group of senior Iraqis to make sure that the new channel was functioning).[73] The United States also encouraged France to extend new loans to Iraq, urged Egypt to continue its arms shipments to Baghdad and, through the provision of Commodity Credit Corporation (CCC) finance, became one of Saddam's best sources of essential funds after Saudi Arabia and Kuwait.

It now seems plain that Saudi Arabia 'figured prominently in the Iraqi war plans ... the Gulf rulers, including the Saudi monarch, had tired of trying to establish rapprochement with Iran's revolutionary regime ...'.[74] Moreover, the war enabled the United States, similarly hostile to the ayatollahs, to pressure Riyadh into the formation of a joint Saudi–American military committee, something that the Saudis had been keen to resist in the past. Doubtless this new arrangement facilitated increased American involvement in the war. Saddam Hussein was happy to welcome the support being provided from a variety of Arab and Western sources, though sometimes churlish about the scale of aid being offered by Saudi Arabia and Kuwait: their contributions were, he complained, 'much less than what duty dictates'.[75] None the less Riyadh remained Saddam's most important regional ally. In March 1983 the Saudi Crown Prince Abdullah ibn Abdul Aziz commented that 'Iran cannot enter Baghdad because that would mean an all-out war with Iran [by us]'.[76] During 1983 there were a dozen official exchange visits between Riyadh and Baghdad, with Saddam himself visiting Riyadh on 15 January when he secured permission to pump oil through a pipeline across Saudi territory. At the same time the Saudis, with Washington, were encouraging France to support the Iraqi war effort – in this case by supplying five sophisticated Super-Etendard warplanes to Saddam. Riyadh agreed to pay for the aircraft in oil: now, because of falling oil prices and the Saudi reduced OPEC quota, Saudi Arabia was feeling the burden of the war.

On 1 June 1984 the UN Security Council responding to a GCC (Gulf Co-operation Council) complaint, passed a resolution (13 votes to nil) condemning attacks on ships trading with Saudi Arabia. Since this represented indirect support for Iraq, even the United Nations was now showing sympathy with the cause of Saddam Hussein. Two days later the Iraqis sank a Turkish-registered tanker in the Gulf, an act that failed to provoke a Security Council resolution. On 5 June Saudi aircraft, helped by US-operated AWACS, brought down an Iranian fighter in Gulf waters, so making Saudi Arabia an active belligerent in the war, whereupon a dispute ensued between Riyadh and Tehran as to whether the downed aircraft had been flying in Saudi or international airspace. Three days later President Ali Khamanei of Iran declared: 'We do not want to fight Saudi Arabia, Bahrain and others ... but this is on condition that they do not get mixed up in this war.'[77] Then Iranian planes, still prepared to strike at vessels aiding Iraq, hit a Kuwaiti supertanker off the Qatari coast. None the less there were still signs that Riyadh and Tehran were reluctant to be dragged into a direct confrontation with each other. Thus Fahd sent a note to Tehran (8 July) expressing his commitment to 'quiet diplomacy'.[78] Then the Saudi *hajj* officials invited the Iranian parliamentary speaker, the influential Ali Akbar Hashemi Rafsanjani, to make the pilgrimage; and agreed to increase the number of Iranian pilgrims by 50 per cent.

The war continued for the best part of the decade, expending vast quantities of treasure and involving human casualties (dead, wounded, traumatised, orphaned and dispossessed) numbered in the millions. Saudi Arabia, Kuwait and the Western powers (mainly the United States) fuelled the years-long process of slaughter and destruction; by their efforts Iraq was allowed to continue a futile war that in the end had no territorial gains to show, no enhanced regional security, nothing beyond death and devastation. By late 1987, with the help of its allies, Iraq was exporting an estimated 2.7 million barrels of oil a day, to service a current carnage and to lay the ground for a future one. On 31 July 1987, at the start of the *hajj*, a protest by about 100,000 Iranians and non-Iranians in Mecca began peacefully but then – under the provocation of police using electrified batons, tear gas, rubber bullets and live ammunition – ended in chaos, stampede and 402 fatalities.[79] The Saudi and Kuwaiti embassies in Tehran were attacked, with the Ayatollah Khomeini encouraging the growing belief, in Iran, that the United States bore ultimate responsibility for the Mecca massacre. The developing communications between Riyadh and Tehran were abruptly terminated; and the United States was allowed to deepen its military penetration of Saudi Arabia and Kuwait. On 25 August, Prince Naif ibn Abdul Aziz, revealing the mounting hostility to Iran, declared: 'The Kingdom hopes to remove from Iran the authority which sends the people of Iran to their deaths'; and Saudi Arabia offered Saddam, Hussein an immediate grant of $2 billion.

It was in 1987 that Iran lost control of events, and so hastened the end of the pointless Gulf conflagration. The riots in Mecca had failed to expose 'any internal weaknesses in Saudi Arabia, or any significant signs of pro-Khomeini support among the Shi'ites in Saudi Arabia's Eastern Province ...' The massacre had drastically weakened the position of Tehran, forcing Saudi Arabia into taking a 'firm and decisive line in opposition to Iran' and into providing 'more direct and comprehensive military cooperation' with the United States.[80] Now there was a catalyst for increased US arms sales to Saudi Arabia. In August, sources within the Reagan Administration leaked a plan to sell a fresh arms package to the Saudis: including F-15s, upgrades to existing US-supplied F-15s, 1600 Maverick missiles, armoured artillery support vehicles, and other items. On 14 April 1988, 58 US Senators and 187 members of the House issued a demand to Reagan that the $450 million AWACS support package be blocked. Even in the changed situation towards the end of the Iran–Iraq War many of the same contentious issues remained unresolved; and now further troubles were brewing in the wings.

The extent to which Saudi Arabia and other countries had helped Iraq during the war became clearer years afterwards, following various investigations into such issues as government dissembling, illegal arms sales and illicit arms transfers in the 1980s. One of the most celebrated of these investigations was conducted by Lord Justice Sir Richard Scott in the United Kingdom: the resulting Scott Report[81] – a disappointment to many because of its failure to include coherent conclusions – did none the less come close to forcing a number of ministerial resignations from the British government. For our purposes the extent to which the Scott Report reveals government sensitivity to Saudi opinion and the scale of Saudi arms transfers to Iraq during the 1980s, is of particular interest. For example, it is significant that even when the Tory government decided to revise its guidelines on the supply of arms to Iraq, 'MOD [Ministry of Defence] officials felt, however, that the revised guidelines should not be published because they would give misleading encouragement to Industry and alarm Gulf States, particularly Saudi Arabia'.[82] It was felt by many observers that government failure to inform Parliament of such 'revised guidelines' was a serious reflection on government probity.

The Report noted also that 'Substantial quantities of arms were licensed for export to Saudi Arabia, Jordan, Kuwait and the United Arab Emirates. These countries were supportive of Iraq during the Iran/Iraq war and, to a lesser extent, in the period that followed the ceasefire ... The papers disclosed and the evidence given to the Inquiry have raised the question whether, and to what extent, British arms ... may have been diverted to Iraq.'[83] In fact a Secret Intelligence Service (SIS) intelligence note (14 March 1986) records an informant as saying that 'the Iraquis have no problems over obtaining equipment thanks to the willingness of countries such as Saudi Arabia and Jordan to act as the notional end-user'.[84] The Report subsequently considers the scale of arms transfer from Saudi Arabia to Iraq (a Saudi prince is quoted as admitting 'openly ... that military equipment received into Saudi Arabia was re-routed to Iraq').[85] There was no doubt that British-made equipment had been fed via Saudi Arabia and other countries to Iraq for use in the Iran–Iraq War, and as potential assets for any other future military conflict (including the 1991 Gulf War); the real debate was about how much equipment had been supplied to Saddam Hussein in this fashion, and precisely how much the various Tory ministers knew about the matter. Similarly, other questions have yet to be answered: for example, the extent to which Saudi Arabia supported Iraq's efforts to build a nuclear weapon.[86]

With both sides tiring of an indecisive war the belligerents became increasingly receptive to UN ceasefire efforts through 1987. On 20 July the Security Council unanimously passed Resolution 598 calling for a ceasefire and a withdrawal of the warring parties. Iran accepted the resolution, with Khomeini still prepared to say: 'God knows that were it not that all our honour and prestige should still be sacrificed for Islam, I would never have consented ... I repeat that accepting this [resolution] was more deadly to me than taking poison': Khomeini submitted himself 'to God's will and drank this drink for His satisfaction. ... Accepting the UN resolution does not mean that the question of war has been solved. We should be prepared for jihad ...'.[87] Agreement had been reached but hostilities dragged on into 1988. Iraq continued to wage war, while declaring itself in favour of Resolution 598; at the same time the Iranians denounced Baghdad and also the United States for keeping its warships in the Gulf. Said Iran's Deputy Foreign Minister: 'the USA needs the intensification of tension ... as an excuse for keeping its fleet in the region.'[88]

The final ceasefire of August 1988 brought an end to the war. Some Western estimates put the number of war dead at 367,000 (262,000 Iranian and 105,000 Iraqi); with some 700,000 injured, many badly. Figures based on estimates made in NATO capitals put the number of Iranian fatalities at between 420,000 and 580,000 (many of them teen-aged youths promised paradise for a glorious death), with some 300,000 Iraqi dead (to these 1985 figures should be added the casualties for three further years of war). The Iran–Iraq War had cost in excess of $1,000,000,000,000, expended by many powers involved either directly or indirectly. Saudi Arabia was one of the principal belligerents in the war: mostly as an indirect but powerful participant but occasionally as an active combatant. Beyond the massive expenditure of human life and treasure the war had accomplished nothing, except to prepare the way for another Gulf war that would soon convulse the region.

Saudi Arabia – by providing prodigious support to Iraq in its prosecution of the Iran–Iraq War, and by subsequently helping to compound Baghdad's economic and political problems – bears significant responsibility (with Saddam Hussein, Kuwait and the United States) for the 1991 Gulf War. Here too the feudal rulers of Saudi Arabia would show their willingness to conspire in a vast slaughter of Muslims.

THE 1991 GULF WAR

The Iraqi claims to Kuwait in 1990 did not begin with Saddam Hussein. To understand the origins of the war, and the part played by Saudi Arabia, it is useful to glance at the historical circumstances.

The frontiers that define the twentieth-century Middle East were drawn up by Britain and France with the (overt or covert) agreement of some other states. The cynical definition of the territorial boundaries had inevitable consequences for ethnic rivalries, for spheres of influence and sovereignty, and the likelihood of war in the years to come. Kuwait was established as an independent state by Britain as an easy mechanism for ensuring continued British influence in the Gulf. On 23 January 1899 Sheikh Mubarak of Kuwait, who possessed the finest natural harbour in the Gulf, was brought into treaty relations with Britain under the direction of Lord Curzon.[89] Mubarak had often asked for British protection but it had always been recognised that Kuwait was a part of Iraq under the sovereignty of the Turkish sultan. Thus in 1892 Lord Curzon wrote: 'Northward from Port Ujair, Ottoman dominion is established (on the Arab coast of the Gulf) without dispute as far as Fao.' In the same vein Sir A. T. Wilson wrote in 1928 that, until 1986, Kuwait was 'regarded at home [that is, in Britain] as under the exclusive influence of Turkey'.[90] For these reasons Mubarak was regarded as a 'usurper', hoping to carve off a piece of land and to establish its sovereign independence.[91] It came to suit Britain to support this manifest usurpation.

In 1899 Germany had obtained a concession to build a railway from Constantinople to Baghdad, and since Kuwait might serve as a suitable terminal for such a project, this was quite enough to alarm the British. In December 1901 the Turkish sloop *Zuhaf* arrived off Kuwait demanding that Sheikh Mubarak abandon his claims for independence – but, by now confident of British support, he ignored the Turkish ultimatum and the *Zuhaf* withdrew without taking action. Then British troops were landed in Kuwait to forestall an anticipated Turkish attack from Basra; and in a subsequent action the British sloop intercepted a Turkish force and captured 150 men. Thereafter the Kuwaiti–British links were strengthened and there were no further threats from the Ottoman Empire, already in a moribund state. Now Mubarak was prepared to grant trade concessions exclusively to the British, agreeing (July 1911) that sponge and pearl concessions would be granted only with British consent, and agreeing the same (October 1913) on oil concessions. There still remained the possibility of territorial disputes between Kuwait and Saudi Arabia.

In November 1915 the Ajman rebelled against Ibn Saud, whereupon, with the Saudi forces besieged at Hufuf, Mubarak sent a force to aid Ibn Saud. When Sheikh Salim, Mubarak's second son, offered sanctuary to the surviving Ajman, Ibn Saud immediately accused Kuwait of acting against Saudi interests. Jabir, Mubarak's eldest son, set to rule for only one year, ejected the Ajman and tried to restore the earlier satisfactory relationship with the Saudis; but now there was the likelihood of more frontier disputes, with Britain placed to adjudicate between the respective claims of Sheikh Salim, Jabir's successor, and the Saudi Ikhwan, led by Faisal Dawish. On 27 February Salim died, to be succeeded by Sheikh Ahmad al-Jabir, giving Ibn Saud the chance to make placatory overtures. Sir Percy Cox, unhappy with the course of events, called the Ujair Conference (1922), already mentioned, in the hope of reaching a final boundary settlement for Kuwait, Iraq and Saudi Arabia.

The resulting settlement, shaped by the whim of Percy Cox, confirmed the separation of Kuwait from Iraq. It had suited Britain to detach Kuwait from the Ottoman *vilayet* of Basra – as a matter of no more than *realpolitik* calculation. Later (1930) the British High Commissioner in Baghdad commented that 'Britain should encourage the gradual absorption of Kuwait into Iraq', with representatives of the British government contending that '*Kuwait was a small and expendable state which could be sacrificed without too much concern if the power struggles of the period demanded it.*'⁹² Saddam Hussein could not have put it better himself. The 1922 Cox settlement was far from the only cause of the 1991 Gulf War but it made a contribution.

The Iraqi government, in contemplating an invasion of Kuwait, was not concerned only with frontier questions: if it had not been for other matters the Iraqi claim on the territory of Kuwait would not have been repeated by Saddam Hussein in 1990. In the aftermath to the Iran–Iraq War, with Iraq massively in debt and needing vast infrastructure investment, there was mounting concern in Baghdad with diminishing oil revenues. It was well known that the main barriers to higher oil prices were overproduction and other manifestations of producer indiscipline within the OPEC cartel. The United Arab Emirates (UAE) typically produced more oil than its OPEC allocation, and this – and other departures from OPEC protocols – served as a precedent for Kuwaiti non-compliance. By July 1990 it was plain that, whereas Iran and Iraq had achieved a measure of agreement on oil production, Kuwait was flooding the oil market in violation of the agreed OPEC production quotas; and Saudi Arabia, concerned with Iraq at falling oil revenues, was urging OPEC self-discipline. Now Kuwait and the UAE, refusing to heed the warnings (but perhaps working to another calculated agenda), were causing a massive drop in oil prices which 'in turn, hurt Iraq, which was already short on funds'.⁹³ By any reckoning, Iraq, with a sudden slump in oil revenue of $7 billion, 'was facing economic suffocation'.⁹⁴

Moreover, it now appeared that Kuwait, along with Saudi Arabia, was unwilling to consider 'forgiving' the massive war debt (a total of $35 billion) that Baghdad had incurred through the Iran–Iraq War. Iraq was to be squeezed but with an ever diminishing chance of paying its debt. Kuwait, backed by the West, was saying in effect: 'We'll continue to act to diminish your revenues but you must pay your debts'. This interpretation of events was not unique to Baghdad and the pro-Iraq lobby throughout the Arab world. Sir Alan Munro, the British ambassador to Saudi Arabia from 1989 to 1993, has been able to acknowledge a degree of Kuwaiti responsibility for the deteriorating circumstances leading to the 1991 Gulf War:

In some measure Kuwait herself contributed to Saddam Hussein's search for a pretext for his design upon his neighbour. During their three decades of independence since 1961, the Kuwaitis acquired something of a reputation for the pursuit of self-interest which was at odds with their generosity towards their partners within the Arab community ... stirrings of domestic discontent provided issues which Saddam Hussein would seek to exploits ... In regional matters, too, the Kuwaitis had sometimes chosen to go their own way ... they showed themselves lukewarm over the process of closer integration with their neighbours in the Gulf Co-operation Council ... in the eyes of other Gulf states there was an overconfidence to Kuwaiti foreign policy.[95]

In this context King Faisal of Saudi Arabia is said to have commented 'with some exasperation in the 1970s that there were not two but three superpowers in the world: the USA, the USSR and Kuwait'.[96*]

The impression of Kuwait's 'shortsighted pursuit of self-interest was enhanced in 1990' by an increase in its oil production in excess of the OPEC quota. The other OPEC members, 'not least Saudi Arabia', were irritated by this departure from the agreed levels: 'Above all the Kuwaiti action afforded a source of particular grievance to Iraq, already in the mood to find cause for affront, and faced with a calamitous economic situation and a need to maximise oil revenue ...'.[97] Iraq had assumed the burden of defending the Gulf states from Iranian expansion, to the advantage of Kuwait and Saudi Arabia as much as to Iraq's benefit. Now it was easy to understand how the Kuwaiti attitude – shown in illicit oil production and a broadcasting of the Iraqi debt ($12 billion to Kuwait alone) – was seen as particularly provocative.

On 30 May 1990 Saddam Hussein commented to participants at an extraordinary Arab summit in Baghdad on 'the failure by some of our Arab brothers to abide by the OPEC decisions when they flooded the world market with more oil than it needed, thereby enabling clients to buy below the fixed price?. He added:

> ... for every US dollar drop in the price of a barrel of oil, the Iraqi loss amounted to $1 billion annually ... War is fought with soldiers and harm is done by explosions, killing and coup attempts, but it is also done by economic means sometimes. I say to those who do not mean to wage war on Iraq, that this is in fact a kind of war against Iraq. Were it possible we would have endured ... But I say that we have reached a point where we can no longer withstand pressure.[98]

Saddam emphasised that Iraq wanted to return to the pre-war economic situation: '... we urgently need $10 billion, as well as the cancellation of the $30 billion worth of debts to Kuwait, the Arab Emirates and Saudi Arabia that we incurred

---

* There is evidence that in 1990 King Fahd came to believe that '*the Kuwaitis had brought the invasion upon themselves by being too inflexible ...*' (Heikel, 1993, p. 273).

during the war ... we are today living through another conflict ... War doesn't mean just tanks, artillery or ships. It can take subtler and more insidious forms, such as the overproduction of oil, economic damage and pressures to enslave a nation.'[99]

On 11 July 1990 the oil ministers of Iraq, Kuwait, Qatar, the UAE and Saudi Arabia moved some way towards agreement on the Iraqi demand of $25 a barrel; there was unanimous agreement on an OPEC production ceiling that would help raise the barrel price to the $18 target set in November 1989. Two days later the Kuwaiti oil minister unilaterally repudiated the agreement. This and other developments, including the American 'green light',[100] were now conspiring for war. At the time Assistant Secretary John Kelly was declaring that the United States had no commitment to help Kuwait in the event of an Iraqi invasion, Kuwaiti and Iraqi officials were preparing for high-level talks in Jeddah. Hours before the planned meeting, the emir of Kuwait declared that he would not be attending, a rebuff that Saddam took as a slap in the face (a 'deadly insult'). In response Saddam too declared that he would not be attending and Izzat Ibrahim, his Number 2 in the Baath leadership, would be sent in his stead. In this atmosphere the talks were bound to fail. After some desultory talk King Fahd announced that he would pay a disputed $1 billion to Iraq, 'with no strings attached'; but this was insufficient to prevent a confrontation between the Iraqis and the Kuwaitis, now insisting that the Iraqis repay all their debts: 'Kuwait has very powerful friends. We too have allies. You'll be forced to pay back all the money you owe us.' Soon afterwards, the two delegations parted in total discord.

On 2 August 1990 the Iraqi military invaded Kuwait. The Kuwaiti emir, Sheikh Jabir Ahmad al-Sabah, tipped off an hour before the invasion, fled to Saudi Arabia where he set up a provisional government in exile. Now the escalated crisis was quickly polarising the Arab world: Jordan, the PLO, and many popular factions with little voice in the various Arab states supported Saddam Hussein; Saudi Arabia, its GCC allies, Egypt and Syria opposed the Iraqi aggression. (One week before the invasion, Saudi Arabia officially revived its claim to a piece of Kuwaiti territory: the island of Qaruh, briefly occupied by Saudi forces in 1989.[101] The Iraqis were not the only ones who believed that they had legitimate claims against Kuwait.) Now the United States embarked upon a massive diplomatic and political campaign, most of it planned in advance, to impose comprehensive sanctions on Iraq, to win (by bribery and intimidation) international support for the US interpretation of events, and to convince the Saudis that unless they allowed a vast influx of American troops and equipment into their territory they were doomed. The question hinged on whether Saddam Hussein was satisfied with his occupation of Kuwait. Did he now intend to invade Saudi Arabia?

Two days after the invasion, reports began arriving that Iraqi troops had entered the so-called 'neutral zone' between Kuwait and Saudi Arabia, and were taking up positions close to the Saudi border. According to the US National Security Agency (NSA), satellite photographs were showing 100,000 Iraqi soldiers massing near the border. A secret NSA report passed to key members of the Bush Administration indicated the dangers posed:

> An Iraqi invasion of Saudi Arabia would involve a much more extensive military operation than those so far conducted by Baghdad's ground forces. The key objectives of the invasion would be the ports and airfields near Dharan (one of the main petroleum centres), about 175 miles from the Kuwaiti border, with the capital, Riyadh, as the next objective. This area contains all the vital economic targets whose capture would cut off Saudi access to the Persian Gulf and hamper the arrival of American reinforcements.[102]

It was now plain to the Americans that a US deployment in the Gulf, either to contain or to repel the Iraqi invasion, could not be effective without the support of Saudi Arabia; in particular, without permission to deploy military forces on Saudi territory. It soon became clear that the Saudis were reluctant to agree to any such development: in part because they were hoping for an Arab settlement of the crisis and in part because – as the custodian country for the Muslim Holy Places – they were highly sensitive to the possibility of a massive influx of infidel troops onto Arab land. President Bush would continue to hope that the news (real or fabricated) of Iraqi soldiers massing on the Kuwaiti–Saudi border would be a trump card in any negotiations with King Fahd.

The first Bush–Fahd telephone conversation was, from the American perspective, unhelpful. Fahd commented that while he required some assistance for the Royal Saudi Air Force there was no need for the US army to become involved.[103] Prince Bandar left Washington to join the Saudi discussions in Jeddah, where he learned that Saudi scouts in Kuwait had revealed 'no trace of the Iraqi troops heading towards the kingdom'; Bandar responded by citing the US satellite evidence to the contrary. The satellite photographs were to become the principal weapon of Richard Cheney, US Secretary of Defense, in his efforts 'to persuade King Fahd to invite'[104] American troops onto Saudi land. *In fact when sample photographs were later obtained from Soyuz Karta by an enterprising journalist, no evidence of the alleged troop build-up was discernible.*[105] None the less the photographs, whatever their character, were greatly to assist in the task of badgering King Fahd into 'requesting' US protection. On 6 August Saddam Hussein declared that since 1975 Iraq and Saudi Arabia had enjoyed good relations and there was no reason why the Iraqi–Saudi links should be harmful to American interests: '... there is no danger to Saudi Arabia. If you want to push Saudi Arabia to do something against our interests, that is another thing ... Kuwait was always part of Iraq ... But Saudi Arabia is a completely sovereign state.'

King Fahd, 'by nature pacific, to an extent bordering on meekness', was 'experiencing his most difficult and trying days'.[106] He had always been keen to resist a substantial American military presence on Saudi land, but his reticence was no match for the sustained propaganda onslaught launched from Washington. At first

Fahd, not believing that Saddam was planning an invasion of Saudi Arabia, had refused to accept American assistance 'despite huge American pressure'[107] – and this had led to tensions within the Saudi royal family. Fahd had reminded Bush: 'We have faced countless problems in the past without asking for your help. There was a time in the 1960s, during the civil war in Yemen, when Nasser of Egypt started threatening us, and even then we did not accept American forces.' The Saudi King was aware that the much-hyped satellite photographs could not in fact be interpreted by Prince Bandar or by other Saudis, that the pictures carried no more than black dots on a blank background. Ambassador Bandar had been forced to rely entirely on the Pentagon experts – 'which increased the king's scepticism'.[108] Hindsight suggests that Fahd's doubts were well founded. Apart from the journalistic initiatives that later threw doubts on the veracity of the Pentagon claims, 'CIA officials have privately conceded that at no time was there any evidence that Saddam contemplated such a move [an invasion of Saudi Arabia]'.[109] A US official who closely monitored CIA intelligence reports concluded that the Iraqis never intended to enter Saudi Arabia;[110] and another intelligence official, who received daily intelligence news briefings on the Gulf crisis, told *New York Newsday* (9 August 1990) that the CIA was 'questioning whether they've got the intention. I tend to agree with them [the CIA]. I don't think it was their intention from Day One to invade Saudi Arabia.'[111] Other expert commentary conveys the same impression:

> The swift despatch of American troops was announced as a means of forestalling any Iraqi takeover of the airfields in the eastern province of Saudi Arabia, or a quick drive on to Dhahran. Yet it seems extremely unlikely that Saddam Hussein ever intended to invade Saudi Arabia. He had only recently signed a non-aggression treaty with King Fahd,* but had he seriously intended to seize the Eastern provinces and prevent American aircraft and troops from landing, or to capture the oilfields, he could have done so swiftly and easily. … Iraqi deployments were entirely defensive…[112]

On 6 August 1990 Saudi Arabia was finally 'pushed'[113] to seek US military intervention in the Kingdom. Endless telephone diplomacy, added to pressure on Prince Bandar in Washington via satellite photographs and other blandishments, had finally done the trick. Bandar had recalled Carter's provision of *unarmed* (therefore useless) F-15s on an earlier occasion; Bush had seemed hurt at the recollection, as if there were reason to doubt *his* word (Bush: 'I give my word of honor. I will see this through with you'[114]). Fahd's weary acquiescence was given with three conditions: the US would indicate in writing that it would leave Saudi

---

* In fact it was King Fahd who violated the 1989 non-aggression treaty (Heikel, 1993, p. 171) by conspiring with the United States in 1990/91 to facilitate the war against Iraq.

Arabia once the threat was over; it would seek Saudi approval before launching offensive operations in the region; and Washington should keep quiet about the agreement until US forces began to arrive. Soon it would be impossible to keep the Saudi people and the rest of the world in the dark about such momentous developments.

On 9 August King Fahd addressed the Saudi people, giving royal weight to the unproven and self-serving US propaganda line: 'Painful and regrettable events have taken place since the dawn of last Thursday, 11th Muharram 1141 AH [2 August 1990 AD] in a way that took the whole world by surprise – when the Iraqi forces stormed the sisterly state of Kuwait ...'. Then, Fahd claimed, the Iraqis massed 'huge forces' on the borders, whereupon since he was concerned with the safety of the territory and Saudi interests he invited the participation 'of fraternal Arab forces and other friendly forces'. Then the United States and Britain 'took the initiative' to send forces to back the Saudi armed forces 'in performing their duty to defend the homeland and citizens against aggression'. Then Fahd flew to Cairo for an Arab summit conference, during which was heard a Baghdad Radio statement by Saddam Hussein entitled: 'Save Mecca and the Tomb of the Prophet from Occupation'.[115] This was an astute ploy by Saddam. Already the Americans realised that fighting might endanger the Muslim Holy Sites in Saudi Arabia. At a White House meeting to discuss various military options, Chief of Staff John Sununu asked: 'Where is Mecca?'[116]

On 8 August President Bush appeared on national television to explain to the American people, under instruction from National Security Advisor Brent Scowcroft, that the Saudis had *requested* the US presence. He emphasised also that the US troops being sent to Saudi Arabia would be there in a purely defensive role. No aggressive action would be taken against Iraq: '... our troops ... will not initiate hostilities, but they will defend themselves, the Kingdom of Saudi Arabia, and other friends in the Persian Gulf'.

Once King Fahd had given permission for the basing of foreign troops on Saudi territory a vast logistical exercise was set in motion. It had become necessary to provide food, water and housing for – at the Coalition's peak – well over half a million men in desert and other camps. And for the vast majority of the troops this was a completely alien environment, bleak and inhospitable, and without any of the comforts that have traditionally helped to define US army culture. Thus General Norman Schwarzkopf later recorded that one of his first orders 'was that no alcohol or pornography was to be brought into Saudi Arabia. ("Pornography" meant girlie magazines as well as X-rated stuff.) I knew some of the troops – along with their congressmen – would complain, but liquor and pornography were against the law in Saudi Arabia, and nothing would have ruined our welcome sooner than for us to let it all hang out the way some Americans had in Vietnam.'[117]

General Khaled Bin Sultan, Schwarzkopf's Saudi equivalent, noted that the half a million foreign troops flooding through the Saudi ports and airports would have been overwhelming if it had not been for the experience the Kingdom had gained in handling more than a million *hajj* pilgrims every year, in addition to the hundreds of thousands of Saudis journeying to Mecca at the same time. The feeding, transporting and accommodating of immense numbers of foreigners 'are, in fact, something of a Saudi speciality'. In addition to the foreign military personnel, some 360,000 Kuwaitis had flooded into the Kingdom following Saddam's aggression.[118] In early September Fahd told the Americans that the kingdom would supply and fund the US forces in Saudi Arabia with everything they needed (food, water, fuel, accommodation, local transport and other facilities). Some weeks later a US Department of Defense team was despatched to formalise a Host Nation Support agreement between the two countries. The situation was already leading to friction. Schwarzkopf recalls Major General Dane Starling, his director of logistics, repeatedly complaining that the Saudis were not paying any of the US bills,[119] with Khaled forced to respond: 'The clear implication ... is that the Saudis were poor payers – an astonishing comment. ... The main reason for the delay in signing the Host Nation Support agreement was that the bill for $2.6 billion ... was far too large.'[120] In fact Washington had tried to inflate the bill by $1.9 billion to include US costs in conveying the men and supplies *to* the Kingdom, where Fahd had agreed only to carry the burden of costs *within* Saudi Arabia. According to Khaled it was an acknowledged try-on by the US Department of Defense, but one that was detected by the Saudis and abandoned by the Americans to allow a formal signing of the agreement in mid-November.*

The cost to Saudi Arabia of supporting its military visitors was $10 billion, with the Saudi Ministry of Finance contributing about $14 billion directly to the US Treasury and a further $3.5 billion to the treasuries of various other countries (Britain, France, Egypt, Syria, Morocco, Senegal, Niger, etc.) that made military contributions to the Coalition. The Saudi expenditure met one of its principal tasks in pumping money into the national economy: the war effort was important but so was free enterprise. Khaled is happy to recount just how much the Saudi market economy benefited from the war: some 400 companies had been in difficulties but 592 Saudi firms were given war-linked contracts, so fulfilling Fahd's aim of both stimulating the economy and rallying support for the war.[121] As many companies as possible were allowed to share in the bonanza ('We must give everyone a chance'), including public companies providing many of the

---

* In October 1992 Prince Khaled described the Schwarzkopf version of events (as described in *It Doesn't Take a Hero*, 1992) as 'self-serving' and riddled with inaccuracies: 'I was commanding 200,000 troops, 80 ships and 250–300 planes. Anyone who buys this book will think that Schwarzkopf alone was commanding.' Khaled disputes many other points: for example, Schwarzkopf's claim that Khaled wanted the initial attack on Iraq to be launched from Turkey, the claim that Saudi maps were banned, and Schwarzkopf's account of the battle for Khafji. (See Marie Colvin, 'Prince blasts Schwarzkopf over war book', *The Sunday Times*, London, 25 October 1992.)

required transport facilities. More than 125 Saudi firms became involved in providing food to the Coalition forces, while more than 3000 water tankers were used to bring water from the Saudi desalination plants at Jubail, al-Khobar, Hafr al-Batin and elsewhere.[122]

The massive influx of infidel troops into Saudi Arabia divided the Arab world. The PLO leader Yasser Arafat met with Saddam Hussein on 28 August 1990 and then urged the need to 'fight the American and foreign presence in the region'. Some Arab leaders condemned the American presence on Saudi territory but were still critical of the Iraqi invasion of Kuwait: Libya's Muammar Gaddafi predictably opposed the US influx into the Arab world, as did Tunisia's President Zine at Abidine ibn Ali and Mauritania's Colonel Maayouya Ould Sidi Ahmad Taya. Sudan and South Yemen expressed bitter anti-American feelings, enough to guarantee the punishment of these two desperately poor countries by Washington as events unfolded. In Syria the police shot down hundreds of people demonstrating in favour of Saddam Hussein; and in Egypt the response was mixed, some popular pro-Iraq feeling co-existing uneasily with recollections of the poor treatment of Egyptians in pre-invasion Iraq and televised pictures of Egyptians fleeing from Kuwait and Iraq in the wake of the Iraqi aggression.[123] But the Saudi authorities, sensitive to widespread feeling in the Muslim world, took care not to relax their own brand of Islamic fundamentalism.* The ban on places of worship for Christians and Jews remained in place, forcing the Pentagon to comment: 'Our personnel, whether Jewish, Christian or any other faith, are free to practise their religion as long as they do so in a discreet manner.' In the event this meant that the massive Saudi intolerance of religious diversity was applied even to ordinary soldiers who had arrived on Saudi soil with the nominal intention of saving the Custodian of the Muslim Holy Places from overthrow by a foreign power. American military personnel had to wear their cross or star of David hidden under their clothes; the red crescent replaced the red cross emblem on ambulances and hospital tents; and soldiers were advised not to take bibles outside the US military compounds and to describe their clandestine religious services as 'fellowship meetings'. A Christmas dispensation was allowed, on the condition that any celebrations took place far from the Saudi public.[124]

Over a period of months, beginning in August 1990, the military build-up continued. The Saudis, whatever their Muslim doubts and the subsequent imposed restrictions on foreign personnel, had accepted a massive non-Muslim force on Saudi land. King Fahd had been assured by President Bush that the military plan was purely defensive, and that no military initiative against Iraq was

---

* A slight shift of emphasis, of little practical consequence, is worth recording. In Jeddah a fundamentalist imam complained: 'It is selective Islam now ... the Koran expurgated to suit the present political purposes of the house of Saud and the war aims of General Schwarzkopf' (Karl Waldron, 'Saudi imams toe King Fahds line', *The Independent*, London, 19 January 1991).

contemplated; but once the (essentially) American troops were in place a different impression was created. On 29 November 1990 Washington secured the passage of Resolution 678 through the UN Security Council, the resolution that supposedly authorised the use of force against Iraq but which on close scrutiny was too vague to be credible.[125] On 12 January 1991, after furious lobbying by the White House, the US Congress voted to authorise war in the Gulf – by votes that were far from overwhelming (Senate: 52 to 47; House of Representatives: 250 to 183). By now the Saudis had been forced to contemplate the likelihood of an infidel-launched war against a brother Arab state that would violate not only Fahd's non-aggression pact with Saddam Hussein but also the Saudi interest in maintaining the solidarity of the Arab nation.

The air onslaught on Iraq (Operation Desert Storm) began on 16 January 1991 as the commencement of a war that would last 42 days.[126] The main bombing phase, launched mainly from Saudi territory, involved the dropping of the equivalent of seven Hiroshima-size atomic bombs on Iraq (one a week) – a pace and scale of destruction that has no parallel in the history of warfare. The Saudis, as befitted a brother Arab state, provided no troops for the final four-day ground assault on Iraq, despite the vast Saudi complicity in producing hundreds of thousands of Arab fatalities.[127] The Saudis were, however, directly involved in air attacks on Iraq, presumably more acceptable in Islamic theory than direct participation in land assaults on a Muslim country. The Saudis themselves suffered casualties, in part through Scud missile attacks launched from Iraq and in part through military clashes with the Iraqis on Saudi territory. By 26 January 1991 Iraq had launched 51 Scuds, 25 at Israel and 26 at Saudi Arabia; the casualties included four Israeli and one Saudi killed, and 212 Israeli and 12 Saudis wounded.[128] The most significant Saudi–Iraqi ground battle began on 29 January, when Iraqi troops briefly captured the Saudi border town of Khafji.

Few could doubt that Saudi Arabia had made an immense contribution to the prosecution of the 1991 Gulf War, just as it had to the Iran–Iraq War. It offered funds and strategic territory, as well as personnel in limited but significant roles. The Saudi's flew 7018 air missions (out of the Coalition total of 108,043), inevitably many fewer than the Americans (90,312) but more than any of the other leading combatants: Britain (5546), France (2326) and Canada (1308).

A central role of Saudi finance was to service the *de facto* mercenary Coalition, where not only were major states paid in millions or billions of dollars but where numbers of unemployed men in Arab states were invited onto the Saudi military payroll.[129] At the end of August 1990 the Saudi authorities encouraged increased recruitment of volunteers within the Kingdom and elsewhere; and, for all US talk of *defensive* intent, the suspicion quickly grew that soon there would be a wider military conflict. Early in 1991 the Saudis staged general air-raid practices in Riyadh and the towns of al-Kharj and al-Dalam. On 14 January the journalist Robert Fisk reported from the border town of Khafji, from which most of the women and children had fled but where shops were still open.[130]

On 20 January Iraq launched at least ten Scud missiles at Riyadh and Dhahran, but there were no immediate reports of casualties (the journalist Christopher Bellamy, reporting for *The Independent*, saw little damage in Riyadh). In one listing (*The* Guardian, 24 January 1991), some nineteen Scuds had been launched at Saudi Arabia in the period 18–23 January: Dhahran had received five, Riyadh six, eastern Saudi Arabia seven, with one falling in the water off Dhahran – a scale of attack that scarcely rated against what was being done to Iraq. None the less the Saudis were becoming increasingly disconcerted that they too were in the firing line; and that earlier American assurances that Saudi Arabia would not be used as a launch-pad for an attack on Iraq now counted for nothing: 'In the beginning, there seemed to be no ambiguities ... Saudi officials say both the King and the Crown Prince were led to believe that the Americans would allow sanctions to evict Iraq from Kuwait. Saudi Arabia would not be a launching pad...'.[131]

At the end of January 1991 the Iraqis overran Khafji, some twelve miles inside Saudi Arabia. The Iraqis had driven into the border town with five Soviet T-55 tanks and as many as fifteen armoured personnel carriers in one of several incursions over a broad front. These initiatives, little more than probing raids, were scarcely 'the beginning of the ground war' signalled in press reports. Khafji was retaken in a matter of days (later to become an issue of controversy between Khaled and Schwarzkopf), with US and Saudi casualties but much greater Iraqi losses. In one report some 600 Iraqis held the town for 36 hours before it was recaptured by Saudi and Qatari forces backed by US air and artillery fire. In another, 500 Iraqi troops had been captured, with another 300 (later amended to 30) killed. The Khafji battle had perturbed the Coalition commanders: an extensive inquest was begun 'after serious doubts were raised over allied conduct before and during the first important ground conflict of the war'.[132] But Schwarzkopf's comment that Khafji was 'about as significant as a mosquito on an elephant' was near the truth; it was a trivial detail when set against the vast slaughter planned for the hapless Iraqi conscripts trapped in the desert. The Saudis had taken the principal credit in expelling the Iraqis, which many observers saw as appropriate in the circumstances.[*]

Khafji had been converted by the Saudis into a propaganda triumph. Crown Prince Abdullah took the trouble to immortalise the eighteen Saudi soldiers and national guardsmen killed at Khafji as 'the symbol of valour and courage in the minds of generations to come'. The Press drew up the score-card: Iraq: 30 dead, more than 400 prisoners, 24 tanks destroyed: Saudi Arabia: 18 dead, 29 wounded, 3 personnel carriers destroyed. Other matters soon supplanted Khafji in the attention of the media. Reports began to appear that Syria was using Saudi Coalition-linked aid to expand its own armed forces and to nurture long-held territorial

---

[*] In 1997 the British Ministry of Defence confirmed a police investigation into charges that UK soldiers, in violation of the Geneva Convention, had shot dead Iraqi prisoners captured at Khafji (*The Sunday Times*, 17 August 1997).

ambitions; that the Saudis were seeking a $3 billion loan from foreign banks to help cover their war costs; that Riyadh was supporting two exiled Iraqi generals as possible successors to Saddam Hussein, sure to fall from power as a result of the war; and that the Saudis had penetrated Iraqi defences to collect intelligence in preparation for the imminent ground war. On 25 February an Iraqi Scud missile hit a US army base at Khobar City near Dhahran: at least 12 servicemen died, 25 were injured, and 40 were missing.

In total fewer than 150 Americans were killed (perhaps a half of these by 'friendly fire') in the 1991 Gulf War, with around 340 wounded, out of a 540,000-strong force. Saudi forces suffered about 40 fatalities, with about 175 wounded, out of a 96,000-strong force. These figures can be compared with the 200,000 Iraqis killed during the 42-day Gulf war and the 2,000,000 civilians – babies, children, the old and the sick – killed by sanctions-induced starvation and disease between 1990 and 1998.[133]

THE YEMEN WARS – II

Tensions and conflicts between the Saudis and the Yemenis have persisted through much of the twentieth century, reflecting the confrontations of earlier times. Khaled Bin Sultan noted in 1995 Yemen's sympathies with Iraq, as shown by their membership of the Arab Co-operation Council (Iraq, Jordan, Egypt and North Yemen), created as a response to the Gulf Co-operation Council. He speculates on the possibility of a threat to Saudi Arabia from various quarters ('from Yemen, say ...') and remembers earlier conflicts in Yemen; when, for example, Faisal 'covered himself in glory fighting in Asir, and then in Yemen'.[134] The Litton communication system, installed to provide nationwide security, extends to the southern border with Yemen – a key requirement reflecting the Saudi view that Yemen 'had conspired with Saddam to control the Gulf'. Khaled, against Schwarzkopf, believed that Yemen's President Ali Abdullah Salih was irrevocably committed to Saddam and that 'we should make clear to the Yemenis that they could not gamble with the security of the peninsula'.[135] At the beginning of the 1990 Gulf crisis the Saudis wondered if Yemen might try to exploit the situation by moving across the border to seize Asir; as a prompt defensive measure the Saudi Chief of Staff, General Muhammed al-Hammad sent a Pakistani brigade to reinforce the positions facing Yemen.

Other Saudi commentary has focused on the extent to which Saudi aid to President Salih has induced his Yemeni rivals to regard him as a 'Saudi protégé'.[136] Hundreds of thousands of Yemenis worked in the kingdom, without the need for visas, work permits or residency qualifications. This arrangement, not extended to other Arab and Muslim communities within the kingdom, appeared to the Saudis to be an important privilege; but still the Yemeni–Saudi tensions persisted. Yemen frequently complained about what it considered to be the meagre levels of Saudi aid; and felt excluded, as a poor country, from the Gulf Co-operation Council. In earlier conflicts the Saudis had stolen Yemeni land, making it easy for anti-Saudi factions in Yemen to exploit the impression of Saudi hegemony in the region. Algosaibi himself acknowledges Saudi racial abuse of the Yemenis, dubbed 'Zaidis' (members of the Zaidiyah sect) and 'Abu-Yemen': 'I have tried to explain to a number of ordinary Saudi citizens that the use of a sectarian name to refer to a nationality is unjustified and a form of disparagement for the other party.'[137] In any event – through history, resentment of Saudi power, Baathist sympathies and other factors – Yemen decided to resist the US–Saudi posture on the Gulf crisis, failing to vote for the initial UN Security Council Resolution 660 and thereafter either abstaining or opposing later SC resolutions.

Iraq had supplied military support to North Yemen for many years; and the Marxist state of South Yemen had remained reliably anti-American. A few weeks after the Iraqi invasion of Kuwait an official radio broadcast in Yemen emphasised that 'the main threat to the region is the build-up of US and NATO forces, and the escalation of psychological and propaganda warfare against Iraq and the Arab nation with the objective of pushing our region to the brink of military confrontation'.[138] On 22 November 1990 the US Secretary of State, James Baker, visited Sanaa and threatened President Salih that $70 million worth of American aid to Yemen would be cancelled if Salih refused to support the United States in the Security Council. A few days later, refusing to bow to American pressure, Salih commented: 'I know Iraq is ready for dialogue ... First the United States says it is coming to protect Saudi Arabia from aggression, and now the US says it wants to use force against Iraq ... The entire world was against Iraq's invasion of Kuwait, but the foreign intervention and threats of force are leading some Arabs now to support Iraq.'[139] Now Riyadh was conducting a vendetta against the 1.6 million Yemenis in Saudi Arabia, a further economic strike against an impoverished Yemen.

The refusal of President Salih to be intimidated by Secretary of State Baker meant that Yemen had lost not only the $70 million worth of US aid but also an annual $2 billion to $3 billion remitted from expatriates. Then Sanaa launched a criticism of Riyadh for inviting foreign forces onto Saudi territory, whereupon the Saudi government responded by insisting that every Yemeni resident in the Kingdom must now find a Saudi sponsor or be expelled. Before the two-month deadline expired some 651,000 Yemenis were being forced to leave the kingdom, with a further 150,000 returning to Yemen unofficially. This exodus represented an added burden for a Yemen already deprived of a substantial part of its income. When, on 29 November 1990, Yemen (with Cuba) voted against SC Resolution 678 a senior American diplomat immediately told the Yemeni ambassador: 'That was the most expensive "no" vote you ever cast.' The American aid was blocked, the World Bank and the International Monetary Fund (IMF) moved to hamper further Yemeni loans, and some 800,000 Yemeni workers were expelled from

Saudi Arabia. Abdel Hameed Noaman, a member of the General Association of
Yemeni Immigrants in the United States, subsequently commented on the persecution of Yemenis in Saudi Arabia:

> The Saudi government has forced the Yemeni workers and entrepreneurs to
> sell their belongings and businesses at prices lower than the accustomed
> market price. In consequence, these Yemeni immigrants also had to helplessly
> abandon compensation and ownership rights that they had acquired over
> decades...
>
> Before their departure, the Yemeni immigrants were interrogated and harassed
> by the Saudi officials, police officers, reactionary citizens. Soldiers at the
> Saudi–Yemeni border pushed people through at gun point ... Adolescents and
> children heard name calling and slurs against their families made by the
> Saudis. In the month of September 1990 alone, 140,000 workers including
> thirteen pregnant women were dumped in the desert ...[140]

Yemen had suffered more than any other non-combatant country, with
massive blows to the national economy ($7 billion in debt in November 1990),
Yemen was forced to cope with a final total of more than one million expropriated and demoralised Yemenis thrown out of Saudi Arabia. For months an estimated 600,000 Yemenis had struggled to survive on the hot and desolate Tihama
plain, with cholera still killing 50–60 children every week as late as 1992.[141] It
was inevitable in these circumstances that a feeling of bitterness would be
encouraged against the Saudi royal family: 'Effete, luxury-loving princes who
spend their time in night clubs, and proved incapable of defending their own
country without American help ... a famous Arab pun transforms King Fahd's
religious title, "Protector of the two holy shrines" (Mecca and Medina) into
"Betrayer of the two holy shrines". In the Islamic world, there's scarcely a worse
insult than that.'[142]

This atmosphere of bitterness, contempt and recrimination did nothing to settle
the question of the undefined Yemeni–Saudi border running for almost
1000 miles through mountains and desert; or to resolve other matters that continued to fuel tensions between the two states. The long-standing unease between
Yemen and Saudi Arabia, massively exacerbated by the circumstances of the
1990/91 Gulf crisis, was set to continue in the years that followed.

In July 1992, after the attempted assassination of the Yemeni socialist Anis
Hassan Yahya, fears grew that Saudi Arabia was trying to destabilise Yemen;
other Yemeni politicians had already been killed in similar attacks. In May,
without mentioning Riyadh, President Salih accused 'enemy forces' of conspiring
against Yemen's efforts to establish a democracy in the Arabian peninsula; and
now Yahya was suggesting a conspiracy to prevent the creation of a modern state
so close to the Saudi feudalists. Sheikh Ali Shami, the leader of the moderate

Al-Haq Party, was quoted: 'Saudi Arabia is pouring lots and lots of money into Yemen to promote its own version of Wahhabist Islam. This is actually an irrational and an uncompromising version of our religion which we can do without.'[143] At the same time few doubted that US–Saudi resentment at Yemen's posture during the Gulf War was continuing to present problems for the impoverished Arabian state. Said one Western diplomat: 'Basically the position is that the US is still very angry at Yemen's position during the Gulf crisis ... being nasty to Yemen earns silver stars with the Saudis.'[144] Britain, typically shadowing US foreign policy, also cut its paltry aid to Yemen, with British Petroleum even going so far as to suspend oil prospecting in a Yemeni concession area now being claimed by Riyadh as Saudi territory – an obvious indication of how Britain was prepared to shape its policies in line with US and Saudi sensitivities.

Yemen was now struggling to emerge as a multi-party democracy, following the union of the Marxist South and the free-market North in 1990. With an election scheduled for April 1993, more than fifty parties were preparing to fight for 301 seats in a new parliament. Saudi Arabia was now increasingly alarmed that the establishment of a Western-style democracy on the peninsula would represent a threat to the feudal monarchy. But Yemen had little reason to heed Saudi anxieties. Around the Red Sea port of Hodeida the camps set up by the Yemenis expelled from Saudi Arabia were fast becoming permanent. A new population of dispossessed refugees was struggling to establish adequate conditions for life, but with no electricity and only primitive sanitation. The Saudis, compounding Yemen's problems, had taken the opportunity to expel anyone who might be a burden on the state: the blind, the infirm, beggars, thieves and drug addicts. This was part of the price paid by Yemen's decision to use its sovereign voting right in the UN Security Council.

The April (1993) election produced a parliament that quickly demonstrated a desire to improve relations with Riyadh by electing as its speaker Sheikh Hussein Abdullah al-Ahmar, the pro-Saudi chief of the Hashid confederacy and the leader of the Yemeni Congregation for Reform, which won 62 parliamentary seats. Now it was judged that the new speaker would help to balance the government majority formed by the merger of Salih's People's General Congress and the Yemeni Socialist Party. But the new political structure proved fragile: within months fighting broke out between North and South, threatening the 1990 union. In February 1994 the Yemeni Vice-President, Ali Salem al-Baidh (the South Yemen president until the 1990 unity pact), visited Saudi Arabia to seek better relations: his opponents were quick to criticise a trip to a state with an interest in the collapse of Yemeni democracy.

By April fighting had broken out between rival factions, with a tank battle (27 April) involving rival units of the Yemeni army reportedly causing heavy casualties (said one diplomat: 'Many bodies were brought [to Sanaa] from the battle area'). It now seemed that the hasty ceasefire would not be long sustained. In May the spreading civil war had engulfed much of the country, with five Scud missiles fired at Sanaa (6 May) and Northern forces advancing on the Aden stronghold; five days later a further Scud missile landed in Sanaa, killing 23 adults and children, with a second missile causing civilian casualties in Taiz. Saudi Arabia, alarmed at the mounting conflict on its borders, issued a call for a ceasefire. In an attempt to influence the worsening situation and to impress international Arab opinion, the Saudi Defence Minister Prince Sultan ibn Abdul Aziz declared that Riyadh was engaged in 'constant and serious' contacts with other Arab countries to contain the war and emphasised that Saudi Arabia had 'blessed' the four-year-old union of North and South Yemen. In commentary, it was suggested that Prince Sultan 'was less than straightforward' since the Saudis 'have always been against a strong, united and democratic Yemen in the Arabian peninsula'.[145]

On 7 July 1994 the Yemeni civil war came to an end, two months and three days after it began. The central government, led by President Salih, had finally managed to crush the forces of the (would-be) secessionist Southern rebels. In the official account the last stronghold of the separatists in the Crater district of Aden was brought down by a popular uprising. Now there was mounting speculation that the role of Saudi Arabia would be closely examined. Said a Sanaa newspaper editor: *'They invested heavily in this war [on behalf of the South] and it hasn't worked out the way they wanted. I've talked to several people in other Arab countries, and they seem more cheerful about the result than we are. They feel that Saudi muscle-flexing has been dealt a blow.'*[146] In Jeddah a spokesman for the separatists, Muhsin Farid, was allowed to make a public statement: 'The war is not over. We will regroup and continue the struggle by all possible means.'

Little publicity was given in the West to the scale of Saudi involvement in the Yemeni civil war. According to the American CIA the Saudis paid 'millions of dollars' to hire Russian air force pilots and MiG-29s to fly from Russia to Aden and bomb the advancing Northern forces. Here it is claimed that a full squadron of up to twelve MiG-29s, a sophisticated fighter, was based at the al-Rayan airfield near Mukallah, the second largest city in South Yemen. At first the Russians denied the charges, but later said that if the reported events did take place official permission had not been given.[147] It was known that the Saudis had supported the Southern rebels with cash and arms, a clear sign of Riyadh's bitter resentment of Yemeni democracy. In the 1993 election women had been allowed to vote, and a vigorous debate had taken place in more than 100 local newspapers and magazines – all of this anathema to the feudal Saudi royal family, still intent on banning anything resembling free elections or a free press.

In mid-January 1995 Saudi Arabia was reported to be massing troops, warplanes and missile launchers on the Saudi–Yemeni border; and reports said that border skirmishes with Yemeni forces had already caused the death of a high-ranking Saudi army officer. One diplomat confirmed that the Saudis were moving troops and equipment to the border region of Saada and Mahrah; and now it was being acknowledged that several clashes between Saudi and Yemeni forces had occurred since the end of the Yemeni civil war. The new crisis began when Saudi troops occupied territory vacated by Southern rebel forces, in violation of the mutually agreed border. In one incident Saudi-armed tribesmen occupied a Yemeni border post, hoisted the Saudi flag, and killed as many as a dozen Yemeni troops.[148] Again the issue of the poorly defined border was a point of contention: the Yemenis argue that a 1934 agreement, negotiated in Taif (and renewed in 1954 and 1974), expired in September 1994, and that they are no longer prepared to accept the stipulated ceding of control over Yemeni land to Saudi Arabia.[149] In the event, without a permanent resolution of the dispute, the dangerous tension was resolved by Syrian mediation.

On 27 April 1997 Yemen's ruling General People's Congress won the parliamentary election by securing 187 of the 301 seats. The Islah Party, the government's junior coalition partner, won 53 seats; independents 54; and two opposition parties 5. The election was marred by shooting incidents in which 22 people were killed. Now Saudi Arabia was being forced to tolerate the continued existence of a brave Arab attempt at parliamentary democracy on the Arabian peninsula. This significant advance of human rights on the borders of Saudi Arabia was only one of the growing threats to the traditional dynasty based in Riyadh. Now, at the end of the 1990s, the client feudalism of the House of Saud faces many gathering clouds.

7 The Gathering Clouds

On June 13, 1982 Crown Prince Fahd Ibn Abdulaziz became the new King of Saudi Arabia. His policies and foresight ... brought to the Kingdom of Saudi Arabia great progress and development, the likes of which are unparalleled in the history of mankind.[1]

O believers! surely wine and games of chance ... are an abomination of Satan's work! ... Only would Satan sow hatred and strife among you, by wine and games of chance ... will ye not, therefore, abstain from them?

Koran, Sura 5, Verses 92–3.

How can Fahd, a gambler, a notorious womaniser ... and a great lover of Scotch Whiskey, claim to be the Holy protector ... of Makka and Madina?[2]

PREAMBLE

It is characteristic of autocracies that leaders are constantly praised to excess in the works of sycophantic writers and official propaganda. In this, Saudi Arabia is no exception. Thus, in one account, the Kingdom became 'among the most modern, and perhaps most progressive' nations by virtue of 'miraculous achievements' made possible by great monarchs with no hint of human frailty. King Abdul Aziz (Ibn Saud) was 'a giant of a man', a 'wonderful human being ... Once he set his eyes on a goal he did the impossible to achieve it ... The strength of his mind and the depth of his thoughts were fascinating ... His marvelous depth of mind ...',[3] and so on and so forth. King Fahd, in turn, 'is a man of great wisdom ... While Abdul Aziz was the father of the nation, Fahd ... became the pioneer and founder of the Modern Kingdom of Saudi Arabia.'[4]

In this hagiological theatre there is no space for criticism: immensely talented monarchs move like demigods through a conjured world of extraordinary achievement. And just as the Saudi kings merit praise without qualification, so a feudal and corrupt Saudi Arabia is depicted as among the 'most progressive' of nations. Today, in the late 1990s, it is part of the crisis of the modern Kingdom that the privilege and profligacy of the House of Saud are being forced to confront the mounting pressures of the real world. It seems unlikely that the feudal dynasty will long be able to exploit oil and Islam to preserve its local hegemony; that the House of Saud, as it has historically evolved, will be able to dispel the gathering clouds.

PROBLEMS

The problems facing the Saudi regime derive from many sources – economic, political, religious; and for some years the House of Saud, by its very nature, has seemed increasingly ill-equipped to face the mounting challenges to its survival. It is often acknowledged that the Saudi royal family has overcome, and continues to overcome, many historical and current difficulties: the early Arab wars in the peninsula, the threat from Nasserite socialism, internal religious conflicts, challenges from Iraq and others, revolutionary terrorism, the 1991 Gulf War, and the persistent hostilities of dissident Muslims abroad; but it remains to be seen whether the growing predicament of an outdated dynasty will cause the eventual collapse of the Saudi regime.[5]

The Saudi royal family – through both commission and inertia – has brought many of its problems upon itself. It has been profligate in financial expenditure, both to fund the absurdly luxurious life-styles of individual dynastic members (in the early 1990s Prince Abdul, one of Fahd's young sons, was reportedly receiving some $5 million a week pocket money) and to purchase billions of dollars worth of weapons that added nothing to national security but much to national debt. More billions have been spent on unwise development projects and prestige schemes, often with poor productivity and little return in economic and social terms. Most enterprises have been forced to rely on foreign labour, signalling both the narrow educational base in the Kingdom and the problems faced by an oil-rich state with a relatively small population (less than 13 million): 'The Saudi non-oil industry may have 2000 different enterprises, but most employ expatriates and rely on expensive government subsidies to survive. Most importantly, the Kingdom's economy has failed at one of its most important tasks: the generation of jobs for Saudis.[6] Technical Saudi publications (here more interested in fact than propaganda plaudit) often acknowledge the government's failure to achieve effective 'Saudiization' of the economy:

> 'The labor market in the Kingdom has been characterised by its inflexible response to prevailing economic circumstances ... the number of foreign workers has continued to grow at relatively high rates, regardless of calls ... for a reduction in non-Saudi worker numbers ... Continuous recruitment of non-Saudi workers will increase the difficulties in finding such jobs for poorly qualified Saudi workers, who make up such a high proportion of new entrants to the labor market.[7]

This failure to provide adequate employment opportunities for the Saudi workforce (7.4 million in working-age group '12 years and over', according to a 1993 census) has helped to spread disaffection in the Kingdom, creating dissidents and fuelling racial resentment against foreign workers. At the same time the royal family continues to resist any real attempts to broaden the political base, remaining wholly opposed to the idea of a parliamentary-style democracy in the Saudi context. There are persistent suspicions that the Saudis continue to fund terrorist efforts to destabilise the struggling democracy in Yemen.[8]

The relationship between the House of Saud and Islam continues to be problematic, not only because of the flagrantly dissolute habits of many of the Saudi royals, but also because of the ineluctable schisms within Islam itself. How is any proud 'Custodian of the Muslim Holy Sites' able to straddle the competing claims of Sunnis, Shi'ites, Wahhabists, fundamentalists and a hundred other versions, variants, sub-dialects, bastard offspring, pretenders *inter alia*? (Christianity, despite all its eager ecumenists, faces the same problem – the unchanging godhead is perversely fickle.) It has also been pointed out that the Saudi regime has been keen to fund Islamic institutions within the Kingdom, to the point of a promiscuous lack of discrimination, as a means of advertising Saudi piety. One consequence, as with the funding of foreign fundamentalist groups, has been a surfeit of theological dissidents, often unemployable but keen to cause mischief as a means of showing their own commitment to this or that True Path. At the same time the modernists, keen to equip the Kingdom for the twentieth (if not quite the twenty-first) century, have been keen to rail against excess of religious devotion. Perhaps, after all, the Word conveyed by Muhammed is *not* sacrosanct. Perhaps endless infernal torture is *not* the mark of 'God, the compassionate, the merciful'. Perhaps, after all, women *should* be treated as equal to men.

In the midst of all this confusion the Saudi regime is driven to defend the modernisers against the fundamentalists, and the fundamentalists against any encroachments from the infidel West. In reality, from its deeply reactionary instinct, the House of Saud has tried to entrench a deeply repressive conservatism, where few concessions are offered to the modern world (see Chapter 1): '... too many concessions have been made to hard-line fundamentalists. The latter, for example, have been allowed to express their views in hundreds of mosques and schools, while Saudi progressives and modernists have been muzzled so as not to provoke further religious discord.'[9] This retrenchment has done no more than to fuel the opposition. In response, the *ulema* urges further repression to safeguard what is taken to be the current religious orthodoxy. Preachers and other Wahhabist devotees are given priority on the state-run television programmes; while the official Committee for the Promotion of Virtue and Prevention of Sin censors imported films (sometimes reducing the running time by 80 per cent), spies on private behaviour, and urges beatings and additional religious education for detected miscreants. This situation promotes hypocrisy rather than virtue, at best a reluctant acquiescence rather than enthusiasm for the regime, where many people indulge themselves privately (at risk of exposure) but observe the expected proprieties in public.

The efforts of the regime to resist the encroachments of the dissolute West are not helped by the Kingdom's manifest reliance upon American protection: 'The one *special relationship of paramount importance* is certainly that between the

Kingdom of Saudi Arabia and the United States of America' (original italics).[10] The relationship has provided substantial mutual advantages. Thus William B. Quandt from the US Brookings Institution notes: 'No country has benefited more from relations with Saudi Arabia than the United States. American oil companies have made enormous profits. American businessmen have had a disproportionate share of the Saudi market.[11]

The Saudis, as already noted, have also provided covert funding for US-inspired terrorism that may or may not have accorded with widespread Muslim feeling. Thus the Saudi regime supplied financial and other support to terrorist groups in such war-torn places as Angola, Afghanistan and Nicaragua. At one time Pakistan was the funnel to the Afghan resistance, with Saudi Arabia 'providing more funding than the CIA'.[12] And what could be done with Afghanistan could be done elsewhere. In the early 1980s the Saudis were supporting the rebels against the Marxist government in Ethiopia; and it soon occurred to President Reagan that they might be prepared to fund his beloved 'Contra' terrorists in Nicaragua. At first Riyadh was reluctant: the CIA was offering nothing in return, the Sandinistas in Nicaragua were basically pro-Arab (while the US proxies in Costa Rica and El Salvador had shown signs of anti-Arab diplomacy), and secrets were not secure in the Reagan Administration.

The Americans persisted, with Reagan using the enticement of four hundred Stinger missiles, whereupon the Saudis eventually agreed to contribute $8 million to $10 million to the Contras at the rate of $1 million a month. On Memorial Day weekend (1984) the American President invoked emergency procedures to bypass the Congress, and the converted Stingers were flown secretly to Saudi Arabia.[13] It was not only the missiles, but also – according to Colonel Oliver North – 'the honest-to-God affection that the Saudis ... had for President Reagan'.[14]

The Saudi dilemma was plain. For much of the time Riyadh was prepared to support US-inspired terrorism, even though such covert activities brought the House of Saud uncomfortably close to the infidel West. At the same time the Saudis were prepared to support Arab terrorism; for example, the Palestine Liberation Organisation (PLO) against Israel – as if there were no political contradiction in simultaneous Saudi support for a pro-Jewish Washington and anti-Jewish Arab nationalists. Sometimes the United States compounded the Saudi problems; as when, having failed in a CIA-run plot against Syria in August 1957, Washington assumed that Saudi Arabia would want protection against pro-Soviet Syrian expansion, as if Saudi Arabia would be keen to advertise a split between Riyadh and a brother Arab state. In September, Jordan, Iraq and Saudi Arabia all denied that Syria posed a threat.[15]

Egypt's President Nasser, however, was another case altogether; and this time it was the CIA that offered funds – to support the Saudis in their efforts to eliminate Nasser's influence in Syria and elsewhere. Saudi Arabia was often named as a possible conspirator in assassination attempts against the radical Egyptian leader.[16] The Saudi involvement with the clandestine activities of the CIA was of long standing: 'Saudi Arabia ... thanks to the omnipresent oil consortium, ARAMCO, was under American influence. Moreover, its new king, Saud, and his brother Prince Faisal, had long been on the payroll of the CIA, who had bailed them both out to the tune of several million dollars.'[17]

The attempts of the Saudis to ride simultaneously the horses of Islam, Arab nationalism and US global hegemony were graphically exposed during the 1991 Gulf War and its aftermath. Fahd's trepidation at 'inviting' the infidel – in vast numbers – onto Saudi soil was well founded. Fundamentalist agitation was boosted in the Kingdom and beyond, and incidents of dissident protest and violence once again exposed the tensions at the heart of the Muslim world. Soon after the Gulf War the United States was pressing King Fahd to allow a build-up of US forces in Saudi Arabia, nominally as a response to continued Iraqi intransigence; but Fahd, alarmed at the spreading influence of fundamentalists wanting even stricter Islamic laws, was reluctant to agree a bolstering of American troops in the Kingdom.

Already the fundamentalists were claiming that the regime had been corrupted by the West; and they were secretly circulating videotapes of two royal weddings where alcohol and belly dancers were much in evidence (men are shown dancing with unveiled women, alcohol is present, and a belly dancer evokes much delight). At the same time, with the Wahhabists pressing the regime for an Islamisation of all economic, social, education and administrative systems within Saudi Arabia, there were signs that the influence of the fundamentalists was spreading in the army and the national guard. In November 1991 an unprecedented meeting took place in New York between the Saudi ambassador to Washington, Prince Bandar, and prominent American Jews – providing yet more evidence, from the perspective of the Muslim fundamentalists, that the House of Saud was prepared to betray the Word of the Prophet. A Jewish spokesman, Shoshana Cardin, commented to *The Jerusalem Post*: 'For the first time the barriers were removed'; with Robert Lifton, President of the American Jewish Congress, observing that the Saudis 'have made a decision that they are going to be players in the process'.[18] In practical terms this meant that King Fahd, in manifest betrayal of the traditional Muslim posture, was now willing to contemplate an ending of the Arab boycott of Israel, an end to the Palestinian *intifada*, and Saudi acceptance of American aid to Israel to facilitate the absorption of Soviet Jews.

In early 1992 it was plain that Riyadh was shaping its oil policy to aid the Bush presidential campaign, despite some OPEC members being angered by the Saudi move.[19] Such developments were soon to be set against the growing perception that the 'oil bonanza that made the kingdom wealthy is evaporating' and that the House of Saud was having to address 'the thorny question of how far to relinquish its monopoly on political and economic power'.[20] The Saudi regime had increasingly relied upon bribery and religious conservatism to keep afloat 'an ever-precarious federation of different regions, religious groups (Sufi and Sunni) and classes (merchant, Bedouin, technocrats and mullahs)'.[21] In this context of mounting corruption and repression the House of Saud was facing growing opposition from Muslim fundamentalists, liberal Saudi factions (including some disaffected princes), revolutionary dissidents and others. It was easy for commentators in the West to see the similarities between the situation of Saudi Arabia and that of Iran before the violent revolution: undue reliance on the United States, secret-police repression under CIA direction, the progressive alienation of the mass of the people.

Washington also was trying to ride two horses, as always trying to maintain its dominant influence over Saudi affairs while working to appease the Jewish lobby in the United States. In November 1996 Washington informed Saudi Arabia that it would block its application to join the World Trade Organisation (WTO) if Riyadh continued to support the economic boycott of Israel – so signalling American dissatisfaction with the Saudi's slow-moving consideration of this crucial issue. It was not long before world events were putting Saudi Arabia under a countervailing pressure. In March 1997 Yasser Arafat, the Palestinian leader, urged Muslim countries to rescue Jerusalem from 'Zionist clutches'. At an extraordinary summit meeting of the 54 members of the Organisation of Islamic Conference, Arafat denounced the illegal building of Jewish settlements in Arab east Jerusalem and urged the Muslim states to respond: 'It is the religious duty of all Muslims to act to save Islam's holy place from the danger of Judaisation ... Israeli plans to establish Jewish settlements in east Jerusalem are a flagrant violation of the peace agreement brokered by Washington.'[22] Among the Islamic leaders at the conference were President Rafsanjani of Iran, President Demirel of Turkey, and Sultan ibn Abdul Aziz, the Crown Prince of Saudi Arabia.

There was no sign that the Arafat appeal would have the slightest effect on the assembled Muslim leaders. The die had been cast years ago, and the various Islamic states would continue to balance their perceived priorities in an unstable world. There was evidence that Saudi Arabia was continuing to support US-favoured factions in various parts of the world; for example, the Taliban militia in Afghanistan, at once prepared to repress all opposition and to safeguard US interests, was given Saudi support,[23] just as terrorist groups around the world have traditionally attracted cynical American support and Saudi largesse. The US–Saudi relationship, though often uncomfortable, was set to persist on the basis of perceived mutual advantage despite vast cultural differences. In the same way, the UK–Saudi links, despite some economic and human-rights tensions (see Chapter 1), seemed likely to survive in the short term at least. As a British Aerospace (Al-Yamamah) commentary rousingly and optimistically proclaims: '*Over many years there has been a bond of friendship, mutual respect and understanding between Saudi Arabia and the United Kingdom, which continues to flourish in spite of what are undoubtedly wide cultural differences.*' In this happy lexicon King Fahd is a 'wise' ruler of a Saudi Arabia that remains 'a model of stability'. No clue here to the gathering clouds.

The close Saudi links with the West (in particular, the royal affinity for the grosser forms of secular hedonism) continues to pose problems for a state that professes custodianship of spiritual virtue. Public unease over the traditional US–Saudi attachment has grown in recent years, not least because of the American 'invasion' of Saudi Arabia in 1990/91 and other practical ramifications of US policy in the region: 'The United States has ... undermined its own relations with Saudi Arabia, where public hostility to America is growing and where, as a result, Saudi officials are beginning to distance themselves from the United States.'[24] US *tolerance of/support for* Israeli policy in Lebanon, for example, has aroused public Saudi ire. Said one Western diplomat, following an Israeli artillery attack in April 1996 which killed 150 Lebanese civilians: 'The Saudi public was really outraged. They were absolutely enraged.'. On this occasion, as at other times, the 'government-controlled press and speakers at several mosques harshly criticised the United States for not condemning Israel's attacks in Lebanon'.[25] In these circumstances, in conditions of mounting public resentment of US arrogance and brutality, Saudi officials are increasingly emphasising their independence from American policy in the region: 'Saudi leaders, who consider their relationship with the US as a cornerstone of their defence and foreign policy, are not willing to cede to all US demands. A senior Saudi official, who requested anonymity, says: 'We are not American lackeys. We have good relations ... But we are not Guatemala.'[26]

The question remains: will the House of Saud be able to evolve politically – in areas of both domestic administration and foreign policy – to contain the growing pressures of public disaffection, or is Saudi Arabia now irrevocably set on the Iranian path? Is the regime flexible enough to counter the growing influence of the domestic and overseas dissidents (see below), or will uncontainable domestic pressures force the House of Saud to impotence and collapse? The predicament of the regime is not helped by the persistent border disputes with brotherly Arab states.

In October 1992 frontier skirmishes between Qatari and Saudi forces served as yet another reminder of the potential for border disputes in the Arabian peninsula. The situation had not been helped by the role of colonial Britain, keen to draw the coastal sheikhdoms into UK-friendly pacts and to define borders as suited the colonial need. Apart from the British requirement, much of the business of frontier drawing was an arbitrary matter. Thus Philby could write in a letter to the Dicksons, with regard to the territorial relationships between Kuwait and Arabia:

> 'Of course the whole trouble about Kuwait is that it is racially and geographically a part of this country [Arabia], though it is artificially separated from it by a political barrier which the British in their folly prefer to keep up. You might just as well make Hull and its district an independent principality under German protection...'[27]

It was inevitable that the British attitude to frontier drawing – in Ireland, India and elsewhere, as well as in Arabia – should store up problems for the future.

The Qatari–Saudi border dispute dragged on for some months until a deal was signed in Medina in December 1992. The settlement, witnessed by King Fahd of Saudi Arabia, the Emir of Qatar and Egypt's President Hosni Mubarak, had seemingly brought to an end the long-standing frontier dispute; but soon fresh tensions would arise. In early 1996 the new Emir of Qatar, Sheikh Hamed ibn Khalifa al Thani, was alarming the other emirs of the region by proposing the election of a national assembly and by disputing the appointment of a Saudi national to head the Gulf Co-operation Council (GCC). Soon the pressure was mounting on Hamed to 'see the error of his ways' and to fall into line with 'traditional' regional policies. Said one prominent Saudi official: 'This guy in Qatar is pushing it. It's not that we want to overthrow him – that would be too much of a precedent – but we just want him to behave, and see the error of his ways.'[28] In the event, a few weeks later, Emir Hamed was forced to put down a *coup* attempt, in which the Qatari government claimed Saudi Arabia and other GCC states had been involved. Hamed survived, but then found himself embroiled in a dispute with his father, the former Emir Khalifa, about $8 billion of public funds said to be missing from the Qatari treasury. Again the Saudis intervened, this time to prevent the case being publicly aired in the High Court in London.[29] It would have been deeply embarrassing to the House of Saud to have any lawyers picking over the distinctions between royal revenues and state treasuries. Such developments did no more than confirm the fact that the Saudi royal family regarded the state treasury as its personal account.

The various problems faced by the Saudi regime – economic, political, religious – are stimulating a growing dissident response, with protest and violence at home and a growing propaganda offensive from vocal Saudis in exile. It is useful to look in more detail at the characteristic problems facing the House of Saud, and to profile the scope and character of the dissident reply.

AN ECONOMIC PREDICAMENT?

The prodigious energy resources of Saudi Arabia make it difficult to understand why such a country should be facing economic problems. Thus Ghazi Algosaibi, the Saudi ambassador to the United Kingdom, commented in June 1995: 'It is hard to be seriously worried about the long-term economic health of any country which possesses one quarter of the world's proved reserves of oil and gas.'[30] None the less, various circumstances have combined to present Saudi Arabia with a range of economic difficulties, not least the problem of funding profligate royal expenditure at home and abroad. The continuous massive expenditure on armaments and related facilities has put the Saudi economy under mounting pressure, with the US-contrived burden of the 1990/91 Gulf crisis still affecting the health of the economy. In 1991 many analysts were pointing to the strains being inflicted on Saudi finances by the massive scale of the expenditure to meet the war costs: 'Saudi Arabia lost more than it gained from the Persian Gulf crisis in 1990, and staggering costs incurred over the last few months will widen its budget deficit ...'[31] Regional analysts pointed out that Riyadh was continuing to spend more than it earned: 'Saudi Arabia will probably receive an additional $12 billion to $18 billion in 1990 revenue, originally set at around $31.5 billion ... this figure was dwarfed by $30 billion of pledges and payments extending well into 1991 ... the 1990 Saudi budget deficit ... would widen to $8 billion to $10 billion as a result.'[32] Riyadh had funded the supply of food, fuel and housing for more than half a million foreign troops, and in addition had met many of the costs of front-line states hit by UN sanctions against Iraq. Aid was supplied to 300,000 displaced Kuwaitis; Saudi defence costs had increased; and the task of boosting Saudi oil output to compensate world markets for the loss of Kuwaiti and Iraqi supplies had incurred further costs. Riyadh spent $1 billion on US forces alone in 1990; and by January 1991 had donated $6 billion to front-line allies such as Egypt and Syria, with pledges to provide Turkey with $1.1 billion worth of free oil and the moribund Soviet Union with $7 billion in loans and export credits. According to one estimate Saudi Arabia had only $5–10 billion in financial reserves in February 1992 as a result of the 1991 Gulf War and a decade of deficit financing (said one Western economist: 'The kingdom is broke after 10 years in the red'). The war was reckoned to have cost Saudi Arabia an extra $62 billion, with an additional $14.8 billion worth of US arms purchased in the period immediately following the Iraqi invasion of Kuwait.[33]

The massive scale of Saudi expenditure has only been possible because of the vast revenues from oil sales; but the highly lucrative oil industry has-done little to support the development of the economy. The industry, self-contained and specialist, relies heavily on foreign expertise and employs relatively few people. There is little scope for technology transfer to other industrial sectors; and oil-funded government expenditure, rather than diversified free enterprise, has remained the principal engine of economic activity. At the same time the oil industry had encouraged wide-ranging infrastructure developments, though many of these have been focused on the oil installations themselves. For example, ARAMCO itself constructed roads, housing, port facilities, water systems, clinics, schools and power plants to establish an autonomous fiefdom within the Saudi state.

The 1946 national budget indicated £13.2 million revenue and £17.5 million expenditure, with £2 million allocated for servicing existing debt, £2 million earmarked for the royal garage, £1 million set aside for court hospitality and entertaining, and a miserable £150,000 reserved for education. From the end of the Second World War to Ibn Saud's death in 1953 the sum total of development had included the Dhahran-to-Riyadh railway, a jetty in Jeddah, a few roads and some water wells.[34] When his son Talal sought permission in 1949 to build a public hospital in Riyadh, Ibn Saud 'could not imagine what the boy was getting at'.[35] Ibn Saud's successor, Saud ibn Abdul Aziz, by contrast wanted to be remembered for providing social facilities for the Saudi people. Under Saud, work began on the construction of highways, schools, hospitals and two universities; at Riyadh, now the new focus of government administration, rows of monolithic structures were built to house the ministries. The oil revenues continued to represent the backbone of the national economy: by 1955 oil was providing the government with more than three-quarters of its income, two-thirds of the gross national product (GNP), and almost all the government's foreign exchange. But the expanding oil revenues were also funding massive corruption and royal profligacy. Crown Prince Faisal then imposed a period of austerity to relieve the near-bankrupt Treasury, and these measures plus the rising oil revenues brought some improvement in the national finances. In 1970 a Five-Year Plan, devised by the Kingdom's new Central Planning Organisation under advice from Western specialists, was launched to lay the basis for future economic development.

The 1973 Arab–Israeli War and the associated oil boycott saw a quintupling in the price of oil to nearly $17 a barrel by December 1973. This development yielded soaring revenues for Saudi Arabia, though the oil revenues were to vary widely – causing financial uncertainty – in the years to come (see Table 7.1). The unexpected revenues gave the Saudi planners the opportunity to expand the Second Five-Year Plan, due to begin in 1975. Now fresh emphasis was given to infrastructure development, with new investment made available for roads,

Table 7.1   Saudi oil revenues (1973–94)

Year	Total revenue (US $ billion)	Year	Total revenue (US $ billion)
1973	4.34	1984	31.47
1974	22.57	1985	18.32
1975	25.68	1986	13.55
1976	30.75	1987	17.49
1977	36.54	1988	16.64
1978	32.23	1989	20.24
1979	48.44	1990	31.50
1980	84.47	1991[a]	43.70
1981	101.81	1992[b]	42.30
1982	70.48	1993[c]	37.40
1983	37.35	1994[c]	30.50

Source: Saudi Arabian Monetary Agency (SAMA) Annual Reports.

[a] *Economist Intelligence Unit* estimate.
[b] *Middle East Monitor* estimate.
[c] Estimate: Wilson and Graham (1994).

Source: Wilson and Graham (1994).

schools, hospitals, military bases, seaports and airports. Cement factories, oil refineries, oil pipelines, water desalination plants and other installations were built; and billions more were soon being invested in defence and the security apparatus of the state. Much of the new expenditure was profligate and unnecessary; for example, the King Abdul Aziz International Airport covered an area as large as the five biggest airports in America put together.[36] Substantial funds were provided for education and health, and subsidies were used to significantly reduce the price of food staples (bread, rice, sugar, meats, cooking oil, etc.). In the same way the expensively desalinated water was subsidised (consumer charge only 8 cents per cubic meter; cost to government, $1.20), with subsidies also made available for electricity, gasoline, cooking gas, trains, buses and Saudi Arabian Airlines (Saudia).[37] Land was given to favoured subjects (the House of Saud theoretically owned all land) and was then repurchased as a means of channelling oil revenue to supporters, friends and relatives. Over the period of the first four Five-Year Plans the government spent more than $776 billion. But the massive revenues and vast expenditure could not be indefinitely sustained.

The high price of Saudi oil encouraged the exploitation of fields elsewhere (for example, in Alaska and the North Sea). With the increased competition and a fresh consumer emphasis on conservation, the price of oil began to fall, whereupon the Saudis cut their production in a vain attempt to bolster the price: in six years the barrel price fell, from $40 to $10 in 1986, so reducing Saudi oil revenues to only $13.55 billion and causing a current-account deficit for the period 1983–87 of $54 billion. Now Riyadh was forced to cut back on government-funded projects; late payments forced many small companies into bankruptcy, employees into redundancy, and foreign firms into withdrawing staff from industrial and other programmes in the Kingdom; and government support for welfare, food subsidies and international aid was speedily reduced. In a desperate attempt to increase government revenues a range of taxes and other charges were introduced early in 1988: new taxes for both domestic and international flights, a surcharge on electricity and water bills, a surcharge on patients relying on government hospitals and health clinics, a higher tariff on most imports, a vehicle road tax and a real-estate transfer fee.[38] A new income tax on expatriates caused thousands to resign, forcing the government to repeal the tax four days after it had been introduced. The issuing of SR (Saudi Riyal) 30 billion worth of development bonds by 1989 (and a total of SR 116 billion worth in the period 1988–92), judged a moderately successful policy, was still not able to cover the deficit. In the event various government agencies, such as the Public Investment Fund (PIF) and the General Organisation for Social Insurance (GOSI), were driven to take up many of the issued bonds: the government had introduced the novel idea of borrowing from itself.[39]

Now Riyadh, still reeling from the financial burden of supporting Saddam Hussein through the entire period (1980–8) of the Iran–Iraq War, was forced to shoulder the immense financial burden of the 1990 Gulf crisis and the 1991 war that followed. In the event the Saudi expenditure on the war ($64 billion) produced a budget deficit of between $20 billion and $30 billion in 1991; now Saudi Arabia was pledging, via loans or direct grants, in excess of $1 billion to each of the Soviet Union, Egypt, Syria, Turkey and the United States, and smaller amounts to Djibouti, Lebanon, Somalia, Bahrain and Morocco. Riyadh made an appeal to Kuwait to use some of its overseas deposits and investments to defray the Saudi costs, but the request was turned down.[40] In these circumstances it was not surprising that the Saudis were having difficulties paying US corporations for purchases of arms and related services. Washington, sensitive as always to the Saudi predicament, then began pressuring Riyadh to repay some $500 million owed to fourteen American companies.[41]

Various obvious factors have been identified as contributing to the Saudi economic predicament. While Riyadh, through massive propaganda efforts, struggles to project an optimistic view of its financial affairs, international criticism has focused on:

- Riyadh's inability to live within its means: the extravagant expenditure on armaments and related facilities, largely inappropriate to Saudi defence requirements, that add little to national security but preserve Saudi indebtedness to Western manufacturers;
- The inadequacies of the Saudi banking system, constrained by the illegality of interest (usury) in Islamic doctrine;
- The monarchical system, giving immense licence to corruption, nepotism and personal profligacy – in turn stimulating dissident demonstrations, public disaffection and revolutionary violence;
- The inflexibility of the traditional *sharia* legal system (see also Chapter 1), again trapped in old Islamic categories that are poorly suited to the economic and human-rights obligations of a modern state;
- The inefficient bureaucracy, linked to the disproportionate power of the House of Saud, where corruption and waste are endemic.

In 1994 Saudi Arabia's inability to achieve a balanced budget was continuing to alarm many international observers.[42] Since 1983 Riyadh had run eleven consecutive years of deficit budgeting, with hints by outsiders that due to the characteristic inaccuracies of Saudi accounting the figures were even worse than those published. In addition, there is the further complication that the Saudi royals have often chosen to hide embarrassing personal spending and secret arms deals in obscure accounts, further distorting the publicly-accessible figures. The persistent deficits have in turn forced Riyadh to deplete its reserves: around $120 billion in 1981, as little as $7 billion in 1994.[43] The vast loans to Iraq (in one estimate, $26 billion) were now irrecoverable due to the US-inspired block on Iraqi oil sales, Baghdad's main source of revenue. This debt and others to various Arab countries have in effect been written off. The Saudi Arabian Monetary Agency

(SAMA) has always been secretive about certain aspects of the national economy (for example, regarding the distribution of development bonds), so information supplied to foreign companies and to the International Monetary Fund (IMF) has sometimes been regarded as suspect.

Riyadh has also moved into substantial medium- and long-term debt, occasioned in large part by its war involvements through the 1980s and 1990/91. After the 1991 Gulf War the Saudi Ministry of Finance, ARAMCO (now a largely Saudi-owned concern) and Vela (the ARAMCO tanker subsidiary) all approached the international markets in order to raise loans. For example, the Ministry of Finance borrowed $4.5 billion from a J. P. Morgan banking consortium in May 1991; ARAMCO raised $2 billion and Vela $900 million in March 1992.[44] The debt burden continued to rise thereafter as Riyadh renegotiated repayment obligations for past armaments deals that it could no longer honour. Doubts have been expressed about Saudi credit-worthiness by the Bank of England, various US government credit agencies and the International Monetary Fund. At the same time Riyadh's substantial reliance on borrowing has represented competition with its own private sector for international funds, so restricting free-market expansion.

The wide fluctuations in Saudi economic fortunes have also intensified the problems of the banks, already contending with the peculiarities of Islamic orthodoxy.[45] (*'They who swallow down usury, shall arise in the resurrection only as he ariseth whom Satan hath infected by his touch. ... God hath allowed selling, and forbidden usury'* – Koran, Sura 2, Verse 6.) Where banks had charged interest they were often denounced by the *sharia* courts, exacerbating the banking problems at times when borrowers were striving to delay repayments or to otherwise escape their obligations. Without government support some of the largest Saudi banks would have been forced into bankruptcy. It is also significant that Riyadh has borrowed increasingly from the commercial banking sector, incurring long-term debt without the deposits to match: 'The resulting mismatch of assets and liabilities could result in serious liquidity problems for the Kingdom's financial system.'[46]

By 1994 the combined foreign and domestic debts of the Saudi government were reckoned at around $70 billion, not counting a further $10 billion owed by various state agencies. Riyadh, keen to counter the growing international alarm, pointed out that in relation to Gross Domestic Product (GDP) the debt was comparable to that of some European countries. But it was not only the size of the Saudi debt that was causing disquiet in the international markets: it was the fact that the debt had rapidly escalated and shown every sign of further growth. Saudi finances, suggested more than one observer, were quickly running out of control. The government had tried to increase taxes and reduce subsidies, but the resulting clamour from both public and employers had caused a hasty reversal of many of the reform measures. A central problem is that the House of Saud has been happy to cultivate an image of the 'Great Provider', as if the prodigious but finite oil revenues can sustain an *in*finite domestic and extraterritorial largesse. In such an atmosphere the very discussion of financial retrenchment, let alone any practical implementation, can be seen as an abject and humiliating government failure.

For years it has been possible to ask: 'Is Saudi Arabia, the world's largest oil exporter, richest of the Gulf super-rich, going bust?'[47] After the 1991 Gulf War, despite the financial and other restrictions on the private sector, the market economy was thriving. Now the Saudis were even exporting grain, with Saudi flour being used in Swiss croissants and Holland receiving two plane cargoes of Saudi roses every day. Such things (the state-of-the-art grain mills and silos, the new focus on cultivating fruit and vegetables) have helped to disguise the parlous state of Saudi finances, the fact that economic management had remained loose and short-sighted for too long. Said one newspaper editor: 'There are two budgets here, the secret one which only the King and a handful of technocrats know about, and the public one which we can write about'; in the same vein a foreign expert commented: 'We are talking about a government which 10 years ago could lay its hands on real, realisable reserves of a good $100 billion, but now it is down to $12 or $15 billion.'[48]

The profligate foreign policies have always been mirrored by the endemic royal extravagance (see also Chapter 1). In August 1993, for example, a dozen Saudi princes and the vast entourages were occupying the luxury hotels in Cannes; some lounged in their oppulent palaces above the bay; while Prince Talal steamed the Mediterranean in a 264-foot yacht chartered for a mere $230,000 a week. Sheikh Eynani, an intimate of King Fahd, has lost $8.8 million on a single night of gambling at the Cannes roulette wheels; and when Fahd's personal 508-foot yacht docks, it is customary to trundle his portable garden down an immense gangway.[49] One estimate suggests that over a period of one decade the House of Saud managed to squander national assets of more than $120 billion, leading the US Federal Reserve Bank to propose a lowering of Saudi Arabia's credit rating. Financial advisors to the Bank of England have commented on the increasing instability of the Saudi financial sector, noting especially the massive debts of the largest Saudi bank, the National Commercial Bank of Saudi Arabia. In July 1993 Lloyd Bentsen, the US Treasury Secretary, called a meeting of the CIA and the State Department to discuss the impending crisis. Said one Arab consultant, regarding the debts of the National Commercial: 'They have huge non-performing debts. A very large part of that is believed to be owed by the king and senior members of the royal family. Nobody at the bank dares to demand repayment from them.' A minister associated with the bank commented: 'The problem is that the royal family thinks it owns the country.'[50]

By 1994 international concern that the Saudis were living far beyond their means was undermining the Saudi Riyal on foreign exchange markets and raising questions about Riyadh's ability to borrow at prime lending rates. Now it was being widely suggested that only a radical change in Saudi policies would enable Saudi Arabia to cope with its twin current-account and budget deficits. The possible consequences of failure were wide-ranging – nothing less than the undermining of foreign banks, arms manufacturers and the International Monetary Fund. The IMF itself was now declaring that – as a result of high import costs, mounting debt service bills and relatively low oil prices – the current-account deficit for Saudi Arabia (1992–96) would total an unsustainable $74.2 billion, five times higher than the 1991 IMF estimate. Again it was easy for foreign observers to note the reasons for anxiety about the future of Saudi finances: the incomplete picture of the Kingdom's financial position, the dwindling reserves, the soaring debt, massive domestic subsidies, and the failure of the House of Saud to confront the pressures and problems of the modern world.[51] In early 1994 it was reported that Riyadh had experienced problems in meeting the latest payment on its US arms contracts; and later in the year the Dutch-controlled NCM Credit Insurance company, providing 80 per cent of the short-term export credit in the United Kingdom, decided to restrict its cover for firms doing business in Saudi Arabia – because of Riyadh's 'very grave' financial situation and payment delays.[52] Said an NCM spokesman: 'We recognise the seriousness of these measures and their likely impact on the business of many of our customers. However, the situation in Saudi is very grave and continues to deteriorate. It is therefore vital that we take action to protect not only our own position but, in the final analysis, that of our customers.'[53] It was revealed that 'repeated promises' of payment, including promises to UK ministers, had not been honoured; and that there were no signs of an improvement in the situation.

Throughout 1994, in addition to constant efforts to refute growing international criticism, the Saudis and their Western economic advisors worked on the Sixth Development Plan (to cover the years 1995–2000).[54] The earlier Plans, begun in 1970, all emphasised the same underlying themes (despite changes in emphasis):[55]

- to maintain the religious values of Islam;
- to assure the defence of the religion and the country and to maintain internal security and social stability within the Kingdom;
- to continue balanced growth by developing the country's resources, by increasing the income from oil over the long term and by conserving depleted resources;
- to reduce dependence on the production of crude oil as the primary source of national income.

The development process (Figure 7.1) has been adapted for the specific requirements of the Sixth Development Plan. In contrast to the earlier Plans, the Sixth has been forced to attempt a reduction in public sector involvement and to place a greater reliance on the private sector and free enterprise. According to the planners Saudi Arabia is now 'firmly in stage 2 of the development process ... and this is reflected in the nature of the Sixth Development Plan'; the new Plan

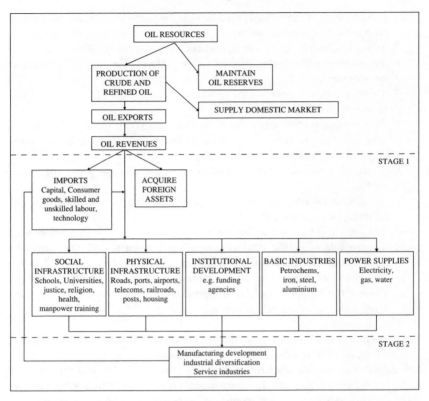

Figure 7.1   The Development Process – Saudi economy
Source: *Sixth Development Plan '96*, Saudi–British Bank

describes what Riyadh 'would like to see happen' over the next five years in the Saudi economy.[56] It is at best 'indicative' since circumstances are likely to force deviations from the Plan.

Thirteen objectives are specified:

1 To safeguard Islamic values by duly observing, disseminating and confirming Allah's *sharia* (God's Divine Law);
2 To defend the Faith and the nation and to uphold the security and social stability of the Kingdom;
3 To form the productive national citizen through providing him with the appropriate means and sources of income, and ascertaining his reward on the basis of his work;
4 To develop human resources and to continually ensure an increasing supply of manpower, upgrading its efficiency sufficiently to meet the

requirements of the national economy, and replacing non-Saudi manpower with suitably qualified Saudis;

5   To achieve balanced growth throughout all regions of the Kingdom;
6   To continue encouraging private sector participation in socio-economic development;
7   To reduce dependence on the production and export of crude oil as the main source of national income;
8   To continue restructuring the Kingdom's economy through continuing diversification of the economic base, particularly through laying more emphasis on industry and agriculture;
9   To develop mineral resources and to encourage discovery and utilization thereof;
10 To concentrate on qualitative development of already-existing utilities and facilities by improving their level of performance;
11 To complete infrastructure projects necessary to achieve overall development;
12 To promote scientific activity and to raise cultural and informational standards to keep pace with the Kingdom's development;
13 To achieve economic and social integration among the Gulf Cooperation Council (GCC) countries, and to support economic cooperation with Arab, Islamic and other friendly countries.[57]

Such (wish-list) aims should be set against the actual character of Saudi society (Chapter 1), and the likelihood that the bad financial habits of decades will be speedily abandoned over the brief period of the Sixth Development Plan. It is of course possible to argue that the international criticisms of Saudi Arabia are no more than journalistic invention, contrived for reasons best known to its authors. It is useful to quote the views of one specialist Saudi-observer:

The conviction that the true conditions in Saudi Arabia are being distorted by the international media is shared by the business community. Visitors say that Saudi Arabia continues to be a calm and well-ordered society. They argue that concerns about recent economic developments have to be set against the kingdom's prosperity, the extent to which all sections of the community have benefited from the economic development programme and the bright prospects the kingdom's huge oil reserves promise ... In international affairs the kingdom is recognised for consistently moderate policies that are seasoned with principled positions about issues of concern to the Arab and Islamic world ...[58]

We must presume that Riyadh's 'consistently moderate policies' have included vast aid for Iraqi aggression through the 1980s, military intervention in Yemeni affairs, the failure to pay due bills in the context of massive royal profligacy, and the periodic support for US terrorism around the world.

The planning for the new five-year programme did little to stem the criticism of Saudi financial mismanagement. Forecasts of increased world demand for oil in 1995 presented Saudi Arabia with further dilemmas. Should the Saudis increase production? And what, if they did, would be the consequences for oil revenues? Already Riyadh had negotiated a new repayment scheme for US arms, a hiring freeze had been imposed on government agencies, privatisation was being considered for many state enterprises, and the domestic subsidy situation was again under review. Again the imposition of new financial restrictions would be likely to disturb both the public and royal constituencies. One leading diplomat commented that if Riyadh were to remove the accustomed goodies the House of Saud would be overthrown in a military *coup* before the century was out.[59] In such fraught circumstances the Saudis were clearly desperate for an increase in their oil revenues but were not sure which way to turn. Now some Saudis were apt to comment, anonymously, on the 'drifting feeling ... New policies are needed, but as the money has dried up, the silence has become more deafening.'[60] There were still no clear signs that King Fahd was addressing the central question of royal profligacy, and the vexed topic of late payment on both domestic and foreign contracts was still taxing the patience of creditors. The Saudi Ministry of Defence and Aviation, under pressure from the United States and other foreign powers, seemingly continued to ignore any policy of restraint; while many observers continued to look to privatisation and free enterprise to offer the economic miracles that the country needed. Still little had been done, despite the various Development Plans, to address the endemic labour shortage. Of the little more than 17 million people living on Saudi territory, some 5 million were foreign workers repatriating £10 billion a year; and still ordinary Saudi workers continued to shun jobs considered 'unclean'. A young Saudi government employee commented: 'In 10 years there will be a working class here. It will be another 150 years before we can run our own country.'[61]

The persistent foreign pressures for Riyadh to buy inappropriate volumes of arms persisted, as if the economic problems of the United States, Britain and France could be solved by the endless exploitation of the Saudi milch-cow. Thus a European diplomat in Riyadh commented on the Western arms trade with Saudi Arabia: 'It's cynically about money and not about regional security. The Saudis are being sold equipment that is over-priced, over-sophisticated and frankly of little use to them in a real military crisis.' Another said: '*Look at the air force – they don't even have the pilots to fly all those planes that you British are selling them ... the Americans are worse – one moment the Treasury Secretary is telling King Fahd to cut his budget and the next day Clinton is on the phone persuading him to buy more weaponry.*'[62] This is all far removed from the worthy aim of *arms limitation* promulgated by virtuous Western politicians at the end of the 1991 Gulf War.

The 1995 Saudi budget – despite the far-reaching reforms outlined in the Sixth Development Plan – came as a disappointment to economists and bankers urging truly radical economic reforms. The proposed budget cuts were small (6 per cent),' with the associated measures (increased charges on petrol and electricity, a fee on visas for foreign workers, etc.) judged to be *minimal*, signalling nervousness in a government reluctant to increase public disaffection. The huge backlog of payments owed to contractors remained, forcing some suppliers to take out extra loans (so paying a *de facto* surcharge for trading with Riyadh); but Fahd had urged this matter to be given priority. Western commentators were in little doubt that the basic problems of the feudal and profligate Saudi state remained: '*There are reasons for alarm about the world's biggest oil producer, which is economically enfeebled, politically decrepit and beset by Islamic dissent.*'[63]

Other commentary suggested that the new budget was a positive move in the right direction, likely to 'reduce the deficit and set the economy on a sustainable footing'; the previous year's budgetary targets had been missed 'by a wide margin' – but perhaps now there was reason for optimism. Riyadh had shown its 'customary caution'; it remained to be seen whether it would succeed where it had failed in earlier years. In at least one sense the budget was innovatory: it was the first annual budget in modern times that was designed to reduce the living standards of many Saudi Arabians, perhaps not altogether cautious in circumstances of growing dissent. Where most observers continued to view the Saudi scene with alarm it was generally acknowledged that a strike at subsidies was a 'revolutionary' move in a nominally wealthy country accustomed to rising living standards.[64]

Through 1995 a fall in oil prices – one of the circumstances apt to force deviations from the Sixth Development Plan – led to 'a downward revision in growth and export earnings forecasts ... The current account is projected to record a balance instead of a $1500 million surplus as forecast' in June 1995.[65] The outlook for Riyadh continued to be bleak: 'The outlook for 1996 is clouded by prospects for the oil market and how OPEC and Saudi Arabia will cope with the rise in non-OPEC crude oil production.'[66] At the same time the foreign reserves had climbed to $8.9 billion by the end of May (1995), Fahd had introduced a radical cabinet reshuffle, the long-standing border disputes looked near to a solution (in line with GCC talks), and in June the Yemeni president, Ali Abdullah Salih, visited Riyadh for a mutual reaffirmation of the Memorandum of Understanding (MoU), signed in February after the border skirmishes. Now optimists could point to Fahd's efforts to refresh the political scene and to an improved diplomatic picture on the Arabian peninsula.[67] But few doubted that Riyadh was still faced with serious economic problems. In November 1995 a bomb blast in Riyadh (see below) showed that King Fahd's regime was 'far from stable'.[68]

It was soon plain that the relative prudence evident in Riyadh's 1995 budgetary policies was insufficient to cope with the seriousness of the Saudi financial position. Thus an IMF staff report for September, based on masses of new data on the Saudi economy, includes a projection of economic trends for the years to

2000. The report is more positive than the 1994 analysis but the projections '*show the worrying financial trends seen in the early 1990s will continue through to the end of the decade unless there are new measures to deal with the domestic deficit and public spending*'.[69] Three key conclusions were reached:

- *The current-account deficit* is projected to average $8 billion to $10 billion a year to 2000 after falling to $5 billion in 1995;
- *The budget deficit* is projected to rise steadily to SR 52 billion in 2000 from an estimated SR 23 billion in 1995;
- *Government debt* (net outstanding stock) is projected to rise to 110 per cent of Gross Domestic Product (GDP) in 2000 from 77 per cent of GDP in 1994.

To counter these dire projections the IMF proposes a mix of measures: basically an increase in taxes and duties, price rises, and a cut in the government wage bill.

By 1997 it was possible for the optimists to note improvements in Saudi finances. The new economic disciplines, though moderate in their scope, suggested that King Fahd and his advisors had at last shown a willingness to grasp the economic and political nettles, without which resolution no solution to the Saudi economic plight would have been possible. Thus pro-Saudi commentators were happy to proclaim that the economic outlook had been transformed, that the deficit could be eliminated and that the current account could show a surplus for the first time since the early 1980s.[70] At the same time, despite consigning talk of economic crisis to history, it was still too early to believe that the Saudis had found a 'sustainable' development path: '… more than two decades after Saudi Arabia committed itself to a strategy of diversifying away from dependence on oil, the energy market continues to determine the health of its economy … the kingdom today remains in the final years of the 1990s essentially an oil-based economy'.[71] From this perspective the overall financial position 'should remain satisfactory', but there were still reasons for concern: '… it will take several years of prudent government behaviour to rebuild investor confidence in the long-term prospects for the kingdom'.[72] Some observers judged that the economic reforms would be 'patchy', with the current-account deficit set to widen again in 1997–98.[73]

Most observers agreed that the 1996 surge in oil prices, coupled with new elements of Saudi financial discipline, had helped to improve the Kingdom's economic status. At the same time many of the deep-seated problems remained: the massive domestic subsidy, the likelihood that prolonged financial stringency would stimulate internal dissent, the vast burden of debt, the constant pressures – essential to Western economies – to overspend on arms, the endemic profligacy of the House of Saud. The trade commentators, generally keen to promote short-term commercial activity, took care to emphasise any positive signs in the Saudi economy – so the 'feelgood factor' was hitting Saudi Arabia in early 1997,[74] and the Kingdom was 'back on track'.[75] In such commentary there is no need to voice doubts about the long-term health of the Saudi economy, to question the political stability of a vast and growing dynasty rooted in feudal repression, or to consider the accumulating evidence of domestic and external dissent. Saudi political credibility has been weakened by many factors that have developed through the 1990s, not least by the ubiquitous infidel presence (substantial US forces) newly entrenched in most of the GCC countries.

It is useful to emphasise that a healthy economy is essential to national stability; and that, even if this were to be accomplished in the problematic context of Saudi Arabia, there are additional gathering clouds that need to be considered. In particular, there are the problems of political succession within the royal family; and the growing tensions in the turbulent and fragmented world of Islam. Such problems are fuelling growing public disaffection and dissent, contained increasingly by state repression. This is not a recipe for social stability.

FEUDALISM OR CHANGE?

Saudi Arabia is typically defined as a monarchy 'with strong historical links between the Government and the Islamic religion'.[76] If anything, this particular formulation understates the nominal place of Islam. In fact the Koran is regarded by Riyadh as the actual *de facto* and *de jure* constitution of Saudi Arabia, with the powers and duties of the King defined according to Koran-based *sharia* law. Thus Article 1 of the Articles of Government (Appendix III) for Saudi Arabia states: 'The Kingdom of Saudi Arabia is an Arab and Islamic sovereign state, its religion is Islam, and its constitution the Holy Quran and the Prophet's Sunnah. Its language is Arabic and Riyadh its capital.' Article 5 emphasises the hereditary nature of the monarchy, with rulers 'enthroned ... under the guidance of the Holy Quran and the Prophet's Sunnah'; Article 6 demands the allegiance of citizens 'before the Monarch in line with the Holy Quran and the Prophet's Sunnah'; and Article 11 declares that Saudi society 'is based on dependence on Almighty God ...'. Hence Saudi Arabia is not a theocracy (that is, a state ruled by priests) but an hereditary monarchy with massive theological underpinning.

In this context there is no semblance of political democracy. Political parties are prohibited; and any extraterritorial moves to establish elements of democracy elsewhere on the Arabian peninsula (for example, in Qatar or Yemen) are bitterly opposed. Riyadh makes much of the Consultative Council (*Majlis Al-Shura*), whereby the King is supposed to take advice in a public forum of members drawn from the religious, business, government and academic communities. Ibn Saud, who created the first Consultative Council in 1927, commented: 'We have to follow what is stated in the Holy Quran and the *Sunnah* in implementation of Allah's orders to consult others in the affairs of the moment.' On 21 August 1993 King Fahd announced reforms to the Consultative Council (see Appendix IV). Again there is nothing of democracy in this constitutional arrangement. The membership and deliberations of the Council remains entirely subject to the will and whim of the King (see Articles 3, 5, 6, 7, 9, 10, etc.).

The Council of Ministers is similarly subject to royal decision: the King appoints the Council's members and approves all their decisions. Article I of the General Rules of the Council of Ministers declares: 'The Council of Ministers is an organisational body presided over by the King'; Article 4 stipulates that no Minister can assume his post before swearing: '*I swear by Allah the Great to be loyal to my religion, my king and my country, and never to divulge any of the secrets of the state, and to uphold the interests and the systems, and to perform my duties truthfully, faithfully and loyally*'; and Article 7 declares that Council resolutions only become final 'after the King has approved them' (see Appendix V). Thus the principal constitutional organs of the Saudi state remain completely subject to Royal Decree and royal whim, a circumstances that affects every aspect of the legal system and the state bureaucracy.

The Saudi legal system has been represented as 'one of the main impediments to the Kingdom's future economic growth'.[77] In 1928 Ibn Saud established the main elements of the court system, with subsequent Royal Decrees (Civil Procedures Rules, 1936 and 1952; Board of Grievances, 1955; Ministry of Justice, 1970) making some effort to modernise the system. However, such Decrees (with Faisal's 1962 Ten-Point Programme and Fahd's 1992 Basic Law reform) have been no more than piecemeal and arbitrary changes to an essentially archaic system that remains entirely subject to royal diktat. It is still substantially the case that the House of Saud – including thousands of princes and princesses with vast land holdings and immense economic power – remains above the law; where a criminal financial institution that has been closed by the Saudi Arabian Monetary Agency (SAMA) can be re-opened by the defence minister, Prince Sultan; where Fahd can in effect sack the chairman-elect of the Saudi American Bank; and where court decisions can be overruled by Prince Naif 'on a whim'.[78]

A central problem is the rooting of the judicial system in the Koran – which leads to inevitable tensions between religious devotion and the secular needs of a modern society, and which duplicates in *sharia* jurisprudence all the conflicting Koranic interpretations represented by the various Islamic factions. The Saudi *ulema* have inevitably resisted all attempts at legal modernisation, with the successive kings equally reluctant to countenance any effective erosion of royal prerogative. Even where reform was introduced it was generally partial and relatively inconsequential. Thus the Committee for the Settlement of Commercial Disputes (CSCD), created in 1967 as a commercial reform measure, was kept under-staffed until abolished in 1987/88) in favour of the Board of Grievances, already considered part of the King's executive staff. In the early 1990s the Saudi fundamentalists redoubled their efforts to ensure that all legal cases, not only criminal ones, be heard in *sharia* courts. At the same time the often cumbersome judicial process is subject to endemic corruption (royal bribes used to block court proceedings) and the practice of commercial hostage-taking, where expatriates have been imprisoned for years because of unresolved disagreements between their company and the Saudi partner.[79]

In the same way the Saudi bureaucracy has been criticised as grossly inefficient, bedevilled by nepotism, absenteeism and incompetence. Again there are the inevitable costs of a grossly venal system, with favouritism and corruption endemic. In such circumstances the bureaucracy, like the *sharia* legal system, has been widely depicted as a powerful impediment to Riyadh's attempts to operate as a principal industrial player in the modern world. It seems unlikely that the necessary radical reforms in law and state administration will be best accomplished by a feudal dynasty characteristically reliant upon repression in order to survive.

In the 1990s, following the 1991 Gulf War, the House of Saud became increasingly sensitive to the domestic and external pressures for democratic reform and the mounting problems of an unaccountable dynastic succession. The vast influx of infidel troops in 1990/91 had inevitably prised open the closed and heavily repressed Saudi society, encouraging the world's media to focus on the cultural and ideological peculiarities of a world that seemed to belong to another age. These developments, unwelcome to Saudi traditionalists, gave fresh impetus to exiles and reformers struggling to urge Riyadh into the modern age. In fact various Saudi monarchs had long hinted at the possibility of real reform; in the 1980s a 'parliamentary' building was erected in Riyadh but, with no political will for real change, it has remained empty ever since. In March 1992 King Fahd was reportedly ready to nominate 60 leading citizens to a reformed Consultative Council, though some commentators were rightly predicting that even this minor shift in emphasis would be delayed.

In July 1993 Saudi officials were suggesting that the King was ready to announce a cabinet reshuffle, an inconsequential response to democratic critics of the regime; and again there were predictions that the new composition of the Consultative Council would soon be announced. It was not expected that the revamped Council would contain any members of the radical opposition but that new appointees would include professionals, tribal chiefs and religious leaders. From one perspective, any change to cabinet or Council could be perceived as deeply significant, a clear acknowledgement from Riyadh that some reform (or appearance of reform) had to be attempted. A senior Saudi royal was prepared to comment that the cabinet reshuffle was designed to 'repair relations between the royal family and the people', with the unprecedented admission that a number of ministers had not been sensitive to popular needs.[80] It was still necessary for Fahd to emphasise that any constitutional changes did not represent the birth of democracy: the Saudi people had 'unique qualities' that rendered them 'different from ... the rest of the world'; free elections were neither Islamic nor 'suited to our country'.[81] No political favours would be wrested from the House of Saud; if they were granted at all they would be conferred by royal decision. In fact few commentators imagined that the reformed Council – if it were even to begin deliberations – would do anything but consolidate the power of the monarch. Now the regime was becoming more rather than less intolerant; for example, with more rein being given to religious police (*Mutawa*), some of whom were killing people in an excess of Muslim zeal. In August 1993 Riyadh announced that King Fahd had appointed sixty men to the new Consultative Council, a forum with no power and chaired by Fahd himself. Said one critic: 'Nobody in the Council is going to rock the boat. They've all been chosen because of their loyalty.' It was Saudi political business as usual.

Reforms were also being introduced for regional administration. In September 1993 royal decrees were issued to divide the country into thirteen provinces, each administered by a royally-appointed representative assembly run by royally-appointed emirs. King Fahd named 210 members to the new Provincial Councils and declared: '*We are confident that the system, with the grace of God, will be beneficial in the achievement of the well-being, progress and prosperity of the Saudi citizen, his country and his Islamic and Arab nation. The Saudi citizen is the main pillar of the main development and progress of his country, and we shall spare no effort to achieve his happiness and welfare.*' Articles 2, 3 and 4 of the Provincial System emphasise that the new arrangements will remain completely subject to Royal Decree; with Article 6 requiring the governor and his deputy to be sworn in before the King before assuming their duties. Three months later the new Consultative Council was sworn in, before meeting for the first time in Riyadh. King Fahd, having appointed all the members of the Council, took trouble to assure them that they had his full support: 'You will find all the support from me personally and from the cabinet. We are a country that follows the book of God and will not deviate from that in any way. So we are not bothered in any way by those who object and say "Why not have elections?" '

The Consultative Council, however impotent, has been seen as a reluctant royal concession in conditions of growing public disquiet; and also as a sign of unease in the House of Saud. *No* change would have been forthcoming unless Riyadh was now sensing internal threats and instabilities; but, whatever image the Council would be expected to convey, King Fahd would work hard to maintain control. No public sessions of the Council would be allowed; recalcitrant members, if such were ever to emerge, would be promptly discharged; and no deliberations or resolutions would be permitted without royal approval. A journalist describes the atmosphere in the new forum represented by Riyadh as an important opportunity for public debate:

Accommodated within a lavish purpose-built palace clad in white marble, the 61 members of the Majlis Al-Shura, all appointed by King Fahd, pursue their deliberations amid a surreal calm. No hue and cry of debate echoes to the vast dome of the assembly chamber. The padded comfort of the committee rooms would hush the timbre of any argument. A handful of dedicated functionaries pass along pristine carpeted corridors to empty reception rooms as splendid as Versailles.[82]

We learn that this palatial building – perhaps 'the beginning of a parliament ... then again, it may be just a mirage' – has some 270 rooms, vast corridors, ceilings festooned with chandeliers, a reference library of virgin books, thousands of yards of thick carpets, and 'hardly any people'.[83] Said the Council's deputy chairman, in apt summary: 'We have no-one to satisfy but God and the King.'[84]

By 1995, with the 73-year-old Fahd in deteriorating health, there were growing doubts within the Kingdom that he might not be up to the job, that the King was becoming increasingly blind to the needs of his people in the modern global environment. Nor were commentators reassured to learn that King Fahd was resorting to witches and soothsayers in order to stay in power.[85] One soothsayer evidently warned Fahd that he would die unless he viewed the face of one of his sons, the 22-year-old Abdul Aziz, at least once a week. In early 1995 Abdul was appointed a special advisor with ministerial status, a pay rise of £4 million, and exclusive right to the revenue from a million barrels of oil a day (in addition to income from a £70 million endowment and Fahd's bequest to Abdul of some £40 billion). Nor is it only the King who employs soothsayers, though such are supposedly prohibited in Islam. The Saudi princes typically have a witch or wizard in residence, sometimes advising on business matters and sometimes helping favourite football teams by casting spells on their opponents.[86] Individual princes may also expect their soothsayers to advise on the looming issue of the royal succession, another matter that often advertises the uncertainties and instabilities of the Saudi regime.

In August 1995 King Fahd reshuffled his government, moving 15 of his 28 ministers in the biggest shake-up for thirteen years. The new ministers were mostly pro-West technocrats, though Saudi princes continued to hold key ministries in the areas of defence, internal affairs and foreign affairs. At the same time Fahd removed all but one of the presidents of Saudi Arabia's universities, since the 1991 Gulf War a breeding ground for religious dissidents. In responding to academic dissent – in, for example, King Saud University and Imam Muhammed Ibn Saud University – King Fahd was clearly trying to reassert central control. But increasingly it seemed that any such efforts would be more likely to benefit Fahd's successor than Fahd himself. At the end of November 1995 the King entered hospital in Riyadh for (in some reports) an 'ordinary medical check-up' or (in others) treatment for an undisclosed medical condition; Fahd was overweight, a diabetic, and prone to a painful knee condition (in 1994 he underwent gall bladder surgery). In speculation it was widely assumed that the 71-year-old Crown Prince Abdullah, a sufferer from heart disease, would be the most likely successor, though opposition from some of the 6000 Saudi princes had not been ruled out. Part of Abdullah's claim derived from his command of the Saudi Arabian National Guard, an obvious counterweight to the army controlled by the defence minister, the 67-year-old Prince Sultan.

The deteriorating health of King Fahd was soon causing anxiety in Riyadh and in the international oil markets. On 4 December it was confirmed in Washington that Fahd, weakened by a life of chain-smoking and over-eating, had suffered a stroke but was 'doing well'. Increasingly the spotlight swung onto Crown Prince Abdullah, who had already assumed a number of Fahd's royal duties. Observers were noting that Abdullah, though 'a lesser intellect' than Fahd, was 'not overly corrupt'; the fact that he was less pro-West than Fahd was doubtless causing minor agitation among Washington strategists. It was also uncertain that Abdullah supported Fahd's modest reforms or entertained any sympathies with critics of the House of Saud. Said one expert, Abdullah's instinct, faced with dissent, will be 'to break heads'. A harder line on Israel was anticipated, but there was hope also that he had the moral clout to force the profligate Saudi princes 'to tighten their belts in the face of public revulsion at their privileges and greed'.[87]

On 5 December Fahd was reportedly receiving ministers and family relatives in a Dubai hospital – doubtless selected following a soothsayer's prediction that Fahd would die in Riyadh. His return to Jeddah, having apparently recovered, failed to quell the growing belief that Fahd's 13-year reign was effectively at an end and that a new phase in the history of the Saudi dynasty had begun. But the uncertainties remained. A 1992 Royal Decree had emphasised that Fahd was able to choose his successor, that he was entitled to change his mind, and that the successor should be the 'wisest' of the descendants of Ibn Saud. Abdullah had then been named Crown Prince, but now there were intense family meetings to discuss the succession. Here Prince Sultan, Fahd's full brother and one of the 'Sudeiri Seven', was pressing his own claims, doubtless encouraged by Washington in recollection of his pro-US stance during the 1991 Gulf War; Prince Bandar, the Saudi ambassador to Washington (who was helpful in convincing Fahd that the doctored satellite photos of Iraqi troops were genuine), would also have been acceptable to the United States.

Abdullah was said to trust nobody, knowing that significant powers had also been delegated to Sultan: were Fahd and Sultan planning to drop him? At the same time it was known that Abdullah was well prepared to use his command of the 77,000 National Guard to win power; that, being less corrupt than Sultan, he may enjoy greater popular support. Said the Saudi diplomat defector Mohammed al-Khilewi, on the question of the succession: 'The royal family is facing the worst crisis since Fahd came to power in 1982. They face not only the problem of filling the king's seat but also the political and economic disasters left by Fahd.'[88] It is also the case that Sultan and Abdullah are both elderly, and that Saudi Arabia may be facing the sequence of ageing despots that plagued the moribund Soviet Union before running through its last years under Gorbachev.

In the event Abdullah's anxieties were groundless. On 1 January 1996 the official Saudi Press Agency released an excerpt from a letter from King Fahd to Crown Prince Abdullah: '*Because we wish to spend some time resting and recuperating and because of your highness's good character ... we entrust you in this decree to take over management of government affairs while we enjoy rest and recuperation.*'[89] Abdullah has no full brothers but one of his sons is Prince Mutib, a deputy commander of the Saudi National Guard and already establishing his own power base. If the transfer of authority were to become permanent then few changes in policy would be expected; Abdullah's Syrian wife is from the same Alawite minority as Syria's President Hafez Al-Assad, and Abdullah is known for his strong pan-Arab sentiments. Abdullah was said also to be relatively pious, a man who is patient with petitioners, and a keen horseman (founder of the Riyadh Equestrian Club). He is known to have argued against the resort to non-Muslim forces for Saudi defence in 1990/91. It has been remarked that Abdullah never speaks English, uncommon among leading Saudi royals; has long championed the cause of the Palestinians; and is likely to adopt a hawkish posture on oil matters. In one commentary, Abdullah 'could be the man to clean up the family firm … if Prince Abdullah set about lessening the resentment that Saudis feel for their rulers, the West would be wise to back him, quietly'.[90]

On 13 January 1996 King Fahd presided over a cabinet meeting, suggesting that he might be close to taking back the reins of government temporarily ceded to Abdullah. A week later Fahd announced that he was resuming full powers ('I have finished my recuperative period'). The statement did not come as a complete surprise: Fahd had recently been seen on television hosting a reception for princes and officials, and leading prayers at the Grand Mosque at Mecca to mark the end of Ramadan. Some observers were now speculating that Fahd had again taken up the reins to prevent internal chaos within the House of Saud as the various factions struggled for the succession. Now there were signs that the royal family was closing ranks to protect the regime, with Sultan now being prepared to depict Abdullah as Fahd's 'right arm' – 'Those who wish to detect splits in the Saudi royal family will be greatly disappointed.' But Fahd's return to effective power seemed only a temporary solution: soon the question of the succession would have to be addressed again.

In late February there were rumours among Arab diplomats of an unexpected temporary state of alert recently in the Saudi military, with suggestions of mounting conflict between the princes. Fahd himself was now presiding over government business, and little indication was given of possible tensions within the royal family (Fahd: 'Having spent a period of rest and convalescence, God has bestowed on me a cure and good health'). For his part, Abdullah continued to perform a range of royal duties, not least a weekly *Majlis* (open court) to meet Saudis of every class and to examine petitions. Here there was no hint of an incipient royal power struggle, but many commentators in Saudi Arabia and elsewhere were continuing to ask questions about Fahd's health. There were now reports that he had suffered two severe strokes, and many rumours that he was unfit for office. It was known that Prince Salman had all but deserted his post as governor of Riyadh to attend Fahd, and was acting as a filter between the King and the rest of the world. Said one loyalist critic of the regime: 'When I heard that Abdullah had taken over, I was elated, because it showed the royal family could handle a difficult succession … So imagine my pessimism when I heard that the jack-in-the-box had sprung back again.' By June the calls were yet again growing for Fahd to abdicate in favour of Abdullah.

The ailing King was now delaying plans for a recuperative trip abroad as tension again mounted over the question of the succession. Part of the problem was that there was no precedent for abdication in the entire history of modern Saudi Arabia. Would Fahd really want to be remembered as the only Saudi monarch to abandon his full royal duties? One leading Saudi analyst commented: 'A lot of people in the kingdom are saying that King Fahd should this time hand over power permanently and relinquish all claim to the throne, regardless of whether he recovers or not.' Now there were American reports that the King was suffering periods of dementia following his stroke; and that, when lucid, he was resisting pressure to convalesce abroad, knowing that the succession struggle would intensify in his absence. It now seemed that already various minor princes were jostling for the position of Crown Prince, once Abdullah had been appointed the new Saudi King. Again there was the unmistakable feeling that Saudi Arabia was in transition; that the departure of Fahd would not be long delayed; and that, even with no significant shift in policy, a new political atmosphere would engulf Riyadh.

The months dragged by through the period of a *de facto* interregnum. King Fahd, still clearly ailing with no complete recovery in prospect, remained committed to the management of state business. Abdullah continued to perform a growing range of royal duties, with increasing speculation about how he would behave once he was king. In June 1997 Abdullah visited three key Arab capitals, signalling there and to the wider world community that he favoured an active pro-Arab role over the Palestinian issue and other matters; in Cairo, Damascus and Beirut Abdullah indicated that he would support a boycott of a forthcoming conference in Qatar that would be attended by Israel, and that America should be warned about its uncritical support of Israel over the so-called peace process. At the same time Saudi commentators were emphasising that Abdullah's remarks were intended as criticism of Israel rather than its ally, the United States. Again Saudi Arabia was facing the dilemma that had perplexed Riyadh over the decades. How was the Arab nation to be supported when *realpolitik* demanded a pragmatic accommodation with Washington, with all the consequences that flowed from such an imperative?

Perhaps, through 1997, the power struggle in the House of Saud had shifted to the matter of the future Crown Prince under the future King Abdullah. But in the second half of 1997 the question of the succession had still not been resolved. Commentators were speculating on a fresh pro-Arab stance, on the possibility of a new Saudi approach to Iran, and on possible changes in the cabinet and the Consultative Council.[91] But the problems of a grossly expanded dynasty remained largely unaddressed in Riyadh and through the various Saudi provinces. There were no clear routes to the modernisation of an archaic feudal state that increasingly depended upon repression rather than popular support. Abdullah, committed to the protection of the dynasty above all, was poorly equipped from the start for the radical vision needed in the global commercial environment. And Islam, like fervent religion in whatever shape, remained a substantial part of the problem.

CUSTODIAN OF ISLAM?

The King of Saudi Arabia also carries the title of Prime Minister, suggesting a practical role with a strong secular responsibility for the running of a functioning state in the modern world. In addition, the King bears the sacred title of *The Custodian of the Two Holy Mosques*, indicating the unique links between the Saudi royal family and the holy sites of Mecca and Medina. It is in this way – assigning the King a religious role, and stipulating the Koran and the Sunna as the sacred heart of the constitution – that the House of Saud attempts to claim a special status in the Muslim world. Today this ambitious claim is being widely disputed, both within Saudi Arabia and beyond, with competing Islamic groups each urging a particular Koranic exegesis while protesting at the demonstrable hypocrisies and carnalities of the House of Saud.

In an official Saudi publication we learn that 'King Fahd's dedication to his nation is surpassed only by his commitment to Islam.' As The Custodian of the Two Holy Mosques of Mecca and Medina, he has personally supervised a number of plans to facilitate the *hajj* for more than two million pilgrims who visit the holy sites every year: 'This is a great responsibility which we are honoured to bear and we must always be equal to the task.' In 1985 Fahd launched a major scheme to expand the two Holy Mosques to enhance the comfort and safety of the pilgrims: the Holy Mosque at Mecca (Makka) was almost doubled in size and the Prophet's Mosque at Medina (Madinah) was increased tenfold. Fahd has also provided funds for the Al-Aqsa Mosque in Jerusalem, the third holiest site of Islam, and for the Dome of the Rock and Omar Ibn Al-Khattab mosques.[92] Against such manifestations of piety the numerous critics of the House of Saud point to the high-profile venalities of the Saudi princes, the tolerance of infidel military forces on Saudi territory, the non-Islamic resort to soothsayers, Fahd's drinking and gambling, and countless other evident violations of the Koran and Islamic doctrine.

Apologists for Saudi Arabia argue that the Koran, correctly interpreted, is more suitable as a political ideology than any secular constitution. Many non-Saudi Muslims would agree with such a judgement, but would then discuss the crucial issue of *interpretation* and whether the House of Saud was living up to its obligations (see also Chapter 1). (In this there is a surprising text in the Koran itself that is manifestly unhelpful to any Muslim seeking a correct interpretation. Consider Sura 3, Verse 5: '*Some of its [the Koran's] signs are of themselves perspicuous – these are the basis of the Book – and others are figurative ... yet none knoweth its interpretation but God.'* In short, only God knows whether a particular Koranic text is to be taken literally or figuratively. How, in such circumstances, can any human exegete confidently claim that this or that interpretation is the true one?) Saudi Arabia, in trying to implement its own version of Islam, allows no churches, synagogues, temples or shrines of other religions – a circumstance that caused problems for foreign Christians and Jews on Saudi territory during the 1990/91 Gulf crisis.

The unique status of Islam, despite the problems of interpretation, has often been emphasised in the Saudi context. Thus a former Saudi Minister of Pilgrimage and Endowments, Al Sa'yed Hassan Kutbi, commented in 1975 that the text of the Koran had remained unchanged, 'for God has undertaken to safeguard it'. By contrast, other sacred scriptures 'have undergone many influences that have led to discrepancies between their texts as well as division among their followers'. Thus Islam governed by the Holy Koran is not just another religious doctrine; rather it is unique as it 'penetrates into the whole spirit of its adherents through the Holy Koran whether individually or collectively, for it has put together authority in the form of the political state. It has been protected against division between religious affairs and state affairs. Religion has been given the authority for legislation and jurisprudence.'[93] (We need not discuss here the circular argument that bedevils all creeds that rely solely on a sacred text. *How do we know that the text is true? – Because God says so. How do we know that God exists? – Because the text says so.*)

The suggestion that, because God has safeguarded the Koran, there are no divisions among the followers of Islam is abundantly contradicted by events in the real world. On 20 November 1979 more than 40,000 Muslim pilgrims had assembled at the Grand Mosque in Mecca, the largest Islamic shrine on earth and one off limits to all unbelievers. Suddenly armed men appeared, shots were fired, and then a voice over the minaret microphones declared that the Grand Mosque had been seized and that a long-awaited 'Mahdi' had arrived to 'cleanse' Islam. The proclaimed Mahdi and his Sunni fundamentalist supporters then sealed off the Mosque and reiterated their call for a new age of Islam, one untainted by corruption and betrayal of the Prophet's Word. Riyadh was slow to react. Five days later, bolstered by a *ulema* ruling that the use of weapons would be permitted at the holy shrine, some 2000 police, army and National Guard troops stormed the Mosque to crush the rebellion. It took a further nine days for the armed Saudis, guided by French military advisors, to retake the Mosque including its 270 vaults and chambers. Of the 255 fatalities and 560 injured, some 127 Saudi troops were killed and 451 injured.

Then, with Ayatollah Khomeini denouncing 'American imperialism and international Zionism' as responsible for the occupation of the Mosque, anti-American demonstrations, many of them violent, took place in the Philippines, Turkey, Bangladesh, India, the United Arab Emirates, Pakistan, Kuwait and Libya. With the turmoil in Mecca not yet contained, Shi'ite fundamentalists began rioting in Saudi Arabia as a violent accompaniment to the emotional festival of Ashura, involving bloody self-flagellation and nominally outlawed by Riyadh. Saudi troops confronted the fanatical Ashura devotees, with a violent eruption the inevitable consequence. In one account Riyadh rushed a further 20,000 troops to crush rebellions in various parts of the country and to seal off a number of towns on the eastern oil coast.[94] Now, in the face of the growing (Sunni and Shi'ite) fundamentalist threat, there was mounting concern in Riyadh and Washington that Saudi Arabia would go the way of Iran, undermined by fanatical religious groups committed to the overthrow of a self-serving and repressive regime that had lost touch with the people.

There had long been a fundamentalist challenge to the House of Saud: despite the rigours of Wahhabism there were always factions prepared to espouse harsher forms of Islam. In 1969 Sheikh Abdul Aziz al-Baz, the blind rector at the University of Medina and a man keen to disparage infidel pretensions, denounced the American moon landing as a hoax. It was he who became the main influence on the Sunni fundamentalist Juhaiman Saif al-Otaiba, a former member of the National Guard, who was one of the principal architects of the Grand Mosque seizure. In the mid-1970s Juhaiman even outstripped Baz in fervour, urging a return to pure Islam, denunciation of all Western influences, an end to education for women, the abolition of television, the expulsion of all non-Muslims from Saudi territory, and the use of oil revenues for religious purposes rather than personal and state profligacy.[95] He denounced the House of Saud for spending money on palaces and not on Islam: 'If you accept what they say, they will make you rich. Otherwise, they will persecute and even torture you.' In a pamphlet entitled 'Rules of Allegiance and Obedience: The Misconduct of Rulers', Juhaiman declared:

> Our belief is that the continued rule [by the House of Saud] is a destruction of God's religion even if they pretend to uphold Islam. We ask God to relieve us of them all … Anyone with eyesight can see today how they represent religion as a form of humiliation, insult and mockery. These rulers have subjected Muslims to their interests and made religion into a way of acquiring their material interests. They have brought upon the Muslims all evil and corruption.[96]

In 1978 Juhaiman and 98 of his followers were arrested and interrogated; then released six weeks later. After the Grand Mosque seizure there would be no reprieve for the guilty men: 63 Sunni fundamentalists – 41 Saudis (including Juhaiman), 10 Egyptians, 6 South Yemenis, 3 Kuwaitis, one North Yemeni, one Sudanese and one Iraqi – were tried in secret to avoid all publicity, and then dispersed to eight different cities for public beheading. Thousands of Shi'ites in the eastern province were detained, so signalling Riyadh's willingness to combat the excesses of fundamentalism while at the same time cracking down on any perceived violations of Islam: shopkeepers were compelled to close during the five daily prayer periods; newspapers were urged to be more vigilant about provocative photographs; women were denied scholarships for foreign universities; and the Saudi royals redoubled their efforts to bribe tribal elders. Any tentative steps towards cultural liberalisation were thrown into reverse: since in Islam dogs are regarded as 'unclean', dog food was prohibited in supermarkets; dolls, considered idolatrous, were removed from shops; and the *Mutawa* patrolled with a new vigilance.[97]

With the outbreak of the Iran–Iraq War in 1980, in circumstances where Saudi Arabia was quick to show its support for Saddam Hussein, the tensions grew between Riyadh and Tehran. Now the Saudis were increasingly worried about the *hajj*, the sacred pigrimage whereby hundreds of thousands of potentially hostile Muslims had to be allowed into the Kingdom. In 1981 the governor of Mecca pledged an 'iron fist' response to anyone who tried to break the law. It was known that Iran was sending some 75,000 pilgrims to Hejaz, and also funding sympathetic Shi'ites from states other than Iran to make the journey to the holy sites. In Medina there were some protests, with one Iranian Shi'ite reportedly urging his compatriots to 'trigger the long-overdue reawakening of Muslims all over the world'. Some Iranians found carrying subversive pamphlets were banned from the holy sites, one of several incidents that provoked a denunciatory response from Ayatollah Khomeini. In 1981 the Saudis' Palestinian peace plan evoked fury in Tehran: thousands marched to denounce Crown Prince Fahd as 'an enemy of Islam', with the Saudi press responding with condemnation of Khomeini's 'antireligious' posture. Further incidents involving thousands of Iranians in both Mecca and Medina marred the 1982 pilgrimage: fundamentalists holding political rallies were attacked by the Saudi security forces, and many of the pilgrims, some with arms, were injured. Now Riyadh was accusing Hojatoleslam Mohammed Hossein Musawi Khoeiny, Khomeini's personal representative, of instigating the riots. In response to Saudi appeals he reportedly declared: 'Do slogans such as "Death to Israel" and "Death to the US" create disorder? Do such slogans bring discomfort to Muslims? ... We do not intend to violate security, rather we intend to invite Muslims to unite against the US, Israel and the Soviet Union. We are surprised that you opposed this action, as we expect you to lead the way.'[98]

In 1984 some 154,000 Iranian pilgrims visited Mecca and Medina, in the face of Saudi efforts to segregate them from other worshippers. With the Iran–Iraq War far from its end, Iraqi pilgrims carrying posters of Saddam Hussein confronted Iranians in Medina; in the ensuing fighting one Iranian was killed and several were wounded. Tehran was quick to charge that the Saudis had turned a blind eye to the violence, failing to provide the protection that pilgrims should expect. Riyadh responded at once, denying any failure to take prompt action and claiming that many demonstrations had been blocked. It was now clear that the *hajj* necessarily exposed the Saudis to all sorts of problems: as Custodian of the

Holy Mosques, Fahd could never deny other Muslims access to Mecca and Medina or fail to protect the pilgrims; but here was a route for all dissident Muslims and anti-Saudi factions, their right to enter Saudi territory enshrined at the heart of Islam.

One consequence of the Iranian pressure was to encourage the Saudis to maintain at least the appearance of an austere Islam. But the contradictions remained. While the *Mutawa* were encouraged to enforce cultural repression at home, in the name of Muslim virtue, the dissolute princes were happy to drink, gamble and womanise around the world. It was not a contrast set to impress the pious proponents of religious orthodoxy. Saudi Arabia, royal profligacy apart, has been represented as sufficiently austere to deny the fundamentalists a propaganda opportunity; but the inevitable tensions remained and in the early 1990s the fundamentalists were again posing a significant challenge to the House of Saud.

King Fahd's contentious decision to 'invite' American forces into Saudi Arabia in 1990, following his sceptical response to the fake satellite photographs, quickly added fuel to the fundamentalist fires. Why was the infidel being allowed into a Muslim land? Why was the Custodian of the Holy Mosques not prepared to insist on a Muslim solution to a Muslim problem? Was Islam bound to yield to pressure from the Christian West? The flood of non-Muslims into Saudi Arabia in 1990/91 did much to erode the Muslim authority of King Fahd; and, with the war over, the fundamentalist challenge did not abate. In June 1991 it was reported that Saudi Arabia was facing massive unrest among its own puritan element. Wahhabist preachers had been suspended by Fahd's half-brother, stimulating protests in Al Qasim, near Riyadh. Said one Saudi source: 'There is no means of judging its strength, but there is a built-in explosive charge in the increased power of the religious movement, particularly as it has spread to the army.' Twelve years on, the shadow of Juhaiman was still evident.

During the 1991 Gulf War, sermons had been preached against both the infidel West and Saudi domestic abuses. On 18 May 1991 a group of Saudi clerics presented a memorandum to King Fahd demanding not only a move to a full-blooded theocracy but also the necessary corollary, heavy restrictions on the power of the House of Saud. Now the parlous financial situation was stimulating religious dissent, signalling the growing awareness of Saudi economic mismanagement by a profligate royal family. It now seemed plain that the fundamentalists were being aided by the Saudi policy of repression. Said one Saudi liberal: 'If we had real freedom of speech, as opposed to the artificial assembly now planned, the religious minority would be isolated, since the vast majority of Saudis oppose them.'[99] The fundamentalists, by contrast, were claiming that they had the support of a majority of the population. Thus Ali Namleh, a lecturer at the Iman Mohammad bin Saud University, near Riyadh, commented in 1992 that in his estimation 10 per cent of people were happy with Saudi society as it was, 20 to 25 per cent wanted liberal changes, and 65 per cent wanted a shift to a more Islamic state.[100] In the judgement of one specialist observer, this 65 per cent is the result of Riyadh's decision to back the Muslim Brotherhood in the 1960s and to install pro-Brotherhood staff throughout the education system. The upshot was a call for more *sharia* colleges, more religious faculties in the universities, and the subsequent building of the Iman Mohammad bin Saud University, which has spawned further *sharia* colleges in other cities. Many of the graduates, pious and self-important, have emerged as disaffected Islamist agitators, active in the *Mutawa* or, in the 1980s, with the Afghan *mujahiddin*.

Again many of Riyadh's problems in responding to the fundamentalist challenge can be seen to derive from Saudi Arabia's reliance on American protection. Thus the Saudi regime is quite likely to adopt an anti-Arab and anti-Muslim posture when the alternative causes offence to Washington – as when Riyadh banned an Arab Libyan flight carrying *hajj* pilgrims. The Libyans were quick to point out that UN Security Council Resolution 748, imposed to punish Gaddafi, does in fact exclude all humanitarian and religious cases from the air ban. Thus in practice and in law the embargo on Arab Libyan Airlines derived from a Saudi government wanting to placate the Americans rather than from the requirements of Resolution 748. Commented the Arab affairs editor of the Jamahiriya News Agency (JANA) in June 1993:

> We were not shocked as we have become accustomed to such contrary stances on the part of the Saudis. On the one hand, they claim that their responsibility is restricted to the reception of pilgrims arriving from any Islamic country and on the other hand they refuse to receive Libyan airlines transporting pilgrims.
>
> Unfortunately, the Saudi government has embroiled the Holy Shrines in the complexities and intricacies of international affairs. This is a definite contradiction of a statement made by one of its officials to Reuters on June 29th. 'Our duty states that politics is not to be involved with haj', the official claimed.[101]

In 1991 fundamentalist pressure in Saudi Arabia had succeeded in blocking American plans to expand its forces in the aftermath of the Gulf War.[102] Fahd urged Washington to station helicopters in Kuwait or to seize territory inside Iraq: 'The whole thing must not look like a Saudi–American operation.' In June 1992 a statement by Fahd to two million Muslims at Mecca suggested that 'Islam negates all other faiths', implying support for the views of the extremist *Gamaat el-Islamia* in Egypt that Christians should be treated as pagans and not as protected 'People of the Book' (as in the Koran). King Fahd's speech, representing a reinterpretation of basic doctrine, and possible support for a murderous terrorist group, further stimulated debate within the Saudi religious community and beyond. What authority had Fahd, even following Wahhabist doctrine that Christians were beyond redemption, to rewrite Koranic doctrine in such a fashion? Was this yet another sop to the extremists, perhaps to deflect fundamentalist pressure away from the House of Saud? Now it seemed plain that

Wahhabism was serving as a link between the Saudis and the Egyptian *Gamaat* and extremist Algerian factions that condemned Arab governments for supporting the infidel West in the 1991 Gulf War.[103]

Saudi Arabia has continued to fund extremist Muslim groups in various countries, and to use its custodianship of Mecca and Medina as a political weapon (for example, in early 1994 the Saudis hinted that the PLO chairman, Yasser Arafat, might soon be allowed into the Kingdom to perform a pilgrimage – so signalling improved PLO–Saudi relations). Later in 1994, despite massive Saudi precautions, the *hajj* pilgrimage was subject to another disaster: in May about 270 pilgrims were killed in a stampede at Mecca. The pilgrimage had been largely trouble-free, despite the presence of a 60,000-strong Iranian contingent (the Iranians had planned a 'disavowal of pagans' rally but had cancelled it at the last minute). The tragedy had happened in a large cavern where pilgrims were throwing pebbles at three stone pillars (at which Muhammed is said to have thrown rocks) representing the devil. The stampede occurred on the narrow paths leading to the cavern, to which ambulances could not gain speedy access. The official Saudi Press Agency subsequently quoted a Health Ministry official as saying that 829 pilgrims had died during the 1994 *hajj* – an unspecified number during the 'stoning the devil' ritual, and many more through old age and heart ailments. The disastrous stampede did little to enhance the Saudi custodianship of the pilgrimage; once again the Saudis, prepared to spend billions on largely useless armaments, showed themselves incapable of ensuring the safety of Muslim pilgrims fulfilling their spiritual duties. In the traumatic aftermath the Saudis appeared reluctant to convey the truth about what had happened, and no effort was made to inform the countries from which the bulk of the pilgrims came.[104]

The Libyans, denied landing rights in Saudi Arabia because of US pressure, decided to travel to Mecca by camel, if only to demonstrate the arbitrary West-inspired restrictions on the *hajj*. The journey is described in essentially political terms:

> After a long arduous journey we undertook by camel from our country, we arrived today in Mecca to perform the *Hajj*. During our journey, some of our fellow travellers died as a result of the hardship we endured, conditions on the road, and a lack of water and medical treatment. We even travelled by foot for part of the journey in order to perform our religious rites after having been prevented for three years...
>
> When we left Egypt for Jordan, the journey became even more strenuous because of the Israeli occupation of the region of Um Al Rashash (formerly part of Egypt), which the Israelis call 'Eilat' ... The back of the Arab world was broken ... The Israelis continue to occupy this region as part of their joint plans with the Christians to destroy this nation and to prevent it from becoming unified, from developing, establishing its presence and preserving its sovereignty...[105]

The following year, with some softening in the Saudi position, the Libyans made plans to fly from airports in Libya directly to Jeddah, in order to perform the *hajj*. On 1 April 1995 the Libyan Secretary of the General People's Committee for Unity met with the Saudi Chargé d'Affaires to discuss the option of planned flights, despite the attitude of the US-dominated Security Council. By 4 April more than one thousand Libyans had responded to President Gaddafi's call for volunteers to fly to Saudi Arabia for the *hajj*. One would-be pilgrim, Yasser Abdou Rabu, the editor of the Paris-based *Al-Shahr* magazine, cabled Gaddafi: 'I am happy to volunteer to go to the Holy places with the Libyan brothers in defiance of the blockade so that the whole world will know that your call echoes through the Arab homeland and Europe.'[106]

On 19 April the first group of Libyan and non-Libyan Arab pilgrims (150 Muslims in all), having flown from Tripoli International Airport in Libya, landed in Jeddah, doubtless causing some trepidation among Saudis aware of the resentment in Washington at this nominal breach of the US-orchestrated Security Council sanctions. Celebratory rallies were held in the Libyan cities of Tripoli, Benghazi, Mesrata, Sabha, Azawia and Al-Baidaa when the pilgrims arrived in Jeddah; while the Jeddah-based Organisation of Islamic Conference (OIC) issued a statement confirming the right of Libyan-Arab pilgrims to fly directly from Libya to Jeddah.

Several more groups of Libyan and non-Libyan Arab pilgrims flew from Libya to Jeddah on 22 April, using the Egypt Air airline. Three days later, five flights left Tripoli with a total of 1227 pilgrims on board, with 247 Libyans and non-Libyan Arabs flying from Benghazi. On 27 April some 1480 more pilgrims flew out of Tripoli, while preparations were being made for yet more flights. In these fresh circumstances the United States could not refrain from condemning both Libya and Saudi Arabia, though such a response was obviously counterproductive. On 2 May, in an unusually robust statement that received little publicity in the West, the Saudi interior minister, Naif Bin Abdel Aziz, denounced Washington's criticism of Saudi Arabia over the issue. Naif asserted that the American accusations were an interference in the internal affairs of Saudi Arabia, and that the reception of the pilgrims' aircraft was a matter for Saudi alone. It seemed that under calculated pressure from Gaddafi the Saudis had not been prepared to betray their custodianship of the *hajj*.

On 6 May the Emir of Mecca welcomed the Libyan-Arab pilgrims in the Muslim holy land, emphasising that Saudi Arabia had never prevented, and would never prevent, any Muslim from performing his *hajj* duty. Saudi Arabia, he declared, had welcomed the Libyan pilgrims when they had come on camels and it welcomed them when they came by air. Saudi Arabia would not abdicate its decision-making powers with regard to the Holy Places, and they would always be accessible to all Muslims. On 22 May the first batch of Libyan pilgrims flew back to Tripoli, where huge receptions were held in their honour. Thereafter other flights followed. With the co-operation of Egypt and Saudi Arabia the

Libyans and the non-Libyan Arab volunteers had flown out of Libya to perform the *hajj*. An incensed Washington had not dared to take any military action against the religious flights. The episode had as much political as religious significance for Tripoli, Riyadh and Washington. On 19 April 1996 President Gaddafi recalled the successful 'flight of challenge': from now on, for the purposes of the *hajj*, the air embargo would be ignored. Libyans would fly through the Egyptian, Sudanese and Saudi skies to perform their religious duties.

In April 1997 the *hajj* suffered a further disaster. At least 217 Muslim pilgrims were killed and 1290 injured when a fire swept through 70,000 tents near Mecca. Most of the dead were Indians, Pakistanis and Bangladeshis, with hundreds of thousands of pilgrims stranded on the plains of Mina. Yet again the Saudi government had been embarrassed at its seeming inability to fulfil its self-proclaimed custodianship duties. The fundamentalist Omar Bakri Mohammed, leader of the extremist al-Muhajiroun group, commented: 'This is yet more proof that the House of Saud is incompetent in its task. Just compare the money spent on the *hajj* with the money that these princes spend on belly dancers in the nightclubs of Egypt.'[107] Afzal Amanullah, the Indian Consul-General, said in Jeddah that the Indian victims of the fire could have escaped if their Saudi guides had not insisted on locking them in their compounds. At the final count, aid workers and diplomats were estimating that at least 500 pilgrims had died. This was not all: three other fires were reported at the 1997 *hajj*.

It seemed that the House of Saud was unable to manage even the matters that it constantly claimed were closest to its heart. The *hajj* disasters over the years had come to represent a potent symbol of Saudi failure, the plight of an archaic and repressive regime unable either to adjust to the demands of the modern age or to accommodate what many Muslim observers regard as the essential elements of true Islam. It is useful to glance at the character of the dissident response.

THE DISSIDENT REVOLT

It is easy to find non-Saudi critics of Saudi Arabia: many people throughout the world are unsympathetic to hand choppings, royal profligacy, the abuse of women, and grotesque hypocrisy. But it is possible also to find a growing number of Saudi critics of the House of Saud, whether such critics are boldly voicing their dissent within the Kingdom or from the confines of the Saudi diaspora of exiles and defectors around the world. And in addition to verbal protest a campaign of violence is being waged against the regime from within the country (see below). We may debate the extent to which there is overlap between the worlds of verbal dissent and violent protest.

Of the many exiled Saudi dissidents few are more active than the human-rights worker Mohammed Siddiq. Born in Medina, he was educated in economics and government in the United States, before working for sixteen years in Saudi government service. He has produced books, articles and a stream of letters with the aim of exposing 'the degree of inequality and the gap of injustice in the current Saudi governmental system and to help establish a new system with at least the beginnings of democracy'. In a Preface (addressed to a Saudi prince) to one of his books Siddiq appeals to both the demands of justice and the imperatives of self-interest: 'It is urgent that you speak strongly against the injustices and inequalities of your system, and act, in union with your brother-citizens, to create a fair and equitable system. You know what happened to Nicolae Ceausescu and his family.'[108] This appeal, like many from the dissident Saudi community, derives essentially from an Islamic perspective ('You know, too, that ISLAM urges you to treat Muslims with equality, dignity, and respect').

Activists such as Siddiq recognise that the Saudi problem is part of a wider predicament in the Arab world: 'Today's Arab leaders are either self-elected or inheritors of old regimes. Some Arab governments did not bother to write a constitution. The Koran is said to be the constitution ... There is no reason whatever to heed the demands of 21 Arab leaders who can't stomach the idea that the Arab world cannot become a democracy.' And again it is necessary to confront the baleful role of the West, well prepared to support oppression in Arab lands; and to address such issues as women's rights and racial exclusion.[109] It would be impossible for such ideas to circulate freely in Saudi Arabia, where public debate is massively curtailed and censorship the norm. Thus a typical *Confidential Telex Statement* (4 March 1991) sent from a provincial governor's office 'To All The Major Public & Secret Police, And Religious Offices In The Province' urges a ban on the religious scholar Salman Bin Fahd Al-Aouda: he had been 'going out of the confines of giving public advice and guidance in many of his speeches, and addressing many matters that do not concern him'; so 'do take the proper measures to ban him from giving any religious sermon or lecture ...'.

The Saudi opposition leader, Tawfiq al-Shaikh, noting Fahd's 1992 plans for the new Consultative Council, declared: 'I don't think it will protect individual liberty because there is no system to protect people. No free press, no parliament, no independent judiciary.' Shaikh, who had been forced to flee Saudi Arabia in 1986, pointed out that none of the proposed reforms allowed people even to set up a magazine of their own. His Committee for the Defence of Human Rights in Saudi Arabia would continue to press for democratic reform; but in 1992 the best that could be said was that the House of Saud was being forced to recognise that an element of political change was necessary.[110] In the same vein Mohammed Siddiq commented that the reforms were 'minimal but significant because they are being made at all'; but in reality they were 'not reforms at all but codification of the existing structure ... a case of King Fahd placating his critics and assuaging his supporters at the same time, giving with one hand and taking back with the other':

It is to be hoped that the reforms blow up in the royal family's face by becoming the real beginning of democratic action, and there is a potential for this in spite of the weakness of the provisions and the desire on the part of King Fahd to protect his own rights above all else. The reforms do increase participation in the political process and could bring new voices into the political arena ... Fahd has sown the wind, and Fahd shall reap the whirlwind.[111]

In September 1992 a group of more than a hundred Islamic scholars and university professors petitioned King Fahd to introduce political change. The 45-page *nasiha* (memorandum) covered most areas of the country's political life, including foreign relations, monetary policies, social services, and the current oil production rates. The petition demanded that Saudi Arabia end its special relationship with the United States, put more emphasis on relations with Muslim countries, and stop supplying aid to those governments which oppose the more revolutionary Islamic movements in the Arab world. In addition, the royal family was criticised, with accusations of corruption in the handling of state finances; an annual audit of government expenditure to check 'embezzlement and corruption' was demanded.[112] In response the Supreme Ulema Council, the official body of Muslim clergymen, accused the petitioners of sedition and 'serving the interests of the enemies' of Saudi Arabia. A Saudi commentator close to the petitioners (who included fundamentalist Salafis, members of the Muslim Brotherhood, and Wahhabist scholars) declared: 'The wheel is beginning to turn after 60 years. Even the liberals are now admitting that the Islamic movements are setting the pace for reform in our country.'

The petition was the fourth of its kind submitted to King Fahd by 1993, signalling the widespread concern and disaffection throughout the Kingdom. Fahd himself showed no willingness to respond to any of the demands. In December 1992 he dismissed half the members of the Council of Senior Ulema, the highest religious body, because of discernible support among the *ulema* for aspects of the latest petition. Fahd announced that seven members of the Council were clearly too ill to perform their duties, and that they would be replaced by seventeen clerics who could be trusted. To most observers Fahd's response was predictable. The petitioners had blamed the government for the 'total chaos of the economy and society, administrative corruption, widespread bribery, favouritism and the extreme feebleness of the courts'; they had also denounced the lack of political freedoms and 'torture by security and police'. The government had attempted to block the circulation of the petition, whereupon the authors had sent it through the mail and had copies printed in the foreign Arab press.[113]

It was now plain that substantial areas of dissent existed within the Kingdom – among religious minorities, the 'approved' *ulema*, and the general public. Riyadh, as usual, was reacting with denial, censorship and other forms of repression. In September 1994 a further round-up of Saudi dissidents provided more evidence that the legitimacy of the regime was continuing to erode following the reverberations of the 1991 Gulf War: 'Nor is an erosion of legitimacy the only weakness exposed by these developments. The country's financial institutions are suffering;

the bureaucracy is corrupt.'[114] Among the 110 dissident clerics arrested were Safar al-Hawali and Salman al-Aouda, well known in the Muslim world. At first Prince Naif, Minister of the Interior, denied that the arrests had taken place, he then admitted them and claimed that the dissidents were backed by Iran. In fact many of the disaffected protesters were young men keen to participate in Saudi affairs but restricted by their non-membership of the Saud clan. Instead of nepotism and tribal connection, the so-called 'oil generation' is advocating education and Islam as routes to real advancement. Mamoun Fandy, a US-based academic, comments: 'The best choice for preserving order in Saudi Arabia is a systematic overhaul that begins to establish power sharing and responsibility sharing between all the social groups ... the Saudi government does not seem to have considered this option. It has chosen repression instead.'[115]

Now at least one former Saudi minister was beginning to pose a significant threat to the regime. Sheikh Yamani, the former oil minister sacked by King Fahd in 1986, was returning to prominence in late 1994, attracting disaffected religious leaders and concerned members of the business elite. Yamani, without joining any organised opposition faction, was gathering around him prominent critics of the royal family. He was now holding *diwaniyahs* (meetings) in Jeddah, under surveillance by the Saudi secret police, which in turn led to further acts of repression by the authorities: two Yamani associates at the meetings, the journalist Mohamed Salahadeen and the businessman Mohamed Tayeb, were arrested and jailed. In addition, Yamani was issuing reports from his London-based Centre for Global Energy Studies, contradicting the official Saudi line on energy policy and other matters.[116] By now the House of Saud was facing growing opposition on many fronts: for example, from Yamani, with support from the Hejaz-based Sunni Muslims; from the eastern Shi'ites; from various liberal factions; and from the London-based Wahhabist Committee for the Defence of Legitimate Rights (CDLR).

By early 1995 the prisons were swelling as the Saudi authorities cracked down on any public manifestations of dissent. In Riyadh a businessman was quoted: 'There are now more than 400 political prisoners, most of them being held for nothing at all. They are held in solitary confinement. They are given their food and water through a hole in the door. Really, it is like Siberia.'[117] At the same time the mounting repression was not stopping public protest: some 10,000 demonstrators were reported to have gathered outside the Buraida mosque when Salman Aouda was arrested in September 1994 (130 people were rounded up and taken into custody, with around two dozen remaining in detention; Islamic activists told of police knocking on their doors and taking them away). In March 1995 various militant Muslim groups made an unprecedented call for co-ordinated demonstrations in Riyadh, Jeddah and Hail, to coincide with the visit of US Defense Secretary William Perry to the Gulf region. In London a CDLR spokesman was urging Muslims to hold a vigil at mosques in the cities 'just to read the Koran and to show their anger'. Saudi law does not permit freedom of assembly but the activists judged that the authorities might be reluctant to inter-vene within mosque precincts. On 19 May Mohammed Siddiq wrote to the US Vice President Albert Gore, complaining about the lack of free speech in Saudi Arabia, the scale of repression, Saudi propaganda lies, and the extent to which King Fahd and his brothers had looted the country: 'Sir, my mood turns instantly grim every time I see you shaking hands with King Fahd, who during the past 30 years has committed outrages including arbitrary executions, torture, kidnapping, and jailed hundreds of Saudis who disagreed with his policies.' After his meeting with King Fahd on 22 March, Vice President Gore said the discussions had been excellent ('We concentrated on the concrete and deep-rooted ties between the United States and the Kingdom of Saudi Arabia').

On 10 September 1994 hundreds of cars had escorted Sheikh Salman Aouda as he returned to Riyadh, in order to prevent his arrest or 'disappearance'. The following day, the security police surrounded his house in force, but Aouda's massed followers prevented them from taking action. The governor then demanded – in vain – that Aouda renounce his activities and cease his campaign against the regime. On 13 September the 30-year-old sheikh addressed a crowd outside the mosque and recited a poem, 'They Have Forbidden Speech', written by Abdullah Hamid al-Hamid, an assistant lecturer at the University of Riyadh:

They forbid writing and speech.
Shut up! And injustice remains.
If the tongue is mute, it will burn in the fire like a butterfly.
Because opinions become rubbish hidden and thrown in the trash.
The word became a crime. Beware the instigator of discussion.[118]

At dawn the next day, Aouda and many of his supporters were arrested, stimulat-ing further demonstrations in Riyadh and elsewhere. Two years after the 'uprising at Buraida', Aouda was still in jail. By 1997 it was becoming increasingly plain that a policy of repression could not contain the growing level of dissent. Thus one study concluded: '... the points of active dissent are multiplying. The minor-ity Shia have recently renewed their active opposition to the royal family, while a renegade businessman, Osama bin Laden, has called for a *jihad* (holy war) to flush US troops from the country.'[119] At the same time the capacity of the opposi-tion to wage a sustained campaign was 'questionable', not least because of the divisions in the movement.

The Saudi authorities were also finding it necessary to clamp down on the aca-demic community. In early May 1993 Mohammed al-Masari, a physics professor at a Riyadh university, had founded the Committee for the Defence of Legitimate Rights (CDLR), an organisation that was immediately pronounced illegal by the Supreme Council of Ulema. Liberals too were opposed to the Committee, arguing that it was no more than a moderate mask for ambitious clerics and radical preachers. On 15 May police raided the campus and arrested Masari and some of his followers, releasing him after seven months, during which time he was frequently tortured. In April 1994 he arrived in Britain seeking political asylum and calling for elections in Saudi Arabia, an end to royal corruption and an end to the Kingdom's close relationship with the United States. Without reform, he declared, the dissidents could lose patience: 'There are 10,000 Saudi veterans of the Afghan war and they are all armed to the teeth. At the moment, the religious scholars are persuading them to remain patient and work quietly for reform. But they are getting more and more frustrated. We don't want violence or a situation like Egypt, which is a mess. But the fuse is burning through. The dissident demands were not excessive: 'We want the right to elect our government, to have a free press and hold meetings, and habeas corpus.' Soon it was being reported that the Saudi authorities were taking action against Masari's family in Riyadh.[120] Now Masari's CDLR and Osama bin Laden's Advisory and Reformation Committee, both ensconced in London, were waging a vigorous propaganda war against the Saudi regime: one estimate suggested that both groups were each sending up to 1000 faxes a day to the Kingdom, these in turn being copied and passed on, to publicise their dissident views. The CDLR denies charges that its members are ultra-religious zealots, insisting that the aim is open, representative government accountable to the people. There would be strict application of *sharia* law, but efforts would be made to uphold the independence of the judiciary from the executive. A purer form of Islam would usher in an end to corruption, petty tribal customs, and the Western exploitation of Saudi oil resources.[121]

The arrival of Masari demanding political asylum was problematic for a British government with a nominal commitment to human rights but keen also to protect its lucrative Saudi connection. Masari knew where he stood: *'The House of Saud are like dinosaurs. They should die out. The government is the monarchy, is the state, is the family, is the mafia.'* This was less than comforting to nervous Tory ministers well prepared to massage away the asylum commitment in the interest of useful foreign tyrannies. Masari was now aligning himself with two Buraida clerics (Salman bin Fahd al-Aouda and Safar Abdul Rahman al-Hawali) detained since September 1994, with another 300 or so political prisoners arrested for protesting against the clerics' incarceration. But not all Saudi opposition observers were prepared to take Masari at face value. Said one academic: 'The sheikhs are just a façade.' Said another: 'We admire his courage but he is not for human rights. His constituency here wouldn't accept that. Neither is his Islamic clothing real.? An Islamic moderate was prepared to admit: '... the sentiment is growing that the government is no longer the glue holding the country together, but the problem ... A modern country should realise it is natural to have reformers and sensible to let them express themselves in an organised way.'[122]

It was not long before the British government laid plans for the expulsion of Masari, not to Saudi Arabia – that would have been too blatantly supine, even for a Tory administration – but to a third country. Already the Home Office had informed him that his asylum application was invalid because he had spent a month in Yemen before arriving in London (Yemen was quick to assert that it would not welcome any opposition figure from 'sisterly countries'). By now the Saudi royal family, in the figure of Prince Naif, Minister of the Interior and one of Fahd's brothers, was declaring that Masari's activities in London could call into question the 'deep political and economic relationship' between Britain and Saudi Arabia. In May 1995 Masari addressed a day-long conference at the House of Commons, arranged by the Labour MP George Galloway, where Masari was introduced as the 'Leader of the Saudi Opposition'. Said Masari, with characteristic confidence: 'My presence in Britain may be publicly embarrassing, but secretly I think the government does not mind having someone here who may be influential in the future. They can build bridges to me.' The judgement seemed unduly optimistic. In October the government was charged with sabotaging a press conference at which Masari was scheduled to speak on Saudi human-rights abuses: suddenly a room booked at the Foreign Press Association (FPA), whose lease is paid by the Foreign Office, had become unavailable; and now there were signs that the Saudis were prepared to block multi-billion-pound armaments deals as a way of punishing the British government.[123]

A deeply alarmed British cabinet quickly made arrangements for Masari to be expelled to the tiny Caribbean island of Dominica. If an appeal against the decision failed, he would be placed on an aircraft for deportation on 19 January 1996. It was enough to provoke George Galloway into denouncing this 'sordid act of obeisance to the arms dealers in Britain and the dictators in Riyadh'. Then it emerged that Britain's biggest arms companies had secretly collaborated with ministers, Whitehall officials and the CIA to find a way of 'stifling' Masari.[124] And there were other plots afoot. On 6 January Masari revealed at a press conference that he had reason to believe that the Saudi government was planning to kill him in London; a colleague of Masari, Abdalla al-Hudhaif, had already been beheaded in Riyadh, partly because of his known CDLR connections. Tory MPs were now backing virulent propaganda attacks on Masari being launched by the pro-Saudi Gulf Centre for Strategic Studies. At a seminar organised by the Centre the Tory Lady Olga Maitland was happy to praise the Middle East's hereditary rulers, declaring that they represented 'stability, tradition and legitimacy'.

In the event, Masari's court appeal against deportation was successful. Lawyers at the Joint Council for the Welfare of Immigrants (JCWI) produced a dozen grounds for challenging the legality of the deportation notice. The Council's director, Claude Moraes commented: 'The government is making a mockery of the law and Britain's international treaty obligations.' And he suggested that Dominica might have been chosen because it had not signed UN conventions on torture and extradition. Prince Sultan declared that Britain had a 'viper in its bosom'; but now Britain would have to live with it – Masari was to be allowed to stay in Britain for two years, despite all the government's efforts to have him deported. Babcock International complained that the Masari affair had lost the company £200 million worth of Saudi orders; and Vickers, having plotted to silence Masari, was now uncertain about the future of Saudi orders.

Masari's problems were far from over: he was almost prosecuted for urging the killing of Jews in Palestine;[125] he was accused of condoning the Dhahran bombing (see below);[126] he faced schism within the CDLR, with Sa'ad al-Faqih breaking away in March 1996 to form the Islamic Reform Movement; and in 1997 he was facing mounting financial problems.[127] In late 1996 the Tory government failed to secure the passage of a new dissident bill designed to tackle the problem of Masari-type asylum seekers. And in the run-up to the 1997 British general election the Al-Muhajiroun Islamic group, headed by Sheikh Omar Bakri Muhammed, a close associate of Masari, urged Britain's two million Muslims not to vote – on the ground that it was against the teaching of Allah for Muslims to participate in the election of any government not committed to Islam.

While Masari was beginning his struggle for asylum in Britain in April 1994, the Saudis were stripping the wealthy Osama bin Laden of citizenship 'because of his irresponsible behaviour that contradicts the interests of Saudi Arabia and harms sisterly countries'. His assets in Saudi Arabia were frozen, though he was believed to have substantial funds in foreign bank accounts. Osama bin Laden had spent much of the previous two years in Khartoum where he provided financial backing for the leading fundamentalist Hassan Turabi. Bin Laden was reputed to have placed his wealth at the disposal of many Islamic causes around the world. In June 1996 Bin Laden had reportedly left Sudan in his private jet, accompanied by several wives and children and twenty of his militant supporters. His destination was unknown but various Arabic-language newspapers were reporting sightings of him in London, Ethiopia, Somalia and Afghanistan. Said one US intelligence officer in Washington: 'There isn't one Western government who wouldn't like to talk to Osama.'

In July 1996 Bin Laden, 'the fiercest opponent of the Saudi regime and of America's presence in the Gulf', was tracked down in Afghanistan.[128] In interview he insisted that the killing of the American troops in Dhahran (see below) demonstrated the depth of hatred for the Americans in Saudi Arabia: 'Not long ago, I gave advice to the Americans to withdraw their troops from Saudi Arabia. Now let us give some advice to the governments of Britain and France to take the troops out – because what happened in Riyadh and Khobar [Dhahran] showed that the people who did this have a deep understanding in choosing their targets. They hit their main enemy which is the Americans. They killed no secondary enemies, nor their brothers in the army or the police of Saudi Arabia ... I give this advice to the government of Britain.'[129] He blamed the Saudi government for promising *sharia* laws while allowing the Westernisation of Saudi Arabia and the exploitation of the economy, for supporting Saddam Hussein in the Iran–Iraq War (to the tune of $25 billion) and for supporting the West in the 1991 Gulf War (to the tune of $60 billion), and for buying useless military equipment while creating unemployment, high taxes and a bankrupt economy. In September 1996, to the dismay of many of his supporters, Bin Laden was calling for a *jihad* against the United States in Saudi Arabia: '... pushing out this American occupying army is the most important duty after the duty of belief in God'.[130]

In November Bin Laden suggested that he might consider moving his base from Afghanistan to Yemen, whatever the views of the Yemeni government ('I would rather die than live in a European state. I have to live in a Muslim country ...'). Yemeni officials in London declared that if Bin Laden arrived he would be deported ('We are in the business of improving our relations with Saudi Arabia'). In an interview with the London-based *Al-Quds al-Arabi* newspaper Bin Laden reportedly claimed that Riyadh had offered to allow him back into Saudi Arabia, provided that he announced that King Fahd was a good Muslim; he refused ('... the regime has ... made itself a law-giver and co-legislator with God, which has been recognised by religious scholars as idolatry').[131]

In June 1994 another wealthy Saudi, Mohammed al-Khilewi, a high-flyer in the Saudi bureaucracy, broke ranks to denounce the royal family as being corrupt and oppressive. To support his charges, and to justify his demands in New York for political asylum, he brandished some of many documents he had secretly gathered with the help of other dissident Saudi officials. Soon he was claiming a kidnapping attempt against him, offers of millions of dollars to stifle his criticism, and veiled death threats.[132] On 17 May 1994 he sent a letter of protest to Crown Prince Abdullah, and also made a copy available to the CDLR. His demands, supported with copious cables and other documents, are familiar: an end to sectarian divisions among the Saudi people, the fair distribution of wealth and power, political freedom, the release of political prisoners, and just treatment for women. Prince Bandar, the Saudi ambassador to Washington, offered to meet Khilewi; he refused fearing a kidnapping attempt. Then Prince Salman, governor of Riyadh, despatched members of Khilewi's family to New York, instructing them not to return without him: 'Tell your relative we can get him in the United States, we can get him even if he goes to the moon'.[133]

Then Khilewi went underground, fearing Saudi reprisals. He claimed that the documents prove that Saudi government officials transferred funds and bomb-making details to the militant Islamic group Hamas, and that the Saudi embassy arranged wiretaps on Jewish organisations in the United States.[134] Now there was every sign that Washington faced deep embarrassment. If Saudi sponsorship of terrorism were to be proven in a public forum, as opposed to any covert US–Saudi deals, it seemed that the United States – always strong on rhetoric about Arab terrorism – would have to take some action. But sanctions against Saudi Arabia? In August 1994 Mohammed al-Khilewi, already mentioned in connection with revelations about Saudi nuclear activities (see p. 254), was granted political asylum in the United States: 'My plan is to fight for the right to live under a democratic system.' In July the FBI had warned of a plot to kidnap Khilewi and return him to Riyadh.

At the same time as Khilewi's defection, another Saudi diplomat, Ahmed Zakrany, the Vice-Consul at the Saudi-Arabian consulate-general in Houston, applied for political asylum in Britain. Now yet another comfortable Saudi official was declaring that he could no longer tolerate human-rights abuses in Saudi Arabia. Needless to say, this served as further embarrassment to Britain, rarely preoccupied with human-rights concerns but always committed to the protection of lucrative commercial accommodations. At the beginning of October 1994 Zakrany began a hunger strike in London, protesting at the refusal of the British government to grant him political asylum. Already he had been summoned to return to Riyadh to assist in 'correcting' a book he had published about Saudi foreign policy. Now he feared that he faced jail or 'disappearance' on his arrival. Yet another Saudi academic now found it impossible to live in the country of his birth.

Most of the dissidents mentioned above – with the notable exception of Osama bin Laden – have been committed to peaceful political change, though some are clearly not pacifists and would support a resort to *jihad* and *coup d'état* in appropriate circumstances (in this they do not differ from the vast majority in any national population). But some activists have already resorted to force in an attempt to destabilise the Saudi state and to expel the Western infidel from Saudi territory. In the closed society of Saudi Arabia, today marginally exposed by trade and in the aftermath of the 1991 Gulf War, many incidents of dissident violence go unreported in the Saudi or Western media. Some, because of their magnitude and their involvement of foreign personnel, have been too graphic to disguise from the eyes of the world. They signify a turbulent political atmosphere, the gathering clouds of instability and dissolution ...

THE VIOLENT OPTION

Saudi Arabia, like most states, was born in violence. Unlike most states, its constitution – the Koran – enshrines and celebrates violence: for example, against thieves, infidels and apostates. The sword of Ibn Saud is revered in tradition; just as a sword, accompanied by a pious accolade, is carried on the national flag. Throughout its history the House of Saud has striven to consolidate its power and ensure its survival by the use of force: against competing clans, religious minorities and political reformers. This approach to the use of secular and religious power has been underwritten by the West, principally the United States, over some decades; partly because the House of Saud has been seen as a bulwark against the radical politics of communism and Arab nationalism, but primarily to safeguard the exploitation of Saudi Arabia as a source of cheap energy and a commercial milch-cow. In response to this programme of US-supported violence and state security, Saudi political and religious radicals have been encouraged to resort to force as the only practical engine of change in the Kingdom. Non-Saudi radicals, committed to alternative versions of Islam or to the unification and political independence of the Arab nation, have been well prepared to adopt the violent option.

Soon after the creation of Israel in 1948, radical Palestinians began campaigning to retake what they considered to be Arab land under illegal occupation. For example, the Palestinian George Habash, a member of the American University of Beirut (AUB) soon after the Second World War, commented in interview on the Jewish occupation of Arab land and homes:

> ... I have seen with my own eyes the Israeli army entering the town [Lydda, where Habash was born and was a student] and killing its inhabitants. I am not exaggerating ... They have killed our people and expelled us from our homes, towns and land. On the way from Lydda to Ramalla I have seen children, young men and old people dying. What can you do after you have seen all this? You cannot but become a revolutionary and fight for the cause. Your own cause as well as that of your own people.[135]

In 1950 Habash was elected president of *al-Urwa*, a mouthpiece for Arab aspirations, before 1958 known as the Arab Nationalist Youth and thereafter as the Arab Nationalists' Movement (*Harakat al-Qawmiyyin al-Arab*). Before leaving Beirut towards the end of 1952 Ahmad al-Khatib, one of the Movement's main activists, resolved to found new radical groups in Saudi Arabia and elsewhere in the Gulf area. Most of his initiatives came to nothing. In Bahrain his attempts to form underground groups were suppressed by the authorities in 1959, 1963 and 1965; while a 1962 AUB attempt to establish a radical group in Saudi Arabia soon collapsed.

A conference of the Movement (Kuwait, 1962) resolved that because of Saudi Arabia's unique status in the Arabian peninsula emphasis should be given to the Kingdom as a focus for radical politics. Key Movement figures were then despatched from Kuwait, Bahrain and Qatar to establish a new branch in Saudi Arabia. A small group was subsequently formed in Dhahran but it quickly faced the same problems that had defeated the earlier initiatives. Then a number of politicised Saudi students, members of the Movement in Beirut, established a radical group in Riyadh and built up ties with the Dhahran organisation. At a joint meeting (Beirut, 21–2 January 1966) a number of decisions were adopted:

1   To prepare studies on the social, economic and political situation in Saudi Arabia;
2   To combine the two groups in Saudi Arabia under a joint leadership;
3   To secure permanent contact with the centre of the Movement through Kuwait;
4   To hold an annual conference for the region;
5   To recruit Saudi students in Cairo, Beirut, Damascus and Baghdad.[136]

Saudi students were subsequently recruited into the ranks of the Movement, but until 1968 the Movement's branch in Saudi Arabia remained under the control of the Regional Command of Kuwait. Then it was decided that a separate Political Bureau should be established in Saudi Arabia, which would subsequently meet with the Movement's leadership for the rest of the Gulf region to form a Central Committee.

All these plans and initiatives came to very little. The revolutionary activities in South Yemen were more successful: the armed uprising that began in late 1963 resulted in the triumph of Qahtan al-Shabi when the final withdrawal of the British on 30 November 1967 caused an immediate collapse of the archaic regimes in the area. The situation in South Yemen had exposed the competing interests of Britain and Saudi Arabia; but, as was to happen repeatedly in the decades that followed, the House of Saud was able to survive bouts of domestic agitation and the revolutionary turmoil on the borders of the Kingdom.

The role of Saudi Arabia as a pro-West obstacle to Arab-nationalist ambitions continued to attract the attention of both Saudi and non-Saudi political radicals. One route to the possible destabilising of the House of Saudi was to strike at Saudi targets outside the Kingdom. Thus one Palestinian activist, code-named Hussein Jorde Abdallah, has related his activities in Abu Nidal's terrorist organisation.[137] In September 1988 Jorde was preparing to confront the Saudi presence in Bangkok. He had been instructed to learn the language and to compile a report and photographic record of the diplomatic staff of the Saudi embassy. Jorde assumed that Abu Nidal probably intended to mount an assassination against a Saudi target.[138] Abu Nidal had launched an assault on the Saudi embassy in Paris in September 1973 and would have mounted further attacks against Saudi interests had his state sponsors, Iraq (1970s) and Syria (1980s), allowed such actions. A possible accommodation between the Saudis and Abu Nidal, that would probably have entailed characteristic royal bribes to protect the House of Saud, was aborted when Washington pressured Riyadh to end the tentative relationship.

On 25 October 1988 the second secretary at the Saudi embassy in Ankara was shot dead, presumably according to Abu Nidal's orders. On 27 December the Saudi vice-consul in Karachi, Hasan al-Amri, was assassinated. On 4 January 1989, with Jorde now seemingly ignored by the Abu Nidal organisation, the third secretary at the Saudi embassy in Bangkok, tracked and photographed by Jorde, was shot. Jorde was arrested as an Arab but, in the absence of incriminating evidence, soon released. At a time when the Abu Nidal organisation was torn by schism Jorde's predicament in Thailand was simply ignored. Abu Nidal had demonstrated the vulnerability of Saudi interests, at least of the 'soft' targets that could be relatively easily attacked. And he had also shown that terrorist successes could bring substantial rewards: it is estimated that blackmail of the Saudis and the other Gulf rulers had brought him around $50 million between 1976 and 1988, despite any efforts that the Americans might have made to block such deals.[139] But it has always been the possibility of terrorist attacks *within* the

Kingdom that has caused the House of Saud most concern: the mounting opportunities and incentives for domestic violence, and the possibility of infiltration of hostile foreign elements through normal day-to-day travel or the mechanism of the *hajj*.[140]

Where the Saudis are unable to eliminate a terrorist threat they are happy to offer bribes, as with Abu Nidal. Thus the fundamentalist Muslim Sheikh Fadlallah, leader of the Party of God, Hizbollah, was known to be involved in attacks on American targets in Beirut in the 1980s and to be posing a threat to Saudi interests. On 8 March 1985 a car bomb in Beirut, orchestrated by an Englishman appointed by the Saudis, failed to assassinate Fadlallah, though killing eighty people and wounding two hundred. An 'after-action' deception had been organised to distance the Saudis and the Americans from the clear assassination attempt. Fadlallah escaped without injury and his Hizbollah followers hung a massive 'MADE IN USA' banner in front of a building that had been blown out by the bomb.[141] Now it was time for the Saudis to try bribery. Fadlallah was approached and offered $2 million cash to act as a Saudi early-warning system for terrorist attacks on Saudi and American targets. He was happy to oblige though insisting that the payment be in food, medicine and education expenses – to impress his followers. Said Prince Bandar, the Saudi ambassador to Washington: 'It was easier to bribe him than to kill him.'[142] It was also cheaper: the Saudis had spent $3 million on the Beirut car bomb that had killed eighty innocent people.

It was still impossible for the Saudis to buy off *all* threats to their interests. In March 1997 Osama bin Laden warned that there would be further attacks on targets within the Kingdom as a way of driving the Americans out of Saudi Arabia. In January letter bombs were sent to the Saudi-owned *Al-Hayat* newspaper at its offices in Riyadh, London, New York and elsewhere.[143] Said editor Jihad Khazen: 'We have been criticising extremism in the Arab world for the last eight years. I hope and pray there will be no more attacks. We will not change. We will maintain our moderate position on Arab and international affairs.' There was no discussion of the possible relevance of the fact that *Al-Hayat* is owned by Prince Khaled Bin Sultan, the senior Saudi commander during the 1991 Gulf War and one of the principal Saudi leaders responsible for the close US–Saudi relationship.

On 13 November 1995 a bomb explosion in Riyadh destroyed a building housing Saudi and American military personnel, killing at least six people and wounding sixty. The blast set off a fire that engulfed the modern, three-storey building, a training facility for the Saudi National Guard; cars were damaged and windows blown out in nearby buildings. Of the casualties, there were four US fatalities and thirty-four American wounded. Kenneth Bacon, a US Defense Department spokesman in Washington, said that a preliminary report indicated that two explosions had taken place about five minutes apart; and President Clinton pledged that 'an enormous effort' would be devoted to finding out who was responsible. King Fahd convened an emergency cabinet meeting which, according to the Saudi Press Agency, 'expressed its condemnation of this criminal act, which is foreign to our society, beliefs and religion'. At least two groups – the *Islamic Change Movement* and *Tigers of the Gulf* – claimed responsibility for what Clinton dubbed 'this cowardly act', though US officials said that they had no confirmation that either was involved.

Now politicians and journalists were asking how such a catastrophe could have been allowed to happen. Why had the $5.6 billion scheme to modernise the National Guard not been better protected? Said Nicholas Burns of the US State Department: 'Certainly part of the investigation that the United States government has now launched will encompass a lot of questions about what security measures were in place and what security measures should now be put in place.' Reports suggested that security was being intensified at various other US installations, but not in a visible manner. Burns, speaking to reporters, emphasised that the outrage would not deter the United States from continuing with its plans to maintain a large number of US troops in Saudi Arabia and elsewhere in the Middle East. Few observers expected the bombing attack to encourage political reform in the Kingdom. *The New York Times*, noting 'Tremors in Saudi Arabia', commented:

> The attack is a reminder of the inherent vulnerability of the American position in Saudi Arabia ... the regime, while it remains firmly in control, has seen its grip challenged in recent years by the radical brand of political Islam that is sweeping the Middle East ... The regime faces increasing challenge at home as well as from abroad ... To reduce the risk of future upheavals Washington needs to encourage a more open political system and more prudent economic management ... to avoid provoking Islamic sensitivities, it needs to keep its advice and its presence low-key.[144]

Here was the bland admission, if such were needed, that the Saudi regime was both undemocratic and incompetent; but with no suggestion that the United States should distance itself from the feudal autocracy ('Washington has little choice but to maintain close relations with the Saudi monarchy'). In short, the United States – in the interests of cheap oil and arms sales – would do what it could to protect the repression, corruption and abuse of human rights.

The price of oil increased slightly on the international markets, a development that seemed as much to do with the possibility of sanctions against Nigeria for human-rights abuses as with any events in Saudi Arabia. Some experts noted that the bombing was an isolated incident and not like a *coup* attempt that could disrupt the Saudi regime. The US Federal Bureau of Investigation signalled that it would be sending a team to the Kingdom to investigate the explosion. Asserted the expert commentator Said Aburish: 'I've been expecting violence in the Kingdom for a long time. There are now small Islamic groups who are committed to changing the regime by force.'[145] Some observers noted that the choice of the

Saudi National Guard, headed by Crown Prince Abdullah, may have been intended to signify a deliberate strike at the anticipated King of Saudi Arabia.

More than twenty US investigators and hundreds of Saudi security officials were soon searching the rubble of the destroyed building. Now it was being asserted that at least one bomb made of 150 to 225 pounds of high explosives had been set off in a van. No suspects had as yet been identified. Said Raymond Mabus, the US ambassador to Saudi Arabia: 'The only way people like this win is if you're intimidated or deterred, and we won't be intimidated or deterred.' But it was plain that the Riyadh regime and its American advisors on terrorism and security had been made to look incompetent. Hermann F. Eilts, who was US ambassador from 1965 to 1970, spoke for many: 'The Saudi government must be very embarrassed by all this since it suggests an element of internal instability and an inability to maintain security. They will go after this in a major way.'[146] In international commentary a consensus was emerging that the bombing had plunged Saudi Arabia into 'a new period of uncertainty',[147] a growing 'sense of unease'.[148] The inevitable economic adjustments undertaken to bring the Saudi finances back on track were encouraging public disaffection; with the regime no longer able to buy the loyalty and silence of the public, there was a fresh questioning of the government's legitimacy and competence. Said one Riyadh-based economist: '... when you are struggling to survive and the royal family lives high, that fuels resentment'.[149]

In early February 1996 Pakistan handed over to the Saudi Arabian authorities a Saudi wanted in connection with the November bombing. This man, Hassan al-Sarai, was landed at Jeddah and taken away for interrogation. On 22 April four Saudis confessed on state television to involvement in the bombing and admitted that they had been planning further attacks, adding that they had been influenced by various Muslim groups outside the country and in particular by the dissident Mohammed al-Masari. In mid-May the US embassy in Riyadh received a threat that if the four suspects were convicted and punished there would be further retaliation against American interests in Saudi Arabia. Few independent observers believed that the guilt of the four men had been adequately demonstrated; or that the threat of further bombings had been removed.

On 25 June a massive truck bomb exploded at a military compound housing American, British and French servicemen near Dhahran. Early reports suggested that there were about a dozen fatalities with up to 160 men injured. Most of the casualties were American, though some French troops had been hurt. A lorry packed with gasoline had been detonated near the King Abdul Aziz base, in al-Khobar, where the United States has F-15 and F-16 fighter aircraft. A British spokesman said that none of the 200 Royal Air Force airmen and support staff stationed at the base were among the casualties. President Clinton was quick to announce that he was 'outraged'; said he: 'The cowards who committed this murderous act must not go unpunished. America takes care of its own.' FBI investigators were again despatched to Saudi Arabia to help in the case. To some observers this new bombing came as no surprise. The four men convicted of the Riyadh bombing had been executed in public, despite the anonymous threats that further dire consequences would follow any punishment.

Soon it was being announced that as many as nineteen American servicemen had died; with Clinton surmising that the explosion appeared 'to be the work of terrorists'. Secretary of State Warren Christopher declared that those responsible would be 'hunted down' and that Washington 'will not be deterred from fulfilling its duties around the world'. Now it was being suggested that a 5000-pound bomb had been responsible for the 35 ft-deep crater and shock waves felt 40 miles away in Bahrain. This further disaster again focused attention on the US role in Saudi Arabia, inducing Clinton to go out of his way to applaud the Saudis for their help, stressing that the American troops in the Kingdom were the lynchpin of US forward defence in the Gulf region; the Saudis, noted Clinton, had made the Americans 'very welcome'. At the same time Washington was well aware of how sensitively Riyadh viewed the massive American presence (some 40,000 Americans now working in the defence and technology sectors, with precise numbers of military personnel never given). The growing pressures of Muslim fundamentalism and Arab nationalism were combining to force the Americans in the Kingdom to behave as unobtrusively as possible.

Again the United States was not sure who had committed the outrage. Zealous pundits were quick to declare that Iran was responsible, but by now it was clear that many radical groups were working within the Kingdom to destabilise the regime. In particular, Afghan veterans were seen as threatening the governments of Algeria, Egypt, Jordan and other Arabs states, including Saudi Arabia. These *jihadis* remain committed to expelling infidel forces from the holy land of Islam, the land of Mecca and Medina; and to the necessary political corollary, the overthrow of the corrupt pro-West regime that has betrayed the Word of the Prophet. Declared one Saudi expert on Islamic groups: 'The *jihadis* are the lunatic fringe of Islamic fundamentalism. They reject modernism, democracy as *kaffir* (heathen). They are very dangerous.' It came as no surprise to some commentators that one of the convicted Riyadh bombers had frequently visited Abu Mohamed al-Maqdisi, a *jihadi* leader jailed in Jordan. The Riyadh bombing, like the Dhahran attack, was preceded by warnings that Western forces in Saudi Arabia were vulnerable and would be bombed. And again some experts speculated on the possible role of Osama bin Laden in the two outrages.

The Dhahran bombing again thrust the issue of terrorism before the world's leaders, with proposals at the June (1996) G7 summit in Lyon focusing on a possible international response. British premier John Major made a useful contribution to in-depth debate by branding the Dhahran outrage 'an act of pure evil'; while the foreign minister Malcolm Rifkind knew equally where Britain stood: 'The British government condemns in the strongest possible terms the appalling terrorist attack.' For its part, Saudi Arabia pledged 'very harsh and very swift' punishment and offered a £1.7 million reward for help in finding the culprits.

Fresh doubts were also being raised about the stability of the Kingdom, not only because of the Dhahran bombing but also because of the deteriorating health of King Fahd. Said one senior American intelligence official: 'He moves in and out of lucidity. He'll be in the middle of a meeting and all of a sudden will say, "Where am I? What am I doing here?"'[150] This problem at the highest reaches of the Saudi government was not helping the battle against militant fundamentalism. An editorial in *The New York Times* (27 June 1996) noted: '*The presence of American forces in Saudi Arabia remains a sensitive and volatile issue ... The synchronization of American and Saudi interests and customs has always been difficult ... The interests that bring together the United States and Saudi Arabia are powerful and undeniable, but as Washington mourns its dead it must not overlook the differences.*' So there are differences as well as common interests. What is to be done?

Now fresh doubts were being raised about the culpability of the four convicted Riyadh bombers. Washington was reportedly horrified that they had been executed so quickly, so preventing extensive interrogation; and many observers believed that the men's public confessions – using identical language in a spectacle that one diplomat branded as 'almost surreal' – were scripted by the Saudi authorities. It may be, opined one diplomat, that the men had been guilty, but had they acted alone? If the Riyadh and Dhahran bombings were linked then clearly the four men had been part of a wider group.[151] Soon FBI and CIA officials were complaining that the Saudis were refusing to co-operate in the search for the Dhahran bombers: 'The Saudis are very sensitive about this and their inclination is to keep what they know to themselves. It's making life very difficult.'[152] At the same time, aware of Fahd's health problems, Washington was reportedly reassessing the prospects for stability in Saudi Arabia.

At the Khobar complex a new boundary wall was built to better protect the 2000 American troops living there, and various other unremarked security measures were introduced. At the same time no-one doubted that the bombings had given unwelcome publicity to the US presence. Thus a correspondent from Riyadh noted 'confirmation of the fact' that large numbers of Saudis resented the invasion of their land by infidel forces, an attitude that had begun with the arrival in 1990 of hundreds of thousands of Western troops.[153] Perhaps it was also significant that neither the Saudi authorities nor the United States were making progress in apprehending the culprits. In consequence Washington was driven to offering a reward of $2 million (in addition to the Saudi $3 million) for help in finding the bombers; while Malcolm Rifkind was proposing a change to the 1951 UN Convention on Refugees whereby anyone 'aiding and abetting terrorism' would not be entitled to claim asylum. And who would say what is a terrorist? King Fahd?

Again it was easy to ask the question: how safe is the Saudi regime, in the light of the Dhahran bombing? Nicholas Burns was admitting that the United States had 'no leads whatever', but it was assumed that the bombers were home-grown Saudis rather than foreign infiltrators.[154] In these circumstances the militant fundamentalists had little to fear, knowing that all the billions of dollars that Riyadh had spent on weapons had done nothing to improve the security of the military bases at Riyadh and Dhahran. And perhaps there was worse to come: 'Rebellions may be brewing out in the desert that foreigners haven't even heard of yet. It's impossible to predict whether the royal family will be able to handle the challenge indefinitely.'[155] Now the Americans had reason to feel increasingly insecure in their Saudi bases (a cartoon in the *Orlando Sentinel* showed an Arab sheikh telling an American soldier: 'No, you don't understand. The deal is that you get to defend us. We don't have to defend you'). In July 1996 there were reports of fresh bombing threats to US personnel in Saudi Arabia, with the US embassy urging all Americans in the Kingdom to use 'extreme caution', to reduce their travel in the country, and to inspect their mail closely ('Unfortunately the sophistication of the June 25 bombing suggests that additional attacks are quite possible'). In these circumstances tensions between US personnel and the Saudi authorities continue to grow, an atmosphere of unease exacerbated by Riyadh's refusal to contemplate a Pentagon suggestion that US troops be moved from Dhahran to a safer location.

In July/August there was mounting talk of crisis in Riyadh–Washington relations. The Saudis had been tardy in supplying information gleaned, or blocked it altogether; they had been unsympathetic to US suggestions for enhanced security; and there were proposals that American dependents would be allowed to leave the Kingdom at Washington's expense (this last a measure usually introduced in Third World states on the brink of revolution or civil war). The Clinton Administration appeared split on what course to adopt in Saudi Arabia, with the US intelligence agencies reporting that the Kingdom was about to enter a lengthy period of political and financial instability. Again the similarities with Iran were blindingly obvious: '... the CIA failed to predict accurately that the Shah was going to fall. The CIA finds itself in the same position today. For decades it has relied on the Saudi royal family and the secret police to keep it informed. Now, when real intelligence is at a premium, there is none to be found.'[156]

It was now emerging that hundreds – possibly as many as 1000 – Muslim radicals had been detained in Saudi Arabia in connection with the Dhahran bombing. Some were detained for hours, some for weeks, and some indefinitely. The London-based Arabic *Al-Quds al-Arabi* reported that six Arab Afghans had been extensively tortured until they confessed to the bombing, and that US investigators had been allowed no contact with the accused men. In October the Beirut daily *Al-Bayrak* reported that eleven people had been arrested and that the Saudi authorities were claiming to have 'dismantled a sabotage network and arrested the saboteurs who planned or carried out the blast'; in early November, reports appeared that 40 Saudi suspects were being interrogated. The US Defense Secretary William Perry responded to these reports with scepticism ('We have reached no conclusion about who was responsible'), while the FBI was signalling its withdrawal from the joint enquiry because of the Saudis' failure to co-operate, despite earlier assurances on this aspect from King Fahd himself: Saudi officials 'had routinely withheld information ... arrested and interrogated dozens of suspects and had decided who was responsible, but had not told the FBI or shared information on how they had reached their conclusions ... Perry seemed to express the changed atmosphere and impatience within the Administration...'.[157]

It was not long before fresh alerts were being called at American bases in Saudi Arabia as new threats were received of imminent bomb attacks. Now Riyadh, familiar with pressures from Iran, was moving to underwrite American wishes to identify an Iranian hand in the Dhahran bombing. At the same time the Clinton administration was hinting that a new campaign might be launched against Iran in view of the 'highly persuasive' evidence of Iranian involvement. Now the Saudis, according to sources within the US administration, were suggesting joint US–Saudi air strikes against selected military targets in Iran. Nor was the possible involvement of other regional powers ruled out: both Riyadh and Washington were prepared to consider a Syrian connection with the Dhahran bombing.[158] None of the Saudi findings could be checked by the American investigators. Suspects were being rounded up, interrogated and accused in various parts of the Kingdom, but any incriminating evidence – if such there was – remained solely within the purview of the Saudi police and officials.

In early 1997 the Americans were again criticising the Saudi authorities for failing to supply 'very important information' about the Dhahran enquiry, while fresh alerts were still being called at US bases in the Kingdom. By April, the Clinton administration seemed sufficiently convinced of an Iranian connection to hint yet again at the possibility of US air strikes against selected Iranian targets. At the same time some US officials were stressing that they had seen no evidence linking Iran to the bombing – a position maintained through 1997 (*Guardian*, 17 October 1997). No matter, the American Right favoured a military strike: Newt Gingrich, Republican House Speaker, urged that serious consideration be given to 'certain very high-value targets in Iran'.

Nothing, in any of these developments, had served to improve the security of the tens of thousands of US and other foreign personnel in Saudi Arabia. Much less had any real attempt been made to address the basic causes of the growing political and religious instability in the Kingdom.

The multifaceted and deepening predicament of the Kingdom of Saudi Arabia is now plain. In none of the three great areas essential to the Muslim state – economic, political, religious – is the Kingdom secure. The economy is bedevilled by corruption, reliance on foreign labour, and royal (private and state) profligacy; the politics by an unrepresentative feudalism indifferent to human rights; the religion by superstition, dogma and a bitter factionalism with deep historical roots. All this, in a shrinking world increasingly committed to ideological consensus, is a recipe for political turmoil and social instability.

Change is inevitable but largely unpredictable. Political turmoil in Saudi Arabia is as likely to produce an obscurantist Muslim fundamentalism trapped behind the prison bars of a narrow tract as it is an open and humane democracy. But, whatever the change, it is probable that Saudi Arabia – possibly renamed in escape from the tyranny of a single clan – will remain dominant in the Gulf Co-operation Council (GCC), on the Arabian peninsula, and in the Organisation of Petroleum Exporting Countries (OPEC): it will remain sited above some of the largest oil and gas reserves in the world. For all these reasons, another undemocratic plutocracy, still militarily unassailable and the most resource-profligate on earth, will maintain a keen interest in the course of events.

If developments in Saudi Arabia are not congenial to the United States then, to protect perceived American interests, there may follow a comprehensive military intervention, according to custom and practice – to accomplish whatever resource management and imperial slaughter is judged necessary to appease a jealous Christian god and to protect the American Way. The future of Saudi Arabia is uncertain.

Appendix I

International Human Rights Instruments Signed or Ratified by Arab and Islamic Countries but not by Saudi Arabia

The International Covenant on Civil and Political Rights and the International Covenant on Economic, Social and Cultural Rights have been ratified by Afghanistan, Algeria, Cameroon, Egypt, Gabon, Gambia, Guinea, Iran, Iraq, Jordan, Lebanon, Libya, Mali, Morocco, Niger, Senegal, Somalia, Sudan, Syria, Tunisia, and Yemen. The International Covenant on Civil and Political Rights has also been ratified by Uganda.

The International Convention on the Elimination of All Forms of Racial Discrimination has been ratified by Afghanistan, Algeria, Bangladesh, Benin (s), Burkina Faso, Cameroon, Chad, Democratic Yemen, Egypt, Gabon, Gambia, Guinea, Iran, Iraq, Kuwait, Jordan, Lebanon, Libya, Maldives, Mali, Mauritania, Morocco, Niger, Nigeria, Pakistan, Qatar, Senegal, Sierra Leone, Somalia, Sudan, Syria, Turkey (signed but not yet ratified), Uganda, the United Arab Emirates, and Yemen.

The Convention on the Elimination of All Forms of Discrimination against Women has been signed or ratified by Afghanistan (s), Bangladesh, Benin (s), Burkina Faso, Cameroon (s), Egypt, Gabon, Gambia (s), Guinea, Guinea-Bissau, Indonesia, Iraq, Jordan (s), Libya, Mali, Nigeria, Senegal, Sierra Leone, Turkey, Uganda, and Yemen.

The Convention against Torture and Other Cruel, Inhuman or Degrading Treatment or Punishment has been signed or ratified by Afghanistan, Algeria, Cameroon, Egypt, Gabon (s), Gambia (s), Guinea, Indonesia (s), Libya, Morocco (s), Nigeria (s), Senegal, Sierra Leone (s), Somalia, Sudan (s), Turkey, and Uganda.

The Convention on the Political Rights of Women has been ratified by Afghanistan, Albania, Democratic Yemen, Egypt, Gabon, Guinea, Indonesia, Lebanon, Libya, Mali, Mauritania, Morocco, Niger, Nigeria, Pakistan, Senegal, Sierra Leone, and Turkey.

The Convention on the Nationality of Married Women has been ratified by Albania, Guinea (s), Libya, Malaysia, Mali, Pakistan (s), Sierra Leone, and Uganda.

The Convention on Consent to Marriage, Minimum Age for Marriage and Registration of Marriages has been ratified by Benin, Burkina Faso, Democratic Yemen, Guinea, Mali, and Niger.

The Convention for the Suppression of the Traffic in Persons and of the Exploitation of the Prostitution of Others has been ratified by Afghanistan, Albania, Algeria, Bangladesh, Burkina Faso, Cameroon, Djibouti, Egypt, Guinea, Iran (s), Iraq, Jordan, Kuwait, Libya, Mali, Mauritania, Morocco, Niger, Pakistan, Senegal, Syria, and Yemen.

The Freedom of Association and Protection of the Right to Organise Convention (ILO Convention No. 87) has been ratified by Albania, Algeria, Bangladesh, Benin, Burkina Faso, Cameroon, Chad, Comoros, Egypt, Gabon, Guinea, Kuwait, Mali, Mauritania, Niger, Nigeria, Pakistan, Senegal, Sierra Leone, and Yemen.

The Right to Organise and Collective Bargaining Convention (ILO Convention No. 98) has been ratified by Albania, Algeria, Bangladesh, Cameroon, Comoros, Democratic Yemen, Egypt, Gabon, Guinea, Guinea-Bissau, Indonesia, Iraq, Jordan, Lebanon, Libya, Malaysia, Mali, Morocco, Niger, Nigeria, Pakistan, Senegal, Sierra Leone, Sudan, Syria, Turkey, Uganda, and Yemen.

Appendix II

The Cairo Declaration on Human Rights in Islam

The Member States of the Organization of the Islamic Conference.

Reaffirming the civilizing and historical role of the Islamic Ummah which God made the best nation that has given mankind a universal and well-balanced civilization in which harmony is established between this life and the hereafter and knowledge is combined with faith; and the role that this Ummah should play to guide a humanity confused by competing trends and ideologies and to provide solutions to the chronic problems of this materialistic civilization.

Wishing to contribute to the efforts of mankind to assert human rights, to protect man from exploitation and persecution, and to affirm his freedom and right to a dignified life in accordance with the Islamic Shari'ah;

Convinced that mankind which has reached an advanced stage in materialistic science is still, and shall remain, in dire need of faith to support its civilization and of a self motivating force to guard its rights;

Believing that fundamental rights and universal freedoms in Islam are an integral part of the Islamic religion and that no one as a matter of principle has the right to suspend them in whole or in part or violate or ignore them in as much as they are binding divine commandments, which are contained in the Revealed Books of God and were sent through the last of His Prophets to complete the preceding divine messages thereby making their observance an act of worship and their neglect or violation an abominable sin, and accordingly every person is individually responsible – and the Ummah collectively responsible – for their safeguard.

Proceeding from the above-mentioned principles,

Declare the following:

Article 1:

(a) All human beings form one family whose members are united by submission to God and descent from Adam. All men are equal in terms of basic human dignity and basic obligations and responsibilities, without any discrimination on the grounds of race, colour, language, sex, religious belief, political affiliation, social status or other considerations. True faith is the guarantee for enhancing such dignity along the path to human perfection.

(b) All human beings are God's subjects, and the most loved by Him are those who are most useful to the rest of His subjects, and no one has superiority over another except on the basis of piety and good deeds.

Article 2:

(a) Life is a God-given gift and the right to life is guaranteed to every human being. It is the duty of individuals, societies and states to protect this right from any violation, and it is prohibited to take away life except for a Shari'a-prescribed reason.

(b) It is forbidden to resort to such means as may result in the genocidal annihilation of mankind.

(c) The preservation of human life throughout the term of time willed by God is a duty prescribed by Shari'a.

(d) Safety from bodily harm is a guaranteed right. It is the duty of the state to safeguard it, and it is prohibited to breach it without a Shari'a-prescribed reason.

Article 3:

(a) In the event of the use of force and in case of armed conflict, it is not permissible to kill non-belligerents such as old men, women and children. The wounded and the sick shall have the right to medical treatment; and prisoners of war shall have the right to be fed, sheltered and clothed. It is prohibited to mutilate dead bodies. It is a duty to exchange prisoners of war and to arrange visits or reunions of the families separated by the circumstances of war.

(b) It is prohibited to fell trees, to damage crops or livestock, and to destroy the enemy's civilian buildings and installations by shelling, blasting or any other means.

Article 4:

Every human being is entitled to inviolability and the protection of his good name and honour during his life and after his death. The state and society shall protect his remains and burial place.

Article 5:

(a) The family is the foundation of society, and marriage is the basis of its formation. Men and women have the right to marriage, and no restrictions stemming from race, colour or nationality shall prevent them from enjoying this right.

(b) Society and the State shall remove all obstacles to marriage and shall facilitate marital procedure. They shall ensure family protection and welfare.

Article 6:

(a) Woman is equal to man in human dignity, and has rights to enjoy as well as duties to perform; she has her own civil entity and financial independence, and the right to retain her name and lineage.

(b) The husband is responsible for the support and welfare of the family.

Article 7:

(a) As of the moment of birth, every child has rights due from the parents, society and the state to be accorded proper nursing, education and material, hygienic and moral care. Both the fetus and the mother must be protected and accorded special care.

(b) Parents and those in such like capacity have the right to choose the type of education they desire for their children, provided they take into consideration the interest and future of the children in accordance with ethical values and the principles of Shari'a.

(c) Both parents are entitled to certain rights from their children, and relatives are entitled to rights from their kin, in accordance with the tenets of the Shari'a.

Article 8:

Every human being has the right to enjoy his legal capacity in terms of both obligation and commitment, should this capacity be lost or impaired, he shall be represented by his guardian.

Article 9:

(a) The quest for knowledge is an obligation and the provision of education is a duty for society and the State. The State shall ensure the availability of ways and means to acquire education and shall guarantee educational diversity in the interest of society so as to enable man to be acquainted with the religion of Islam and the facts of the Universe for the benefit of mankind.

(b) Every human being has the right to receive both religious and worldly education from the various institutions of education and guidance, including the family, the school, the university, the media, etc., and in such an integrated and balanced manner as to develop his personality, strengthen his faith in God and promote his respect for and defence of both rights and obligations.

Article 10:

Islam is the religion of unspoiled nature. It is prohibited to exercise any form of compulsion on man or to exploit his poverty or ignorance in order to convert him to another religion or to atheism.

Article 11:

(a) Human beings are born free, and no one has the right to enslave, humiliate, oppress or exploit them, and there can be no subjugation but to God the Most-High.

(b) Colonialism of all types being one of the most evil forms of enslavement is totally prohibited. Peoples suffering from colonialism have the full right to freedom and self-determination. It is the duty of all States and peoples to support the struggle of colonized peoples for the liquidation of all forms of colonialism and occupation, and all States and peoples have the right to preserve their independent identity and exercise control over their wealth and natural resources.

Article 12:

Every man shall have the right, within the framework of Shari'a, to free movement and to select his place of residence whether inside or outside his country and if persecuted, is entitled to seek asylum in another country. The country of refuge shall ensure his protection until he reaches safety, unless asylum is motivated by an act which Shari'a regards as a crime.

Article 13:

Work is a right guaranteed by the State and Society for each person able to work. Everyone shall be free to choose the work that suits him best and which serves his interests and those of society. The employee shall have the right to safety and security as well as to all other social guarantees. He may neither be assigned work beyond his capacity nor be subjected to compulsion or exploited or harmed in any way. He shall be entitled – without any discrimination between males and females – to fair wages for his work without delay, as well as to the holidays allowances and promotions which he deserves. For his part, he shall be required to be dedicated and meticulous in his work. Should workers and employers disagree on any matter, the State shall intervene to settle the dispute and have the grievances redressed, the rights confirmed and justice enforced without bias.

Article 14:

Everyone shall have the right to legitimate gains without monopolization, deceit or harm to oneself or to others. Usury (*riba*) is absolutely prohibited.

Article 15:

(a) Everyone shall have the right to own property acquired in a legitimate way, and shall be entitled to the rights of ownership, without prejudice to oneself, others or to society in general. Expropriation is not permissible except for the requirements of public interest and upon payment of immediate and fair compensation.

(b) Confiscation and seizure of property is prohibited except for a necessity dictated by law.

Article 16:

Everyone shall have the right to enjoy the fruits of his scientific, literary, artistic or technical production and the right to protect the moral and material interests stemming therefrom, provided that such production is not contrary to the principles of Shari'a.

Article 17:

(a) Everyone shall have the right to live in a clean environment, away from vice and moral corruption, an environment that would foster his self-development and it is incumbent upon the State and Society in general to afford that right.

(b) Everyone shall have the right to medical and social care, and to all public amenities provided by society and the State within the limits of their available resources.

(c) The State shall ensure the right of the individual to a decent living which will enable him to meet all his requirements and those of his dependants, including food, clothing, housing, education, medical care and all other basic needs.

Article 18:

(a) Everyone shall have the right to live in security for himself, his religion, his dependants, his honour and his property.

(b) Everyone shall have the right to privacy in the conduct of his private affairs, in his home, among his family, with regard to his property and his relationships. It is not permitted to spy on him, to place him under surveillance or to besmirch his good name. The State shall protect him from arbitrary interference.

(c) A private residence is inviolable in all cases. It will not be entered without permission from its inhabitants or in any unlawful manner, nor shall it be demolished or confiscated and its dwellers evicted.

Article 19:

(a) All individuals are equal before the law, without distinction between the ruler and the ruled.

(b) The right to resort to justice is guaranteed to everyone.

(c) Liability is in essence personal.

(d) There shall be no crime or punishment except as provided for in the Shari'a.

(e) A defendant is innocent until his guilt is proven in a fair trial in which he shall be given all the guarantees of defence.

Article 20:

It is not permitted without legitimate reason to arrest an individual, or restrict his freedom, to exile or to punish him. It is not permitted to subject him to physical or psychological torture or to any form of humiliation, cruelty or indignity. Nor is it permitted to subject an individual to medical or scientific experimentation without his consent or at the risk of his health or of his life. Nor is it permitted to promulgate emergency laws that would provide executive authority for such actions.

Article 21:

Taking hostages under any form or for any purpose is expressly forbidden.

Article 22:

(a) Everyone shall have the right to express his opinion freely in such manner as would not be contrary to the principles of the Shari'a.

(b) Everyone shall have the right to advocate what is right, and propagate what is good, and warn against what is wrong and evil according to the norms of Islamic Shari'a.

(c) Information is a vital necessity to society. It may not be exploited or misused in such a way as may violate sanctities and the dignity of Prophets, undermine moral and ethical values or disintegrate, corrupt or harm society or weaken its faith.

(d) It is not permitted to arouse nationalistic or doctrinal hatred or to do anything that may be an incitement to any form of racial discrimination. ...

Article 24:

All the rights and freedoms stipulated in this Declaration are subject to the Islamic Shari'a.

Article 25:

The Islamic Shari'a is the only source of reference for the explanation or clarification of any of the articles of this Declaration.

Cairo, 14 Muharram 1411 AH
5 August 1990

Appendix III

Articles of Government

CHAPTER ONE: THE GENERAL PRINCIPLES

Article 1:

The Kingdom of Saudi Arabia is an Arab and Islamic sovereign state, its religion is Islam, and its constitution the Holy Quran and the Prophet's Sunnah. Its language is Arabic and Riyadh its capital.

Article 2:

The festivals of the state are Eid Al-Fitr and Eid Al-Adha and its calendar is the Hijri calendar.

Article 3:

The flag of the state is as follows:
  A – Its colour is green
  B – Its width is equal to a third of its length.
  C – It will carry 'La Ilah Illah Allah Mohammad Rasoul Allah'
(There is but one God and Mohammad is His Messenger).

Article 4:

The emblem of the state is two intersected swords and a palm tree.

The system determines the national anthem and its medals.

CHAPTER TWO

Article 5:

  (a) The system of the Kingdom of Saudi Arabia is a Monarchy.

  (b) Its rule is confined to the sons of the Kingdom's founder, Abdulaziz Ibn Abdulrahman Al-Faisal Al-Saud, and grandsons. The most suitable of these is enthroned to rule under the guidance of the Holy Quran and the Prophet's Sunnah.

  (c) The King chooses his Crown Prince and relieves him of his duties by Royal Order.

(d) The Crown Prince is to devote his time to his duties as Crown Prince and to the duties delegated to him by the King.

(e) When the King dies, the Crown Prince succeeds him until enthronement.

Article 6:

The citizens will take allegiance before the Monarch in line with the Holy Quran and the Prophet's Sunnah.

Article 7:

The rule in the Kingdom depends on the Holy Quran and the Prophet's Sunnah.

Article 8:

The rule in the Kingdom is based on justice, consultation and equality in accordance with the Islamic Shariah.

CHAPTER THREE: THE CONSTITUENTS OF SAUDI SOCIETY

Article 9:

The family is the nucleus of Saudi society and its members will be brought up on the basis of the Islamic creed and obedience to Almighty God, the Prophet and rulers and have respect of the system, love of the homeland and pride in its history.

Article 10:

The state is keen on enhancing relations among members of the family, preserving Arab and Islamic values and taking care of all members, enabling them to develop their skills.

Article 11:

Saudi society is based on dependence on Almighty God and co-operation.

Article 12:

The state is keen on enhancing national unity and preventing all kinds of sedition.

Article 13:

State education aims to implant the Islamic creed in new generations, developing their skills to enable them to contribute to the building of their society.

CHAPTER FOUR: THE ECONOMIC PRINCIPLES

Article 14:

All the wealth under the ground, or on its surface, or in the territorial waters, or in the land and maritime domains, as well as all resources of this wealth, is owned by the state as will be shown by the system.

The system defines means for the exploitation of the wealth, its protection and development in a manner that serves the interests of the state, its security and economy.

Article 15:

There will be no concessions or investment of the resources of the country, except those allowed according to the system.

Article 16:

The state will protect the public funds and citizens and residents are to safeguard them.

Article 17:

Ownership, capital and labour are basic constituents of the Kingdom's economic and social system.

Article 18:

The state allows the freedom of personal property, which will not be expropriated except in the public interest and after fair compensation.

Article 19:

Confiscation of public property is prohibited. Confiscation is only according to judicial verdict.

Article 20:

Taxes and fees are levied only on the basis of justice and only when the need arises. They are not levied, amended or cancelled except in accordance with the system.

Article 21:

Zakat (alms) shall be collected and spent according to the Shariah teachings.

Article 22:

Economic and social development is carried out in the light of a scientific and just plan.

CHAPTER FIVE: DUTIES AND RIGHTS

Article 23:

The state protects the Islamic creed and carries out its Shariah and undertakes its duty towards the Islamic call.

Article 24:

The state services the Two Holy Mosques and ensures the security and safety of their visitors, enabling them to perform their rituals in comfort and ease.

Article 25:

The state is keen on realisation of the hopes of the Arab and Muslim nation in solidarity and unity and at the same time enhances its relations with friendly states.

Article 26:

The state protects the rights of the people in line with the Islamic Shariah.

Article 27:

The state ensures the rights of the citizens and their families, in case of emergency, disease, disability and old age, supports the social insurance system and encourages establishments and individuals to contribute to charitable works.

Article 28:

The state helps all able people to obtain work and enacts laws to protect the worker and the employer.

Article 29:

The state takes care of science, arts and culture and encourages scientific research, preserves Arab and Islamic heritage and contributes to the Arab, Islamic and human civilisation.

Article 30:

The state makes education available and adheres to the principle of illiteracy eradication.

Article 31:

The state takes care of public health and makes healthcare available.

Article 32:

The state works for the preservation, protection and improvement of the environment, and for the prevention of pollution.

Article 33:

The state establishes the armed forces and enables them to take up their responsibility for the defence of the Islamic creed, the Two Holy Mosques, society and the homeland.

Article 34:

Defence of the Islamic creed, society and the homeland are the responsibility of all. The system clarifies the rules of military service.

Article 35:

The system clarifies the rules of Saudi Arabian nationality.

Article 36:

The state ensures the security of all citizens and residents. No-one has the right to restrict, arrest or imprison anyone except under the rules of the system.

Article 37:

No-one is allowed to enter private homes without the permission of their owners, and no-one has the right to probe private homes except in accordance with the system.

Article 38:

Penalties will be personal, with no crime or penalty except in accordance with the Shariah or the regulations, and no penalty except in accordance with the regulations.

Article 39:

The information and publication media should express themselves in a courteous manner and abide by the regulations of the state and contribute to the education of the nation and support its unity, All acts that lead to sedition and disunity or undermine the state's security and public relations or insult the dignity and rights of the people will be prohibited. The regulations will clarify this.

Article 40:

No-one has the right to confiscate delay or interfere with cables, postal items or telephone calls and other means of telecommunications, except according to the regulations set by the system.

Article 41:

The residents of the Kingdom of Saudi Arabia will adhere to its regulations and should respect the values of Saudi society, its traditions and feelings.

Article 42:

The state gives political asylum if the public interest necessitates, and regulations and international agreements will clarify the procedures pertaining to the extradition of criminals.

Article 43:

The council of the King and the council of the Crown Prince are open to all citizens and everyone has the right to clarify his problem.

CHAPTER SIX: THE STATE'S AUTHORITIES

Article 44:

The authorities of the state comprise the Judicial authority, the Executive authority and the Organisational authority.

All these authorities co-operate in discharging their responsibilities. The King is the point of reference of all these authorities.

Article 45:

The source of Ifta in the Kingdom of Saudi Arabia is the Holy Quran and the Prophet's Sunnah and the system clarifies the hierarchy of the senior Ulema and the administration of the scientific researches and Ifta and their responsibilities.

Article 46:

The Judicial authority is an independent organ and no-one has authority over Judges, other than the authority of the Islamic Shariah.

Article 47:

All people, whether citizens or residents in the Kingdom, have the right to litigation on an equal basis. The system will clarify the required procedures.

Article 48:

The system of Judges is applied on all cases presented before the Shariah rules according to the teachings of the Holy Quran and Sunnah and the regulations set by the ruler, provided that they do not contradict the Holy Quran and Sunnah.

Article 49:

In the light of what has been stipulated in article 53 of this system, the courts will arbitrate in all disputes and crimes.

Article 50:

The King, or whomsoever he may deputise will be responsible for the implementation of the judicial rules.

Article 51:

The system will determine the formation of the Supreme Judicial Council and its prerogative as well as the organisation and prerogatives of various courts.

Article 52:

Judges will be appointed and relieved of their duties by Royal Decree, according to a proposal by the Supreme Judicial Council and according to the system's regulations.

Article 53:

The system will determine the organisation and prerogatives of the Board of Grievances.

Article 54:

The system will determine the organisation and prerogatives of the Department of Investigations and Public Prosecution.

Article 55:

The King will rule the nation, according to the rulings of Islam, and supervise the application of Shariah (Islamic laws), the state's general policy and the protection and defence of the country.

Article 56:

The King acts as Prime Minister and is assisted in the performance of his duties by members of the Council of Ministers, according to the rulings of this and other systems. The system of the Council of Ministers will determine the authorities of the council, in connection with internal and external affairs, the organisation of government authorities and the co-ordination of their work. It will also determine the qualities that are required of ministers, the authorities invested in them, the method of questioning them and all their affairs. The system and prerogatives of the Council of Ministers will be modified according to this system.

Article 57:

   (a) The King will appoint Deputy Prime Ministers and Cabinet Ministers and relieve them of their duties by Royal Decree.

   (b) The Deputy Prime Ministers and Cabinet Ministers are responsible before the King for the application of the Islamic Shariah, systems and the state's general policy.

   (c) The King has the right to dissolve the Council of Ministers and restructure it.

Article 58:

The King will appoint Ministers, Deputy Ministers and officials of the excellent grade, and relieve them of their duties by Royal Decree and according to the rulings of the system.

Ministers and heads of independent authorities are responsible to the Prime Minister for their Ministries or authorities.

Article 59:

The system will determine the rules of the civil service, including salaries, rewards, compensation, privileges and retirement pensions.

Article 60:

The King is the Supreme Commander of all the armed forces and appoints officers or terminates their service according to the system.

Article 61:

The King has the right to declare a state of emergency, general mobilisation and war. The system will determine relevant rulings.

Article 62:

If a danger threatens the safety of the Kingdom, the unity of its lands or impedes the state institutions' performance of their duties, the King has the right to take the necessary speedy measures to face this danger. If the King decides that these measures should be continuous, he will implement the necessary regulations to this end

Article 63:

The King will receive heads of states, appoint his representatives in other countries and accept accreditation of the representatives of other countries in the Kingdom.

Article 64:

The King will award medals according to the relevant clauses of the system.

Article 65:

The King has the right to delegate prerogatives to the Crown Prince by Royal Decree.

Article 66:

In case of his travelling abroad, the King issues a Royal Decree to deputise the Crown Prince to run the affairs of state and look after the interests of the people as stated in the Royal Decree.

Article 67:

The organisational authority will draw up systems and regulations to protect state interests or eliminate corruption in the affairs of the state, according to the rulings of the Islamic Shariah, and exercise its functions according to this system and the systems of the Council of Ministers and Shura.

Article 68:

The system of the Shura Council will determine the method of its formation, the exercise of its powers and the selection of its members.

The King has the right to dissolve the Shura Council and restructure it.

Article 69:

The King has the right to call the Council of Ministers and Shura for a joint meeting and invite whoever he wishes to attend this meeting and discuss whatever issues he raises.

Article 70:

Systems, treaties, international agreements and privileges will be issued and modified by Royal Decree.

Article 71:

Systems will be published in the official gazette and deemed effective as of the date of their publication, unless another date is specified.

CHAPTER SEVEN: FINANCIAL AFFAIRS

Article 72:

The system will determine the rulings of the state revenues and their delivery to the State Treasury:

Article 73:

No obligation should be made to pay funds from the State Treasury except in accordance with the provisions of the budget. Should the provisions of the budget not be sufficient for paying such funds, a Royal Decree must be issued for their payment.

Article 74:

The assets of the state should not be sold, rented or dealt with except in accordance with the system.

Article 75:

The systems will determine the rulings of monetary agencies, banks, standards, measures and weights.

Article 76:

The system will determine the state's fiscal year. The budget will be issued by a Royal Decree and will include an estimate of the year's revenues and expenditures at least one month before the beginning of the fiscal year. Should emergency reasons arise and prevent its issuance before the beginning of the new fiscal year, the budget of the previous fiscal year will be followed until a new one has been issued.

Article 77:

The concerned authority will prepare the state's final accounts for the ending fiscal year and submit it to the Prime Minister.

Article 78:

The budgets and final accounts of corporate bodies will be subject to the rulings of the state budget and its final account.

CHAPTER EIGHT: CONTROL AUTHORITIES

Article 79:

All revenues, expenditures and fixed and mobile assets of the state will be controlled to ensure that they are well-utilised. An annual report on this control will be submitted to the Prime Minister.

The system will determine the relevant control authority and its specialisations.

Article 80:

Government authorities will be controlled to ensure their good performance and the application of systems. Financial and administrative violations will be investigated and an annual report on them submitted to the Prime Minister.

The system will determine the relevant authority and its specialisations.

CHAPTER NINE: GENERAL RULINGS

Article 81:

The implementation of this system does not violate treaties and agreements for which the Kingdom is committed in respect of other countries, international organisations and institutions.

Article 82:

Noting that the seventh article of this system should not be violated, none of the rulings of this system should, in any way, be obstructed, unless it is a temporary measure during a time of war and as shown in the system.

Article 83:

No amendment of this system should be made except in the same manner of its issuance.

Appendix IV

Articles of the Shura (Consultative Council)

Referring to the system of the Consultative Council (*Majlis Al-Shura*) issued under the Royal Decree in 1347 AH, we order the following:

Firstly:

Issue of the council's system with the enclosed formula.

Secondly:

This system will replace the system of the Shura Council of 1347 AH and the affairs of this council will be regulated by a Royal Decree.

Thirdly:

All regulations, instructions and resolutions valid until the implementation of this system will continue until they are accordingly amended.

Fourthly:

This system will be implemented within a period of six months from the date of its issue.

Fifthly:

This system will be published in the official gazette.

In the name of God, most gracious, most merciful: the system of Majlis Al-Shura (Consultative Council):

Article 1:

In accordance with the words of Almighty God: 'It is part of the mercy of God that thou dost deal gently with them, wert thou severe or harsh-hearted, they would have broken away from about thee. So pass over their faults, and ask for God's forgiveness for them, and consult them in affairs of moment, then when thou art resolved put they trust in God, and God's saying: "Those who hearken to their Lord and establish regular prayer, who conduct their affairs in mutual consultation who spend out of what we bestow on them for sustenance".'

And in line with the tradition of the Messenger of Allah (peace be upon him), in consulting his companions and persuading the nation to do the same.

The consultative council has been set up to undertake proper tasks in compliance with this system and the basic system of ruling in adherence to the book of God and the tradition of his messenger, preserving the bonds of brotherhood, co-operation and righteousness.

Article 2:

The council is based on holding fast to the rope which God stretches out – in other words, strict adherence to the sources of Islamic legislation. Council members should devote themselves to serve the common interest and preserve the unity of the people, the entity of the state and the interests of the nation.

Article 3:

The council will consist of a speaker, and 60 well-educated and qualified members selected by the King. The rights and duties of the members and their affairs will be identified by Royal Decree.

Article 4:

A member of the council should be:
  (a) A Saudi national in terms of origin and by birth.
  (b) Well-qualified and of good reputation.
  (c) No younger than 30 years of age.

Article 5:

A member of the council has the right to apply for exemption to the speaker and in turn the speaker should submit the matter to the King.

Article 6:

If a member of the council neglects his duties, investigation should be made and he should be judged in accordance with the rules and procedures to be issued by Royal Decree.

Article 7:

If, for any reason, a seat of a member of the council falls vacant, the King will name a replacement by a Royal Decree.

Article 8:

A member of the council should not exploit membership to serve his own interests.

Article 9:

Membership of the council should not be joined with any other private or public undertaking unless the King sees a need for it.

Article 10:

The speaker of the council may appoint his deputy and the secretary general of the council. Their resignations, salaries, rights and duties and various affairs will be determined by Royal Decree.

Article 11:

The speaker, members and the secretary general of the council should take the following oath before undertaking their work in the council:

> I swear by Almighty Allah, that I shall be faithful to my religion, then to my King and country, and never uncover a secret of the state, and shall preserve the interests of state, its regulations and perform my duties with truth, honesty, justice and faithfulness.

Article 12:

The city of Riyadh will be the headquarters of the consultative council, but the council may hold meeting at any other place inside the Kingdom if approved by the King.

Article 13:

The term of the Shura Council will be four years (Hijri calendar) as of the date set in the Royal Decree on the formation of the council. The new council should be formed at least two months ahead of the expiry date of the preceding one. If the term finished before the formation of a new council, the old one should perform its duties until a new one is formed. When a new council is formed, at least half the members of the council should be new members.

Article 14:

The King or whomsoever he delegates to serve on the council, should deliver an annual royal speech before the council on the domestic and foreign policies of the state.

Article 15:

The council will express opinions on the general policy of the state, which are referred to it by the Council of Ministers. In particular, it may do the following:

(a) Discuss the general plan of economic and social development.
(b) Study international laws, charters, treaties and agreements, and concessions and make appropriate suggestions regarding them.
(c) Interpret laws.
(d) Discuss annual reports by Ministries and other government bodies, and make appropriate suggestions regarding them.

Article 16:

The council's meeting will not be considered in order without the attendance of at least two-thirds of its members, including the chairman or whoever deputises for him. Decisions will not be in order unless they are approved by a majority in the council.

Article 17:

Resolutions of the council should be submitted to the Prime Minister, who will refer them to the Councils of Ministers for discussion and, if viewpoints of the two councils are identical, a royal approval will be issued. If the viewpoints differ, however, the King will undertake a proper decision.

Article 18:

Regulations, conventions, international agreements, and privileges will be only issued and amended by Royal Decree after being reviewed by the council.

Article 19:

The council will assign specialised committees of its members. It also has the right to form specialised committees of its members to discuss items on its agenda.

Article 20:

The council's affiliated committees may seek the help of whoever it deems suitable from non-members after the approval of the speaker of the council.

Article 21:

A General Commission should be set up for the council comprising the speaker, his deputy and heads of specialised committees of the council.

Article 22:

The speaker of the council should submit to the Prime Minister an application if any official is required to attend the council's sessions, provided that the council is discussing concerned matters and the official has the right of discussion but not the right of voting.

Article 23:

Every group of 10 members of the council, has the right to propose a new system, or amendment of an implemented one and to submit the matter to the speaker of the council who, in turn, should raise the proposal to the King.

Article 24:

The speaker of the council must submit an application to the Prime Minister for governmental documents and statements that the council sees necessary to facilitate its functions.

Article 25:

The council's speaker should submit an annual report to the King on the council's activities in line with its internal regulations.

Article 26:

Civil service regulations are applied to the personnel of the council's bodies unless internal regulations stipulate otherwise.

Article 27:

The council will have a special budget ratified by the King to be spent within regulation and rules issued by Royal Decree.

Article 28:

Organisation of financial affairs of the council, financial control and final accounts will be made in line with special rules to be identified by a Royal Decree.

Article 29:

The internal regulations of the council should organise the duties of its speaker and his deputy, the council's secretary general, the bodies of the council, management of the sessions, work process, functions of committees; method of voting; discussion regulations, and answer rules besides all matters that would provide contol and perfection inside the council so that it can exercise its duties in the best interests of the Kindom and its people. Such regulations will be issued by a Royal Decree.

Article 30:

Amendment of this system will not be made except in the method it has been issued.

Appendix V

Council of Ministers – Rules

The following are the key decrees issued in 1993 about the operations of the council of ministers.

Council of Ministers Rules

Royal decree A/13, which sets out a council of ministers system, says that the council's term of office will not exceed four years 'during which it will be reshuffled by a royal decree'. The council of ministers will comprise the Prime Minister King Fahd, the deputy premiers Prince Abdullah and Prince Sultan, ministers, state ministers appointed council members by royal decree and king's advisers appointed council members by royal decree. Valid council of ministers meetings will require a quorum of two-thirds of its membership. Its decisions become law only when a majority vote in favour. The Prime Minister has the casting vote.

The government cannot conclude a loan prior to obtaining the approval of the council of ministers and the issue of a royal decree. The council will review and approve the annual state budget.

Ministerial Appointment Rules

Royal decree A/14, which sets out the rules governing individual cabinet members, says that membership of the council will be for four years. The service of a minister or an official on the excellent grade in the government salary scale will be terminated after two years, unless it is extended by a royal decree for no more than another two years.

The Council of Ministers System General Rules:

Article 1: The Council of Ministers is an organisational body presided over by the king.

Article 2: The Council of Ministers' headquarters is based in Riyadh city and it can hold its sessions anywhere else in the kingdom.

Article 3: A Council of Ministers member should be:

    A – A Saudi by nationality and origin.
    B – A person of mightiness and competence.
    C – Should not have been sentenced for a crime in violation of religion and honour.

Article 4: A Council of Ministers member shall not assume his post before swearing to the following:

> *I swear by Allah the Great to be loyal to my religion, my king and my country, and never to divulge any of the secrets of the state, and to uphold the interests and the systems, and to perform my duties truthfully, faithfully and loyally.*

Article 5: A Council of Ministers member cannot hold another government post unless the Prime Minister deems it necessary to do so.

Article 6: The Council of Ministers member cannot directly, through a mediator or in a public tender, purchase or lease any of the state properties and should not sell or let any of his properties to the state, and he must not practice any commercial or financial work or accept membership of the board of any company in the course of the term of his office.

Article 7: The Council of Ministers' sessions will be held under the chairmanship of the king, the prime minister, or any of the deputy premiers. Council resolutions become final after the king has approved them.

Article 8: Council of Ministers members are appointed and relieved of their duties by royal decrees, and their responsibilities are decided in accordance with articles 57 and 58 of the basic system of government. The Council's internal system spells out their rights.

Article 9: The Council's term will not exceed four years during which it will be reshuffled by a royal decree. If the duration expires before the reshuffle, it will continue to perform its duties until the reshuffle is carried out.

Article 10: A minister is the direct head of and final authority on the affairs of his ministry and will undertake his duties in accordance with the provisions of the bylaws of this system and other systems and regulations.

Article 11:

A. Only a minister can act in lieu of another minister and in accordance with an order by the premier.
B. The deputy minister will practice the authorities of the minister in his absence.

The Formation of the Council of Ministers

Article 12: The Council of Ministers consists of the following:

A   The Prime Minister.
B   Deputy Premiers.
C   Ministers.
D   State Ministers appointed members of the council by a royal decree.
E   The king's advisers who are appointed cabinet members by a royal decree.

Article 13: Only the members and the Secretary-General of the Council of Ministers have the right to attend its sessions, at the request of the premier or a cabinet minister, and pursuant to the approval of the premier, an official or an expert can attend the sessions to submit information or clarifications. However, the right to vote is unique to the Council members only.

Article 14: A Council of Ministers meeting is not considered valid unless two-thirds of the members are present and its decisions become legal by winning the votes of a majority of attending members. In the case of equal votes (for or against a decision), the premier will cast the deciding vote. In exceptional cases, the Council session can be valid if half the members are present but its decisions only become legal by the approval of two-thirds of the present members. The premier has the right to evaluate the exceptional cases.

Article 15: The Council of Ministers will not make a decision on an issue concerning the works of a ministry unless the concerned minister or his deputy is present, unless urgency necessitates it.

Article 16: Council deliberations are confidential but its decisions are made public, with the exception of those deemed secret by the council.

Article 17: Council members are tried for offences they commit in official works by virtue of a special law outlining the violations, determining the accusation procedures and the formation of the court panel.

Article 18: The Council of Ministers may form committees from its members or others to discuss an issue included in the agenda to submit a special report on this issue. The Council's internal system will decide the number and work of the committees.

Specialisations of the Council of Ministers

Article 19: With consideration of the basic system of government and the Shura Council system, the Council of Ministers will draw up the internal, external, monetary, economic, educational, and defence policies as well as all public affairs of the state and will supervise their implementation. It will review Shura Council resolutions. It has the executive authority and will act as the reference to financial and administrative affairs in all ministries and other government bodies.

Organisational Affairs

Article 20: With consideration of the Shura Council system, rules, treaties, international conventions and privileges are issued and amended by the royal decree after review by the cabinet.

Article 21: The Council of Ministers will study the draft laws and regulations submitted to it and vote on them article by article and then vote on all of them as per the procedures spelled out in the Council's internal system.

Article 22: Each minister has the right to propose a draft law or regulation concerning the works of his ministry. Each member can propose what he deems useful to study by the council after the approval of the prime minister.

Article 23: All decrees must be published in the official gazette and shall be effective from the date of their publication, unless another date is set for it.

Executive Affairs

Article 24: As the district executive authority, the Council seizes complete control of the affairs of execution and administration and the following matters fall under its executive powers:

1 Control over the application of laws, regulations and resolutions.

2 Setting up and arranging public interests.

3 Following up of the Public Development Plan.

Financial Affairs

Article 25: The government cannot conclude a loan prior to obtaining the approval of the Council of Ministers and the issuance of a royal decree to this effect.

Article 26: The Council of Ministers will study the state budget and will vote on it chapter by chapter and issue it by a royal decree.

Article 27: Any increase in the budget is to be made by royal decree.

Article 28: The minister of finance and national economy will submit the state's final account for the past fiscal year to the prime minister for submission to the council for approval.

Presidency of the Council of Ministers

Article 29: The King is the prime minister and he steers the state's general policy, guarantees co-ordination and co-operation among various government bodies and ensures coherence, consistency and unity in the works of the Council of Ministers. He supervises and controls the Council of Ministers, ministries and government bodies and observes the implementation of rules, regulations and decisions.

All ministries and cabinet bodies have to submit to the prime minister within 90 days of the beginning of the fiscal year a report of their achievements in comparison with the provisions of the general development plan for the previous fiscal year, the difficulties which faced them and their proposals for improving their performance.

Administrative Structure of the Council of Ministers

Article 30: The following bodies fall within the administrative formation of the Council of Ministers:

First, the cabinet of the Council of Ministers Presidency.

Secondly, the Council of Ministers General Secretarial.

Thirdly, the Experts Board.

The Council's internal system spells out the formations, specialisations and methods of work of these bodies.

Article 31: The internal system of the Council of Ministers is issued by a royal decree.

Article 32: This system cannot be amended except in the same manner as its issuance.

Notes

Notes to Chapter 1: Islam, Law and Human Rights

1. Patrick Cormack, 'Enlightened leadership', *First*, Special Report for National Day of Saudi Arabia (First Magazine, London).
2. Alan Munro, *Enterprise Al Yamamah* (Preston, UK: British Aerospace, November 1991).
3. John Casey, 'Friend of Islam given a hero's welcome', *The Daily Telegraph*, London, 8 March 1997.
4. Jean P. Sasson, *Princess* (London: Bantam, 1993). I have no other documentation to support this charge but Sasson is reliable in other details.
5. *Shame in the House of Saud: Contempt for Human Rights in the Kingdom of Saudi Arabia*, Minnesota Lawyers International Human Rights Committee, Minneapolis, Minnesota, USA, May 1992, p. vii.
6. *Ibid.*, pp. vii–viii.
7. *Saudi Arabia*, Human Rights Report, State Department, Washington, DC, USA, 1996, p. 1.
8. Aziz Abu-Hamad, 'Human rights and constitutional change in Saudi Arabia', *Arabia Monitor*, October 1992, p. 3.
9. *Ibid.*, pp. 3–4.
10. Mohammed H. Siddiq, *Saudi Government Analyzed* (Lincoln, Nebraska, USA, 18 October 1994).
11. Rashed Aba-Namay, 'The dynamics of individual rights and their prospective development under the new constitution of Saudi Arabia', *Journal of South Asian and Middle Eastern Studies*, Volume 18, Number 3 (Spring 1995), pp. 25–6.
12. *Ibid.*, p. 28.
13. *Ibid.*, pp. 39, 40.
14. Associate Press Report, *The Daily Telegraph*, London, 23 August 1997.
15. *The Observer*, London, 3 July 1994.
16. David Sapsted, 'Nike says sorry to Muslims over "Allah" shoes', *The Daily Telegraph*, London, 26 June 1997.
17. *Saudi Arabia*, Human Rights Report, *op. cit.*, p. 7.
18. James P. Piscatori, 'Ideological politics in Saudi Arabia', in Piscatori (ed.), *Islam in the Political Process* (New York: Cambridge University Press, 1983), p. 62.
19. Leon Barkho, 'Saudis "starved Iraqi pilgrims"', *The Independent*, London, 10 June 1992.
20. Ian Black, Deborah Pugh, Simon Tisdall, Kathy Evans and Leslie Plommer, 'Militant Islam's Saudi paymasters', *The Guardian*, London, 29 February 1992.
21. *Ibid.*; Kathy Evans, 'Fundamental difficulties', *The Guardian*, London, 15 May August 1993.
22. David Hirst, 'Kingdom where God is everywhere', *The Guardian*, London, 16 August 1993.
23. Quoted in David Hirst, 'Royal shepherd tussles with his restless flock', *The Guardian*, London, 17 August 1993.
24. Quoted in David Hirst, 'Saudi reformers fight culture of orthodoxy', *The Guardian*, London, 11 April 1996.

25. 'The role of Saudi Arabia in Islamic affairs world-wide', *Saudi Arabian Bulletin*, Royal Embassy of Saudi Arabia, London, September 1996, p. 5.

26. *Crescent International*, 16 March 1993.

27. Mohammed H. Siddiq, 'Monarchy melancholy', *Lincoln Journal*, Nebraska, USA, 9 March 1994.

28. See, for example, Muhammad Iqbal Siddiqi, *Model of an Islamic Bank* (Lahore, Pakistan: Kazi Publications, 1986); Allama Yusuf al-Qardawi, *Economic Security in Islam* (Lahore, Pakistan: Kazi Publications, 1981).

29. Ibrahim ibn Ali al-Wazir, 'Islamic notions about the dialogue of civilizations', *The Diplomat*, 15 February 1996, pp. 27–30.

30. Paul Stokes, 'Koran bishop has no regrets', *The Daily Telegraph*, London, 1 April 1997.

31. Sayed Hassan Amin, *Middle East Legal Systems* (Glasgow, Scotland: Royston, 1985), pp. 310–13.

32. Piscatori (ed.), *op. cit.*, p. 62.

33. Fouard Al-Farsy, *Modernity and Tradition: The Saudi Equation* (London: Kegan Paul, 1990), p. 36.

34. Quoted in *Shame in the House of Saud*, *op. cit.*, p. 19.

35. Quoted in *ibid.*, p. 21.

36. *Ibid.*, p. 24.

37. *Ibid.*, p. 26.

38. Muhammad Yusuf Guraya, *Islamic Jurisprudence in the Modern World* (Lahore, Pakistan: Sh. Muhammad Ashraf, 1992), pp. 50–51.

39. *Saudi Arabia*, Human Rights Report, *op. cit.*, p. 6.

40. King Fahd, press conference, 8 November 1990; reprinted in *BBC Summary of World Broadcasting*, 10 November 1990, ME/0918 A/1.

41. Michael Field, *Inside the Arab World* (London: John Murray, 1994), p. 175.

42. Abdul Bari Atwan, in Abdul Bari Atwan and Jihad Khazen, 'In the Saudi pocket', *Index on Censorship*, London, Number 2 (1996), p. 50.

43. *Ibid.*, p. 51.

44. Jihad Khazen, in Atwan and Khazen, *op. cit.*, p. 52.

45. Cited in *Shame in the House of Saud*, *op. cit.*, p. 25.

46. *Silent Kingdom: Freedom of Expression in Saudi Arabia*, Article 19, International Centre Against Censorship, London, 24 October 1991.

47. Kathy Evans, 'Saudi cleric rules out criticism of king', *The Guardian*, London, 25 May 1993.

48. Annika Saville, 'Saudi move to take over critical Arab press', *The Independent*, London, 27 November 1993.

49. Marie Colvin, 'Saudi ambassador risks royal wrath', *The Sunday Times*, London, 5 December 1993.

50. Hani Ahmed Zaki Yamani, *To Be a Saudi* (London: Janus Publishing, 1997).

51. David Hirst, 'How Riyadh stifled a free Arab voice', *The Guardian*, London, 21 April 1995.

52. Quoted in Owen Boycott and David Hirst, 'War of words with Saudis forces BBC to shut down Arabic TV channel', *The Guardian*, London, 9 April 1996; Fred Halliday, 'Saudi bigots lack door to truth', *The Observer*, London, 14 April 1996.

53. David Holden and Richard Johns, *The House of Saud* (London: Sidgwick and Jackson, 1981), p. 180.

54. José Arnold, *Golden Pots and Swords and Pans* (London: Gollancz, 1964), pp. 143, 222–6.

55. Holden and Johns, *op. cit.*, p. 180.

56. *Ibid.*, p. 181.

57.   *Ibid.*, p. 413.
58.   *Financial Times*, London, 9 April 1980.
59.   Holden and Johns, *op. cit.*, p. 535.
60.   *Muslim Chronicle*, March 1990; reprinted in Haroon M. Jadhakhan (ed.), *The Thieves of Riyadh: Lives and Crimes of the Al Sauds and the Al-Nahyans* (London: Muslim Chronicle, 1992), pp. 24–9.
61.   Quoted in *ibid.*, p. 27.
62.   G. J. Church, 'An exquisite balancing act', *Time*, 24 September 1990, p. 45.
63.   'Two Saudi Arabian aides packing', *Omaha World Herald*, 7 November 1990.
64.   G. Brooks, 'Saudi diplomat seeks asylum in US, putting Washington, Riyadh on the spot', *The Wall Street Journal*, 15 June 1994; Patricia Dane Rogers, 'Saudis dig deep into diplomatic bag to house prince's expanding family', *The Guardian*, London, 10 September 1994.
65.   Jonathan Freedland, 'Saudi splurge stuns Arizona', *The Guardian*, London, 8 July 1966.
66.   Mohammed H. Siddiq, *Saudi Arabia: A Country Under Arrest* (Lincoln, Nebraska, USA, 1991), p. 24.
67.   Said K. Aburish, *The Rise, Corruption and Coming Fall of the House of Saud* (London: Bloomsbury, 1995), p. 68.
68.   Quoted in David Hirst, 'Power struggle looms for a desert kingdom-in-waiting', *The Guardian*, London, 6 April 1996.
69.   Aburish, *op. cit.*, p. 295.
70.   *Ibid.*, p. 64.
71.   Quoted in Marie Colvin, 'Stolen papers prove Saudi corruption', *The Sunday Times*, London, 12 June 1994.
72.   Paul Halloran and Mark Hollingsworth, *Thatcher's Gold: The Life and Times of Mark Thatcher* (London: Simon and Schuster, 1995), p. 167.
73.   Quoted in *ibid.*, p. 179.
74.   Quoted in *ibid.*, p. 181.
75.   *Ibid.*, p. 184.
76.   Michael Sheridan, 'Our friends the Saudis', *Independent on Sunday*, London, 16 April 1995; David Leigh, 'We've had the lies. Where's the truth?', *The Observer*, London, 22 June 1997; Maurice Chittenden, *The Sunday Times*, London, 22 June 1997; Marie Colvin and Maurice Chittenden, 'Mystery of the missing £25m', *The Sunday Times*, London, 29 June 1997.
77.   Fred Halliday, *Arabia Without Sultans* (London: Penguin, 1974), p. 65.
78.   *Area Handbook for Saudi Arabia*, American University, Washington DC; quoted in *ibid.*, pp. 65–6.
79.   *BBC Summary of World Broadcasts*, 13 April 1967; quoted in *ibid.*, p. 67.
80.   Duncan Campbell, 'BP sets up Saudi secret police', *New Statesman*, London, 23 April 1979.
81.   *Saudi Arabia: Detention Without Trial of Suspected Political Opponents*, Amnesty International, London, MDE 23/04/89, January 1990.
82.   *Shame in the House of Saud*, *op. cit.*, pp. 39–41.
83.   Cited in *ibid.*, pp. 99, 101.
84.   *Saudi Arabia: Religious intolerance: the arrest, detention and torture of Christian worshippers and Shi'a Muslims*, Amnesty International, London, MDE 23/06/93, 14 September 1993. In October 1993 Fahd released some Shi'a Muslims in return for pledges of support. In one view this was an attempt to neutralise the Shi'a opposition while pressing the campaign against the Sunni activists, a larger faction (*The Washington Post*, 16 October 1993).
85.   *Saudi Arabia*, 1993, *op. cit.*, p. 1.

86. *Saudi Arabia: Unwelcome 'guests': the plight of Iraqi refugees*, Amnesty International, London, MDE 23/01/94, 10 May 1994; Kathy Evans, 'Nowhere to hide between Saddam and the emirate', *The Guardian*, London, 21 October 1994.
87. 'Saudi arrests', *The Daily Telegraph*, London, 20 September 1994.
88. 'Saudi Arabia: Human Rights Developments', *Human Rights Watch World Report, Events of 1995*, Human Rights Watch, New York, December 1995.
89. *Ibid.*, p. 306.
90. Quoted in *ibid.*, p. 307
91. *Saudi Arabia*, Amnesty International, London, 1996.
92. *Ibid.*
93. 'Saudi Arabia: Human Rights Developments', *Human Rights Watch World Report 1997*, Human Rights Watch, New York, December 1996, p. 297.
94. *Ibid.*
95. 'UN accuses "torture" nations', *The Guardian*, London, 27 March 1997.
96. J. M. Rodwell translation of the Koran (London: Dent, 1937), p. 490(n).
97. Robert Fisk, 'Scarred by the savage lash of Islamic justice', *The Independent*, London, 13 October 1995.
98. Quoted in *ibid.*
99. Quoted in *ibid.*
100. Quoted in John Ware, 'The virtuous circle', *Index on Censorship*, London, Number 4 (1996), p. 62.
101. *Ibid.*
102. 'How is James Rebenito now?', *Kanlungen Migrant Alert*, Philippines, Number 8 (December 1995).
103. Robert Fisk, 'A friendship that corrupts', *Independent on Sunday*, London, 7 January 1996.
104. *Ibid.*
105. 'Saudi Arabia', *Torture in the Eighties*, Amnesty International, London, 1984.
106. 'Saudi Arabia', *Amnesty International Report 1983*, covering period January-to-December 1982, Amnesty International, London, 1983, p. 327.
107. *Saudi Arabia: Torture, Detention and Arbitrary Arrests*, Amnesty International, London, MDE 23/09/90, November 1990, p. 3.
108. *Ibid.*, p. 4.
109. Quoted in *ibid.*
110. *Shame in the House of Saud*, *op. cit.*, pp. 41–2; it is nominally acknowledged that for a confession to be valid certain conditions have to be satisfied: 'The confessor must be of age, mature, sane, capable of self-expression, and acting of his own free will' (Salma, 'General Principles of Criminal Evidence in Islamic Jurisprudence', in M. C. Bassiouni (ed.), *The Islamic Criminal Justice System*, Oceana Publications, 1982).
111. *Shame in the House of Saud*, *op. cit.*, pp. 42–3.
112. *Ibid.*, pp. 43–4.
113. *Ibid.*, pp. 46–7.
114. See, for example, the individual Amnesty International annual reports, and such individual Amnesty reports as *Saudi Arabia: Religious intolerance*, *op. cit.*; *Saudi Arabia – Behind Closed Doors: Unfair Trials in Saudi Arabia*, Amnesty International, London, MDE 23/08/97, November 1997, pp. 13–16.
115. Jadhakhan (ed.), *op. cit.*, pp. 135–40.
116. 'Women behind the iron curtain in Saudi Arabia', *Arabia Monitor*, July 1993, p. 7.
117. Judith Vidal-Hall, 'Oil, arms and immunity', *Index on Censorship*, London, Number 4 (1996), p. 67.
118. 'Saudi Arabia: Human Rights Developments', 1996, *op. cit.*, p. 308.

119. Adam Raphael, 'How £20 billion buys a blind eye to torture', *The Observer*, London, 17 May 1992; Richard Norton-Taylor, 'Illegal batons "sold by UK to Saudis"', *The Guardian*, London, 11 January 1995; David Pallister, 'Minister admits "torture" baton export licence', *The Guardian*, London, 12 August 1995; Alexander Cockburn and Ken Silverstein, *Washington Babylon* (London: Verso, 1996), p. 180.

120. Pallister, *op. cit.*; *Arming the Torturers: Electro-shock Torture and the Spread of Stun Technology*, Amnesty International, London, ACT 40/01/97, March 1997.

121. Quoted in *Arming the Torturers, op. cit.*, p. 8.

122. *Saudi Arabia: Unwelcome 'guests', op. cit.*, p. 9.

123. *Saudi Arabia*, Amnesty International Report, Amnesty International, London, 1996.

124. See accounts in, for example, Aburish, *op. cit.*, pp. 79–82; John Dickie, *Inside the Foreign Office* (London: Chapmans, 1992), pp. 175–8; Edward W. Said, *The Politics of Dispossession: The Struggle for Palestinian Self-Determination 1969–1994* (London: Chatto and Windus, 1994), pp. 236–41.

125. *Saudi Arabia: An upsurge in public executions*, Amnesty International, London, MDE 23/04/93, 15 May 1993, p. 4.

126. Quoted in Charles Richards, 'Saudi envoy rejects execution dossier', *The Independent*, London, 2 July 1993.

127. James McCredie, 'I feel numb. I have seen Islamic justice firsthand', *The Guardian*, London, 27 April 1995.

128. Quoted in 'Saudis defend executions', *The Guardian*, London, 28 April 1995; see also Con Coughlin, 'Pilgrims face sword of Islam on the road to Mecca', *The Sunday Telegraph*, London, 30 April 1995.

129. Steve Boggan, 'Nurses made confessions "under extreme pressure"', *The Independent*, London, 28 December 1996; Marie Colvin, 'British nurses say Saudi police abused them', *The Sunday Times*, London, 25 May 1997; Laurence Donegan, 'Confessions by nurses to Saudi murder obtained by coercion, claim scientists', *The Guardian*, London, 6 June 1997; Tim Reid, 'British nurse "condemned to death" for Saudi killing', *The Daily Telegraph*, London, 31 August 1997. An earlier case concerned the mysterious death, still not resolved, of the British nurse Helen Smith who allegedly fell from a balcony in Jeddah in 1979 during a drinks party. See Paul Foot, *The Helen Smith Story* (London: Fontana, 1983); Martin Wainwright, 'Body in morgue for 18 years "holds key to Saudi death of British nurse"', *The Guardian*, London, 31 May 1997.

130. This and the subsequent sources are cited in Hermann Heinrich Ploss, Max Bartels and Paul Bartels, *Woman: An Historical Gynaecological and Anthropological Compendium* (London: Heinemann, 1935).

131. Elizabeth Gould Davis, *The First Sex* (London: Dent, 1973), p. 154.

132. T. Bell, *Kalogynomia* (London: Stockdale, 1821), p. 177; quoted in *ibid.*, p. 156.

133. Richard Burton, *Love, War and Fancy: Notes to the Arabian Nights* (London: Kimber, 1954), p. 108.

134. Deborah Pugh, 'Egypt to end genital mutilation', *The Guardian*, London, 28 March 1994.

135. Shyam Bhatia, 'Women battle for ban on mutilation in name of God', *The Observer*, London, 30 July 1995.

136. Kathy Evans, 'Egypt court backs female circumcision', *The Guardian*, London, 25 June 1997; 'Circumcision approved', *The Daily Telegraph*, London, 25 June 1997.

137. Sasson, *op. cit.*, pp. 159–62.

138. *Ibid.*, p. 160.

139. Fernando Henriques, *Prostitution and Society: A Survey, Volume 1, Primitive, Classical and Oriental* (London: MacGibbon and Kee, 1962), p. 336.
140. R. Patai, *Sex and Family in the Bible and the Middle East* (New York, 1949), pp. 138–9.
141. C. Snouk Hurongronje, *Mekka* (The Hague, 1888–9), Volume 1, pp. 60f.
142. J. S. Buckingham, *Travels in Assyria, Media and Persia* (London, 1830), Volume 1, pp. 110f.
143. F. W. Lane, *An Account of the Manners and Customs of the Modern Egyptians (1833–5)* (London, 1896), p. 387. A detailed account of sexual behaviour in the Middle East is given in Allen Edwardes, *The Jewel in the Lotus: A Historical Survey of the Sexual Culture of the East* (London: Blond, 1961).
144. *Saudi Arabia*, Human Rights Report, *op. cit.*, p. 10.
145. *Ibid.*
146. *Ibid.*, p. 11.
147. *Shame in the House of Saud*, *op. cit.*, p. 94.
148. Mona Al Munajjed, *Women in Saudi Arabia Today* (London: Macmillan, 1997), p. 107.
149. *Ibid.*
150. Sasson, *op. cit.*, p. 15.
151. *Ibid.*, pp. 21–2.
152. *Ibid.*, pp. 214–16.
153. *Ibid.*, pp. 263–6; see also the sequel, Jean Sasson, *Daughters of Arabia* (London: Bantam, 1995).
154. Linda Blandford, *Oil Sheikhs* (London: Weidenfeld and Nicolson, 1976), p. 48.
155. *Ibid.*, p. 73.
156. Jehan Sadat, *A Woman of Egypt* (London: Coronet, 1987), p. 368.
157. *Ibid.*, pp. 387–8.
158. *Ibid.*, p. 388.
159. Quoted in Yusuf Al-Qaradawi, *The Lawful and the Prohibited in Islam (Al-Halal Wal-Haram fil Islam)* (Indianapolis, USA: American Trust Publications,) p. 85.
160. *Ibid.*, p. 90.
161. Abdul Malik Mujahid, in Muhammad bin Abdul-Aziz al-Musnad (compiler), *Islamic Fatawa Regarding Women*, translated by Jamaal Al-Din Zarabozo (Darussalam, Saudi Arabia, 1996).
162. *Ibid.*
163. Atwan, *op. cit.*, p. 78; another account of the episode talks of '48 veiled women' drivers.
164. Khaled Bin Sultan, *Desert Warrior* (London: HarperCollins, 1996), p. 211.
165. *Ibid.*, p. 302.
166. Ghazi Algosaibi, *The Gulf Crisis: An Attempt to Understand* (London: Kegan Paul, 1993), pp. 96–7.
167. *Ibid.*, p. 97.
168. Carol Berger, 'Sheikhs to show Islam Mecca is in good hands', *The Independent*, London, 14 February 1991.
169. Ahmed Versi, 'Why Islam is really a women-friendly religion', *The Guardian*, London, 16 November 1996.
170. Jamal A. Badawi, *The Status of Women in Islam*, Islamic Propagation Centre International (UK), Birmingham, England.
171. Mostafa Mahmoud, *Dialogue with an Atheist* (London: Dar Al Taqwa, 1994), p. 68.
172. Mai Yamani, 'Some observations on women in Saudi Arabia', in Mai Yamani (ed.), *Feminism and Islam: Legal and Literary Perspectives* (Reading, England: Ithaca Press, 1996), pp. 263–81.

173. *Ibid.*, p. 280; see also Maria Holt, 'A tangle of meanings; women and the contemporary Islamic movement', talk given to Middle East Society, Cambridge University, England, 7 May 1996, published as Arab World Briefing Number 3, CAABU, London; 'Saudi Arabia: silent revolution', *The Economist*, London, 4 February 1995; Mai Yamani, 'The power behind the veil', *Index on Censorship*, London, Number 4 (1996), pp. 80–83.
174. Quoted in Kathy Evans, 'Grand Mufti says yes to "pop-in marriage"', *The Observer*, London, 15 December 1996.
175. Quoted in Thomas Lippman, 'Albright makes women's rights her priority', *The Guardian*, London, 26 March 1997.
176. Mohammed H. Siddiq, *Crescent International*, 1–15 May 1995.
177. Reported by Alistair Cooke, *The Manchester Guardian*, Manchester, England, 30 January 1957.
178. Robert Lacey, *The Kingdom* (London: Fontana, 1982), p. 177.
179. Quoted in *ibid.*, p. 345.
180. *The Daily Telegraph*, London, 3 June 1963; cited in Holden and Johns, *op. cit.*, p. 230.
181. Mohamed Awad (Special Rapporteur on Slavery), *Report on Slavery*, United Nations, New York, 1966, pp. 120–21.
182. John Osman, *The Sunday Telegraph*, London, 17 March 1963.
183. Awad, *op. cit.*, p. 121.
184. *Ibid.*, p. 122.
185. *Ibid.*, p. 123.
186. *Ibid.*, p. 173.
187. Aburish, *op. cit.*, p. 88.
188. *Ibid.*, p. 90.
189. *Ibid.*, p. 91.
190. *Shame in the House of Saud*, *op. cit.*, p. 54.
191. *Ibid.*, pp. 57–8.
192. *Ibid.*, pp. 59–60.
193. *Ibid.*, pp. 60–76.
194. Robert Fisk, 'Gulf maids in slavery to a reign of terror', *The Independent*, London, 12 October 1995.
195. Michael Sheridan, 'Manila issues sex warning to migrant maids', *The Sunday Times*, London, 2 February 1997.
196. See, for example, Bridget Anderson, *Britain's Secret Slaves: An Investigation into the Plight of Overseas Domestic Workers*, Anti-Slavery International, Kalayaan, and The Migrant Domestic Workers, London, 1993.
197. 'Remy's story', *1995 Slavery Still Alive*, Kalayaan, Justice for Overseas Domestic Workers, London, 1995, p. 10.
198. Rajeev Syal, 'London maids sue Saudi royals over abuse claims', *The Sunday Times*, London, 5 January 1997; Luke Harding, 'Maids can sue Saudi princess', *The Guardian*, London, 21 May 1997.

Notes to Chapter 2: Religious Roots

1. Andrew Crichton, *The History of Arabia*, Volume 1 (New York: Harper and Brothers, 1838), pp. 36–7.
2. J. Zarins, N. Whalen, M. Ibrahim, A. Morad and M. Khan, 'Preliminary Report on the Central and Southwestern Provinces Survey', *Atlal* 4, Riyadh (1980), pp. 9–36.
3. William Facey, *Riyadh, The Old City* (London: IMMEL Publishing, 1992), p. 29.

4. *Ibid.*, p. 33.
5. Crichton, *op. cit.*, pp. 82–96.
6. *Ibid.*
7. Frederich Engels, letter to Karl Marx, Manchester, England, 24 May 1853; in K. Marx and F. Engels, *On Religion* (Moscow, 1955), pp. 119–20.
8. Crichton, *op. cit.*, p. 96.
9. *Ibid.*, p. 108; lists 19 Kings of Yemen (noting also four anonymous kings) who reigned between 175 and 529.
10. Alfred Guillaume, *Islam* (Harmondsworth, England: Penguin, 1954), p. 1. In another view it is the southern Arabs who are the 'true Arabs' (see Peter Mansfield, *A History of the Middle East* (London, England: Penguin, 1991), p. 6.
11. From the Arab word 'Badawiyin', meaning 'people who appear in open country', such as the desert expanses.
12. Guillaume, *op. cit.*, p. 2.
13. Peter Mansfield, *The Arabs* (Harmondsworth, England: Penguin, 1980), p. 16.
14. See, for example, P. J. Parr, L. Harding and J. Dayton, 'Preliminary Survey in North-West Arabia, 1968', *Bulletin of the Institute of Archaeology* 8 and 9, London (1970); P. J. Parr, 'North-West Arabia from *c.*1200 BC to AD 106', unpublished paper produced for Local Museums research project, Department of Antiquities and Museums, Riyadh, Saudi Arabia, 1984. Both, with more, cited by Facey, *op. cit.*, 1992.
15. See, for example, the brief profile in Facey, *op. cit.*, pp. 36–7.
16. *Ibid.*, p. 37.
17. R. A. Nicholson, cited by W. Montgomery Watt, *Muhammad at Mecca* (London: Oxford University Press, 1953), p. 20.
18. Karen Armstrong, *A History of God* (London: Mandarin, 1993), p. 157.
19. Watt, *op. cit.*, p. 23.
20. Hisham ibn Muhammad al-Kalbi, *The Book of Idols*, trans. from Arabic by Nahim Amin Faris (Princeton University Press; Series Princeton Oriental Studies, 1952), pp. 16–17, 19–20, 23–4, 27–9.
21. *Ibid.*
22. *Ibid.*
23. Paul Tabori, *Taken in Adultery* (London: Aldus, 1949), p. 166.
24. Allen Edwardes, *The Jewel in the Lotus, A Historical Survey of the Sexual Culture of the East* (London: Anthony Blond, 1961), pp. 45–6.
25. *Ibid.*, p. 99.
26. Muhammad Mazheruddin Siddiqi, *Women in Islam* (Lahore: Institute of Islamic Culture, 1959).
27. Cited in Allen Edwardes and R. E. L. Masters, *The Cradle of Erotica* (London: Odyssey Press, 1970), p. 96.
28. W. Montgomery Watt, *Muhammad at Medina* (London: Oxford University Press, 1956), pp. 272–4.
29. Watt (1953), *op. cit.*, pp. 5–8.
30. *Ibid.*, pp. 10–11.
31. *Ibid.*, p. 9.
32. Robert L. Playfair, *A History of the Arabia Felix or Yemen* (Bombay, 1859; reprinted St Leonards Ad Orientem, Amsterdam Philo Press, 1970), p. 67.
33. *Ibid.*, p. 71.
34. *Ibid.*, p. 77.
35. The main sources for the life of Muhammed are the Koran and historical works of the third and fourth centuries of the Muslim era: the *Sira* (or life of Muhammed) by Mohammed Ibn Ishaq (d. 768); the part of the *Annals* of Abu Jafar al-Tabari

(d. 922) that covers the life of Muhammed; the *Maghazi* (or History of Muhammed's Campaigns) by Umar al-Waqidi (d. 822); and the *Tabaqat* of Mohammed Ibn Sa'd (d. 845), a vast compilation on Muhammed, his chief Companions and later 'bearers of Islam'. *The Traditions* (anecdotes about the sayings and doings of Muhammed) are collected in the *Sahih* of al-Bukhari and in the *Musnad* of Ahmad ibn Hanbal. Biographical dictionaries of the Companions are given in the *Usd al-Ghabah* by Ibn al-Athir (d. 1234) and the *Isabah* by Ibn Majar (d. 1447).

36. Mohammed Ibn Ishaq, *The Life of Mohammed*, trans. by A. Guillaume (Lahore: Oxford University Press, 1955), pp. 68–72, 104–7, 493–7.
37. Source cited in Watt (1953), *op. cit.*, p. 40.
38. Cited in *ibid.*, pp. 40–1; sources given.
39. Thomas Kiernan, *The Arabs* (London: Sphere, 1978), p. 119.
40. John Bagot Glubb, *A Short History of the Arab Peoples* (London: Quartet, 1980), pp. 36–7.
41. Quoted in Albert Hourani, *A History of the Arab Peoples* (London: Faber and Faber, 1991), p. 18.
42. Glubb, *op. cit.*, p. 38.
43. Watt (1956), *op. cit.*, pp. 66–7.
44. Hourani, *op. cit.*, p. 19.
45. Watt (1956), *op. cit.*, discusses, for example, the 'Constitution of Medina' (preserved by Ibn Ishaq), pp. 221–8.
46. Watt (1956), *op. cit.*, pp. 393–9.
47. See Norman Daniel, *Islam and the West: The Making of An Image* (Edinburgh, 1960); and R. W. Southern, *Western Views of Islam in the Middle Ages* (Cambridge, MA, 1980); cited by Rana Kabbani, *Letter to Christendom* (London: Virago, 1992).
48. Rana Kabbani, *Letter to Christendom* (London: Virago, 1992), p. 8. See also Rana Kabbani, *Europe's Myths of Orient, Devise and Rule* (London: Macmillan, 1986).
49. Karen Armstrong, *Muhammad, A Biography of the Prophet* (London: Victor Gollancz, 1991), pp. 9–44.
50. *Ibid.*, pp. 10–12.
51. Winwood Reade, *The Martyrdom of Man* (London: Watts, 1925), p. 211.
52. *Ibid.*, pp. 211–13; Watts (1953) *op. cit.*, pp. 49–50, discusses Muhammed's fear, despair and thoughts of suicide.
53. *Ibid.*, p. 213.
54. Armstrong (1991), *op. cit.*, p. 83.
55. *Ibid.*, p. 84.
56. Crichton, *op. cit.*, p. 202.
57. *Ibid.*, pp. 202–3.
58. *Ibid.*, p. 218.
59. *Ibid.*, p. 220.
60. Armstrong (1991), *op. cit.*, p. 138.
61. Quoted by J. M. Rodwell, Preface to *The Koran*, trans. by Rodwell (London: Dent, 1st edition, 1909), p. 1.
62. *Ibid.*
63. Some commentators have not been impressed by how Zaid set about his task. Thus Rodwell (*Ibid.*, p. 2): 'Zaid and his coadjutors ... do not appear to have arranged the materials ... upon any system more definite than that of placing the longest and best known Suras first ... even this rule, artless and unscientific as it is, has not been adhered to with strictness. Anything approaching to a chronological arrangement was entirely lost sight of ... The text ... necessarily assumes the form of a most unreadable and incongruous patchwork ...'.

64. Rodwell (*ibid.*, pp. 2–7) conveys well some of the problems of Koranic exegesis (without beginning to explore the underlying difficulties of religious philosophy). See also Watt (1953), *op. cit.*, pp. 60–72.

65. Crichton, *op. cit.*, p. 275.

66. *Ibid.*

67. N. J. Dawood, Introduction to his translation of the Koran (London: Penguin, 1956), p. 9.

68. Mostafa Mahmoud, *Dialogue with an Atheist* (London: Dar Al Taqwa, 1994), p. 92.

69. *Ibid.*

70. Harold Nicolson, in a letter (9 August 1961) to Vita Sackville-West, writing of the Koran being 'diffuse, repetitive and superficial' and of the 'thinness' of Muhammed's teaching, represents a typical Western response (*Diaries and Letters, 1945–1962* (London: Collins, 1968), p. 397). In the same vein the novelist Anthony Powell comments in his *Journals, 1990–1992* (London: Heinemann, 1997), 11 May 1992: 'I read with considerable skipping, the Koran (tr. N. J. Dashwood). Repetitive, lacking in narrative powers, in short not a patch on the Bible.'

71. Crichton, *op. cit.*, pp. 286–7.

72. The Bible too, like all substantial sacred texts, is replete with superstition, absurdity and contradiction. See G. W. Foote and W. P. Ball, *The Bible Handbook* (London: Pioneer Press, 1961).

73. This means that the supposed Word of God is inevitably defined by human beings. People, rather than divinities, are the *de facto* authorities behind all 'sacred' texts. From this logico-empirical circumstance there can be no escape.

74. G. W. Murray, *Sons of Ishmael, A Study of the Egyptian Bedouin* (London: Routledge, 1935), pp. 150–56.

75. Yusuf Al-Qaradawi, *The Lawful and the Prohibited in Islam (Al-Halal Wal-Waram Fil Islam)* (Indianapolis, US, 1960).

Notes to Chapter 3: Conquest and Decline

1. Robert L. Playfair, *A History of Arabia Felix or Yemen* (Bombay, 1859; reprinted St Leonards Ad Orientem, Amsterdam Philo Press, 1970), p. 80.

2. Quoted in *ibid.*, pp. 80–1.

3. Philip K. Hitti, *History of the Arabs* (London: Macmillan, 1970), p. 141.

4. J. J. Saunders, *A History of Medieval Islam* (London: Routledge and Kegan Paul, 1965), p. 42.

5. Hitti, *op. cit.*, p. 149; sources cited.

6. Quoted in *ibid.*, p. 150.

7. Quoted in *ibid.*, p. 151.

8. Quoted in *ibid.*, p. 152.

9. Quoted in *ibid.*, pp. 156–7.

10. Saunders, *op. cit.*, p. 56.

11. John Bagot Glubb, *A Short History of the Arab Peoples* (London: Quartet, 1980), p. 64.

12. Andrew Crichton, *The History of Arabia*, Volume 1 (New York: Harper and Brothers, 1838), pp. 366–7.

13. Joel Carmichael, *The Shaping of the Arabs* (London, 1967), p. 118.

14. Saunders, *op. cit.*, p. 103.

15. Andrew Crichton, *The History of Arabia*, Volume 2 (New York: Harper and Brothers, 1838), p. 10.

16. Muhammed ibn Jarir al-Tabari, *Tarikh*, ed. M. Ibrahim, Volume 7 (Cairo, 1966), pp. 614–22, trans. J. A. Williams, *Al-Tabari, the Early Abbasi Empire, I: The Reign of al-Ja'far al-Mansur* (Cambridge, 1988), p. 145; quoted by Albert Hourani, *A History of the Arab Peoples* (London: Faber and Faber, 1991), p. 33.

17. Crichton (Vol. 2), *op. cit.*, p. 13.

18. Some historians remember al-Mamum as the Octonary, since he was the *eighth* caliph of his family, the *eighth* in descent from Abbas; he gained *eight* distinguished victories; *eight* sons of princes were enrolled in his service; he possessed *8000* male and *8000* female slaves; he had *eight* sons and *eight* daughters; he owned *80,000* horses; he left in his coffers *eight* million gold dinars, with *18* million drachms of silver.

19. There is debate (see, for example, Glubb, *op. cit.*, p. 110) about the extent to which such remarkable cultural advances were Arab (as opposed to Persian, Greek or Armenian). Such doubts, sometimes smacking of European racism, are largely sterile. What is beyond doubt is that this amazing cultural progress was made at the heart of the Muslim empire.

20. William D. Phillips, *Slavery from Roman Times to the Transatlantic Trade* (Manchester University Press, England, 1985), pp. 76–7. Some authorities (for example, M. A. Shaban, *Islamic History: A New Interpretation*, Cambridge, 1971) question whether the Zanj were slaves.

21. Saunders, *op. cit.*, pp. 125–40.

22. Amin Maalouf, *The Crusades through Arab Eyes*, trans. Jon Rothschild (London: Al Saqi Books, 1984), p. 6.

23. Joachim Kahl, *The Misery of Christianity*, trans. N. D. Smith (Harmondsworth, England: Penguin, 1971), p. 47.

24. Glubb, *op. cit.*, Chapter 14.

25. Quoted by Maalouf, *op. cit.*, pp. 235–6.

26. Stanford J. Shaw, *History of the Ottoman Empire and Modern Turkey, Volume 1, Empire of the Gazis: The Rise and Decline of the Ottoman Empire, 1280–1808* (Cambridge, England: Cambridge University Press, 1976), pp. 83–5.

27. *Ibid.*

28. *Ibid.*, p. 95.

29. Alan Palmer, *The Decline and Fall of the Ottoman Empire* (London: John Murray, 1992), p. 3.

30. *Ibid.*, pp. 5–6.

31. Shaw, *op. cit.*, p. 194.

Notes to Chapter 4: Saudi Ascendancy

1. Edward G. Browne, *A Year Among the Persians* (London: Adam and Charles Black, 1893), p. 306.

2. R. Bayly Winder, *Saudi Arabia in the Nineteenth Century* (London: Macmillan, 1965), pp. 6–8.

3. John Bagot Glubb, *War in the Desert* (London: Hodder and Stoughton, 1960), p. 42.

4. David Holden and Richard Johns, *The House of Saud* (London: Sidgwick and Jackson, 1981), p. 20.

5. Winder, *op. cit.*, p. 9.

6. Wilfred Cantwell Smith, *Islam in Modern History* (Princeton, 1957), p. 42.

7. Winder, *op. cit.*, pp. 10–11.

8. *Ibid.*

9. Quoted in Winder, *op. cit.*, p. 13.

10. *Ibid.*
11. William Facey, *Riyadh: The Old City* (London; IMMEL Publishing, 1992), p. 100.
12. *Ibid.*, pp. 99–100.
13. Husain ibn Ghannam; quoted by Facey, *ibid.*, p. 102.
14. Reinand, responding to questions asked by the German scholar Ulrich Seetzen in Aleppo in 1805, remarked that Diriyah was a small town 'beautifully built in the Arabian style'; and that Abdul Aziz, then about 60 years old, was a 'slim, lean man, very educated for a savage Arab'.
15. Robert L. Playfair, *A History of Arabia Felix or Yemen* (Bombay, 1859; reprinted St Leonards Ad Orientum Ltd, Amsterdam Philo Press, 1970), p. 132.
16. *Ibid.*, p. 133.
17. George Foster Sadleir, *Diary of a Journey Across Arabia* (Bombay, 1866; reprinted, Cambridge, 1977), pp. 77–9.
18. A cholera epidemic broke out in India in 1817, reached the Gulf in 1821, and reached Astrakhan on the Volga in September 1823. Bahrain suffered 4000 cholera deaths in 1821.
19. Quoted by Winder, *op. cit.*, p. 57.
20. W. G. Palgrave, *Narrative of a Year's Journey through Central and Eastern Arabia (1862–63)*, Volume 2 (London, 1865), p. 18.
21. Winder, *op. cit.*, p. 91.
22. Harry St John Bridger Philby, *Arabia* (London, 1930), p. 114.
23. Louis Pelly, *Report on a Journey to the Wahabee Capital of Riyadh in Central Arabia* (Bombay, 1866), p. 7.
24. *Ibid.*
25. Winder, *op. cit.*, p. 228.
26. Ibn Isa, *Iqd al-Darar fima Waqa'a fi Najd* (Riyadh, 1954/5), translated Winder, *op. cit.*, p. 251; quoted by Facey, *op. cit.*, p. 171.
27. J. G. Lorimer, *Gazetteer of the Persian Gulf, Oman and Central Arabia*, Volume 1 (Calcutta, 1908–15), p. 983; cited by Winder, *op. cit.*, p. 263.
28. Harry St John Bridger Philby, *The Heart of Arabia* (London, 1922), pp. 100–1.
29. This successful offensive action has been copiously described as the historical start of the modern Saudi state. Facey (*op. cit.*, p. 344) cites a dozen representative accounts. There are many more.
30. Quoted by Facey, *op. cit.*, p. 187.
31. Letter to Sheikh Mubarak of Kuwait, archives of India Office, London; quoted in Robert Lacey, *The Kingdom* (London: Fontana, 1982), p. 72.
32. Lacey, *op. cit.*, p. 72.
33. H. V. F. Winstone, *Captain Shakespear* (New York: Quartet Books, 1978), p. 38.
34. Quoted in D. Howarth, *The Desert King* (London, 1964), p. 70.
35. C. M. Helms, *The Cohesion of Saudi Arabia* (London, 1980), p. 289.
36. A. Hirtzel of the India Office, minute, 2 April 1914; quoted in G. Troeller, *The Birth of Saudi Arabia* (London, 1976), p. 7, n. 97.
37. Quoted by Leslie McLoughlin, *Ibn Saud, Founder of a Kingdom* (London: Macmillan, 1993), p. 45.
38. The text of the treaty is included in Troeller, *op. cit.*
39. Peter Mansfield, *A History of the Middle East* (Harmondsworth: Penguin, 1991), p. 152.
40. Jeremy Wilson, *Lawrence of Arabia* (London: Mandarin, 1989), p. 235.
41. David Fromkin, *A Peace to End all Peace: Creating the Modern Middle East 1914–1922* (Harmondsworth: Penguin, 1991), p. 219.

42. Holden and Johns (*op. cit.*, p. 53) note that the Hashemites were given about £1 million in gold (sources cited); G. M. Gathorne-Hardy (*A Short History of International Affairs, 1920–1938* (London: Oxford University Press, 1939), p. 126) highlights the subsidy to Hussain and Faisal of £2.4 million a year.
43. Holden and Johns, *op. cit.*, p. 53.
44. H. V. F. Winstone and Zahra Freeth, *Kuwait: Prospect and Reality* (London: George Allen and Unwin, 1972), p. 87.
45. Quoted in *ibid.*, p. 90.
46. Holden and Johns, *op. cit.*, p. 80.
47. Quoted in McLoughlin, *op. cit.*, pp. 68–9.
48. Hafiz Wahba, *Arabian Days* (London: Arthur Barker, 1964), p. 20; quoted by Holden and Johns, *op. cit.*, p. 84.
49. Holden and Johns, *op. cit.*, p. 85.
50. J. Lunt, *Glubb Pasha* (London, 1984), pp. 49–50.
51. Quoted in McLoughlin, *op. cit.*, p. 106.
52. A. Ryan, *The Last of the Dracomans* (London, 1951), p. 278.
53. Said K. Aburish, *The Rise, Corruption and Coming Fall of the House of Saud* (London: Bloomsbury, 1995), p. 24.
54. *Ibid.*
55. *Ibid.*, p. 27.
56. Philby is said to have benefited from Ibn Saud's generosity in this regard.
57. Quoted by Aburish, *op. cit.*, p. 32.

Notes to Chapter 5: The Oil State

1. Ibn Saud, quoted in M. Asad, *The Road to Mecca* (London, 1954), p. 178.
2. Ibn Saud, quoted in K. Zirikli, *Arabia in the Time of Abdul-Aziz*, 4 volumes, in Arabic – see Note 11 (Beirut, 1970), p. 984.
3. Harold St John Bridger Philby, *The Empty Quarter* (London: Century, 1986). The many appendices cover such topics as meteorites, flora and fauna (ostrich eggs, mammals, reptiles, insects, etc.).
4. Another explorer, Bertram Thomas, crossed the Empty Quarter from south to north in 1931 without obtaining Ibn Saud's permission.
5. The only significant non-Anglo-American company allowed within the Red Line area was France's Compagnie Française des Pétroles, given the Deutsche Bank's interest in the Turkish Petroleum Company as part of the settlement following the Great War. See Anthony Sampson, *The Seven Sisters* (London: Hodder and Stoughton, 1980), p. 84.
6. Robert Lacey, *The Kingdom* (London: Fontana, 1982), p. 236.
7. *Ibid.*, pp. 236–7.
8. Leslie McLouglin, *Ibn Saud: Founder of a Kingdom* (London: Macmillan, 1993), pp. 128–9.
9. *Ibid.*
10. Quoted in *ibid.*, p. 131.
11. Khair al-Din Zirikli, *Shibh al-Jazira fee Ahd al-Malik Abdul-Aziz*, 4 volumes (Beirut, 1970), p. 1100; quoted by McLouglin, *op. cit.*, p. 137.
12. At the inauguration of the Arabic service of the BBC (August 1938), attended by Ibn Saud and Bullard, the first report was of a young Palestinian hanged by the British for possessing arms (Ibn Saud: 'If it had not been for the Zionist policy of the British government that Arab would be alive today').
13. Lacey, *op. cit.*, pp. 254–5.

14. Quoted in *ibid.*, p. 257.
15. David Holden and Richard Johns, *The House of Saud* (London: Sidgwick and Jackson, 1981), p. 126.
16. Quoted by Lacey, *op. cit.*, p. 257.
17. In 1937 Ibn Saud declared to Harold Dickson that a Muslim who killed a Jew in war would be assured 'an immediate entry to Heaven ...'.
18. Harold St John Bridger Philby, *Arabian Highlands* (Cornell, 1952), pp. 75ff.
19. Quoted by Lacey, *op. cit.*, p. 261.
20. Lacey, *op. cit.*, p. 264.
21. There were other matters, noted by Lacey (*op. cit.*, p. 274). Ibn Saud gave Churchill robes, a jewelled sword, dagger and diamond rings (all valued at £3500). The Prime Minister of the British Empire responded with a £100 case of scent. Roosevelt gave Ibn Saud his own wheelchair and a DC3 aircraft. Later the British provided the King with a special Rolls Royce, with right-hand drive, meaning that Ibn Saud would be forced to sit on the left of his driver, a position of dishonour.
22. J. B. Kelly, *Eastern Arabian Frontiers* London: Faber and Faber, 1964).
23. Lacey, *op. cit.*, p. 292.
24. Little mention was made of the reasons for earlier Saudi enthusiasm for Buraimi; namely, to collect revenues from slave sales.
25. These sons were Abdul-Majeed (1940), Sattam (1940), Ahmad (1940), Mamduh (1941), Hidhlul (1941), Mashdur (1942), Abdul-Salaam (between 1942 and 1944), and Maqrin (1943), bringing the total to well over forty sons. The similar number of daughters was always given minimum publicity.
26. Lacey, *op. cit.*, p. 300.
27. Slade-Baker, unpublished papers: 'Middle East Diary No. 5', entry for 31 May 1956; quoted by William Facey, *Riyadh: The Old City* (London: IMMEL Publishing, 1992), p. 318.
28. Lacey, *op. cit.*, p. 301.
29. Quoted in *ibid.*, p. 305.
30. Kelly, *op. cit.*, pp. 266–7.
31. Mark W. Zacher, *Dag Hammarskjöld's United Nations* (London: Columbia University Press, 1970), p. 98.
32. Lacey, *op. cit.*, p. 309. When Philby, now over 70, refused to apologise, Saud sent trucks round to Philby's Riyadh house to empty it of the possessions that Philby had collected over a lifetime in Arabia. Then Philby was exiled to Lebanon.
33. Peter Mansfield, *The Arabs* (London: Penguin, 1983), p. 401.
34. Quoted by Said K. Aburish, *The Rise, Corruption and Coming Fall of the House of Saud* (London: Bloomsbury, 1995), p. 45.
35. *Ibid.*, p. 45.
36. Faisal's anti-semitism was well known. He once proclaimed the mediaeval view that the Jews used the blood of Gentile babies to make bread for the Passover (Mansfield, *op. cit.*, p. 402, n.).
37. R. T. Naylor, *Hot Money and the Politics of Debt* (London: Unwin, 1988), p. 35.
38. Mansfield, *op. cit.*, p. 406.
39. George Corm, *Fragmentation of the Middle East* (London: Hutchinson, 1988), p. 84.
40. Aburish, *op. cit.*, pp. 46–51.
41. Jeffrey Robinson, *Yamani: The Inside Story* (London: Fontana, 1988).
42. Aburish, *op. cit.*, p. 48.
43. *Ibid.*, p. 49.
44. Lacey, *op. cit.*, p. 423.
45. Aburish, *op. cit.*, p. 50.

46. Holden and Johns, *op. cit.*, p. 329.
47. J. B. Kelly, *Arabia, the Gulf and the West* (New York: Basic Books, 1980), p. 244.
48. Robinson, *op. cit.*, pp. 215–17. There were many theories as to why Faisal ibn Musaid had murdered the King. Suggested elements included the CIA, Libya's Muammar Gaddafi, anti-American groups in Saudi Arabia, Marxists, and simple revenge for a dead brother.
49. Lacey, *op. cit.*, pp. 423–8.
50. Aburish, *op. cit.*, p. 51.
51. Holden and Johns, *op. cit.*, pp. 384–5.
52. Aburish, *op. cit.*, p. 52.
53. Lacey, *op. cit.*, p. 430.
54. Robinson, *op. cit.*, pp. 266–7.
55. Robinson (*op. cit.*, pp. 259–74) and others discuss the so-called 'Sudeiri conspiracy' in detail.
56. Quoted by Aburish, *op. cit.*, p. 54.
57. *Ibid.*, pp. 58–9.
58. Mansfield, *op. cit.*, p. 241.
59. F. William Engdahl, *A Century of War: Anglo-American Oil Politics and the New World Order* (Concord, Massachusetts: Paul and Company, 1993), p. 60.
60. From the Trenchard Papers, quoted in Philip Knightley and Colin Simpson, *The Secret Lives of Lawrence of Arabia* (London, 1969), p. 139. C. Townshend, 'Civilization and Frightfulness', 148, Wg/Cdr to CAS, 19 February 1920, Trenchard Papers MFC 76/1/36; Martin Gilbert, *Winston S. Churchill*, Volume IV (London: Heinemann, 1975), pp. 494, 810; Companion IV ii, pp. 1066–7, 1083, 1170; quoted in David E. Omissi, *Air Power and Colonial Control: The Royal Air Force 1919–1939* (Manchester, England: Manchester University Press, 1990), p. 160.
61. Anton Mohr, '*The Oil War*' (New York: Harcourt, Brace and Company, 1926).
62. Dwight D. Eisenhower, *Mandate for Change, 1953–1956: The White House Years* (London: Heinemann, 1963), pp. 163–6.
63. Mordechai Abir, *Oil, Power and Politics: Conflict and Arabia, the Red Sea and the Gulf* (London: Frank Cass, 1974), pp. 14–19.
64. Holden and Johns, *op. cit.*, p. 125.
65. *Ibid.*
66. Nor were such past pre-war British betrayals of Arab aspirations – the Hussain–McMahon correspondence on Arab independence, the Sykes–Picot Agreement carving up Arab land between Britain and France, and the Balfour Declaration signalling a Jewish right to Arab territory – forgotten by Arab observers newly seduced by US claims to an anti-imperialist posture.
67. William Blum, *The CIA: A Forgotten History* (London: Zed Books, 1986), pp. 103–7.
68. Nasser himself had the option of supporting the Eisenhower Doctrine but would neither willingly enter the sphere of influence of any Great Power nor deprive himself of Soviet aid (Robert Stephens, *Nasser: A Political Biography* (London: Allen Lane, 1971), p. 238).
69. Dwight D. Eisenhower, *Waging Peace, Volume II, The White House Years* (New York: Doubleday, 1963–5), Appendix D, pp. 669–70, 680–81.
70. Stephens, *op. cit.*, pp. 258–9.
71. Patrick Seale, *The Struggle for Syria: A Study of Post-War Arab Politics, 1945–1958* (London: I. B. Tauris, 1965), p. 289.
72. Ibid., pp. 302–3.
73. *Al-Sha'b* (Damascus), 28 September 1957; quoted by Seale, *op. cit.*, pp. 303–4.
74. *New York Times*, 4 October 1957.

75. According to Nasser himself, speech, 6 March 1958; quoted in Keith Wheelock, *Nasser's New Egypt: A Critical Analysis* (London: Atlantic Books, Stevens and Sons, 1960), p. 259. The money was said to have been offered to the head of Syrian military intelligence, Colonel Abdul Hamid Sarraj (Stephens, *op. cit.*, pp. 261–2).
76. Robert Engler, *The Politics of Oil* (Chicago, 1967), p. 254.
77. Aburish, *op. cit.*, p. 148.
78. *Ibid.*, pp. 156–7.
79. Richard Nixon, *Memoirs* (London: Arrow Books, 1979), pp. 1012–13.
80. Naylor, *op. cit.*, p. 397.
81. *Ibid.*
82. Aburish, *op. cit.*, pp. 169–70.
83. *Ibid.*, p. 170.
84. Naylor, *op. cit.*, p. 403.
85. K. S. Twitchell, *Saudi Arabia* (Princeton, New Jersey: Princeton University Press, 1953), p. 139.
86. In *ibid* is the Ibn Saud accolade: 'To the memory of Charles R. Crane, the great American whose practical philanthropy was the foundation of the present development of the kingdom of his esteemed friend.'
87. *Ibid.*, p. 148.
88. *Ibid.*, p. 150.
89. *Fortune Magazine*, June 1944; quoted in *ibid.*, p. 153.
90. Harold St John Bridger Philby, *Arabian Jubilee* (London, 1962), p. 179.
91. Sampson, *op. cit.*, p. 91.
92. Senate Multinational subcommittee: *A Documentary History of the Petroleum Reserves Corporation, 1943–1944* (Washington, 1974) pp. 4–5; quoted by Sampson, *op. cit.*, pp. 95–6.
93. Sampson, *op. cit.*, p. 104.
94. *Ibid.*, p. 110.
95. *Ibid.*, p. 112.
96. Peter Mansfield, *A History of the Middle East* (London: Viking, 1991), p. 285.
97. Document Research and Translation Office, *Middle East Economic Survey*, Beirut, Lebanon; quoted in Leonard Mosley, *Power Play* (London: Weidenfeld and Nicolson, 1973), p. 219.
98. Quoted in Mosley, *op. cit.*, p. 221.
99. Aburish, *op. cit.*, p. 288.
100. *Ibid.*, p. 289.
101. *Ibid.*, p. 290.
102. Stephens, *op. cit.*, pp. 385–7.
103. Interview with William Attwood, *Look*, 4 March 1968; quoted in *ibid.*, p. 391.
104. Anthony Nutting, *Nasser* (London: Constable, 1972), p. 322.
105. *Ibid.*, p. 338.
106. It was not difficult to analyse Washington's support for a peaceful settlement. The Americans judged that a protracted Saudi–Yemeni struggle might destabilise the Saudi monarchy and so threaten US oil interests.
107. Nutting, *op. cit.*, p. 342.
108. *Ibid.*, p. 353.
109. Fred Halliday, *New Left Review*, September–October 1970, pp. 17–19; J. J. Malone, 'Yemen Arab Republic's "Game of Nations"', *World Today*, December 1971, p. 543.
110. Andrew and Leslie Cockburn, *Dangerous Liaison* (London: Bodley Head, 1992), pp. 127–30.

111. W. Montgomery Watt, *Muhammad at Medina* (London: Oxford University Press, 1956), pp. 192–220.
112. The Koran itself (Sura 20, Verse 112) notes that God chose Arabic in which to impart the divine message to mankind. The 'Arabic Koran' is depicted as a verbatim copy of the eternal Koran preserved in heaven (Sura 56, Verses 76/77).
113. Bernard Postal and Henry V. Levy, *And the Hills Shouted for Joy: The Day Israel was Born* (New York: David McKay, 1973), pp. 302–3.
114. To these five wars should be added the 1991 Gulf War, which supposedly did not involve active Israeli combatants but during which Iraq fired Scud missiles at Israel.
115. Cockburn and Cockburn, *op. cit.*, p. 329.
116. Lacey, *op. cit.*, p. 398.
117. *Ibid.*, p. 402.
118. Cranford D. Goodwin et al., 'Energy Policy in Perspective' (Washington, DC: The Brookings Institute, 1981).
119. Engdahl, *op. cit.*, p. 154.
120. Cockburn and Cockburn, *op. cit.*, p. 329. Other sources (for example, Aburish, *op. cit.*, p. 169) suggest that the United States tried to stop the 1982 invasion of Lebanon.

Chapter 6: Wars, Rumours of Wars

1. Quoted by James Chace, *Time*, 4 August 1997, p. 31.
2. Ronald Steel, *Temptations of a Superpower* (Cambridge, Massachusetts: Harvard University Press, 1995).
3. I have profiled some of these devices in *Vietnam Syndrome: Impact on US Foreign Policy* (London: Macmillan, 1998), Chapter 7.
4. *New York Times*, 4 February, 2 July, 27 July 1987; Thomas Bodenheimer and Robert Gould, *Rollback! Right-wing Power in US Foreign Policy* (Boston: South End Press, 1989), pp. 56–8.
5. Noam Chomsky, 'International Terrorism: Image and Reality', in Alexander George (ed.), *Western State Terrorism* (Cambridge, England: Polity Press, 1991), p. 15.
6. S. Anderson and J. Anderson, *Inside the League* (New York: Dodd Mead, 1986), p. 47.
7. *Ibid.*, Chapter 9.
8. Bodenheimer and Gould, *op. cit.*, p. 78.
9. Anderson and Anderson, *op. cit.*, pp. 163, 170–4.
10. Joe Stork and Martha Wenger, 'From Rapid Deployment to Massive Deployment', in Micah L. Sifry and Christopher Cerf (eds), *The Gulf War Reader* (New York: Random House, 1991), p. 36.
11. Quoted in *ibid*.
12. *Ibid*.
13. Quoted in *ibid.*, p. 37.
14. *The New York Times*, 5 September 1985, quoting US State Department study prepared for congressional leaders by Secretary of State Richard Murphy.
15. William E. Burroughs and Robert Windrem, *Critical Mass* (New York: Simon and Schuster, 1994), pp. 330–1.
16. *Ibid*.
17. Mohamed Heikel, *Illusions of Triumph: An Arab View of the Gulf War* (London: Fontana, 1993), p. 115.
18. Helen Lackner, *A House Built on Sand: A Political Economy of Saudi Arabia* (London: Ithaca Press, 1978), p. 131.

19. George Thayer, *The War Business* (London: Paladin, 1970), pp. 213–14.
20. International Institute for Strategic Studies, cited in *Proposed Sales and Upgrades of Major Defence Equipment to Saudi Arabia*, Hearing before the Subcommittee on Arms Control, International Security and Science and on Europe and the Middle East of the Committee on Foreign Affairs, 19 June 1990, p. 28.
21. Russell Warren Howe, *Weapons* (London: Abacus, 1981), p. 561.
22. *Ibid.*, p. 562.
23. 'Missile Madness', *Near East Report*, American–Israel Public Affairs Committee, 15 September 1976.
24. Quoted in Howe, *op. cit.*, p. 563.
25. Jimmy Carter, responding to Ford proposal before Congress to sell 650 Maverick missiles to Saudi Arabia, 30 September 1976; quoted in *ibid.*, p. 564.
26. Anthony Sampson, *The Arms Bazaar* (London: Coronet, 1978), p. 173.
27. Howe, *op. cit.*, pp. 566–7.
28. Khaled Bin Sultan, *Desert Warrior* (London: HarperCollins, 1996), Chapter VII ('Taming the Company [Raytheon]').
29. *Ibid.*, p. 87.
30. *Ibid.*, p. 105.
31. Sheila Ryan, 'Countdown for a decade: The US build-up for war in the Gulf', in Phyllis Bennis and Michel Moushabeck (eds), *Beyond the Storm: A Gulf Crisis Reader* (London: Canongate, 1992), pp. 98–9.
32. *Ibid.*, p. 99.
33. Anthony H. Cordesman, *The Gulf and the West: Strategic Relations and Military Realities* (Boulder: Westview Press, 1988), pp. 265–6.
34. The AWACS deal was associated with a secret provision for the establishment of a joint US–Saudi fund in Geneva (amounting to between $1 billion and $2 billion) for the clandestine financing of various terrorist groups, such as UNITA in Angola and the MNR in Mozambique (see citations in Sean Gervasi and Sybil Wong, 'The Reagan Doctrine and the Destabilization of Southern Africa', in George (ed.), *op. cit.*, pp. 227–8).
35. General Norman Schwarzkopf commented to a congressional committee in 1989 that the restriction on sales had lost the United States $43 billion in arms deals over a 4-year period.
36. Details about Al-Yamamah are derived mainly from the British Offset Office, 77–91 New Oxford Street, London, WC1A 1DS.
37. General H. Norman Schwarzkopf, *It Doesn't Take a Hero* (New York: Bantam Press, 1992), p. 275.
38. There were also other slights. In October 1987, early in the 'tanker war' between Iran and Iraq, US Central Command had sent an uninvited 2-star general to Riyadh to direct a joint force of Saudi and US aircraft. Thus Schwarzkopf found the Saudi Defence Minister Prince Sultan ibn Abdul Aziz al-Saud 'unavailable' (*ibid.*).
39. Burrows and Windrem, *op. cit.*, pp. 392–5.
40. *Ibid.*, p. 393.
41. Adel Darwish and Gregory Alexander, *Unholy Babylon* (London: Victor Gollancz, 1991), p. 89.
42. Khaled Bin Sultan, *op. cit.*, Chapter X.
43. *Ibid.*, p. 142.
44. *Ibid.*, p. 143.
45. Quoted in James Adams, *Trading in Death: The Modern Arms Race* (London: Pan, 1991), p. 124.
46. Andrew and Leslie Cockburn, *Dangerous Liaison* (London: Bodley Head, 1992), pp. 194–5.

47. Larry Black, 'US defence industry on a high', *The Independent*, London, 26 January 1991.
48. *Ibid.*
49. Patrick Tyler, 'Gulf alliance plan stalled as Saudis step up demands', *The Guardian*, London, 14 October 1991
50. Rupert Cornwell, 'Saudi deals in US weapons strain American goodwill', *The Independent*, London, 22 April 1992.
51. '£40 bn Saudi defence deal "in jeopardy", *The Guardian*, London, 19 October 1992.
52. Andrew Lorenz, 'BAe pulls it off: Saudi contract seals revival', *The Sunday Times*, London, 31 January 1993.
53. Marie Colvin, 'How an insider lifted the veil on Saudi plot for an "Islamic bomb"', *The Sunday Times*, London, 24 July 1994; Marie Colvin, 'CIA starts enquiry on nuclear plot by Saudis', *The Sunday Times*, London, 31 July 1994; Marie Colvin and Peter Sawyer, 'Saudis bargained with Chinese for nuclear reactors', *The Sunday Times*, London, 7 August 1994.
54. Colvin (31 July 1994), *op. cit.*
55. Leslie Plommer, 'Weapon-toting West bleeds Saudis dry', *The Guardian*, London, 17 December 1994.
56. Quoted in *ibid.*
57. George Paloczi-Horvath, 'Saudi Arabians open credibility gulf', *The Engineer*, 25 January 1996.
58. Richard Norton-Taylor, 'Weapons exports "costing taxpayers £384m a year"', *The Guardian*, London, 22 May 1995.
59. Said K. Aburish, *A Brutal Friendship: The West and the Arab Elite* (London: Victor Gollancz, 1997).
60. *Ibid.*
61. *Ibid.*
62. Quoted in Kenneth R, Timmerman, *Death Lobby: How the West Armed Iraq* (London: Fourth Estate, 1992), p. 74.
63. Ghazi A. Algosaibi, *The Gulf Crisis: An Attempt to Understand* (London: Kegan Paul–International, 1993), p. 28.
64. *Ibid.*
65. *Ibid.*, p. 29.
66. For a full account of the Iran–Iraq War see Dilip Hiro, *The Longest War: The Iran–Iraq Military Conflict* (London: Paladin, 1990); Shahram Chubin and Charles Tripp, *Iran and Iraq at War* (London: I. B. Tauris, 1989).
67. Efraim Karsh and Inari Rautski, *Saddam Hussein: A Political Biography* (London: Futura, 1991), p. 158.
68. Algosaibi, *op. cit.*
69. Reports appeared in the West that the Iranians had captured Western military hardware supplied to Saudi Arabia.
70. The Scott Report: Sir Richard Scott, *Report of the Inquiry into the Export of Defence Equipment and Dual-Use Goods to Iraq and Related Prosecutions* (London: HMSO, 15 February 1996).
71. Cited in Said K. Aburish. *The Rise, Corruption and Coming Fall of the House of Saud* (London: Bloomsbury, 1995), p. 140.
72. Interview with Richard Murphy, 7 March 1991; quoted in Timmerman, *op. cit.*, p. 130.
73. Bob Woodward, *Veil: The Secret Wars of the CIA 1981–1987* (New York: Simon and Schuster, 1987), p. 480.
74. Hiro, *op. cit.*, p. 75.
75. Saddam Hussein, Baghdad Radio, 21 July 1981; quoted in Hiro, *op. cit.*, p. 79.

76. Foreign Broadcast Information Service, 23 March 1983; quoted in Hiro, *op. cit.*, p. 114.
77. *Washington Post*, 9 June 1984.
78. Quoted in Hiro, *op. cit.*, p. 154.
79. Dilip Hiro, *Islamic Fundamentalism* (London: Paladin Books, 1988), pp. 217–19.
80. Cordesman, *op. cit.*, pp. 370–2.
81. The Scott Report, *op. cit.*
82. *Ibid.*, Volume I, D3.64, p. 398.
83. *Ibid.*, Volume II, E1.1, p. 817.
84. *Ibid.*, E2.14, p. 823.
85. *Ibid.*, Chapter 6, pp. 869–75; Chapter 8, pp. 887–92.
86. Kathy Evans, 'Red faces as defector tells of Saudi billions in backing for Saddam's nuclear programmes', *The Guardian*, London, 25 July 1994.
87. BBC World Service, 20 July 1988; *The Independent*, London, 21 July 1988.
88. Teheran Home Service, 21 May 1988; quoted in Jabr Muhsin, George Harding and Fran Hazelton, 'Iraq in the Gulf War', in *Saddam's Iraq: Revolution or Reaction?* (London: Zed Books and CARDRI, 1989), p. 239.
89. *Parliamentary Debates*, House of Lords, London, 5th Series, Volume III, 1911, p. 587.
90. A. T. Wilson, *Persian Gulf* (London, 1928), p. 251.
91. Philip Willard Ireland, *Iraq* (London: Jonathan Cape, 1937), p. 40.
92. H. V. F. Winstone and Zahra Freeth, *Kuwait: Prospect and Reality* (London: George Allen and Unwin, 1972), p. 111.
93. Bishara A. Bahban, 'The crisis in the Gulf – why Iraq invaded Kuwait', in Bennis and Moushabeck (eds), *op. cit.*, p. 52.
94. Heikel, *op. cit.*, p. 175.
95. Alan Munro, *An Arabian Affair: Politics and Diplomacy Behind the Gulf War* (London: Brassey's, 1996), p. 19.
96. *Ibid.*
97. *Ibid.*, p. 20.
98. Baghdad Radio, 18 June 1990; Cited in Dilip Hiro, *Desert Shield to Desert Storm: The Second Gulf War* (London: Paladin, 1992), pp. 77–8.
99. Pierre Salinger and Eric Laurent, *Secret Dossier: The Hidden Agenda Behind the Gulf War* (Harmondsworth, England: Penguin, 1991), pp. 32–3.
100. Geoff Simons, *Iraq: From Sumer to Saddam* (London: Macmillan, 2nd edition, 1996), pp. 345–51.
101. *The Independent*, London, 26 January 1991.
102. Quoted in Salinger and Laurent, *op. cit.*, p. 119.
103. Hiro (1992), *op. cit.*, p. 111.
104. *Ibid.*
105. Maggie O'Kane, *The Guardian*, London, 16 September 1995.
106. Algosaibi, *op. cit.*, pp. 34–5.
107. Heikel, *op. cit.*, p. 268.
108. *Ibid.*, p. 272.
109. Cockburn and Cockburn, *op. cit.*, p. 353.
110. Knut Royce, 'A trail of distortion against Iraq', *New York Newsday*, 21 January 1991.
111. *Ibid.*
112. Darwish and Alexander, *op. cit.*, pp. 285–6.
113. Hiro (1992), *op. cit.*, p. 116.
114. Quoted in Bob Woodward, *The Commanders* (New York: Simon and Schuster, 1991), p. 241.

115. Hiro (1992), *op. cit.*, p. 126.
116. Quoted in Woodward (1991), *op. cit.*, p. 251.
117. Schwarzkopf, *op. cit.*, p. 312.
118. Khaled Bin Sultan, *op. cit.*, p. 291.
119. Schwarzkopf, *op. cit.*, p. 363.
120. Khaled Bin Sultan, *op. cit.*, p. 291.
121. *Ibid.*, pp. 292–3.
122. *Ibid.*, pp. 294–5.
123. Hiro (1992), *op. cit.*, pp. 162–3.
124. *Ibid.*, pp. 288–9
125. See Simons (2nd edn, 1996), *op. cit.*, p. 369.
126. *Ibid.*, pp. 372–8. The conduct of the war is described in contrasting terms by Khaled Bin Sultan (*op. cit.*), Schwarzkopf (*op. cit.*), Hiro (1992, *op. cit.*), Rick Atkinson, *Crusade: The Untold Story of the Gulf War* (London: HarperCollins, 1994) and General Sir Peter de la Billiére, *Storm Command: A Personal Account of the Gulf War* (London: HarperCollins, 1992).
127. I have surveyed the character of the war and the impact of economic sanctions on Iraq in *The Scourging of Iraq: Sanctions, Law and Natural Justice* (London: Macmillan, 2nd edition, 1998).
128. *The Independent on Sunday*, London, 27 January 1991; *Jane's Defence Weekly*, 2 February 1991, p. 134.
129. Carol Berger, 'Mecca and money compete to lure Egypt's volunteers', *The Independent*, London, 15 August 1990.
130. Robert Fisk, 'Illusions of normality ride the wind on the Saudi front', *The Independent*, London, 14 January 1991.
131. Robert Fisk, 'Arab against Arab for how long?', *The Independent*, London, 24 January 1991.
132. John Cassidy, 'Khafji reveals allied flaws', *The Sunday Times*, London, 3 February 1991.
133. Simons, Scourging of Iraq (1998), *op. cit.*
134. Khaled Bin Sultan, *op. cit.*, p. 49.
135. *Ibid.*, p. 209.
136. Algosaibi, *op. cit.*, p. 54.
137. *Ibid.*, pp. 56–7.
138. *The Independent*; London, 30 August 1990; quoted in Hiro (1992), *op. cit.*, pp. 162–3.
139. *International Herald Tribune*, 23 November 1990.
140. Abdel Hameed Noaman, 'Yemen: A Victim of the Bribery and Corruption of the UN', in Ramsey Clark et al., *War Crimes: A Report on United States War Crimes Against Iraq* (Washington DC: Maisonneuve Press, 1992), pp. 193–4.
141. Brian Whitaker, 'Anguish in the land of Sheba', *The Guardian*, London, 2 January 1992.
142. *Ibid.*
143. Deborah Pugh, 'Murder attempt fuels Yemeni fear of Riyadh', *The Guardian*, London, 10 July 1992.
144. *Ibid.*
145. Charles Richards, 'Arab League keeps its distance over Yemen', *The Independent*, London, 13 May 1994.
146. Brian Whitaker, 'Yemeni war ends as rebel leaders flee', *The Guardian*, London, 8 July 1994.
147. James Adams, 'Riyadh hired Russian MiGs for Yemen war', *The Sunday Times*, London, 7 August 1994.

148. Marie Colvin, 'Saudi forces mass on border with Yemen', *The Sunday Times*, London, 15 January 1995.
149. Assem Abdul Mohsen, 'Saudi–Yemen border tense as troops mass', *The Independent*, London, 16 January 1995.

Notes to Chapter 7: The Gathering Clouds

1.   Nasser Ibrahim Rashid and Esber Ibrahim Shaheen, *King Fahd and Saudi Arabia's Great Evolution* (Joplin, Missouri, USA: International Institute of Technology, 1987), p. 56.
2.   Haroon M. Jadhakhan (ed.), *The Thieves of Riyadh: Lives and Crimes of the Al Sauds and the Al Nahyans*, essays from the *Muslim Chronicle* (London, 1992) p. 24.
3.   Rashid and Shaheen, *op. cit.*, pp. 44–5.
4.   *Ibid.*, p. 56.
5.   See, for example, Peter W. Wilson and Douglas F. Graham, *Saudi Arabia: The Coming Storm* (New York: M. E. Sharpe, 1994); Michael Field, *Inside the Arab World* (London: John Murray, 1994), Chapter 16 ('The Problems of Saudi Arabia').
6.   Wilson and Graham, *op. cit.*, p. 267.
7.   *Sixth Development Plan, 1995–2000 A.D.*, Ministry of Planning, Riyadh, Kingdom of Saudi Arabia, 1996, p. 171.
8.   'Yemen blames foreign cash', Reuters, *The Independent*, London, 18 August 1997.
9.   Wilson and Graham, *op. cit.*, pp. 267–8.
10. Rashid and Shaheen, *op. cit.*, p. 148.
11. Quoted in *ibid.*
12. Bob Woodward, *Veil: The Secret Wars of the CIA 1981–1987* (New York: Simon and Schuster, p. 104.
13. *Ibid.*
14. Oliver L. North, *Under Fire: An American Story* (London: Fontana, 1992), p. 243.
15. William Blum, *The CIA: A Forgotten History* (London: Zed Books, 1986), p. 99.
16. *Ibid.*, p. 101.
17. Leonard Mosley, *Dulles* (London: Hodder and Stoughton, 1978), p. 348.
18. Quoted in Michael Sheridan, 'Breakthrough as Saudi envoy meets Jews in US', *The Independent*, London, 20 November 1991.
19. Martin Walker, 'Saudis "boost oil output to elect Bush"', *The Guardian*, London, 4 January 1992.
20. James Bruce, Jacques de Lestapis, Carol Reed and Barbara Starr, 'Saudis at a turning point', *Jane's Defence Weekly*, 6 May 1995.
21. Adrian Hamilton, 'By doing nothing to offend the Saud family, we will also go down if they fall', *The Observer*, London, 7 January 1996.
22. Zahid Hussain, 'Islam told of duty to rescue Jerusalem', *The Times*, London, 24 March 1997.
23. Robert Fisk, 'Circling over a broken ruined state', *The Independent on Sunday*, London, 14 July 1996.
24. Eric Watkins, 'The unfolding US policy in the Middle East', *International Affairs*, Volume 73, Number 1 (January 1997), p. 5.
25. 'Strains in US – Saudi alliance', *APS Diplomat Recorder Predicasts, Newsletter*, 7 July 1996.
26. *Ibid.*
27. Quoted in H. V. F. Winstone and Zahra Freeth, *Kuwait: Prospect and Reality* (London: George Allen and Unwin, 1972), p. 125.

28. Kathy Evans, 'Gulf rulers seek to rein in Qatar's maverick emir', *The Guardian*, London, 7 February 1996.
29. Kathy Evans, 'Saudi ruler ends Qatari emir's feud', *The Guardian*, London, 16 September 1996.
30. Interview with Ghazi A. Algosaibi, *CAABU Briefing*, Council for the Advancement of Arab–British Understanding (CAABU), The Arab–British Centre, London, June 1995.
31. Miriam Isa, 'Saudis said to lose more than they gain from crisis', *The Washington Report on Middle East Affairs*, February 1991; first appeared in *The Washington Times*, 28 December 1990.
32. *Ibid.*
33. Patrick Cockburn, 'Saudi Arabian finances hit by Gulf war', *The Independent*, London, 27 February 1992.
34. Robert Lacey, *The Kingdom* (London: Fontana, 1982), p. 279.
35. *Ibid.*
36. Wilson and Graham, *op. cit.*, p. 178.
37. *Ibid.*, pp. 178–9.
38. *Middle East Economic Digest*, 13 February 1988.
39. Wilson and Graham, *op. cit.*, p. 187.
40. *Business Week*, 18 March 1991.
41. *Middle East Economic Digest*, 5 June 1992.
42. Wilson and Graham, *op. cit.*, p. 191.
43. *Saudi Arabia: Staff Report*, International Monetary Fund, 1991; quoted in *ibid.*, p. 192.
44. Wilson and Graham, *op. cit.*, pp. 194–5.
45. Muhammad Iqbal Siddiqi, *Model of an Islamic Bank* (Lahore, Pakistan; Chicago, USA: Kazi Publications, 1986).
46. Wilson and Graham, *op. cit.*, p. 200.
47. David Hirst, 'Heads in the Sand', *The Guardian*, London, 14 August 1993.
48. Quoted in *ibid.*
49. Marie Colvin, 'The squandering sheikhs', *The Sunday Times*, London, 29 August 1993.
50. Quoted in *ibid.*
51. Peter Torday, 'Clouds over Riyadh', *The Independent*, London, 11 November 1993.
52. Roger Matthews, 'Insurer restricts business with Saudi Arabia', *Financial Times*, London, 26 October 1994.
53. Quoted in *ibid.*
54. *Sixth Development Plan, op. cit.*
55. The earlier Plans are briefly summarised in *ibid.* The *Sixth Development Plan* (which runs to 431 large-format pages) is summarised in *Sixth Development Plan '96*, prepared by John Presley, Economic Advisor to The Saudi–British Bank, London and Riyadh.
56. *Sixth Development Plan '96, op. cit.*, pp. 8–9.
57. *Sixth Development Plan, op. cit.*, pp. 87–8.
58. Edmund O'Sullivan, 'Riyadh reacts to a changing landscape', *Middle East Economic Digest*, 11 November 1994, p. 34.
59. Quoted in Irwin Steizer, 'An oil crisis knocks on recovery's door', *The Sunday Times*, London, 11 December 1994.
60. Quoted in Leslie Plommer, 'Deserted by its erstwhile super-riches, Saudi Arabia is forced to go to work', *The Guardian*, London, 12 December 1994.
61. Quoted in *ibid.*

62. Michael Sheridan, 'Security haunts ruling Saudis', *The Independent*, London, 14 December 1994; see also Leslie Plommer, 'Weapon-toting West bleeds Saudis dry', *The Guardian*, London, 17 December 1994.

63. Angus Hindley, 'Bold moves to balance the books', *Middle East Economic Digest*, 10 March 1995, p. 25.

64. James Bruce, Jacques de Lestapis, Carol Reed and Barbara Starr, 'Saudis at a turning point', *Jane's Defence Weekly*, 6 May 1995, p. 21.

65. Saudi Arabia, *Middle East Economic Digest*, Quarterly Report, September 1995.

66. *Ibid.*

67. *Saudi Arabia*, Country Report, The Economist Intelligence Unit, London, 3rd quarter 1995.

68. 'Chairman Fahd', *The Economist*, London, 18 November 1995.

69. *Saudi Arabia: Staff Report*, International Monetary Fund, 6 September 1995; summary in *Middle East Economic Digest*, December 1995, pp. 18–19.

70. Peter Kemp, 'The winds of change blow more gently', *Middle East Economic Digest*, 8 November 1996, p. 29.

71. Edmund O'Sullivan, 'Crisis talk ends, calm descends', *Middle East Economic Digest*, 8 November 1996, p. 32.

72. *Ibid.*, p. 35.

73. *Saudi Arabia*, Country Report, The Economist Intelligence Unit, London, 4th quarter 1996; see also Saudi Arabia, *Middle East Economic Digest*, Quarterly Report, December 1996.

74. Dan Bloch, 'The feelgood factor hits Saudi Arabia', *Gulf Marketing Review*, January 1997, pp. 40–42.

75. 'Back on track in the desert', *DTI/FCO Magazine for UK Exporters*, February 1997, pp. 10–11.

76. *Saudi Arabia*, The HSBC Group: Business Profile Series, The Saudi-British Bank, London and Riyadh, Fourth Quarter 1996, p. 4.

77. Wilson and Graham, *op. cit.*, p. 200.

78. *Middle East Economic Digest*, 24 January 1992.

79. Wilson and Graham (*op. cit.*, pp. 203–4) cite the case of Neville Norton, a British citizen held for 16 years (arrested 17 times, 5 years in Saudi jails), because of commercial disputes between his employer and Prince Naif.

80. Kathy Evans, 'Saudi regime to revamp image with cabinet shuffle', *The Guardian*, London, 2 July 1993.

81. David Hirst, 'Royal shepherd tussles with his restless flock', *The Guardian*, London, 17 August 1993.

82. Michael Sheridan, 'Saudi rulers learn to live with fewer millions', *The Guardian*, London, 13 December 1994.

83. Leslie Plommer, 'Saudi Arabia's paper parliament seeks a role under God and king', *The Guardian*, London, 29 December 1994.

84. Quoted in *ibid.*

85. 'Government by clairvoyance: the House of Saud resorts to witchcraft to stay in power', *Crescent International*, 16–31 March 1995, p. 6.

86. For the pro-US Saudi royals, Ronald Reagan's reliance on a fortune-teller was a useful model (as is perhaps Boris Yeltsin's consultations with soothsayers).

87. Leslie Plommer, 'Fears mount for ailing King Fahd', *The Guardian*, London, 5 December 1995.

88. Quoted in Marie Colvin, 'Saudi princes view for crown', *The Sunday Times*, London, 10 December 1995.

89. Quoted in Richard H. Curtis, 'With Saudi changing of the guard there will be no "Crash of '79"', *The Washington Report on Middle East Affairs*, February/March 1996.

90. 'Saudi Arabia needs a face-lift', *The Economist*, London, 6 January 1996.

91. Kathy Evans, 'Silent Saudi begins to stir', *The Guardian*, London, 4 July 1997.

92. *King Fahd: The Years of Devotion*, Saudi Arabian Information Centre, London, 1996, pp. 20–21.

93. Al Sa'yed Hassan Kutbi, speech in South Korea, 1975; quoted in Fouad Al-Farsy, *Modernity and Tradition: The Saudi Equation* (London: Kegan Paul, 1990), pp. 40–41.

94. Robin Wright, *Sacred Rage: The Wrath of Militant Islam* (London: André Deutsch, 1986), p. 150.

95. *Ibid.*, p. 152.

96. Juhaiman Saif al-Otaiba, 'Rules of allegiance and obedience: the misconduct of rulers'; quoted in *ibid.*, p. 153.

97. Wright, *op. cit.*, p. 155.

98. Quoted in *ibid.*, p. 168.

99. Quoted in Helga Graham, 'Shadow of a martyr stalks the Sauds', *The Observer*, London, 2 June 1991.

100. Field, *op. cit.*, p. 337.

101. *News Bulletin*, Jamahiriya News Agency (JANA), London, 9 June 1993, p. 1.

102. Andrew Hogg, 'Islamic zealots stop Bush reinforcing the Saudi forces', *The Sunday Times*, London, 6 October 1991.

103. Karim Alrawi, 'Extremists' unholy war', *The Guardian*, London, 3 July 1992.

104. Charles Richards, 'Hundreds die as Muslim pilgrimage turns to tragedy', *The Independent*, London, 25 May 1994.

105. *News Bulletin*, Jamahiriya News Agency (JANA), London, 25 May 1994.

106. *News Bulletin*, Jamahiriya News Agency (JANA), London, 12 April 1995.

107. Quoted in Christopher Lockwood, 'Anger over *hajj* deaths turns on House of Saud', *The Daily Telegraph*, London, 17 April 1997.

108. Mohammed H. Siddiq, *Agonies of a Native Son of Saudi Arabia* (Lincoln, Nebraska, USA, 1990), p. 5.

109. Mohammed H. Siddiq, articles in *Lincoln Journal*, Nebraska, USA, 28 July 1988, 12 December 1988 and 11 September 1989.

110. Patrick Cockburn, 'Saudi dissident cool on royal reforms', *The Independent*, London, 3 March 1992.

111. Mohammed H. Siddiq, 'King Fahd's new reform: an old song made by an old pate', Lincoln, Nebraska, USA, May 1992; see also Siddiq, *Crescent International*, 16–30 September 1992.

112. Kathy Evans, 'Petitioners press Saudi leaders', *The Guardian*, London, 23 September 1992.

113. Marie Colvin, 'Fundamentalists threaten to wage holy war on Saudi royal family', *The Sunday Times*, London, 13 December 1992.

114. Mamoun Fandy, 'Discontent is rising among Saudi "oil generation"', *The Christian Science Monitor*, 13 October 1994.

115. *Ibid.*

116. Marie Colvin, 'Yamani poses threat to Saudi's embattled royals', *The Sunday Times*, London, 27 November 1994.

117. Quoted in Kim Murphy, 'Dissent grows in the secretive kingdom', *The Guardian*, London, 7 January 1995.

118. Quoted in Alain Gresh, 'The most obscure dictatorship', *Middle East Report*, November/December 1995.

119. *Saudi Arabia*, Country Report, The Economist Intelligence Unit, London, 4th quarter 1996, p. 6.

120. Kathy Evans, 'Saudi refugees fear for families', *The Guardian*, London, 26 April 1994.

121. 'Challenge to the House of Saud', *The Economist*, London, 8 October 1994.
122. Quoted in Leslie Plommer, 'Royal family vulnerable to Islamists', *The Guardian*, London, 28 November 1994.
123. Andrew Lorenz, '£3bn army order threatened by Saudi tensions', *The Sunday Times*, London, 12 November 1995; Lorenz, 'Saudis freeze new contracts', *The Sunday Times*, London, 3 December 1995.
124. Seumas Milne and Ian Black, 'Arms bosses' secret plot', *The Guardian*, London, 8 January 1996.
125. Andrew Malone and Chris Dodd, 'Masari may be charged over "kill Jews" call', *The Sunday Times*, London, 16 June 1996.
126. John Lichfield, 'Massari denies condoning bomb', *The Independent*, London, 28 June 1996.
127. Kathy Evans, 'I'm broke says dissident thorn in Saudis' side', *The Guardian*, London, 11 January 1997.
128. Robert Fisk, 'Arab rebel leader warns the British: "Get out of the Gulf"', *The Independent*, London, 10 July 1996.
129. Quoted in *ibid.*; see also Robert Fisk, 'Why we reject the West – by the Saudis' fiercest Arab critic', *The Independent*, London, 10 July 1996; Fisk, 'Small comfort in Saudi rebel's dangerous exile', *The Independent*, London, 11 July 1996; Fisk, 'A pilgrimage through a broken and dangerous land of death', *The Independent*, London, 23 March 1997.
130. Robert Fisk, 'Saudi calls for jihad against US "crusader"', *The Independent*, London, 2 September 1996.
131. Christopher Lockwood, 'Afghan cave exile rejects Saudi deal', *The Daily Telegraph*, London, 30 November 1996.
132. Marie Colvin, 'An unlikely Saudi rebel pleads for political asylum', *The Sunday Times*, London, 12 June 1994.
133. Quoted in *ibid.*
134. Geraldine Brooks, 'Saudi diplomat seeks asylum in US, putting Washington, Riyadh on the spot', *The Wall Street Journal*, 15 June 1994.
135. Interview in Lebanese daily *Al-Anwar*, 13 August 1973, quoted in Walid Kazziha, *Revolutionary Transformation in the Arab World: Habash and his Comrades from Nationalism to Marxism* (London: Charles Knight, 1975), pp. 17–18.
136. Internal Circular for confidential use of Movement members, 'A Study on Saudi Arabia' (*Dirasa Hawl al-Saudia*), 1967, cited in Kazziha, *op. cit.*, p. 36.
137. Experiences related in 1990 to Patrick Seale (*Abu Nidal: A Gun for Hire* (London: Hutchinson, 1992), pp. 9–31).
138. *Ibid.*, p. 27.
139. *Ibid.*, p. 204.
140. R. T. Naylor, *Hot Money and the Politics of Debt* (London: Unwin, 1987), p. 415.
141. Woodward, *op. cit.*, p. 197.
142. Quoted in *ibid.*, p. 397.
143. Sarah Lyall, '2 hurt at Arabic paper as bombs are mailed to London and UN', *The New York Times*, 14 January 1997; John Steele and David Sapsted, 'Two hurt in letter bomb attack on newspaper', *The Daily Telegraph*, London, 14 January 1997.
144. 'Tremors in Saudi Arabia', *The New York Times*, 14 November 1995.
145. Quoted in Peter Waldman, 'Saudi bombing prompts fears for nation', *The Wall Street Journal*, 14 November 1995.
146. Quoted in Eric Schmitt, 'FBI agents join search in Saudi blast', *The New York Times*, 15 November 1995.
147. Louise Lief, Brian Duffy and Richard Z. Chesnoff, 'Telling friend from foe', *US News and World Report*, 27 November 1995.

148. 'A dangerous spark in the oil fields', *Business Week*, 27 November 1995.
149. Quoted in *ibid*.
150. Quoted in Elaine Sciolino, 'Bombing attack raises questions about stability of Saudi government', *The New York Times*, 27 June 1996.
151. Douglas Jehl, 'Envoys are skeptical on 4 Saudis' confessions', *The New York Times*, 29 June 1996.
152. Quoted in James Adams, 'Secretive Saudis block US hunt for bombers', *The Sunday Times*, London, 30 June 1996; Melinda Liu, 'Kept in the dark', *Newsweek*, 15 July 1996.
153. 'Dhahran episode exposes kingdom's ugly reality', *Crescent International*, 1–15 July 1996.
154. Bruce W. Nelan, 'Gulf shock waves', *Time*, 8 July 1996.
155. C. Dickey, 'Target: America', *Newsweek*, 8 July 1996.
156. James Adams, 'Americans face rerun of Iran as Saudi wobbles', *The Sunday Times*, London, 28 July 1996.
157. David Johnston, 'FBI pulls out of joint enquiry on fatal blast in Saudi Arabia', *The New York Times*, 2 November 1996.
158. Con Coughlin, 'The Syrian connection', *The Sunday Telegraph*, London, 19 January 1997.

Bibliography

Abir, Mordechai, *Oil, Power and Politics: Conflict and Arabia, the Red Sea and the Gulf* (London: Cass, 1974).

Aburish, Said K., *A Brutal Friendship: The West and the Arab Elite* (London: Gollancz, 1997).

Aburish, Said K., *The Rise, Corruption and Coming Fall of the House of Saud* (London: Bloomsbury, 1995).

Adams, James, *Trading in Death: The Modern Arms Race* (London: Pan, 1991).

El-Affendi, Abdelwahab, *Who Needs an Islamic State?* (London: Grey Seal, 1991).

Algosaibi, Ghazi, *The Gulf Crisis: An Attempt to Understand* (London: Kegan Paul, 1993).

Almana, Mohammed, *Arabia Unified: A Portrait of Ibn Saud* (London: Hutchinson, 1980).

Amin, Sayed Hassan, *Middle East Legal Systems* (Glasgow, Scotland: Royston, 1985).

Anderson, Bridget, *Britain's Secret Slaves: An Investigation into the Plight of Overseas Domestic Workers* (London, 1993).

Anderson, S. and Anderson, J., *Inside the League* (New York: Dodd, 1986).

Armstrong, Karen, *A History of God* (London: Mandarin, 1993).

Armstrong, Karen, *Muhammad: A Biography of the Prophet* (London: Gollancz, 1991).

Arnold, José, *Golden Pots and Swords and Pans* (London: Gollancz, 1964).

Asad, M., *The Road to Mecca* (London, 1954).

Atkinson, Rick, *Crusade: The Untold Story of the Gulf War* (London: HarperCollins, 1994).

Badawi, Jamal A., *The Status of Women in Islam* (Birmingham, England: Islamic Propagation Centre).

Beling, Willard A. (ed.), *King Faisal and the Modernization of Saudi Arabia* (London: Croom Helm, 1980).

Bell, T., *Kalogynomia* (London: Stockdale, 1821).

Benn, Tony, *Out of the Wilderness: Diaries 1963–67* (London: Hutchinson, 1987).

Bennis, Phyllis and Moushabeck, Michel (eds), *Beyond the Storm: A Gulf Crisis Reader* (London: Canongate, 1992).

de la Billière, Peter, *Storm Command: A Personal Account of the Gulf War* (London: HarperCollins, 1992).

Blandford, Linda, *Oil Sheikhs* (London: Weidenfeld and Nicolson, 1976).

Blum, William, *The CIA: A Forgotten History* (London: Zed Books, 1986).

Bodenheimer, Thomas and Gould, Robert, *Rollback! Right-wing Power in US Foreign Policy* (Boston: South-End Press, 1989).

Browne, Edward G., *A Year Among the Persians* (London: Black, 1893).

Buckingham, J. S., *Travels in Assyria, Media and Persia* (London, 1830).

Burroughs, William E. and Windrem, Robert, *Critical Mass* (New York: Simon and Schuster, 1994).

Burton, Richard, *Love, War and Fancy: Notes to the Arabian Nights* (London: Kimber, 1954).

Burton, Richard, *Pilgrimage to Al-Madinah and Meccah* (London: George Bell, 1898).

Butler, Rohan and Bury, J. P. T. (eds), *Documents on British Foreign Policy 1919–1939, 1st Series, Volume XIII, The Near and Middle East, January 1920–March 1921* (London: HMSO, 1963).

Carmichael, Joel, *The Shaping of the Arabs* (London, 1967).

Chubin, Shahram and Tripp, Charles, *Iran and Iraq at War* (London: Tauris, 1989).

Clark, Ramsey et al., *War Crimes: A Report on United States War Crimes Against Iraq* (Washington DC: Maisonneuve Press, 1992).

Cockburn, Andrew and Cockburn, Leslie, *Dangerous Liaison* (London: Bodley Head, 1992).

Cordesman, Anthony H., *The Gulf and the West: Strategic Relations and Military Realities* (Boulder: Westview Press, 1988).

Corm, George, *Fragmentation of the Middle East* (London: Hutchinson, 1988).

Crichton, Andrew, *The History of Arabia* (New York: Harper, 1838).

Daniel, Norman, *Islam and the West: The Making of an Image* (Edinburgh, 1960).

Darwish, Adel and Alexander, Gregory, *Unholy Babylon* (London: Gollancz, 1991).

Davis, Elizabeth Gould, *The First Sex* (London: Dent, 1973).

Dickie, John, *Inside the Foreign Office* (London: Chapmans, 1992).

Dickson, Violet, *Forty Years in Kuwait* (London: Allen and Unwin, 1971).

Doughty, Charles M., *Travels in Arabia Deserta* (London: Penguin, 1956).

Edwardes, Allen, *The Jewel in the Lotus: A Historical Survey of the Sexual Culture of the East* (London: Blond, 1961).

Edwardes, Allen and Masters, R. E. L., *The Cradle of Erotica* (London: Odyssey Press, 1970).

Eisenhower, Dwight D., *Mandate for Change, 1953–1956: The White House Years* (London: Heinemann, 1963).

Eisenhower, Dwight D., *Waging Peace, Volume II, The White House Years* (New York: Doubleday, 1963–5).

Engdahl, F. William, *A Century of War: Anglo-American Oil Politics and the New World Order* (Massachusetts: Paul, 1993).

Engler, Robert, *The Politics of Oil* (Chicago, 1967).

Facey, William, *Riyadh: The Old City* (London: IMMEL Publishing, 1992).

Al-Farsy, Fouard, *Modernity and Tradition: The Saudi Equation* (London: Kegan Paul, 1990).

Field, Michael, *Inside the Arab World* (London: John Murray, 1994).

Field, Michael, *The Merchants: The Big Business Families of Arabia* (London: John Murray, 1984).

Foot, Paul, *The Helen Smith Story* (London: Fontana, 1983).

Fromkin, David, *A Peace to End All Peace: Creating the Modern Middle East 1914–1922* (Harmondsworth: Penguin, 1991).

Gathorne-Hardy, G. M., *A Short History of International Affairs, 1920–1938* (London: Oxford University Press, 1939).

De Gaury, Gerald, *Faisal: King of Saudi Arabia* (London: Barker, 1966).

George, Alexander (ed.), *Western State Terrorism* (Cambridge, England: Polity Press, 1991).

Glubb, John Bagot, *A Short History of the Arab Peoples* (London: Quartet, 1980).

Glubb, John Bagot, *The Great Arab Conquests* (London: Quartet, 1980).

Glubb, John Bagot, *War in the Desert* (London: Hodder and Stoughton, 1960).

Graves, Robert, *Lawrence and the Arabs* (London: Cape, 1935).

Guillaume, Alfred, *Islam* (Harmondsworth: Penguin, 1954).

Guraya, Muhammad Yusuf, *Islamic Jurisprudence in the Modern World* (Lahore: Sh. Muhammad Ashraf, 1992).

Habib, John S., *Ibn Saud's Warriors of Islam: The Ikhwan of Najd and their Role in the Creation of the Saudi Kingdom, 1910–1930* (New Jersey: Humanities Press, 1978).

Halliday, Fred, *Arabia without Sultans* (London: Penguin, 1974).

Halloran, Paul and Hollingsworth, Mark, *Thatcher's Gold: The Life and Times of Mark Thatcher* (London: Simon and Schuster, 1995).

Hamidullah, Muhammad, *The Muslim Conduct of State* (Lahore: Sh. Muhammad Ashraf, 1987).

Hartshorn, J. E., *Oil Companies and Governments* (London: Faber and Faber, 1962).
Heikel, Mohamed, *Illusions of Triumph: An Arab View of the Gulf War* (London: Fontana, 1993).
Helms, C. M., *The Cohesion of Saudi Arabia* (London, 1980).
Henriques, Fernando, *Prostitution and Society: A Survey, Volume 1, Primitive, Classical and Oriental* (London: MacGibbon and Kee, 1962).
Herzog, Chaim, *The Arab–Israeli Wars: War and Peace in the Middle East* (London: Arms and Armour Press, 1982).
Hiro, Dilip, *Desert Shield to Desert Storm* (London: Paladin, 1992).
Hiro, Dilip, *Islamic Fundamentalism* (London: Paladin, 1988).
Hiro, Dilip, *The Longest War: The Iran–Iraq Military Conflict* (London: Paladin, 1990).
Hitti, Philip K., *History of the Arabs* (London: Macmillan, 1970).
Holden, David and Johns, Richard, *The House of Saud* (London: Sidgwick and Jackson, 1981).
Hourani, Albert, *A History of the Arab Peoples* (London: Faber and Faber, 1991).
Howarth, D., *The Desert King* (London, 1964).
Howe, Russell Warren, *Weapons* (London: Abacus, 1981).
Hurongronje, C. Snouk, *Mekka* (The Hague, 1888–9).
Ireland, Philip Willard, *Iraq* (London: Cape, 1937).
Jadhakhan, Haroon M. (ed.), *The Thieves of Riyadh: Lives and Crimes of the Al Sauds and the Al Nahyans* (London: Muslim Chronicle, 1992).
James, Lawrence, *Imperial Rearguard: Wars of Empire, 1919–85* (London: Brassey's, 1988).
Kabbani, Rana, *Europe's Myths of Orient, Devise and Rule* (London: Macmillan, 1986).
Kabbani, Rana, *Letter to Christendom* (London: Virago, 1992).
Kahl, Joachim, *The Misery of Christianity* (Harmondsworth: Penguin, 1971).
Karsh, Efraim and Rautski, Inari, *Saddam Hussein: A Political Biography* (London: Futura, 1991).
Kazziha, Walid, *Revolutionary Transformation in the Arab World: Habash and his Comrades from Nationalism to Marxism* (London: Knight, 1975).
Kelly, J. B., *Arabia, the Gulf and the West* (New York: Basic Books, 1980).
Kelly, J. B., *Eastern Arabian Frontiers* (London: Faber and Faber, 1964).
Khaled Bin Sultan, *Desert Warrior* (London: HarperCollins, 1996).
Kiernan, Thomas, *The Arabs* (London: Sphere, 1978).
King Fahd: The Years of Devotion (London: Saudi Arabian Information Centre, 1996).
Knightley, Philip and Simpson, Colin, *The Secret Lives of Lawrence of Arabia* (London, 1969).
The Koran, translated by J. M. Rodwell (London: Dent, 1937); translated by N. J. Dawood (London: Penguin, 1988).
Lacey, Robert, *The Kingdom* (London: Fontana, 1982).
Lackner, Helen, *A House Built on Sand: A Political Economy of Saudi Arabia* (London: Ithaca Press, 1978).
Lane, F. W., *An Account of the Manners and Customs of the Modern Egyptian (1833–5)* (London, 1896).
Lawrence, T. E., *Seven Pillars of Wisdom* (London: Cape, 1935).
Lunt, J., *Glubb Pasha* (London, 1984).
Mahmoud, Mostafa, *Dialogue with an Atheist* (London: Dar Al Taqwa, 1994).
Malouf, Amin, *The Crusades through Arab Eyes* (London: Al Saqi Books, 1984).
Mansfield, Peter, *A History of the Middle East* (London: Penguin, 1991).
Mansfield, Peter, *The Arabs* (Harmondsworth: Penguin, 1980).
McLoughlin, Leslie, *Ibn Saud: Founder of a Kingdom* (London: Macmillan, 1993).

McNeil, William H. and Waldman, Marilyn Robinson (eds), *The Islamic World* (Chicago: University of Chicago Press, 1973).

Minnesota Lawyers International Human Rights Committee, *Shame in the House of Saud: Contempt for Human Rights in the Kingdom of Saudi Arabia* (Minneapolis, 1992).

Mosley, Leonard, *Dulles* (London: Hodder and Stoughton, 1978).

Mosley, Leonard, *Power Play* (London: Weidenfeld and Nicolson, 1973).

Al Munajjed, Mona, *Women in Saudi Arabia Today* (London: Macmillan, 1997).

Munro, Alan, *An Arabian Affair: Politics and Diplomacy Behind the Gulf War* (London: Brassey's, 1996).

Murray, G. W., *Sons of Ishmael: A Study of the Egyptian Bedouin* (London: Routledge, 1935).

al-Musnad, Muhammed bin Abdul-Aziz (compiler), *Islamic Fatawa Regarding Women* (Darussalam, Saudi Arabia, 1996).

Naylor, R. T., *Hot Money and the Politics of Debt* (London: Unwin, 1988).

Nixon, Richard, *Memoirs* (London: Arrow, 1979).

North, Oliver F., *Under Fire: An American Story* (London: Fontana, 1992).

Nutting, Anthony, *Nasser* (London: Constable, 1972).

Omissi, David E., *Air Power and Colonial Control: The Royal Air Force 1919–1939* (Manchester, England: Manchester University Press, 1990).

Palgrave, W. G., *Narrative of a Year's Journey through Central and Eastern Arabia 1862–63* (London, 1865).

Palmer, Alan, *The Decline and Fall of the Ottoman Empire* (London: Murray, 1992).

Patai, R., *Sex and Family in the Bible and the Middle East* (New York, 1949).

Pelly, Louis, *Report on a Journey to the Wahabee Capital of Riyadh in Central Arabia* (Bombay, 1866).

Petran, Tabitha, *Syria: A Modern History* (London: Benn, 1972).

Philby, Harry St John Bridger, *Arabia* (London, 1930).

Philby, Harry St John Bridger, *Arabian Highlands* (Cornell, 1952).

Philby, Harry St John Bridger, *Arabian Jubilee* (London, 1962).

Philby, Harry St John Bridger, *The Empty Quarter* (London: Century, 1986).

Philby, Harry St John Bridger, *The Heart of Arabia* (London, 1922).

Phillips, William D., *Slavery from Roman Times to the Transatlantic Trade* (Manchester, England: Manchester University Press, 1985).

Piscatori, James P. (ed.), *Islam in the Political Process* (New York: Cambridge University Press, 1983).

Playfair, Robert L., *A History of the Arabia Felix or Yemen* (Bombay, 1959).

Ploss, Hermann Heinrich; Bartels, Max; and Bartels, Paul, *Woman: An Historical Gynaecological and Anthropological Compendium* (London: Heinemann, 1935).

Postal, Bernard and Levy, Henry V., *And the Hills Shouted for Joy: The Day Israel was Born* (New York: McKay, 1973).

Al-Qaradawi, Yusuf, *The Lawful and the Prohibited in Islam (Al-Halal Wal-Haram fil Islam)* (Indianapolis: American Trust Publications).

al-Qardawi, Allama Yusuf, *Economic Security in Islam* (Lahore: Kazi Publications, 1981).

Rashid, Nasser Ibrahim and Shaheen, Esber Ibrahim, *King Fahd and Saudi Arabia's Great Evolution* (Missouri: International Institute of Technology, 1987).

Reade, Winwood, *The Martyrdom of Man* (London: Watts, 1925).

Robinson, Jeffrey, *Yamani: The Inside Story* (London: Fontana, 1988).

Ryan, A., *The Last of the Dracomans* (London, 1951).

Sadat, Anwar, *In Search of Identity: An Autobiography* (London: Fontana, 1978).

Sadat, Jehan, *A Woman of Egypt* (London: Coronet, 1987).

Sadleir, George Foster, *Diary of a Journey Across Arabia* (Bombay, 1866).

Said, Edward W., *The Politics of Dispossession: The Struggle for Palestinian Self-Determination 1969–1994* (London: Chatto and Windus, 1994).

Salinger, Pierre and Laurent, Eric, *Secret Dossier: The Hidden Agenda Behind the Gulf War* (Harmondsworth: Penguin, 1991).

Sampson, Anthony, *The Arms Bazaar* (London: Coronet, 1978).

Sampson, Anthony, *The Seven Sisters: The Great Oil Companies and the World They Made* (London: Hodder and Stoughton, 1975).

Sasson, Jean P., *Daughters of Arabia* (London: Bantam, 1995).

Sasson, Jean P., *Princess* (London: Bantam, 1993).

Saunders, J. J., *A History of Medieval Islam* (London: Routledge and Kegan Paul, 1965).

Schwarzkopf, Norman H., *It Doesn't Take a Hero* (New York: Bantam, 1992).

Seale, Patrick, *Abu Nidal: A Gun for Hire* (London: Hutchinson, 1992).

Seale, Patrick, *The Struggle for Syria: A Study of Post-War Arab Politics, 1945–1958* (London: Tauris, 1965).

Shaban, M. A., *Islamic History: A New Interpretation* (Cambridge, England, 1971).

Shaw, Stanford J., *History of the Ottoman Empire and Modern Turkey, Volume 1, Empire of the Gazis: The Rise and Decline of the Ottoman Empire, 1280–1808* (Cambridge, England: Cambridge University Press, 1976).

Siddiq, Mohammed H., *Saudi Arabia: A Country under Arrest* (Nebraska, 1991).

Siddiq, Mohammed H., *Saudi Government Analysed* (Nebraska, 1994).

Siddiqi, Muhammad Iqbal, *Model of an Islamic Bank* (Lahore: Kazi Publications, 1986).

Siddiqi, Muhammed Mazheruddin, *Women in Islam* (Lahore: Institute of Islamic Culture, 1959).

Sifry, Micah L. and Carf, Christopher (eds), *The Gulf War Reader* (New York: Random House, 1991).

Simons, Geoff, *Iraq: From Sumer to Saddam* (London: Macmillan, 2nd edition, 1996).

Simons, Geoff, *The Scourging of Iraq: Sanctions, Law and Natural Justice* (London: Macmillan, 1996; 2nd edition, 1998).

Simons, Geoff, *Vietnam Syndrome: Impact on US Foreign Policy* (London: Macmillan, 1998).

Smith, Wilfred Cantwell, *Islam in Modern History* (Princeton, 1957).

Southern, R. W., *Western Views of Islam in the Middle Ages* (Cambridge, MA, 1980).

Steel, Ronald, *Temptations of a Superpower* (Cambridge, MA: Harvard University Press, 1995).

Stephens, Robert, *Nasser: A Political Biography* (London: Allen Lane, 1971).

Tabori, Paul, *Taken in Adultery* (London: Aldus, 1949).

Taheri, Amir, *The Cauldron: The Middle East Behind the Headlines* (London: Hutchinson, 1988).

Thayer, George, *The War Business* (London: Paladin, 1970).

Timmerman, Kenneth R., *Death Lobby: How the West Armed Iraq* (London: Fourth Estate, 1992).

Troeller, Gary, *The Birth of Saudi Arabia: Britain and the Rise of the House of Saud* (London: Frank Cass, 1976).

Twitchell, K. S., *Saudi Arabia* (Princeton, 1953).

Wahba, Hafiz, *Arabian Days* (London: Barker, 1964).

Watt, W. Montgomery, *Muhammad at Mecca* (London: Oxford University Press, 1953).

Watt, W. Montgomery, *Muhammad at Medina* (London: Oxford University Press, 1956).

Wheelock, Keith, *Nasser's New Egypt: A Critical Analysis* (London: Stevens, 1960).

Wilson, A. T., *Persian Gulf* (London, 1928).

Wilson, Jeremy, *Lawrence of Arabia* (London: Mandarin, 1989).

Wilson, Peter W. and Graham, Douglas F., *Saudi Arabia: The Coming Storm* (New York: Sharpe, 1994).

Winder, R. Bayly, *Saudi Arabia in the Nineteenth Century* (London: Macmillan, 1965).

Winstone, H. V. F., *Captain Shakespear* (New York: Quartet, 1978).

Winstone, H. V. F. and Freeth, Zahra, *Kuwait: Prospect and Reality* (London: Allen and Unwin, 1972).

Woodward, Bob, *The Commanders* (New York: Simon and Schuster, 1991).

Woodward, Bob, *Veil: The Secret Wars of the CIA 1981–1987* (New York: Simon and Schuster, 1987).

Wright, Robin, *Sacred Rage: The Wrath of Militant Islam* (London: Deutsch, 1986).

Yamani, Hani Ahmed Zaki, *To Be a Saudi* (London: Janus Publishing, 1997).

Yamani, Mai (ed.), *Feminism and Islam: Legal and Literary Perspectives* (Reading, England: Ithaca Press, 1996).

Zacher, Mark W., *Dag Hammarskjöld's United Nations* (London: Columbia University Press, 1970).

Index